21ST CENTURY

FRENCH-ENGLISH
ENGLISH-FRENCH
DICTIONARY

D1358825

Produced by The Philip Lief Group, Inc.

A LAUREL BOOK
Published by
Dell Publishing
a division of
Bantam Doubleday Dell Publishing Group, Inc.
1540 Broadway
New York, New York 10036

Published by arrangement with
The Philip Lief Group, Inc.
6 West 20th Street
New York, NY 10011

ISBN: 0-440-22088-2

Printed in the United States of America

Published simultaneously in Canada

September 1996

10   9   8   7

OPM

Contents

Introduction

The *21st Century French-English/English-French Dictionary* is an invaluable reference source for today's students, business people, and travelers. Rather than wasting space on verbose, overly complicated definitions, the *21st Century French-English/English-French Dictionary* provides essential information in a brief, easy-to-use format.

The dual format of the *21st Century French-English/English-French Dictionary* eliminates the need to use two dictionaries: one volume for looking up words in French; and a separate one for looking up words in English. A student, for example, can use this dictionary to find the English translation to an unfamiliar French word—*and* to discover the correct way to express a certain English phrase in French. Because each entry is listed in both French and English, this dictionary is useful for every situation. Whether you are a business person checking the terms of a contract on an international deal, a foreign exchange student getting settled into a French dormitory, or a tourist trying to understand the items on a menu, the *21st Century French-English/ English-French Dictionary* will help you find quick, clear translations from French to English—*and* from English to French.

Each entry in the *21st Century French-English/English-French Dictionary* appears in a concise, easy-to-follow format. The headwords are listed in alphabetical order, with a separate A-to-Z section for both the French-English and the English-French. The pronunciation, complete with syllable markings, appears in brackets after each headword, followed by its part of speech. (See Pronunciation Guide.) Entries for nouns also include an indication of gender, with *M* signifying a masculine word, *F* indicating a feminine word, and *MF* representing a neuter word. Verbs are marked either *vt* (verb transitive) or *vi* (verb intransitive). Finally, a clear, succinct translation of each word appears, followed by a list of related forms and common phrases.

Reflecting current attitudes and ever-changing sensitivities in its choice of word list, definitions, translations, and pronunciations, the *21st Century French-English/English-French Dictionary* provides the most reliable and up-to-date information available. Whether for speaking, writing, or understanding, the *21st Century French-English/ English-French Dictionary* successfully combines a simple, concise format with a contemporary slant, and will serve as an indispensable tool for every occasion.

Pronunciation Guide

This dictionary represents a unique approach to phonetic pronunciation. It relies on plain, or readily understood, symbols and letters. There are no Greek symbols, and most people, whether English-speaking or French-speaking, should be able to easily sound out the words using this guide.

For English words, the pronunciation is based on conventional (unaccented) American English. The most common pronunciation has been chosen in any instance where there is more than one acceptable pronunciation.

The French language is very consistent with the sounds of its vowel groupings as well as consonants. This outline has very few, if any, exceptions. Accents are noted. Vowel sounds are generally pure. The groupings in the left column are the French language; the English counterparts are in the right hand column.

VOWELS	ENGLISH EQUIVALENT
a = ah	c*o*p, m*o*p
à = a unique sound between "bag" and "bug"	b*a*g
â = a softer version of ah	p*a*lm
e = eh	*e*h, h*e*fty, h*ea*ther
é = ay	cl*a*y
è = uh, closer with lips rounded	*ea*rth
I = ee	s*ee*n, k*ee*n, m*ea*n
î = ee, but shorter than plain I	b*ee*s
ì = ee, shorter than I or î	b*ee*f
o = oh	ph*o*ne, h*o*pe
ò = aw	b*o*ss
ô = o, but without a final u diphthong	s*o*
u = oo	h*oo*p, l*oo*p, s*ou*p

CONSONANTS		ENGLISH EQUIVALENT	
b		b	*b*at, *b*e, a*b*le
d	(tongue next to teeth in French)	d	*d*ip, see*d*
f		f	*f*all, *ph*ysic, laug*h*
g		g	*g*ap, bi*g*
h	(never sounded in French)	h	*h*eat
		j	*j*ob, e*dg*e
k		k	*c*at, ti*ck*, *k*in, *q*uit
l		l	*l*ip, pu*ll*, he*l*p
m		m	ha*m*, *m*at, li*m*p
n		n	*n*o, ha*n*g, bi*n*
_	a nasal n after vowels, keep the passage between the nose and throat closed		
p		p	*p*ut, u*p*
r	(in French pronounced with a slight roll)	r	ta*r*, *r*ipe, pa*r*t
s		s	*s*it, *c*ite, hi*ss*
t	(tongue next to teeth in French)	t	ha*t*, *t*in, bu*tt*er
v		v	*v*ine, ha*v*e
w		w	*w*hy, *w*it
y	(usually)		yes
y	(at end of word in French, elongated)		
z		z	*z*oo, hi*s*, read*s*
		ch	*ch*in, i*tch*
		sh	a*sh*, a*c*tion
		th	*th*e, *th*at
		zh	vi*s*ion
		ng	ba*n*k, a*n*ger

Liaison

In most cases in French, when a word begins with a vowel (or a mute, aspirated h), it is joined with the last consonant sound of the preceding word, even when the consonant is followed by a mute e. The liaison only occurs when the two words are closely connected and pronounced in the same breath.

Basic pronunciation in this dictionary

Traditional English phonetics	Becomes	As in

VOWELS

æ	a	cat, ask
e	ai	gate, they, air
a, a:	ah	hot, father
	au	bought, haunt, war, fall
	e	fell, head
I, I:	ee	see, tea
	I	lid, damage
aï	uy	buy, lie, height, I
o	o	no, foe, road
u	oo	loop, chute, poor
	ou	now, out, town
	oi	boy, void
	uh	but, mother, hunt
	u	bird, aloof, alert, debris, book, put, could

This neutral *u* sound is one of the most common vowel sounds in English, and it is used for many unstressed syllables.

Introduction

Le *dictionnaire Français/Anglais-Anglais/Français du 21ème siècle* est une source de référence précieuse pour les étudiants d'aujourd'hui, les hommes d'affaires, et les voyageurs. Plutôt que de remplir les pages de définitions verbeuses et compliquées, le *dictionnaire Français/Anglais-Anglais/Français du 21ème siècle* vous donne l'information essentielle et d'une manière concise.

Le format double fonction du *dictionnaire Français/Anglais-Anglais/Français du 21ème siècle* élimine le besoin d'avoir à utiliser deux dictionnaires: l'un pour chercher le mot en Français, et l'autre pour chercher le mot en Anglais. Un étudiant, par exemple, peut utiliser ce dictionnaire pour trouver la traduction anglaise d'un mot français qui ne lui est pas familier—**et aussi** pour découvrir la façon correcte d'exprimer une phrase anglaise en Français. Chaque mot étant listé à la fois en Français et en Anglais, ce dictionnaire peut être utilisé en toute occasion.Quelle que soit votre situation: homme d'affaires vérifiant les termes d'un contrat international, étudiant d'un programme d'échange s'installant dans un dortoir Français, ou un touriste essayant de déchiffrer un menu, le *dictionnaire Français/Anglais-Anglais/Français du 21ème siècle* vous aidera à trouver des traductions claires, de façon rapide, de Français en Anglais—et d'Anglais en Français.

Dans le *dictionnaire Français/Anglais-Anglais/Français du 21ème siècle*, chaque mot est listé de manière concise, facile à suivre. Les entrées sont par ordre alphabétique, et les parties Français-Anglais et Anglais-Français ont chacune leur section de A à Z. La prononciation détaillée de chaque mot (comprenant la marque de chaque syllabe) apparaît entre parenthèses, suivie des parties du discours du mot (Voir Guide de Prononciation). Les entrées pour les noms communs comprennent le genre, M indiquant le genre masculin. F signifiant le genre féminin, et N représentant le genre neutre. Les verbes transitifs possèdent l'indication *vt* et les verbes intransitifs se reconnaissent à l'indication *vi*.

Une traduction claire et précise du mot suit ainsi qu'une liste de phrases courantes.

Reflétant les idées actuelles et les éternels changements des sensibilités par son choix de mots, de définitions, de traductions, et de prononciations, le *dictionnaire Français/Anglais-Anglais/Français du 21ème siècle* vous apporte l'information la plus correcte et la plus récente. Quel que soit votre besoin: conversation, écriture, ou compréhension, le dictionnaire Français/Anglais-Anglais/Français du 21ème siècle allie brillamment un format simple et concis avec une tendance contemporaine, se révélant ainsi un outil indispensable pour toute occasion.

Guide de Prononciation

Ce dictionnaire dévoile une approche unique concernant la prononciation phonétique. Il fait usage de symboles et de lettres simples et compris de tout le monde. Il n'y a aucun symbole grec et la plupart des gens, qu'ils soient de langue Française ou Anglaise, devraient pouvoir prononcer les mots avec l'aide de ce guide.

Pour les mots anglais, la prononciation a pour base l'Anglais Américain courant. Dans le cas où un choix entre plusieurs prononciations était à faire, la plus courante a été sélectionnée.

La langue Française est très cohérente en ce qui concerne ses groupements de voyelles et de consonnes. Cette règle possède très peu d'exceptions. Les accents sont indiqués. Les sons de voyelles sont en général purs. Les groupements de la colonne de gauche représentent la langue Française; l'équivalent anglais se trouve dans la colonne de droite.

VOYELLES	ANGLAIS ÉQUIVALENT
a = ah	c*o*p, m*o*p
à = son unique, entre "bag" et "bug"	b*a*g
â = une version plus douce de ah	p*a*lm
e = eh	*e*h, h*e*fty, h*ea*ther
é = ay	cl*a*y
è = uh, avec bouche arrondie	*ea*rth
i = ee	s*ee*n, k*ee*n, m*ea*n
î = ee, plus court que i	b*ee*s
o = oh	ph*o*ne, h*o*pe
ò = aw	b*o*ss
ô = o, sans la diphtongue finale du u	s*o*
u = oo	h*oo*p, l*oo*p, s*ou*p

CONSONNES		ANGLAIS ÉQUIVALENT	
b		b	*b*at, *b*e, a*b*le
d	(langue près des dents)	d	*d*eep, see*d*
f		f	*f*all, *ph*ysic, lau*gh*
g		g	*g*ap, bi*g*
h	(toujours muet en Français)	h	*h*eat
j		j	*j*ob, e*dg*e
k		k	*c*at, ti*ck*, *k*in, *q*uit
l		l	*l*ip, pu*ll*, he*l*p
m		m	ha*m*, *m*at, li*m*p
n		n	*n*o, ha*ng*, bi*n*

-pour un son n nasal après une voyelle, fermer le conduit entre le nez et la gorge.

p		p	*p*ut, u*p*
r	(en Français, prononcer avec léger roulement)	r	ta*r*, *r*ipe, pa*r*t
s		s	*s*it, *c*ite, hi*ss*
t	(langue près des dents)	t	ha*t*, *t*in, bu*tt*er
v		v	*v*ine, ha*v*e
w		w	*w*hy, *w*it
y	(en général, si placé à la fin du mot en Français, son étiré)	y	*y*es
z		z	*z*oo, hi*s*, read*s*
		ch	*ch*in, it*ch*
		sh	a*sh*, a*c*tion
		th	*th*e, *th*at
		zh	vi*si*on
		ng	ba*nk*, a*ng*er

Liaison

En Français, dans la plupart des cas, lorsqu'un nom commence par une voyelle (ou un h muet ou aspiré), il est lié à la dernière consonne du mot précédent, même si celle-ci se termine par un e muet. La liaison a lieu lorsque les deux mots sont annexés et prononcés dans la même haleine.

Prononciation de base utilisée dans ce dictionnaire:

Anglais Phonétique Traditionnel	Devient	Exemple

VOYELLES

ae	a	c*a*t, *a*sk
e	ai	g*a*te, th*e*y, *ai*r
a, at	ah	h*o*t, f*a*ther
	au	b*ou*ght, h*au*nt, w*a*r, f*a*ll
	e	f*e*ll, h*ea*d
I	ee	s*ee*, t*ea*
	l	l*i*d, dam*a*ge
aï	uy	b*uy*, l*ie*, h*eigh*t, *I*
o	o	n*o*, f*oe*, r*oa*d
u	oo	l*oo*p, ch*u*te, p*oo*r
	ou	n*ow*, *ou*t, t*ow*n
	oi	b*oy*, v*oi*d
	uh	b*u*t, m*o*ther, h*u*nt
	u	b*i*rd, *a*loof, al*e*rt
		d*e*bris, b*oo*k, p*u*t, c*ou*ld

Ce son *u* neutre est un des sons de voyelles les plus utilisés en Anglais, et est utilisé par beaucoup de syllabes inaccentuées.

A

à [ah] *prép* to; at; in; from; of; on; for; by; with

A.M. du matin; A.M.(ante meridiem)

abaisser [ah•bai•SAI] *vt* abase; lower; drop; reduce; debase

abandoner [ah•bahn•dau•NEH] *vt* waive (rights); give up; forsake; abandon

abandonné [ah•bahπ•dau•NAI] *adj* forsaken; desolate

abasourdir [ahb•soor•deer] *vt* dumbfound

abat-jour [ah•BAH•ZHOOR] *n* M lamp shade

abattoir [ah•bah•TWAR] *n* M slaughterhouse

abattre [ah•BAHTR] *n* M *vt* laughter

abattu [ah•bah•TEW] *adj* dejected; downcast; haggard

abbaye [ah•BAIEE] *n* F abbey

abdomen [ahb•dau•MEN] *n* M abdomen

abécédaire [ah•BEH•ceh•DEHR] *n* M spelling book

abeille [ah•BEY] *n* F bee

abhorrer [ah•bau•RAI] *vt* abhor; loathe; detest

abîme [ah•BEEM] *n* M abyss; F chasm

abolir [ah•bau•LEER] *vt* abolish

abominable [ah•BAU•mee•NAHBL] *adj* abominable

abondant [ah•bauπ•DAHπ] *adj* M abundant; plentiful; profuse

abonnée [ah•bau•NEH] *adj; n* MF subscriber

abonnement [ah•BAU•nah•MAHπ] *n* M subscription

abord [ah•BOR] *n* M approach; access; *npl* surroundings

aborder [ah•bor•DEH] *vt* land; approach

aboyer [ah•boi•YEAH] *vt* bark (as a dog)

abréger [ah•brai•ZHAI] *vt* abbreviate; abridge

abreuver [ah•brœ•VEH] *vt* water (plants)

abreuvoir [ah•brœ•VWAHR] *n* M trough

abréviation [ah•BRAI•vyah•SYAUπ] *n* F abbreviation

abri [ah•BREE] *n* M shelter ; *vt* abriter

abricot [ah•bree•KO] *n* M apricot

absent [ahp•SAHπ] *adj* M absent

absolu [ahp•sau•LEW] *adj* M
absolute; complete; total;
utter; ~ prononcer un mot ou
des mots *vt* utter

absolument
[ahp•sau•lew•MAHπ] *adv* M
absolutely

absorber [ahp•saur•BAI] *vt*
absorb

absurde [ahp•SEWRD] *adj*
absurd; ludicrous; preposterous

absurdités [—dee•TEH] *fpl*
nonsense

académie [ah•kah•dai•MEE] *n*
F academy

acajou [ah•kah•ZHOO] *n* M
mahogany

accablant [ah•kah•BLAHπ] *adj*
overwhelming; accabement
adj overwhelming

accabler [ah•kah•BLAI] *vt*
overwhelm

accélérateur
[ak•SEH•leh•rah•TœR] *n* M
throttle (moteur)

accélerer [ahk•SAI•lu•RAI] *vt*
quicken; *vi* s'accélérer

accent [ahk•SAHπ] *n* M accent;
emphasis; ~ léger régional *n*
comp M twang

accepter [ahk•sep•TAI] *vt*
accept

accès [ahk•SE] *n* M access

accessoire [ahk•se•SWAHR]
adj M additional

accessoires [ahk•seh•SWAHR]
npl M trappings

accident [ahk•see•DAHπ] *n* M
accident

accidentel [ahk•see•dahπ•TEL]
adj M accidental

acclamations
[ah•klah•mah•SYAUπ] *spl* F
cheering

acclamer [ah•klah•MAI] *vt*
cheer

accommodant -e
[ah•KAU•mau•DAHπ] *adj;*
accommodating; easy-going;
tractable

accomoder [ah•CAU•mau•DAI]
vt accommodate

accompagner
[ah•KAUπ•pah•NYAI] *vt*
accompany

accomplir [ah•kauπ•PLEER] *vt*
accomplish

accord 1 [ah•KAUR] *n* M
agreement; accord

accord 2 *n* M chord; MF tuning

accorder [-DEH] *vt* reconcile;
grant; concede

accoster [ah•kau•STAI] *vt* come
along-side; accost

accouchement
[ah•koo•SHMAHπ] *n* M
childbirth

accoutumer [ah•koo•tew•MAI]
vt accustom; get used to; *vi*
s'accoutumer

accrochage [ah•krau•SHAZH]
n F skirmish

accrocher [ah•kro•SHAI] *vi* refl
cling

accumuler [ah•KEW•mew•LAI]
vi accumulate; *vt/vi* refl
s'accumuler

accuser [ah•kew•ZAI] *vt* accuse;
impeach (un haut
fonctionnaire); indict

acerbe [ah•SERB] *adj* scathing;
sour bitter

achat [ah•SHAH] *n* M purchase

achats *mpl* shopping; aller faire
ses ~ *vt* go shopping

acheter [ahsh•TAI] *vt* buy;
purchase

acheteur [ahsh•TUR] *n* M
buyer

acide [ah•SEED] *adj n* M acid

acier [ah•seey•EH] *n* M steel; ~
inoxydable M\ stainless
steel

acompte [ah•KAUπT] *n* down
payment; installment payment

acquérir [ah•kai•REER] *vt*
acquire

acquiescer [ah•kye•SAI] *vi*
acquiesce

acquitter [ah•kee•TAI] *vt* acquit

acre [ah•kr] *n* F acre

âcre [ah•kr] *adj* M acrid

acrylique m [ah•kree•LEEK]
adj n M acrylic

acte [ahkt] *n* F action; act

actif -vif [ahk•TEEF] *adj* active

action [ahk•TSYUπ] *n* F action;
deed

actionnaire
[AHK•seey•au•NEHR] *n* MF
stockholder

actions *fpl* [ahk•SYAUπ] *n*
doings

actrice [ahk•TREES] *n* F actress

actuel [ahk•tew•EL] *adj* real;
current; present

actuellement
[AHK•tew•el•MAHπ] *adv*
presently; really; actually

adapter [ah•dahp•TAI] *vi* adapt;
vi refl s'adapter

addition 1 [ah•dee•SYAUπ] *n*
F addition

addition 2 [ah•dee•SYAUπ] *n*
F check (bill)

additonner
[ah•DEE•syauπ•NEH] *vt* add

adhésion [ah•dai•ZYAUπ] *n*
membership

adieu [ah•DYØ] *n* M farewell

adjectif [ahd•jek•TEEF] *n* M
adjective

admettre [ahd•METR] *vt* admit

administration
[ahd•MEE•nee•strah•SYAUπ]
n F management

administrer
[ahd•MEE•nee•STRAI] *vt*
administer

admirablement
[ahd•mee•rah•bl•MAHπ] *adj*
wonderfully

admirer [ahd•mee•RAI] *vt*
admire

admission [ahd•mee•SYAUπ] *n*
F admission

admonester
[ahd•mau•ne•STAI] *vt*
admonish

adolescence
[ah•DAU•le•SAHπS] *n* F
adolescence

adolescent; -e
[ah•DAW•leh•SAHπ]; [-sahnt]
n MF youngster

adopter [ah•daup•TAI] *vt* adopt

adoption [ah•daup•SYAUπ] *n*
F adoption

adorable [ah•dau•RAHBL] *adj*
lovable

adorateur; -trice
[ah•daur•ah•TœR]; [-TREES]
n MF worshipper

adorer [ah•dau•RAI] *vt* adore;
worship

adoucir [ah•doo•SEEUR] *vt*
soften

adresse [ah•DRES] *n* F address;
~ de l'expéditeur *n* F return
address

adresser [ah•dre•SAI] *vt*
address; ~ à *vt* refer

adroit [ah•DRWAH] *adj* deft;
clever

adulte [ah•DEWLT] *n* M
adult; *adj* adulte; (material
subject) pour adultes\ for
adults only

adultère [ah•dewl•TAIR] *n* M
adultery

adverbe [ahd•VERB] *n* M
adverbe

adversaire [ahd•ver•SER] *n* MF
opponent

adversité [ahd•VER•see•TAI] *n*
F adversity

aérer [ah•ehr•EH] *vt* ventilate;
air; air out

aéroport [ah•ai•ro•PAUR] *n* M
airport

affaiblir [ah•feh•BLEEUR] *vt*
weaken; impair

affaire [ah•FAIR] *n* F affair

affaires [ah•FAIR] *npl* F
business

affamé [ah•fah•MAI] *adj*
famished;

affamer [ah•fah•MEH] *vt* starve

affecter [ah•fek•TAI] *vt* affect

affection [ah•fek•SYAUπ] *n* F
affection; liking; ailment

affectueux [ah•fek•tew•Ø] *adj*
endearing; ~ tendre\ fond

affiche [ah•FEESH] *n* F poster

afflux [ah•FLEWKS] *n* M
influx

affranchier [ah•frahπ•SHEER]
vt to free; frank (postage)

affranchissement
[ah•frahπ•shees•MAHπ] *n* M
liberartion; postage

affreux [ah•FRU] *adj* awful;
lurid; ghastly

Afghanistan
[ahf•gah•nee•STAHπ] *n* M
Afghanistan

Afrique [ah•FREEK] *n* F Africa

agacer [ah•gah•seh] *vt* annouy;
irritate; *adj* agaçant; *adv*
agacement

âge [ahzh] *n* M age; quel ~
as-tu?\ how old are you?; ~
d'homme *n* manhood; ~ d'or;
apogée *n* M heyday

âgé [ah•ZHAI] *adj* M aged

agence [ah•ZHAHπS] *n* F
agency; ~ de voyages\ travel
agency

agencement
[ah•zhahπs•MAHπ] *n* M
layout; plan

agent [ah•ZHAHπ] *n* M M
agent; ~de change *n* M
stockbroker; ~ de police *n* M
policeman; ~ immobilier *n* M
realtor

agrafe [ah•GRAHF] n; MF
staple; *vt* agrafer

aggraver [ah•grah•VAI] *vt*
aggravate; *v refl* s'aggraver\
grow worse

agile [ah•ZHEEL] *adj* nimble

agir [ah•ZHEER] *vt* act

agitation 1
[ah•zhee•tah•SYAUπ] *n* F
restlessness

agitation 2 *n* F ferment;
fermentation agité -e
[ah•zhee•teh] *adj* turbulent

agité -e [ah•zhee•EH] *adj*
restless; les enfants étaient ~a
au dîner\ the children are
eager for dinner; ~
mouvementé\ *adj* hectic

agneau [ah•NYO] *n* M lamb

agrandir; *vi* s'agrandir
[ah•grahπ•DEER] *vt* enlarge

agréable [ah•grai•YAHBL] *adj*
agreeable; likable; palatable;
pleasant; refreshing (drink); ~
enjoyable

agressif [ah•gre•SEEF] *adj*
aggressive

agriculture
[ah•GREE•cewl•TEWR] *n* F
agriculture; F farming

agripper [ah•gree•PAI] *vt/vi refl*
clutch

aide 1 [ed] *n* F aid

aide 2 *n* M assistant; helper

aider [eh•DEH] *vt* help; succor

aigle [e•GL] *n* M eagle

aigre [ehgr] *adj* sour; tart

aigu [ai•GEW] *adj* M sharp;
pointed; keen; shrill;
criticalacute

aiguille [e•GEEY] *n* F needle

aiguiser [eh•gee•ZEH] *vt*
sharpen; whet

ail [ahy] *n* M garlic

aile [ehl] *n* F wing

ailé; -e [eh•LEH] *adj* winged

ailleurs [ah•YœR] *adv*
elsewhere

aller [ah•LEH] *vt* go; walk;
move; run; ~ à pied\ walk; ~
speed;\ zoom; ~ chercher\
fetch; ~ vite\ whisk; ~ avec\
go with

allusion (of flavor) soupçon m;
vt insinuer que; *vi* faire
allusion

aimant [e•MAHπ] *n* M magnet

aimer [e•MAI] *vt* love; like; ~
mieux\ prefer; ne pas ~\
dislike

aine [en] *n* F groin

aîné [e•NAI] *adj n* M elder

ainsi [aπ•SEE] *adv* thus; pour ~
dire\ so to speak

air [air] *n* M air; avoir ~\
appear; se donner des ~\ put
on airs

aisance [e•ZAHπS] *n* F fluency

aisé; -e [eh•ZEH] *adj* well-to-do

ajourner [ah•joor•NAI] *vt vi
refl* adjourn; postpone; delay

ajouter [ah•joo•TAI] *vt* add

ajuster [ah•zhew•STAI] *vt*
adjust; set; adapt;

ajusteur [ah•zhew•STœR] *n* M
adjuster; fitter

akteur [ahk•TœR] *n* M actor

alarme [ah•LAHRM] *n* F alarm;
vt alarmer

Albanie [ahl•bah•NEE] *n* F
Albania

album [ahl•BAUM] *n* M
album

alcool [ahl•KOOL] *n* M alcohol

alcoolique [ahl•coo•LEEK] *adj
n* MF alcoholic

alentours [ahn•lahn•TOOR] *npl*
M vicinity

alerte [ah•LEHRT] *adv* alert; sprightly; ~ à la bombe\ *n* bomb scare

algèbre [ahl•ZHEBR] *n* F algebra

Algérie [ahl•zhai•REE] *n* F Algeria

alibi [ah•lee•BEE] *n* M alibi

alimenter [ah•lee•mahπ•TAH] *n* M diet; *vt* augment; ~ un feu\ stoke

aliments [ah•lee•MAHN] *npl* viands

alizé [ah•lee•ZEH] *n* M tradewind

allée [ah•LAI] *n* F aisle

allégation [ah•lai•gah•SYAUπ] *n* F allegation

Allemagne [ah•le•mah•NYU] *n* F Germany

allemand [ah•le•mahπ] *n* M Allemand (person); M allemand (language) *adj* German

allergie [ah•ler•ZHEE] *n* F allergy

allergique [ah•ler•ZHEEK] *adj* F allergic

alliance [ah•lee•YAHπS] *n* F alliance

allumer [ah•lew•MEH] *vt* kindle

allumette [ah•lew•METT] *n* F match (fire)

allusion [ah•lew•ZHAUπ] *n* F allusion; allusion f; (of flavor) soupçon; faire ~ à\ hint

alouette f [ah•loo•et] *n* lark; (joke) blague

aloyau [ah•lwah•YO] *n* M sirloin

alphabet [ahl•fah•BE] *n* M alphabet

alpiniste [ahl•pee•NEEST] *n* MF mountaineer

altérer [ahl•teh•REH] *vt; vi* alter; tamper

alterner (avec) [ahl•ter•NAI] *vi* alternate (with)

amadou [ah•mah•DOO] *n* M tinder

amande 1 [ah•MAHπD] *n* F almond

amande 2 [ah•MAHπD] *n* F kernel

amant [ah•MAHπ] *n* M lover (of sports, nature, etc)

amateur [ah•mah•TœR] *adj n* M amateur

ambassade [ahπ•bah•SAHD] *n* F embassy

ambassadeur (F -drice) [ahm•bah•sah•DœR] *n* M ambassador

ambigu [ahm•bee•GEW] *adj* ambiguous (f -ë)

ambitieux [ahm•bee•SYØ] *adj* ambitious

âme [ahm] *n* F soul

amélioration [ah•MAI•lyau•rah•SYAUπ] *n* F improvement

améliorer (un produit) [ah•meh•lyaur•EH] *vt* upgrade; improve; s'améliorer\ improve

amender (loi) [ah•mahπ•DAI] *vt* amend (law); *n* M amendement

amer (ère) [ah•MER] *adj* bitter

Amérique [ah•mai•REEK] *n* America

amérique du sud
[ah•meh•REEK dew sewd] *n*
F South America

Amérique du Nord *n* F North
America

Amérique latine *n* M Latin
America

amertume [ah•mer•TEWM] *n*
F bitterness

ami [ah•MEE] *n* M friend

amiable [ah•mee•ah•BLUH] *adj*
amicable; friendly

amical [ah•mee•KAHL] *adj*
friendly

amidon [ah•mee•DAUπ] *n*
starch

amidonner [ah•mee•dau•NEH]
vt M starch; ~ une chemise

amitié [ah•mee•TYAI] *n* F
friendship; fellowship;
association

amnistie [ahm•nee•STEE] *n* F
amnesty

amortisseur [ah•maur•tee•SœR]
n shock absorber

amour [ah•MOOR] *n* M
love

amoureux (de) [ah•moo•RU]
adj in love (with)

ample [ahm•PLUH] *adj*
broad; ample; wide; *n* F
ampleur breadth; width;
intensity

ampoule [ahπ•POOL] *n* F
blister; bulb (elec); vial

amusant [ah•mew•ZAHπ] *adj*
fun

amuse-gueule *n* M appetizer

amusement [ah•mewz•MAHπ]
n M entertainment

amuser [ah•mew•ZAI] *vt*
amuse; s'amuser have fun

amygdale(s) [ah•mee•DAHL] *n*
F tonsil

an [ahπ] M year; avoir six ~s
be six years old; l'~ dernier\
last year; année bissextile\
leap year; année scolaire *n*\
school year

analogie [ah•nah•lau•ZHEE] *n*
F analogy

analyse [ah•nah•LEES] *n* F
analysis; ~ de sang *n* F\ blood
test

analyser [ah•nah•lee•ZAI] *vt*
analyze

anarchie [ah•nahr•SHEE] *n* F
anarchy

ancêtre [ahπ•SAITR] *n* M
ancestor; forefather

ancien [ahπ•SYAπ] *adj* antique;
ancient; old; elder; former;
senior

ancienneté
[ahπ•SYAHπ•nu•TAI] *n* F
seniority

ancre [AHπ•kr] *n* F anchor

âne [ahn] *n* donkey

ange [ahnzh] *n* M angel

anglais [ahπ•GLAI] *adj*
English; *n* M Anglais ; *npl* les
Anglais

angle [AHπ•gl] *n* M angle

Angleterre [ahπ•glu•TER] *n* F
England

angoisse [ahπ•GWAHS] *n* F
anguish; *vt* angoisser

anguille [ahπ•GEEY] *n* eel

animal [ah•nee•MAHL] *n* M
animal

animé [ah•nee•MAI] *adj*
animated; spirited

animer [ah•nee•MAI] *vt* liven;
enliven; animate

animosité
[ah•nee•mau•see•TAI] *n* F ill
will

anneau [ahn•NOH] *n* MF ring;
link; ringlet

annexe [ah•nehks] *n* MF rider;
annex

anniversaire
[ah•NEE•ver•SER] *n* F
anniversary; birthday

annonce [ah•nauπ•SUH] *n* F
announcement; advertise-
ment; ~ publicitaire\
commercial;

annoncer [ah•nauπ•SAI] *vt*
announce; advertise

annuaire [ahn•nyoo•AIR] *n* M
directory

annuel [ah•new•EL] *adj* annual;
n plante F annuelle (plant);
publication F annuelle\
(periodical)

annuler [ah•new•LAI] *vt*
cancel; nullify; repeal

anormal [ah•naur•MAHL] *adj*
M abnormal

anse [ahπs] *n* F handle

antérieur [ahπ•tai•RYœR] *adj*
prior

anthologie [ahπ•tau•lau•ZHEE]
n F anthology

antique [ahπ•TEEK] *adj*
ancient; old

antisocial
[ahπ•tee•sau•SYAHL] *adj*
antisocial

antre [ahπ•tr] *n* M lair

anxiété [ahπk•see•yai•TAI] *n* F
anxiety

anxieux [ahπk•SYØ] *adj*
anxious; inquiet

aôut [oo] *n* M August

apaiser [ah•peh•ZEH] *vt* soothe;
placate; pacify (politics)

aparemment
[ah•pah•rah•MAHπ] *adv*
apparently

aperçu [ah•per•SEW] *n* M
glimpse; insight; outline;
rough estimate

apercevoir [ah•per•ser•VWAR]
vt catch sight of; glimpse

aplatir [a•plah•TEER] *vt* flatten

apogée [ah•pau•ZHAI] *n* M
climax

apparaître [ah•pah•RAITR] *vi*
appear

appareil [ah•pah•RUY] *n* M
camera; device; ~ de
chauffage\ heater

appareiller [ah•pah•ruy•EH] *vt*
install; fit up

apparemment
[ah•pah•re•MAHπ] *adv*
seemingly; apparently

apparence [ah•pah•RAHπS] *n*
F guise; appearance;
semblance

apparition
[ah•pah•ree•SYAUπ] *n* F
appearance

appartement [ah•pahrt•MAHπ]
n M apartment; ~ de luxe *n*\
penthouse

appât [a•PA] *n* M bait; lure; *vt*
appâter

appeler (s'appel M)
[ah•pu•LAI] *vt* call; name;
summon; *v reflx* s'apeler; en ~
à\ call on; appeal to

appentis [ah•pahπ•TEE] *n* M
outhouse

appétit [ah•pai•TEE] *n* M
appetite

applaudir [ah•plo•DEER] *vt*
applaud; clap

applaudissements
[ah•pla•dee•SMAHπ] *spl* M
clapping; applause

application
[ah•plee•kah•SYAUπ] *n* F
application

appliqué [ah•plee•KEH] *adj*
diligent

appliquer [ah•plee•KAI] *vt*
apply

apprécier [ah•prai•SYAI] *vt*
appreciate; appraise; estimate

**apprendre; apprendre à faire
qqch** [ah•PRAHNDR] *vt vi*
learn; ~ par cœur *vt*\
memorize

approbation
[ah•prau•bah•SYAUπ] *n* F
approval

approcher [ah•prau•SHAI] *vi*
approach

approfondir
[ah•prau•fauπ•DEER] *vt*
deepen; *vi* s'approfondir

approprié [ah•prau•pree•AI] *adj*
appropriate

approuver [ah•proo•VAI] *vt*
approve

approximativement
[ah•PRAUK•see•tee•VMAHπ]
adv approximately; loosely

appui [ah•PWEE] *n* M support;
backing; prop; être sans ~\ be
without support; ~ d fenêtre\
window-sill; ~ -tête M\
headrest

appuyer [ah•pwee•YAI] *vt*
endorse

après; [ah•PRE] *prep adv* after;
adv afterwads; *conj* après que
after; après tout\ after all;
après vous!;\ after you

après-midi [ah•PRE•mee•DEE]
n M afternoon

aquarelle [ah•kah•REHL] *n* F
watercolor

Arabie Saoudite
[ah•rah•BEE•sow•DEET] *n* F
Saudi Arabia

araignée [ah•reh•NYEH] *n* F
spider

arbitraire [ahr•bee•TRER] *adj*
arbitrary

arbitre [ahr•BEETR] *n* M
umpire; referee; *vt* arbiter; *vi*
être arbitre

arbre [ahrbr] *n* M tree; ~
généalogique\ family tree ; ~
à feuilles persistantes\
evergreen

arbuste [ahr•BEWST] *n* M
shrub

arc [ahrk] *n* M arch

arc-en ciel [ahr•kahπ•SYEL] *n*
M rainbow

archaïque [ahr•kah•YEEK] *adj*
archaic

archéologie
[ahr•kai•yau•lau•ZHEE] *n* F
archaeology

architecte [ahr•shee•TEKT] *n*
M architect

architecture
  [ahr•SHEE•tek•TEWR] *n* F
  architecture

ardu -e [ahr•DEW] *adj*
  strenuous; steep; abrupt;
  knotty

argent 1 [ahr•ZHAHπ] *n* M
  money; gagner de l'~\ earn
  money

argent 2 [ahr•ZHAHπ] *n* M
  silver; *adj* argenté (color); de
  or en ~ (in substance)

argenterie [ahr•zhaπt•REE] *n* F
  silverware

argile [ahr•ZHEEL] *n* F clay

argot [ahr•GO] *n* M slang

aride [ah•REED] *adj* arid

arme [ahrm] *n* F weapon

armée [ahr•MAI] *n* F army

armer [ahr•MAI] *vt* arm; equip;
  provision; cock (a gun)

armure [ahr•MEWR] *n* F armor

arnaquer [ahr•nah•KEH] *n* M
  slicker; raincoat

arôme [ah•ROM] *n* M aroma

arracher [ah•rah•SHEH] *vt* tear
  out; tear away; extract; wrest

arranger [ah•rahπ•ZHAI] *vt*
  arrange; adult; set in order

arrêt [ah•REH] *n* M stop;
  stoppage; arrest; ~ du mort\
  death sentence; maison d'~\
  prison; prononcer un ~\ pass
  sentence

arrêter [ah•reh•TAI] *vt* stop;
  arrest; *vi* s'arrêter

arrière [ah•ree•YER] *adj* rear; *n*
  M rear end; buttocks; backward

arrière-cour [ah•RYER•koor] *n*
  F backyard

arrière-grand-mère *n* F
  great-grandmother

arrière-grand-père *n* M
  great-grandfather

arrière-grands-parents *mpl n*
  great-grandparents

arrière-petit-fils *n* M
  great-grandson

arrière-petite-fille *n* F
  great-granddaughter

arrière-plan (à l')
  [ah•RYER•plahπ] *n* M
  background (in the)

arrivée [ah•ree•VAI] *n* F arrival

arriver [ah•ree•VAI] *vi* arrive

arrogant [ah•rau•GAHπ] *adj*
  arrogant

arroser [ah•ro•SAI] *vt* baste;
  water (plants)

art [ahrt] *n* M art; skill;
  artfulness; artificiality

article [ahr•TEEKL] *n* M
  article; item; ~s de Paris\
  fancy goods; faire l'~ \show
  off; à la ~ de la mort \at the
  point of death

articulation
  [ahr•tee•cew•la•SYUπ] *n* F
  joint; articulation; coupling; ~
  du doigt\ knuckle

articuler [ahr•tee•cew•LAI] *vt/vi*
  articulate; link; pronounce;
  utter

artificiel [ahr•tee•fee•CYEL] *adj*
  artificial

artiste [ahr•TEEST] *n* MF artist

ascendant -e [ah•sahπ•DAHπ]
  [-DAHπT] *adj* upward

ascenseur [ah•sahπ•SœR] *n* M
  elevator

aspect [ah•SPE] *n* M aspect; sight; appearance; look; point of view

asperges [ah•SPERZH] *spl* F asparagus

aspirant [ah•spee•RAHπ] candidate; officer

aspirateur [ah•spee•rah•TœR] *n* M vacuum; suction

aspirine [ah•spee•REEN] *n* F aspirin

assaisonnement [ah•se•zaun•MAHπ] *n* M seasoning

assassinat [ah•sah•see•NAH] M assassination

assassiner [ah•sah•see•NAI] *vt* assassinate

assemblée [ah•sahπ•BLAI] *n* F congregation

assembler; *vi* s'assembler [ah•sahπ•BLAI] *vt* assemble

asservir [ah•ser•VEER] *vt* enslave

assez [ah•SAI] *adj* enough; *adv* rather, quite; de; *pron* assez; *adv* assez; *excl* ~!\ enough!

assidu [ah•see•DEW] *adj* diligent

assiduité [ah•see•dwee•TAI] *n* F diligence

assiéger [ah•syai•ZHAI] *vt* besiege

assiette [ah•SYET] *n* F plate; seat (horse)

assigner [ah•see•NYAI] *vt* assign; allot; fix; appoint

assistance [ah•sees•TAπS] *n* F audience; spectators; bystanders

assister [ah•see•STAI] *vi* assist; help; ~ à\ attend

association [ah•sau•syah•SYAUπ] *n* F association; partnership

associer [ah•sau•SYAI] *vt* associate; *n* M associé

assombrir [ah•sauπ•BREER] *vt* darken; sadden ; *vi* s'assombrir

assourdir [ah•soor•DEER] *vt* deafen; tone down

assourdissant [ah•soor•dee•SAHπ] *adj* deafening

assujettir [ah•sew•jeh•teeur] *vt* subjugate

assurance [ah•sew•RAHπS] *n* F insurance

assurer [ah•sew•RAI] *vt* ensure; insure

asthme [ahs•MUH] *n* M asthma

asthmatique [ahs•mah•TEEK] *adj* asthmatic; wheezy

asticoter [ah•stee•koh•TEH] *n* F needle

astrologie [ah•strau•lau•ZHEE] *n* F astrology

astronaute [ah•strau•NOT] *n* MF astronaut

astronomie [ah•strau•nau•MEE] *n* F astronomy

astuce [ah•STEWS] *n* F guile

astucieux [ah•stew•SYØ] *adj* shrewd

atelier [ah•tehl•EEYEH] *n* M studio; workshop

athée 1 [ah•TCH] *adj* godless

athée 2 [ah•TEH] *n* MF unbeliever

atomiseur [ah•tau•ee•ZHœR] *n*
'M sprayer

atout [ah•TOO] *n* M courage;
setback; trump (cards)

atrocité [ah•trau•see•TAI] *n*
outrage

attacher [ah•tah•SHAI] *vt*
attach

attaque [ah•TAHK] *n* F attack;
onslaught; ~ d'apoplexie\
stroke

attaquer [ah•tah•KEH] *vt*
waylay; attack; tackle (sports)

attelle [ah•TEHL] *n* F splint

attendre [ah•TAHπDR] *vt* wait

attente [ah•TAHπT] *n* F
waiting; salle d'~\ waiting
room

attentif [ah•tahπ•TEEF] *adj*
attentive

attentif -ive [ah•tahπ•TEEF]
[-TEEV] *adj* thoughtful

attention [ah•tahπ•SYAUπ] *n*
F attention; plein d'~
thoughtful; faire ~ à\ pay
attention to; ~! look out!

atténuant [ah•tai•new•AHπ]
adj mitigating

attester [ah•teh•STEH] *vt*
vouch

attirail [ah•tee•REY] *n*
paraphernalia

attirant [ah•tee•RAHπ] *adj*
attractive

attirant attrayant
[ah•tee•rah•yahπ] *adj* enticing

attirer [ah•tee•RAI] *vt* attract

attitude [ah•tee•TEWD] *n* F
attitude; outlook

attraction [ah•trahk•SYAUπ] *n*
F attraction; variety
entertainment

attraper [ah•trah•PAI] *vt* catch;
nab; trick

attrayant [ah•trah•YAHπ] *adj*
inviting

attribut [ah•tree•BEW] *adj n* M
predicate

attrister [ah•tree•STAI] *vt*
sadden

aubaine [o•BEN] *n* F godsend

aube 1 [ob] *n* F dawn

aube 2 [ob] *n* F paddle; float

auberge [o•BERZH] *n* F inn;
tavern

aubergine [o•ber•ZHEEN] *n* F
eggplant

aubergiste [o•ber•ZHEEST] *n*
MF innkeeper

aucun [o•Kœπ] *pron* none; not
any; d'aucune some

au-dessous [o•du•SEWS] *adv*
below

au-dessus [o du•SEW] *adv*
prep above; over

audacieux [o•dah•SYØ] *adj*
daring; audacious

auditeur [o•dee•TœR] *n* M
listener; prosecutor (law)

audition [o•dee•SYAUπ] *n* F
audition; hearing

augmentation
[og•mahπ•tah•SYAUπ] *n*
increase; raise (wages)

augmenter [og•mahπ•TAI] *vt*
vi increase

augure [o•GEWR] *n* M omen;
de bon ~\ auspicious

aujourd'hui [au•zhoor•DWEE]
adv; *n* M today

aumônier [o•mo•NYE] *n* M
chaplain

auréole [o•rai•AUL] *n* M halo

aurore [o•ROHR] *n* F dawn

aussi [o•SEE] *adv* also; too; as; therefore; ~ bien\ besides; for that matter; moi ~\ me too; so am I

austère [au•STEHR] *adj* stark

automne [au•TAUN] *n* M fall (saison)

Australie [o•strah•LEE] *n* F Australia

ausucieux; -euse [ah•stew•SYØ]; [-SYØZ] *adj* wily

auteur [o•TœR] *n* M author

authentique [o•tahπ•TEEK] *adj* authentic; genuine

authorité [o•tau•ree•TAI] *n* F authority; power

auto-stoppeur [o•to•stau•PœR] *vi* M hitchhiker

autobiographie [o•tau•byau•grah•FEE] *n* F autobiography

autobus [o•to•BEWS] *n* M bus

autodéfense [o•to•dai•FAHπS] *n* F self-defense

autodidacte [o•to•dee•DAHKT] *adj* self-taught

autodiscipline [o•to•dee•see•PLEEN] *n* F self-discipline

autographe [o•tau•GRAF] *n* M autograph

automatique [o•tau•mah•TEEK] *adj* automatic

automne [o•TAUHN] *n* F autumn

autoportrait [o•to•paur•TREH] *n* M self-portrait

autorisation [au•tau•ree•za•SYAUπ] *n* F clearance; authorization; warrant

autoritoire [o•tau•ree•TWAHR] *adj* overbearing

autoroute [o•to•ROOT] *n* F highway

autre [otr] *adj pron;* other; another; different; further; else; quel qu'un d'~\ someone else; ; l'un et l'~\ both; l'un ou l'~\ either; ni l'un ni l'~\ neither; ~ chose\ something else

autrement; *conj* sinon [o•tr•MAHπ] *adv* otherwise

Autriche [o•TREESH] *n* F Austria

autruche [au•TREWSH] *n* F ostrich

auxiliaire [ok•seel•YER] *adj n* MF auxiliary

av. J.-C. abbr B.C. Before Christ

avaler [ah•vah•LEH] *vt* swallow; gulp

avali [ah•vah•LEE] *vt* debase

avance [ah•VAHπS] *n* F advance; avoir l'~ de\ be head of; d'~\ beforehand; être en ~\ be fast

avancer [ah•vahπ•SAI] *vi* proceed; *vt vi* refl s'avancer\ advance

avant [ah•VAHπ] *prep* before; in front of; *adv* beforehand; previously; en ~\ forward; plus ~\ further;

avant-bras *n* M forearm

avant-hier *n* M the day before yesterday

avant-première *n* F preview

avant-propos *n* M foreword

avantage [ah•vahπ•TAHZH] *n* M advantage; profit; benefit

avantageux [ah•vahπ•tah•ZHœ] *adj* advantageous

avare [ah•VAHR] *n* MF miser; tightwad; *adj* miserly; stingy

avarice [ah•vah•REES] *n* F stinginess

avec [ah•VEK] *prep* with

avec impunité F [aπ•PEW•nee•TAI] *n* impunity

avec modération [mau•dai•rah•SYAUπ] *n* moderation

avec plaisir [ple•ZEER] *adv* gladly

avec reconnaissance [ruh•kau•nee•SAHNS] *prép comp* F thankfully

l'Avent [(l)ah•VAHπ] M Advent

aventure [ah•vahπ•TEWR] *n* F adventure; risk

aventurer [ah•vahπ•tew•RAI] *vt* risk; adventure; *vi refl* s'aventurer take risks

aventureux [ah•vahπ•tew•Rœ] *adj* adventurous; risky; reckless

avenue [ah•veh•NEW] *n* F avenue

aversion [ah•VERZYAUπ] *n* F dislike

avertir [ah•vehr•TEER] *vt* warn

aveugle [ah•VUGL] *adj* blind

aveuglément [ah•vu•glai•MAHπ] *adv* blindly

avide [ah•VEED] *adj* grasping; greedy; ~ impatient; ~ de\ eager

avidité [ah•VEE•dee•TAI] *n* F greed

avion [ah•VYOπ] *n* F airplane

avis [ah•VEE] *n* M news; warning; opinion; advice; à mon ~\ in my opinion; changer d'~\ change one's mind

avoine [ah•VWAHπ] *n* F oats

avoir 1 [ah•VWAHR] *n* M property; possession

avoir 2 [ah•VWAHR] *vi* have; possess; hold; ~ de la chance\ be lucky; ~ heureux\ charming; ~ faim\ hungry; ~ grand besoin de; ~ un besoin de\ crave; ~ l'intention de\ intend; ~ le cafard\ mope; ~ le coup pour\ knack; ~le droit à\ entitled; ~ le mal de mer\ seasick; ~ le trac\ stage fright; ~ les moyens d'acheter qqch\ afford; ~ mal à l'estomac\ queasy; ~ sommeil\ sleepy; ~ tort\ wrong

avorton [ah•vaur•TAUπ] *n* M runt

avortement [ah•vaurt•MAHπ] *n* M abortion

avorter [ah•vaur•TAI] *vt* abort; *vi refl* se faire avorter\ have an abortion

axe [ahks] *n* M axis; axle

azote [ah•ZAUT] *n* M nitrogen

azur [ah•ZOOR] *n* M azure; blue

B

babillard -e [bah•BYAHR];
[-BYAHRD] *n* MF tattle-tale

babiller [bah•bee•YAI] *vi*
babble; tattle

bâche [bahsh] *n* F tarpaulin

badge [bahzh] *n* M badge

badinage [bah•dee•NAHZH] *n*
M banter; joking

badiner [bah•dee•NAI] joke;
banter

bagages [bah•GAZH] *spl* M
baggage; luggage

bagarre [bah•GAHR] *n* F fight;
scuffle; brawl

baie [bai] *n* F bay; F berry

baigneur [be•NYUR] *n* M
bather

baignoire [be•NYWAHR] *n* F
bathtub

bail [bel] *n* M lease

bâiller [bah•YEH] *vi* yawn;
gape

bâillon [bah•YAUπ] *n* M joke;
gag

bain [beπ] *n* M bath; tub
prendre un ~\ take a bath

baïonette [bah•yu•NET] *n* F
bayonet

baiser [be•ZAI] *n* M kiss;
donner un ~\ give a kiss

baisser [beh•SEH] vi lower; let
down; subside

balai [bah•LAHY] *n* M broom;
brush; windshield wiper (auto)

balancement
[bah•lahπs•MAHπ] *n* M
rocking

balancer [bah•lahπ•SEH] *vt*
swing; *vi* se balancer

balançoire [bah•lahπ•SWHAR]
n F swing

balayer [bah•lehy•EH] *vt* sweep

balayeur -euse [bah•lehy•œR];
[-ØZ] *n* MF sweeper

balcon [bahl•KAUπ] *n* M
balcony

baldaquin [bahl•dah•KAπ] *n* M
canopy

baleine [bah•LAN] *n* F whale

ballade [bah•LAHD] *n* F ballad

balle 1 [bahl] *n* F ball; bullet; ~
perdu\ stray bullet

balle 2 [bahl] *n* F pack; bale
(cotton)

ballerine [bahl•REEN] *n* F
ballerina

ballet [bah•LEH] *n* M ballet

ballon [ba•LOπ] *n* M balloon;
ball; football; envoyer un ~
d'essai\ float a trial ballon; put
out a feeler

bambou [bahπ•BOO] *n* M
bamboo

ban [baπ]˙ *n* M proclamation;
applause; metter au ~\ banish

banal [bah•NAHL] *adj* banal;
commonplace; mundane; trite;
hackneyed

banane [bah•NAHN] *n* F
banana

banc [bahπ] *n* M bench; ~
d'eglise\ pew

bandage [bahπ•DAHZH] *n* M
bandage

bande [bahπduh] *n* F band;
party; gang; ~ noire\
terrorists; ~ dessinée\ comics
(comic strip)

bandeau [bahπ•DO] *n* M
headband; blindfold

banderole [bahπ•de•ROL] *n* F
banner; streamer

bandit [bahπ•DEE] *n* MF thief ;
robber; bandit

banni [bah•NEE] *n* M outcast;
outlaw

bannir [bah•NEER] *vt* banish

banque [bahnk] *n* F bank

banquet [bahπ•KE] *n* M
banquet

banquier [bahπ•KYE] *n* M
banker

baptême [bahp•TEM] *n* M
baptism

baptiser [bahp•tee•ZAI] *vt*
baptize; christen

bar [bahr] *n* M bar (hotel, café,
etc.)

baraque [bah•RAHK] *n* F
booth; shed; shanty

baratter [bah•rha•TAI] *vt* churn

barbare [bahr•BAHR] *adj* inv
barbaric; uncultured

barbe [barb] *n* F beard

barbelé [bahr•bu•LAI] *adj*
barbed

barbouiller [bahr•bwee•YAI] *vt*
deface

barman [bahr• K] *n* M
bartender

baromètre [bah•ro•METR] *n* M
barometer

baroque [bah•ROK] *adj n* M
baroque; curious; odd; strange

barrage [bah•RAHZH] *n* M
dam; barring; closing; ~ de
route\ roadblock

barre [bahr] *n* F rod; bar; helm
(naut) paraître à la ~\ appear
at court; ~ de plage\ surf

barricade [bah•ree•KAHD] *n* F
barricade

barrière [bah•RYER] *n* F
barrier; gate

bas [bah] *n* M loer part; bottom;
stocking; *adj* low; small;
mean; à ~ .!\ down with.!;
~-fonds\ underworld; ~-côte\
aisle

du bas; *adv* en basdownstairs

basané -e [bah•zah•NEH] *adj*
swarthy

bascule [bah•SKEWL] *n* F
seesaw

basculer [bah•skew•LEH] *vi*
topple

base [bas] *n* F base; bottom;
basis; foundation; ~ de
données\ database; ~ on *vi*
baser

base-ball [bez•BAUL] *n* M
baseball

basilic [bah•see•LEEK] *n* M
basil

basket [bah•SKET] *n* M
basketball

basse [bas] *n* F bass (mus)

basson [bah•SOπ] *n* M bassoon

bastion [bah•steey•AUπ] *n* MF
stronghold

bataille [bah•TAHY] *n* F battle;
livrer ~ à\ *vt* join (the) battle

bataillon [bah•tah•YOπ] *n* M
battalion

bâtard [bah•TAR] *n* M *adj*
bastard

bâteau [bah•TO] *n* M boat;
ship; ~ à vapeur\ steamboat;
~à voile voilier\ sailboat

bâtiment [bah•tee•MAHπ] *n* M
building

bâtir [bah•TEER] *vt* build;
construct

bâton [bah•TAUπ] *n* M wand

battage [bah•TAZH] *n* M
beating; threshing

battement [bah•ta•MEπ] *n* M
beating; ~ de cœur\ *n*
heartbeat

battre [bahtr] *vt* beat; thresh; *vi*
se ~\ fight

bavard [bah•VAHR] *n* M
chatterbox

bavardage f [bah•vahr•DAJ] *n*
F gossip; chatter; chat

bavarder [bah•vahr•DAI] *vi*
gossip; chat

baver [bah•VAI] *vi* drool;
slobber

bavette [bah•VET] *n* F bib

bazar [bah•ZAHR] *n* M bazaar

beagle *n* M beagle

beau [bo] *adj* beautiful; *adj*
good-looking

béant [bai•AHπ] *adj* gaping

beau-fille [bo•FEEY] *n* F
stepdaughter

beau-fils [bo•FEES] *n* M
stepson

beau-fils; belle-fille
[bo•FEES]; [behl•FEEY]ˈ *n*
MF stepchild

beau-frère *n* M brother-in-law

beau-père *n* M father-in-law

beau-père [bo•PEHR] *n* M
stepfather

beaucoup [bo•KOO] many;
much ; ~ de plenty;\ a lot

beauté [bo•TAI] *n* F beauty

bébé [bai•BAI] *n* M baby

bec [bek] *n* M beak; spout

beffroi [be•FRWAH] *n* M
belfry

bégaiment [beh•geh•MAHπ] *n*
M stutter

bégayer [beh•geh•YEH] *vt;vi*
M stutter

beige [bezh] *adj n* M beige

bel-esprit [behl eh•SPREE] *n*
wiseacre

belette [buh•LEHT] *n* F weasel

belge [belzh] *adj* Belgian

Belgique [bel•ZHEEK] *n* F
Belgium

belier [be•lee•YAI] *n* M ram;
battering ram

belle-famille *n* F in-laws

belle-famille beaux-parents
MPL *n* in-laws

belle-fille *n* F daughter-in-law

belle-mère [bel•MER] *n* F
mother-in-law; stepmother

belle-sœur *n* F sister-in-law

bénédiction
[bai•NAI•deek•SYOπ] *n* F
benediction; blessing

bénéfice [beh•neh•FEES] *n* M
benefit; gain; profit

bénin [bai•NAπ] *adj* benign

bénir [bai•NEER] *vt* bless;
consecrate

béquille [bai•KEEY] *n* F
crutch; stand; shore

berceau [ber•SO] *n* crib; cradle

bercer [ber•SEH] *vt* rock; soothe

berceuse [ber•SØZ] *n* F lullaby

berét [bai•RAI] *n* M beret

béret écossais [beh•REH eh•kau•SEH] *n* M tam o' shanter

berger [ber•ZHAI] *n* M shepherd; F bergère shepherdess

besoin [be•SWAHπ] *n* M need; *vt* avoir ~ de\ have need of

bestial [be•STYAL] *adj* beastly; brutish

bestiaux [be•sty•OH] *npl* M livestock

bétail [bai•TAHY] *n* M cattle; livestock

bête 1 [bet] *n* F beast

bête 2 [bet] *adj* silly; stupid; faire la ~\ play the fool

bêtise [beh•TEEZ] *n* F stupidity

betterave [bet•RAHV] *n* F beet

bêtises [beh•TEES] *n* F nonsense

beurre [bur] *n* M butter; *vt* beurrer; ~ de cacahuète\ peanut butter

bibelot [beeb•LO] *n* M trinket

Bible [BEE•bl] *n* F Bible

bibliothécaire [BEE•blyau•tai•KER] *n* MF librarian

bibliothèque [BEE•blyau•TEK] *n* F library

biche [beesh] *n* F doe

bicyclette [bee•see•KLET] *n* F bicycle

bien [byeπ] *adv* well; good; proper; really; many; alright (in answer); faire du ~\ do good; être ~\ be comfortable/good-looking; ~ que\ although; tant ~ que mal\ so-so

bien disposé *adj* willing bien elevé; -e [~ ehlu•VEH] *adj* well-bred

bien en chair *adj* plump

bien être [byeπ ehtr] *n* M well-being

bien-aimé [byahπ•nai•MAI] *adj* beloved

bienfaiteur [byahπ•fai•TUR] *n* benefactor

biens immobiliers *npl* M real estate

bientôt [byahπ•TO] *adv* shortly; soon; à ~\ see you soon/shortly

bienveillant [byahπ•ve•YAHπ] *adj* kindly; avec ~\ with kindness

bienvenue [byen•vehn•NEW] *adj* welcome

bienviellant -e [byaπ•veh•ẎAHπ] [-YAHπT] *adj* understanding (envers qq'un)

bière [byer] *n* F beer

bifteck [beef•TEHK] *n* M steak

bigamie [bee•gah•MEE] *n* F bigamy

bigarré -e [bee•gah•REH] *adj* variegated (vêtement, fleur)

bijou [bee•ZHOO] *n* M jewel

bijoutier [bee•zhoo•TYE] *n* M jeweler; bijouterie F (shop)

bijoux [bee•ZHOO] *npl* M jewelry

bikini [bee•kee•NEE] *n* M bikini

bilan [bee•LAHπ] *n* M
balance-sheet
bile [beel] *n* F bile
bilingue [bee•LANG] *adj*
bilingual
billard [bee•YAHR] *n* M
billiards
billet [bee•YEH] *n* M note;
ticket; letter; notice; ~ de
banque\ bank note; ~ doux\
love letter; ~ simple\ single
ticket; ~ a ordre\ I.O.U.;
promissory note
biographie [byo•grah•FEE] *n* F
biography
biologie [byo•lo•ZHEE] *n* F
biology
birman [beer•MAHπ] *adj*
Burmese
Birmanie [beer•mah•NEE] *n* F
Burma
bis [bees] *adv* twice, again;
repeat; ditto; encore!
biscuit [bee•SKWEE] *n* M
cookie; biscuit
bistro [bee•STRO] *n* M pub;
dive; cheap café
bizarre [bee•ZAHR] *adj* kinky;
bizarre
bizzarrerie [bee•ZAH•ru•REE]
n F oddity; peculiarity; whim
blague [blahg] *n* joke; tobacco
pouch; humbug; nonsense;
sans ~?\ you don't say?
blaguer [blah•GœR] *vt* joke;
chaff; *n* M joker; wag; *adj*
scoffing
blâmer [blah•MAI] *vt* blame
blanc 1 [blaπ] *n* M blank
blanc 2 [blaπ] *n* M breast (of
bird)

blanc blanche 3 [blahπ]
[blahπsh] *adj* white; ; ~ de
chaux *n* M\ whitewash
blancheur [blahπ•SHœR] *n* F
whiteness
blanchir [blahπ•SHEER] *vt*
launder; whitewash; *vt vi*
whiten; ~ à la chaux *vi*\
whitewash
blasphémer [blahs•fai•MAI] *vt*
vi blaspheme
blé [bleh] *n* M wheat
blême [blehm] *adj inv* pale;
wan
blessant [ble•SAHπ] *adj*
hurtful; offensive (remarque)
blessé [ble•SAI] *adj* hurt
blesser [ble•SAI] *vt* injure; hurt
blessure [ble•SEWR] *n* F
injury; wound
bleu 1 [blØ] *adj; n* M blue;
bruise; conte ~\ fairy tale;
rester ~\ be flabbergasted
bloc [blauk] *n* MF block;
memorandum; pad; slab
blocage [blo•KAZH] *n* M
blockage; rubble
blocus [blo•KEW] *n* M
blockade
blond [blauπ] *adj* blonde; fair
bloquer [blo•KAI] *vt* block;
block up; blockade
bobard [bau•BAHR] *n* M fib;
tall story; *vi* raconter des
bobards
bobine [bau•BEEN] *n* F spool;
reel
bobiner [bau•bee•NEH] wind
bœuf [bœf] *n* M beef; ox; steer
boire [bwahr] *n* M drink;
drinking; *vt* drink; absorb; ~

comme un trou\ drink like a fish; chanson à ~\ drinking song

bois [bwah] *n* M wood; ~ de charpente *n comp* M\ timber; lumber; ~ de chauffage *n* M\ firewood

boisseau [bwah•SO] *n* M bushel

boisson [bwah•SOπ] *n* F beverage; drink

boîte [bwaht] *n* F box; ~ aux lettres\ mailbox; ~ de nuit\ nightclub; en ~\ canned; mettre en ~\ pull one's leg; ~ en fer\ tin can

boiter [bwah•TEH] *adj* limp; *vi* boiter\ go limp

boiteux [bwah•TØ] *adj* lame; crippled

boitiller [bwah•tee•YAI] *vi* hobble

bol [baul] *n* M bowl; basin

bombardement [bauπ•bahrd•MAHπ] *n* M bombing

bombarder [bauπ•bahr•DAI] *vt* bombard; bomb

bombardier [bauπ•bahr•DYE] *n* M bomber (avion)

bombe [bauπb] *n* F bomb

bon [bauπ] bonne [baun] *n* M order; voucher; bond; draft; *adj* well; good; pour de ~\ in earnest

bon marché *adj* cheap

bon sens *n* M common sense

bon-mot [bauπ mo] *n* M wisecrack; witticism

bonbon [bauπ•BAUπ] *n* M candy

bondir [bauπ•DEER] *vi* pounce; ~ sur\ capture

bonheur [bau•NœR] *n* F happiness; good luck

bonjour [bauπ•ZHOOR] *n* M good day; good morning; good afternoon

bonn de garantie [baun duh GAH•rahπ•TEE] *n* voucher

bonne [baun] maid; servant

bonne aubaine [baun au•BEHN] *n* F windfall

bonne volonte [baun vau•lauπ•TEH] *n* F willingness

bonnet [bau•NE] *n* M bonnet; cap; gros ~\ big shot

bonneterie [baun•te•REE] *n* F hosiery

boomerang *n* M boomerang

bord [baur] *n* M rim; edge (blade) au ~ de la mer\ by the sea

bordeaux 1 [baur•DO] *adj* maroon

bordeaux 2 [baur•DO] *n* M Bordeaux wine; claret

bordel [baur•DEL] *n* brothel

borné [baur•NAI] *adj* narrow-minded

bosniaque [bauz•NYAHK] *adj n* M Bosnian

Bosnie [bauz•NEE] *n* F Bosnia

bosquet [bau•SKE] *n* M grove

bosse [baus] *n* F bulge

bosse *n* F bump

bosselure [bau•SLEWR] *n* M dent

bossu [bau•SEW] *n* M hunchback

botanique [bo•tah•NEEK] *n* F
botany

botte; [baut] *n* F boot

bouc émissaire *n* M scapegoat

bouche [boosh] *n* F mouth;
opening; ~ d'incendie
hydrant; faire la petite ~\ be
picky

bouchée [boo•SHAI] *n* F
mouthful; gulp

boucher 1 [boo•SHAI] *n* M
butcher;

boucher 2 [boo•SHAI] *vt/vi refl*
clog; stop up

boucherie [boo•she•REE] *n* F
butcher (shop)

boucheur [boo•SHER] *n* M
butcher

bouchon [boo•SHAUπ] *n* M
stopper

boucle [bookl] *n* F buckle;
loop; ~ d'oreille\ earring

boucler [boo•KLER] *vt* buckle

bouddhisme [boo•DEESM] *n*
M Buddhism

boue [boo] *n* F mud

bouée [boo•AI] *n* F buoy

boueux [boo•Ø] *adj* muddy

bouffée [boo•FEH] *n* F whiff

bouffi [boo•FEE] *adj* bloated

bouger [boo•ZHAI] *vi* budge;
vt faire ~

bougie [boo•ZHEE] *n* F candle;
spark plug (voiture)

bouillir [boo•YEER] *vi* boil

bouilloire [bweey•WAHR] *n* F
teakettle; kettle

bouillon [bwee•YAUπ] *n* M
broth

boulanger [boo•lahn•ZEH] *n* M
baker

boulangerie
[boo•LAHπ•zhe•REE] *n* F
bakery

boule [bool] *n* F ball; bowl; ~
de neige\ snowball; fourer aux
~\ bowl (sport)

bouleau [boo•LO] *n* M birch

bouledogue [bool•DAUG] *n* M
bulldog

boulette [boo•LET] *n* F pellet;
blunder; ~ de viande\ meatball

bouleversement
[booul•vehrs•MAHπ] *n* M
upset; overthrow

bouquet [boo•KAI] *n* M bunch;
cluster; aroma (vin)

bourbier [boor•BYAI] *n*
quagmire

bourdon [boor•DAUN] *n* M
bumblebee

bourdonnement
[boor•dauπ•MAHπ] *n* M buzz
(of insect)

bourgeon [boor•ZHAUπ] *n* M
bud; *vi* bourgeonner

bourre [boor] *n* F floss; wad;
stuffing

bourreau [boo•RO] *n* M
executioner; hangman; torturer

bourrer [boo•REH] *vt* stuff;
cram (école)

bourru [boo•REW] *adj* gruff

bourse [burs] *n* F Stock
Exchange; stock market

boursoufflé -e;
[boor•soo•FLEH] *adj* bloated;
inflated; bombastic; turgid

boussole [boo•SAUL] *n* M
compass (math)

bout [boo] *n* M end; extremity;
tip; ~ d'une\ cigarette butt; ~
du doigt\ fingertip

bouteille [boo•TAIY] *n* F
bottle; *vt* mettre en ~

bouton [boo•TOπ] *n* M button;
pimple

bovin [bo•VAπ] *adj* bovine

bowling *n* M bowling

boxe [bauks] *n* F boxing

boxer [bauk•SAI] *vi* F box

boxeur [bauk•SUR] *n* M boxer

boycott [boi•CAUT] *n* boycott;
vt boycotter

bracelet [brah•SLET] *n* bracelet

braille [brayl] *n* M braille

brailler [brah•YAI] *vt vi* bawl

braire [brair] *vi* bray

braises [brez] *npl* F embers

brancard [brahπ•KAHR] *n* M
stretcher (méd)

branche [brahπsh] *n* F branch;
stick

branchies [brahπ•SHEE] *n* FPL
gills

brandir [brahπ•DEER] *vt* wield;
brandish

bras [brah] *n* M arm

brasse [brahs] *n* F fathom

brasserie [brah•su•REE] *n* F
brewery; restaurant

brasseur [brah•SUR] *n* M
brewer

brave [brahv] *adj* brave; *vt*
braver

bravoure [brah•VOOR] *n* F
bravery

brebis [bre•BEE] *n* F ewe

brèche [bresh] *n* F breach (in
wall); *vt* faire une ~ dans

bref [bref] *adj* brief

brendille [brahπ•DY] *n* F twig
(d'un arbre)

bretelles [bruh•TEHL] *npl* F
suspenders

breuvage [brØ•VAHZH] *n* M
potion

bric-à-brac [bree•kah•BRAHK]
n M junk

brièvement [bryev•MAHπ] *adv*
briefly

brièveté [bryev•i•TAI] *n* F
brevity

brillant [bree•YAHπ] *adj*
bright; shiny; brilliant

briller [bree•YAI] *vt* shine

brin [braiπ] *n* M sprig; shoot;
blad (herbes)

brique [breek] *n* F brick

briquet [bree•KEH] *n* M lighter

brise [brees] *n* F breeze

briser [bree•ZAI] *vt* shatter;
break open

britannique [bree•tah•NEEK]
adj British

brocart [bro•KAHR] *n* M
brocade

broche [braush] *n* F brooch;
skewer; spindle

brochure [brau•SHEWR] *n* F
brochure; pamphlet

brocoli [brau•ko•lee] *n* M
broccoli

broderie [brau•de•ree] *n* F
embroidery

bronzage [brauπ•ZAHZH] *n* M
tan

bronze [braunz] *n* bronze; *adj*
bronzé

brosse 1 [braus] *n* F hump

brosse 2 [braus] *n* F brush *vt vi*
refl brosser; ~ de chevaux\
hairbursh; ~ à dents\
toothbrush

brouillard [brwee•YAHR] *n* M
fog

brouillé [broo•YAI] *adj* blurry

brouillon [broo•YAUπ] *n* M
rough draft

bruine [brween] *n* F drizzle; *vi*
bruiner

bruissement [brew•ehs•MAHπ]
n M whir

bruit [brwee] *n* M noise; report;
rumor; ~ lourd\ thump

brûlant [brew•LAHπ] *adj* fiery

brûler [brew•LAI] *vi vt* burn;
scorch ; ~ légèrement\ singe

brûleur [brew•LUR] *n* M
burner

brume [brewm] *n* F haze; mist

brumeux [brew•MØ] *adj* misty;
vague; hazy

brun [brœn] *adj n* M brown

brunette [brew•NET] *n* F
brunette

brusque [brewsk] *adj* M abrupt;
impolite; curt; gruff

brutal [brew•TAHL] *adj* brutal

brute [brewt] *n* F brute

Bruxelles [brewk•SEL] *n* F
Brussels

bruyant [brew•YAHπ] *adj*
boisterous; noisy; loud
(vêtements)

bruyère [brew•YER] *n* F
heather

bûche [bewsh] *n* F log

bûcheron [bewsh•RAUπ] *n* M
lumberjack

budget [bew•JAI] *n* M budget

buffet [bew•FAI] *n* M buffet

buffle [BEW•fl] *n* M buffalo

buisson [bwee•SOπ] *n* M bush

Bulgarie [BEWL•gah•REE] *n* F
Bulgaria

bulldozer [bewl•dau•ZAIR] *n*
M bulldozer

bulle [bewl] *n* F bubble; *vi*
bouilloner

bulletin [bew•lu•TAπ] *n* M
bulletin; newsletter

bureau [bew•RO] *n* M bureau;
office; desk (école); ~ de
location\ *n* box office; ~ de
poste\ post office

bureaucratie
[bew•RO•krah•TEE] *n* F
bureaucracy

burette [bru•EHT] *n* F
wheelbarrow

buste [bewst] *n* M bust (of
statue)

but [bew] *n* M aim; goal

butin [bew•TAπ] *n* M booty;
loot

C

ça [sah] *adv* here; ~ et là\ here
and there

cabane [kah•BAHN] *n* F cabin;
shack

cabine [kah•BEEN] *n* F booth;
~ téléphonique\ phone booth

cabinet [kah•bee•NAI] *n* M
cabinet; office

câble [KAH•bl] *n* M cable; vi/vt câbler\ send a cable

cacahuète [kah•kah•WET] *n* F peanut

cacao [kah•KAH'O] *n* M cocoa

cache [kahsh] *n* F hiding place

caché [kah•SHAI] *adj* hidden

cacher [kah•SHEH] *vt* hide; conceal; *vi* se cacher\ avoid

cachette [kah•SHET] *n* F hiding place

cachot [ka•SHO] *n* M dungeon

cactus [kahk•TEW] *n* M cactus

cadavre [kah•DAHVR] *n* M cadaver; corpse

cadeau [kah•DO] *n* M gift; present

cadenas [kah•de•NAH] *n* M padlock

cadet [kah•DAI] *n* M cadet

cadran [kah•DRAHπ] *n* M dial

cadre [kahdr] *n* M setting; frame

cafard [kah•FAHR] *n* M cockroach

café [kah•FAI] *n* M coffee; coffee shop; diner

cafétéria [kah•FAI•tai•RYA] *n* F cafeteria

cafetière [kah•fe•TYER] *n* F coffee pot

cage [kahzh] *n* F cage; ~ de oiseau\ bird cage

cageot [kah•ZHO] *n* M crate

cahier [kah•YE] *n* notebook

caille [key] *n* F quail

cailler [kah•YAI] *vi* curdle; *vi* se cailler

caisse [kehs] *n* F till; ~ enregistreuse *n* F cash register

caissier -ère [keh•SYEH]; [kuh•SYEHR] *n* MF teller

calcium [kahl•CYEWM] *n* M calcium

calculatrice [KAHL•kew•lah•TREES] *n* F calculator

calculer [kahl•kew•LAI] *vt* calculate

cale [cahl] *n* F wedge

calendrier [kah•lahπ•DRYER] *n* M calendar

câliner [kah•lee•NAI] *vt* cuddle

calmant [kahl•MAHπ] *n* M painkiller

calme 1 [kahlme] *adj* calm; placid; *adj* inv untroubled; ~ froid\ dispassionate

calme 2 [kahlm] *n* M poise

calmement [kahl•mu•MAHπ] *adv* quietly

calmer [kahl•MAI] *vt vi refl* calm down

calomnie [KAH•laum•NEE] *n* F slander; *vt* calomnier

calomnieux [KAH•lauπ•NYØ] *adj* scurrilous

camarade [kah•mah•RAHD] *n* MF comrade; ~ de chambre\ roommate

Camboge [kahm•BOZH] *n* M Cambodia

cambrioleur [kahm•bryau•LUR] *n* M burglar

camée [kah•MAI] *n* M cameo

caméléon [kah•MAI•lai•AUπ] *n* M chameleon

cameraman [kah•mrah•MAHπ] *n* M cameraman

camion [kah•MYAUπ] *n* M
truck

camionnette
[kah•mee•au•NEHT] *n* F van

camionneur [-œr] *n* M truck
driver

commune [kau•MEWN] *n* MF
township

camp [kahmp] *n* M camp; *vi*
camper

campagne [kahm•PAHNYU] *n*
campaign; *vi* faire ~

campement [kahπp•MAHπ] *n*
M encampment

camping [kahm•PING] *n* M
campground

Canada [kah•nah•DAH] *n* M
Canada

canal [kah•NAHL] *n* M canal

canaliser [kah•NAH•lee•SEH]
vt channel; dig a channel

canapé [kah•nah•PAI] *n* F
couch; sofa

canard 1 [kah•NAHR] *n* M
duck

canard 2 [kah•NAHR] *n* M
hoax; false news;
sensationalism

canari [kah•nah•REE] *n* M
canary

cancer [kahπ•SER] *n* M cancer

cancre [kahπ•KR] *n* M dunce

candidat [kahn•dee•DAH] *n* M
candidate

caniche [kah•NEESH] *n* M
poodle

canif [kah•NEEF] *n* pocketknife

canin [kah•NAπ] *adj* canine

canne [kahn] *n* F cane

canneberge [kahn•BERZH] *n*
F cranberry

cannelle [kah•NEL] *n* F
cinnamon

cannibale [kah•nee•BAHL] *n*
MF cannibal

canoë [kah•NO] *n* M canoe

canon 1 [kah•NAUπ] *n* M
cannon

canon 2 [kah•NAUπ] *n* M
canon; law (eccles)

cañon [kah•NYAUπ] *n* canyon

canot [kah•NO] *n* M boat; ~ de
sauvetage\ lifeboat; ~ glisseur\
speedboat

canotage [kah•no•TAZH] *n* M
boating; *vt* faire du ~

canton [kahπ•TAUπ] *n* MF
township (Suisse)

canular 1 [kah•new•LAHR] *n*
M hoax

canular 2 [kah•new•LAHR] *vt*
vi bore (coll)

caoutchouc [kah•ou•CHOOK]
n M rubber

cap [kahp] *n* M cape (geog); de
pied en ~\ from head to toe;
mettre le ~ sur\ head for

capable [kah•pah•BL] *adj* able

capacité [kah•PAH•cee•TAI] *n*
F capacity; ability

cape [kahp] *n* F cape (clothing);
cloak

capitaine [kah•pee•TEN] *n* M
captain; skipper

capital [kah•pee•TAHL] assets;
capital

capitale [kah•pee•TAHL] *n* F
capital (ville, lettre)

capitalisme
[kah•pee•tah•LEEZM] *n* M
capitalism

câpre [kahpr] *n* F caper

caprice [kah•PREES] *n* M whim

capricieux; -euse [kah•pree•SYØ]; [-SYØZ] *adj* whimsical

capsule [kahp•sewl] *n* F capsule

captif [kahp•TEEF] *n* M captive

capturer [kahp•tew•RAI] *vt* capture; *n* F capture

capuchon [kah•pew•SHAUπ] *n* M hood

capucine [kah•pew•SEEN] *n* F nasturtium

caqueter [kah•ku•TAI] *vi* cackle

carafe [kah•RAHF] *n* F decanter

carcasse [kahr•KAHS] *n* F carcass

cardiaque [kahr•DYAHK] *adj* cardiac

cardigan [kahr•dee•GAHπ] *n* cardigan

cardinal [kahr•dee•NAHL] *adj; n* M cardinal

carectère [kah•rahk•TER] *n* M character

Carême [kah•REM] *n* M Lent

caresser [kah•re•SAI] *vt* fondle; stroke; pet; *n* F caresse

cargaison [kahr•gai•SAUπ] *n* M cargo

carillon [kah•ree•YAUπ] *n* M chime; *vi* carilloner

carnaval [kahr•nah•VAHL] *n* M carnival

carnivore [kahr•nee•VOR] *adj* carnivorous

carpe [kahrp] *n* F carp; wrist

carré [kah•REH] *adj; n* M square; tête ~\ obstinate person

carreau [kahr•o] *n* M tile; pane

carrefour [kah•ru•FOOR] *n* crossroads

carrière1 [kah•RYER] *n* F career

carrière 2 [kah•RYER] *n* F quarry

carrotte [kah•RAUT] *n* F carrot; trick; hoax

carte [kahrt] *n* F card; map;~ de crédit *n*\ credit card; ~ postale\ post card

cartilage [kahr•tee•LAHZH] *n* M gristle; cartillage

carton [kahr•TAUπ] *n* M cardboard; carton

cas [kah] *n* M case; en ~ de\ in case of; en tout ~\ in any case; in case au ~ où\ in case of

caserne [kah•SERN] *n* F barracks; ~ de pompiers\ fire station

casque [kahsk] *n* F headphones; helmet

casquette [kah•SKET] *n* F cap

casse-cou [kahs•KOO] *n* M daredevil

casse-noix; casse-noisette [kahs•NWAH] [-nwah•ZET] *npl* M nutcrackers

casserole [kah•su•RAUL] *n* F pan

cassette [kah•SET] *n* cassette

castor [kah•STOR] *n* M beaver

catalogue [kah•ta•LAUG] *n* M catalogue; *vt* cataloguer

catapulter [kah•tew•PEWL•TAI] *vt* catapult; *n* F catapulte

cataract [kah•tah•RAHKT] *n* F
cataract

catastrophe [kah•tah•STRAUF]
n F catastrophe

catégorie [kah•TAI•gau•REE] *n*
F category

catégorique
[kah•TAI•gau•REEK] *adj*
categorical; outright; *adv*
catégoriquement

cathédrale [kah•tai•DRAHL] *n*
F cathedral

catholique [kah•tau•LEEK] *adj*
n MF Catholic

cauchemar [kosh•MAHR] *n* M
nightmare

causer [KO•zai] *vt* cause; *n* F
cause

caustique [ko•STEEK] *adj*
caustic

caution [ko•SYOπ] *n* F bail;
sous ~\ on bail

cavalerie [kah•vahl•REE] *n* F
cavalry

cavalier 1 [kah•vah•LEEYEH]n
MF rider; horseman/woman

cavalier 2 [kah•vah•LYEH] *adj*
offhand; haughty; *adv*
cavalièrement

cave [kahv] *n* F cellar; wine
cellar

caverne [kah•VERN] *n* F cave

cavité [kah•vee•TAI] *n* F cavity

ce [suh] *dem pron* (c' with être)
he; she; it; this; that; they;
those; c'est un livre\ it is a
book; ce sont des hommes\
they are men; ç'a été vrai\ it
was true

ce; cette [suh]; [seht] *prép dém*
this; these; them (cet before
vowel)

céder [sai•DAI] *vt vi* cede;
yield; give way

cédille [sai•DEEY] *n* F cedilla

cèdre [sedr] *n* M cedar

ceinture [saπ•TEWR] f F belt;
girdle

célébration
[sai•lai•brah•SYAUπ] *n* F
celebration

célèbre [sai•LEBR] *adj* famous;
celebrated

célébrer [sai•lai•BRAI] *vt*
celebrate

célébrité [sai•lai•bree•TAI] *n* F
celebrity

celestial [se•le•STYAHL] *adj*
heavenly

célibataire 1
[sai•LEE•bah•TAIR] *n* M
bachelor

célibataire 2
[sai•LEE•bah•TAIR] *adj*
celibate

cellule [se•LEWL] *n* F cell

celte [selt] *adj* Celtic

celui/celle qui [sehl•WEE/sehl
kuh/] *pron*; *adj* he, she, it,
whom; whichever; celui qui
parle\ he who speaks

celui ci/celui là *pron* this one;
that one

cendre [sahπdr] *n* F ash; cinder

cendrier [sahπ•dree•AI] *n* M
ashtray

Cendrillon [sahπ•dree•YAUπ] *n*
F Cinderella

censeur [sahπ•sewr]
[sahπ•su•rai] *n* M censor; F
censorship; *vt* censurer

cent 1 [sahπ] *n* M penny

cent 2 [sahπ] *num* hundred

centenaire [sahπ•tu•NAIR] *n* M centennial

centième (see also fifth) [sahπ•TYEM] *num* hundredth

centigrade [sahπ•tee•GRAHD] *adj* centigrade

centimètre [sahπ•tee•METR] *n* M centimeter

central [sahπ•TRAHL] *adj* central

centre [sahπtr] *n* M center; hub; ~\ commercial shopping center

cependant [su•pahπ•DAHπ] *conj* however; yet; *adv* meanwhile

céramique [sai•rah•MEEK] *adj* ceramic

cerceau [ser•KO] *n* M hoop

cercle [serkl] *n* M circle

cercueil [ser•kœy] *n* M casket; coffin

céréale [sai•rai•ahl] *n* F cereal

cérémonie [sai•rai•mo•nee] *n* F ceremony

cerf [sehrf] *n* M deer; stag

cerf-volant [serf•váu•LAHπ] *n* M kite

cerise [se•REEZ] *n* F cherry

certain [ser•TEπ] *adj* certain; chose certaine\ a sure thing

certes [sert] *adv* to be sure; indeed

certainement [ser•teπ•MAHπ] *adv* certainly

certificat [ser•TEE•fee•KAH] *n* M certificate

certifier [ser•tee•FYAI] *vt* certify

certitude [ser•tee•TEWD] *n* F certainty

cerveau [ser•VO] *n* M brain; mind

cervelle [ser•VEHL] *n* F brains (anat)

cesser [se•SAI] *vt vi* cease; *vi* desist; cessez-le-feu\ cease-fire

chacal [shah•KAHL] *n* M jackal

chagrin [shah•GRAπ] *n* M grief

chaîne [shen] *n* F channel; chain

chair [sher] *n* flesh

chaire [sher] *n* F pulpit

chaise [shes] *n* F chair; seat ~ longue\ reclining chair

châle [shahl] *n* M shawl

chaleur [sha•LœR] *n* F warmth; heat; en ~ angry (coll)

chaleureux [shah•lœ•RØ] *adj* glowing; warm

chamailler [shah•mah•YAI] *vi refl* bicker

chambre [shahmbr] *n* F bedroom; chamber; lodgings; ~ d'amis\ guestroom; ~ d'enfants\ nursery

chameau [shah•MO] *n* M camel; dirty dog (coll)

champ [shahπ] *n* M field

champagne [shahπ•pan•YU] *n* M champagne

champignon [shahπ•pee•NYAUπ] *n* M fungus; mushroom

champion [shahπ•PYAUπ] *n* M champion

chance [shahs] *n* F luck; chance; opportunity; bonne ~!\ good luck; mal ~\ bad luck

chanceler [shahπs•LEH] *vi* stagger; reel; falter; *adj* chancelant

chancelier [shahπ•su•LYE] *n*
chancellor

changement [shahπzh•MAHπ]
n M shift; change; alteration;
vi refl changer

chanson [shahπ•SAUπ] *n* F
song

chantage [shahπ•TAZH] *n* M
blackmail; *vt* faire chanter

chanter [shahπ•TAI] *vt vi* sing

chaos [kah•aus] *n* M chaos

chapeau [shah•PO] *n* M hat

chapelle [shah•PEL] *n* F chapel

chapitre [shah•PEETR] *n* M
chapter

chaque [shahk] *adj* each; every;
~ fois\ whenever; each time

charabia [shah•rah•BYAH] *n* M
gibberish

characteristique
[kah•rahk•te•ree•STEEK] *n*
adj characteristic

charançon [shar•auπ•SOπ] *n* M
weevil

charbon [shahr•BAUπ] *n* M
coal

charbon de bois *n* M charcoal

charbone [shahr•BAUN] *n* M
carbon

chardon [shahr•DAUπ] *n* M
thistle

charge [sahr•ZHAI] *n* F burden;
vt charger

chariot [shah•ree•O] *n* M
trolley; ~ au supermarché\
shopping cart

charité [shah•ree•TAI] *n* F
charity

charmant [shahr•MAHπ] *adj*
charming; lovely

charme [shahrm] *n* M charm;
glamor; *vt* charmer

charmé [shahr•MEH] *adj*
spellbound; enchanted;
charmed

charnel [shahr•NEL] *adj* carnal

charnière [shahr•NYER] *n* F
hinge

charnu [shahr•NEW] *adj* fleshy

charpentier [shahr•pahπ•TYE]
n M carpenter

charpie [shahr•PEE] *n* F lint

charrette [shah•RET] *n* F cart

charrotte [shah•RAUT] *n* F
cart

charrue [shah•REW] *n* F plow

chasse [shahs] *n* F hunt; *vt*
chasser

chasse-neige [shahs-nehzh] *n*
M snowplow

chasseur [shah•SœR] *n* M
hunter

chaste [shahst] *adj* chaste

chasteté [shah•stu•TAI] *n* F
chastity

chat [shah] *n* M cat

chat matou [shah mah•TOO] *n*
M tomcat

châtaigne [shah•te•NYU] *n* F
chestnut

château [shah•TO] *n* M castle;
mansion

châtier [shah•TYAI] *vt* chastise

châtiment [sha•tee•MAUπ] *n*
M punishment

chaton [shah•TAUπ] *n* M kitten

chatouillement
[shah•tweey•MAHπ]: *n* M
tickle

chatouiller [shah•tweey•EH] *vt*
vi tickle

chaud; -e [sho]; [shod] *adj*
warm; spicy; j'ai ~\ I'm hot;
il fait ~\ it's hot

chauffage [sho•FAHZH] *n M*
heating

chauffé au rouge brûlant *adj*
red-hot

chauffe-plats [shof•PLAH] *n*
M hot-plate

chauffeur [sho•FUR] *n M*
chauffeur

chaume [shaum] *n M* thatch;
stubble (agriculture)

chaussette [shau•SEHT] *n F*
sock

chaussure [sho•SEWR] *n M*
shoe

chauve [shov] *adj* bald

chef [shef] *n M* chief; ~ de
cuisine\ chef; leader (pol)

chef-d'œuvre [she•DœVR] *n*
M masterpiece

chemin [she•MAπ] *n M* way;
road; path; course; ~ de fer\
railroad; ~ sentier\ pathway;
path; *vt* faire son ~\ thrive; à
mi-~\ halfway

cheminée [she•mee•NAI] *n F*
chimney; fireplace;
mantlepiece

chemise [she•MEEZ] *n F* shirt;
~ de nuit\ nightgown

chemisier [she•mee•SYE] *n M*
blouse

chenal [shu•NAHL] *n M*
channel

chêne [shen] *n M* oak; *adj* en
chêne

chenille [she•NEEY] *n F*
caterpillar; track; chenille
(textile)

cheque [sheck] *n F* check
(currency)

chéquier [shai•KYAI] *n M*
checkbook

cher [sher] *adj* dear; precious
valuable; ~ coûteux\
expensive; *vi* rendre ~\ endear

chercher 1 [sher•SHAI] *vt* seek;
look for; aller ~\ go look for;
envoyer ~\ send for

chéri [shai•REE] *adj n M*
darling

chérir [shai•REER] *vt* cherish

cheval [she•VAHL] *n* horse;
horse-power (auto); aller à ~\
go on horseback

chevalier [sheh•vahl•YEH] *n M*
knight; horseman; *vt* straddle

chevaucher [sheh•vau•SHEH]
vt ride horseback

cheveux [she•VØ] *n npl M*
hair; *vi* faire coupler le ~\ cut
one's hair; ~d'ange\ angel
hair; tinsel

chèvre [shevr] *n F* goat

chevron [she•VRAUπ] *n M*
rafter

chez [shai] *pre* at; with; to; in
among; at someone's home; ~
moi\ at my house; ~
Corneille\ in (the works of)
Corneille; je viens de ~ mon
oncle\ I am coming from my
uncle's house

chic [sheek] *n M* chic; high
style; *adj* chic stylish; smart

chicane [shee•KAHN] quibble;
argument; *vi* chicaner

chien [shyaπ] *n M* dog; cock; ~
de garde\ watch dog; ~ de
chasse/~courant\ hound

chiendent [shyen•DAHπ] *n* F
weed

chienne [shyen] nF bitch

chiffon [shee•FAUπ] *n* M rag

chiffre [sheefr] *n* M digit;
numeral; ~ d'affaires revenue

Chili [chee•LEE] *n* M Chile

chimie [shee•MEE] *n* F
chemistry

chimique [shee•meek] *adj*
chemical; produit M chimique

chimiste [shee•MEEST] *n* MF
chemist

chimpanzé [shanπ•pahπ•ZAI] *n*
M chimpanzee

Chine [sheen] *n* F China

chinois [shee•NWAH] *adj*
Chinese

chiot [shau] *n* M puppy

chlore [klaur] *n* M chlorine

chlorophylle [klau•rau•FEEL] *n*
F chlorophyll

choc [shauk] *n* M

chocolat [shau•kau•LAH] *n* M
chocolate

chœur [kœr] *n* M choir; chorus

choisi [shwah•ZEE] *adj* choice;
select

choisir [shwah•ZEER] *vi vt*
choose

choix [shwah] *n* M choice; au
~\ by choice; de ~\ first-class

choléra [kau•le•RAH] *n* M
cholera

chômage [sho•MAHZH] *n* M
unemployment

chômeur -euse [sho•MœR]
[ØZ] *adj; n* unemployed

choquer [shau•KEH] *vt* stun;
shock; clink (verres); *vi* se
choquer\ take offense

chose [shoz] *n* F thing

chou [shoo] *n* M cabbage

chou-fleur [shoo•FLUR] *n* M
cauliflower

chouette 1 [shweht] *n* F owl

chouette 2 [shweht] *adj* terrific;
swell

chrétien [krai•TYEπ] *adj n*
Christian

Christ [kreest] *n* M Christ

christianisme
[kree•styah•NEEZM] *n* M
Christianity

chrome [kraum] *n* M chrome

chronique 1 [krau•NEEK] *adj*
chronic

chronique 2 [krau•NEEK] *n* F
chronicle

chronologique
[krau•NAU•lau•ZHEEK] *adj*
chronological

chronomètre
[krau•nau•MEHTR] *n* M
stopwatch

chrysanthème
[kree•zahπ•TEM] *n* M
chrysanthemum

chucotement [shoo•co•TMEπ]
n M whisper

chucoter [shoo•co•TEH] *vt; vi*
whisper

chute [shewt] *n* F fall; drop;
downfall; ~ d'eau\ waterfall;
~ de neige\ snowfall; ~ de
pluie\ rainfall; *vt* faire une ~\
fall; tumble

ci [see] dem *pron* this; *adv* here;
herein; cet; homme-ci this
man; par-ci par-là here and
there; ci-après below;

ci-contre\ opposite; ci-dessus above

cible [seebl] *n* F target

cicatrice [see•kah•TREES] *n* F scar

cidre [see•dr] *n* M cider

ciel [syel] *n* M sky; heaven; paradise; arc en ~\ rainbow; à ciel ouvert\ uncovered; outdoors

cigare [see•GAHR] *n* M cigar

cigarette [see•gah•RET] *n* F cigarette

cigogne [see•GAUNY] *n* F stork

cil [seel] *n* M eyelash

cimenter [see•mahπ•TAI] *vt* cement; *n* M ciment

cimitière [see•mee•TYER] *n* M cemetery

cinéma [see•nai•MAH] *n* M cinema

cinglant [saπ•GLAπ] *adj* scathing

cinglé [saπ•GLAI] *adj* loony; out of it (coll)

cinq [saπk] *num* five

cinquante [saπ•KAHπT] *num* fifty

cinquantième [saπ•kahπ•TYEM] *num* fiftieth

cinquième (see also eighth) [saπ•KYEM] *num* fifth

cintre [saπ•tr] M hanger

cirage [see•RAHZH] *n* M shoe polish

circoncision [seer•kaun•see•ZYAUπ] *n* F circumcision

circonférence [seer•KAUπ•fai•RAHπS] *n* F circumference; girth

circonflex [seer•kauπ•FLEKS] *adj* circumflex

circonstance [seer•kauπ•STAπS] *n* F circumstances; de ~\ special; fit for the occasion

circuit [seer•KWEE] *n* M circuit

circulaire [seer•kew•LAIR] *adj* circular

circulation [seer•kew•lah•SYAUπ] *n* F circulation

circuler [seer•kew•LAI] *vt* circulatevi; *vi* faire circuler

cire [see•ur] *n* F wax; *vt vi* cirer

cirque [seerk] *n* F circus

ciseau [see•ZO] *n* M chisel

ciseler [see•ZLEH] *vt* cut; chisel; chase (argent)

ciseaux *mpl* [see•ZO] *n* scissors

citation [see•tah•SYAUπ] *n* F quotation; estimate; subpoena (loi)

citer [see•TAI] *vt* quote; estimate; cite

citerne [see•TEHRN] *n* F tank

cithare [see•TAHR] *n* F zither

citoyen [see•twah•YEπ] *n* M citizen

citron [see•TRAUπ] *n* M lemon

citronnade [see•trau•NAHD] *n* F lemonade

civil [see•VEEL] *n* M civilian; *adj* civil; polite

civilisation [see•VEE•lee•sah•SYAUπ] *n* civilization

civiliser [see•VEE•lee•ZAI] *vt* civilize

civique [see•VEEK] *adj* civic

civoulette [see•voo•LET] *n* F chive

clair [klair] *adj* clear; light; transparent; obvious; *n* M clarity; light; ~ de lune\ moonlight; *vi* s'éclaircir (become clear)

clairement [kler•MAHπ] *adv* clearly; plainly

clairon [clai•RAUπ] *n* M bugle

clan [klahπ] *n* M clan

clandestin [klahπ•de•STAπ] *adj* clandestine; covert

clapier [klah•PYE] *n* M hutch

claque [klahk] *n* F whack; hired applauders (theat.)

claquer [klah•KEH] *vt* clap; slap; ~ la porte au nez de qq'un\ slam

clarifier [klah•ree•FYAI] *vt* clarify

clarinette [klah•ree•NET] *n* F clarinet

clarté [klahr•TAI] *n* F clarity

classe [klahs] *n* F class; *vt* classier

classifier [klah•see•FYAI] *vt* classify

classique [kah•SEEK] *adj n* M classic; classical

clause [kloz] *n* F clause

clavecin [klah•ve•SAπ] *n* M harpsichord

clavier [klah•VYE] *n* M keyboard

clé [kleh] *n* F key; wrench; sous ~\ under lock and key

clef de sol [kleh duh SAUL] *n* F treble clef

clergé [kler•ZHAI] *n* M clergy

client [klee•AHπ] *n* M client; customer; patron

clientèle [klee•ahπ•TEL] *n* F clientele

clignoter [klee•nyo•TAI] *vi* blink

climat [klee•MAH] *n* M climate

climatisation [klee•MAH•tee•za•SYOπ] *n* F air•conditioning

climatisé [klee•MAH•tee•ZAI] *adj* air-conditioned

clin [klaπ] *n* M twinkling; ~ d'oeil\ wink

clinique [klee•NEEK] *n* F clinic; *adj* clinical

clivage [klee•VAHZH] *n* F cleavage

cliver [klee•VEH] *vt* split

clochard -e [klau•SHAHR] [-SHAHRD] *n* MF tramp

cloche [klaush] *n* F bell

clocher 1 [klau•SHEH] *vt* limp, hobble

clocher 2 [klau•SHEH] *n* M steeple; belfy

cloison [clwah•ZAUπ] *n* M partition

cloître [klwah•TR] *n* M cloister

clôture [klo•TEWR] *n* F fence

clou [kloo] *n* M nail; spike; *vt* clouer

clown [kloon] *n* M clown; *vi* faire le clown

cobaye [kau•BAHY] *n* M guinea pig

cocaïne [ko•kah•EEN] *n* F cocaine

cochon [kau•SHAUπ] *n* M hog; pig

cocktail [kauk•TEL] *n* M cocktail

cocon [kau•KAUπ] *n* cocoon

code [kaud] *n* F cole; law

cœur [kœr] *n* M heart ; courage; feeling; ~ brisé\ broken hearted; par ~\ by heart; un homme de ~\ brave man

coffre [kaufr] *n* M chest; box hamper

coffrer [kau•freh] *vt* lock up

cognac [kau•NYAK] *n* M brandy

cohérent [kau•ai•RAHπ] *adj* coherent

cohue [kau•EW] *n* F rabble

coiffeur [kwah•FEUR] *n* M barber; hairdresser

coiffure [kwah•FEWR] *n* F hairstyle

coin [kwahπ] *n* M corner

coincer [ko•aπ•SEH] *vt* wedge

coïncidence [kau•Aπ•see•DAHπS] *n* F coincidence

coïncider [kau•aπ•see•DAI] *vi* coincide

col [kaul] *n* M collar; neck

colère [koh•LEHR] *n* F wrath; anger; *vt* mettre en ~

colérique [kau•lai•REEK] *adj* hot-tempered

colis [kau•LEE] *n* M package; packet; parcel

collaborer [kah•LAH•bau•RAI] *vi* collaborate

collant [kau•LAHπ] *n* M pantihose

colle [kaul] *n* F glue; *vt* coller

collection [ko•lek•SYUπ] *n* F collection

collectioner [ko•LEK•syuπ•EH] *vt* collect

collègue [kau•LEG] *n* mf colleague

coller [kau•LEH] *vt* stick; paste

colline [kau•LEEN] *n* F hill

colombe [kau•LAUπB] *n* F dove

colonie [kau•lau•NEE] *n* F colony; settlement

colonne [kau•LAUN] *n* F column; ~ vertébrale\ spinal column

coloré [kau•lau•RAI] *adj* colorful

colorer [kau•lau•RAI] *vt* color; dye; tint

colossal [kau•lau•SAHL] *adj* colossal

colporter [kaul•paur•TAI] *vt* peddle; *vi* faire le colportage

coma [kau•MAH] *n* M coma

combat [kauπ•BAH] *n* M bout; combat; battle

combattre [kauπ•BAHTR] *vt vi* fight; battle; combat

combinaison [kauπ•bee•nai•ZAUπ] *n* F combination

combiner [kauπ•bee•NAI] *vt* combine

combustible [kauπ•bew•STEEBL] *n* M fuel; *adj* combustible

comédie [kau•mai•DEE] *n* F comedy

comestible [kau•me•STEEBL] *adj* edible

comète [kau•MET] *n* F comet

comique [kau•MEEK] n M
comic; comedian

comité [kau•mee•TAI] n F
committee

commandant
[kau•mahπ•DAHπ] n M
commander

comme [kaum] adv; as; like;
how; in; the way of; conj as;
faites ~ moi\ do as I do; ~ il
est bon\ how kind he is; ~
mort\ almost dead

commemoratif
[kau•ME•mau•rah•TEEF] adj
memorial; commemorative

commencement
[kau•mœπs•MAHπ] n M
starting; beginning

commencer [ko•mahn•SAI] vt
vi begin; commence (école);
start

comment [kau•MAHπ] adv
how; interj what? why?

commentaire
[kau•mahπ•TAIR] n M
commentary; comment

commérage [kau•mai•RAHZH]
n M gossip

commerçant -e
[kauπ•mehr•SAHπ];
[-SAHNT] n MF storekeeper;
tradesman/-woman

commerce [kau•MERS] n M
commerce; trade; trading

commercial [co•mer•SYAHL]
adj F business

commisariat
[kau•MEE•sah•RYAH] n M
police station

commettre [kau•METR] vt
commit

commissaire [kau•mee•SER] n
M commissioner

commission [kau•mee•SYAUπ]
n commission

commode [kau•MAUD] n F
dresser; chest of. drawers

commodité
[kau•MAU•dee•TAI] n F
convenience

commotion [kau•mau•SYAUπ]
n F commotion

commun; -e [kau•Mœπ];
[-MEWN] adj vulgar;
mediocre; undistinguished

communauté
[kau•MEW•no•TAI] n F
community

communion
[kau•mew•NYAUN] n F
communion

communiquer
[kau•MEW•nee•KAI] vt/vi
communicate

communisme
[kau•mew•NEEZM] n M
communism

communiste
[kau•mew•NEEST] adj n mf
M communist

compact [kauπ•PAHKT] adj
compact

compagnie [kaun•pah•NYEE] n
F company; corporation

compagnon
[kauπ•pah•NYAUπ] n M
companion; F compagne

comparaison
[kaun•pah•rai•ZAUπ] n F
comparison

comparer [kauπ•pah•RAI] vt
compare

compartiment
[kauπ•PAHR•tee•MAHπ] *n* M
compartment

compassion
[kauπ•pah•SYAUπ] *n* F
compassion; sympathy

compatible [kauπ•pah•TEEBL]
adj compatible

compatissant -e
[kauπ•PAH•tee•SAHπ];
[-SAHNT] *adj* sympathetic;
compassionate

compétence [kauπ•pai•TAHπS]
n F proficiency; skill;
competence

compétent [kauπ•pai•TAHπ] *n*
competent

complaisant [kauπ•ple•ZAHπ]
adj complacent

complet complète
[kauπ•PLEH]; [-PLEHT] *adj*
whole

complexe [kauπ•PLEKS] *n* M
complex; hang-up (coll)

complice mf [cauπ•PLEES] *n*
M accomplice

compliqué [kauπ•plee•KAI] *adj*
complicated; intricate

compliquer [kauπ•plee•KAI] *vt*
complicate

complot [kauπ•PLAU] *n* M
plot; conspiracy; scheme; *vi*
comploter

comportement
[kom•POR•tu•MAHπ] *n* M
behavior; demeanor

comporter [kom•por•TAI] *vi*
refl behave

composant [kauπ•pau•ZAHπ] *n*
M component

composé [kauπ•pau•ZAI] *adj*
compound; *n* M compound;
composed (of)

compositeur -trice
[kauπ•PAU•zee•TœR];
[-TREES] *n* MF song-writer;
n M composer

composition
[kauπ•PAU•zee•SYAUπ] *n* F
composition

compréhensible
[kauπ•preh•ahπ•SEEBL] *adj*
inv understandable

comprendre [kauπ•PRAHπDR]
vt comprehend; understand;
include

comprimé [kauπ•pree•MEH] *n*
MF tablet; pill (med)

comprimer [kauπ•pree•MAI] *vt*
compress

comptabilité
[kauπ•tah•bee•lee•TAI] *n* F
bookkeeping

comptable [kauπ•TAHBL] *n*
MF bookkeeper

compte [kauπt] *n* F account;
tally; ~ d'épargne\ savings
account; ~ joint\ joint account

compte-minutes
[kauπt-mee•NEWT] *n* inv M
timer

compter [kauπ•TAI] *vt* reckon;
count; rely

compteur [kauπ•TœR] *n* m
computer; meter

comptine [kauπ•TEEN] *n* F
nursery rhyme

comptoir [kauπ•TWAHR] *n* M
counter

comté [kauπ•TAI] *n* M county

comtesse [kauπ•TES] *n* F
countess

concéder [kauπ•sai•DAI] *vt/vi*
concede

concept [kauπ•SEPT] *n* M
concept

conception erronée *vt* F
misconception

concert [kauπ•SER] *n* M
concert

concession [kauπ•se•SYAUπ] *n*
F concession

concevoir [kauπ•su•VWAHR]
vt/vi conceive; *vt* devise

concierge [kauπ•SYERZH] *n*
M janitor

concis [kauπ•SEE] *adj* concise

conclure [kauπ•KLEWR] *vt/vi*
conclude

concombre [kauπ•KAUπBR] *n*
M cucumber

concourir [kauπ•coo•REER] *vi*
compete; *vt* faire concurrence

concours [kauπ•KOOR] *n*
contest

concret [kauπ•KRE] *adj n* M
concrete

concerner [kauπ•sur•NEH] *vt*
refer

condamnation
[kauπ•DAHπ•nah•SYAUπ] *n*
F condemnation; ~ à
perpétuité\ life sentence

condamner [kauπ•dahπ•NAI]
vt condemn

condenser [kauπ•dahπ•SAI]
vt/vi refl condense

condescendant
[kauπ•DE•sahπ•DAHπ] *adj*
condescending; patrionizing

condiment [kauπ•dee•MAHπ]
n M relish

condition [kauπ•dee•SYAπ] *n*
F condition; state;
circumstans; ~s
atmosphériques *npl*\ weather
conditions

conditionner
[kauπ•DEE•syaπ•NEH] *vi*
condition; season

condoléances
[kauπ•DAU•lai•AHπS] *npl* F
condolences

conduire [kauπ•DWEEUR] *vt*
steer; drive (auto)

conduite [kauπ•DWEET] *n*
duct; *n* M conduit (anat)

cône [kon] *n* F cone

confédération
[kauπ•FAI•dai•rah•SYAUπ] *n*
F confederation

conférence [kauπ•fai•RAHπS]
n F conference; lecture

conférer [kauπ•fai•RAI] *vt*
bestow

confesser [kauπ•fai•SAI] *vt/vi
refl* confess

confession [kauπ•fai•SYAUπ]
n F confession

confiance [kauπ•feey•AHπs]; *n*
F secret; confidence; ~ en soi\
self-confidence; *vt* faire ~ à\
confide in

confident [kauπ•fee•DAHπ] *n*
M confidant

confidentiel
[kauπ•fee•dahπ•SYEL] *adj*
confidential

confier [kauπ•fee•EH] *vt/vi refl*
confide

confiner [kauπ•fee•NAI] *vt*
confine

confirmation
[kauπ•FEER•ma•SYAUπ] *n* F
confirmation

confirmer [kauπ•feer•MAI] *vt*
confirm

confiserie [kauπ•fe•EZREE] *n*
F confectionery

confisquer [kauπ•fee•SKAI] *vt*
confiscate

confiture [kauπ•fee•TOOR] *n* F
preserves; jam; ~ d'oranges\
marmalade

conflit [kauπ•FLEE] *n* M
conflict; *vi* être en conflit

confondre [kauπ•FAUπDR] *vt*
confound;confuse

conformer [kauπ•faur•MAI]
vt/vi conform

conformiste
[kauπ•faur•MEEST] *adj n* MF
conformist

confort m [kauπ•FAUR] *n* M
comfort

confortable
[kauπ•faur•TAHBL] *adj*
comfortable; snug

confrérie [kauπ•frai•REE] *n* F
fraternity

confronter [kauπ•frauπ•TAI] *vt*
confront; compare (texts)

confusion [kauπ•fyoo•SYAUπ]
n F confusion

congé [kauπ•ZHAI] *n* M
holiday; leave (mil)

congédier [kauπ•zhai•DYAI] *vt*
dismiss

congélateur
[kauπ•ZHAI•lah•TœR] *n* M
freezer

congère [kauπ•ZHEHR] *n* F
snowdrift

congestion
[kauπ•zhe•STYAUπ] *n* F
congestion

conjecture [kauπ•zhek•TEWR]
n F guess

conjonction
[kauπ•shauπk•SYAUπ] *n* F
conjunction

conjugaison
[kauπ•ZHOO•gai•ZAUπ] *n* F
conjugation

connaissance [kau•ne•SAHπS]
n F acquaintance; knowledge

conquérant [kauπ•kai•RAHπ]
n M conqueror

conquérir [kauπ•kai•REER] *vt*
conquer

conquête [kauπ•KET] *n* F
conquest

consacrer [kauπ•sah•KRAI] *vt*
consecrate; devote

conscience [kauπ•SYAHπS] *n*
F conscience

consciencieux
[kauπ•syahπ•SYØ] *adj*
conscientious

conscient [kohπ•SYAHπ] *adj*
aware; conscious

consécutif
[kauπ•SAI•kew•TEEF] *adj*
consecutive

conseil [kauπ•SEY] *n* M advice;
counsel; conseil M; (lawyer)
avocat M *n* counsel; counselor

conseiller [kauπ•se•YAI] *vt*
advise

conseils [kauπ•SEY] *npl* M
guidance

consentement
[kauπ•sahπt•MAHπ] *n* M
consent; *vi* consentir

conséquant [kauπ•sai•KAHπ]
adj consistent

conséquence
[kauπ•sai•KAHπS] *n* F
consequence; sequel (film)

conservaduer
[kauπ•ser•vah•DœR] *n* M
conservative

conserver [kauπ•ser•VEH] *vt*
preserve; keep; maintain; *vi* se
conserver

considérable
[kauπ•SEE•dai•RAHBL] *vt*
considerable; extensive

considérer [kauπ•SEE•dai•RAI]
vt consider; ponder

consistance
[kauπ•see•STAHπS] *n* F
consistency

consister [kauπ•see•STAI] *vt*
consist

consolation
[kauπ•SAU•lah•SYAUπ] *n* F
consolation; solace

consoler [kauπ•sau•LAI] *vt*
console

consolider
[kauπ•SAU•lee•DAI] *vt*
consolidate

consommateur
[kauπ•SAU•mah•TœR] *n*
consumer

consommation
[kauπ•SAU•mah•SYAUπ] *n*
consumption

consommer 1 [kauπ•sau•MAI]
vt consume

consommer 2 [kauπ•sau•MAI]
vt consummate

consonne [kauπ•SAUN] *n* F
consonant

conspiration
[kauπ•SPEE•rah•SYAUπ] *n* F
conspiracy

constante [kauπ•STAHπ] *n* F
constant (math); *adj* constant;
steadfast

constellation
[kauπ•STE•lah•SYAUπ] *n*
constellation

consternation
[kauπ•STER•nah•SYAUπ] *n*
dismay; *vi* consterner

constituant
[kauπ•STEE•tew•AHπ] *n* M
constituent

constitution
[kauπ•STEE•tew•SYAUπ] *n* F
constitution

constrainte [kauπ•STRAπT] *n*
F constraint

construire [kauπ•STRWEER]
vt construct

consulat [kauπ•sew•LAH] *n* M
consulate

contageux [kauπ•tah•ZHØ] *adj*
contagious

contaminer
[kauπ•TAH•mee•NAI] *vt*
contaminate

contarier [kauπ•TAH•reey•EH]
vt thwart

conte [kaunt] *n* M tale; story; ~
de fées\ fairy tale

contempler [kauπ•tahπ•PLAI]
vt/vi contemplate

contemporain
[kauπ•TAHπ•pau•RAπ] *adj/n*
contemporary

contenir [kauπ•te•NEER] *vt*
contain

content [kauπ•TAHπ] *adj* glad;
pleased; content

contenu [kauπ•te•NEW] *n* M
contents

contester [kauπ•te•STAI] *vt*
contest

contexte [kauπ•TEKST] *n* M
context

continent [kauπ•tee•NAHπ] *n*
M continent; mainland

continu [kauπ•tee•NEW] *adj*
continuous; continual;
unbroken

continuation
[kauπ•TEE•new•ah•SYAUπ] *n*
F continuation

continuel [kauπ•TEE•new•EL]
adj continual

continuellement
[kauπ•TEE•new•el•MAHπ]
adv continually

contion préalable
[prai•ah•LAHBL] *adj*
prerequisite

contraction
[kauπ•trahk•SYAUπ] *n* F
contraction

contraindre [kauπ•TREπDR] *vt*
coerce; ~ obliger *vt*\ compel

contraire; au contraire
[kauπ•TRAIR] *adj/n* contrary;
~ inverse *n* M\ converse;
reverse

contrairer [kaun•treh•RYEH] *vt*
annoy

contraste [kauπ•TRAHST] *n* M
contrast; par ~ ; avec ~\ in
contrast (to); *vt* contraster

contrat [kauπ•TRAH] *n*
covenant; contract; *vt*
contracter

contre [koπtr] *prép* against; *adv*
near; tout ~\ nearby

contre-cœur [kauπ•tr•KœR] *adj*
reluctant

contrebalancer
[kauπ•TRU•bah•lahπ•SAI] *vt*
counteract

contrecoup [kohπ•truh•COO] *n*
M backlash

contrediction
[kauπ•TRU•deek•SYAUπ] *n* F
contradiction

contredire [kauπ•tru•DEER] *vt*
contradict

contremaître [kauπ•tr•METR]
n M foreman; overseer

contreplaqué
[kauπtr•plah•KAI] *n* M
plywood

contribuable
[kauπ•tree•bew•AHBL] *n* MF
taxpayer

contribution
[kauπ•TREE•bew•SYAUπ] *n*
F contribution

contrôle [kauπ•TROL] *n* M
control; ~ des naissances\
birth control

contrôleur [kauπ•tro•LœR] *n* M
controller

controverse [kauπ•trau•VERS]
n F controversy

convaincant [kauπ•vaπ•KAHπ]
adj convincing

convaincre [kauπ•VAπKR] *vt*
convince

convalescence
[kauπ•vah•lai•SAHπS] *n* F
convalescence

convalescent
[kauπ•vah•lai•SAHπ] *adj/s* M
convalescent

convenable [kauπ•ve•NAHBL]
adj fit; convenient

convention
[kauπ•vahn•SYAUπ] *n* F
convention

converger [kauπ•ver•ZHAI] *vi*
converge

conversation
[kauπ•VER•sah•SYAUπ] *n* F
conversation

converser [kauπ•ver•SAI] *vi*
converse

conversion [kauπ•ver•zyauπ] *n*
F conversion

converti m; *vt/vi refl* convertir
[kauπ•ver•TEE] *n* convert

convexe [kauπ•VEKS] *adj*
convex

convoi [kauπ•VWAH] *n* M
convoy

convoiter [kauπ•vwah•TAI] *vt*
covet

coopération
[kau•AU•pai•rah•SYAUπ] *n*
cooperation

coopérer [kau•AU•pai•RAI] *vi*
cooperate

coordination
[kau•AUR•dee•nah•SYAUπ] *n*
F coordination

copain [kau•PEπ] *n* M pal; F
copine [kay•PEEN]

copie [KAU•pee] *n* F copy

copieux [kau•PYØ] *adj* copious

copyright [kau•pee•RUYT] *n*
M copyright

coq [kauk] *n* M cock

coque [kauk] *n* F hull

coquelicot [kauk•lee•KAU] *n*
M poppy

coquille [kau•KEEY] *n* F shell;
~ Saint-Jacques\ scallop

coquin; -e [kau•KAπ]; [-EEN]
adj villain; scoundrel

corail [kau•RAY] *n* M coral

corbeau [kaur•BO] *n* M raven

corbeille [kor•BEY] *n* F basket;
flower bed; wedding presents;
~ à papier M\ waste-paper
basket

corbillard [kaur•bee•YAHR] *n*
M hearse

corde [kaurd] *n* F rope

corde [kaurd] *n* F cord; M
cordon

cordial [kaur•DYAHL] *adj*
genial; hearty

Corée [kau•RAI] *n* F Korea

corneille [kaur•NEY] *n* crow

cornemuse [kornuh•MEWZ] *n*
F bagpipes

corniche [kaur•NEESH] *n* F
cornice

coroner [kau•rau•NœR] *n*
coroner

corporel [kaur•pau•REL] *adj*
corporal

corps [kaur] *n* M body; matter;
group (mil); ~ législatif\
legislature

corpulent -e [kaur•pew•LAHπ];
[-LAHNT] *adj* stout; portly;
fat

correct [kau•REKT] *adj* correct;
accurate

correctement
[kau•rekt•MAHπ] *adv*
correctly

correctement; convenablement [kau•rekt•MAHπ] *adv* properly

correction [kau•rek•SYAUπ] *n* F correction

correspondance [kau•RE•spauπ•DAHπs] *n* F correspondence

correspondant [kau•RE•spauπ•DAHπT] *n* M correspondent; *adj* corresponding

correspondre [kau•re•SPAUπDR] *vi* correspond

corridor [kau•ree•DAUR] *n* M corridor

corriger [kaur•ree•ZHEH] *vt* correct; reform; adjust; punish

corrompu [kau•rauπ•POO] *adj* corrupt; *vt* corrompre

corrosion [kau•rau•ZYAUπ] *n* F corrosion

corruption [kau•rewp•SYAUπ] *n* F corruption

Corse [kaurs] *n* F Corsica

cosmétique [kau•smai•TEEK] *n* M *adj* cosmetic

cosmopolite [kau•SMAU•pau•LEET] *n* MF *adj* cosmopolitan

cosse [kaus] *n* F pod; husk; shell

costume [kau•STEWM] *n* M costume

côte 1 [kot] *n* F coast; rib; hill; coast; ~ à ~\ side by side

côte 2 [kot] *n* M side; district; aspect; rating

coteau [kau•TO] *n* M hillside; knoll

côtelette [kau•TLET] *n* F cutlet; chop

coton [kau•TAUπ] *n* M cotton

cottage [kau•TAHZH] *n* M cottage

cou [koo] *n* M neck

couche 1 [koosh] *n* M bed; couch

couche 2 [koosh] *n* M social strata; layer; film; coat (peinture)

coucher [koo•SHAI] *n* M night's lodging; *vt* put to be; *vi* se coucher\ go to bed

coude [kood] *n* M elbow; angle

coudre [koodr] *vt vi* sew

coulant [koo•LAHπ] *n* F fluent; running; flowing

couleur [koo•LœR] *n* F color; paint; dye

couloir [kool•WAHR] *n* M hallway

coup [koo] *n* M blow; knock; stroke; hit; thrust; ~ de couteau\ slash; ~ tonnerre\ thunderclap; ~ d'œil furtif\ peep; ~ de feu\ gunshot; ~ de fil\ phone call; ~\ kick; ~ de poing; punch; ~ de veine\ fluke; ~ de vent gale; tout d'un ~\ all at once

coupable [koo•PAHBL] *n* MF culprit; *adj* guilty

coupe [koop] *n* F de cheveux haircut

couper [koo•PAI] *vt* cut; cut off; sever; intercept; *vi* se couper\ contradict oneself; intersect

couperet [koo•pe•RAI] *n* M
cleaver

couple [koopl] *n* M couple; pair
vt coupler

coupon [koo•PAUπ] *n* coupon

cour [koor] *n* F courtyard; ~ de
récréation\ playground

courage [koo•RAHZH] *n* M
courage

courageux [koo•rah•ZHØ] *adj*
courageous; gallant

courant -e [kur•AHπ];
[kur•AHNT] *adj* running; *n* M
stream

courbe [koorb] *n* F curve; *vt*
faire une ~

courbé [koor•BAI] *adj* bent; ~
tordu\ crooked

courber [koor•BEH] *vt* bend;
curve; *vi* se courbe bend;
stoop

coureur [koo•RœR] *n* F runner

courir [kur•EEUR] *vt* run; be
current; pursue; run after; ~ le
monde\ travel the world

couronnement
[koo•raun•MAHπ] *n*
coronation

courrier [koo•RYAI] *n* M
courier

courroie [ku•RWAH] *n* F strap;
belt (mech)

courrone [koo•RAUN] *n* F
crown; *vt* courroner

cours [koor] *n* M course;
stream; avenue; donner libre ~
à\ give free rein

course [koors] *n* F errand; *vt*
faire une ~\ run an errand

coursier [kur•seey•EH] *n* M
steed

courtier [koor•TYE] *n* M
broker

courtois [koor•TWAH] *adj*
gracious; courteous

courtoisie [koor•twah•ZEE] *n* F
courtesy

cousin 1 [koo•ZAπ] *n* M cousin

cousin 2 [koo•ZAπ] *n* M gnat

coussin [koo•SAπ] *n* M cushion

coût [koo] *n* M cost; *npl*
expenses; *vt vi* coûter

couteau [koo•TO] *n* M knife;
coup de ~\ stab

coûteux [koo•TØ] *adj* costly

coutume [koo•TEWM] *n* F
custom; wont

couture [koo•TEWR] *n* F seam;
sewing

couturier [koo•tewr•ee•AI] *n* F
ladies' tailor; fashion designer

couvent [koo•VAHπ] *n* M
convent

couvercle [koo•VERKL] *n* M
lid

couvert 1 [koo•VER] *adj*
overcast

couvert 2 [koo•VER] *n* M table
things (dishes, etc)

couverts [koo•VER] *spl* M
cutlery

couverture [koo•ver•TEWR] *n*
F covering; blanket

couvre-feu [koo•vru•FØ] *n* F
curfew

couvrir [koo•VREER] *vt* cover;
wrap up; protect

cow-boy *n* M cowboy

crabe [krahb] *n* M crab

crachat [krah•SHAH] *n* M spit;
spittle

cracher [krah•SHEH] *vt* spit; cough up

craie [crai] *n* F chalk

craintif [crai π•TEEF] *adj* fearful

cramoisi [krah•mwah•ZEE] *adj* crimson

crampe [krahπp] *n* F cramp; *vt* cramponner

crampon [krahπ•PAUπ] *n* M clamp; *vt* cramponner

crâne [krahn] *n* M skull

crapaud [krah•PO] *n* M toad

craquelin [krah•KLAπ] *n* M cracker

craquer [krah•KAI] *vi* creak

crasse [krahs] *n* F grime

crasseux [krah•SØ] *adj* F grimy

cratère [krah•TER] *n* M crater

cravate [krah•VAHT] *n* F tie; neck-tie

crayon [kre•YAUπ] *n* M crayon; pencil

créateur [krai•ah•TØR] *n* M creator

créatif [krai•ah•TEEF] *adj* creative

création [krai•ah•SYAUπ] *n* F creation

créature [krai•ah•TEWR] *n* F creature

crédit [krai•DEE] *n* M credit; *vt* créditer

crédule [krai•DEWL] *adj* gullible

créer [krai•AI] *vt* create

crème [krem] *n* F cream; ~ à raser\ shaving cream; ~ anglaise\ custard

crémeux [krai•MØ] *adj* creamy

crêpe [krep] *n* M crepe; pancake

crépuscule [krai•pew•sewl] *n* M dusk; twilight

crête [kreht] *n* F ridge; crest; summit

creuser [krØ•ZAI] *vt* excavate; hollow out

creux [krØ] *adj* hollow

crevaison [kru•ve•ZAUπ] *n* F puncture; *vt* crever

crevette [cre•VET] *n* F shrimp

cri [kree] *n* M cry; shout; whoop; le dernier ~\ the latest thing

crier [kreey•EH] *vi* cry; scream; shout; yell

crime [kreem] *n* M crime; felony

criminel [kree•mee•NEL] *adj n* M criminal; felon

crinière [kree•NYER] *n* F mane

crique [kreek] *n* cove; creek

cris [cree] *npl* M clamor

crise [kreez] *n* F crisis; ~ de colère\ tantrum; ~ cardiaque\ heart attack; ~ de nerfs\ hysterics; ~ nerveuse\ nervous breakdown

crisser [kree•seh] *vt; vi* squeal; squeak

cristal [kree•STAHL] *n* M crystal

critère [kree•TER] *n* M criterion

critique [kree•TEEK] *n* M critic; *n* F criticism

critiquer [kree•tee•KAI] *vt vi* criticize

croc [krauk] *n* M fang

crochet [krau•CHAI] *n* M bracket (in writing); crochet; hook (peche)

crocodile [krau•kau•DEEL] *n* M
crocodile

croire [krwahr] *vt vi* believe;
think; ~ à\ believe in; s'en ~\
be conceited

croisade [krwah•SAHD] *n* F
crusade

croisé [krwah•ZAI] *adj*
double-breasted

croiser [krwah•ZAI] *vt* intersect;
vi se croiser

croisière [krwah•ee•AIR] *vi*
cross; meet; *n* F cruise

croissance [krwah•SAHπS] *n* F
growth

croissant [krwah•SAHπ] *n* M
crescent; crescent roll; *adj*
growing; increasing

croix [krwah] *n* F cross; en ~\
crosswise; Croix-Rouge\ Red
Cross

croquer [krau•KAI] *vt vi*
munch; crunch

croquis [krau•KEE] *n* M sketch;
rough draft; outline

croustillant [kroo•stee•YAHπ]
adj crisp

croûte1 [kroot] *n* M crust

croûte 2 [kroot] *n* M scab
(strikebreaker)

croyable [krwah•YAHBL] *adj*
credible; believable

croyance [krwah•YAHπS] *n* F
belief; creed

cru 1 [kroo] *adj* crude; raw

cru 2 [kroo] *n* M wine region;
vineyard; vin du ~\ local wine

cruche [krewsh] *n* F pitcher

crucial [krew•SYAHL] *adj*
crucial

crucifix [krew•see•FEE] *n* M
crucifix; the Crucifixion *n* la
Crucifixion F

cruel [krew•EL] *adj* cruel

Cuba [KEW•bah] *n* M Cuba

cubain [kew•BAπ] *adj n* M
Cuban

cube [kewb] *n* M cube; *vt*
(math) élever au cube

cubique [kew•BEEK] *adj* cubic

cuillère [kewy•EHR] *n* F spoon

cuillère à café [kwee•EHR ah
kah•FEH] *n* F teaspoon

cuillerée [kewy•ehr•EH] *n* F
spoonful

cuir [kweer] *n* M leather; ~
verni\ patent leather

cuire [kweer] *vt* cook; bake;
boil; faire ~\ cook

cuirassé [kwee•rah•SAI] *n* M
battleship

cuisine [kwee•ZEEN] *n* F
cooking; kitchen; *vt* faire la ~\
cook

cuisinier [keww•zee•NYEH] *n*
M cook; chef

cuisse [kwees] *n* F thigh

cuisson [kwee•SAUπ] *n* FM
bakery

cuivre [kweevr] *n* M copper

culbute [kewl•BEWT] *n* F
somersault; *vt* faire la culbute

culinaire [kew•lee•NER] *adj*
culinary

culotte [kew•LAUT] *n* F
trousers; pants; panties

culpabilité
[kewl•PAH•bee•lee•TAI] *n* F
guilt

culte [kewlt] *n* M cult

cultiver [kewl•tee•VAI] *vt*
cultivate

culture 1 [kewl•TEWR] *n* F
culture

culture 2 [kewl•TEWR] *n* F
crop; cultivation; tillage

culturel [kewl•tew•REL] *adj*
cultural

cumulatif
[KEW•mew•lah•TEEF] *adj*
cumulative

cure-dents [kyr-DAHπ] *n* inv
M toothpick

curieux [kew•RYØ] *adj* curious;
inquisitive; peculiar

curiosité [kew•ryo•zee•TAI] *n* F
curiosity

curry [kew•REE] *n* M curry

cuve [kewv] *n* F vat (pour le
blanchissage; réservoir)

cycle [seekl] *n* M cycle; *vi* faire
de la bicyclette

cyclone [see•KLON] *n* M
cyclone

cygne [seeny] *n* M swan

cylindre [see•LAπDR] *n* M
cylinder

cynique [see•NEEK] *adj*
cynical; *n* cynic

cyprès [see•PRE] *n* M cypress

D

dactylographe
[dahk•TEE•lau•GRAHF] *n*
MF typist

daltonien [dahl•tau•NYAπ] *adj*
color-blind

dame [dahm] *n* F lady
(mariée); queen (cartes)

Danemark [Dahn•MAHRK] *n*
M Denmark

danger [dahπ•ZHAI] *n* M
danger; en ~\ in danger

dangereux [dahπ•zhe•RØ] *adj*
dangerous .

dans [dahπ] *prep* in; within;
during; into; from; ~
le sens des aiguilles d'une
montre\ clockwise; ~ les
coulisses\ offstage; ~ les
environs *adv comp*
thereabouts

danse [dahπs] *n* F dance; *vi*
dancer

danseur [dahπ•SœR] *n* M
dancer

date [daht] *n* F date; deadline;
vt dater

dauphin [do•FAπ] *n* dolphin;
dauphin (hist)

de [duh] *prep* (d' before vowel
and mute h) (du = de le;
des = de les) from; by; on;
with; any; some; than; from;
at; de Paris à New York\
from Paris to New York; de
sa poche\ from his pocket;
je bois du thé\ I drink
some tea; d'un côté\ to one
side; de cinq à dix
personnes\ between five and
ten people

dé 1 [deh] *n* M dice; dominos; tee (golf)

dé 2 [deh] *n* M thimble

de/en plein air *adj* outdoor

de cela; en [duh suh•LAH]; [œπ] *adv* thereof

de dessus [duh duh•SEW] *adj* upper

de deuxième ordre *adj* second-rate

de devant; (first) premier; *adv* devant; *n* avant m; (of stucture) de; du (de la) des; en de [du] *prép* of

de fait [duh FEH] *adv* virtually

de laine [lehn] *n* F woolen

de même *adv* likewise

de nuit; d'une nuit; *adv* la nuit *adj* overnight

de or en papier; *n* papier m; (newspaper) journal [pah•pye] *n* paper

de plus *adv* furthermore

de plus *adv* moreover

de plus en plus *adv* increasingly

de premier main *adj adv* firsthand

de temps en temps *adv* occasionally

de toujours *adj* lifelong

de toute façon anyway

débâcle [dai•BAHKL] *n* F debacle

débandade [deh•bahn•DAHD] *n* F confusion; stampede

débandader 1 [deh•bahn•DEH] *vt* disband; disperse

débandader 2 [deh•bahn•DEH] *vi* relax; loosen; unbandage

débat [dai•BAH] *n* M debate; *vt* *vi* débattre

débauche [dai•BOSH] *n* F vice; debauchery; *adj* débauché; *vt* débaucher

débit [dai•BEE] *n* M debit; sale; retail shop

débiter [dai•bee•TEH] *vt* retail; sell; give out; discharge; utter

débiteur [dai•bee•TœR] *n* debtor

déboucher [deh•boo•SHEH] *vt* uncork

débouchoir [dai•boo•SHWAHR] *n* plunger

debout [duh•BOO] *adj; n* F standing

déboutonner [deh•boo•tau•NEH] *vt* unbutton

début [dai•BEW] *n* M beginning; outset; debut; *vi* débuter

débutant [dai•bew•TAHπ] *n* M *adj* beginner

deçà [duh•SAH] *adv* on this side

décadence [dai•kah•DAHπS] *n* F decadence

décadent [dai•kah•DAHπ] *adj* decadent

décapiter [dai•kah•pee•TAI] *vt* behead

décéder [dai•sai•DAI] *adj* deceased

déceler [dai•SLAI] *vt* detect

décembre [dai•SAHπBR] *n* M December

décence [dai•SAHπS] *n* F decency

décennie [dai•se•NEE] *n* F
'decade

décent [dai•SAHπ] *adj* decent

déception [dai•sep•SYAUπ] *n*
F disappointment

décevant [dai•se•VAHπ] *adj*
disappointing; deceptive;
misleading

décevoir [dai•se•VOIR] *vt*
disappoint; deceive; mislead

décharge [dai•SHAHRZH] *n* F
unloading; discharge; release;
dump

décharger [dai•shahrzh•EH] *vt*
unload; discharge; vent;
acquit; dismiss; *vi* se
décharger

décharné [dai•shahr•NAI] *adj*
gaunt

déchiffrer [dai•shee•FRAI] *vt*
decipher; sight read (mus)

déchirer [deh•chee•REH] *vt*
tear; rend; defame

déchirure [deh•chee•RYR] *n* F
tear; rent; defamation

décider [dai•see•DAI] *vt* decide;
settle; rule (loi)

décimale [dai•see•MAHL] *n* F
decimal

décimer [dai•see•MAI] *vt*
decimate

décisif [dai•see•SEEF] *adj*
decisive

décision [dai•see•ZYAUπ] *n*
decision

déclaration
[deh•klahr•ah•SYAUπ] *n* F
statement

déclarer [dai•klah•RAI] *vt*
declare

déclin [deh•KLAπ] *n* M decline;
wane; *vt* décliner

décoder [dai•kau•DAI] *vt*
decode

décolorer [dai•kau•lau•RAI] *vt*
fade; *vi* se décolorer

décombres [deh•KAHMBR]
npl M rubble

décoratif [dai•kau•rah•TEEF]
adj ornamental

décoration
[dai•kau•rah•SYAUπ] *n* F
decoration

décorer [dai•kau•RAI] *vt*
decorate

décorum [dai•kau•REWM] *n* M
decorum

découragé
[dai•KOO•rah•ZHAI] *adj*
despondent; dejected

décourager
[dai•KOO•rah•ZHAI] *vt*
discourage; dishearten

découverte [dai•koo•VERT] *n*
F discovery; detection

découvrir [dai•koo•VREER] *vt*
discover; uncover

décrepit [dai•kre•PEE] *adj*
decrepit

décret [dai•CRE] *n* M decree;
vt décréter

décrire [dai•KREER] *vt*
describe

dédain [dai•DAπ] *n* M disdain

dedans [duh•DANπ] *adv*
within; inside; *n* M inside

dédier [dai•DYAI] *vt* dedicate

déduction [dai•dewk•SYAUπ]
n F deduction

déduire [dai•DWEER] *vt*
deduct; infer

déesse [dai•ES] *n* F goddess

défaillance [dai•fah•YAHπs] *n* F lapse

défaire [deh•FEHR] *vt* undo; unwrap

défaite [dai•FET] *n* F defeat

défaut [dai•FO] *n* M blemish; flaw; default; defect; *vi* faire défection

défauts [dai•FO] *npl* M shortcomings

défectueux [dai•fek•tew•Ø] *adj* faulty

défendre [dai•FAHπDR] *vt* defend

défense 1 [dai•FAHπS] *n* F defense

défense 2 [deh•FAHπS] *n* F tusk (éléphant)

défenseur [dai•fahπ•SœR] *n* M defendant

défensif [dai•fahπ•SEEF] *adj* F defensive; sur la défensive

défi [dai•FEE] *n* defiance; dare

déficit [dai•fee•SEE] *n* M deficit

défier [dai•FYAI] *vt* challenge; defy; défier de faire qqch\ challenge someone to do something

défi [dai•FEE] *n* M challenge

défigurer [dai•FEE•gew•RAI] *vt* disfigure

définir [dai•fee•NEER] *vt* define

définition [dai•fee•nee•SYAUπ] *n* definition

déformer [dai•faur•MAI] *vt* distort

dégager [dai•gah•ZHAI] *vt* disengage

dégénéré [dai•ZHAI•nai•RAI] *adj* degenerate; *vi* dégénérer

dégivrer [dai•zhee•VRAI] *vt* defrost

dégonfler [dai•gauπ•FLAI] *vt* deflate; *vi* se dégonfler

dégoût [dai•GOO] *n* M distaste; disgust

degoûtant [dai•goo•TAHπ] *adj* disgusting

dégoûter [deh•goo•TEH] *vt* repulse; disgust

dégradant [dai•grah•DAHπ] *adj* degrading

degré [du•GRAI] *n* M degree

déguisement [dai•geez•MAHπ] *n* M disguise; *vt* déguiser; *adj* en déguisé

dehors [du•AUR] *n* M outdoors; out; *adv* outside; abroad; in the offing

déjà [dai•ZHAH] *adv* already; before

déjeuner [dai•zhØ•NAI] *n* M lunch *vi* déjeuner

délecter [dai•lehk•TEH] *vt* relish

délégation [dai•LAI•gah•SYAUπ] *n* F delegation

délégué [dai•lai•GAI] *n* M delegate; *vt* déléguer

délibéré [dai•LEE•bai•RAI] *adj* deliberate; *vi* délibérer

délicat [dai•lee•KAKH] *adj* delicate; fragile; dainty; nice; tricky (question)

délicatement [dai•LEE•kaht•MAHN] *adv* delicately; gingerly

délice [dai•LEES] *n* M delight; pleasure

délicieux [dai•lee•SYØ] *adj*
delicious

délinquant [dai•lee•KAHπ]
adj n M delinquent

délirant [dai•lee•RAHπ] *adj*
delirious

délit [dai•LEE] *n* M
misdemeanor; offense; en
flagrant ~\ red-handed (coll)

déloyal [dai•lwah•YAHL] *adj*
disloyal

déluge [dai•LEWZH] *n* M
deluge; downpour

démagogue [dai•mah•GAUG]
n MF demagogue

demain [duh•MAπ] *adv n* M
tomorrow; à demain\ until
tomorrow; après-~\ the day
after tomorrow

demande [du•MAHπD] *n* F
request; question; inquiry;
demand

demander [du•mahπ•DAI] *vt*
ask; inquire; request

démangeaison
[dai•mahπ•zhe•ZAUπ] *n* F
itchf; *vi* (subj part of body)
démanger; mon pied me
démange

démarche [dai•MAHRSH] *n* F
gait; walk; step; strut

dément [dai•MAHπ] *adj*
demented

démérite [dai•mai•REET] *n* M
demerit

demeure [du•MœR] *n* F abode

demi [de•MEE] *adj* half; à ~\
by halves; ~-heure\ half hour;
il est une heure et ~\ it's half
past one

démissionner
[deh•MEE•syauπ•NEH] *vi*
resign

démobiliser
[dai•MAU•bee•lee•ZAI] *vt*
demobilize

démocrate [dai•mau•KRAHT]
n MF democrat

démocratie
[dai•MAU•krah•TEE] *n* F
democracy

démocratique
[dai•MAU•krah•TEEK] *adj*
democratic

démodé [dai•mau•DAI] *adj*
outmoded; outdated;
old-fashioned

demoiselle [dai•wah•ZEL] *n* F
young lade; ~ d'honneur *n*
bridesmaid

démolir [dai•mau•LEER] *vt*
demolish

démon [dai•MAUπ] *n* M fiend

démonstratif
[dai•MAUπ•strah•TEEF] *adj*
demonstrative

démonstration
[dai•MAUπ•strah•SYAUπ] *n*
F demonstration; show

démontrer [dai•mauπ•TRAI] *vt*
demonstrate; show

démoralisé
[dai•MAU•rah•lee•ZAI] *adj*
downcast; depressed;
demoralized

démoraliser
[dai•MAU•rah•lee•ZAI] *vt*
demoralize; dishearten

dénoncer [dai•nauπ•SAI] *vt*
denounce

dénouement [dai•noo•MAHπ]
n M ending

dénouer [deh•NWEH] *vt* untie;
unravel; *vi* se dénouer

dense [dahns] *adj* dense; thick

densité [dahπ•see•TAI] *n* F
density

dent [dahπ] *n* F tooth; prong;
mal au ~s\ toothache; sur les
~\ worn out; dents *npl* F\ teeth

dentaire [dahπ•TER] *adj* dental

dentelé [dahπ•tu•LAI] *adj*
jagged

dentelle [dahπ•TEL] *n* F lace

dentifrice [dahπ•tee•FREES] *n*
M toothpaste

dentiste mf [dahπ•TEEST] *n*
dentist

départ [dai•PAHR] *n* M
departure

département
[dai•pahrt•MAHπ] *n* M
department

dépasser [dai•pah•SAI] *vt*
overstep; protrude; overtake;
exceed

dépeindre représenter
[dai•PAπDR] *vt* portray;
depict

dépendance
[dai•pahπ•DAHπS] *n* F
addiction

dépendre [dai•PAHπDR] *vi*
depend; ~ de\ rely on

dépense [dai•PAHπS] *n* F
expenditure; expense; aux ~
de qqn\ at someone's expense

dépenser [dai•pahπ•SAI] *vt*
spend; expend

dépensier -ère
[deh•pahπ•SYEH] [-SYEHR]
n MF spendthrift

dépit [dai•PEE] *n* M spite;
pique

déplacer [dai•plah•SAI] *vt*
displace

déplaire [dai•PLER] *vt*
displease

déplorable [dai•plau•rah•BL]
adj deplorable

déplorer [dai•plau•RAI] *vt*
deplore

déposer [dai•pau•ZAI] *vt*
deposit; depose

dépôt [dai•PO] *n* M depot

dépression [dai•pre•SYAUπ] *n*
F depression

déprimant [dai•pree•MAHπ]
adj depressing

déprimé [dai•pree•MAI] *adj*
depressed; *vt* déprimer

dénégation
[dai•nai•gah•SYAUπ] *n* F
denial

depuis [de•PWEE] *adj* *prép*
since; from; for after

député [dai•pew•TAI] *n* M
deputy

dérailler [dai•rah•YAI] *vi* derail

déraisonnable
[re•zau•NAHBL] *adj*
unreasonable

dérangé [dai•rahπ•ZHAI] *adj*
deranged

dérangement
[dai•rahπzh•MAHπ] *n* M
disturbance

déranger [dai•rahπ•ZHAI] *vt*
disrupt; disturb

dérapage [dai•rah•PAHZH] *n*
skid; *vi* déraper

dérisoire [dai•ree•ZWAHR] *adj*
paltry

dérivervenir [dai•ree•VAI] *vt*
derive; *vi* dériver (de)

dernier [der•NYE] *adj* last;
final

dérouler [deh•roo•LEH] *vt; vi*
unroll; unwind

derrière [de•RYER] *prép adv n*
behind; *n* M back; rear;
buttocks (coll)

dés [dai] *prep* from; since;
upon; as early as

désaccord [dai•sah•KAUR] *n*
M disagreement

désadvantage
[dai•SAHD•vah π•TAHZH] *n*
F disadvantage; *adj*
désadvantagé

désagréable
[deh•ZAH•greh•AHBL] *adj*
unattractive; disagreeable

désapprobation
[dai•SAH•prau•bah•SYAUπ] *n*
F disapproval

désapprouver
[dai•SAH•proo•VAI] *vt*
disapprove

désarmer [da•sahr•MAI] *vt vi*
disarm

désastre [dai•ZAHSTR] *n* M
disaster

désastreux [dai•za•STRØ] *adj*
disastrous

désavouer [dai•SAH•voo•WAI]
vt disavow

descendant [de•sahπ•DAHπ] *n*
M descendant; *adj* downward

descendre [de•SAHπDR] *vt vi*
descend; dismount; ~ en
piqué\ swoop; ~ en roue libre\
coast

descente [de•SAHπ] *n* F
descent

description [de•skreep•SYAUπ]
n F description

déséquilibre
[dai•ZAI•kee•LEEBR] *n* M
imbalance

deserrer [de•su•RAI] *vt* loosen;
vi se desserrer

désert [dai•zer] *n* M desert; *vt*
vi déserter

déserteur [dai•zer•TœR] *n* M
deserter

désespéré [dai•ze•spai•RAI]
adj desperate; hopeless

désespoir [dai•ze•SPWAHR] *n*
M depair; desperation; *vi* ~
(for) désespérer (de)

déshonneur [dai•zau•NœR] *n*
M dishonor; *vt* déshonorer

déshydrater
[dai•SEE•drah•TAI] *vt*
dehydrate

désigner [dai•see•NYAI] *vt*
designate

désillusion
[dai•ZEE•lew•ZYAUπ] *n* F
disillusion

désinfectant
[dai•ZAπ•fek•TAHπ] *n*
disinfectant

désinfecter [dai•ZAπ•fek•TAI]
vt disinfect

désintéressé
[dai•ZAπ•tai•re•SAI] *adj*
disinterested; selfless

désinvolte [dai•saπ•VOLT] *adj*
casual; flippant; glib

désir [deh•ZEEUR] *n* M
yearning; lust; desire; *vt*
désirer

désirable [dai•zee•RAHBL] *adj*
desirable

désirer [deh•zeeur•REH] *vt*
yearn

désobéir à [dai•zau•bai•EER] *vi*
disobey

désobéissant
[dai•ZAU•bai•ee•SAHπ] *adj*
disobedient

désobligeant
[dai•ZAU•blee•ZHAHπ] *adj*
disparaging

désolé [deh•zau•LEH] *adj*
sorry; stark; desolate

désordonné
[dai•ZAUR•dau•NAI] *adj*
disorganized

désordre [dai•ZAUDR] *n* M
disorder; untidiness

désorienté
[dai•ZAU•ryahπ•TAI] *adj*
disoriented

despote [de•SPAUT] *n* M
despot

desséché [du•sai•SHAI] *adj*
parched

dessécher [dee•sai•SHAI] *vt*
scorch

dessert [de•ZER] *n* M dessert;
~ crémeux\ pudding

dessin [de•SAπ] *n* drawing;
sketch; plan; pattern; ~ animé\
cartoon

dessinateur [de•see•nah•TœR]
n M designer

dessous; au-dessous de
[duh•SOO]; [au-duh•SOO,
duh] *adv; prép comp*
underneath

dessus [duh•SEW] *n* M upside

destin [de•STAπ] *n* M fate;
doom

destination
[de•STEE•nah•SYAUπ] *n* F
destination

destinée [de•stee•NAI] *n* F
destiny

destiner [deh•stee•NEH] *vi*
intend; ~ à destine; slate

destructeur -trice
[de•strewk•TœR] [-TREES] *n*
MF destroyer; *adj* destructive

destruction
[de•strewk•SYAUπ] *n* F
destruction

détacher [dai•tah•SHAI] *vt*
detach; unfasten; undo;
separate

détail [dai•TAHY] *n* M detail;
en ~\ in detail; *vt* détailler;
donner des ~s\ give the details

détaillant -e [deh•tuy•YAHπ]
[-AHπT] *n* MF retailer

détaillé [dai•tah•YAI] *adj*
elaborate; detailed

détailler [dai•tah•YAI] *vt*
itemize; relate in detail

détective [deh•tehk•TEEV] *n*
M detective; sleuth

détendre [deh•TAHπDR] *vt*
slacken; loosen; se détendre\
relax; ease

détendu [dai•tahπ•DEW] *adj*
relaxed

détention [dai•tahπ•SYAUπ] *n*
F detention; imprisonment;
holding

détenu [dai•tu•NEW] *n* M
inmate; detainee

détergent [dai•ter•ZHAHπ] *n*
detergent

détermination
[dai•TER•mee•nah•SYAUπ] *n*
F determination

déterminé [dai•TER•mee•NAI]
n definite

déterminer
[dai•TER•mee•NAI] *vt*
determine

déterrer [deh•tehr•EH] *vt*
unearth

détester [dai•te•STAI] *vt* detest;
loathe

détoner [dai•tau•NAI] *vt*
detonate

détour [dai•TOOR] *n* M detour;
diversion

détourné [dai•toor•NAI] *adj*
devious

détournement
[dai•toorn•MAHπ] *n* M
misappropriation (de fonds)

détourner [dai•tour•NAI] *vt*
embezzle; detour; divert

détremé; -e [deh•traπ•PEH] *adj*
watery

détresse [dai•TRES] *n* F
distress

détritus [dai•tree•TEW] *npl* M
garbage; rubbish; litter

détroit [deh•TRWAH] *n* M
strait; channel

détromper [deh•trauπ•PEH] *vt*
undeceive

détruire [dai•TRWEER] *vt*
destroy

dette [det] *n* F debt

deux [dØ] *adj; n* M two; ~ fois
adj comp twice

deuxième [dØ•zyem] *num*
second

devant [de•VAHπ] *n* M front
adv prép ahead (of); in front
of; ~ la loi\ in the eyes of the
law

dévastateur
[dai•VAH•stah•TœR] *adj*
devastating

dévaster [dai•vah•STAI] *vt*
devastate

développement
[dai•VE•laup•MAHπ] *n* M
development; expansion

développer [dai•VE•lau•PAI]
vt develop; *vi* se developper

devenir [duv•NEER] *vi*
become; grow; turn

devenir [deh•ve•NEER] *vi* grow

dévêtir [deh•veh•TEEUR] *vt; vi*
strip; divest

dévier [dai•VYAI] *vi* deviate;
deflect; swerve

dévier [deh•VEEYEH] *vi*
swerve

devis [du•VEE] *n* M chat;
estimate; ~ approximatif\
rough estimate

devise [de•VEEZ] *n* F motto;
slogan

dévoiler [deh•vwah•LEH] *vt*
unveil

devoir [du•VWAHR] *n* M duty;
exercise; *npl* respects; *vt* owe;
have to must; should; ought;
~ fonctions\ duty

devoirs [du•VWAHR] *npl* M
homework

dévorer [dai•vau•RAI] *vt*
devour

dévot [dai•VO] *adj* devout

dévotion *n* F [dai•vo•SYAUπ]

dévoué [dai•voo•WAI] *adj* devoted

dévouement [dai•voo•MAHπ] *n* M devotion

dextérité; [dehk•STEHR•ee•TEH] *n* F dexterity; sleight

diabète [dyah•BET] *n* M diabetes

diabétique mf [dyah•bai•TEEK] *adj n* diabetic

diable [dyah•BL] *n* M devil; jack-in-the-box\ le Diable Satan

diabolique [dyah•bau•LEEK] *adj* fiendish; devilish

diadème [dyah•DEHM] *n* M tiara

diagnostic [dyahg•nau•STEEK] *adj n* F diagnosis

diagnostiquer [dyahg•NAU•stee•KAI] *vt* diagnose

diagonal [dyah•gau•NAHL] *adj* diagonal; *n* F diagonale

diagramme [dyah•GRAMME] *n* M diagram

dialecte [dyah•LEKT] *n* M dialect

dialogue [dyah•LAUG] *n* M dialog

diamant [dyah•MAHπ] *n* M diamond

diamètre [dyah•METR] *n* M diameter

diatribe [dyah•TREEB] *n* F tirade; diatribe

dictateur [deek•tah•TœR] *n* M dictator

dictature [deek•tah•TEWR] *n* F dictatorship

dictée [deek•TAI] *n* F dictation

dicter [deek•TAI] *vt* dictate; give dictation

dictionnaire [deek•syau•NER] *n* M dictionary

dieu [dyØ] *n* M god; mon Dieu~\ dear me!

diffamation [dee•FAH•mah•SYAUπ] *n* M libel

diffamer [dee•fah•MAI] *vt* defame; libel; slander; ~ calomnier\ malign

différence [dee•fai•RAHπS] *n* F difference

différencier [dee•FAI•rahπ•SYAI] *vt* differentiate

différent [dee•fai•RAHπ] *adj* different

différer 1 [dee•fai•RAI] *vi* differ

différer 2 [dee•fai•RAI] *vt* defer *vi* déférer (à)

difficile [dee•fee•SEEL] *adj* difficult

difficulté [dee•FEE•kewl•TAI] *n* F difficulty

diffimation [dee•FEE•mah•SYAUπ] *n* F defamation

difforme [dee•FAURM] *adj* deformed

diffuser [dee•few•ZAI] *vt* diffuse

digérer [dee•zhai•RAI] *vt vi* digest; *n* M digest

digestion [dee•zhe•STYAUπ] *n* F digestion

digital [dee•zhee•TAHL] *adj* M
digital

digne [DEE•nyu] *adj* dignified;
~ de\ worth; ~ de confiance
sûr\ dependable

dignité [dee•nyee•TAI] *n* F
dignity

dilater; [dee•lah•TAI] *vt* dilate
vi se dilater

dilemme [dee•LEM] *n* M
dilemma

dilué [dee•lwai] *adj* dilute; *vt*
diluer

dimanche [dee•MAHNSH] *n* M
Sunday

dîme [deem] *n* F tithe; offering

dimension [dee•mahπ•SYAUπ]
n F dimension; à trois ~s\
three dimensional

diminuer [dee•mee•NWAI] *vt*
detract; diminish; dwindle;
decrease

dindon [daπ•DAUπ] *n* MF
turkey; dinde (bird)

dîner [dee•NAI] *vi* dine; *n* M
dinner

dinosaure [dee•no•ZAUR] *n* M
dinosaur

diocèse [dyau•SEZ] *n* M
diocese

diplomate [dee•plau•MAHT] *n*
M diplomat

diplomatie
[dee•plau•mah•TEE] *n* M
diplomacy

diplomatique
[dee•plau•mah•TEEK] *adj*
diplomatic

diplôme [dee•PLOM] *n* M
diploma

dire [deeur] *n* M speech; words;
vt tell; recite; order

direct [dee•REKT] *adj* direct;
straight; straightforward

directement [dee•rekt•MAHπ]
adv directly

directeur [dee•rek•TœR] *n* M
director; manager

direction [dee•rek•SYAUπ] *n* F
direction; leadership

discerner [dee•ser•NAI] *vt*
discern

disciple [dee•SEEPL] *n* MF
disciple; follower

discipline [dee•see•PLEEN] *n* F
discipline; *vt* discipliner

discorde [dee•SKAURD] *n* F
discord

discours [dee•SKOOR] *n* M
oratory; talking; discourse;
speech

discrédit [dees•krai•DEE] *n*
discredit; *vt* discréditer

discret [dee•SKRE] *adj* discreet;
inconspicuous

discrétion [dee•skrai•SYAUπ] *n*
discretion; prudence

disculper [dee•skewl•PAI] *vt*
exonerate

discussion [dee•skew•SYAUπ]
n F discussion

discutable [dee•skew•TAHBL]
adj questionable; suspicious

discuter [dee•skew•TAI] *vi*
discuss

disjoindre [dee•ZHWAHNDR]
vt disconnect

disloquer [dees•lau•KAI] *vt*
dislocate

disparaître [dee•spah•RAITR]
vi disappear; *n* F disparition
disappearance

disparu [dee•spah•REW] *adj*
extinct

disperser [dee•sper•SAI] *vt*
disperse; *vi* se disperser

disponible [dee•spau•NEEBL]
adj available; spare; vacant

disposer [dee•spau•ZAI] *vt*
dispose; throw away

disposition
[dee•SPAU•zee•SYAUπ]n F
temperament; nature

dispute [dee•SPEWT] *n* F
argument; quarrel feud

disputer [dee•spyoo•TEH] *vt*
argue; wrangle; *vi* se disputer

disque [deesk] *n* M disk; ~
compact\ compact disc

dissauder [dee•swah•DAI] *vt*
dissuade

disséminer [dee•sai•mee•NAI]
vt disseminate

dissensions [dee•sahπ•SYAUπ]
npl F dissention; strife

dissentiment
[dee•SAHπ•tee•MAHπ] *n*
dissent

disséquer [dee•sai•KAI] *vt*
dissect

dissimulé [dee•SEE•mew•LAI]
adj secretive; dissembling

dissimuler [dee•SEE•mew•LAI]
vt vi dissemble; conceal; hide;
cover up; *vi* se dissimuler

dissiper [dee•see•PAI] *vt* dispel

dissiper [dee•see•PAI] *vt*
dissipate; *vi* se dissiper

dissocier [dee•sau•SYAI] *vt*
dissociate; *vi* se dissocier

dissolu [dee•sau•LEW] *adj*
dissolute

dissolvant [dee•saul•VAHπ] *n*
M solvent

dissoudre [dee•SOODR] *vt*
dissolve; *vi* se dissoudre

dissuader [dee•swah•DAI] *vt*
deter

distance [dee•STAHπS] *n* F
distance

distant [dee•STAHπ] *adj*
remote; distant; far away

distiller [dee•stee•YAI] *vt vi*
distill

distillerie [dee•STEE•ye•REE]
n distillery

distinct [dee•STAπ] *adj* distinct

distinguer [dee•staπ•GAI] *vt*
distinguish; *adj* distingué

distraire [dee•STRER] *vt*
distract

distrait [dee•STREH] *adj*
forgetful; distracted;
absent-minded

distribuer [dee•STREE•bew•AI]
vt distribute; dispense

distributeur
[dee•STREE•bew•TœR] *n* M
dispenser; ~ automatique\
vending machine

distribution
[dee•STREE•bew•SYAUπ] *n*
F distribution

dit -e [dee]; [deet] *adj; vi* (pp
de dire) told

divergence [dee•ver•ZHAHπS]
n discrepancy

diverger [dee•ver•ZHAI] *vi*
diverge

divers [dee•VER] *adj* diverse;
miscellaneous; various

diversifier [dee•VER•see•FYAI]
vt diversify; *vi* se diversifier

diversité [dee•VER•see•TAI] *n*
F diversity

divertir [dee•ver•TEER] *vt*
entertain; divert; amuse

divertissant
[dee•VER•teez•AUπ] *adj*
entertaining; diverting

divertissement
[dee•VER•teez•MAUπ] *n* M
spectacle show; entertainment

divin [dee•VAπ] *adj* divine

divinité [dee•VEE•nee•TAI] *n* F
deity; divinity

diviser [dee•vee•zai] *vt* divide;
spearate; ~ en deux\ halve; *vi*
se diviser

division [dee•vee•ZYAUπ] *n* F
division; branch; portion

divorce [dee•VAURS] *n* M
divorce; *vt* divorcer

divulguer [dee•vewl•GAI] *vt*
divulge

dix [dees] *adj; n* M ten

dix-huit *num* eighteen

dix-huitième; see also eighth
num eighteenth

dix-neuf [dees•nØf] *num*
nineteen

dix-sept [dee•set] *num*
seventeen

dixième [dee•ZYEHM] *adj; n*
MF tenth

docile [dau•SEEL] *adj* docile

dock [dauk] *n* M dock

docker [dau•KEHR] *n* M
stevedore

docteur [dauk•TœR] *n* doctor;
physician

doctorat [dauk•tau•RA] *n* M
doctorate

doctrine [dauk•TREEN] *n* F
doctrine

document [dau•kew•MAHπ] *n*
M document; *vt* documenter

dogme [daugmu] *n* M dogma

doigt [dwah] *n* finger; toe; digit;
monter du ~\ point at

doléance [dau•lai•AHπS] *n* F
grievance

dollar [dau•LAR] *n* M dollar

domaine [dau•MEN] *n* M
domain; realm

dôme [dom] *n* M dome

domestique [dau•me•STEEK]
n F maid; MF servant; *adj*
domestic

domestiqué
[dau•meh•stee•KEH] *adj*
tame; domesticated

dominant [dau•mee•NAHπ] *adj*
dominant; prevailing

dominateur
[dau•mee•nah•TœR] *adj*
domineering

dominer [dau•mee•NAI] *vt*
dominate

dommage [dau•MAHZH] *n* M
damage; injury; loss; quel ~\
what a pity

don [dauπ] *n* M donation;
present

donc [dauπk] *adv conj*
therefore; then; now; so;
nonsense; allons ~\ come on!

données [dau•NAI] *n pl* F data

donner [dau•NAI] *vt* give;
present; attribute; supply; ~
un coup à qq'un\ swipe

doré [dau•RAI] *adj* gilded

dorénavant
[dau•rai•nah•VAHπ] *adv*
henceforth

dorloter |daur•lau•TAI| *vt*
pamper

dormeur |daur•MœR| *n* M
sleeper

dortoir |daur•TWAHR| *n* M
dormitory

dos |dau| *n* M back

dose |doz| *n* F dose

dossier |dau•SYE| *n* file

dot |daut| *n* F dowry

double |doobl| *adj* dual;
double; twice; doubly

doubler |doo•BLEH| *vt* double

doublure |doo•BLEWR| *n* F
lining; (théâtre) *n* F
understudy

doucement |doos•MAHπ| *adv*
gently

douceur |doo•SœR| *n* F
softness

douche |doosh| *n* shower; *vi* se
doucher

doué |doo•AI| *adj* gifted

douille |dweey| *n* F socket

douillet |dwee•YE| *adj* cozy

douleur |doo•LœR| *n* F sorrow;
woe; ache; pain

douloureux |doo•loo•RØ| *adj*
painful; trying

doute |doot| *n* F qualm; doubt;
sans aucun ~\ without a
doubt; *vt* douter doutes |doot|
npl F\ misgivings

douteux |doo•TØ| *adj* dubious;
doubtful

doux |doo| *adj* gentle; mild;
meek; soft; mellow (taste)

douzaine |doo•ZEN| *n* F dozen

douze |dooz| *adj*; *n* M twelve

douzième |doo•ZYEHM| *adj*;
n MF twelfth

doyen |dwah•YAπ| *n* M dean;
doyen; *adj* senior; eldest

dragon |drah•GAUπ| *n* M
dragon

dramatique |drah•mah•TEEK|
adj dramatic

dramatiser |drah•mah•tee•ZAI|
vt dramatize

dramatiste |drah•mah•TEEST|
n MF dramatist

dramaturge
|drah•mah•TEWRZH| *n* M
playwright

drame |drahm| *n* M drama

drapeau |drah•PO| *n* M flag

draper |drah•PAI| *vt* drape

drastique |drah•STEEK| *adj*
drastic

dressage |dreh•SAHZH| *n* MF
training

drogué |drau•GAI| *n* drug
addict

droit -e |drah| |draht| *n* M law;
right; fee; *n* F the right hand;
adj right; upright; straight; les
~s de l'homme\ the rights of
man

drôle |drol| *adj* funny; amusing

dû; due |dew| *pp* devoir; *n* M
what is due; *adj* due; owing

Dublin |dew•BLAπ| *n* Dublin

duc |dewk| *n* M duke

duchesse |dew•SHES| *n* F
duchess

duel |dew•EL| *n* M duel; *vi* se
battre en duel

dune |dewn| *n* F dune

duo |dew•O| *n* M duet

duplicité |dew•PLEE•see•TAI|
n F duplicity

dur [dewr] *adj* hard; tough; difficult; ~ de oreille\ hard of hearing

durable [dew•RAHBL] *adj* lasting; durable

durée [dew•RAI] *n* F duration; ~ de vie\ lifespan

dureté [dew•ehr•TEH] *n* F toughness

duvet [dew•VEH] *n* M fluff

dynamique [dee•nah•MEEK] *adj n* F dynamic

dynamite [dee•nah•MEET] *n* M dynamite; *vt* dynamiter

dynastie [dee•nah•STEE] *n* F dynasty

E

eau [o] *n* F water; rain; juice; wet; perspiration; ~ de savon\ suds; ~ de toilette\ toilet water; ~ de Javel\ bleach; ~ dentifrice\ mouthwash; ~ de mer;\ saltwater; ~ de vie\ brandy; ~-forte\ etching; nitric acid

ébène [ai•BEN] *n* F ebony

éblouir [ai•bloo•EER] *vt* dazzle

éboueur [ai•boo•œR] *n* M scavenger

ébouillanter [ai•BWEE•yah•TAI] *vt* scald

ébrecher [ai•bru•SHAI] *vt* notch; chip

écarlate [ai•kahr•LAHT] *n* F scarlet

écart [ai•KAHR] *n* M deviation; variation; swerve; lurch

eccentrique [ek•sahπ•TREEK] *adj n* MF eccentric

ecclésiastique [e•klai•zyah•STEEK] *adj* ecclesiastic

échafaud [ai•shah•FO] *n* M scaffold

échafaudage [ai•shah•fo•DAHZH] *n* M scaffolding

échange [eh•SHAHπZH] *n* M swap; exchange; interchange; switch; *vt* échanger

échantillon [ai•SHAHπ•tee•YAUπ] *n* M sample; taste

échappatoire [ai•SHAH•pah•TWAHR] *n* F escape; loophole

échapper [ai•shah•PEH] elude; evade; escape; avoid; laisser ~\ overlook

écharde [eh•SHAHRD] *n* F splinter

écharpe [ai•SHAHRP] *n* F scarf; sash; sling

échasse [ai•SHAS] *n* F stilt

échec [ai•SHEK] *n* failure

échecs [ai•SHEK] *spl* M chess

échelle [ai•SHEL] *n* F ladder; scale; ~\ double pair of steps;

faire la courte ~\ give a
helping hand; ~ mobile\
sliding scale

échevelé [ai•shu•VLAI] *adj*
dishevelled; rumpled

écho [ai•KO] *n* echo; *vi* faire
écho

échouer [ai•SHWEH] *vt; vi*
strand (un navire)

éclabousser [eh•klah•boo•SEH]
vt spatter; splash

éclair [ai•KLER] *n* M lightning
flash; éclair (patisserie)

éclairage [ai•klah•RAHZH] *n*
M light; lighting

éclairer [ai•kle•RAI] *vt*
enlighten; illuminate

éclat [ai•KLAH] *n* M burst;
explosion; flash; brightness;
brilliance; faire un ~\ create a
stir

éclater [ai•klah•TEH] *vt* burst;
explode; *vi* faire éclater

éclipse [ai•KLEEPS] *n* F eclipse

éclipser [ai•kleep•SAI] *vt*
overshadow; eclipse

éclore [ai•KLAUR] *vi* hatch

écœurant [ai•kœ•RAHπ] *adj*
sickening

écœurer [ai•kœ•RAI] *vt*
nauseate; sicken

école [ai•KAUL] *n* F school;
school-house; doctine;
instruction; faire ~\ set a
fashion; ~ maternelle\ nursery
school; ~ secondaire\ high
school; ~ professionnelle\
trade school

écologie [ai•kau•lau•ZHEE] *n* F
ecology

économe [ai•kau•NAUM] *adj*
frugal

économie [ai•KAU•nau•MEE]
n F economy; ~ politique\
economics

économies [ai•KAU•nau•MEE]
npl F savings

économique
[ai•KAU•nau•MEEK] *adj*
economic

Écossais [ai•kau•SE] *n* M Scot

écossais [ai•kau•SE] *adj*
Scottish; Scotch; *n* M scotch
whiskey

Écosse [ai•KAUS] *n* F Scotland

écourter [ai•koor•TAI] *vt*
curtail; shorten

écouter [ai•koo•TAI] *vt* listen;
heed; pay attention; *vi*
s'écouter\ indulge oneself

écran [ai•KRAHπ] *n* screen;
filter (photo)

écrasant [ai•krah•SAπ] *adj*
overwhelming

écraser [eh•krah•ZEH] *vt* swat
(une mouche)

écrevisse [ai•kru•VEES] *n* F
crayfish

écrire [eh•KREEUR] *vt* write;
write down; machine à ~\
typewriter

écrit [eh•KREE] *n* M writing;
pamphlet; *adj* written

écriture [ai•kree•TEWR] *n* F
handwriting; writing; Écriture
Sainte\ Scripture

écrivain [eh•kree•VAπ] *n* M
writer

écureuil [eh•kyr•œY] *n* M
squirrel

écurie [eh•kyr•EE] *n* F *adj* stable

édedron [ai•du•DRAUπ] *n* M quilt

éditer [ai•dee•TAI] *vt* edit

éditeur [ai•dee•TœR] *n* publisher

édition [ai•dee•SYAUπ] *n* F edition

éditorial [ai•DEE•tau•RYAHL] *adj n* M editorial

éducation [ai•DEW•kah•SYAUπ] *n* F education

effacer [e•fah•SAI] *vt* obliterate; erase

effectivement [e•fek•teev•MAHπ] *adv* actually

effet [eh•FEH] *n* M effect ; *vt* effectuer; ~ secondaire\ side effect; prendre ~\ take effect

efficace [eh•fee•KAHS] *n* efficient; effective

efficacement [eh•fee•kahs•MAUπ] *adv* effective

efficacité [eh•fee•kah•see•TAI] *n* F efficiency

effiler [eh•fee•LEH] *vt* unravel; fray; taper

effondrer [eh•faun•DREH] *vt* collapse; break up; s'effondrer; collapse from effort; effort [e•faur] *n* M effort; exertion; strain; faire un ~\ make an effort

effrayant [eh•frah•YAHπ] *adj* frightening; scary

effrayer [eh•frah•YAI] *vt* frighten

effréné [eh•freh•NEH] *adj inv* uncontrollable

effronté [ai•frauπ•TAI] *adj* shameless; impudent; brash

égal [ai•GAHL] *adj n* M equal; even; *vt* égaler; ça m'est ~\ it's all the same to me; I don't mind

également [ai•gahl•MAHπ] *adv* equally

égalité [ai•GAH•lee•TAI] *n* F equality

égarer [ai•ga•RAI] *vt* misplace

égayer [ai•gah•YAI] *vi* cheer up

église [ai•GLEEZ] *n* F church

égocentrique [ai•GAU•sahπ•TREEK] *adj* self-centered

égoïsme [ai•gau•EEZM] *n* M selfishness

égoïste [ai•gau•EEST] *adj* selfish

égotiste [ai•gau•TEEST] *n* MF egotist

égout [ai•GOO] *n* M sewer; drain

Égypte [ai•ZHEEPT] *n* F Egypt

égyptien; [ai•zheep•TYAπ] *adj* Egyptian; *n* M Égyptien

éhonté [ai•auπ•TAI] *adj* shameless

élan 1 [ai•LAHπ] *n* M spring; dash; bound; impetus; outburst

élan 2 [ai•LAHπ] *n* M elk

élastique [ai•lah•STEEK] *adj n* M elastic

élection [ai•lek•SYAUπ] *n* election

électricité [ai•lek•TREE•see•TAI] *n* electricity

électrique [ai•lek•TREEK] *adj*
electric

électrocuter
[ai•LEK•trau•kew•TAI] *vt*
electrocute

électronique
[ai•LEK•trau•NEEK] *adj*
electronic; courrier ~\ e-mail

élégance [ai•lai•GAHπS] *n* F
elegance

élégant [ai•lai•GAHπ] *adj* F
elegant

élément [ai•lai•MAHπ] *n*
element; les éléments *npl* M

élémentaire
[ai•lai•mahπ•TEHR] *adj*
elementary

éléphant [ai•lai•FAHπ] *n* M
elephant

élevage [ai•lu•VAHZH] *n*
breeding (plants animals)

élévation [ai•leh•vah•SYAUπ]
n F uplift

élève [ai•LEHV] *n* MF pupil;
student; disciple; F seedling;
~ truant

élever [ai•leh•VAI] *vt* elevate;
nurture; exalt (eccles)

éligible; admissible
[ai•lee•ZHEEBL] *adj* eligible

éliminer [ai•lee•mee•NAI] *vt*
eliminate

élire [ai•LEER] *vt* elect; choose

élite [ai•LEET] *adj* elite

élitiste [ai•lee•TEEST] *adj n*
MF elitist

elle [el] *pr pers* she; *pl* elles;
elle-même herself; itself

éloge [ai•LAUZH] *n* F eulogy

éloigné [eh•lwah•NYEH] *adj*
far away; removed

éloquence [ai•lau•KAHπS] *n* F
eloquence

éloquent [ai•lau•KAHπ] *adj*
eloquent

élu [ai•LEW] *adj* elect; chosen

émacié [ai•mah•SYAI] *adj*
emaciated

émail [ai•MAHY] *n* enamel; *vt*
émailler

émancipation
[ai•MAHπ•see•pah•SYAUπ] *n*
F emancipation; freedom

émaner [ai•mah•NAI] *vi*
emanate; issue; originate

emballage [ahπ•bah•LAHZH] *n*
M packing

embargo [ahπ•bahr•GO] *n* M
embargo; *vt* mettre un
embargo

embarras [ahπ•bah•RAH] *n* M
embarrassment

embarressant
[ahπ•bah•re•SAHπ] *adj*
embarrassing

embarressé [ahπ•bah•reh•SAI]
adj embarrassed

embarresser [ahπ•bah•re•SAI]
vt embarrass

embellir [ahπ•be•LEER] *vt*
embellish

embêtement [ahn•bet•MAHπ]
n M hassle; bother; *vt* embêter

emblème [ahπ•BLEM] *n* M
emblem

embouteillage
[ahπ•BOO•tehy•AHZH] *n* M
tie-up (circulation)

embrouillant
[ahπ•brwee•YAHN] *adj*
confusing

embrouiller [ahπ•brooy•EH] *vt*
tangle; embroil; confuse

embryon [ahn•bree•YAUπ] *n*
M embryo

émeraude [ai•me•ROD] *adj n*
F emerald

émerger [ai•mer•ZHAI] *vi*
emerge; appear; come into
view

émettier [ai•me•TYAI] *vt*
crumble; *vi* s'émettier

émettre [ai•METR] *vt*•emit;
send out; express an opinion

émigré [ai•mee•GRAI] *n* M
emigrant

émigrer [ai•mee•GRAI] *vi* M
emigrate

éminence [ai•mee•NAHπS] *n*
eminence

éminent [ai•mee•NAHπ] *adj*
eminent

émissaire [ai•mee•SAIR] *n* M
emissary

émission [ai•mi•SYAUπ] *n* F
broadcast; emission

emmailloter
[ahπ•mahy•au•TEH] *vt* swathe

emmener [eh•meh•NEH] *vt*
take away; lead away; take

empêchement
[ahπ•PEH•sheh•MAUπ] *n* M
obstacle; hindrance

empêcher [ahπ•peh•SHEH] *vt*
restrain; prevent; ~ de croître\
stunt

empereur [ahπ•PRœR] *n* M
emperor

empiéter sur [ahπ•pyai•TAI] *vi*
encroach

empire [ahπ•PEER] *n* M empire

emplacement
[ahπ•plahs•MAHπ] *n* location;
site

emploi [ahπ•PLWAH] *n* M
employment; *vt.* use

employé [ahπ•plwah•YAI] *n* M
employee; clerk

employer [ahπ•plwah•YAI] *vt*
employ; hire

employeur [ahπ•plwah•YœR] *n*
M employer

empoisonnement
[ahπ•PWAH•zaun•MAHπ] *n*
M poisoning

emporté [ahπ•pau•TAI] *adj*
short-tempered

empreinte [ahπ•PRAπT] *n* F
print; ~ de pied\ footprint; ~
digitale\ fingerprint

emprissonner
[aπ•PREE•sau•NAI] *vt*
imprison

emprunter [ahπ•prœπ•TAI] *vt*
borrow

en 1 [ahπ] *pron*; of/for
him/her/it/them; while within;
from; aller ~ Amerique\ go to
America; ~ un an\ in a year;
tout en riant\ while laughing;
en été\ in summer; agir en
homme\ act like a man

en 2 [ahπ] *pron* of/for
him/her/it/them; from; there;
some; any il ~ parle\ he is
speaking of it ; j'~ ai\ I have
some; il ~ est aimé\ he is
loved by her

en désordre [dai•SAURDR] *n*
disarray

en désordre sale
[de•SAURDR] *adj* messy

en dessous; *prep* sous
au-dessous de *adv* below

en dessous; *prep* sous
au-dessous de *adv* beneath

en effet; *excl* ~! vraiment!
adv indeed

émigrer [ai•mee•GRAI] *vi*
migrate

en entier entirety

en face de *prép* facing

en grande partie *adv* largely

en haillons ragged

en haillons [en ah•YAUπ] *npl*
M rags; tatters

en haut [ahn O] *adv* upstairs

en liberté conditionelle *n*
parole

en losange [-lau•SAHπZH] *adj*
diamond-shaped

en partie *adv* partly

en passant (by the ~) M way

en plus [ahπ•PLEW] *adv* (prép
~ de) besides

en route pour (être); à
destination de (être) bound

en tranches épaisses [œπ
trahπsh eh•pehs] *adv comp*
thickly

enceinte [ahπ•SAπT] *n* F
enclousre; walls; precinct; *adj*
pregnant

encens [ahn•SAHNS] *n* incense

enchaîner [ahn•shen•AI] chain

enchanter [ahπ•shahπ•TAI] *vt*
enchant

enchère [ahπ•SHER] *n* F bid;
vi faire une ~

enclin [ahπ•KLAπ] *adj* prone;
inclined; disposed; apt

encore [ahπ•KOR] *adv* again;
still

encorner [ahπ•kaur•NAI] *vt*
gore

encorse [ahπ•KAUR] *adj* yet

encouragement
[ahπ•KOO•rahzh•MAHπ] *n* M
encouragement

encourager
[ahπ•KOO•rah•ZHAI] *vt*
encourage

encourir [ahπ•koo•REER] *vt*
incur

encre [ahπkr] *n* F ink

encyclopédie
[ahπ•SEE•klau•pai•DEE] *n* F
encyclopedia

endommager
[ahn•DAU•mah•ZHEH] *vt*
impair

endormi [ahπ•daur•MEE] *adj*
asleep; sleeping

endurance [ahπ•dew•RAHπS]
n F endurance; stamina

énergie [ai•ner•ZHEE] *n* F
energy

énergique [ai•ner•ZHEEK] *adj*
energetic; forceful

énerver [ai•ner•VAI] *vt*
unnerve; fluster

enfance [ahπ•FAHπS] *n* F
childhood

enfant [ahπ•FAHπ] *n* F child

enfer [ahπ•FER] *n* M hell

enfin [ahπ•FAπ] *adv* finally; at
last

enflammer [ahπ•flah•MAI] *vt*
inflame

enflure [ahπ•FLYR] *n* F
swelling

enfreindre [ahπ•fraπDR] *vt*
infringe

engageant [ahπ•gah•ZHAHπ]
adj engaging

engagement
[ahπ•gazh•MAHπ] *n* M
engagement; committment

engager [ahπ•gah•ZHAI] *vt*
engage; wage

engendrer [ahπ•zhaπ•DREH]
vt engender; spawn

engloutir [ahπ•gloo•TEER] *vt.*
engulf; gobble

engouement [ahπ•goo•MAHπ]
n M craze; fad

engourdi [ahπ•goor•DEE] *adj*
torpid; numb; *vt* engourdir; *vi*
s'engourdir engrais [ahπ•gre]
n M fertilizer; manure; grass;
pasture

engraisser [ahπ•gre•SAI] *vt*
fatten; fertilize

énigme [ai•NEEGMU] *n* F
enigma; riddle

enjoliveur
[ahπ•ZHAU•lee•VœR] *n*
hubcap

enjoué [ahπ•zhoo•AI] *adj*
playful

enlèvement [ahπ•lev•MAHπ] *n*
kidnaping; removal

enlever [ahπ•lu•VEH] *vt*
remove; abduct

ennemi [en•uh•MEE] *n* M
enemy; foe

ennui [ahπ•NWEE] *n* M
boredom; nuisance

ennuis [ahπ•NWEE] *npl* M
trouble

ennuyer [ahn•wee•AI] *vt* bore;
vex

ennuyeux -euse
[ahπ•nweey•Ø]; [-ØZ] *adj*

annoying; tiresome; tedious;
boring; dull

énorme [ai•NAURM] *adj*
enormous; huge; tremendous

enquête [ahπ•KET] *n*
investigation; probe; inquiry

enragé [ahπ•rah•ZHAI] *n* M
madman; *adj* mad; enraged;
rabid

enregistrement
[ahn•RE•zhee•str•MAHπ] *n* M
recording

enrichir [ahπ•ree•SHEER] *vt*
enrich

enrôler [ahπ•ro•LAI] *vt* enlist *vi*
s'enrôler

enrouler [ahπ•roo•LEH] *vt*
wrap

enseigné [ahπ•seh•NYEH] *adj*
pp enseigner taught

enseigner [ahπ•seh•NYEH] *vt*
teach

enseignment
[ahπ•seh•NYMAHπ] *n* M
teaching

ensemble [ahπ•SAHπBL] *adv*
together

ensorcelant
[ahπ•saur•su•LAHπ] *adj*
bewitching; captivating

ensuite [ahπ•SWEET] *adv* then;
after; afterards; next

entâcher [ahπ•tah•SHEH] *vt*
taint

entaille [ahπ•TAI] *n* F notch;
groove; cut; gash

entailler [ahπ•tai•YEH] *vt*
indent; notch; groove

entendre [ahπ•tahπDR] *vt* hear;
understand; expect; intend;

mean; ~ par hasard\ overhear;
~ parler que\ hear of

enterrement [ahπ•ter•MAHπ]
n M burial; funeral

enterrer [ahπ•te•RAI] *vt* bury

enthousiasme
[ahπ•TOO•zee•AHZM] *n* M
enthusiasm

enthousiaste
[ahπ•TOO•zee•AHST] *adj* M
enthusiastic

entier [ahπ•TYEH] *adj* entire

entièrement
[ahπ•tyehr•MAHπ] *adv*
altogether; entirely; *adj* entire;
wholly

entité [ahπ•tee•TAI] *n* F entity

entonnoir [ahπ•tau•NWAHR] *n*
M funnel

entoure [aπ•TOOR] *adj*
surrounded; enclosed

entourer [ahπ•too•RAI] *vt*
enclose

entracte [ahπ•TRAHKT] *n* M
intermission

entraîner [ahπ•tre•NAI] *vt*
entail

entraîneur -euse
[ahπ•traπ•NœR] [ØZ] *n* MF
trainer

entraves [ahπ•TRAHV] *npl* F
shackles

entre [ahπtr] *prép* between;
among; amid; into; ~ nous\
between us

entrée [ahπ•TRAI] *n* F
entrance; entry; price of entry;
first course

entrelacer [ahπ•tru•lah•SAI] *vt*
intertwine; *vi* s'entrelacer

entreprenant
[ahπ•tr•pre•NAHπ] *adj*
enterprising

entreprendre
[ahπtr•PRAHπDR] *vt*
undertake (une tâche)

entrepreneur
[AHπ•tru•pru•NUR] *n* M
builder; undertaker;
entrepreneur

entrepris [ahπtr•PREE] *adj*
undertaken

entreprise [ahπtr•PREEZ] *n* F
enterprise; undertaking

entrer [ahπ•TRAI] *vi* enter; go
into; take part; ~ dans une
propriété privée sans
autorisation *vi comp*\ trespass;
~ en collision (avec)\ collide
(with); ~ en éruption\ erupt

entrêté [ahπ•treh•TEH] *adj*
wayward

entretenir [ahπtr•tu•NEER] *vt*
sustain

entretien [ahπtr•TYAπ] *n* M
upkeep

entrevue [ahπ•tru•VEW] *n*
interview

entrouvert [ahπ•troo•VEHR]
adj ajar

énumérer [ai•NEW•mai•RAI]
vt enumerate

envahi [ahπ•vah•EE] *adj*
overrun; ~ par les herbes\
weedy

envahir [ahπ•vah•EER] *vt*
invade

enveloppe [ahπ•VLAUP] *n* F
envelope

envelopper [ahπ•vlau•PAI] *vt*
envelop

envie [ahπ•VEE] *n* envy F; *vt*
envier; ~ de dormir\
sleepiness

envieux [ahπ•VYØ] *adj*
envious

environ [ahπ•vee•RAUπ] *adj*
roughly

environnement
[ahπ•VEE•rauπ•MAHπ] *n* M
environment; surroundings

environs [ahn•ee•RAUN] *npl* M
vicinity

envoûté [ahπ•voo•TEH] *adj*
spellbound

envoyé [ahπ•vwah•YAI] *n*
envoy; emmisary

envoyer [ahπ•vwah•YAI] *vt*
send

épais -se [eh•PEH] [eh•PEHS]
adj thick

épaisseur [eh•peh•SœR] *n* F
thickness

épar [eh•PAHR] *adj* sparse

éparpiller [ai•PAHR•pee•YAI]
vt scatter; *vi* se disperser

épaule [ai•POL] *n* F shoulder

épave [ai•PAHV] *n* F waif; M
wreck

épée [ai•PEH] *n* F sword; rapier

épeler [ai•peh•LEH] *vt* spell

éperdu [ai•per•DEW] *adj*
distraught; distracted;
bewildered

éperon [ai•pehr•AUπ] *n* M
spur; ridge; buttress

épice [ai•PEES] *n* F spice

épicerie [ai•PEE•se•REE] *n* F
grocery; ~\ fine delicatessen

épidémie [ai•PEE•dai•MEE] *n*
F epidemic

épinards [ai•pee•NAHR] *npl* M
spinach

épine [ai•PEEN] *n* F thorn

épingle [ai•PAπGL] *n* F pin; *vt*
épingler; ~ à cheveux\
hairpin; ~ de sûreté/~ de
nourrice\ safety pin

épique [ai•PEEK] *adj* epic; *n* F
épopée

épisode [ai•pee•ZAUD] *n* M
episode

épitaphe [ai•pee•TAF] *n* F
epitaph

épître [ai•PEETR] *n* F epistle

éponge [ai•PAUπZH] *n* F
sponge; *vt* éponger

époque [ai•PAUK] *n* epoch

épouser [ai•poo•ZAI] *vt* marry

épousseter [ai•poo•seh•TEH] *vi*
whisk

épouvantable
[ai•poo•vahπ•TAHBL] *adj*
dreadful

épouvante [ai•poo•VAHπ] *n* F
dread

époux -se; [ai•POO] [-POOZ] *n*
MF spouse

épreuves [ai•PRØV] *n* F proof;
trial; test; print; *npl* F
hardship; difficulty; ordeal

épris (de) [ai•PREE] *adj*
enamored (of)

éprouvette [eh•proo•VEHT] *n*
F test tube

épuisé [ai•pwee•ZAI] *adj*
exhausted; used up; run-down

épuisement [ai•pweez•MAHπ]
n M exhaustion

épuiser [ai•pwee•ZAI] *vt*
deplete

épuissant [eh•pwee•ZAHπ] *adj*
wearisome

épuissé [eh•pwee•SEH] *adj*
weary; run-down (pers)

équateur [ai•kwah•TØR] *n* M
equator

équation [ai•kwah•SYAUπ] *n*
F equation

équilibre [ai•kee•LEEBR] *n* M
balance; *vt* mettre en
équilibre; équilibrer; *vi*
s'équilibrer

équipage [ai•kee•PAHZH] *n* M
crew; team; equipment;
carriage; hunt

équipement [ai•keep•MAHπ] *n*
M equipment; gear

équiper [ai•kee•PAI] *vt* equip

équippe [eh•KEEP] *n* F team

équivalent [ai•KEE•vah•LAHπ]
adj n M equivalent;
counterpart

érable [ai•RAHBL] *n* M maple

éradiquer [ai•RAH•dee•KAI] *vt*
eradicate; erase

ère [er] *n* F era

érection [ai•rek•SYAUπ] *n* F
erection

éreintant [ai•raπ•TAHπ] *adj*
grueling; harsh

éreinté [ai•raπ•TAI] *adj* jaded;
critical

ermite [er•MEET] *n* M hermit

éroder [ai•rau•DAI] *vt* erode; *vi*
s'éroder

érosion [ai•rau•ZYAUπ] *n* F
erosion

errant -e; [ehr•AHπ] [-AHNT]
adj n MF stray; errant

errer [ehr•REH] *vi* wander;
stray

erreur [e•RœR] *n* F error;
mistake

érroné [ai•rau•NAI] *adj*
mistaken

érudit [ai•rew•DEE] *adj* erudite;
scholarly; *n* M scholar

éruption [ai•rewp•SYAUπ] *n* F
eruption; outbreak

escabeau [eh•skah•BAU] *n* M
stepladder

escadron [eh•skah•DRAUπ] *n*
MF troop; squadron

escalier; escaliers
[eh•skah•leey•EH] *n; npl* M
stair; escalator

esclavage [eh•sklah•VAHZH] *n*
M bondage

esclave [eh•SKLAHV] *n* MF
slave

escorte [eh•SKAURT] *n* F
escort; *vt* escorter

escouade [eh•SKWAHD] *n* F
squad (mil); section; brigade

escrime [eh•SCREEM] *n* F
fencing (sport)

escroc [eh•SKRAUK] *n* M
crook

escroquerie
[eh•SKRAU•kehr•EE] *n* F
swindle; *vt* escroquer

espace [eh•SPAHS] *n* M space

Espagnol -e [eh•spah•NYAUL]
n MF Spaniard

espagnol -e [eh•spah•NYAUL]
[-NYAULE] *adj* Spanish

espèce [eh•SPEHS] *n* F species

espèces [eh•SPEHS] *spl* F cash

espérance [eh•sper•AUπS] *n* F
hope; expectation; ~ de vie\
life expectancy

espérer [eh•speh•REH] *vt* hope; expect; await (qqn)

espion -nne [eh•speey•AUπ]; [-AUN] *n* MF spy

espionnage [eh•spyau•NAHZH] *n* M espionage

espoir [eh•spwahr] *n* M hope; expectation

esprit [eh•SPREE] *n* M mind; spirit; wit; ~ d'économie\ thrift

esquiver [eh•skee•VAI] *vt* dodge; avoid; *vi* s'esquiver

essai [eh•SEH] *n* M essay; test; try

essayer [eh•sehy•EH] *vt vi* M try

essence [eh•SAHπs] *n* F essence; gasoline

essenciel [eh•sahπ•SYEL] *adj* F essential; *n* M gist

essenciellement [eh•SAHπ•syel•MAHπ] *adv* F essentially

essieu [eh•SYU] *n* M axle

éssoufflé [ai•soo•FLAI] *adj* breathless

essuyer [eh•swee•YEH] *vt* wipe; essuie glace *n* M\ windshield wiper

est [est] *adj* east ; à/vers l'~\ to the east

estime [eh•STEEM] *n* F esteem f; *vt* estimer; ~ de soi *n*\ self-esteem

estimer [eh•stee•MAI] *vt* appraise; estimate

estomac [eh•stau•MAHK] *n* M stomach

estropier [eh•strau•PYAI] *vt* maim

esturgeon [eh•styr•ZHAUπ] *n* M sturgeon

et [ai] *conj* and

établir [ai•tah•BLEER] *vt* establish

établissement; l'Establishment [ai•TAH•blees•MAHπ] *n* M establishment

étage [eh•TAZH] *n* M story; floor; stage; stratum; layer

étager [eh•tazh•EH] *vi* range in tiers

étagère [ai•tah•ZHEHR] *n* F shelf

étain [eh•TAπ] *n* M tin

étalage [ai•tah•LAHZH] *n* display

étalon [ai•tahl•AUπ] *n* M stallion; stud

étanche [ai•TAπSH] *adj* watertight

étang [ei•TAHπ] *n* M pool; pond; *n* F mare

étant [ai•TAHπ] *prep* considering; given

état [ai•TAH] *n* M state; occupation; profession; trade; government; establishment; estate; predicament; estimate; statement of account; l'~ de neuf\ as good as new; hors d'~\ useless; homme d'Etat\ statesman; remettre en ~\ put in order; Etats-Unis\ United States

été [ai•TAI] *n* M summer

éteindre [ai•TAπDR] *vt* extinguish; extend; switch off

étendue [ai•tahπ•DEW] *n* F extent

éternel [ai•ter•NEL] *adj* eternal

éternité [ai•TER•nee•TAI] *n* F
eternity

Éthiopie [ai•tyau•PEE] *n*
Ethiopia

éthique [ai•TEEK] *n* F ethic;
moral; morale

ethnique [et•NEEK] *adj* ethnic

étincelant [ai•taπs•LAHπ] *adj*
sparkling

étinceler [ai•taπs•LEH] *vi*
twinkle

étincellement (étoiles)
[ai•taπ•sehl•mahπ] *n* M
twinkling

étiqueter [ai•teek•TEH] *vt* tag

étiquette 1 [ai•tee•KEHT] *n* F
tab; label; ticket; tag; *vt*
étiquer

étiquette 2 [ai•tee•KEHT] *n*
etiquette; ceremony

étoile [ai•TWAHL] *n* F star; ~
filante\ shooting star

étole [ai•TAUL] *n* F stole

étonment [ai•ton•MAUπ] *n* M
wonder; astonishment

étonnant [ai•tau•NAHπ] *adj*
amazing

étonner [ai•tau•NEH] *vt* startle;
stun

étouffement [ai•toof•MAHπ] *n*
M cover-up

étouffer [ai•too•FEH] *vt* stifle;
cover up; ~ de chaleur *vi*\
swelter

étourdi [ai•toor•DEE] *adj*
giddy; unthinking

étrange [ai•TRAHπZH] *adj*
(inv) strange; odd

étranger -ère [ai•trahπ•ZHEH];
[-ZHEHR] *n* MF stranger;
foreigner

étranger [ai•trahπ•ZHEH] *n* M
outsider; *adj* foreign

étrangeté [ai•trahπzh•TEH] *n* F
strangeness

étrangler [ai•tahπ•GLAI] *vt vi*
refl choke; *vt* strangle;
strangulate

être [ehtr] *n* M being; creature;
existence; *v* be; exist; have;
go; belong; be dressed; ~
allongé\ recline; ~ d'accord\
concur; ~ debout\ be up; ~
humain\ human being; ~
originaire\ originate; ~ relatif
à\ pertain; ~ voué à l'échec\
doomed

étreinte [ai•TRAπT] *n* F
embrace; hug

étrier [ai•treey•EH] *n* M stirrup

étroit -e [ai•TRWAH] [-trwaht]
adj tight; narrow

étudiant -e
[ai•tew•DEEYAHπ]; [-ahnt] *n*
MF student; ~ de seconde
année\ sophomore; ~ qui
prépare sa license\
undergraduate; ~ de première
année\ freshman

étudier [ai•tew•DEEYEH] *vt*
study

étui [ai•TWEE] *n* M holster

euphémisme [Ø•fai•MEEZM]
n M euphemism

Europe [Ø•RAUP] *n* F Europe

européen; Européen
[Ø•rau•pai•Aπ] *n* MF *adj*
European

euthanasie [Ø•tah•nah•ZEE] *n*
F euthanasia

eux elles; les; leur [eØ] [ehl];
[leh]; [lœr] *pron disjonctif;*

pron object direct; pron objet indirect them

eux-mêmes; elles-mêmes [Ø-MEHM] [ehl-MEHM] *pron emphatique* themselves

évacuer; *vi* s'évacuer [ai•vah•kew•AI] *vt* evacuate

évailler [ai•veh•YEH] *vt* waken

évaluation [ai•VAH•lew•ah•SYAUπ] *n* F appraisal; estimate; evaluation

évaluer [ai•vah•lew•AI] *vt* evaluate

évangile [ai•vahπ•ZHEEL] *n* M gospel; the Gospel\ l'Evangile

évaporer [ai•VAH•pau•RAI] *vt* evaporate

évasif [ai•vah•SEEF] *adj* evasive

évasion [ai•vah•ZYAUπ] *n* F escape

événement [ai•vain•MAHπ] *n* M happening; occurence; event

éventualité [ai•VAHπ•tew•ah•lee•TAI] *n* F contingency; eventuality

éventuel [ai•VAHπ•tew•EL] *adj* prospective; eventual

éventuellement [ai•VAHπ•tew•ehl•MAHπ] *adv* ultimately

évêque [ai•VEK] *n* M bishop

évidement [ai•vee•du•MAHπ] *adj* obviously

évident [ai•vee•DAHπ] *adj* evident; obvious

évier [ai•VYEH] *n* M ; sink; kitchen sink

évincer [ai•vaπ•SAI] *vt* oust

éviter [ai•vee•TAI] *vt* avoid; shun

évoluer [ai•vau•lew•AI] *vi* evolve

évolution [ai•vau•lew•SYAUπ] *n* F evolution

évoquer [ai•vau•KAI] *vt* evoke

exact [eg•ZAHKT] *adj* exact

exagération [eg•ZAH•zhai•rah•SYAUπ] *n* exaggeration

exagérer [eg•ZAH•zhai•RAI] *vt* *vi* exaggerate

examen [eg•zah•MAπ] *n* M examination; passer un ~\ take an exam

examiner [eg•ZAH•mee•NAI] *vt* M examine

exaspérer [eg•ZAH•spai•RAI] *vt* exasperate; madden

excédentaire [ek•SAI•dahπ•TEHR] *adj* excess; *n* M excès

excellence [ek•su•LAHπS] *n* excellence

excellent [ek•su•LAHπ] *adj* excellent

exceller [ek•se•LAI] *vi* excel

exception [ek•sep•SYAUπ] *n* F exception

exceptionel [ek•SEP•syau•NEL] *adj* exceptional; outstanding; special

excessif [ek•se•SEEF] *adj* excessive

excité [ek•see•TAI] *adj* excited

exciter [ek•see•TAI] *vt* excite; *vi* s'exciter

exclure [ek•SKLEWR] *vt* preclude; exclude

excrément [ek•skrai•MAHπ] *n*
M excrement

excursion [ek•skewr•ZYAUπ] *n*
F excursion

excuse [ek•SKEWS] *n* F excuse

excuser [eks•kew•ZAI] *vt*
excuse; excusez moi\ excuse
me; *vi refl* apologize

excuses [ek•skew•ZE] *npl* F
apology

exécuter [ek•sai•kew•TAI] *vt*
execute

exécutif [eg•zai•kew•TEEF] *adj*
n M executive

exécution [ek•sai•kew•SYAUπ]
n F execution; performance

exemplaire [eg•zahπ•PLEHR]
adj exemplary

exemple [eg•ZAHπPL] *'n* M
example; instance por ~\ for
example

exemplifier
[eg•ZAHπ•plee•FYAI] *vt*
exemplify

exempt [eg•ZAHπ] *adj* exempt;
vt exempter

exercer [eg•zer•SAI] *vt* exert

exercice [eg•zer•SEES] *n* F
exercise ; *vt* exercer; *vi*
prendre de l'exercice

exhaler [ek•sah•lai] *vt* exhale

exigeant [eg•zee•ZHAHπ] *adj*
fastidious; demanding

exigence [ek•see•ZHAHπS] *n* F
demand; requiremeng

exiger [ehg•zee•ZHEH] *vt*
require

exil [eg•ZEEL] *n* M exile; *adj*
exilé ; *vt* exiler

existence [eg•zee•STAHπS] *n*
F existence

exister [eg•zee•STAI] *vi* exist

exode [eg•ZAUD] *n* M exodus

exotique [eg•zau•TEEK] *adj*
exotic

expéditeur [ek•SPAI•dee•TœR]
n M sender

expédition
[ek•spai•dee•SYAUπ] *n* F
expedition

expérience [ek•spai•RYAHπS]
n F experience

expérimenter
[ek•SPAI•ree•mahπ•TEH] *n*
experiment

expérimenté 1
[ek•SPAI•ree•mahπ•TAI] *adj*
experienced; seasoned

expérimenté 2
[ek•SPAI•ree•mahπ•TAI] *adj*
n M veteran

expert [ek•SPER] *adj n* M
expert; skilled

expirer [ek•spee•RAI] *vi* expire

explication
[ek•splee•kah•SYAUπ] *n* F
explanation

expliquer [ek•splee•KAI] *vt*
explain; *vi* s'expliquer

exploit [ek•SPLWAH] *n* M
feat; exploit; ~ spectaculaire\
stunt

exploitation
[ek•splwah•ta•SYUπ] *n* F
exploitation; mining

exploration
[ek•splau•rah•SYAUπ] *n* F
exploration

explorer [ek•splau•RAI] *vt vi*
explore

exploreur [ek•splau•RœR] *n* M
explorer

exploser [ek•splau•ZAI] *vi*
explode

explosion [ek•splau•ZYAUπ] *n*
outburst; blast

exportation
[ek•spaur•tah•SYAUπ] *n*
export; *vt vi* exporter

exposer [ek•spau•ZAI] *vt*
expose

exposition
[ek•spau•zee•SYAUπ] *n* F
exhibit; *vt* exposer

exprès [ek•SPREH] *adv*
deliberately; *adj* express

expressif [ek•spre•SEEF] *adj*
expressive

expression [ek•spre•shn] *n* F
expression; phrase

expulser [ek•spewl•SAI] *vt*
evict; eject; deport; expel

exquis [ek•SKEE] *adj* exquisite

extase [ek•STAHS] *n* F
ecstasy

extatique [ek•stah•TEEK] *adj*
F ecstatic

extensible [ek•stahπ•SEEBL]
adj (inv) tensile

extension [ek•stahπ•SYAUπ] *n*
F extent; extension

extérieur [ek•stai•RYœR] *adj n*
M exterior; *adj* outer;
outward; outside

exterminer [ek•ster•mee•NAI]
vt exterminate

externe [ek•STERN] *adj*
external

extorquer qqch à qqn
[ek•staur•KAI] *vt* extort

extrader [ek•strah•DAI] *vt*
extradite

extrait [ek•STREH] *n* M
excerpt

extrait [ek•STREH] *n* M
extract; *vt* extraire

extraordinaire
[ek•strau•dee•NEHR] *adj*
extraordinary

extravagance
[ek•strah•vah•GAHπS]
extravagance

extravagant
[ek•strah•vah•GAHπ] *adj*
extravagant

extrême [ek•STREM] *adj*
dire; *adj n* M extreme;
ultimate

extrémiste [ek•strai•MEEST]
adj n M extremist

extroverti [ek•strau•ver•TEE]
adj n M extrovert

exubérant [eg•zew•bai•RAHπ]
adj exuberant

exulter [eg•zewl•TAI] *vi* exult

F

fable [fahbl] *n* F fable
fabricant [fah•bree•KAHπ] *n* M
manufacturer

fabrication
[fah•bree•kah•SYAUπ] *n*
manufacture

fabrique [fa•BREEK] *n* F
factory

fabriquer [fah•bree•KAI] *vt*
fabricate; manufacture

fabuleux [fah•bew•LØ] *adj*
fabulous

façade [fah•SAHD] *n* F facade

facétieux [fah•sai•TYØ] *adj*
facetious

facette [fah•SET] *n* F facet

faché [fah•SHAI] *adj* angry

facile [fah•SEEL] *adj* easy

facilement [fah•seel•MAHπ]
adv easily

facilité [fah•SEE•lee•TAI] *n*
ease; facility; ability

façon [fah•SAUπ] *n* F make;
work; workmanship; manner;
way *npl* ceremeony;
affectation; fuss; de ~ à\ so as
to; de toute ~\ in any case

façonner [fah•sauπ•NEH] *vt*
shape; form; fashion

facteur [fahk•TœR] *n* M factor;
mailman; postman

facture [fahk•TEWR] *n* F
invoice; bill

facultatif [fah•kewl•tah•TEEF]
adj optional

faculté [fah•kewl•TAI] *n* F
faculty; ~ de droit *n*\ law
school

fade [fahd] *adj* bland; tasteless

faseur [fah•SœR] *n* F blandess;
insipidity; pointlessness

faible [fehbl] *adj* feeble; weak

faiblement [feh•bl•MAHπ] *adv*
weakly

failli [fah•YEE] *adj* bankrupt; *vi*
go ~\ faire faillite

faillite [fah•YEET] *n* F
bankruptcy

faim [fehπ] *n* F hunger;
starvation; *vt* avoir ~\ be
hungry

fainéant [faπ•neh•AHπ] *n* M
slacker; idler; sluggard

fair tapisserie [fehr
tah•PEE•sehr•EE] *vt* comp
wallflower

faire [fehr] *n* M doing;
technique; style;
workmanship; *vt* make; cause;
get; do; perform; suit; fit;
manage; say; persuade; wage;
cela fait mon affaire\ that suits
me fine; faites attention\ be
careful; faites-moi le plaisir
de\ do me the favor of; cela
ne se fait pas\ that is not
done; ne vours en faites pas\
don't worry

faire bouillir *vi* boil

faire connaître au public
publicize

**faire de l'auto-stop faire du
stop** *vi* hitchhike

faire détoner detenate

faire dévier *vt* sidetrack

faire don de *vt* donate

faire éclore *vi* hatch

faire purée *vt* mash

faire étalage de flaunt

faire évaporer *vi* evaporate

faire exploser *vi* explode

faire intrusion intrude

faire respecter; imposer *vt*
enforce

faire sécession *vt* secede

faire semblant (faire semblant
de faire qqch) *vi* pretend

faire signe à beckon

faire une enquête sur
investigate

faire une grimace frown

faisable [fe•ZAHBL] *adj*
feasible

fait 1 [feh] *pp de faire*\ did;
done; ~ à la main\ handmade;
~ à la maison\ homemade; ~
au hasard\ random; ~ par
inadvertance\ inadvertent

fait 2 [feh] *n* M fact; deed; act;
feat; en ~\ in fact; au ~ de ~\
indeed; être au ~ de\ be
informed; en venir au ~\ come
to the point (of/that)

falaise [fah•LEZ] *n* F cliff;
bluff

falloir [fah•LWAR] *vi* be
necessary; il faut que\ he
must; comme il faut\ proper;
correct

falsifier [fahl•see•FYAI] *vt*
falsify

familiariser
[fah•MEE•lyah•ree•ZAI] *vt*
familiarize

familier [fah•mee•LYAI] *adj*
colloquial; familiar; informal

famille [fah•MEEY] *n* F
family

famine [fah•MEEN] *n* F
famine

fanatique [fah•nah•TEEK] *n*
MF fanatic; zealot

fanion [fah•NYAUπ] *n* M
pennant; banner

fantastique [fahπ•tah•STEEK]
adj fantastic

fantôme [fahn•TAUM] *n* M
ghost; phantom; spook

faon m; [fahπ] *n* fawn; *vi* ~ en\
flatter

farce 1 [fahrs] *n* F farce; prank;
practical joke

farce 2 [fahrs] *n* F stuffing
(cusine)

farine [fah•REEN] *n* F flour;
meal

farouche [fah•ROOSH] *adj*
wild; fierce

fascinant [fah•see•NAHπ] *adj*
fascinating

fascination
[fah•see•nah•SYAUπ] *n* F
fascination

fasciner [fah•see•NAI] *vt*
fascinate

fascisme [fah•SEESM] *n* M
fascism

fatal [fah•TAHL] *adj* fatal;

fatidique [fah•tee•DEEK] *adj*
fateful

fatigue [fah•TEEG] *n* F fatigue;
tiredness; weariness; *vi*
fatiguer; *adj* fatigant

fatigué [fah•tee•GEH] *adj* tired

faubourgs [fo•BOORG] *npl* M
outskirts

faucille [fo•SEEL] *n* F sickle

faucon [fo•KAUπ] *n* M falcon;
hawk

faune [fon] *n* F fauna; plant life

faussement [fo•SMAUπ] *adj*
adv coy

faute [fot] *n* fault; error;
mistake; ~ d'impression; ~ de
vi\ want; c'est de ma ~\ it's
my fault; ~ professionelle;
négligence;\ malpractice

fauteuil [fo•TœY] *n* M
armchair; ~ roulant\

wheelchair; ~ basculer\rocking chair; ~ pivotant(e)\ swivel chair

faux 1 [fo] *n* M falseood; forgery; *adj* wrong; artificial; fake; false; untrue

faux f 2 [fo] *n* scythe; *vt* faucher

faveur [fah•VœR] *n* F favor; *vt* favoriser

favorable [fah•vau•RAHBL] *adj* favorable

favori [fah•vau•REE] *adj n* M favorite

fédéral [fai•dai•RAHL] *adj* federal

fédération [fai•DAI•rah•SYAUπ] *n* F federation

fée [fai] *n* F fairy

feindre [faπdr] *vt* feign; fake; sham; pretend

félicité [fai•lee•cee•TAI] *n* F bliss; felicity

féliciter [fai•lee•see•TAI] *vt* congratulate

femelle [fai•MEHL] *adj n* F female

féminin [feh•mee•NAπ] *adj* feminine; womanly

fémininité [feh•MEE•nee•nee•TEH] *n* F womanhood; femininity

femme [fahm] *n* F woman; wife; ~ de ménage *n*\ cleaning lady

fenêtre [fuh•NEHTR] *n* F window

fente [fahπt] *n* F slit; crack; fissure; opening

féodal [fai•au•DAHL] *adj* feudal

fer [fer] *n* M iron; sword; horseshoe; flat-iron; ~ forgé\ wrought iron; ~-blanc\ tin; ~ à cheval\ horseshoe; ~ fer à repasser (pour vêtements)

ferme [ferm] *n* F farm; *adj* firm; rigid; steady; fixed; resolved

fermenter [fer•mahπ•TEHI] *vi* ferment

fermer [fer•MAI] *vt* close; shut; fasten; switch off; turn off; *vi* se fermer; *adj* fermé

fermier [fer•MYEHR] *n* M farmer

fermoir [fer•MWAHR] *n* M clasp

fermature à crémaillère [fehr•mah•TOOR ah kreh•mah•YEHR] *n* F zipper

féroce [fai•ROS] *adj* ferocious; wild; fierce

ferry [fe•REE] *n* M ferry

fertile [fer•TEEL] *adj* fertile

fertiliser [fer•tee•lee•ZAI] *vt* fertilize

fertilité [fer•tee•lee•TAI] *n* fertility

fervent [fer•VAHπ] *adj* fervent

ferveur [fehr•VœR] *n* F zeal

fesse [fes] *n* F buttock

fessée [feh•SEH] *n* spanking

fesser [feh•SEH] *vt* spank

festin [feh•STAπ] *n* M feast; banquet

festival [feh•stee•VAHL] *n* M festival

festivités [feh•stee•vee•TEH] *npl* F revelry; festivities

festoyer [feh•stoi•YEH] *vt*
feast; regale

fête [feht] *n F* party; feast;
festival; holiday

fêter [feh•TEH] *vt* feast;
entertain; celebrate

feu [fØ] *n M* fire; flame; heat;
blaze; fireplace; light; spirit;
ardor; ~ en feu\ on fire;
mettre le ~\ set fire to; ~
d'artifice\ fireworks;
donne-moi du ~\ give me a
light; ~ croisé\ crossfire; ~ de
joie\ bonfire

feuillage [fœ•YAHZH] *n M*
foliage

feuille [fœy] *n F* leaf; *vi*
feuilleter\ leaf through

feuilleter [fœy•TEH] *vt* skim
(~ un magazine ou un
journal)

feuilleton [fœ•yu•TAUπ] *n M*
serial

feutre m; *pt* a feel [fØ•TR] *n*
felt

février [fai•vree•AI] *n M*
February

fiable [fyah•BL] *adj* reliable

fiancé [fyahπ•SAI] *n M* fiancé

fiancée [fyahπ•SAI] *n F* fiancée

fibre [feebr] *n F* fiber

ficelle [fee•SEHL] *n F* string;
twine

fiction [feek•SYAUπ] *n F*
fiction

fidèle [fee•DEL] *adj* faithful

fidélité [fee•DAI•lee•TAI] *n F*
fidelity

fier 1 [fyai] *adj* proud

fier 2 [fyai] *vi refl* rely on;
depend upon (se fier)

fierté [fyer•TAI] *n F* pride

fièvre [fye•VR] *n F* fever

fiévreux [fyai•VRØ] *adj F*
feverish

figue [feeg] *n F* fig

figure [fee•GYUR] *n F* visage;
figure; shape; form

figuré [fee•gew•RAI] *adj*
figurative; au ~\ figuratively

fil [feeul] *n M* thread; wire;
edge; grain; clue; course; ~ de
fer; fil métalique\ wire

filé [fee•LEH] *adj* spun

filer [fee•LEH] *vi* spring; draw
out; pay out; flow; run off;
sneak away

filet [fee•LE] *n M* loin;
tenderloin; fillet

fille [feey] *n F* daughter; girl

filleul [fee•YœL] *n M* godson

filleule [fee•YOOL] *n F*
goddaughter

film [feelm] *n M* film; movie; *vt*
filmer

fils [fees] *n M* son

filtre [feeltr] *n M* filter; *vt* filtrer

fin 1 [faπ] *n* finish; end;
termination; umpshot; à la ~\
in the long run; at last; mettre
~ à\ put an end to

fin 2 [faπ] *adj* fine; refined;
pure; subtle; delicate; small

final [fee•NAHL] *adj* final;
eventual

finalement [fee•nahl•MAHπ]
adv finally; eventually

finance [fee•NAHπS] *n F*
finance; *npl* finances fpl; *vt*
financer

financier [fee•nahπ•SYEH] *adj*
financial

fini [fee•NEE] *n* M finishing touch; *adj* over; finished; ended

Finlandais *n* F Finn

finlandais [feen•lah•π•DAI] *n* F Finnish

Finlande [feen•LAHπD] *n* F Finland

finnois [fee•NWAH] *n* M Finnish (langue)

fiscal [fee•SKAHL] *adj* fiscal

fission [fee•SYAUπ] *n* F fission

fissure [fee•SEWR] *n* F crevice; fissure; opening

fixation [feek•sah•SYAUπ] *n* F fixation

fixe [feeks] *n* M fixed salary/price; *adj* fixed; set; firm; regular

fixer [feek•SAI] *vt* fix; fasten; steady; stare at; arrange; decide; *vi* se fixer\ settle down; get fixed

flacon [fla•KAUπ] *n* M flask; bottle

flageller [flah•zhe•LAI] *vt* flog

flagrant [flah•GRAHπ] *adj* blatant; flagrant; obvious

flair [fler] *n* M flair

flamant [flah•MAHπ] *n* M flamingo

flambant [flahm•BAHπ] *adj* flaming; ~ neuf\ brand new

flamber [flahm•BEH] *vi* flame; blaze; singe; sterilize

flambé [flahm•BAI] *adj* flaming; blazing

flamme [flahm] *n* F flame; passion; love

flanc [flahπ] *n* M flank; side; *vt* flanquer; flanqué de

flanelle [flah•NEL] *n* F flannel

flaner [flah•NEH] *vi* stroll; walk

flâner [flah•NEH] *vi* dawdle

flaque [flahk] *n* F puddle; pool

flashback [flahsh•BAHK] *n* M flashback

flatter [flah•tai] *vt* caress; stroke; please

flatterie [flah•te•REE] *n* F flattery

flatteur [flah•TœR] *adj* flattering; pleasing

fléau [flai•O] *n* M scourge

flèche [flesh] *n* F arrow; spire

flèchette [fle•SHET] *n* F dart

fléchir [flai•SHEER] *vt vi* flex; yield

fléchissement [fleh•shee•MAUπ] *n* M yielding; bending

flet [fle] *n* M flounder

flétan [flai•TAHπ] *n* M halibut

flétrir; *vi* se flétrir [flai•TREER] *vt* shrivel

fleur [flœr] *n* M blossom; flower; en ~\ in flower; in bloom

fleurir [flœ•REER] *vi* flower; blossom; bloom

fleuriste [flœ•REEST] *n* MF florist

flexible [flek•SEEBL] *adj* flexible; yielding

flic [fleek] *n* M cop (coll)

flirt [flœrt] *n* M flirt; *vi* flirter

flocon [flau•KAUπ] *n* M flake; ~ de neige\ snowflake; ~ s *mpl* d'acoinen\ oatmeal

flore [flaur] *n* F flora; plants

fluctuer [flewk•tew•AI] *vi* fluctuate

fluide [flew•EED] *adj n* M fluid

fluorescent [flew•au•re•SAHπ] *adj* fluorescent

fluorure [flew•au•REWR] *n* M fluoride

flûte [flewt] *n* F flute

focal [fau•KAHL] *adj* focal; central

fœtus [fœ•TEW] *n* M fetus

foi [fwah] *n* F faith; belief; trust; confidence; evidence; de bonne ~\ in good faith; digne de ~\ reliable; trustworthy

foie [fwah] *n* M liver

foin [fwahπ] *n* M hay

folâtre [fau•LAHTR] *adj* playful; frisky; wanton

folâtrer [fau•lah•TREH] *vi* frolic

folie [fau•LEE] *n* F folly; insanity; madness

follement [faul•MAHπ] *adv* madly; ~ amoureux de\ madly in love with

fomenter [fau•mahπ•TAI] *vt* foment

fonction [fauπk•SYAUπ] *n* function; *vi* fonctionner

fond [fauπ] *n* M bottom; *prep* au ~ de\ on the bottom; à ~\ thoroughly

fondamental [fon•dah•mahπ•TAHL] *adj* basic; fundamental

fondant [fon•DAHπ] *n* M confection ~ de chocalat\ fudge

fondateur [fauπ•dah•TœR] *n* F founder

fondation [fauπ•dah•SYAUπ] *n* F foundation; basis

fondé [fauπ•DAI] *adj* founded; authorized

fonder [fauπ•DEH] *vt* found; establish; ground; base; justify

fondre [fauπdr] *vi* thaw

fonds [fauπ] *n* M land; estate; fund; business; *npl* M cash; capital revenue

fondu [fauπ•DEW] *adj* molten

fontaine [fauπ•TEN] *n* F fountain

football [foot•BOL] *n* M football

forçat [faur•SAH] *n* M convict

force [faurs] *n* F force; strength; vigor; à force de\ on the strength of; ~ majeure\ absolute necessity; circumstances outside one's control *vi*

force [faurs] *n* F kmight

forceps [faur•SEPS] *n* M forceps

forcer 1 [faur•SEH] *vt* force; compel; oblige; break open; break through

forcer 2 [faur•SEH] *vt* drill; bore

forêt [fau•RE] *n* F forest

forge [faurzh] *n* F forge; smithy; *vt* (iron etc) forger;

forgeron [fau•zhu•ROπ] *n* M blacksmith

formalité [faur•mah•lee•TAI] *n* F formality

forme [faurm] *n* F form; *vt* former; *vi* se former; ~ profilée\ streamlined

formidable [faur•mee•DAHBL] *adj* terrific; wonderful; dreadful; swell (coll)

formule [faur•MEWL] *n* F
formula; form; prescription;
phrase

formuler [faur•mew•LEH] *vt*
draw up; formulate; express

fort [faur] *n* M fort; strong man;
strong pont; *adj* strong;
robust; clever; good

fortement [faurt•MAHπ] *adv*
strongly

forteresse [faur•TRES] *n* F
fortress

fortification
[faur•TEE•fee•kah•SYAUπ] *n*
F fortification

fortifier [faur•tee•FYAI] *vt*
fortify; strengthen

fortuit [faur•TWEE] *adj*
fortuitous; lucky

fortune [faur•TEWN] *n* F
fortune; chance; luck; wealth;
adj fortuné

fossé [fau•SAI] *n* F moat;
trench; ditch~ septique\ septic
tank

fossette [fau•SET] *n* F dimple

fossile [fau•SEEL] *n* F fossil

fou; folle [foo] [faul] *adj*
insane; mad; crazy; *n* M
madman; *n* F madwoman;
lunatic; maniac; jester; rendre
~\ drive mad; maison de ~s\
madhouse; être ~ de\ be crazy
about

fouet [foo•EH] *n* M flogging;
whip

fougeux [foo•ZHO] *adj* fiery

fouetter [fewh•TEH] *vt* whip

fougère [foo•ZHER] *n* F fern

fouille [fwee] *n* F excavation;
search

fouiller [fwee•YAI] *vi* excavate;
search; rummage

fouillis [fwee•YEE] *n* muddle;
jumble; mess

fouinard [fwee•NAHR] *adj*
nosy

foule [fooul] *n* F throng; crowd;
mob; venir en ~\ crowd mob

four [foor] *n* M kiln; oven; ~ à
micro-ondes\ microwave

fourche [foorsh] *n* F pitchfork

fourchette [foor•SHET] *n* F
fork

fourmi [foor•MEE] *n* F ant

fourmiller [foor•MYEH] *vi*
tingle

fourneau [foor•NO] *n* M
furnace

fournir [foor•NEER] *vt* provide

fourrage [foo•RAHZH] *n* M
fodder; forage; *vt vi* fourrager

fourrure [foo•REWR] *n* F fur

foyer [fwah•YEH] *n* M hearth;
focus

fraction [frahk•SYAUπ] *n* F
fraction

fracture [frahk•TEWR] *n* M
fracture; *vt* fracturer

fragile [frah•ZHEEL] *adj* fragile

fragment [frahg•MAHπ] *n* M
fragment

fraîcheur [fre•SHœR] *n* F
freshness; coolness

frais 1 [fre] *n* M coolness; *adj*
fresh; il fait ~\ it's fresh
(temps)

frais 2 [fre] *npl* M costs;
expenses; à peu ~\ at little
cost; faire les ~ de\ bear the
costs (of) ; ~ d'inscription\
tuition

fraise [frehz] *n* F strawberry

framboise [frahπ•BWAHZ] *n* F raspberry

franc 1 [frahπ] *adj* candid; frank; outspoken

franc 2 [frahπ] *adj* frank (poste)

français; [frahπ•SAI] *adj* French; *n* M French (language; people)

France [frahπs] *n* F France

franchise [frahπ•SHEES] *n* F franchise; candor

frange [frahnzh] *n* F fringe

frappe [frahp] *n* F minting; strking; *vt* frapper

frappant [frah•PAHπ];*adj* striking

fraternel [frah•ter•NEL] *adj* fraternal

fraude [frod] *n* F fraud

frauder [fro•DAI] *vt* defraud

frauduleux [fro•dew•LØ] *adj* fraudulent

fredonner [fre•dau•NEH] *vt* hum; *vi* fredonner

frein [frain] *n* M brake (voiture); curb; restraint; *vi* freiner

frelon [fre•LAUπ] *n* hornet

frémir [free•sau•NAI] *vi* shudder

frénésie [frai•nai•SEE] *n* F frenzy

frénétique [frai•nai•TEEK] *adj* frantic

fréquence [frai•KAHπS] *n* F frequency

fréquent [frai•KAHπ] *adj* F frequent; *vt* fréquenter

frère [frer] *n* M brother; friar (eccles)

fret [freh] *n* freight

friction [freek•syauπ] *n* F friction

frire [freer] *vt vi* fry

frisé [free•ZAI] *adj* curly

frisson [free•SAUπ] *n* M chill; quiver; shiver; thrill; *vi* frissoner

frites [freet] *npl* F french fries

frivole [free•VAUL] *adj* frivolous; skittish

froid [frwah] *adj* chilly; cold; avoir ~\ be cold; en ~\ on chilly terms; il fait ~\ it's cold (temps)

froissé [frwah•SAI] *adj* huff

froisser [frwah•SEH] *vt* rumple

fromage [frau•MAHZH] *n* F cheese

froncement [frauns•MAUπ] *n* M frown;\ ~ de sourcils; frown *vi*\ froncer les sourcils

front [frauπ] *n* M forehead

frontière [frauπ•TYER] *n* F frontier; border

frotter [frau•TEH] *vt* rub; scrub; polish; strike

fruit [frwee] *n* M fruit; advantag; profit; result

frustration [frew•strah•SYAUπ] *n* F frustration

frustrer [frew•STRAI] *vt* frustrate

fugitif [few•zhee•TEEF] *n* M fugitive

fuir [fweer] *vt vi* flee; escape

fuite [fweet] *n* F leak; flight; escape

fumée [foo•MAI] *n* F smoke; fumes; steam

fumer [foo•MEH] vt smoke;
steam
fumier [few•MYEH] n M dung;
manure
fumiger [few•mee•GEH] vt
fumigate
furet [few•RE] nM ferret
fureur [few•RœR] n F fury;
rage; faire ~\ be all the rage
furieux [few•RYØ] adj furious;
livid; mad

furtif [fewr•TEEF] adj furtive
fusée [few•ZAI] n F rocket;
flare
fusible [few•ZEEBL] n M
fuse
fusil [few•ZEEYL] n M rifle; ~
de chasse\ shotgun
fusion [few•ZYAUπ] n F
fusion; merger
futile [few•TEEL] adj futile
futur [few•TEWR] adj future

G

gâchette [gah•SHEHT] n vt F
trigger
gâchis [gah•SHEE] n mess; vt
gâcher mess up
gadget [gah•ZHEH] n M
gadget
gaélique [gah•ai•LEEK] n M
Gaelic
gaffe [gahf] n F blunder; vi
faire une ~
gagnant [gah•NYAHπ] n MF
winner; adj winning
gagné [gah•NYAI] adj won
gagner [gah•NYEH] vt earn;
win
gai [gai] adj cheerful; jolly;
merry; homosexual (coll)
gain [gaπ] n M gain; vt gagner
galanterie [gah•lahπ•TREE] n
F chivalry
galère [gah•LER] n F galley
galerie [gah•le•REE] n F
gallery

galet [gah•LEH] n pebble; npl
shingle
gallon [gah•LAUπ] n M gallon
galop [gah•LAUP] n gallop; vi
galoper
gangster [gahπg•STEH] n M
gangster
gant [gahπ] n M glove
gantelet [gahπ•TLET] n
gauntlet
garage [gah•RAHZH] n M
garage
garantie [gah•rahπ•TEE] n F
warrant; guarantee; vt
guarantir
garçon [gahr•SAUπ] n M boy;
~ de café\ waiter
garde 1 [gahrd] n M guard;
watchman; keeper; ~ du
corps\ bodyguard; ~ fou\
railing; ~ manger\ pantry
garde 2 [gahrd] n F care; watch;
protection; keeping; ~ à fond

n\ hilt; ~ robe\ wardrobe
(meubles)

garder [gahr•DAI] *vt* keep;
watch; protect

gardien [gahr•DYAHπ] *n* M
keeper; guardian; custodian

gare [gahr] *n* F railroad station;
station

gargouille [gahr•GWEEY] *n* F
gargoyle

gargouiller [gahr•gwee•YAI] *vi*
gurgle

garnison [gahr•nee•ZAUπ] *n*
garrison

garniture [gahr•nee•TEWR] *n*
F garnish; *vt* garnir

gardeboue [gahrd•BOO] *n* M
fender

gaspillage [gah•spee•LAHZH]
n M waste; rubbish; trash

gaspiller [gah•spee•LEH] *vt*
waste

gâteau [gah•TO] *n* M cake;
cookie; ~ de Savoie\ sponge
cake

gâter [gah•TEH] *vt* spoil;
pamper; mar

gâterie [gah•tehr•EE] *n* F treat

gauche [gosh] *n* F left hand;
lef-hand side; *adj* inv left;
crooked; awkward; clumsy;
unwieldy; à ~\ on the left;
tourner à ~\ turn left; tenir à
~\ keep to the left

gaucher [go•SHER] *adj*
left-handed

gauchiste [gosh] *adj n* M leftist

gaufre [gaufr] *n* F waffle

gaufrette [gau•FREHT] *n* F
wafer; biscuit

gaz [gahz] *n* M gas; *vt* gazer

gaze [gahz] *n* F gauze

gazette [gah•ZET] *n* gazette

gazeux [ga•ZØ] *adj* gaseous

gazouillement (d'un oiseau)
[gah•zwee•MAHπ] *n* M
twitter

gazouiller [gah•zwee•YEH] *vi*
warble

gazouillis [gah•zool•LEE] *n* M
warble

geai [zhe] *n* M jay

géant [zhai•AHπ] *adj n* M
giant; mammoth

gel [zhel] *n* M frost; frosting

gélatine [zhai•lah•TEEN] *n* F
gelatin

gelée [zhu•LAI] *n* F jelly

geler [ge•LEH] *vt* freeze

gelure [zhe•LEWR] *n* F
frostbite

gémir [zheh•MEER] *vt* wail;
moan; groan; lament

gémissement
[zheh•mees•MAHπ] *n* M
whimper; groan; moan

gênant [zheh•NAHπ] *adj*
troublesome

gendre [zhahπdr] *n* M
son-in-law

gène [zhen] *n* M gene

gêne [zhen] *n* F torture;
uneasiness; discomfort;
difficulty; sans ~\ free and
easy

gêné [zheh•NAI] *adj* uneasy

gêner [zhe•NEH] *vt* hinder;
impede

général [zhai•nai•RAHL] *adj n*
M general; en ~ in general

généralement
[zhai•nai•rahl•MAHπ] *adv*
commonly; generally

généralisation
[zhai•NAI•rah•lee•zah•SYAUπ]
vt generalization

généraliser
[zhai•nai•RAH•lee•ZAI] *vt*
generalize

génération
[zhai•NAI•rah•SYAUπ] *n* F
generation

généreux [zhai•nai•RØ] *adj*
generous

générosité
[zhai•ṄAI•rau•see•TAI] *n* F
generosity

génétique [zhai•nai•TEEK] *adj*
genetic

génie [zhai•NEE] *n* M genius

génital [zhai•nee•TAHL] *adj*
genital

genou [zhe•NOO] *n* knee

genre [zhahπr] *n* M gender

gens [zhahπ] *npl* M people; folk
(F devant *adj*)

gentil [zhahπ•TEEL] *adj* kind

gentillesse [zhahπ•tee•YES] *n*
F kindness

gentiment [zhahπ•tee•MAHπ]
adv nicely; agreeably

géographie
[zhai•AU•grah•FEE] *n* F
geography

géologie [zhai•AU•lau•ZHEE]
n F geology

géométrie
[zhai•AU•mai•TREE] *n* F
geometry

géométrique
[zhai•AU•mai•TREEK] *n*
geometric

gérer [zhai•RAI] *vt* manage;
administer; mal ~\ mismanage

germe [zherm] *n* M germ

germer [zher•MEH] *vi*
germinate

gerouette [gehr•WHET] *n* F
vane

geste [zhest] *n* gesture; ~ de la\
main wave

gesticuler
[zhe•STEE•kew•LEH] *vi*
gesticulate

gicler [gee•kleh] *vi* spew

gifle [zheefl] *n* F slap

gigantesque
[zhee•gahπ•TESK] *adj*
gigantic

gigue [zheeg] *n* F jig

gilet [gee•LEH] *n* M vest; ~ de
sauvetage\ life jacket

gin [jeen] *n* M gin

gingembre [zhaπ•ZHAHπBR]
n M ginger

girafe [zhee•RAHF] *n* F giraffe

gitan [zhee•TAHπ] *n* M gypsy

glaçage [glah•SAHZH] *n* M
icing

glace [glahs] *n* F ice; ice-cream;
vi se givrer (gateaux)

glacial [glah•SYAHL] *adj* icy;
frigid

glacier [glah•SYEH] *n* glacier

glaçon [glah•SAUπ] *n* M ice
cube

gland [glahπ] *n* M tassel

glande [glahπd] *n* F gland

glaner [glah•NEH] *vt* glean

glissant [glee•SAHπ] *adj*
slippery

glissement [gless•MAHπ] *n* M
slipping; sliding; ~ de terrain\
landslide

glissière [glee•SYER] *n* F chute

globe [glaub] *n* M globe; ~ oculaire\ eyeball

gloire [glwahr] *n* F glory; fame

glorieux [glau•RYØ] *adj* glorious

glorifier [glau•ree•FYAI] *vt* glorify

glossaire [glau•SER] *n* M glossary

glousser [gloo•SEH] *vi* chuckle; cluck; giggle

glouton [gloo•TAUπ] *n* M glutton; *adj* gluttonous

gloutonnerie [gloo•TAU•ne•REE] *n* F gluttony

glucose [glew•KAUZ] *n* M glucose

gobelet [gau•BLEH] *n* M tumbler

golf [gaulf] *n* M golf

gomme [gaum] *n* F eraser; gum

gonfler [gauπ•FLAI] *vt* inflate; blow up; swell

gong [gauπg] *n* M gong

gorge [gaurzh] *n* F throat; neck; breast; bosom

gorger [gaur•ZHEH] *vt* gorge; cram

gorille [gau•REEY] *n* M gorilla

gosier [gau•SYAI] *n* M gullet

gothique [gau•TEEK] *adj* gothic

goudron [goo•DRAUπ] *n* M tar; *vt* goudróner

gourde [goord] *n* F gourd

gousset [goo•SEH] *n* M gusset

goût [goo] *n* M taste; flavor; smell; liking; preference; manner; style

goûter [goo•TEH] *n* M snack; lunch; *vt* M taste; enjoy

goutte [goot] *n* F drop; drip; spot; ~ pluie\ raindrop; *vi* goutter

gouttière [goo•TYER] *n* F gutter

gouvernail [goo•ver•NAI] *n* M rudder

gouvernante [goo•ver•NAHπT] *n* F governess; housekeeper

gouvernement [goo•vern•MAHπT] *n* M government

gouverner [goo•ver•NAI] *vt vi* govern

gouverneur [goo•ver•NœR] *n* M governor

grâce [grahs] *n* grace; gracefulness; charm

gracieux [grah•SYØ] *adj* graceful

graduel [grah•dew•EL] *adj* gradual

grain [graπ] *n* M grain

graine [gren] *n* F seed

graisse [gres] *n* F grease; ~ de rognon\ suet

grammaire [grah•MEHR] *n* F grammar

grammatical [grah•MAH•tee•KAHL] *adj* grammatical

gramme [grahm] *n* M gram

grand [grahπ] *n* M great man; adult; *adj* big; tall; great; large; grand; wide; grand-mère [grahπ•MEHR] *n* F grandmother

grand-père [grahπ•PEHR] *n*
FM grandfather

Grande-Bretagne
[-bre•TAHNYU] *adj* F Great
Britain

grandeur [grahπ•DœR] *n* F
greatness; magnitude

grandiose; pompeux
[grahn•DYAUZ] *adj*
grandiose

grands-parents
[grahπ-pah•RAHπ] *npl* M
grandparents

grange [grahπzh] *n* F barn;
grange

granit [grah•NEE] *n* M granite

granule [grah•NEWL] *n* M
granule

graphique [grah•FEEK] *n* M
chart; graph; graphic

gratitude [grah•tee•TEWD] *n* F
thankfulness

gratte-ciel (inv) [graht-syehl] *n*
M skyscraper

gratter [grah•TEH] *vt* scrape

grattoir [grah•TWAHR] *n* M
scraper

grave [grahv] *adj* grievous;
serious; *n* F grave; tomb

graver [grah•VAI] *vt* engrave

gravier [grah•VYEH] *n* M
gravel; *npl* gravillons

gravillon [grah•vee•YAUπ] *n*
M grit; courage

gravir [grah•VEER] *vt* climb;
scale

gravité [grah•vee•TAI] *n*
gravity

gravure [grah•VEWR] *n* F
engraving

gre [greh] *n* M will

grec [grek] *adj* Greek; *n* M
(preson) Grec (Grecque);
(language)

Grèce [gres] *n* F Greece

greffe [gref] *n* F graft;
transplant *vt* greffer

grêle [grel] *n* hail; *vi* grêler

grêlon [gre•LAUπ] *n* M
hailstone

grenade [gre•NAHD] *n* F
grenade

grenier [gru•NYAI] *n* M attic;
granary; loft

grenouille [gre•NWEEY] *n* F
frog

grésiller [grai•zee•YAI] *vi*
sizzle

gréviste [greh•VEEST] *n* MF
striker

gribouiller [gree•bwee•YEH] *vt*
vi scribble

griffe [greef] *n* F scratch

griffer [gree•FAI] *vt* scratch;
claw (at)

griffonage [gree•fau•NAHZH]
n M scrawl; *vt vi* griffonner

griffoner [gree•fau•NEH] *vi*
doodle; scribble

grignoter [gree•nyau•TAI] *vt*
nibble

gril [gree] *n* M grill; *vt* faire
griller; *vi* griller

grillage [gree•YAHZH] *n* M
grille

grille [greey] *n* F grate; grid;
iron gate; railing

griller [gree•YAI] *vt* broil

grillon [gree•YAUπ] *n* M
cricket

grimace [gree•MAHS] *n* F
grimace; wince

grimacer [gree•mah•SEH] *vi*
wince; duck; grimace

grincer [graπ•SEH] *vt* gnash; ~
les dents\ grin/gnash one's
teeth

grincheux [graπ•SHØ] *adj*
cranky

grippe [greep] *n* F flu; influenza

gris [gree] *adj n* M gray; *vi*
grissonner

grisant [gree•SAHπ] *adj*
exhilarating

grive [greev] *n* F thrush
(oiseau)

Groenland [grau•en•LAHπD] *n*
M Greenland

grognement [grau•nye•MAHπ]
n grunt; growl; snort

grogner [grau•NYEH] *vt* snort;
grunt; growl

grognon [grau•NYAUπ] *n* M
grouch

grommeler [grau•me•LEH] *vi*
grumble

grondement [grauπ•du•MAHπ]
n rumble; boom (affaires)

gronder [grauπ•DEH] *vt* scold;
rumble; boom; ~ harceler\ nag

gros [gro] *adj* fat; ~ lot\
jackpot; ~ morceau\ chunk

grossesse [grau•SES] *n* F
pregnancy

grossier [grau•SYAI] *adj*
coarse; uncouth

grossir [grau•SEER] *vt* magnify;
vi get fat

grotesque [grau•TESK] *adj*
grotesque

grouiller [grwee•YEH] *vi* stir;
swarm; teem

groupe [groop] *n* M group;
cluster; *vt* grouper; *vi* se
grouper

grue [grew] *n* F crane

gué [gai] *n* M ford; crossing;
passer un ~\ ford a river

guépard [gai•PAHR] *n* M
cheetah

guêpe [gehp] *n* F wasp

guérillero [gai•REE•ye•RO] *n*
M guerrilla

guérir [gai•REER] *vt* heal; *vi* se
guérir

guerre [gehr] *n* F war; warfare;
feud; quarrel; faire la ~ à\
make war against

guerrier [gehr•ree•YEH] *adj*
warlike

guerrier; -ière [gehr•ree•EH];
[-ehr] *n* MF warrior

gueule de bois *n* F hangover

guichet 1 [gee•SHEH] *n* M
ticket office

guichet 2 [gee•SHEH] *n* M
wicket

guide [geed] *n* guide; *vt* guider

guilde [geeld] *n* F guild

guillemets [gee•yu•MEH] *npl*
M quotation marks

guillotine [gee•yau•TEEN] *n* F
guillotine

guindé [gaπ•DAI] *adj* prim;
stiff; stilted

guirlande [geer•LAHπD] *n* F
garland; wreath

guitare [gee•TAHR] *n* F guitar

gymnase [zheem•NAHS] *n* M
gymnasium; gym

gymnaste [zheem•NAHST] *n*
FM gymnast

gymnastique
[zheem•nah•STEEK] *n* F
gymnastics

H

habile [ah•BEEYL] *adj* skilled;
skillful; clever

habilité [ah•BEEYL•ee•TAI]
ability; skill

habillement
[ah•BEEL•uh•MAUπ] *n* M
clothes; clothing; dress

habiller [ah•bee•YAI] *vt* clothe;
dress

habit [ah•BEET] *n* M dress;
clothing habit (eccles); *npl*
evening clothes

habitation [ah•bee•tah•SYAUπ]
n F dwelling

habiter [ah•bee•TAI] *vt* inhabit;
vi dwell

habitude [ah•bee•TEWD] *n* F
habit; custom; practice;
comme d' ~\ as usual

habituel [ah•BEE•tew•EL] *adj*
habitual

hache [ahsh] *n* F axe

hacher [ah•SHAI] *vt* mince;
chop

hachette [ah•SHET] *n* F
hatchet

hagard [ah•GAR] *adj* haggard

haie [ey] *n* F hedge; faire la ~\
line up

haine [en] *n* F hatred; hate; *vt*
haïr

Haïti [ah•ee•TEE] *n* M Haiti

halage [ah•LAHZH] *n* MF
towing (barge)

haleter [ah•lu•TAI] *vi* pant;
puff; blow; gasp (from
surprise)

Halloween [alo•WEEN] *n*
Halloween

hallucination
[ah•LEW•see•nah•SYAUπ] *n*
F hallucination

hamac [ah•MAHK] *n* M
hammock

hamburger [AHπ•bewr•GER] *n*
M hamburger

hameau [ah•MO] *n* M hamlet

hanche [ahπsh] *n* F hip

handicap [ahπ•dee•KAHP] *n*
handicap

handicapé [ahπ•dee•kah•PAI]
adj disabled; handicapped

hangar [ang•AHR] *n* M shed;
hangar

hanter [ahπ•TEH] *vt* haunt

harcelement [ahr•sel•MAHπ] *n*
M harassment; ~ sexuel\
sexual harassment

harceler [ahr•se•LAI] *vt* harass;
pester

hardi [ahr•DEE] *adj* bold;
audacious; daring; rash;
impudent

hardiesse [ar•DYES] *n* F
boldness; audacity; daring;
impudence; rashness

hareng [ah•RAHπG] *n* M
herring

haricot [ah•ree•CO] *n* M bean

harmonica
[ahr•MAU•nee•KAH] *n* M
harmonica

harmonie [ahr•mau•NEE] *n* F
harmony

harmonieux [ahr•mau•NYØ]
adj harmonious

harmoniser [ahr•mau•nee•ZAI]
vt F harmonize; *vi*
s'harmoniser

harnais [ahr•NEH] *n* M
harness; *vt* harnacher

harpe [ahrp] *n* F harp

harpon [ahr•PAUπ] *n* M
harpoon; *vt* harponner

hasard [ah•ZAHR] *n* M hazard;
risk; dare; *vt* hasarder

hasardeux [ah•zahr•DØ] *adj*
hazardous

hâte [aht] *n* hurry; haste; rush; à
la ~\ in haste; hastily

hâter [ah•TAI] *vt* hasten; rush;
hurry; *vi* se hâter

hausser [o•SAI] *vt* rise;
heighten; augment; increase

haut [o] *n* M height; top;
summit; *adj* high; tall; lofty;
important; ~-parleur\
loudspeaker

hautain [o•TAπ] *adj* haughty

hauteur [o•TœR] *n* F height;
altitude; hill; arrogance

havre [ah•VR] *n* M haven

hé [ai] *excl* hey

hebdomadaire
[ehb•DAU•mah•DEHR] *adv*
weekly; *n* weekly paper

hélas [ai•LAH] *excl* alas

hélice [ai•LEES] *n* F propeller

hélicoptère
[ai•lee•kaup•TEHR] *n* M
helicopter

hémisphère [ai•mees•FER] *n*
M hemisphere

hémorragie
[ai•mau•rah•ZHEE] *n* F
hemorrhage

hémorroïdes [ai•mau•rau•EED]
npl F hemorrhoids

hennissement [e•nees•MAHπ]
n M neigh; *vi* hennir

héraldique [ai•rahl•DEEK] *n* F
heraldry

héraut [ai•ro] *n* M herald

herbe [erb] *n* F grass; herb;
plant; weed (mauvaise)

herbeux [er•BØ] *adj* grassy

héréditaire [ai•rai•dee•TER]
adj hereditary

hérédité [ai•rai•dee•TAI] *n* F
heredity

hérésie [ai•rai•SEE] *n* F heresy

hérisser [ai•ree•SAI] *vi refl*
bristle

hérisson [ai•ree•SAUπ] *n* M
hedgehog

héritage [ai•ree•TAHZH] *n* M
heritage; inheritance

hériter [ai•ree•TAI] *vt* inherit

héritier [ai•ree•TYEH] *n* M heir

héritière [ai•ree•TYER] *n* F
heiress

hermétique [ehr•mai•TEEK]
adj airtight

hernie [er•NEE] *n* F herniʒ

héroïne 1 [ai•rau•EEN] *n* F
heroine

héroïne 2 [ai•rau•EEN] *n* F
heroin

héroïque [ai•rau•EEK] *adj*
heroic

héroïsme [ai•rau•EEZM] *n* M
heroism

héron [ai•RAUπ] *n* M heron

héros [ai•RO] *n* M hero

hésitant [ai•zee•TAHπ] *adj*
hesitant; wary

hésitation [ai•zee•tah•SYAUπ]
n F hesitation

hésiter [ai•zee•TAI] *vi* falter

hétérosexuel
[AI•tai•RAU•sek•sew•EL] *adj*
n M heterosexual

hêtre [e•tr] *n* M beech

heure [œr] *n* F hour; o'clock;
time; quelle ~ est-il?\ what
time is it; ~s de pointe\
rush-hour; ~s supplémentaires\
overtime; de bonne~\ early;
tout à l'~\ on time

heureusement [œ•rØz•MAHπ]
adv luckily; forutnately;
happily

heureux [œ•RØ] *adj* happy;
glad; pleased

heurtoir [œr•TWAHR] *n* M
knocker

hexagone [ek•sah•GAUN] *n* M
hexagon

hibernation
[ee•ber•nah•SYAUπ] *n* F
hibernation

hiberner [ee•ber•NAI] *vi*
hibernate

hibou [ee•BOO] *n* M owl

hideux [ee•DØ] *adj* hideous;
ugly; gruesome

hier [yehr] *adv* yesterday; ~
soir\ last night

hiérarchie [ee•YAI•rahr•SHEE]
n F hierarchy

hilarant [ee•lah•rahπ] *adj*
hilarious; funny

hindou [aπ•DOO] *adj* Hindu; *n*
M Hindou

hippopatame
[ee•pau•pah•TAHM] *n* M
hippopotamus

hirondelle [eeur•auπ•DEHL] *n*
F swallow (oiseau)

hirsute [eer•SEWT] *adj* shaggy;
hairy

Hispanique; Hispanique
[ee•spah•NEEK] n; *adj* MF
Hispanic

hisser [ee•SAI] *vt* hoist; heave;
lift; heft

histoire [ee•STWAHR] *n* F
history; story; narration;
narrative

historien [ee•stau•RYAHπ] *n*
M historian

historique [ee•stau•REEK] *adj*
historic

hiver [ee•VEHR] *n* M winter

hocher [ho•SHEH] *vt* wag (la
queue d'un chien)

hockey [au•KEE] *n* M hockey

hollandais [au•lahπ•DAI] *adj*
Dutch; les Hollandais *npl* M
(gens)

Hollande [au•LAHπD] *n* F
Holland

holocauste [au•lau•KOST] *n* M
holocaust

homard [au•MAHR] *n* lobster

homicide [au•mee•SEED] *n* M
homicide; ~ involontaire\
manslaughter

homme [aum] *n* M man; ~
d'Etat\ statesman; ~
d'affaires\ businessman; ~ des
cavernes\ caveman; ~
politique\ politician

homosexuel
[o•mau•sek•sew•EL] *adj n* M
homosexual

Hongrie [auπg•GREE]* *n* F
Hungary

hongrois [auπg•GRWAH] *adj*
Hungarian; *n* M Hongrois
(gens); (language) hongrois

honnête [au•NEHT] *adj*
truthful; honest; upright;
decent; becoming; courteous

honnêteté [au•ne•tu•TAI] *n* F
honesty; truthfulness

honneur [au•NœR] *n* F honor;
en ; ~ de

honorable [au•nau•RAHBL]
adj honorable; trustworthy;
reputable

honoraire [au•nau•REHR] *adj*
honorary

honorer [au•nau•RAI] *vt*
dignify; honor; respect

honte [auπt] *n* F shame;
disgrace; discredit; avoir ~\ be
ashamed; disgraced,
stigmatized; faire ~ à\
disgrace

honteux [auπ•TØ] *adj*
disgraceful; shameful

hoquet [au•KEH] *n* M hiccup
m; avoir le ~\ have the
hiccups; *vi* hoqueter

horaire [au•REHR] *n* M
timetable

horizon [au•ree•ZAUπ] *n*
horizon

horizontal [au•ree•zauπ•TAHL]
adj horizontal; level

horloge [aur•LAUZH] *n* F
timepiece; clock

hormone [aur•MAUN] *n* F
hormone

horoscope [au•rau•SKOP] *n* M
horoscope

horreur [au•RœR] *n* F horror

horrible [au•REEBL] *adj*
horrible; horrid

horrifier [au•ree•FYAI] *vt*
horrify

hors [or] *prep* out of; outside
of; without; but; except; ~
taxe\ duty-free; ~-la-loi M;
mettre ~ la loi\ outlaw

hôspital [o•pee•TAHL] *n* M
hospital

hospitalier [au•spee•tah•LYEH]
adj hospitable

hospitalité
[au•spee•tah•lee•TAI] *n* F
hospitality

hostile [au•STEEL] *adj* hostile

hostilité [au•stee•lee•TAI] *n* F
hostility

hot-dog *n* M hot dog

hôte [ot] *n* M host; innkeeper;
landlord

hôtel [o•TEL] *n* M hotel; inn;
mansion; ~ de ville\ city hall

hôtesse [o•TESS] *n* F hostess;
innkeeper; landlady;
stewardess

houe [oo] *n* hoe

houx [oo] *n* M holly

hublot [ew•BLAU] *n* M
porthole

huées [wee•AI] *npl* F boos

huer *excl* hue! [wee•AI] *vt vi*
boo; jeer

huile [weel] *n* F oil

huileux [wee•LØ] *adj* oily

huit [weet] *num* eight; le ~\
eighth

huitième; [wee•TYEM] *num*
eighth

huître [weetr] *n* M oyster

humain [ew•MAπ] *adj n* M
human; *adj* humane

humanitaire
[ew•MAH•nee•TEHR] *adj*
humanitarian

humanité [ew•MAH•nee•TAI]
n F humanity; mankind

humble [aumbl] *adj* lowly;
humble

humecter [ew•mek•TAI] *vt*
dampen; moisten

humeur [ew•MœR] *n* F mood;
de bonne ~\ in a good mood

humide [ew•MEED] *adj* damp;
humid

humidité [ew•MEE•dee•TAI] *n*
F humidity; moisture

humiliation
[ew•mee•lyah•SYAUπ] *n* F
humiliation

humilier [ew•mee•LYAI] *n* F
humiliate; humble

humilité [ew•mee•lee•TAI] *n* F
humility

humoristique
[ew•mau•ree•STEEK] *adj*
humorous

humour [ew•MOOR] *n* M
humor

huppe [ewp] *n* F tuft

hurlement [ewr•lu•MAHπ] *n*
M howl; shriek; screech; *vi*
hurler; hurler des cris plaintifs
vt\ wail

hutte [ewt] *n* F hut

hybride [ee•BREED] *adj n* M
hybrid

hydraulique [ee•dro•LEEK] *adj*
hydraulic

hydrogène [ee•drau•ZHEN] *n*
M hydrogen

hyène [ee•EN] *n* F hyena

hygiène [ee•ZHEN] *n* F
hygiene

hymne [eem•NU] *n* M hymn

hyperactif [ee•per•ahk•TEEF]
adj hyperactive

hypersensible
[ee•PEHR•sahπ•SEEBL] *adj*
squeamish

hypnose [eep•NAUZ] *n* F
hypnosis

hypnotique [eep•nau•TEEK]
adj hypnotic

hypnotiser [eep•nau•tee•ZEH]
vt hypnotize; mesmerize

hypocrisie [ee•pau•kree•ZEE] *n*
F hypocrisy

hypocrite [ee•pau•KREET] *n*
MF hypocrite; *adj* hypocritical

hypothèque [ee•pau•TEK] *n* F
mortgage; *vt* hypothèquer

hypothèse [ee•pau•TEZ] *n* F
hypothesis

hypothétique
[ee•pau•tai•TEEK] *adj* MF
hypothetical

hystérique [ee•stai•REEK] *adj*
hysterical

I

iceberg [ees•BERG] *n* M
iceberg

ici [ee•SEE] *adv* here; now; at
this point

iconsideré
[aπ•KAUπ•see•de•RAI] *adj*
inconsiderate

idéal [ee•dai•AHL] *adj n* M
ideal; imaginary; visionary

idéalisme [ee•dai•ah•LEEZM] *n*
M idealism

idéaliste [ee•dai•ah•LEEST] *adj*
idealistic

idée [ee•DAI] *n* F idea; notion;
concept; mind; intention;
purpose; ~ centrale\ thrust

idem [ee•DEM] *adv* ditto

identification
[ee•DAHπ•tee•fee•kah•SYAUπ]
n identification

identifier [ee•dahπ•tee•FYAI]
vt identify

identique [ee•dahπ•TEEK] *adj*
identical; alike

identité [ee•dahπ•tee•TAI] *n*
identity

idéologie
[ee•DAI•au•lau•ZHEE] *n* F
ideology

idiot [ee•DYAU] *adj* idiotic;
absurd; *n* M idiot; dope;
imbecile; fool

idioties [ee•dyau•TEE] *npl* F
drivel

idolâtrer [ee•dau•lah•TRAI] *vt*
idolize; worship

idole [ee•DAUL] *n* F idol

ignition [eeq•nee•SYAUπ] *n* F
ignition

ignorance [ee•nyau•RAHπS] *n*
F ignorance

ignorant [ee•nyau•RAHπ] *adj*
ignorant; unaware

il; ils [eel] *pron* he; she; it; *pl*
they

il y a [eel•YAH] there is; ago; ~
longtemps\ a long time ago

île [eel] *n* F island; isle

illégal [ee•lai•GAHL] *adj* illegal

illégitime [ee•lai•zhee•TEEM]
adj illegitimate

illetré [ee•le•TRAI] *adj* illiterate

illetrisme [ee•le•TREEZM] *n* M
illiteracy

illicite [ee•lee•SEET] *adj* illicit

illimité [ee•lee•mee•TAI] *adj*
unbounded; unlimited

illogique [ee•lau•ZHEEK] *adj*
illogical

illusion [ee•lew•ZYAUπ] *n* F
delusion; illusion

illustration
[ee•lew•strah•SYAUπ] *n* F
illustration

illustre [ee•LEWSTR] *adj*
illustrious; famous

illustrer [ee•lew•STREH] *vt*
illustrate; depict

image [ee•MAHZH] *n* F image;
picture; idea; impression

images [ee•MAHZH] *npl* F
imagery

imaginaire
[ee•MAH•zhee•NEHR] *adj*
imaginary

imaginatif
[ee•MAH•zhee•nah•TEEF] *adj*
imaginative

imagination
[ee•MAH•zhee•nah•SYAUπ]
n F imagination

imaginer [ee•MAH•zhee•NEH]
vt visualize; imagine; *vi* s`~\
imagine oneself; delude
oneself

imbécile [an•bai•SEEL] *n* MF
imbecile

imitateur [ee•mee•tah•TœR] *n*
M mimic

imitation [ee•mee•tah•SYAUπ]
n F imitation

imiter [ee•mee•TAI] *vt* emulate;
imitate; impersonate

immédiat [ee•mai•DYAH] *adj*
immediate; right away

immédiatement
[ee•mai•dyaht•MAHπ] *adv*
immediately

immense [ee•MAHπS] *adj*
immense

immensité [ee•mahπ•see•TAI]
n F vastness

immerger [ee•mer•ZHEH] *vt*
immerse

immeuble [ee•MØBL] *n* M real
estate; property; building; ~
ancien\ tenement

immigration
[ee•mee•grah•SYAUπ] *n* F
immigration

immigré [ee•mee•GRAI] *n*
immigrant

imminent [ee•mee•NAHπ] *adj*
imminent; pending

immobile [ee•mau•BEEL] *adj*
immobile; still; unmoving

immobiliser
[ee•MAU•bee•lee•ZAI] *vt*
immobilize; stop

immobilité
[ee•MAU•bee•lee•TAI] *n* F
stillness; immobility

immoral [ee•mau•RAHL] *adj*
immoral

immoralité
[ee•mau•RAH•lee•TAI] *n* F
immorality

immortalité
[ee•maur•TAH•lee•TAI] *n* F
immortality

immortel [ee•maur•TEL] *adj*
immortal; undying

immuable [ee•mew•AHBL] *adj*
inv unchangeable

immunisé [ee•mew•nee•ZAI]
adj immune

immuniser [ee•mew•nee•ZEH]
vt immunize

immunité [ee•mew•nee•TAI] *n*
F immunity

impact [anπ•PAHKT] *n* M
impact

imparfait [anπ•pahr•FEH] *adj*
imperfect

impartial [anπ•pahr•SYAHL] *adj*
impartial; open-minded;
unbiased

impassible [anπ•pah•SEEBL] *adj*
inv stolid

impatience [anπ•pah•SYAHπS]
n F impatience

impatient [anπ•pah•SYAHπ] *adj*
impatient; *vi* s'impatienter\
become impatient

impeccable [anπ•pe•KAHBL]
adj immaculate

impératif [aπ•PAI•rah•TEEF]
adj n M imperative

impératrice
[aπ•PAI•rah•TREES] *n* M
empress

impérial [aπ•pai•RYAHL] *adj*
imperial

impérieux [aπ•pai•RYØ] *adj*
imperious

imperméable
[aπ•PER•mai•AHBL] *adj*
impervious; waterproof; *n* M
trench coat

impersonel [aπ•PER•sau•NEL]
adj impersonal

impertinent
[aπ•PER•tee•NAHπ] *adj*
impertinent

impétueux [aπ•pai•tew•Ø] *adj*
impetuous

impie [aπ•PEE] *adj* profane;
ungodly; blasphemous; *n* M
unbeliever

impitoyable
[aπ•pee•twah•YAHBL] *adj*
merciless; pitiless; ruthless

implacable [aπ•plah•KAHBL]
adj relentless

implanter [aπ•plahn•TEH] *vt*
implant

implicite [aπ•plee•SEET] *adj*
implicit

impliquer [aπ•plee•KAI] *vt*
implicate

implorer [aπ•plau•RAI] *vt*
implore

impoli [aπ•pau•LEE] *adj*
impolite; uncivil; rude

importance [aπ•paur•TAHπS]
n F importance

important [aπ paur•TAHπ] *adj*
important; momentous

importation
[aπ•paur•ta•SYAUπ] *n* F
import; *vt* importer

importun [aπ•paur•Tœπ] *adj*
unwelcome; importune;
bothersome

impossible [aπ•pau•SEEBL]
adj impossible

imposteur [aπ•pau•STœR] *n* M
impostor

impôt [aπ•PO] *n* M levy; tax; ~
sur le revenu\ income tax

impression [aπ•pre•SYAUπ] *n*
F impression; printing; avoir
l'~ have\ the impression (that)

impressionant
[aπ•pre•syau•NAHπ] *adj*
awesome; impressive

impressionner
[aπ•pre•syau•NAI] *vt* impress

imprimeur [aπ•pree•MœR] *n* M
printer

improbable [aπ•prau•BAHBL]
adj improbable

impromptu [aπ•prahπ•TEW] *n*
MF skit

impropre [aπ•PRAUPR] *adj*
improper; unfit; unsuitable

improviser [aπ•pro•vee•ZAI] *vt*
vi improvise

imprudence [aπ•prew•DAHπS]
n recklessness; imprudence

imprudent [aπ•prew•DAHπ]
adj imprudent; unwary;
unwise; reckless

impudent [aπ•pew•DAHπ] *adj*
impudent; rude

impuissant [aπ•pwee•ZAHN]
adj F helpless; powerless;
impotent

impulsif [aπ•pewl•SEEF] adh
impulsive

impulsion [an•pewl•SYAUπ] n
F impetus; urge

impur [aπ•PEWR] adj impure

impureté [aπ•pew•re•TAI] n F
impurity

inabordable
[een•ah•baur•DAHBL] adj inv
unapproachable

inaccoutumé
[een•ah•koo•too•MAI];adj
unaccustomed; unused

inactif [ee•nahk•TEEF] adj
inactive

inadapté [ee•nah•dahp•TAI] n
M misfit

inanimé [ee•nahk•nee•MAI]
inanimate

inauguration
[ee•no•gew•rah•SYAUπ] n F
inauguration

incapable [aπ•kah•PAHBL] adj
incapable; unable

incapacité
[aπ•kah•pah•see•TAI] n
inability

incarner [aπ•kahr•NAI] vt
embody; incarnate

incassable [aπ•kah•SAHBL]
adj inv unbreakable

incendie [aπ•sahnπ•DEE] n F
blaze; fire

incertain [aπ•sehr•TAπ] adj
uncertain; undecided

incessant [aπ•se•SAHπ] adj
incessant; unceasing

incident [aπ•see•DAHπ] n
incident

inciter [aπ•see•TEH] vt incite;
impel; instigate; rouse

inclinaison
[aπ•klee•nai•SYAUπ] n F
inclination; slope; slant; bent;
propensity

incliner [aπ•klee•NAI] vt vi
bow; refl s' ~\ be inclined to;
vt tilt

inclure [aπ•KLEWR] vt include;
encompass

incomparable
[an•kauπ•pah•RAHBL] adj
incomparable

incompatible
[aπ•kauπ•pah•TEEBL] adj
incompatible

incompétent
[aπ•kauπ•pai•TAHπ] adj
incompetent

incomplet [aπ•kauπ•PLE] adj
incomplete; unfinished

inconcevable
[aπ•kauπs•VAHBL] adj inv
unthinkable

inconditionnel
[aπ•kauπ•DEE•syau•NEHL]
adj unconditional

inconfortable
[aπ•kauπ•faur•TAHBL] adj
inv uncomfortable

inconscience
[aπ•kauπ•SYAHπS] n F
unconsciousness

inconscient [aπ•kauπ•SYAHπ]
adj unconscious; unaware

inconsidéré
[aπ•kauπ•see•deh•RAI] adj
thoughtless; inconsiderate

inconsistant
[aπ•kauπ•see•STAHπ] adj
inconsistent

inconstant [aπ•kauπ•STAHπ]
adj inconstant; fickle

incontestable
[aπ•kauπ•tehs•TAHBL] *adj*
inv undeniable

incontrôlé [aπ•kauπ•tro•LAI]
adj uncontrolled

inconvenable
[aπ•kauπv•NAHBL] *adj inv*
unsuitable

incorporer [aπ•kaur•pau•REH]
vt incorporate; embody; mix

incorrect [aπ•kau•REKT] *adj*
incorrect; wrong

incrédule [aπ•krai•DEWL] *adj*
incredulous; unbelieving

incriminer [aπ•kree•mee•NAI]
vt incriminate

incroyable [aπ•krwah•YAHBL]
adj incredible; unbelievable

inculte [aπ•KEWLT] *adj inv*
uncultured

incurable [aπ•kew•RAHBL] *adj*
incurable

incursion [aπ•kur•ZYAUπ] *n F*
incursion

Inde [aπd] *n F* India

indécent [aπ•dai•SAHπ] *adj*
indecent

indefini [aπ•de•fee•NEE] *adj*
indefinite; unclear

indemnité [aπ•dem•nee•TAI] *n*
F indemnity; allowance

indépendence
[aπ•dai•pahπ•DAHπS] *n F*
independence

indépendent
[aπ•dai•pahπ•DAHπ] *adj*
independent

indestructible
[aπ•de•strewk•TEEBL] *adj*
indestructible

index [aπ•DEKS] *n* M index;
index finger

indicateur [aπ•dee•kah•TœR] *n*
indicator

indice [aπ•DEES] *n* M clue

indien [aπ•DYAHπ] *adj* Indian;
n Indien

indifférance
[aπ•dee•fai•RAHπS] *n F*
indifference; disregard

indifférent [aπ•dee•fai•RAHπ]
adj indifferent

indigène 1 [aπ•dee•ZHEN] *adj*
indigenous; original; native; *n*
MF native

indigent [aπ•dee•ZHAHπ] *adj*
destitute

indigestion
[aπ•dee•zhe•STYAUπ] *n F*
indigestion

indigne [aπ•DEENY] *adj* inv
unworthy

indigné [aπ•dee•NYAI] *adj*
indignant; *vi* s'indigner

indigo [aπ•dee•GO] *adj n*
indigo

indiquer [aπ•dee•KEH] *vt*
indicate; point out; denote

indirect [aπ•dee•REKT] *adj*
indirect; oblique

indiscret [aπ•dee•SKRE] *adj*
indiscreet; prying; nosy (coll)

indispensable
[aπ•dee•spahπ•SAHBL] *adj*
indispensable; vital

indisponible
[aπ•dee•spauπ•NEEBL] *adj*
inv unavailable; indisposed

indisposer [aπ•dee•spau•ZEH]
vi indispose

indistinct [aπ•dee•STAπ] *adj*
indistinct; unclear

individu [aπ•dee•vee•DOO] *n*
M individual; person; fellow;
guy

individuel
[aπ•dee•VEE•doo•EL] *adj*
individual; personal; private

indoctriner [aπ•dauk•tree•NAI]
vt indoctrinate

indolore [aπ•dau•LAUR] *adj*
painless

Indonésie [aπ•dau•nai•ZEE] *n*
F Indonesia

industrie [aπ•dew•STREE] *n* F
industry

industriel [aπ•DEW•stree•EL]
adj industrial

industrieux [aπ•DEW•stree•Ø]
adj industrious

inébranable
[een•eh•brahπ•NAHBL] *adj*
inv unassailable; steadfast

inefficace [ee•ne•fee•KAHS]
adj ineffective

inégal [een•eh•GAHL] *adj*
unequal

inégalité [ee•nai•GAH•lee•TAI]
n F inequality

inepte [ee•NEPT] *adj* inane;
absurd; stupid

inépuisable
[een•eh•pwee•ZAHBL] *adj*
inv tireless

inestimable
[ee•ne•stee•MAHBL] *adj*
invaluable; inestimable;
priceless

inévitable [een•ai•vee•TAHBL]
adj inevitable; unavoidable

inexact [ee•neg•ZAHKT] *adj*
inaccurate; inexact

inexpérimenté
[ee•nek•spai•ree•mahπ•TAI]
adj inexperienced; green

inexplicable
[een•ek•splee•KAHBL] *adj*
inv unaccountable;
inexplicable

inexploré [een•ek•splaur•RAI]
adj uncharted; unexplored

infaillible [aπ•fah•YEEBL] *adj*
foolproof; infallible

infâme [aπ•FAHM] *adj*
infamous; notorious

infanterie [an•fahπ•TREE] *n* F
infantry

infatigable
[aπ•fah•tee•GAHBL] *adj* inv
untiring

infecter [aπ•fek•TEH] *vt* infect;
contaminate; pollute

infection [aπ•fek•SYAUπ] *n* F
infection; illness; sickness

infectueux [aπ•fek•tew•Ø] *adj*
infectious

inférieur [aπ•fai•RYœ] *adj n* M
inferior; poor

infernal [aπ•fer•NAHL] *adj*
hellish; infernal

infidelité [aπ•fee•de•lee•TAI] *n*
F infidelity; untruthfulness

infini [aπ•fee•NEE] *adj* infinite;
unending

infinité [aπ•fee•nee•TAI] *n* F
infinity

infinitif [aπ•fee•nee•TEEF] *adj*
n M infinitive

infirmière [aπ•feer•MYEHR] *n*
F nurse

infirmerie [aπ•feer•meh•REE] *n*
F infirmary; sick-room

infirmité [aπ•feer•mee•TAI] *n* F
infirmity

inflammable [aπ•flah•MABL]
adj M flammable

inflation [aπ•flah•SYAUπ] *n* F
inflation

inflexible [aπ•flehk•SEEBL] *adj*
inv unbending; unyielding

inflexion [aπ•flek•SYAUπ] *n* F
inflection

infligir [aπ•flee•ZHEER] *vt*
inflict

influence [aπ•flew•AHπS] *n*
influence; pull

influencer [aπ•flew•ahπ•SEH] *n*
influence

informations
[an•faur•mah•SYAUπ] *npl* F
newscast

informatiser
[aπ•faur•mah•tee•ZAI] *vt*
computerize

informer [aπ•faur•MEH] *vt*
inform

infrastructure
[aπ•frah•strewk•TYR] *n* F
infrastructure; under structure

ingénierie [an•zhai•nyu•REE] *n*
engineering

ingénieur [aπ•zhai•NYœR] *n* M
engineer

ingénieux [aπ•zhai•NYØ] *adj*
ingenious; clever

ingrat [aπ•GRAH] *adj*
thankless; ungrateful;
unproductive

ingratitude
[aπ•grah•tee•TEWD] *n* F
ingratitude; thanklessness

ingrédient [aπ•grai•DYAHπ] *n*
M ingredient

inhaler [een•ah•LAI] *vt* inhale

inhérent [een•ai•RAHπ] *adj*
inherent; intrinsic

inhiber [een•ee•BAI] *vt* inhibit

inhumain [een•ew•MAπ] *adj*
inhuman

initial [ee•nee•SYAHL] *adj*
initial; starting; *n* F initiale

initier [ee•nee•seey•AI] *vt*
induct; initiate

injecter [aπ•zhek•TAI] *vt* inject

injustesse [aπ•zhew•STES] *n* F
injustice

injustifiable
[aπ•ZHEW•stee•FYAHBL]
adj inv undue; unjustifiable

injustifié
[aπ•ZHEWS•tee•FYAI] *adj*
unwarranted; unjustified

inné [ee•NAI] *adj* innate;
inherent

innocence [ee•nau•SAHπS] *n* F
innocence

innocent [ee•nau•SAHπ] *adj*
innocent; harmless

innombrable
[ee•naum•BRAHBL] *adj*
countless

innovation
[ee•nau•vah•SYAUπ] *n* F
innovation

inoculer [ee•nau•kew•LAI] *vt*
inoculate

inondation
[ee•nauπ•dah•SYAUπ] *n* F
flood; unundation; *vt* inonder

inonder [ee•nauπ•DEH] *vt*
inundate

inopportun [een•o•paur•Tœπ]
adj inconvenient; *adj adv*
untimely

inorganique
[ee•naur•gah•NEEK] *adj*
inorganic

inouï [ee•NWEE] *adj* untold;
uncounted

inoxydable
[een•AUK•see•DAHBL] *adj*
stainless

inquiétant [aπ•kyai•TAHπ] *adj*
disturbing; troubling

inquiétude [aπ•kee•eh•TOOD]
n F worry; disquiet; concern;
vi refl inquieter

insatiable [aπ•sah•syah•bl] *adj*
insatiable

inscription
[aπ•skreep•SYAUπ]
n F inscription; matriculation;
registration

inscrire [aπ•SKREER] *vt* enroll;
vi s'inscrire

insecte [aπ•SEKT] *n* M insect;
pest

insecticide [aπ•sek•tee•SEED] *n*
M insecticide

insensible [aπ•sahπ•SEEBL]
adj insensitive; senseless

inséparable
[aπ•sai•pah•RAHBL] *adj*
inseparable

insérer [aπ•sai•RAI] *vt* insert

insignifiant
[an•see•nyee•FYAHπ] *adj*
immaterial; insignificant

insinuation
[aπ•see•new•ah•SYAUπ] *n* F
innuendo; insinuation;
implication; suggestion

insinuer [aπ•see•new•AI] *vt*
imply; suggest

inspecter [aπ•spek•TEH] *vt*
inspect; examine

insipide [aπ•see•PEED] *adj* inv
insipid; vapid

insistant [aπ•see•STAHπ] *adj*
insistent

insistance [aπ•see•STAHπS] *n*
F emphasis

insister [aπ•see•STAI] *vi* insist;
~ sur souligner\ emphasize

insitut [aπ•stee•TEW] *n* M
institute; *vt* instituer

insolent [aπ•sau•LAHπ] *adj*
insolent; rude; harsh

insomnie [aπ•saum•NEE] *n* F
insomnia

insonorisé -e
[aπ•sau•naur•ee•ZAI] *adj*
soundproof

insouciant [aπ•soo•CYAHπ]
adj carefree; careless;
unconcerned

insoupçonné
[aπ•soop•sau•NAI] *adj*
unsuspected

inspecteur [aπ•spek•TœR] *n* M
inspector

inspection [aπ•spek•SYAUπ] *n*
F inspection

inspiration
[aπ•spee•rah•SYAUπ] *n* F
inspiration

inspirer [aπ•spee•RAI] *vt*
inspire

installation
[aπ•stah•lah•SYAUπ] *n* F
installation

installations
[aπ•stah•lah•SYAUπ] *npl* F
facilities

installer [aπ•stah•LAI] *vt* install

instamment [aπ•stah•MAHπ] *adv* urgently; instantly

instantané [aπ•STAHπ•tah•NAI] *adj* instant; *n* M *n* instant

instiller [aπ•stee•YEH] qqch à qqn *vt* instill

instinct [aπ•STAπ] *n* M instinct

instituteur [an•stee•tew•TœR]ʹ *n* M schoolteacher

instructeur [aπ•strewk•TœR] *n* M instructor

instruction [aπ•strewk•SYAUπ] *n* F instruction

instruire [aπ•STRWEER] *vt* educate; instruct

instrument [aπ•strew•MAHπ] *n* M instrument

insuffisant [aπ•soo•fee•SAHπ] *n* deficient; insufficient; inadequate

insultant [aπ•sewl•TAHπ] *adj* insulting; rude; offensive

insulte [aπ•SEWLT] *n* F insult

insulter [aπ•sewl•TEH] *vt* insult; revile

insupportable [aπ•sew•paur•TAHBL] *adj* unbearable; insupportable

intact [aπ•TAHKT] *adj* intact; untouched

intégral [aπ•tai•GRAHL] *adj* integral

intégration [aπ•tai•grah•SYAUπ] *n* F integration

intégrité [aπ•tai•gree•TAI] *n* F integrity

intellectuel [aπ•te•lek•tew•EL] *adj n* M intellectual

intelligence [aπ•te•lee•ZHAHπS] *n* F intelligence

intelligent [aπ•te•lee•ZHAHπ] *adj* intelligent

intense [aπ•TAHπS] *adj* intense; loud; heavy

intensif [aπ•tahπ•SEEF] *adj* intensive

intensifier [aπ•tahπ•see•FYEH] *vt* intensify; escalate

intensité [aπ•tahπ•see•TAI] *n* F intensity

intenter [aπ•tahπ•TEH] *vt* initiate; bring suit (loi)

intention [aπ•tahπ•SYAUπ] *n* F intention

intentionnel [aπ•tahπ•syau•NEL] *n* F intentional; *adj* willful

interculer [aπ•tehr•kah•LEH] *vt* layer; sandwich

intercepter [aπ•ter•sep•TEL] *n* intercept

interdiction [aπ•ter•deek•SYAUπ] *n* F ban; prohibit; forbit; *vt* interdire

intéressant [aπ•tai•ru•SAHπ] *adj* interesting

intérêt [aπ•tai•REH] *n* M interest; *npl* M intérêts business; *vt* intéresser; *vi* s'intéresser de\ be interested in; intérêt\ personnel self-interset

intérieur [aπ•tai•RYœR] *adj n* M interior; inner; inside

intermédiaire [aπ•ter•mai•DYEHR] *n* MF

go-between; intermediate; *adj*
intermediate

interminable
[aπ•ter•mee•NAHBL] *adj*
interminable; endless;
unending

internat [aπ•ter•NAH] *n* M
boarding school

international
[aπ•ter•nah•syau•NAHL] *adj*
international

interne 1 [aπ•TERN] *adj*
internal

interne 2 [aπ•TERN] *n* MF
intern; *vt* interner

interpeller [aπ•ter•pe•LAI] *vt*
heckle; hassle

interphone [aπ•ter•FAUN] *n* M
intercom

interprétation
[aπ•ter•prai•tah•SYAUπ] *n* F
interpretation

interprète [aπ•ter•PRET] *n* MF
interpreter

interpréter [aπ•ter•prai•TAI] *vt*
construe; intepret; *vi* faire
l'interprète

interrogatatoire
[aπ•TE•rau•gah•TWAHR] *n*
M interrogation; *n* F
interrogation

interroger [aπ•te•rau•GAI] *vt*
interrogate; question

interrompre [aπ•te•RAUπPR]
vt vi interrupt

interruption
[aπ•te•rewp•SYAUπ] *n* F
interruption

intersection
[aπ•ter•sek•SYAUπ] *n* F
intersection

intervalle [aπ•ter•VAHL] *n* M
interval

intervenir [aπ•ter•vu•NEER] *vt*
intervene

intervention
[aπ•ter•vahπ•SYAUπ] *n*
intervention

intestin [aπ•te•STAπ] *n* M
intestine; gut

intestins [aπ•te•STAπ] *npl* M
bowels

intime [aπ•TEEM] *adj* intimate

intimidant [aπ•tee•mee•DAHπ]
adj daunting

intimité [aπ•tee•mee•TAI] *n* F
intimacy; privacy

intolérable [aπ•tau•lai•RAHBL]
adj intolerable

intolérance [aπ•tau•lai•RAHπS]
n F intolerance

intolérant [aπ•tau•lai•RAHπ]
adj intolerant

intransigeant
[aπ•trahπ•zee•ZHAHπ] *adj*
uncompromising

intraveineux [aπ•trah•ve•NØ]
adj intravenous

intrépide [aπ•trai•PEED] *adj*
fearless; intrepid

intrigue [aπ•TREEG] *n* F
intrigue; *vt* intriguer

introduction
[aπ•TRAU•dewk•SYAUπ] *n* F
introduction; présentation

introverti [aπ•trau•ver•TEE] *n*
M introvert; *adj* introverted

intrus [aπ•TREW] *n* M intruder;
MF trespasser

intrusion [aπ•trew•ZYAUπ] *n* F
intrusion; interference

intuition [aπ•tew•ee•SYAUπ] *n*
F intuition

inutile [ee•new•TEEL] *adj inv*
needless; useless; pointless

inutilité [ee•new•tee•lee•TAI] *n*
F uselessness

invaincu [aπ•vaπ•KEW] *adj*
unconquered; undefeated

invariablement
[aπ•vah•ryah•bl•MAHπ] *adv*
invariably

invasion [aπ•vah•ZYAUπ] *n* F
invasion

inventaire [aπ•vahπ•TER] *n* M
inventory

inventer [aπ•vahπ•TEH] *vt*
invent; create

inventeur [aπ•vahπ•TœR] *n* M
inventor

inventif [aπ•vahπ•TEEF] *adj*
inventive; creative

invention [aπ•vahπ•SYAUπ] *n*
F invention

investigation
[aπ•ve•stee•gah•SYAUπ] *n* F
inquisition

investir [aπ•vahπ•TEER] *vt vi*
invest

investissement
[aπ•ve•stees•MAHπ] *n* M
investment

investisseur [aπ•ve•stee•SœR]
n M investor

invincible [aπ•vahπ•SEEBL]
adj invincible; unbeatable

invisible [aπ•vee•ZEEBL] *adj*
invisible

invitation [aπ•vee•tah•SYAUπ]
n F invitation

invité [aπ•vee•TAI] *n* M guest

inviter [aπ•vee•TEH] *vt* invite

involontaire
[aπ•vau•lauπ•TEHR] *adj*
involuntary

invoquer [aπ•vau•KAI] *vt*
invoke; call up call down

iode [yaud] *n* M iodine

iota [yo•TAH] *n* M title; iota

Irak [ee•RAHK] *n* M Iraq

irakien; *n* Irakien m
[ee•rah•KYAHπ] *n* M Iraqi

Iran [ee•RAHπ] *n* M Iran

iranien; Iranien
[ee•rah•NYAHπ] *adj n* M
Iranian

iris [ee•REE] *n* M iris

irlandais [eer•lahπ•DEH] *adj*
Irish; *n* M Irlandais Irishman;
(language) irlandais

Irlande [eer•LAHπD] *n* F
Ireland

Irlande du Nord *n* F Northern
Ireland

ironie [ee•rau•NEE] *n* F irony

ironique [ee•rau•NEEK] *adj*
ironic

irascible [ee•rah•SEEBL] *adj*
hot-tempered

irrationel [ee•rah•syau•NEL]
adj irrational

irrégularité
[ee•RAI•gew•lah•ree•TAI] *adj*
F irregularity

irrégulier [ee•rai•gew•LYEH]
adj irregular; erratic; broken

irremplaçable
[ee•rahπ•plah•SAHBL] *adj*
irreplaceable

irréparable
[ee•rai•pah•RAHBL] *adj*
irreparable

irrésistible
[eer•rai•zee•STEEBL] *adj*
compelling; irresistible

irresponsable
[ee•re•spauπ•SAHBL] *adj*
irresponsible

irrigation [ee•ree•gah•SYAUπ]
n F irrigation

irriguer [ee•ree•GAI] *vt* irrigate

irritable [ee•ree•TAHBL] *adj*
irritable

irritant [ee•ree•TAHπ] *adj*
irritating

irriter [ee•ree•TAI] *vt* irritate

islam [eez•LAHM] *n* M Islam

Islande [ees•LAHπD] *n* F
Iceland

isolation 1 [ee•sau•lah•SYAUπ]
n F isolation

isolation 2 [ee•sau•lah•SYAUπ]
n F insulation

isoler 1 [ee•sau•LAI] *vt*
insulate

isoler 2 [ee•sau•LAI] *vt* isolate

issue [ee•SEW] *n* F issue; end;
upshot; outcome

italien [ee•tah•LYAHπ] *adj*
Italian; *n* M (person) Italien;
(language) italien

italique [ee•tah•LEEK] *n* italic;
npl F italiques italics

itinéraire [ee•tee•nu•REHR] *n*
M itinerary; MF route

ivoire [ee•VWAHR] *n* ivory

ivre [ee•VR] *adj* inebriated;
intoxicated; drunk

ivresse [ee•VRES] *n* F
drunkenness

J

jacinthe [zhah•SAπT] *n* F
hyacinth; blue-bell

jaillir [juyyr] *vi* spurt; gush;
shoot forth

jaillisement [zhah•yees•MAHπ]
n M gush

jalousie [zhah•loo•ZEE] *n* F
jealousy

jaloux [zhah•LOO] *adj* jealous

jamais [jah•ME] *adv* ever;
never; ne ~\ never; not ever
à ~\ forever

jambe [zhaπb] *n* leg; shank

jambon [zhahπ•BAUπ] *n* ham

janvier [zhahπ•VYE] *n* M
January

Japon [zhah•PAUπ] *n* M Japan

japonais [zhah•pau•NEH] *adj*
Japanese; *n* M (person)
Japonais; (language) japonais

jardin [zhahr•DAπ] *n* M yard;
garden; ~ d'enfants\
kindergarten

jardiner [zhahr•dee•NEH] *vt*
garden

jargon [zhahr•GAUπ] *n* M
jargon; lingo

jaser [zhaseh] *vt* blab; chatter;
gossip; prattle

jauge [zhozh] *n* gauge; *vt*
jauger

jaun [zhaun] *adj; n* F yellow

jaune [zhaun] *n* M yolk
(d'oeuf)

jaunisse [zho•NEES] *n* F
jaundice

javelot [zhah•VLAU] *n* M
javelin

jazz [zhahz] *n* M jazz

je; (before vowel) **j'** [zhØ] *pron
pers* I; ~ vais bien\ I am well

je-sais-tout *n* MF know-it-all

jeep [zheep] *n* F jeep

jet [zhet] *n* M jet; throw; cast; ~
d'eau\ fountain spray

jetée [zhe•TAI] *n* F jetty; pier

jeter [zheh•TEH] *vt* throw;
fling; cast; hurl; ~ un coup
d'œil furtif\ peek

jeton [jeh•TAUπ] *n* M token;
gamepiece

jeu [zhØ] *n* M toy; game; sport;
play (theat); acting (theat); ~
de dames\ checkers; ~ de
mots\ pun

jeudi [zhØ•DEE] *n* M Thursday

jeune [zhœn] *adj* young; *adj*
inv youthful; *adj* junior; ~
arbre\ sapling; ~ paysan\
swain

jeunes [zhœn] *npl* MF teens

jeunesse; [zhœ•NEHS] *n* F
youth

jeux nautiques *npl* M water
sports

jockey [zhau•KEE] *n* M jockey

jogging [zhau•GEENG] *n* M
jogging

joie [zhwah] *n* F glee; joy

joindre [zhwahπdr] *vt* connect;
join; link; unite; bring
together

joint [zhwahπ] *n* M gasket;
joint

joli [zhau•LEE] *adj* pretty

jongler [zhauπ•GLAI] *vi* juggle

jongleur [zhauπ•GLœR] *n* M
juggler

jonquille [zhauπ•KEEL] *n* F
daffodil

joue [zhoo] *n* F cheek; coucher
en ~\ aim at

jouer [zhoo•EH] *vt vi* play; toy;
speculate; ~ à\ play a part

jouet [zhoo•e] *n* M plaything;
toy

joueur [zhoo•œR] *n* M player
(theater) acteur

joug [zhoo] *n* M yoke

jour [zhoor] *n* M day; daybreak;
daylight; aperture; opening; ~
de semaine\ weekday; ~ férié\
holiday

journal [zhoor•NAHL] *n* M
journal; newspaper; tabloid;
diary

journalisme
[zhoor•nah•LEEZM] *n* M
journalism

journaliste [zhoor•nah•LEEST]
n MF journalist

journée de travail *n* F
workday

jovial [zhau•VYAHL] *adj*
jovial

joyeusement
[zhwah•yØz•MAHπ] *adv*
happily; joyfully

joyeux [zhwah•YØ] *adj* joyful;
~ de fête\ festive

judas [zhew•DAH] *n* M
peephole

judiciaire [zhew•dee•SYEHR] *adj* judicial

judicieux [zhew•dee•SYØ] *adj* judicious

juge [zhewzh] *n* M judge; ~ de paix\ Justice of the Peace

juger [zhew•ZHAI] *vt* judge; estimate; deem

Juif [zhweef] *n* M Jew

juif [zhweef] *adj* Jewish

juillet [zhwee•YEH] *n* M July

juin [zhwaπ] *n* M June

juke-box [zhewk•BAUKS] *n* jukebox

jumeau; jumelle [zhew•MO] [zhew•MEHL] *n* MF twin

jumelles [zhew•MEL] *spl* F binoculars

jument [zhew•MAHπ] *n* M mare

jungle [zhauπgl] *n* F jungle

jupe [zhewp] *n* F skirt

juré [zhew•RAI] *n* M juror

jurer [zhy•REH] *vi* swear; vow

juridiction [zhew•ree•deek•SYAUπ] *n* F jurisdiction

jury [zhew•REE] *n* M jury

jus 1 [zhew] *n* M juice

jus 2 [zhew] *n* M gravy (de viande)

jusqu'à [zhews•KAH] *prép* unto; ~ ce point-ci; jusqu'ici *adv comp*\ thus far; hiherto; ~ ce que *prép*\ until; till

juste [zhewst] *adj* righteous; just; fair

justesse [zhew•STES] *n* F justice

justifier [zhew•stee•FYAI] *vt* justify

juteux [zhew•TØ] *adj* juicy

juvénile [zhew•vu•NEEL] *n* juvenile; childish; immature

juxtaposer [ZHEWK•stah•pau•ZAI] *vt* juxtapose

K

kaki; *n* (color) kaki m [kah•kee] *adj* khaki

kaléidoscope *n* M kaleidoscope

kangourou [kahπ•goo•ROO] *n* M kangaroo

kasher [kah•SHEH] *adj* kosher

Kenya *n* M Kenya

kérosène [kai•rau•SEN] *n* M kerosene

ketchup [ke•CHEWP] *n* M ketchup

kidnapper [keed•nah•PEH] *vt* kidnap

kilogramme [kee•lau•GRAHM] *n* M kilogram

kilomètre [kee•lau•METR] *n* M
kilometer

kilowatt [kee•lau•WAHT] *n*
kilowatt

kilt [keelt] *n* M kilt

klaxonner [klahk•sau•NEH] *vi*
honk

Koweït [koo•WAI] *n* M Kuwait

krête [kret] *n* F crest

kyste [keest] *n* M cyst

L

là; là-bas [lah]; [lah-BAH] *adv*
there; over there; cet homme
~\ that man there; yonder

là-dessus [lah-duh•SEW] *adv*
thereon; thereupon

labo [lah•bo] *n* M lab

laboratoire
[lah•bau•rah•TWAHR] *n* M
laboratory

labyrinthe [lah•bee•RAπT] *n* M
maze

lac [lahk] *n* M lake

lâche [lahsh] *adj* cowardly;
slack; careless; *n* MF coward

lâcheté [lahsh•TAI] *n*
cowardice

laconique [lah•kau•NEEK] *adj*
terse

lacque [lahk] *n* M lacquer; *vt*
lacquer

lagune [lah•GEWN] *n* F lagoon

laid [leh] [lehd] *adj* ugly;
homely

laideur [leh•DœR] *n* F ugliness

laine [lehn] *n* F woof (wool)

laineux; -euse [leh•NØ]; [-ØZ]
adj woolly

laisse [les] *n* F leash

laisser [leh•ZAI] *vt* let; leave;
allow; permit; quit; abandon;

~ aller *n* M carelessnes;
slackness; ~ tomber\ jilt;
fumble

lait [le] *n* M milk

laitier; *n* laiterie f [le•TYEH]
adj dairy

laiton [lai•TAUπ] *n* M brass

laitue [le•TEW] *n* F lettuce

lame [lahm] *n* M blade; ~ de
rasoir\ razor blade

lamentation
[lah•MAHπ•tah•SYAUπ] *n*
lament

lamentations
[lah•MEπ•ta•SYON] *vt* F wail

lamenter [lah•meπ•TAI] *vt*
lament; mourn

laminer [lah•mee•NAI] *vt*
laminate

lampadaire [lahπ•pah•DEHR] *n*
M lamp-post

lampe [lahπp] *n* F lamp; ~ de
poche\ flashlight

lampe [lahπ•PEH] *vt* guzzle

lance [lahπs] *n* F lance; spear

lancement [lahπs•MAHπ] *n*
launch; beginning

lancer [lahπ•SAI] *vt* cast;
launch; fling; hurl

lande [lahπd] *n* F moor;
wasteland; heath

langage [lahπ•GAHZH] *n* M
parlance; language

langue [lahπg] *n* F tongue;
language; strip of land;
mauvaise ~\ backbiter;
scandalmonger

languissant [lahπ•gee•SAHπ]
adj languid; listless

lanière [lah•NYEHR] *n* F
thong; lash

lanterne [lahπ•TERN] *n* F
lantern

lapin [lah•PAπ] *n* M rabbit

laquais [lah•KAI] *n* M flunky;
stooge

laque [lahk] *n* F hairspray

lard [lahr] *n* M bacon

large [lahrzh] *adj* broad; wide;
generous; ample; great; grand

largement [lahrzh•MAHπ] *adv*
widely; wide; far

largeur [lahr•ZHUR] *n* F
breadth; width

larme [lahrm] *n* F tear

latent [lah•TAHπ] *adj* latent;
hidden

latin [lah•TAπ] *adj n* M Latin

latitude [lah•tee•TEWD] *n* F
latitude

latte [laht] *n* F slat; lath

laurier [lo•RYEH] *n* M laurel

lavage [lah•VAHZH] *n* M
washing; scrubbing; dilution

lave [lahv] *n* F lava

lave-vaisselle [lahv•vai•SEL] *n*
M dishwasher

laver [lah•VEH] *vt* wash

laxatif [lahk•sah•TEEF] *n* M
laxative

le/la/les [luh] [lah] [leh] *article*
(gramm) the

lécher [lai•SHEH] *vt* lick

leçon [le•SAUπ] *n* F lesson

lecteur [lek•TœR] *n* M reader;
~ de disques\ disk drive

lecture [lek•TEWR] *n* F reading

légal [lai•GAHL] *adj* lawful;
legal

légaliser [lai•GAH•lee•ZAI] *vt*
legalize

légendaire [lai•zhahπ•DEHR]
adj legendary

légende 1 [lai•ZHAHND] *n* F
caption

légende 2 [lai•ZHAHND] *n* F
legend

léger [leh•ZHEH] *adj* slight;
light; lit

légèrement [lai•zher•MAHπ]
adv lightly; slightly

légèreté [lai•zher•TAI] *n* F
lightness

législation
[lai•zhee•slah•SYAUπ] *n* F
legislation

légitime [lai•zhee•TEEM] *adj*
legitimate

legs [leg] *n* legacy; bequest

léguer [lai•GAI] *vt* bequeath;
leave

légume [leh•GEWM] *n* F
vegetable; *npl* M greens

lehvure [leh•VYUR] *n* F yeast

lentille [lahπ•TEEL] *n* lens

léopard [lai•au•PAHR] *n* M
leopard

lèpre [le•pr] *n* F leprosy

lépreux [lai•PRØ] *n* M leper

lequel [lu•KEHL] *pron* who;
whom; which; that; which
one; of whom

lesbienne [lez•BYEN] *n* F
lesbian

léthargie [lai•tahr•ZHEE] *n* F
lethargy; sluggishness

Lettonie [lu•tau•NEE] *n* F
Latvia

lettre [letr] *n* F letter; *npl*
literature; letters

leur -s [lœr] *pron possessif* their

leurre [lØr] *n* decoy; lure

lever [lu•VEH] lift; raise; ~ du
jour\ daybreak; *vi* se lever\
rise; get up

levier [lu•VYAI] *n* M crowbar;
lever

lèvre [levr] *n* F lip

lévrier [laiv•RYEH] *n* M
greyhound

lézard [lai•ZAHR] *n* M lizard

liaison [lye•ZAUπ] *n* F liaison;
love affair

Liban [lee•BAHπ] *n* M Lebanon

libellule [lee•be•LEWL] *n* F
dragonfly

libéral [lee•bai•RAHL] *adj n* M
liberal

libération
[lee•BAI•rah•SYAUπ] *n* F
liberation; release

libérer [lee•bai•RAI] *vt* M
liberate; free; let go

liberté [lee•ber•TAI] *n* F
freedom; liberty; ~ de la
parole\ free speech

librairie [lee•bre•REE] *n* F
bookstore

libre [leebr] *adj* free; open; ~
arbitre\ free will; ~-échange\
free trade

Libye [lee•BYU] *n* F Libya

licou [lee•KOO] *n* M halter

lié [lee•AI] *adj* related; linked

liège [lyezh] *n* F cork

lien [lyaπ] *n* M bond

lierre [lyer] *n* M ivy

lieu [lyØ] *n* venue; place; avoir
~\ take place; ~ saint\ shrine

lieutenant [lyØ•tu•NAHπ] *n* M
lieutenant

lièvre [lyevr] *n* M hare

ligament [lee•gah•MAHπ] *n* M
ligament

ligne [lee•NYU] *n* line

ligoter [lee•gau•TEH] *vt* truss

ligue [leeg] *n* F league

limbes [laπb] *np* M limbo

limitation
[lee•MEE•tah•SYAUπ] *n* F
limitation; restriction;
constraint; ~ de vitesse\ speed
limit

limite [lee•MEET] *n* M limit;
restriction; boundary

limiter [lee•mee•TEH] *vt* limit;
constrain; restrict

limousine [lee•moo•ZEEN] *n* F
limousine

lin [laπ] *n* M flax

linge [laπ] *n* F linen

linceul [laπ•SØL] *n* shroud

linge [laπzh] *n* M laundry

linguistique [laπ•gee•STEEK]
n F linguistics

lion [lyauπ] *n* M lion

lionne [lyaun] *n* F lioness

liquide [lee•KEED] *adj n* M
liquid

liquider [lee•kee•DEH] *vt*
liquidate

lire [leer] *vi* read; ~ sur les
lèvres\ lip-read

lis [lee] *n* M lily

lisible [lee•ZEEBL] *adj* legible

liste [leest] *n* F list; roll; roster

lit [lee] *n* M bed; bedstead; stratum; ~s superimposés\ bunk beds

litige [lee•TEEZH] *n* M litigation

litre [leetr] *n* M quart; litre

littéraire [lee•tai•REHR] *adj* literary

littéral [lee•tai•RAHL] *adj* literal

littérature [lee•TAI•rah•TEWR] *n* F literature

livraison [lee•vreh•ZAUπ] *n* F delivery

livre 1 [leevr] *n* M book; ~ de poche\ paperback

livre 2 [leevr] pound (poids)

livrée [lee•VRAI] *n* F livery

livrer [lee•VREH] *vt* deliver; distribute

lobe [laub] *n* M lobe; ~ de l'oreille\ earlobe

local [lau•KAHL] *adj* local

locataire [lau•kah•TEHR] *n* MF lodger; tenant

locomotive [lau•KAU•mau•TEEV] *n* F locomotive

locuste [lau•KEWST] *n* F locust

logement [lauzh•MAHπ] *n* M housing; dwelling; place (coll)

logique [lau•ZHEEK] *n* F logic; *adj* logical

logo [logo] *n* M logo

loi [lwah] *n* law; rule

loin [lwahπ] *adj adv* far; removed; de ~\ at a distance

lointain [lwahπ•TAπ] *adj* distant

loisir [lwah•ZEER] *n* M leisure; à ~ at leisure

Londres [lauπdr] *n* London

long; longue [lauπ] *adj* long; slow; *n* M length; le ~ de\ along; à la ~\ in the long run

longe [lauπzh] *n* F loin

longeur [lauπ•GœER] *n* F length; ~ d'onde\ wavelength

longitude [lawn•zhee•TEWD] *n* F longitude

loquace [lo•KAHS] *adj* inv verbose; talkative

loquet [lau•KEH] *n* M latch

loterie [lau•tu•REE] *n* raffle; lotter; mettre en ~\ play the lottery

lotion [lau•SYAUπ] *n* F lotion

louange(s) [loo•AHπZH] *n* F praise

louche [loosh] *n* ladle

louer 1 [loo•AI] *vt* rent; hire; book; reserve

louer 2 [loo•AI] *vt* commend

loup; louve [loo]; [loov] *n* MF wolf; ~ garou\ werewolf

loupe [loop] *n* magnifying glass

louer [loo•EH] *vi* lease

lourd [loor] *adj* weighty; heavy

lourdement [loord•MAHπ] *adv* heavily

loutre [lootr] *n* F otter

loyal [lwah•YAHL] *adj* loyal; staunch; trusty

loyauté [lwah•yo•TAI] *n* F loyalty

loyer [lwah•YEH]; *vt* rent

lubrifiant [lew•bree•FYAHπ] *n* M lubricant

lubrifier [lew•bree•FYAI] *vt*
lubricate

lubrique [lew•BREEK] *adj*
lecherous

lucarne [lew•KAHRN] *n* F
skylight

lucide [lew•SEED] *adj* lucid;
clear

lueur [lew•œR] *n* F gleam;
glimmer; glow; *vi* luire

luge [lewzh] *n* F sledge;
toboggan

lugubre [lew•GEWBR] *adj*
dismal

luisant -e [lwee•ZAHπ];
[-ZAHπTE] *adj* sleek

lumineux [lew•mee•NØ] *adj*
luminous

lunaire [lew•NER] *adj* lunar

lundi [lewn•DEE] *n* M Monday

lune [lewn] *n* F moon

lune [lewn] *n* F moon; ~ de
miel\ honeymoon

lunettes fpl [lew•NET] *n*
glasses; spectacles; goggles

lustre [lewstr] *n* M gloss; shine;
sheen; luster

lustré [lew•STRAI] *adj* M
glossy; shiny; lustrous

lutin [lew•TAπ] *n* goblin; imp

lutte [lewt] *n* F struggle; tussle;
fight

lutter [lew•TEH] *vi* wrestle;
struggle; grapple

luxueux [lewk•SWØ] *adj*
luxurious

luxe [lewks] *n* M luxury

lyncher [laπ•SHAI] *vt* lynch

lyrique [lee•REEK] *adj* lyric;
lyrical

M

m'as-tu-vu [mah•tew•VEW] *n*
M show-off

macabre [mah•KAHBR] *adj*
grisly

macaroni [mah•kah•rau•NEE] *n*
M macaroni

mâcher [mah•SHAI] *vt* chew

machette [mah•SHET] *n* F
machete

machin [mah•SHIN] *n* M thing;
gadget; gimmick

machine [mah•SHEEN] *n* F
machine; engine; *npl*
machinery; ~ à écrire F\
typewriter; ~ à laver\

washing-machine; ~ à coudre
n\ sewing machine

machinerie
[mah•SHEE•ne•REE] *n* F
machinery

mâchoire [mah•SHWAHR] *n* F
jaw; clamp

maçon [mah•SAUπ] *n* mason

maçonnerie
[mah•saun•REE] *n* F
stonework; masonry

madame [mah•DAHM] *n* F
madam; married lady

mademoiselle
[mah•DU•mwah•ZEL] *n* F

miss; unmarried lady; young lady

magasin [mah•gah•ZAπ] *n* M warehouse; store; shop

magicien [mah•zhee•SYAHπ] *n* magicien

magique [mah•zheek] *adj* magic; magical; *n* enchantment M

magistrat [mah•zhee•STRAH] *n* magistrate; judge

magnétique [ma•nyai•TEEK] *adj* magnetic

magnificence [mah•nyee•fee•SAHπS] *n* F magnificence

magnifique [mah•nyee•FEEK] *adj* magnificent; splendid; gorgeous

mai [mai] *n* M May

maigre [megr] *adj* meager; skinny; lean

maille [mahy] *n* mesh; stitch; link

maillet [mah•YEH] *n* M mallet

maillot [mahy•o] *n* M swimsuit; bathing suit

main [maπ] *n* f hand; handwriting; donner un coup de ~\ help; give a hand; ~-d'œuvre\ manpower

maintenant [maπ•tu•NAHπ] *adv* now; à partir de ~\ from now; *conj* maintenant que

maintenir [maπ•te•NEER] *vt* maintain

maintien [maπ•TYAHπ] *n* M maintenance (of machine etc); *n* F maintenance

maire [mer] *n* M mayor

mais [mai] *conj* but; ~ oui!\ of course!

maïs [mah•EES] *n* corn; maie

maison [me•ZAUπ] *n* F home; house; house (theat); à la maison\ at home

maître [maitr] *adj n* M master; *vt* maîtriser; ~ d'hotel\ butler

maîtresse [me•TRES] *n* F mistress; teacher; *adj* chief

maîtrise de soi *n* self-control

maîtriser [meh•tree•ZEH] *vt* subdue; control

majesté [mah•zhe•STAI] *n* F majesty; Sa Majesté le Roi; Sa Majesté la Reine

majéstueux [mah•zhai•STEWØ] *adj* majestic; stately

majeur [mah•ZHœR] *adj* major; *n* M major; middle finger

majorité [ma•ZHAU•ree•TAI] *n* F majority

mal [mahl] *n* M evil; hurt; harm; *adj* bad; *adv* badly; ~ à l'aise\ ill at ease; ~ à propos\ inappropriate; ~ à tort\ wrong; ~ comprendre\ misunderstand; ~ compter\ miscount; ~ de dents; ~ aux dents\ toothache; ~ à la tête\ headache; ~ équilibré\ unbalanced; ~ interpréter\ misconstrue; ~ dommage\ mischief; ~ nourri\ underfed; malnourished; ~ orthographier\ misspell; ~ renseigner\ misinform; ~ stuffy

malade [mah•LAHD] *adj* sick; ill; *vt* tomber ~\ fall ill; sick

maladie |mah•la•DEE| *n* F
    disease; illness; sickness;
    malady

maladif |mah•lah•DEEF| *adj*
    sickly

maladroit |mah•lah•DRWAH|
    adj awkward; clumsy

malaise |mah•LEZ| *n* M
    discomfort; malaise; unease

malchance |mahl•SHAHπS| *n*
    F misfortune

malchanceux |mahl•shahπ•SØ|
    adj hapless; unfortunate

mâle |mahl| *n* M *adj* male;
    mate

malédiction
    |mah•LAI•deek•SYUπ| *n* F
    curse

malentendu
    |mahl•ahπ•tahπ•DEW| *n* M
    misunderstanding

malgré |mahl•GRAI| *prép*
    despite

malheureur; -euse
    |mahl•lœr•Ø|; |-Øz| *n* MF
    wretch; grouch

malheureux |mah•lØ•RØ| *adj*
    unhappy; forlorn

malheurs |mahl•œR| *npl* M
    tribulation

malhonnête |mah•lau•NET|
    adj dishonest; impolite;
    indecent; crooked

malicieux |mahl•lee•SØ| *adj*
    mischievous; malicious

malin |mah•LAπ| *adj*
    malignant; cunning; sharp; F
    maligne

mallette |mah•LEHT| *n* F
    valise; suitcase

malsain |mahl•SAπ| *adj*
    unwholesome; unhealthy

maltraitement
    |mahl•trait•MAHπ| *n* M
    abuse; mistreatment

maltraiter |mahl•tre•TEH| *vt*
    mistreat; abuse

maman |mah•MAUπ| *n* F
    mother; mama

mamelon |mah•me•LAUπ| *n* M
    nipple; hill; boss

mammifère |mah•mee•FER| *n*
    M mammal

manant |ma•NAπ| *n* M villain

manche |mahπsh| *n* F sleeve;
    hose; air shaft; La Manche\
    the English Channel

manchette |mahπ•SHET| *n* F
    headline

manchot |mahπ•SHAU| *n* M
    penguin

mandarine |mahπ•dah•REEN|
    n F tangerine

mandat |mahπ•DAH| *n* M
    mandate; ~ de perquisition\
    search warrant

manège |mah•NEZH| *n*
    merry-go-round

manger |mahπ•ZHAI| *vt vi* eat;
    squander; fret

manie |mah•NEE| *n* F mania;
    hysteria; craze

manière |mah•NYER| *n* F
    manner; *npl* ~s manners

manifeste |mah•nee•FEST| *adj*
    manifest; *n* M patent;
    manifesto

manipuler
    |mah•NEE•pew•LAI| *vt*
    manipulate; connive

manivelle [mah•nee•VEHL] *n* F
winch; crank

mannequin [mah•ne•KAπ] *n* M
dummy; fashion model

manœuvre 1 [mah•NœVR] *n*
M laborer

manœuvre 2 [mah•NœVR] *n* F
maneuver; *vt vi* manœuvrer

manoir [mah•NWAHR] *n* M
manor

manque [mahπk] *n* M shortage;
lack; insufficiency; deficiency;
~ de respect\ disrespect

manque d'enthousiasme *n*
comp M unwillingness

manque de prévanance *n* M
thoughtlessness

manquer [mahn•KEH] *vt* want;
miss; cela me ~\ I am missing
that

manteau [mahπ•TO] *n* M
topcoat; coat; mantle

manucure [mah•new•KEWR] *n*
F manicure

manuel [mah•new•ÉL] *adj n* M
manual; ~ scolaire; textbook

manuscrit [mah•new•SKREE] *n*
M manuscript

maquereau 1 [mah•ku•RO] *n*
M mackerel

maquereau 2 [mah•ku•RO] *n*
M pimp

maquillage [mah•kee•YAHZH]
n M make-up; cosmetics

marais [mah•RAI] *n* M bog;
marsh; swamp

marathon [mah•rah•TAUπ] *n*
M marathon

marchand [mahr•SHAHπ] *n* M
dealer; merchant; ~ ambulant\

street vendor; ~ de tabac\
tobacconist

marchander
[mahr•shahπ•DEH] *vi* haggle

marchandise
[mahr•chahπ•DEES] *n* F
commodity

marchandises
[mahr•shaπ•DEEZ] *npl* F
ware; wares; merchandise

marche [mahrsh] *n* F step; stair;
walk; march

marché [mahr•SHAI] *n* M deal;
bargain; market; ~ noir\ black
market

marcher [mahr•SHEH] *vt* walk;
march; step; ~ dans l'eau\
wade; ~ en chien\ tread water;
dog padde; ~ péniblement\
trudge

mardi [mahr•DEE] *adv*; *n* M
Tuesday; Mardi Gras\ Shrove
Tuesday

marécageux
[mah•rai•kah•ZHØ] *adj*
marshy; swampy

maréchal [mah•rai•SHAHL] *n*
M marshal

marée [mah•REH] *n* M tide

margarine [mahr•zhah•REEN]
n F margarine

marge [mahrzh] *n* F margin;
edge; border

marginal [mahr•zhee•NAHL]
adj marginal

marguerite [mahr•gu•REET] *n*
F daisy

mari [mah•REE] *n* M husband

mariage [mah•RY•AHZH] *n* M
marriage; matrimony

marié [mah•RYAI] *n* M groom; bridegroom; *adj* married; wed; wedded

mariée [mah•RYAI] *n* F bride

marijuana [mah•REE•wah•NAH] *n* F marijuana

marin [mah•RAπ] *n* sailor; mariner; seaman; *adj* marine

marine [mah•REEN] *adj n* M marine

marionette [mah•ryau•NET] *n* puppet

marmite [mahr•MEET] *n* F pot; casserole; ~ à vapeur\ steamer

marmonner [mahr•mau•NEH] *vt vi* mutter; grumble

marmotter [mahr•mau•TAI] *vt vi* mumble

Maroc [mah•RAUK] *n* M Morocco

marquant [mahr•KWAHπ] *adj* conspicuous; marked; striking

marque [mahrk] *n* F mark; brand; ~ de fabrique\ trademark; *vt* marquer; ~ au fer rouge\ brand (animaux)

marraine [mah•REN] *n* F godmother

mars [mahrs] *n* M March

Mars [mahrs] *n* F Mars

marsouin [mahr•SWAπ] *n* M porpoise

marteau [mahr•TO] *n* M hammer; ~ -piqueur\ jackhammer

martial [mahr•SYAHL] *adj* martial; military

martyr [mahr•TEER] *n* M martyr; *vt* martyriser

mascara [mah•skah•RAH] *n* M mascara

mascarade [mah•skah•RAHD] *n* F masquerade

masculin [mah•skew•LAπ] *adj* masculine

masque [mahsk] *n* M mask; *vt* masquer

massacre [mah•SAHKR] *n* M massacre; slaughter; *vt* massacrer

massage [mah•SAHZH] *n* M massage; *vt* masser

masse [mahs] *n* F mass ; heap; *vi* se masser

massif [mah•SEEF] *adj* massive; huge; enormous

mastic [mah•STEEK] *n* M putty

mastiquer [mah•stee•KEH] *vt* chew; masticate

mât [mah] *n* M flagpole; mast; pole; ~ de hune\ topmost

matelas [mah•tu•LAH] *n* M mattress

matérialiste [mah•TAI•ryah•LEEST] *adj* materialistic; *n* MF materialist

matériel [mah•tai•RYEL] *n* M working stock; aparatus *adj* material; ~ de pêche\ fishing tackle ; ~ nautique\ rigging

maternel [mah•ter•NEL] *adj* maternal; motherly

maternité [mah•TER•nee•TAI] *n* F motherhood

mathématiques [mah•TAI•mah•TEEK] *npl* F mathematics

matière [mah•TYER] *n* F material; matter; subject; ~ première\ raw material

matin 1 [mah•TAπ] *n* morning

matin 2 [mah•TAπ] *n* mastif

matinée [mah•tee•NAI] *n* F
morning; forenoon; afternoon
performance (theat)

matraquer [mah•trah•KAI] *vt*
bludgeon; beat

matrice 1 [mah•TREES] *n* F
matrix

matrice 2 [mah•TREES] *n* F
womb

maturité [mah•tew•ree•TAI] *n*
F maturity

Maure [maur] *n* M Moor

maussade [mo•SAHD] *adj*
grumpy; crabby

mauvais [mo•VAI] *adj* bad;
wicked; evil; il fait ~\ it's bad
weather

mauvaise conduite *n* F
misconduct

maximum [mahk•see•MEWM]
adj n M maximum

mayonnaise [mah•yau•NEZ] *n*
F mayonnaise

mécanicien
[mai•kah•nee•SYAHπ] *n* M
mechanic; *n* F mécanique; *adj*
mechanical

mécanisme [mai•kah•NEEZM]
n M mechanism; device;
apparatus

méchanceté [meh•shaπs•TEH]
adj wickedness; malice; evil;
ill will

méchant [mai•SHAHπ] *adj*
malicious; wicked; unpleasant

mèche [mehsh] *n* F wick
(bougie); strand; tress (de
cheveux)

mécontent [mai•kauπ•TAHπ]
adj disgruntled; displeased

mécontenter
[mai•KAUπ•tahπ•TAI] *vt*
dissatisfy; displease

médaille [mai•DAHY] *n* F
medal; prize; award

médaillon [mai•dah•YAUπ] *n*
M medallion

médecin [maid•SAπ] *n* M
physician; doctor

médias [mai•DYAH] *npl* M
media

médiateur [mai•dyah•TœR] *n*
M mediator

médical [mai•dee•KAHL] *adj*
medical

médicament
[mai•dee•kah•MAHπ] *n* M
drug

médicamenter
[mai•DEE•kah•mahπ•TAI] *vt*
medicate

médicine [mai•dee•SEEN] *n* F
medicine

médiéval [mai•dyai•VAHL] *adj*
medieval

médiocre [mai•dy•AUKR] *adj*
mediocre; so-so;
undistinguished

méditer [mai•dee•TEH] *vt vi*
meditate

médium *n* M psychic

méduse [mai•DEWZ] *n* F
jellyfish

méfait [mai•FEH] *n* M
misdeed

méfiance [mai•FY•AHπS] *n* F
distrust; mistrust; *vt* se
méfier de

méfiant [mai•FY•AHπ] *adj*
distrustful; mistrusting

méfier (de) [mai•FYAI] *vi* refl
beware (of)

mégot [mai•GO] *n* M butt (of
cigarette)

meilleur [me•YUR] *adj* better

méjuger [mai•zhew•ZHEH] *vt*
misjudge

mélancolique
[mai•lauπ•kau•LEEK] *adj*
melancholy; *n* F mélancolie

mélange [mai•LAHπZH] *n* M
mixture; mix; combination

mélanger [mai•lahπ•ZHAI] *vt*
blend; mix

mélasse [mai•LAHS] *n* F
molasses

mêlée [meh•LAI] *n* F scramble;
fight; tussle

mélodie [mai•lau•DEE] *n* F
melody; tune

melon [me•LAUπ] *n* M melon

membre [mahπbr] *n* member;
limb (anat)

mémé [mai•MAI] *n* F grandma

même [mem] *adj* same; *pron* le
même (la même); les mêmes;
faire de ~\ do the same; *adv*
de la ~ manière\ the same

mémoire [mai•MWAHR] *n* F
memory

mémoires [mai•MWAHR] *npl*
F memoirs

menaçant [me•nah•SAHπ] *adj*
menacing; ominous;
threatening

menace [me•NAHS] *n* F threat;
menace

menacer [meh•nah•SEH] *vt*
threaten; menace

ménage [mai•NAHZH] *n* M
housekeeping; housework

ménagère [mai•nah•ZHER] *n* F
housewife

mendiant [mahn•DYAHπ] *n* M
beggar

mendier [mahπ•DYAI] *vt*
beg

ménopause [mai•nau•POZ] *n* F
menopause

mensonge [mahπ•SAUπZH] *n*
lie

mensonges [mahπ•SAUNZH]
npl F lying

menstruation
[MAHπ•strew•ah•SYAUπ] *n*
F menstruation

mensuel [mahπ•sew•EL] *adj*
monthly; *adv* mensuelment

mental [mahπ•TAHL] *adj*
mental

mentalité [mahπ•TAH•lee•TAI]
n F mentality

menteur [mahπ•TœR] *n* M liar;
adj lying

menthe [mahπth] *n* F mint

mentionner [mahπ•syau•NAI]
vt mention; remark upon

menton [mahπ•TAUπ] *n* M
chin

menu [me•NEW] *n* M menu

menuisier [muhn•wee•ZYEH] *n*
M woodworker

menusierie [muhn•wee•ZREE]
n F woodwork

mépris [mai•PREE] *n* M scorn;
contempt

méprisable [mai•pree•ZABL]
adj contemptible;
despicable

mépriser [mai•pree•ZAI] *vt*
despise

mer [mer] *n* F sea; mal
de ~\ seasick; Mer des
Caraïbes [~ kah•rah•eeb] *n*
Caribbean (Sea)

mercenaire [mer•su•NEHR] *adj*
n M mercenary

merci [mehr•SEE] *n* M thanks;
thank you

mercredi [mehr•kruh•DEE] *n* M
Wednesday

mercure [mer•KEWR] *n*
mercury (element) ; *n* F
Mercury

merde! [merd] *excl* shit

mère [mer] *n* mother; *adj*
motherly

méritant [mai•ree•TAHπ] *adj*
deserving

mérite [mai•REET] *n* M merit

mériter [mai•ree•TAI] *vt*
deserve; merit

merle [merl] *n* M blackbird

merveille [mer•VEY] *n* F
marvel; wonder; *vi*
s'émerveiller (de); marvel'
wonder (at)

merveilleux [mer•veh•YØ] *adj*
marvelous

mésaventure
[mai•zah•vahπ•TEWR] *n* F
mishap

mesquin [me•SKAπ] *adj* mean;
shabby; paltry; nasty

message [me•SAHZH] *n* M
message

messager [me•sah•ZHER] *n* M
messenger

mesure [me•ZEWR] *n* F
measurement

mesuré [muh•zyr•AI] *adj*
temperate

mesure [me•ZEWR] *n* measure;
vt vi mesurer

métal [mai•TAHL] *n* M metal

métallique [mai•tah•LEEK] *adj*
metallic

métaphore [mai•tah•FAUR] *n*
F metaphor

météore [mai•tai•AUR] *n* M
meteor

météorologie
[mai•tai•AU•rah•lau•ZHEE] *n*
F meteorology

méthode [mai•TAUD] *n*
method; system

méticuleux [mai•TEE•kew•LØ]
adj meticulous; fussy

métier [meh•TYEH] *n* M *vi*
comp trade; *n* MF professsion;
occupation

mètre [mehtr] *n* M meter;
yardstick (coll)

métrique [mai•TREEK] *adj*
metric

métro [meh•TRO] *n* M subway

métropolitain
[mai•trau•PAU•lee•TAπ] *adj*
metropolitan

mettre [metr] *vt* put; lay; place;
position; ~ de côté\ discard;
set side; ~ en danger\
endanger; jeopardize; ~ en
rage\ enrage; ~ mettre le feu
à\ ignite

meuble [mØbl] *n* M furniture;
npl M furnishings; ~ de
famille\ heirloom

meubler [mØ•BLAI] *vt*
furnish

meuglement [mØ•glu•MAHπ]
n M moo; *vi* meugler

meule [mØl] *n* F millstone;
grindstone; stack; haystack

meurtre [mœr•TR] *n* F
murder;

mignon [mee•NYAUπ] *adj*
cute; sweet; dainty; tiny;
darling

migraine [mee•GREN] *n* F
migraine

migrateur [mee•grah•TœR] *adj*
migrant

mile [meel] *n* M mile

milice [mee•LEES] *n* F militia

militaire [mee•lee•TER] *adj*
military; *npl* M les
militaires

militant [mee•lee•TAHπ] *adj n*
M militant

mille [meeil] *adj; n* MF
thousand

mille-pattes *n* M centipede

millénaire [mee•lai•NEHR] *n*
M millenium

milliard [mee•YAHRD] *num* M
billion

millième [meeil•YEHM] *adj n*
MF thousandth

million [mee•YAUπ] *num* M
million

millionaire [mee•yau•NER] *n*
MF millionaire

mince [maπs] *adj* slim; thin

minceur [maπ•SœR] *n* F
thinness

minéral [mee•nai•RAHL] *adj n*
M mineral; ore

mineur [mee•NœR] *adj n* M
minor

miniature [mee•nyah•TEWR]
adj n F miniature

minime [mee•NEEM] *adj* tiny;
minimal; minute

minimiser [mee•nee•mee•ZAI]
vt minimize

minimum [mee•nee•MEWM]
adj n M minimum

miniscule [mee•nee•SKEWL]
adj minute; miniscule

ministère [mee•nee•STEHR] *n*
M ministry; ministry office;
agency; ~ des finances;
treasury

ministre [mee•NEESTR] *n*
minister; clergyman

minorité [mee•NAU•ree•TAI] *n*
F minority

minuit [mee•NWEE] *n* M
midnight

minus [mee•NEW] *n* moron;
idiot; cretin

minutieux -euse
[mee•new•SYØ] [-ØZ] *adj*
thorough; meticulous

mioche [myaush] *n* MF brat;
urchin; tot

miracle [mee•RAHKL] *n* M
miracle

miraculeux
[mee•RAH•kew•LØ] *adj* M
miraculous

mirage [mee•RAHZH] *n* M
mirage

miroir [mee•RWAHR] *n* mirror

miroiter [mee•rwah•TAI] *vi*
shimmer

misanthrope
[mee•sahn•TRAUP] *n* MF
misanthrope

misérable [mee•zehr•AHBL]
adj inv wretched; miserable;
unhappy

misère [mee•ZEHR] *n* F
misery; sorrow

miséricordiaux
[mee•ze•REE•kaur•DYO] *adj*
merciful

missile [mee•SEEL] *n* M
missile

mission [mee•SYAUπ] *n* F
mission

missionaire [mee•syau•NEHR]
n MF missionary

miteux [mee•TØ] *adj* seedy;
shabby; run-down; dingy

mitraillete [mee•trahy•EHT] *n*
F submachine gun

mitrailleuse [mee•trah•YØZ] *n*
F machine gun

mobile [mau•BEEL] *adj*
mobile; movable

mobiliser [mau•bee•lee•ZAI] *vt*
mobilize; liquidate

mocassin [mau•kah•SAπ] *n* M
loafer

mode [maud] *n* M mode;
fashion

modèle [mau•DEL] *n* M
pattern; epitome; fashion/art
model; *adj* model

modération
[mau•DEH•rah•SYAUπ] *n* F
temperance; moderation

modéré [mau•dai•RAI] *adj n* M
moderate; *vt* modérer; *vi* se
modérer

moderne [mau•DERN] *adj*
modern; contemporary

moderniser
[mau•DER•nee•ZAI] *vt*
modernize

modeste [mau•DEST] *adj*
dèmure; modest; unassuming

modestie [mau•de•STEE] *n* F
modesty

modifier [mau•dee•FYAI] *vt*
modify; change; alter

moelle épinière [mwahl
eh•pee•NYEHR] *n* M spinal
cord

moi [mwah] *pron* me; I; myself;
n M self; ego

moindre [mwaπdr] *adj* lesser;
à un degré ~\ a little less

moine [mwahn] *n* M monk

moineau [mwah•NO] *n* M
sparrow (oiseau)

moins [mwaπ] *adj n* M moins
less; *prep* minus; ~ que\ less
than

mois [mwah] *n* M month

moississure [mwah•see•SEWR]
n F mold; mildew

moisson [mwah•SAUπ] *n*
harvest; reap; *vt* moissonner

moite [mwaht] *adj* moist

molaire [mau•LEHR] *n* F
molar

mollusque [mau•LEWSK] *n* M
mollusk

moment [mau•MAHπ] *n* M
moment; pour le ~\ for the
time being

momentané
[mau•MAHπ•tah•NAI] *adj*
momentary

momie [mau•MEE] *n* F
mummy

mon; ma; mes [mauπ] *adj* my

monarchie [mau•nahr•SHEE] *n*
F monarchy

monarque [mau•NAHRK] *n* M
monarch

monastère [mau•nah•STER] *n*
M monastery

monde [maund] *n* M world;
family; crowd; tout le ~\
everybody; recevoir le ~\
entertain

monétaire [mau•nai•TEHR] *adj*
monetary

monnaie [mau•NAI] *n* F
currency; money; ~ légale\
legal tender

monologue [mau•nau•LAUG]
n M monologue

monopole [mau•nau•PAUL] *n*
M monopoly

monopoliser
[mau•NAU•pau•lee•ZAI] *vt*
monopolize

monotone [mau•nau•TAUN]
adj monotonous; boring; dull

monotonie
[mau•NAU•tau•NEE] *n*
monotony

Monsieur [mu•SYØ] *n* M
mister (addresse)

monsieur [mu•SYØ] *n* M sir;
gentleman

monstre [mauπstr] *n* M freak;
monster

monstrueux [mauπ•strew•Ø]
adj F monstrous

monstruosité
[mauπ•strew•AU•see•TAI] *n* F
monstrosity

mont [mauπ] *n* M mount;
mountain; par ~ et par vaux\
up hill and down;
mont-de-piété\ pawnshop

montagne [mauπ•tah•NYU] *n*
F mountain

montaigneux [mauπ•te•NYØ]
adj mountainous

montée [mauπ•TAI] *adj*
mounted; on horseback

monter [mauπ•TEH] *vt* climb;
ascend; mount; ~ à cheval\
ride horseback; ~ en flèche\
soar; ~ sur une bicyclette\ ride
a bicycle

montre [mauπtr] *n* F watch

monument [mau•new•MAHπ]
n monument

monumental
[mau•new•mahπ•TAHL] *adj*
monumental

moquer [mau•KEH] *vt* mock;
make fun of

moquerie [mau•ku•REE] *n* M
mockery

moral [mau•RAHL] *adj* ethical;
moral; *n* M morale; *npl* F ~s\
morals

moralité [mau•RAH•lee•TAI] *n*
F morality

morbide [maur•BEED] *adj*
morbid

morceau [mor•SO] *n* M bit;
piece; morsel; strip; scrap; ~
de sucre\ sugar cube

mordre [mordr] *vt* bite

morgue [maurg] *n* F morgue

morne [maurn] *adj* dreary;
gloomy

mort [maur] *adj* dead; lifeless;
stagnant

mort [maur] *n* F death; *npl* F
~s\ the dead; jour des ~s\ All
Saint's Day; peine de ~\ pain
of death

mortalité [maur•TAH•lee•TAI] *n* F mortality

mortier [maur•TYEH] *n* mortar

mortifier [maur•tee•FYEH] *vt* mortify; humiliate; hang (execution)

morue [mau•REW] *n* F cod

mosaïque [mau•zah•EEK] *n* F mosaic

Moscou [mau•SKOO] *n* Moscow

mosquée [mau•SKAI] *n* F mosque

mot [mau] *n* M word; letter; note; bon ~\ witticism; joke; mots croisés\ crossword puzzle

moteur [máu•TœR] *adj* motive; propulsive; *n* M motor; engine; ~ à vapeur\ steam engine

motif [mau•TEEF] *n* M motif; motive

motivation [mau•TEE•vah•SYAUπ] *n* F motivation; incentive

motiver [mau•tee•VAI] *vt* motivate

moto [mau•TAU] *n* M motorcycle

motte [maht] *n* F sod; mound; clump

mou [moo] *adj* limp; F molle

mouchard -e [moo•SHAHR]; [moo•SHAHRD] *n* MF stool pigeon

mouche [moosh] *n* F fly; beauty spot; button; ~ du coche\ busybody; prendre la ~\ take offense

moucheron [moo•she•RAUπ] *n* M gnat

moucheture [moo•shu•TEWR] *n* fleck; particle

mouchoir [moo•SHWAHR] *n* M handkerchief

moudre [moo•dr] *vt* grind

moue [moue] *n* F pout

mouette [moo•ET] *n* F gull

moufette [moo•FEHT] *n* F skunk (animal)

moufle [moofl] *n* F mitten

mouillé [mwee•YAI] *adj* wet; *vt* mouiller

moule [mool] *n* F mussel

moulin [moo•LAπ] *n* M grinder; mill; ; *vt* moudre; ~ à vent\ windmill

mourant [moo•RAHπ] *adj* dying

mourir [moo•REER] *vi* die; se mourir; ~ d'envie\ die of envy

mousse [moos] *n* F moss; mousse; foam; *vi* mousser; ~ de savon\ lather

mousson [moo•SAUπ] *n* M monsoon

moustache [moo•STAHSH] *n* F moustache

moustaches [moo•STAHSH] *npl* F whiskers

moustique [moo•STEEK] *n* mosquito

moutarde [moo•TAHRD] *n* F mustard

mouton [moo•TAUπ] *n* M mutton; sheep

mouvement [moov•MAHπ] *n* M movement; motion

mouver [moo•VEH] *vt* move

mouvement m; (proposal)
motion

moyen [mwah•YAπ] *adj*
average; medium; mean
(math); moyen-âge M Middle
Ages

Moyen-Orient *n* M Middle
East

moyens [mway•EHπ] *n* M
wherewithal; means

mucus [mew•KEW] *n* M
mucous

muet [mew•EH] *adj n* M
mute

muffin [mew•FAπ] *n* M
muffin

mugir [mew•ZHEER] *vi*
bellow

mule [mewl] *n* F mule

multiple [mewl•TEEPL] *n* M
multiple

multiplication
[mewl•tee•PLEE•kah•SYAUπ]
n F multiplication

multiplier [mewl•tee•PLYAI] *vt*
multiply; *vi* se multiplier

multitude [mewl•tee•TEWD] *n*
F multitude

municipal
[mew•nee•see•PAHL] *adj*
municipal

municipalité
[mew•nee•see•PAH•lee•TAI]
n F borough; municipality

mûr [myr] *adj* ripe; mature

mur [myur] *n* M wall

mûre [mewr] *n* F blackberry

mûrir [mewr] *vi* mature; ripen

murmure [muhr•MOOR] *n* M
whisper; murmur; *vt vi*
murmurer

muscle [mewskl] *n* M brawn;
muscle; *adj* musclé

musculaire; [mew•skew•LEHR]
adj muscular

muse [mews] *n* F muse

museau (d'un animal)
[mew•ZO] *n* M snout; muzzle

musée [mew•ZAI] *n* M
museum

musical [mew•zee•KAHL] *adj n*
F musical

musicien [mew•zee•SYAHπ] *n*
musician

musique [mew•ZEEK] *n* F
music

musulman; *n* Musulman M
[mew•zl•MAHπ] *adj* Muslim

muet [mew•AI] *adj* dumb; mute

mutiler [mew•tee•LAI] *vt*
mutilate

mutinerie [mew•TEE•ne•REE]
n F mutiny

mutuel [mew•tew•EL] *adj*
mutual

myope [myaup] *adj*
near-sighted

myrtille [meer•TEEY] *n* F
blueberry

mystère [mee•STER] *n* M
mystery

mystérieux [mee•stai•RYØ] *adj*
mysterious; uncanny

mystique [mee•STEEK] *n* M
mystic; *adj* mystical

mythe [meet] *n* M myth

mythique [mee•TEEK] *adj* F
mythical

mythologie
[mee•TAU•lau•ZHEE] *n* F
mythology

N

nage [nazh] *n* F swimming; rowing; stroke; en ~\ sweaty

nager [nah•ZHEH] *vi* swim; row; pull; scull

nageur -euse [nah•ZHœR]; [-Øz] *n* MF swimmer

naïf [nah•EEF] *adj* naive

nain [naπ] *n* M dwarf; midget; pygmy; run; *adj* dwarfish shrimpy (coll)

naissance [nai•SAπS] *n* F birth; beginning; extraction

naître [naitr] *vi* born (to be)

naiveté [nai•veh•TAI] *n* F artlessness; simplicity; naivety

nanifestant [nah•nee•fe•STAHπ] *n* M protester

nantissement [nahπ•tee•SMAHπ] *n* M collateral

narcotique [nahr•kau•TEEK] *adj n* M narcotic

narine [nah•REEN] *n* F nostril

narrateur [nah•rah•TœR] *n* M narrator; story-teller

narratif [nah•rah•TEEF] *adj* narrative

narration [nah•rah•SYAUπ] *n* narration

nasal [nah•ZAHL] *adj* nasal; twanging

natation [nah•tah•SYAUπ] *n* F swimming

nation [nah•SYAUπ] *n* F nation

national [nah•syau•NAHL] *adj* national

nationalalité [nah•syau•NAH•lee•TAI] *n* F nationality

nationaliser [nah•syau•NAH•lee•ZAI] *vt* nationalize

Nativité [nah•TEE•vee•TAI] *n* F Nativity

naturaliser [nah•tew•RAH•lee•ZAI] *vt* naturalize; stuff

nature [nah•TEWR] *n* F nature

naturel [nah•tew•REL] *adj* natural; unaffected; native; innate; illegitimate (enfant)

naturellement [nah•tew•rahl•MAHπ] *adj* naturally

nausée [no•ZAI] *n* F nausea

nauséeux [no•zai•Ø] *adj* nauseous

naval [nah•VAHL] *adj* naval; nautical

navet [nah•VEH] *n* M turnip

navette [nah•VET] *n* F shuttle; shuttle bus

navigateur [nah•vee•gah•TœR] *n* navigator

navigation [nah•vee•gah•SYAUπ] *n* navigation

navire [nah•VEEUR] *n* M ship; vessel; ~ à vapeur\ steamship; ~-citerne; tanker

navré [nah•VRAI] *adj* heartbroken; grieved; sorry

ne [nuh] *adv* no; not; ~ jamais\
never

né [nai] *adj* born; il est ~\ he
was born

néanmoins [nai•ahπ•MWAHπ]
adv nevertheless; nontheless;
notwithstanding

nécessaire [ne•se•SEHR] *adj*
necessary

nécessité [nai•se•see•TAI] *n* F
necessity

nécessiteux [nai•se•see•TØ] *adj*
needy; in need of

nécrologie
[nai•KRAU•lau•ZHEE] *n* F
obituary

négatif [nai•gah•TEEF] *adj*
negative

négation [nai•gah•SYUπ] *n* F
negation

négligence [nai•glee•ZHAHπS]
n F negligence; neglect; *vt*
négliger

négligent [nai•glee•zhahπ] *adj*
negligent; remiss

negoce [nuh•GAUS] *n* M
business; trade

négociant -e [neh•gau•SYAHπ]
[-AHπt]; *n* MF trader

négociation
[nai•GAU•syah•SYAUπ] *n* F
negotiation

négocier [nai•go•SYAI] *vt vi*
negotiate

nègre [negr] *adj n* M Negro

neige [nehzh] *n* F snow; *vt*
neiger; ~ fondue\ sleet

Neptune [nep•TEWN] *n* F
Neptune

nerf [nerf] *n* M nerve

nerveux [ner•VØ] *adj* nervous;
wiry

net nette [neht]; *adj* tidy; neat;
~ en ordre\ neat

nettoyer [ne•twah•YAI] *vt*
clean; faire la nettoyage

nettoyeur [ne•twah•YœR] *n* M
cleaner

neuf 1 [nØf] *num* nine

neuf 2 neuve [nØf] [nØv] *adj*
new; unused

neutraliser
[nØ•TRAH•lee•ZAI] *vt*
neutralize

neutralité [nØ•TRAH•lee•TAI]
adj F neutrality

neutre [nØtr] *adj* neutral; *adj*
neuter

neuvième [nØ•vyem] *num*
ninth

neveu [ne•VØ] *n* M nephew

névrose [nai•VRAUZ] *n* F
neurosis

névrosé [nai•vrau•ZAI] *adj n* M
neurotic

nez [neh] *n* M nose; snout; bow
(bateau); ~ à ~\ face to face

ni [nee] *conj* or; nor; neither

niche [neesh] *n* F niche; kennel

nicotine [nee•kau•TEEN] *n* F
nicotine

nid [nee] *n* M nest; *vi* nicher

nide-poule [need•pool] *n* M
pothole

nièce [nyes] *n* F niece

nier [nyai] *vt* deny; repudiate

noble [naubl] *adj* noble; stately;
n M nobleman

noblesse [nau•BLES] *n* F
nobility

noce [naus] *n* F wedding; spree

noces [naus] *npl* F marriage;
nuptials

nocif [nau•SEEF] *adj* noxious

nocturne [nauk•TEWRN] *adj*
nocturnal; *n* M nocturne
(mus)

Noël [no•EL] *n* M Christmas;
Yuletide

nœud [nœd] *n* M bow; knot; ~
coulant\ noose; ~ papillon\
bow tie

nouer [nœ] *vt* knot

noir [nwahr] *adj n* M black

noircir [nwahr•SEER] *vt*
blacken

noisette [nwah•ZET] *n* F
hazelnut

noix [nwah] *n* F walnut

noix de coco *n* M coconut

noix-sette *n* MF bolt; écrou
M\ bolt; dingue M\ nut; crazed
person

nom [nauπ] *n* M name; noun; *vt*
nommer; ~ de famille\ last
name; ~ de jeune fille\ maiden
name

nombre [nauπbr] *n* M number;
bon ~ de\ a good many; ~
entier\ integer

nombreux [nauπ•BRØ] *adj*
numerous; many

nombril [nauπ•BREEL] *n* navel

nominal [nau•mee•NAHL] *adj*
nominal; titular

nommer [no•MEH] *vt* appoint;
name; mention

non [nauπ] *adv* no; not

nord [nor] *n* M north; perdre le
~\ become confused

normal [naur•MAHL] *adj*
normal; usual; natural;
standard

normalement
[naur•mahl•MAHπ] *adv*
normally

normalisation
[naur•MAH•lee•zah•SYAUπ]
n (normalisation des prix) F
standardization

normaliser [naur•mah•lee•ZEH]
vt standardize; normalize

norme [naurm] *n* F norm

Norvège [naur•VEZH] *n* F
Norway

norvègien [naur•ve•ZHAHπ]
adj Norwegian; *n* M
Norvègien (langue)

nostalgie [nau•stahl•ZHEE] *n* F
nostalgia

nostalgique
[nau•stahl•ZHEEK] *adj*
homesick

notable [nau•TAHBL] *adj*
notable

notaire [nau•TEHR] *n* M notary

notamment [nau•tah•MAHπ]
adv notably

note
n F memo; note; footnote

noter [no•TEH] *vt* note; notice;
mark; jot

notice [no•TEES] *n* F notice;
account; review

notoire [nau•twahr] *adj*
notorious

notoriété [nau•TAU•ryai•TAI]
n notoriety

notre nos *pl* [nautr] [no] *adj*
poss our

noueux [noo•Ø] *adj* gnarled;
knotty

nouilles [nweey] *npl* F noodles

nourrir [noo•REER] *vt* feed;
nourish

nourrissant [noo•ree•SAHπ]
adj nourishing

nourriture [noo•ree•TEWR] *n*
F food; nourishment;
sustenance

nous [noo] *pron* pl us; we

nouveau [noo•VO] *adj* new;
recent; fress; novel; another;
additona; F nouvelle
[noo•vehl]

nouveauté [noo•vo•TAI] *n* F
novelty

nouvelle [noo•VEL] *n* F short
story; novella

nouvelles [noo•VEL] *npl* F
news; ~ joyeuses\ tidings;
glad tidings

nouvellement
[noo•vel•MAHπ] *adv* newly

novembre [nau•VAHπBR] *n* M
November

novice [nau•VEES] *n* MF
novice; apprentice

noyau [nwah•YO] *n* M nucleus

noyer [nwah•YAI] *vt* drown; *vi*
se noyer

nu [new] *adj* bare; naked; nude;
plain; *n* M nude; nudity

nuage [nwahzh] *n* F cloud

nuageux [nwah•Gœ] *adj* cloudy

nuance [new•AHπS] *n* F
nuance; shade; gradation;
subtlety

nucléaire [new•klai•EHR] *adj*
nuclear

nudiste [new•DEEST] *n* MF
nudist

nudité [new•dee•TAI] *n* F
nakedness; nudity

nuisible [nwe•ZEEBL] *adj*
harmful

nuit [nwee] *n* night

nul nulle [newl] *adj* no; not
one; nu; void; *pron* no one;
nobody; not one; ~ nowhere

nullité [new•lee•TAI] *n*
nonentity

numéro [new•mai•RO] *n* M
number issue (périodique); ~
de téléphone\ telephone
number

nuptial [newp•SYAHL] *adj*
nuptial; bridal

nutritif [new•tree•TEEF] *adj* F
nutritious

nutrition [new•tree•SYAUπ] *n*
F nutrition

nylon [nee•LAUπ] *n* M nylon

nymphe [naπf] *n* F nymph

O

oasis [au•ah•ZEES] *n* F oasis

obéir [au•bai•EER] *vi* obey

obéissance [au•bai•ee•SAHπS]
n F obedience

obéissant [au•bai•ee•SAHπ] *adj*
obedient

obèse [au•BEZ] *adj* obese

objectif [aub•zhek•TEEF] *adj n*
M objective

objection [aub•zhek•SYAUπ] *n*
F objection

objet [aub•ZHEH] *n* object

obligation
[au•blee•gah•SYAUπ] *n* F
obligation; duty; bond

obligatoire
[au•blee•gah•TWAHR] *adj*
obligatory; mandatory

obligeant [au•blee•ZHAHπ] *adj*
obliging; accommodating;
kind; civil

obliger [au•blee•ZHAI] *vt*
oblige; constrain

oblique [au•BLEEK] *adj*
oblique

obscène [aub•SEN] *adj* lewd;
obscene

obscénité [aub•SAI•nee•TAI] *n*
F obscenity

obscur [aub•SKEWR] *adj*
obscure; *vt* obscurcir

obscurité [aub•SKEW•ree•TAI]
n F darkness; obscurity

obsédant [aub•sai•DAHπ] *vt*
obsessive

obséder [aub•sai•DAI] *vt*
obsess

obséquieux -euse
[aub•seh•KYØ]; [-KYØZ] *adj*
subservient

observateur
[aub•ZER•vah•TœR] *adj*
observant; *n* M observer

observation
[aub•zer•vah•SYAUπ] *n* F
observance; observation

observatoire
[aub•ZEHR•vah•TWAHR] *n*
M observatory

observer [aub•serh•VEH] *vt*
observe; view; notice

obsession [aub•se•SYAUπ] *n*
obsession

obsolète [aub•sau•LET] *adj*
obsolete; outmoded;

obstacle [aub•STAHKL] *n* M
impediment; obstacle; hurdle

obstination
[aub•STEE•nah•SYAUπ] *n* F
obstinacy; obstinance;
stubbornness

obstiné [aub•stee•NAI] *adj*
obstinate; stubborn

obstruction
[aub•strewk•SYAUπ] *vt*
obstruction; impediment

obstruer [aub•strew•EH] *vt*
obstruct

obtenir [aub•te•NEER] *vt* elicit;
obtain; get; procure

obtus [aub•TEW] *adj* obtuse

occasion [au•kah•ZYAUπ] *n* F
opportunity; occasion; bargain

occasionné [o•kah•syau•NAI]
adj incidental

occasionnel
[au•KAH•zyau•NEL] *n*
occasional

Occidental
[ahk•SEE•dahπ•TAHL] *adj*
westerner

occulte [au•KEWLT] *adj* occult

occupant [au•kew•PAHπ] *n* M
occupant; *adj* engrossing

occupé [o•kew•PAI] *adj* busy

occuper [au•kew•PAI] *vt*
occupy; s'occuper de qqch\ be
occupied with something

océan [au•sai•AHπ] *n* M ocean

octagone [auk•tah•GAUN] *n* M
octagon

octobre [auk•TAUBR] *n* M
October

odeur [au•DœR] *n* F odor;
aroma; smell

odieux [au•DYØ] *adj* hateful;
odious; loathsome; obnoxious

œil m [œy] pl. yeux [yØ] *n* eye;
opening; hole; coupe d'~\
glance; fair de l'~\ stare; en
un clin d'~\ in the blink of an
eye

oeillere [œ•YEHR] *n* M blinker
(car)

œillet [œ•YEH] *n* M carnation

œuf [sing. œf pl. Øf] *n* M egg;
roe; spawn (biol); ~ à la
coque\ boiled egg

oeuvre [œvr] *n* F work;
production; society;
institution; M wall;
foundation; complete works

offense [au•FAHπS]·*n* offense
(criminel)

offenser [au•fahπ•SAI] *vt*
offend

officiel [au•fee•SYEL] *n* MF
official

officier [au•fee•SYEH] *n* officer

offre [aufr] *n* F offer; offering;
vt offrir

oie [wah] *n* F goose

oignon [wah•NYAUN] *n* M
onion

oiseau [wah•ZO] *n* M bird; ~
chanteur\ song-bird; ~ bleu\
blue bird; ~ -mouche\
hummingbird

oisillon [wah•see•YAUπ] *n*
chick

olive [au•LEEV] *adj n* F olive

ombilic [auπ•beeil•EEK] *n* M
umbilicus

ombrage [auπ•BRAHZH] *n* M
umbrage; offense; shade
(arbre); shady (pers)

ombre [auπbr] *n* F shadow;
shade

ombrelle [auπ•BREL] *n* F
parasol

omelette [aum•LET] *n* F
omelet

omettre [au•METR] *vt* omit

omission [au•mee•SYAUπ] *n* F
omission

omnipotent
[aum•NEE•pau•TAHπ] *adj*
omnipotent

on [auπ] *pron* one; people; they;
we; you; men; somebody; ~
dit\ they say

once [auπs] *n* F ounce

oncle [auπkl] *n* M uncle

onction [auπk•SYAUπ] *n* F
unction

onctueux -euse [auπk•tew•Ø]
[-ØZ] *adj* unctuous; oily

ondulation
[auπ•dew•LAH•SYAUπ]*n* F
ripple ; *vt* onduler

ondulé [auπ•dew•LAI] *adj*
wavy

onduler [auπ•dew•LEH] *vt/vi*
undulate

ongle [auπgl] *n* M nail;
fingernail; ~ de pied\ toenail

onze [auπz] *num* eleven

onzième [auπ•ZYEM] *num*
eleventh

opale [au•PAHL] *n* F opal

opaque [au•PAHK] *adj* opaque

opéra [au•pai•RAH] *n* M opera

opérateur [au•PAI•rah•TœR] *n* M operator

opération [au•PAI•rah•SYAUπ] *n* F operation

opérer [au•pai•RAI] *vt* operate

opinion [au•pee•NYAUπ] *n* opinion

opinionâtre [au•PEE•nyau•NAHTR] *adj* opinionated

opportun [au•paur•Tœπ] *adj* opportune; fortunate

opportuniste [au•paur•tew•NEEST] *n* MF opportunist

opposé [au•pau•ZAI] *adj* opposite; opposing; opposed

opposition [au•pau•zee•SYAUπ] *n* opposition; par ~ à\ opposed

oppressif [au•pre•SEEF] *adj* oppressive

oppression [au•pre•SYAUπ] *n* F oppression

oppresser [au•pre•SEH] *vt* oppress

oprimer [au•pree•MEH] *vt* oppress

opter [aup•TEH] *vi* opt; ~ pour\ opt for

opticien [aup•tee•SYAHπ] *n* M optician

optimisme [aup•tee•MEEZM] *n* M optimism

optimiste [aup•tee•MEEST] *n* MF optimist

optimistique [aup•tee•mee•STEEK] *adj* optimistic

option [aup•SYAUπ] *n* F option; choice

optique [aup•TEEK] *adj* optical

opulence [au•pyew•LAHπS] *n* F opulence

opulent [au•pyew•LAHπ] *adj* opulent

or [aur] *n* M gold; en ~; d'~\ made of gold

oracle [au•RAHKL] *n* M oracle

orage [au•RAHZH] *n* M storm; thunderstorm

orageux -euse [au•rah•ZHØ]; [-ØZ] *adj* stormy; tempestuous

orange [au•RAHπZH] *adj* orange; *n* M orange (coleur); *n* F orange (fruit)

orateur [au•rah•TœR] *n* M orator; speaker

orbite [aur•BEET] *n* F orbit; sur ~\ in orbit; *vt* orbiter

orchestral [aur•ke•STRAHL] *adj* M orchestral

orchestre [aur•KESTR] *n* M orchestra; band

orchidée [aur•shee•DAI] *n* orchid

ordinaire [aur•dee•NEHR] *adj* ordinary; usual; commonplace; *n* M custom; daily fare; mess (mil)

ordinairement [aur•DEE•nehr•MAHπ]; *adv* ordinarily; usually

ordinateur [aur•dee•nah•TœR] *n* M computer

ordonnance [aur•dau•NAHπS] *n* F writ; order; arrangement; disposition; judgment

ordonné [aur•dau•NAI] *adj*
orderly

ordre [aurdr] *n* MF order;
neatness; tidiness; sequence en
~\ in order; ~ du jour\
agenda; *n* M order;
commandment

ordures [aur•DOOR] *npl* F
trash

oreille [au•RAI] *n* F ear; être
toutes ~s\ be all ears; prêter
l'~\ listen attentively; lend an
ear

oreiller [au•re•YAI] *n* M pillow

oreillons [ao•re•YAUπ] *npl* M
mumps

organe [aur•GAHN] *n* M organ
(anat); voice; agent; means
medium

organique [aur•gah•NEEK] *adj*
organic

organisateur
[aur•GAH•nee•zah•TœR] *n* M
promoter; organizer

organisation
[aur•GAH•nee•zah•SYAUπ] *n*
F organization

organiser [aur•GAH•nee•ZAI]
vt organize; form; arrange

organisme [aur•gah•NEEZM] *n*
M organism

orgasme [aur•GAHZM] *n* M
orgasm

orge [orzh] *n* F barley

orgelet [aurzh•LEH] *n* M sty (à
l'oeil)

orgie [aur•ZHEE] *n* F orgy

oriental [au•ryahπ•TAHL] *adj*
oriental

orientation
[au•ryahπ•tah•SYAUπ] *n* F
orientation; bearings

orienter [au•ryahπ•TEH] *vt*
orientate; direct

orifice [au•ree•FEES] *n* M
orifice; opening; hole

origan [au•ree•GAHN] *n* M
oregano

original [au•REE•zhee•NAHL]
adj n M original; inventive;
eccentric

originalité
[au•ree•zhee•NAH•lee•TAI] *n*
M originality

originallement
[au•REE•zhee•nahl•MAHπ]
adv originally

origine [au•ree•ZHEEN] *n* F
origin

orme [aurm] *n* M elm

ornée [aur•NAI] *adj* ornate;
lavish

ornement [aur•nu•MAHπ] *n* M
ornament

ornière [aur•NYEHR] *n* rut;
suivre l'~\ be stuck in a rut

orphelin [aur•fu•LAπ] *n* M
orphan

orphelinat [aur•fe•lee•NAH] *n*
M orphanage

orteil [aur•TEHY] *n* M toe

orthodoxe [aur•tau•DAUKS]
adj orthodox

ortie [aur•TEE] *n* F nettle

os [aus] *n* M bone

osciller [au•see•LAI] *vi*
oscillate; sway; swing; rock

osier [o•ZYEH] *n* M wicker

ostentatoire
[au•STAHπ•tah•TWAHR] *adj*
ostentatious; pretentious

otage [au•TAHZH] *n* M
hostage

où [oo] *adv* where; ~ se trouve\
whereabouts

oubli [oo•BLEE] *n* M oblivion;
forgetfulness

oublier [oo•BLYAI] *vt* forget;
neglect; overlook; ~ de
fair qqch\ forget to do
something; s'oublier \forget
oneself

oublieux [oo•BLYØ] *adj*
oblivious; forgetful

ouest [west] *n* M west; *adj*
western; à l'~\ to the west

oui [wee] *adv* yes; yeah

ouï-dire [wee•DEER] *n* M
hearsay

ouïe [wee] *n* F hearing

ouragan [oo•rah•GAHπ] *n* M
hurricane

ourlet [oor•LEH] *n* M hem; *vt*
ourler

ours [oors] *n* M bear

oursin [oor•SAπ] *n* MF urchin
(child); *n* M sea-urchin

ouste! [oost] *excl* shoo; go
away!

outil [oo•TEE] *n* M tool;
implement

outre [ootr] *pre* beyond; in
addition; to; *adv* further;
en ~\ besides; moreover;
passe ~\ to go on; ignore;
overrule

ouvert [oo•VER] *adj* open;
opened

ouvertement [oo•vert•MAHπ]
adv openly

ouverture [oo•ver•TEWR] *n*
overture; opening

ouvrage [oo•VRAJ] *n* M work

ouvrages romanesques
[oo•VRAHZH
rau•mah•NEHSK] *npl* M
nonfiction

ouvreir [oo•vree•EH] *n* M
workman; worker

ouvrir [oo•VREER] *vt* open;
unfaten; unlock; turn on
(lumière); begin; s'ouvrir\
open; unburden oneself

ovaire [au•VER] *n* M ovary

ovale [au•VAHL] *adj n* M oval;
egg-shaped

ovation [au•vah•SYAUπ] *n* F
ovation

oxygène [auk•see•ZHEN] *n* M
oxygen

P

pacte [pahkt] *n* M pact

pacifier [pah•see•FYEH] *vt*
pacify

page [pahzh] *n* page; à la page\
up to date

paie [pey] *n* F paycheck; wages;
pay

paiement [pahy•MAHπ] *n* M
payment

païen [pah•YAHπ] *adj n* M
pagan; heathen

paillard [pah•YAHR] *adj*
bawdy

paillasson [pah•yai•SAUπ] *n* M
doormat

paille [pahy] *n* F straw

pain [peπ] *n* M bread; loaf;
cake; petit ~\ roll; ~ complet\
whole wheat; ~ grillé\ toast; ~
d'épice\ gingerbread

pair [per] *n* M peer

paisible [peh•ZEEBL] *restful*;
peaceful

pais [pai•EE] *n* F country

paître [petr] *vt* graze

paix [peh] *n* F peace; faire la ~\
make peace

Pakistan [pah•kee•STAHπ] *n* M
Pakistan

palais 1 [pah•LEH] *n* M palace

palais 2 [pah•LEH] *n* M palate

pâle [pahl] *n* pale; *vi* pâlir

Palestine [pah•lu•STEEN] *n* F
Palestine

palette [pah•LET] *n* F palette

palissade [pah•lee•SAHD] *n* F
stockade; fence; palisade

palourde [pah•LOORD] *n* F
clam

palpable [pahl•PAHBL] *adj*
palpable

pamplemousse
[pahπ•pl•MOOS] *n* M
grapefruit

panacée [pah•nah•SAI] *n* F
panacea

panais [pah•NEH] *n* M parsnip

Panama [pah•nu•MAH] *n* M
Panama

panda [pahπ•DAH] *n* M panda

panique [pah•NEEK] *n* panic;
vi paniquer; *vt* scare

panne [pahn] *n* F breakdown
(machine); mishap; en ~\ out
of order; on the blink

panneau [pah•NO] *n* F panel;
snare; net

pantalon [pahπ•tah•LAUπ] *n*
M pants; trousers

panthère [pahπ•TEHR] *n* F
panther

pantoufle [pahπ•TOOFL] *n* F
slipper

paon [paoπ] *n* M peacock

papa [pah•PAH] *n* M dad; papa

papal [pah•PAHL] *adj* papal

pape [pahp] *n* M pope

papeterie [pahp•tehr•EE] *n* F
stationery

papier [pah•PYEH] *n* M paper;
document; ~ cadau\ wrapping
paper; ~d'aluminium\ tin foil;
~ d'emballage\ wrapper; ~ de
soie\ tissue-paper; ~
hygiénique\ toilet paper; ~
d'aluminium\ foil; ~ de verre\
sandpaper; ~ peint\ wallpaper

papillon [pah•pee•YOπ] *n* M
butterfly; ~ de nuit\ moth

Pâques [pahk] *n* M Easter

paquet [pah•KEH] *n* M packet;
pack; package; mail

paquet M; (bag) sac F; (of
dogs) meute F; (of wolves)
bande F; *vt* faire ses par

[pahr] *prép* by; through; via;
~ example\ for example; ~ la
porte\ out the door ~ ici\ this
way; ~ trop\ far too much; ~
égard pour\ for the sake of

par brise [pahr BREEZ] *n* M
windshield

par la suite [pahr lah SWEET]
adv comp thereafter
par le (la) *pr* hereby
par où [pahr OO] *adv comp*
wherever
par-dessus bord *adv* over;
overboard
parabole [pah•rah•BAUL] *n* F
parable
parachute [pah•rah•SHEWT] *n*
parachute; *vi* sauter en
parachute
parade [pah•RAHD] *n* parade;
show *vt* parader
paradis [pah•rah•DEE] *n* M
paradise; top gallery; cheap
seats; ~ ciel m; the heaven
paradoxe [pah•rah•DAUKS] *n*
M paradox
paragraphe [pah•rah•GRAHF]
n M paragraph
Paraguay [pah•rah•GAI] *n* M
Paraguay
parallèle [pah•rah•LEL] *n*
parallel; comparison
paralyser [pah•RAH•lee•ZAI]
vt paralyze
paralysie [pah•RAH•lee•SEE] *n*
F paralysis
paranoïaque
[pah•RAH•nwah•YAHK] *adj*
paranoid
parapluie [pahr•ah•PLWEE] *n*
M umbrella
parasite [pah•rah•SEET] *n* M
parasite; sponger
parc à bestiaux [pahrk ah
beh•steey•AU] *n* M stockyards
parc [pahrk] *n* park; enclosure
parce que [par•SKUH] *conj*
because

parchemin [pahrsh•MAπ] *n* M
parchment
parcourir [pahr•cur•EEUR] *vt/vi*
roam; travel through; go over
pardessus [pahr•du•SEW] *n* M
overcoat
pardon [pahr•DAUπ] *n* pardon;
forgive; *vt* pardonner
pare-chocs [pa•ru•SHAUKS] *n*
M bumper (of car)
pareil [pah•RAI] *adj* alike
parent [pah•RAUπ] *n* M
relative; *npl* ~s\ parents; *adj*
parenté
paresseux [pah•ru•SØ] *adj*
lazy; idle; *n* M loafer; idler
parfait [pahr•FEH] *adj* perfect;
prize
parfaitement [pahr•fet•MAHπ]
adv F perfectly
parfois [pahr•FWAH] *adv*
sometimes; at tomes; now and
then
parfum [pahr•FEWM] *n* M
fragrance; perfume; scent *vt*
parfumer
parfumé [pahr•few•MAI] *adj*
fragrant
pari [pah•REE] *n* M wager; bet;
vt parier
paria [pah•ree•AH] *n* M outcast;
pariah
parjure [pahr•ZHEWR] *n* M
perjury
parking [pahr•KEENG] *n* M
parking; parking lot
parlement [pahr•lu•MAHπ] *n*
M parliament
parlementaire
[pahr•lu•mahπ•TEHR] *adj* M
parliamentary

parler [pahr•LEH] *vi* talk;
speak; converse; *n* M speech;
accent; dialect

parmi [pahr•MEE] *prép* among

parodie [pah•rau•DEE] *n* F
parody; *vt* parodier

paroisse [pah•WHAHZ] *adj*
parish

paroissial [pah•rah•SWAHL]
adj parochial

parole [pah•RAUL] *n* F word;
utterance; promise; *npl* lyrics;
avoir la ~\ have the floor

parrain [pah•REπ] *n* M
godfather

parsemer [pahr•su•MEH] *vt*
sprinkle; strew; stud

partenaire [pahr•tu•NEHR] *n*
MF partner

part [pahr] *n* F share; part;
portion; autre ~\ elsewhere;
d'une ~\ on one hand

parti [pahr•TEE] *n* M party;
side; choice; course; prendre
son ~ de\ resign oneself; ~
travailliste\ Labor Party

partial [pahr•CYAHL] *adj*
partial; one-sided; biased

participant
[pahr•TEE•see•PAHπ] *n* M
participant

participation
[pahr•TEE•see•pah•SYAUπ] *n*
F participation; involvement

participer [pahr•TEE•see•PEH]
vi participate

particule [pahr•tee•KEWL] *n* F
particle

particulier
[pahr•tee•kew•LYEH] *adj*
particular

particulièrement
[pahr•TEE•kew•lyer•MAHπ]
adv particularly

partie [pahr•TEE] *n* F part;
party; game; match; parcel; ~
null\ tie score

partiel [pahr•SYEL] *adj* partial

partiellement
[pahr•syel•MAHπ] *adv*
partially

partir [pahr•TEER] *vi* depart;
leave à ~ de\ starting with

partisan [pahr•tee•ZAHπ] *adj n*
M partisan

partout [pahr•TOO] *adv*
everywhere; all over

parvenu -e [pahr•vuh•NEW] *n*
MF upstart

pas 1 [pah] *n* M footstep; step;
stride

pas 2 [pah] *adv* not; no; none

pas 3 [pah] *n* M pace

passager [pah•sah•ZHAI] *n*
passenger

passant [pah•SAHπ] *n* M
passerby; *adj* busy frequent

passé [pah•SAI] *adj* past

passe-passe [pahs•PAHS] *n* M
hocus-pocus

passe-temps [pahs•TAHπ] *n* M
hobby; pastime

passeport [pas•PAUR] *n* M
passport

passif [pah•SEEF] *adj* passive

passion [pah•SYAUπ] *n* F
passion

passionnant
[pah•seey•au•NAHπ] *adj*
stirring; thrilling; fascinating;
exciting

passioné [pah•syau•NAI] *adj*
passionate; impassioned

passoire [pah•SWAHR] *n* F
strainer

pastel [pah•STEL] *adj n* M
pastel

pasteur [pah•STœR] *n* M
parson; pastor; reverend

pasteuriser [pah•STœ•ree•ZAI]
vt pasteurize

pastiche [pah•STEESH] *n* MF
travesty; pastiche

patate [pah•TAHT] *n* F potato;
~ douce\ sweet potato;
yam

pâte 1 [paht] *n* F batter; dough;
pastry

pâte 2 [paht] *n* paste; glue

pâté [pah•TAI] *n* M pâté

paternel [pah•ter•NEL] *adj*
fatherly; paternal

paternité [pah•TER•nee•TAI] *n*
F paternity

pâtes [paht] *npl* F pasta

pathologie
[pah•TAU•lau•ZHEE] *n* F
pathology

paticulièrement
[pahr•TEE•kew•lyer•MAHπ]
adv especially; particularly

patience [pah•SYAHπS] *n* F
patience

patient [pah•SYAHπ] *n* M
patient

patin [pah•TAπ] *n* M skate

patinage [pah•tee•NAHZH] *n*
M skating; ~ sur glace\ ice
skating

patineur [pah•tee•NœR] *n*
skater

patinoire [pah•tee•NWAHR] *n*
F rink; skating rink

pâtiserrie [pah•TEE•su•REE] *n*
F pastry shop

patrie [pah•TREE] *n* F
fatherland; homeland

patriote [pah•TRYAUT] *n* MF
patriot

patriotique
[pah•TREE•au•TEEK] *adj*
patriotic

patriotisme
[pah•tree•au•TEEZM] *n* M
patriotism

patron [pah•TRAUπ] *n* M
boss

patronner [pah•trau•NEH] *vt*
patronize

patrouille [pah•TRWEEY] *n* F
patrol *vt* patrouiller dans

patte [paht] *n* F paw

pâturage [pah•tew•RAHZH] *n*
M pasture

paupière [po•pyer] *n* F eyelid

pause [pauz] *n* F rest; pause; ~
de\ lunch hour; ~ -café\ coffee
break

pauvre [povr] *adj* poor; needy;
n M pauper; beggar; *npl* M
les pauvres

pauvreté [po•vr•TAI] *n* F
poverty; wretchedness

pavé [pah•VAI] *n* M pavement;
street; paved; *vt* paver

pavés [pah•VAI] *npl* M
cobblestones

pavillon [pah•vee•YAUπ] *n* M
pavilion; lodge

payable [pah•YAHBL] *adj*
payable

payer [pai•YEH] *vt* pay; ~ d'avance\ prepaid; ~ de sa personne; risk; *vi* se ~\ be paid

pays [pai] *n* M country; land; region; home; mal de ~\ homesickness

Pays-Bas [pahy•BAH] *npl* M Netherlands

paysan [pahy•ZAHπ] *n* M peasant; countryman

péage [peh•AZH] *n* M toll-bridge

peau [po] *n* F skin; rind; peel

pêche 1 [pesh] *n* F peach

pêche 2 [pesh] *n* F fishing; catch

péché [pais•SHAI] *n* F sin; *vi* pécher

pêcher [peh•SHEH] *vt* fish; drag up

pécheur 1 [pai•SHœR] *n* M sinner

pêcheur 2 [pe•SHœR] *n* M fisherman

pédagogique [pai•dah•gau•ZHEEK] *adj* educational

pédale [pai•DAHL] *n* F pedal; *vi* pédaler

pédant [pai•DAHπ] *n* M pedant; *adj* pedantic

pègre [pehgr] *n* F underworld

peigne [pe•NYU] *n* M comb; *vt* peigner

peignoir [peh•NYWAHR] *n* M robe

peine [pehn] *n* F punishment; penalty; *vi*; se peiner\ grieve; fret; à ~ ad\ barely; hardly

peintre [peπtr] *n* M painter

peinture [peπ•TEWR] *n* paint; painting *vt vi* peindre

pèlerin [pel•RAπ] *n* M pilgrim

pèlerinage [pe•LU•ree•NAHZH] *n* M pilgrimage

pelle [pel] *n* F scoop; ~ à poussière\ dustpan

pelle [pel] *n* F shovel ; *vt* pelleter

pellicules [pe•lee•KEWL] *n* pl F dandruff

pelouse [pu•LOOZ] *n* F lawn

pénal [pai•NAHL] *adj* penal

pénalité [pai•NAH•lee•TAI] *n* F penalty

penchant [pahπ•SHAHπ] *n* MF penchant; inclination; bent

pendant [pahπ•DAHπ] *prep* while

pendentif [pahπ•dahπ•TEEF] *n* M pendant

pendre [pahπdr] *vt* hang

pendule [pahπ•DEWL] *n* pendulum

pénétrer [pai•nai•TRAI] *vi* penetrate

pénible [peh•NEEBL] *adj; adv* uphill

péniche [pai•NEESH] *n* F barge

pénicilline [pai•NEE•see•LEEN] *n* F penicillin

péninsule [pai•naπ•SEWL] *n* F peninsula

pénis [pai•NEE] *n* M penis

pénitence [pai•nee•TAHπS] *n* F penance

pensée 1 [pahπ•SAI] *n* F pansy

pensée 2 [pahπ•SAI] *n* F
thinking; thought

penser [pahπ•SEH] *vt; vi* think;
penser à\ think of; think about

penseur -euse [pahπ•SœR]
[-ØZ] *n* MF thinker;
philosopher

pensif; -ve [pahπSEEF];
[-SEEV] *adj* wistful

pension [pahπ•SYAUπ] *n* F
pension

pente [pahπt] *n* F slope

Pentecôte [pahπt•uh•KOT] *n* F
Whitsuntide

pépé [pai•PAI] *n* M grandpa

pépier [pai•PYAI] *vi* chirp

perçant [per•SAHπ] *adj* shrill

perceptible [per•sep•TEEBL]
adj noticeable

perception [per•sep•SYAUπ] *n*
F perception

perspicacité *n* F
[per•SPI•ka•si•TAI] *n* F
perspicacity

percer [per•SAI] *vt* pierce

perceuse [per•SØZ] *n* drill; *vt*
percer

percevoir [per•su•VWAHR] *vt*
perceive; (notice) s'apercevoir
de

perchoir [pehr•SHWAHR] *n* M
roost; *vi* se percher

perdre [perdr] *vt* lose; *vi* se
perdre ; ~ sa langue\
tongue-tied

perdrix [per•DREE] *n* F
partridge

perdu; [per•DEW] *adj* lost

père [per] *n* M father; parent

perfection [per•fek•SYAUπ] *n*
F perfection

perfectionniste
[per•fek•syau•NEEST] *n* MF
perfectionist

perforer [per•fau•REH] *vt*
perforate

péril [pai•REEL] *n* M peril

périmètre [pai•ree•METR] *n* M
perimeter

période [pai•RYAUD] *n* period;
~ de travail\ stint

périodique [pai•ryau•DEEK]
adj periodic; *n* M periodical;
recurring

périr [pai•REER] *vi* perish

perle 1 [perl] *n* F bead

perle [2 perl] *n* F pearl

permanent [per•mah•NAHπ]
adj F permanent

permanente [per•mu•NAHπt]
n F perm (hair)

permettre [per•METR] *vt*
allow; *vt* enable

permis [per•MEE] *n* license;
permit

permission [per•mee•SYAUπ]
n F permission

perpendiculaire
[per•PAHπ•dee•kew•LER] *adj*
n F perpendicular

perpétrer [per•pai•TREH] *vt*
perpetrate

perpétuel [per•pai•tew•EL] *adj*
perpetual; perennial

perplexe [per•PLEKS] *adj*
perplexed

perroquet [pe•rau•KEH] *n* M
parrot

perruche [pe•REWSH] *n* F
parakeet

perruque [pehr•EWK] *n* F wig

persécuter [per•sai•kew•TAI] *vt* persecute; torture

persécuteur -trice [pehr•seh•kew•TœR] [-TREES] *n* MF tormentor

persévérance [per•SAI•vai•RAHπS] *n* F perseverance

persévérer [per•SAI•vai•RAI] *vi* persevere

persil [per•SEEL] *n* M parsley

persistance [per•see•STAHπS] *n* F persistence

persistant [per•see•STAHπ] *n* F persistent

persister [per•see•STAI] *vi* persist

personnalité [per•SAU•nah•lee•TAI] *n* F personality

personne [per•saun] *n* person; nobody; ~ agée\ senior citizen

personnel [per•sau•NEL] *adj* personal; *n* M personnel

perspective [per•spek•TEEV] *n* F perspective

perspicacité [per•SPEE•kah•see•TAI] *n* F insight

persuader [per•swah•DAI] *vt* persuade; lure; ~ par des cajoleries\ coax

persuasif [per•swah•SEEF] *adj* persuasive

persuasion [per•swah•ZYAUπ] *n* persuasion

perte [pert] *n* loss

pertinent [per•tee•NAHπ] *adj* pertinent

pervers [per•VEHR] *adj* perverse

pervertir [per•ver•TEER] *vt* pervert

perverti; -e [pehr•vehr•TEE] *adj* warped

péser [peh•ZEH] *vt* weigh

pessimisme [pe•see•MEEZM] *n* M pessimism

pessimiste [pe•see•MEEST] *adj* pessimistic; *n* MF pessimist

peste [pest] *n* plague

pétale [pai•TAHL] *n* M petal

pétillement [pai•teey•MAHπ] *n* fizz; *vi* pétiller

petit [puh•TEE] *adj* small; little; short; petty; slight; ~ enfant *n* MF tot; infant; ~ lit *n* M cot; ~ peu\ whit; ~ rien\ trifle; ~ somme\ nap

petit-fils [pe•TEE•FEES] *n* M grandson

petite amie *n* F girlfriend

petite annonce *npl* F classified ad

petite enfance *n* F infancy

petite gorgée *n* F sip

petite noblesse *n* F gentry

petite promenade *n* F stroll

petite-fille *n* F granddaughter

pétition [pai•tee•SYAUπ] *n* F petition

petrifié [pe•tree•FYAI] *adj* petrified

pétrir [pai•TREER] *vt* knead

pétrole [pai•TRAUL] *n* M petroleum; oil

peu [pØ] *n* M little; few

peupler [pØ•PLAI] *vt* populate

peuplier [pØ•PLYAI] *n* M poplar

peur [pœr] *n* F fright; fear; avoir ~\ be afraid

peut-être [pØt etr] *adv*
perhaps; possibly

phare [fahr] *n* M headlight;
lighthouse

pharmacie [fahr•mah•SEE] *n* F
pharmacy

pharmacien [fahr•mah•SYAπ]
n M druggist; pharmacist

phase [fahz] *n* phase

phénomène [fai•nau•MEN] *n* F
phenomenon

philosophe [fee•lau•SAUF] *n*
MF philosopher

philosophie
[fee•LAU•sau•FEE] *n* F
philosophy

philosophique
[fee•LAU•sau•FEEK] *adj*
philosophical

phonétique [fau•nai•TEEK] *n*
F phonetics

photagraphie
[fau•TAU•grah•FEE] *n*
photography

photo [fau•TAU] *n* M photo

photocalque [fo•to•CAHLK] *n*
M blueprint

photographe [fau•tau•GRAHF]
n MF photographer

photographie
[fau•TAU•grah•FEE] *n*
photograph; *vt* photographier

phrase [frahz] *n* sentence

physicien [fee•zee•SYAHπ] *n*
physicist

physique [fee•ZEEK] *n* F
physics; M physique; physical

pianiste [pyah•NEEST] *n* MF
pianist

piano [pyah•NAU] *n* M piano

pic [peek] *n* M woodpecker

pickle [peekl] *n* M pickle

pickpocket [peek•po•KEH] *n* M
pickpocket

pièce [pyes] *n* F coin; piece

pied [pye] *n* M foot; à pied; ~
nus; nu-pieds\ barefoot

piédestal [pyai•du•STAHL] *n*
M pedestal

piège [pyehzh] *n* M trap; *vt*
piéger

pierre [peey•EHR] *n* F stone; ~
précieuse\ gem; ~ tombale\
tombstone

pierreux -euse [peey•ehr•Ø]
[-ØZ]; [kahy•oo•tØ] [-tØz] *adj*
stony; rocky

piétiner [pyeh•tee•NEH] *vt*
trample

piéton [pyai•TAUπ] *n* M
pedestrian

pieu [pee•Ø] *n* M stake

pieuvre [pyØvr] *n* F octopus

pieux [pyØ] *adj* pious

pigeon [pee•ZHAUπ] *n* M
pigeon

pigment [peeg•MAHπ] *n* M
pigment; tint

pignon [pee•NYAUπ] *n* gable

pile [peel] *n* F battery

pilier [pee•LYEH] *n* M pillar; *vt*
ransack

piller [pee•YAI] *vt* plunder

pilote m; *vt* piloter [pee•LAUT]
n pilot

pilule [pee•LEWL] *n* F pill

pin [paπ] *n* pine

pince [paπs] *n* M tweezers

pinceau [paπ•SO] *n* M
paintbrush

pincement [paπs•MAHπ] *n*
pinch; *vt* pincer

pincer [paπ•SAI] *vt* nab; pinch; lift; steal

pinces [paπs] *npl* F pliers; tongs

pinson [paπ•SAUπ] *n* M finch

pinte [paπt] *n* pint

pion [pyauπ] *n* pawn

pionnier [pyau•NYAI] *n* M pioneer

pique [peek] *n* MF spade

pique-nique m [peek•NEEK] *n* picnic; *vi* piqueniquer

piquer [pee•KEH] *vt* bite; prick (insect, snake)

piquet [pee•KEH] *n* picket

piqûre [pee•KRE] *n* F sting; *vt* piquer [pee•kyr]

pire [pee•ur] *adj* inv worse; worst

pis [pee] *n* MF udder

piscine [pee•SEEN] *n* F swimming pool

pissenlit [pee•sahπ•LEE] *n* M dandelion

pisser [pee•SEH] *vi* urinate; piss (coll)

piste [peest] *n* F runway; racetrack

pistolet [pee•stau•LEH] *n* M pistol

piston [pee•STAUπ] *n* M piston

pitié [pee•TYAI] *n* mercy; pity; *vt* plaindre

pitoyable [pee•twah•YABL] *adj* pathetic; piteous; pitiful

pittoresque [pee•tau•RESK] *adj* picturesque; quaint

pivot [pee•VAU] *n* M pivot

pivoter [pee•vau•TEH] *vt; vi* swivel

placage [plah•KAHZH] *n* M veneer

placard [plah•KAHR] *n* M closet; cupboard; placard

place [plahs] *n* F place; position; stead

placer [plah•SEH] *vt* usher; place

plage [plahzh] *n* beach

plaid [ple] *n* M plaid; *adj* de plaid

plaider [ple•DAI] *vt* plead

plaignant [ple•NYAHπ] *n* M prosecutor; plaintiff

plaindre [plaπdr] *vi refl* complain

plainte [plaπt] *n* F complaint; gripe

plaire [plehr] *vi* please

plaisant [pleh•ZAHπ] *adj* pleasing; enjoyable

plaisanterie [pleh•zahπ•TREE] *n* F jest

plaisir [pleh•ZEER] *n* pleasure; avec ~\ with pleasure

plan [plahπ] *n* plan; plane

planche [plahπsh] *n* F plank; ~ à roulettes\ skateboard

planer [plah•NAI] *vi* hover

planète [plah•NET] *n* F planet

planification [plah•NEE•fee•kah•SYAUπ] *n* F planning

plantation [plahπ•tah•SYAUπ] *n* F plantation

plante [plahπt] *n* plant; *vt* planter; (bomb)

plaque [plahk] *n* F plaque; plate; ad plaqué ; ~ d'or\ gold-plated

plastique [plah•STEEK] *adj n* M plastic

plat [plah] *n* M platter; dish; ~ principal\ main course; *adj* flat

plateau [plah•TO] *n* M plateau; tray

platine 1 [plah•TEEN] *n* M platinum

platine 2 [plah•TEEN] *n* F turntable

plâtre [plahtr] *n* plaster; *vt* plâtrer;

playboy *n* M playboy

plein [plaπ] *adj* full; ~ d'espoir\ hopeful; ~ de suie\ sooty; ~ lune\ full moon

pleurer [plœ•RAI] *vt* mourn; grieve

pleureur [plœr•UHR] *adj* weeping; crying

pleurnicherie [pluhr•NEE•shuh•REE] *n* F whine

pleuvoir [plœ•VWAHR] *vt* rain; shower il pleut\ it's raining

pli [plee] *n* M fold; pleat *vt* plier; plisser

pliable [ply•AHBL] *adj* pliable

plisser [plee•SAI] *vt* pucker

plomb [plaum] *n* M lead

plombier [plauπ•BYAI] *n* plumber

plomberie f [plauπ•bu•REE] *n* F plumbing

plongeon [plauπ•ZHAUπ] *n* M dive; plunge; *n* F plongée f; *vi* plonger

plouf [ploof] *n* M splash

pluie [plwee] *n* F rain; shower

plume [plewm] *n* F feather; plume

plurer [plœr•EH] *vi* weep; cry

pluriel [plew•RYEL] *n* M plural

plus [plew] *adj* more; *n* M more most; ~ âgé\ older; ne ~\ no longer; de ~\ futhermore; non ~\neither; ~ loin\ futher; ~ lointain\ farther

plusieurs [plew•ZYœR] *adj* several; many

plutôt [plew•TO] *adv* quite; rather; ~ que rather

pluveux [plew•VØ] *adj* rainy

pneu [nœ] *n* M tire (auto) ~ de rechange\ spare; tire; ~ dégonflé ou à plat\ flat tire

pneumonie [pnØ•mau•NEE] *n* F pneumonia

poche [paush] *n* pocket; *vt* empocher

poêle [pwahl] *n* M stove; ~ à frire *n* F\ skillet

poème [pau•EM] *n* F poem

poésie [pau•ai•ZEE] *n* F poetry

poète [pau•et] *n* poet

poétique [pau•ai•TEEK] *adj* poetic

poids [pwah] *n* M weight; pound; ~ à vide tare; ~ total tonnage

poignée [pwah•NYAI] *n* F handful; ~ de main\ handshake

poignet [pwah•NYEH] *n* M fist; wrist; cuff

point [pwahπ] *n* M point; speck; dot; stitch; pain (med); period; *adv* not; no; none; ~ ébullition\ boiling point; ~ de départ\ starting point; ~ suture\ suture; ~ culminant\ highlight; ~ d'exclamation\ exclamation point; ~ d'interrogation\ question

mark ~ de repère *n*\
landmark; ~ de vue\ point of
view

pointiller [pwahπ•tee•YEH] *vt*
dot; stipple

point-virgule *n* M semicolon

pointe [pwaπt] *n* F point cape;
tip; peak; witticism; ~ des
pieds\ tiptoe

pointu [pwaπ•TEW] *adj*
pointed

poire [pwahr] *n* F pear

poireau [pwah•RO] *n* M leek

pois [pwah] *n* M pea; polka dot

poison [pwah•ZAUπ] *n* poison;
vt empoisonner

poisson [pwah•SAUπ] *n* M
fish; ~ rouge\ goldfish

poitrine [pwah•TREEN] *n* F
breast; chest; bosom

poivre [pwahvr] *n* M pepper; *vt*
poivrer

polaire [pau•LEHR] *adj* polar

Polande [pau•LAHπD] *n* F
Poland

pôle Nord [paul NOR] North
Pole

pôle Sud [paul SOOD] South
Pole

poli [pau•LEE] *adj* polite; civil;
courteous; *n* M polish; gloss

police [pau•LEES] *n* police;
agent de ~\ policeman; cop;
faire la ~\ keep order

policier [pau•lee•SYAI] *n* police
officer

polisson [pau•lee•SAUπ] *n* M
rascal; scamp

politesse [pau•lee•TES] *n* F
politeness

politique 1 [pau•lee•TEEK] *n* F
politics; *adj* political

politique 2 [pau•lee•TEEK] *n*
policy

pollen [pau•LAHπ] *n* M pollen

polluer [pau•lew•AI] *vt* pollute

pollution [pau•lew•SYAUπ] *n*
F pollution

polo [pau•LO] *n* M polo

polonais [pau•lau•HAI] *n* M
Polish; polish (lang)

Polonais m [pau•lau•HAI] *n* M
Pole

Polynésie [pau•LEE•nai•ZEE] *n*
F Polynesia

pommade [pau•MAHD] *n* F
ointment

pomme [pom] *n* F apple; ~ de
terre\ potato

pompe 1 [pauπp] *n* F pomp

pompe 2 [pauπp] *n* pump; *vt*
pomper

pompeux [pauπ•PØ] *adj*
pompous

pompier [pauπ•PYE] *n* M
fireman

ponctuation
[pauπk•twah•SYAUπ] *n* F
punctuation

ponctuel [pauπk•TWEL] *adj*
punctual

poney [pau•NEE] *n* M pony

pont [pauπ] *n* M bridge; deck
(bateau)

populaire [pau•pew•LEHR] *adj*
popular

populariser
[pau•pew•LAH•ree•ZAI] *vt*
popularize

popularité
[pau•pew•LAH•ree•TAI] *n* F
popularity

population
[pau•pew•lah•SYAUπ] *n* F
population

porc [paurk] *n* M pork

porc-épic [paur•kai•PEEK] *n* M
porcupine

porcelaine [paur•su•LEN] *n* F
china; porcelain

porche [paursh] *n* M stoop;
porch

porcherie [paursh•REE] *n* F
pigsty; sty

pore [paur] *n* M pore

poreux [pau•RØ] *adj* porous

pornagraphie
[paur•NAH•grah•FEE] *n* F
pornagraphy

porridge [pau•REEZH] *n*
porridge

port 1 [paur] *n* M harbor

port 2 [paur] *n* M port (wine)

portatif [paur•tah•TEEF] *adj*
portable

porte [paurt] *n* door; front door;
gate; gateway; ~ a tambour\
revolving door; metter à la ~\
eject; evict; show the door

porté 1 [paur•TEH] *adj*
inclinde; disposed; *prone*;
carried; worn;

porté 2 [paur•TEH] *n* F
bearing; span; litter;
projection; reach; scope; à ~
de la main\ within reach

porter [paur•TEH] *vt* carry;
bear; war; take; bring; strike a
deal

porte feuille [paurt FØY] *n* M
wallet

porte-clés [paurt•KLAI] *n* M
key ring

porte-parole
[paurt-pah•RAUL] *n* M
spokesperson

porte-voix [paurt•VWAH] *n* M
megaphone

portefeuille [paurt•FœY] *n*
portfolio (artist)

porteur [paur•TœR] *n* M porter

portfolio [paur•fœ•LYO] *n* M
portfolio (stock)

portion [paur•SYAUπ] *n* F
portion

portrait [paur•TREH] *n* M
portrait; portrayal

portugais [paur•tew•GAI] *n* M
Portuguese; (gens) Portugais
(language) portugais

Portugal [paur•tew•GAHL] *n* M
Portugal

pose [pauz] *n* F pose; attitude;
posture' *vt vi* poser

posé [pau•ZAI] *adj* sedate

positif [pau•zee•TEEF] *adj*
positive

position [pau•zee•SYAUπ] *n*
position; place

posséder [pau•sai•DAI] *vt*
possess; own

possession [pau•ze•SYAUπ] *n*
F ownership; possession;
holding

possibilité
[pau•see•BEE•lee•TAI] *n* F
possibility; prospect

possible [pau•SEEBL] *adj*
possible

postal [pau•STAHL] *adj* postal

postdater [paust•dah•TAI] *vt*
postdate

poste [paust] *n* F post office; ~
aérienne\ airmail; ~ de
télévison\ television set

postérieur [pau•stai•RYœR] *adj*
n M posterior; behind; back

posthume [paus•TEWM] *adj*
posthumous

posture [pau•STEWR] *n* F
posture

pot [pau] *n* M jar; jug; ~
-de-vin\ bribe

potassium [pau•TA•see•UM] *n*
M potassium

potelé [pau•tu•LAI] *adj* chubby;
pudgy; fat

potence [pau•TAHπS] *n* F
gallows

potentiel [pau•tahπ•SYEL] *adj*
n M potential

potentiellement
[pau•TAHπ•syel•MAHπ] *adv*
M potentially

poterie [pau•tu•REE] *n* F
pottery; ~ de gres\ stoneware

potiron [pau•tee•RAUπ] *n*
pumpkin

pou [poo] *n* M louse

poubelle [poo•BEL] *n* F bin;
garbage can

pouce 1 [poos] *n* M thumb

pouce 2 [poos] *n* M inch
(centimètres)

poudre [poodr] *n* powder; *vt*
poudrer; ~ à canon\
gunpowder

poudrier [poo•dree•eh] *n* M
compact (cosmetics)

pouffer [poo•FEH] *vi* puff; ~
de rire\ guffaw

poulailler [poo•lah•YEH] *n* M
hen-house

poulain [poo•LAπ] *n* M colt

poule [pool] *n* F hen

poulet [poo•LAI] *n* M chicken

poulie [poo•LEE] *n* F pulley

pouls [pool] *n* M pulse

poumon [poo•MAUπ] *n* M
lung

poupée [poo•PAI] *n* F doll;
puppet

pour [poor] *prép* for; on
account of; as for; in order to
~ ainsi dire\ as it were; ~
que\ so that; ~ quel raison\
wherefore; ~ cent\ percent; ~
toujours\ forever

pourboire [poor•BWAHR] *n* M
gratuity; tip

pourcentage
[poor•sahπ•TAHZH] *n* M
percentage

pourquoi [poor•KWAH] *adv*
why

pourri -e [pur•EE] *adj* rotten

pourrir [pur•EEUR] *vt* spoil;
rot; go bad

pourriture [poo•ree•TEWR] *n*
decay; rot; spoilage

poursuite [poor•SWEET] *n* F
chase; pursuit; *vt* poursuivre

poursuites [poor•SWEET] *npl*
F prosecution (law)

poursuivre [poor•swee•vr] *vt*
pursue; prosecute

pourvu [poor•VEW] *conj*
providing; provided

poussée [poo•SAI] *n* F push; *vt*
pousser

pousser [poo•SEH] *vt* prod;
push; poke; induce; shove

poussière [poo•SYEHR] *n* dust;
vt épousseter

poutrelle [poo•trel] *n* F girder

pouvoir 1 [poo•VWAHR] *vt*
attend to; see to; provide for;
vt be able to

pouvoir 2 [poo•VWAHR] *n* MF
strength

prairie [pre•REE] *n* F prairie

pratique 1 [prah•TEEK] *adj*
practical; handy

pratique 2 [prah•TEEK] *n* F
practice; custom

pré [prai] *n* M meadow

précaire [prai•KEHR] *adj*
precarious

précaution [prai•kau•SYAUπ]
n F precaution

précédent [prai•sai•DAHπ] *n*
precedent; *adj* previous

précéder [prai•sai•deh] *vt*
precede

précepteur -trice
[preh•sehp•TœR] [-TREES] *n*
MF tutor

prêcher [pre•SHAI] *vt vi* preach

précieux [prai•SYØ] *adj*
precious

précipitamment
[prai•SEE•pee•tah•MAHπ]
adv hurriedly

précipitation
[prai•SEE•pee•tah•SYAUπ] *n*
F precipitation

précipité [prai•SEE•pee•TAI]
adj hurried

précipiter [prai•SEE•pee•TEH]
vt precipitate

précis [prai•SEE] *adj* precise;
accurate

précisément
[prai•SEE•zai•MAHπ] *adv*
precisely; accurately

précision [prai•see•ZYAUπ] *n*
F precision

précoce [prai•KAUS] *adj*
precocious; early

précurseur [prai•kewr•SœR] *n*
forerunner; precursor

prédateur [prai•dah•TœR] *n* M
predator

prédécesseur
[prai•DAI•se•SœR] *n* M
predecessor

prédestiné [prai•DE•stee•NAI]
adj predestined

prédicateur
[prai•DEE•kah•TœR] *n* M
preacher

prédiction [prai•deek•SYAUπ]
n F prediction

prédire [prai•DEER] *vt* foretell;
predict; prophesy

prédisposé -e;
[preh•dee•spo•ZEH] *adj*
susceptible; predisposed

prédisposition
[preh•dee•SPO•zee•SYAUπ] *n*
F susceptibility; predisposition

prédominant
[prai•dau•mee•NAHπ] *adj*
predominant

préface [prai•FAHS] *n* F
preface

préférable [prai•fai•RAHBL]
adj preferable

préférence [prai•fai•RAHπs] *n*
F preference; like

préférentiel
[prai•FAI•rahπ•SYEHL] *adj*
preferential

préférer [prai•fai•REH] *vt*
prefer

préfixe [prai•FEEKS] *n* M
prefix

préjudiciable
[prai•zhew•dee•SYAHBL] *adj*
detrimental

préjugé [prai•zhew•ZHAI] *n* M
bias; prejudice

préliminaire
[prai•lee•mee•NEHR] *adj*
preliminary; opening

prélude [prai•LEWD] *n* M
prelude

prématuré
[prai•MAH•tew•RAI] *adj*
premature

premier [pre•MYEH] *adj* first;
foremost; premiere; ~ ministre
premier\ prime minister; ~
plan\ foreground; ~ principal\
primary election; ~ maiden
voyage **premièrement**
[pru•myer•MAHπ] *adv*
primarily

premiers secours *mpl n* first
aid

prémisse [prai•MEES] *n*
premise

prémonition
[prai•mau•nee•SYAUπ] *n* F
premonition

prendre [prahπdr] *vt* take; get;
seize; buy (billet) catch
(froid); à tou ~\ on the whole;
~ amitié\ befriend; ~ plaisir à\
enjoy; ~ sa retraite\ retire;
retirement

prénom [prai•NAUπ] *n* first
name

préoccupé [prai•AU•kew•PAI]
adj preoccupied

préparation
[prai•PAH•rah•SYAUπ] *n*
preparation

préparer [prai•pah•RAI] *vt*
prepare; ~ des repas pour\
cater; *vi* se préparer

préposition
[prai•PAU•zee•SYAUπ] *n* F
preposition

prérogative
[prai•RAU•gah•TEEV] *n* F
prerogative

près [preh] *adv* near; close; à
peu ~\ near; ~ de\ close

présage [prai•SAHZH] *n* M
omen

présager [prai•sah•ZHAI] *vt*
foreshadow; presage

presbytère [prez•bee•TEHR] *n*
M rectory; presbytery

prescription
[pre•skreep•SYAUπ] *n* F
prescription

prescrire [pre•SKREER] *vt*
prescribe

préséance [prai•sai•AHπS] *n* F
precedence; favoir la
préséance sur\ have
precedence

présence [prai•ZAHπS] *n* F
presence

présentable
[prai•zahπ•TAHBL] *adj*
presentable

présentation
[prai•ZAHπ•tah•SYAUπ] *n*
presentation

présenter [prai•zahπ•TAI] *vt*
introduce; present

préservation
[prai•ZER•vah•SYAUπ] *n* F
conservation

président [prai•zee•DAHπ] *n*
M chairman; president

présidentiel
[prai•ZEE•dahπ•SYEL] *adj*
presidential

présomption
[prai•zauπ•SYAUπ] *n* F
presumption

presque [presk] *adv* almost;
nearly

presser [preh•seh] *vt* urge

pression [pre•SYAUπ] *n* F
pressure; *vt* faire pression sur

prestige [pre•STEEZH] *n* M
prestige; glamor

présumer [prai•zew•MEH] *vt*
presume

prêt 1 [pre] *n* M loan; *vt* prêter

prêt 2 [pre] *adj* ready

prétendu [prai•tahπ•DEW] *adj*
ostensible

prétentieux [prai•tahπ•SYØ]
adj pretentious

prétention [prai•tahπ•SYAUπ]
n F pretension

prêter [pre•TAI] *vt* lend; ~ sur
gages\ pawnbroker

prétexte [prai•TEKST] *n* M
pretext

prêtre [pre•tr] *n* M priest

preuve [prØv] *n* proof;
evidence

prévaloir [prai•vahl•WAHR] *vi*
prevail

prévanance [preh•vah•NAHπS]
n F thoughtfulness

prévenant [prai•ve•NAHπ] *adj*
considerate

préventif [prai•vahπ•TEEF] *adj*
preventive

prévisible [prai•vee•ZEEBL]
adj F predictable

prévision [prai•vee•ZYAUπ] *n*
forecast; *vt* prévoir; ~s
météorologique

prévoir [prai•VWAHR] *vt*
foresee

prévoyance
[prai•vwah•YAHπS] *n* F
foresight

prier [pryai] *vi* pray

prière [pryer] *n* F prayer

primate [pree•MAHT] *n*
primate (eccles)

prime [preem] *n* M bonus;
premium

primevère [preem•VEHR] *n* F
primrose

primitif [pree•mee•TEEF] *adj*
primitive

primordial
[pree•maur•DYAHL] *adj*
primordial; prime

prince [praπs] *n* M prince

princesse [praπ•SES] *n* F
princess

principal [praπ•see•PAHL]
adj leading; principal;
main

principe [praπ•SEEP] *n* M
principle

priorité [pryau•ree•TAI] *adj*
priority

prise [preez] *n* grasp; grip;
hold

prisme [preezm] *n* M prism

prison [pree•ZAUπ] *n* F
prison; jail *vt* emprissonner

prisonnier [pree•zau•NYAI] *n*
prisoner

privation [pree•vah•SYAUπ] *n*
F privation

privé [pree•VAI] *adj* F private;
en ~\ in private

priver [pree•VEH] *vt* deprive

privilège |pree•vee•LEZH| *n* M
privilege

prix |pree| *n* M price; award; ~
du billet\ fare; *vt* fixer le prix
de

probabilité
|prau•bah•bee•lee•TAI| *n* F
probability

probable |prau•BAHBL| *n* F
probable; likely

probablement
|prau•bah•bl•MAHπ| *adv*
probably

problème |prau•BLEM| *n* M
problem; pas de ~!\ no
problem!

procédure |prau•sai•DEWR| *n*
F procedure

procès |prau•SEH| *n* M lawsuit;
trial

procession |prau•se•SYAUπ| *n*
M procession

processus |prau•se•SEW| *n* M
process

prochain |prau•SHAπ| *adj* next;
~ à venir\ coming; ~ suivant\
following

proche |praush| *adv* près *adj*
nearby; near

proclamer |prau•klah•MAI| *vt*
proclaim

procurer |prau•kew•REH| *vt*
procure; se procurer

prodige |prau•deezh| *n* M
prodigy

prodigieux -eùse
|prau•dee•ZHEEYØ|
|-ZHEEYØZ| *adj* stupendous;
prodigious

prodigue |prau•DEEG| *adj*
prodigal

productif |prau•dewk•TEEF|
adj productive

production
|prau•dewk•SYAUπ| *n* F
output; production

produit |prau•DWEE| *n* M
product; *npl* M ~s\ produce

produire |prau•DWEER| *vt*
produce; create; make

proéminent
|prau•AI•mee•NAHπ| *adj*
prominent

professeur |prau•fe•SœR| *n* M
professor; teacher

profession |prau•fe•SYAUπ| *n*
F profession; occupation; job

pro |prau| *n* pro

professionnel
|prau•FE•syaun•NEL| *adj n* M
professional

profil |prau•FEEL| *n* M profile

profit |prau•FEE| *n* M profit; *vi*
profiter

profond |prau•FAUπ| *adj*
profound

profond |prau•FAUπ| *adj* deep;
adv profondément

profondeur |prau•fauπ•DœR| *n*
M depth

programme |prau•GRAHM| *n*
M program; *vt* programmer

progrès |prau•GRE| *n* M
headway; progress

progresser |prau•gre•SEH| *n*
progress

prohibition
|prau•ee•bee•SYAUπ| *n* F
prohibition

proie |prwah| *n* F prey

projecteur |prau•zhek•TœR| *n*
floodlight; projector

projection [prau•zhek•SYAUπ]
n F projection

projet [prau•ZHEH] *n* scheme;
project

prolétariat
[prau•LAI•tah•RYAH] *n* M
proletariat

prolongement
[prau•lauπzh•MAHπ] *n* M
extension

prolonger [prau•lauπ•ZHAI] *vt*
prolong; extend

promenade [prau•mu•NAHD]
n F promenade; drive;

promesse [prau•MES] *n* F
pledge; promise; *vt vi*
promettre

prometteur [prau•mu•TœR] *adj*
promising

promotion [prau•mau•SYAUπ]
n F promotion

promouvoir
[prau•moo•VWAHR] *vt*
promote

prompt [prauπ] *adj* prompt

promptement
[prauπ•tu•MAHπ] *adv*
promptly

pronom [prau•NAUπ] *n* M
pronoun

prononcé [prau•nauπ•SAI] *adj*
pronounced

prononcer [prau•nauπ•SAI] *vt*
pronounce; declare; pass
judgment

prononciation
[prau•NAUπ•syah•SYAUπ] *n*
F pronunciation

propagande
[prau•pau•GAHπD] *n* F
propaganda

prophète [prau•FET] *n* M
prophet; visionary

prophétie [prau•fai•TEE] *n* F
prophecy

proportion [prau•paur•SYAUπ]
n F ratio

proposer [prau•pau•ZAI] *vt*
propose; nominate

proposition
[prau•PAU•zee•SYAUπ] *n* F
proposition; nomination;
proposal

propre 1 [praupr] *adj* clean

propre 2 [praupr] *adj* own

propriété [prau•pryai•TAI] *n* F
property

propreté [pro•pre•TAI] *n* F
cleanliness

propriétaire [prau•pryai•TEHR]
n M landlord; owner;
proprietor; F landlady; ~ d'un
domaine\ squire

propulser [prau•pewl•SEH] *vt*
propel; propulse

prose [prauz] *n* F prose

prospère [prau•SPEHR] *adj*
prosperous; well off; wealthy

prospérer [prau•spai•RAI] *vi*
prosper; thrive; flourish

prospérité [prau•SPAI•ree•TAI]
n F prosperity; wealth

prostituée [prau•stee•TWAI] *n*
F prostitute

protecteur [prau•tek•TœR] *adj*
protective

protection [prau•tek•SYAUπ] *n*
F protection

protéger [prau•tai•ZHAI] *vt*
protect; preserve

protéine [prau•tai•EEN] *n* F
protein

protestant [prau•tu•STAHπ] *adj n* M Protestant

protestation [prau•te•stah•SYAUπ] *n* protest

protester [prau•teh•STEH] *vi* protester

prouesse [proo•ES] *n* F prowess

prouver [proo•VEH] *vt* prove

proverbe [prau•VERB] *n* M proverb

province [prau•VAπS] *n* F province

provincial [prau•vaπ•SYAHL] *adj* provincial

provision [prau•vee•ZYAUπ] *n* F provision

provisions [pro•vee•SYAWπ] *npl* F victuals; food; groceries

provisoire [prau•vee•ZWAHR] *n* M temporary; interim; *adj* temporary; tentative

provocateur; -trice [prau•vau•kah•TœR] [-TREES] *n* MF trouble maker

provoquer [prau•vau•KAI] *vt* provoke

proximité [prauk•SEE•mee•TAI] *n* F proximity

prude [prewd] *n* F prude; *adj* F prudish

prudenc [prew•DAHπS] *n* F prudence; caution

prudent [prew•DAHπ] *adj* cautious; prudent

prune [prewn] *n* F plum

pruneau [prew•NO] *n* prune

psalmodie [sahl•mau•DEE] *n* F chant; *vt vi* psalmodier

psaume [psom] *n* M psalm

pseudonyme [psØ•dau•NEEM] *n* M pseudonym

psyché [psee•KAI] *n* F psyche

psychiatre [psee•KYAHTR] *n* MF psychiatrist; F psychiatry

psychologie [psee•kau•lau•ZHEE] *n* psychology

psychologique [psee•KAU•lau•ZHEEK] *n* psychological

psychologue [psee•kau•LAUG] *n* MF psychologist

psychotique [psee•kau•TEEK] *adj n* MF psychotic

puanteur [pew•ahπ•TœR] *n* F stench; stink

pub [puhb] *n* M pub

puberté [pew•ber•TAI] *n* F puberty

public [pew•BLEEK] *adj* public

publication [pew•BLEE•kah•SYAUπ] *n* F publication; periodical

publicité [pew•BLEE•see•TAI] *n* F publicity

publier [pew•BLYAI] *vt* publish

puce 1 [pews] *n* F flea

puce 2 [pews] *n* F microchip

puer [pweh] *vt* reek

puéril [pwai•REEL] *adj* childish

puissance [pwee•SAπS] *n* F strength

puissant [pwee•SAHπ] *adj* mighty; powerful; potent

puits [pwee] *n* M well; ~ de pétrol\ oil well

pull-over [pewl-au•VEHR] *n* M
sweater

pulpe [pewlp] *n* F pulp

pulsation [pewl•zah•SYAUπ] *n*
F throb

pulvériser [pewl•VAI•ree•ZAI]
vt pulverize

punaise [pew•NEHZ] *n* F
thumbtack

punaise; clouer [pew•NEHZ];
[kloo•eh] n; *vt* F tack

punir [pew•NEER] *vt*
punish

punition [pew•nee•syauπ] *n* F
punishment

punk [pauπk] *n* MF punk

pupille [pew•PEE] *n* F ward

pur [pewr] *adj* pure

pur-sang [pyr-SAHπ] *n* MF
thoroughbred

pureté [pew•ru•TAI] *n* F purity

purgatoire
[pewr•gah•TWAHR] *n* M
purgatory

purge [pewrzh] *n* F purge; *vt*
purger

purifier [pew•ree•FYAI] *vt*
purify

puritain [pew•ree•TAπ] *adj n*
M puritan

putain [pew•TAπ] *n* F whore

putride [pew•TREED] *adj*
putrid

puzzle [pewzl] *n* M jigsaw
(puzzle)

pyjama [pee•zhah•MAH] *n*
pajamas

pyramide [pee•rah•MEED] *n* F
pyramid

python [pee•TAUπ] *n* python

Q

quadrupler [kah•drew•PLAI] *vt*
vi quadruple

quadruplés mpl
[kah•drew•PLAI] *n*
quadruplets

quai [keh] *n* M quay; wharf

qualification
[kah•LEE•fee•kah•SYAUπ] *n*
F qualification

qualifier [kah•lee•FYAI] *vi*
qualify; se qualifier

qualité [kah•lee•TAI] *n* F
quality; grade; quality;

quand [kahn] *adv* when; ~
même\ regardless

quantité [kahπ•tee•TAI] *n* F
amount; quantity

quarantaine [kah•rah•π•TEHN]
n quarantine; *vt* mettre
en ~

quarante [kah•RAHNT] *num*
forty

quart [kahr] *n* M quarter; m;
(coin) pièce de 25 cents; cinq
heures et ~\ quarter past five;
; ~ to cinq heures moins ~\
quarter to five

quartiers [kahr.•TYEH] *npl* M
quarter' ~-maître\ yeoman

quartz [kahrts] *n* M quartz

quatorze [kah•TAURZ] *num*
fourteen

quatre [kahtr] *num* four

quatre-vingts [kahtr-VAπ]
eighty

quatre-vingts-dix
[kahtr•vaπ•DEE] *num* ninety

quatrième [kah•tryem] *num*
fourth

quatuor [kah•TWAHR] *n* M
quartet

que [kuh] *conj* than; that;
which;

quel; quelle; quelles [kehl] *adj*
what

quelqu'un quelqu'une
[kehl•Kœπ]; [kehl•KEWN]
pron MF somebody; someone

quelque chose [kehlk•SHAUZ]
pron indef inv M something;
anything

quelque part [kehlk•PAHR]
adv M somewhere; anywhere

quelquefois [kehlk•FWAH]
adv sometimes

querrelle [ke•REL] *n* F quarrel;
vi se quereller

question [ke•STYAUπ] *n* F
query; question; issue; *vt*
questioner

questionnaire
[ke•styau•NEHR] *n* F
questionnaire

quête [ket] *n* F quest

queue [kØ] *n* F tail; stalk ;
stem; file; line; en ~\ in the
rear; faire ~\ stand in line; ~
de-cheval *n* M ponytail

qui [kee] *pron* who; whom; à ~
est-ce?\ whose is it? ~ que ce
soit\ anyone; whatever

quiche [keesh] *n* F quiche

quincaillerie
[kan•SAH•ye•REE] *n* M
hardware

quinine [kee•NEEN] *n* F
quinine

quintelle [kaπ•TEL] *n* F quintet

quintuplés [kaπ•tew•PLAI] *npl*
M quintuplets

quinzaine [laπ•ZEHN] *n* F
fortnight

quinze [kaπz] *num* fifteen

quinzième [kaπ•ZYEM] *num*
fifteenth

quitter [kee•TEH] *vt* vacate;
leave (un lieu)

quiz [keez] *n* quiz

quoi [kwah] *pron* what; ~\ que
whatever

quoique [kwahku] *adv* though

quota [kau•TAHḷ *n* M quota

quotidien [kay•tee•DYEHπ]
adj everyday; daily

quotient [kau•SYAHπ] *n* M
quotient

R

rabais [rah•BEH] *n* M rebate;
reduction; discount; fall

rabaisser [rah•be•SAI] *vt*
cheapen; discount; rebate

rabbin [rah•BAπ] *n* M rabbi

raccourci [rah•koor•SEE] *n* M
shortcut; precis; digest; *adj*
shortened; obridged; sloppy

raccourcir [rah•koor•SEER] *vt*
shorten; abridge

raccrocher [rah•kro•SHEH] *vt*
hang up; retrieve

race [rahs] *n* F breed (animals);
stock; blood line

racine [rah•SEEN] *n* F root

racisme [rah•SEEZM] *n* M
racism

raciste [rah•SEEST] *n* MF racist

racketteur [rah•ku•TœR] *n* M
racketeer

raclée [rah•KLAI] *n* F beating
(thrashing)

raconter [ra•kauπ•TEH] *vt*
relate; tell; narate; recount

racquette [rah•KET] *n* M
racket (bruit) (illegal)

rade [rahd] *npl* F roads

radeau [rah•DO] *n* raft

radiateur [rah•dyah•TœR] *n* M
radiator

radiation [rah•dyah•SYAUπ] *n*
F radiation

radical [rah•dee•KAHL] *adj n*
M radical

radieux [rah•DYØ] *adj* radiant;
beaming (sourire)

radio [rah•DYAU] *n* M radio

radioactif [rah•dyau•ahk•TEEF]
adj radioactive

radiodiffuser
[rah•DYAU•dee•few•ZEH] *vt*
broadcast

radiographie
[rah•dyo•grah•FEE] *n* F X-ray

radiologie
[rah•DYAU•lau•ZHEE] *n* F
radiology

radis [rah•DEE] *n* M radish

raffiné [rah•fee•NAI] *adj*
refined

raffiner [rah•fee•NAI] *vt* refine

raffinerie [rah•fee•nu•REE] *n* F
refinery

rage 1 [rahzh] *n* F rage; fury;
violent pain; passion; mania

rage 2 [rahzh] *n* F rabies

ragoût [rah•GOO] *n* M stew;
ragout; relish; seasoning

raide [rehd] *adj* steep

raide [rehd] *adj* (inv) stiff;
steep; rigid; tight

raideur [reh•DœR] *n* F
stiffness; tightness

raidir [reh•DEEUR] *vt; vi*
stiffen; se raidir\ tense up

raie [reh] *n* F stripe; parting;
line; stroke; furrow

raifort [re•FAUR] *n* M
horseradish

raillerie [rah•yehr•EE] *n* F
taunt; *vt* railler

rainure [re•NEWR] *n* groove;
slot; notch

raisin [re•ZAπ] *n* M grape; ~
sec\ currant; raisin

raison [re•ZAUπ] *n* F purpose;
reason

raisonnable [re•zau•NAHBL]
adj sensible; reasonable

raisonnablement
[re•zau•NAH•bl•MAHπ] *adv*
reasonably; sensibly

raisonnement [re•zaun•MAHπ]
n M reasoning; sensible

raisonnnable [re•zau•NAHBL] *adj* reasonable

rajuster [rah•zhew•STAI] *vt* readjust

rallonger [rah•lauπ•zhai] *vt* lengthen; prolong

ramasser [rah•mah•SAI] *vt* gather; collect; assemble

rame [rahm] *n* M oar

rameau [rah•MO] *n* M bough; branch; Climanche des Rameaux\ Palm Sunday

ramener [rah•meh•NAI] *vt* bring back; restore

rampe [rahπp] *n* ramp; slope; incline

ramper [rahπ•PAI] *vi* grovel; slither; crawl

rance [rahπs] *adj* rancid; sour

rançon [rahπ•SAUπ] *n* M ransom; hold; ~ mettre à ~\ hold for ransome; *vt* rançonner

rancune [rahπ•KEWN] *n* F grudge spite; *adj* racunier

randonnée [rahπ•dau•NAI] *n* F hike; circuit

rang [rahπ] *n* M tier; layer; line; row; column; rank (mil)

rangé -e; [rahπ•ZHEH] *n* F row; range; file; line; tier

ranger [rahπ•ZHEH] *vi* stow; put in order; tidy up; arrange

ranimer [rah•nee•MEH] *vt* resuscitate

râpe [rahp] *n* F grater; rasp stalk

râpé [rah•PAI] *adj* threadbare; grated; shabby

rapide [rah•PEED] *adj* fast; rapid; quick; speedy; *npl* M rapids

rapidement; vite [rah•pee•duh•MAHπ] *adv* speedily; quickly

rapidité [rah•pee•dee•TEH] *n* F swiftness

rappel [rah•PEL] *n* encore; recall; reminder; *vt* rappeler; se rappeler\ recall

rapport [rah•PAUR] *n* M rapport; report; account; proceeds; profit; revenue

rapporter [rah•paur•TEH] *vt* bring back; report; repeal; report; quote

rapporteur -euse [rah•paur•TœR] [-ØZ] *adj; n* MF reporter; stenographer; telltale

rapports [rah•PAUR] *npl* M intercourse; ~ (sexuelle) sexual intercourse

rare [rahr] *adj* scarce; rare; uncommon

rarement [rah•ru•MAHπ] *adv* seldom; rarely

rareté [rah•ru•TAI] *n* F rarity

rasage [rah•SAHZH] *n* M shaving

raser [rah•ZAI] *vt* raze; shave; *vi* se raser

rasoir [rah•SWAHR] *n* M razor; shaver

rassemblement [rah•SAHπ•blu•MAHπ] *n* M gathering; assembly

rassembler [rah•sahπ•BLAI] *vi* congregate; gather; assemble; muster (mil)

rassis [rah•SEE]; *adj* stale (du pain rassis)

rassurer [rah•sew•REH] *vt* reassure

rat [rah] *n* M rat; taper (bougie)

rate [raht] *n* F spleen (anat)

raté [rah•TEH] *adj* unsuccessful; *n* M failure; flop; wash-out-flash-in-the-pan (coll)

râteau [rah•to] *n* rake

rater [rah•TAI] *vi* misfire; miss; fail in; bungle; muff (coll)

ratifier [rah•tee•FYAI] *vt* ratify

ration [rah•SYAUπ] *n* ration; *vt* rationer

rationnel [rah•syau•NEL] *adj* rational

raton laveur [ra•TAUπ lah•VœR] *n* M raccoon

rauque [rok] *adj* husky; hoarse (voix)

ravage [rah•VAHZH] *n* M ravage; *vt* ravager

ravages [rah•VAHZH] *npl* M havoc

ravi [rah•VEE] *adv* overjoyed; delighted

ravin [rah•VAπ] *n* M gully; ravine

ravir [rah•VEER] *vt* ravish; abduct; charm; delight

ravissant [rah•vee•SAHπ] *adj* ravishing; delightful

ravissement [rah•vees•MAHπ] *n* M rapture

ravisseur [rah•vee•SœR] *n* M kidnapper

rayon [rah•YAUπ] *n* M radius; ray; spoke

raz [rah] *n* M strong current; tide; ~ de marée\ tidal wave

réaction [rai•ahk•SYAUπ] *n* F reaction; response

réactionnaire [rai•AHK•syau•NEHR] *adj n* MF reactionary

réagir [rai•ah•ZHEER] *vi* react; respond

réalisation [rai•ah•lee•zah•SYAUπ] *n* F realization; fulfillment

réaliser [rai•AH•lee•ZEH] *vt* fulfill; realize

réalisme [rai•ah•LEEZM] *n* M realism

réaliste [rai•ah•LEEST] *n* MF realist; *adj* realistic

réalité [rai•AH•lee•TAI] *n* F reality

réapparaître [rai•AH•pah•RETR] *vi* reappear

réapprovisionner [reh•AH•prau•vee•zyau•NEH] *vt* replenish

rebattu [re•bah•TEW] *adj* hackneyed

rebelle [ru•BEL] *adj* rebellious; *n* MF rebel; *vi* rebeller

rébellion [rai•bal•YAUπ] *n* F rebellion

rebond [ru•BAUπ] *n* M bounce; rebound

rebondir [ru•bauπ•DEER] *vi* bounce; rebound; *vt* faire ~

rebord [re•BAUR] *n* M sill; ~ de fenêtre\ windowsill

rebuffade [ru•bew•FAHD] *n* F snub

récemment [rai•su•MAHπ] *adv*
recently

recensement
[ru•sahπ•SMAHπ] *n* M
census; inventory; count

récent [rai•SAHπ] *adj* recent;
late; new; fresh

réception [rai•sep•SYAUπ] *n* F
reception; receiving; welcome;
receipt

récession [rai•se•SYAUπ] *n* F
recession

recette 1 [ru•SET] *n* F
proceeds; receivables;
returns

recette 2 [ru•SET] *n* F recipe

recevoir [ru•se•VWAHR] *vt*
receive; get; accept; admit;
welcome; entertain

recherche [ru•SHEHRSH] *n* F
research; *vt* rechercher

rechute [re•SHOOT] *n* F
relapse; set-back

récif [rai•SEEF] *n* M reef

récipient [rai•see•PYAHπ] *n*
receptacle; recipient; reservoir;
container

récipiendaire mf
[rai•SEE•pyahπ•DEHR] *n*
recipient

réciproque [rai•see•PRAUK]
adj reciprocal

récital [rai•see•TAHL] *n* recital

réciter [rai•see•TAI] *vt* recite

réclamer [rai•klah•MEH] *vt*
reclaim

reclus [re•KLEW] *n* M recluse

recommandation
[ru•KAU•mahπ•dah•SYAUπ]
n F recommendation

recommander
[ru•KAU•mahπ•DEH] *vt*
recommend

récompense [reh•kauπ•PAHπS]
n F reward

réconciliation
[rai•kauπ•SEE•lyah•SYAUπ]
n F reconciliation

réconfortant
[rai•KAUπ•faur•TAHπ] *adj*
heartwarming; cheery; *vt*
véconforter

reconnaissable
[re•KAU•ne•SAHBL] *adj*
recognizable

reconnaissance
[re•KAU•ne•SAHπS] *n* F
gratitude; recognition;
reconnaissance

reconnaissant
[re•KAU•ne•SAHπ] *adj*
grateful; thankful

reconnaître [ru•kau•NETR] *vt*
acknowledge; recognize

reconsidérer
[ru•KAUπ•see•dai•RAI] *vt*
reconsider; mull over

reconstruire
[ru•kauπ•STRWEER] *vt*
rebuild; reconstruct

reconstituer
[ru•KAUπ•stee•TWAI] *vt*
reconstruct; reconsitute

recours [ru•KOUR] *n* M
recourse; resort

récréation [rai•krai•ah•SYAUπ]
n F recreation

récrire [rai•KREEUR] *vt* rewrite

recrue [re•KREW] *n* F recruit;
vt recruter

rectangle |rek•TAHπGL| *n* M
rectangle

rectifier |rek•tee•FYAI| *vt*
rectify

reçu |reh•SOO| *adj* received;
admitted; recognized; au ~ de\
upon receipt of\ être-~\ pass
(exam)

reculer |ru•kew•LAI| *vi* cringe

récuperation
|raih•KEW•pehr•ah•SYAUπ|
F revival; recouperation

redressement;
|rai•dre•SMAHπ| *n* recovery;
redress

récurer |rai•kew•REH| *vt* scour

rédemption |rai•dahπ•SYAUπ|
n redemption

redevable |re•de•VAHBL| *adj*
indebted

redoutable |re•doo•TAHBL|
adj formidable

redresser |ruh•dreh•SEH| *vt*
straighten

réduction |rai•dewk•syauπ| *n* F
reduction

réduire |rai•DWEER| *vt* reduce;
lessen

refaire |ru•FEHR| *vt* redo

référendum
|rai•fai•rahπ•DAUM| *n* M
referendum

réfléchir |rai•flai•sheer| *vt*
reflect; think

refléter |rai•flai•TEER| *vt*
reflect

réflexion |rai•flek•SYAUπ| *n* F
reflection; ~ faite\ second
thought

reflux |re•FLEWKS| *n* ebb; *vi*
refluer

réforme |rai•FAURM| *n* F
reform; *vt* réformer

refraîchir |ru•fre•SHEER| *vt*
refresh; freshen

refraîchissant
|ru•fre•shee•SAHπ| *adj*
refreshing

refraîchissements
|ru•FRE•shees•MAHπ| *npl* M
refreshments

refrain |re•FRAπ| *n* refrain;
abstain

réfrigérateur
|rai•FREE•zhai•rah•TœR| *n*
refrigerator

refroidissements
|re•FRWAH•dec•SMAHπ| *npl*
M chills (méd)

refuge |re•FEWZH| *n* refuge;
hiding; shelter; protetion se
réfugier

refus |re•FEW| *n* M refusal;
denial; rejection

refuser |ruh•few•ZEH| *vt*; *vi*
withhold; deny; refus

réfuter |rai•few•TEH| *vt*
disprove; refute

regard |re•GAHR| *n* glance;
look; base; stare; frown; en ~\
opposite

regarder |re•gahr•DEH| *vt* *vi*
look; glance at; watch

régime |rai•ZHEEM| *n* M
regime

régiment |rai•zhee•MAHπ| *n*
M regiment

région |rai•ZHAUπ| *n* F region;
locality; area; ~ boisé *n* F
woodland

registre |rai•ZHESTR| *n*
register; record; account book

réglage [reh•GLAHZH] *n* M
tuning

règle [regl] *n* F rule

réglementation
[raigl•MAHπ•tah•SYAUπ] *n* F
regulation

régler [rai•GLAI] *vt* regulate;
settle

règne [re•nyu] *n* M reign; *vi*
régner

regret [re•GREH] *n* regret; *vt*
regretter

régulier -ière
[reh•gew•leey•EH];
[-leey•EHR] *adj* steady

régulier [rai•gew•LYAI] *adj*
regular

régulièrement
[rai•GEW•lyer•MAHπ] *adv*
regularly; steadily

rehausser [ru•o•SAI] *vt*
enhance

rein [raπ] *n* M kidney (anat)

reine [ren] *n* F queen

réitérer [rai•EE•tai•RAI] *vt*
reiterate

rejet [re•ZHEH] *n* M rejection

rejeter [ru•jeh•TEH] *vt* spurn;
throw out; reject

rejeton [ru•zhe•TAUπ] *n* M
offspring

rejeunir [re•zhØ•NEER] *vt*
rejuvenate

réjoui [rai•zhoo•EE] *adj*
jubilant

relâché [ru•lah•SHAI] *adj* lax

relatif [re•lah•TEEF] *adj*
relative

relations [re•lah•SYAUπ]
npl F relationship; dealings;
liaison

relativement
[re•LAH•teev•MAHπ] *adv*
relatively

relaxation
[re•LAHK•sah•SYAUπ] *n* F
relaxation

religieux [re•lee•ZHØ] *adj*
religious

religion [re•lee•ZHAUπ] *n* F
religion

remarquable
[ru•mahr•KAHBL] *adj*
noteworthy; remarkable

remarque [re•MAHRK] *n* F
remark; *vt* faire remarquer

rembourrage
[rahπ•boo•RAHZH] *n* M
padding; stuffing; upholstery

rembourrer [rahπ•boor•EH] *vt*
upholster

remboursement
[RAHπ•boors•MAHπ] *n* M
refund

rembourser [RAHπ•bour•SAI]
vt reimburse; refund; repay;
redeem

remède [ru•MED] *n* M cure;
remedy; *vt* remédier à

remercier
[ruh•MEHR•see•YEH] *vt*
thank

remettre [ru•METR] *vt*
postpone; remit; put back;
rely; s'en ~\ rely upon

remise [re•MEEZ] *n* shed; ~ de
diplômes *n* graduation

remodeler [ru•mau•DLEH] *vt*
remodel

remords [ru•MAUR] M
remorse; regret; sadness

remorque [ruh•MAURK] *n* F
trailer

remplacer [rahπ•plah•SEH] *vt*
replace

remplir [rahπ•PLEER] *vt* fill;
refill; replenish; cram; hold;
stuff

remuer [ruh•mew•EH] *vt; vi*
stir; move; rouse; turn; ~
-ménagen *n* M bustle; to-do
(coll)

renaissance [ru•ne•SAHπs] *n* F
rebirth; renaissance

renard [re•NAHR] *n* M fox

rencontre [rahπ•KAUπTR] *n* F
meeting; encounter;
engagement; coincidence

rencontrer [rahπ•kauπ•TREH]
vt meet; encounter;
experience; chance upon

rendez-vous *n* M engagement;
meeting; appointment; date

rendre [rahπdr] *vt* render;
return; restore; give back;
repay; vomit; pay (visite); ~
furieux\ infuriate; ~ perplexe\
perplex

renforcement
[rahπ•faurs•MAHπ] *vt*
reinforcement

renforcer [rahπ•faur•SEH]
vt reinforce; strengthen;
toughen

renier [ru•NYAI] *vt* disown;
repudiate

renne [ren] *n* M reindeer

renommé [ru•nau•MAI] *adj*
famed; renowned; famous

renommée [ru•nau•MEH] *n* F
renown; fame

renoncer [ruh•nauπ•SEH] *vt*
waive; forego; renounce; skip
over

renouvelement
[ru•NEW•vehl•MAHπ] *n* M
renewal

renouveler [ru•noo•VLEH] *vt*
renew

renouvellement
[ruh•NOO•vehl•MAHπ] *n* M
turnover (de personnel)

rénover [reh•nau•VEH] *vt*
renovate

renseignements
[rahπ•se•nyu•MAHπ] *npl; M*
information

rentrée [rahπ•TRAI] *n* F
comeback; re-entrance; return;
reappearance; collection

rentrer [rahπ•TREH] *vi*
re-enter; return; reopen;
resume; tuck

renverser [rahπ•ver•SAI] *vt*
overthrow; turn upside down;
upset; confuse; amaze; stupefy

renvoi [rahπ•VWAH] *n* M
dismissal; firing; adjournment

renvoyer [rah•vwoy•EH] *vt*
send back; return; dismiss;
fire; discharge

repaire [re•PEHR] *n* M lair;
hide-out

répandre [reh•PAHπDR] *vt*
pour; shed; stress; distribute

répandu [reh•pahπ•DEW] *adj*
widespread; ~ courant\
prevalent

réparation
[reh•pah•rah•SYAUπ] *n* F
reparation

réparer [reh•pah•REH] *vt; vi* M
repair; mend

repas [re•PAH] *n* M meal;
repast

repassage [ru•pah•SAHZH] *n*
M ironing; pressing; *vt*
repasser

répéter [rai•pai•TAI] *vt vi*
rehearse; repeat

répétition
[rai•PAI•tee•SYAUπ] *n* F
rehearsal; M repetition

répit [rai•PEE] *n* MF respite;
pause; break

réplique [reh•PLEEK] *n* F
reply; answer; response;
retort; replica (art); repeat
(mus)

répondre [rai•PAUπDR] *vi*
respond; answer; *vi* répondre à

réponse [reh•PAUπS] *n* F
response; answer; reply

reporter [re•paur•TEH] *n* M
reporter

repousser [ru•poo•SEH] *vt*
repel; repulse

reprendre [ru•PRAHπDR] *vt*
resume; restart

représailles [reh•preh•ZUYY] *n*
F retaliation; vengence

représentatif -ive
[ru•PREH•zahπ•tah•TEEF]
[-IVE] *n* MF representative

représentation
[ru•PREE•zahπ•teh•SYAUπ] *n*
F representation

représenter
[ru•PREH•zahπ•TEH] *vt*
represent; depict

réprimande [rai•pree•MAHπD]
n F rebuke; reprimand; *vt*
réprimander

réprimer [rai•pree•MAI] *vt*
quell; repress

repriser [ru•pree•ZAI] *vt* darn

reproche [ru•PRAUSH] *n* MF
reproof; reproach; reprove; *vt*
reprocher

reproduction
[ru•PRAU•dewk•SYAUπ] *n* F
reproduction

reproduire [ru•prau•DWEEUR]
vt reproduce

reptile [rehp•TEEIL] *n* M
reptile

républicain
[reh•PEW•blee•KAπ] [-KAN]
n; adj MF republican

république [reh•pew•BLEEK]
n F republic

répugnant [rai•pew•NYAHπ]
adj loathsome; repugnant;
repulsive

réputation
[reh•PEW•teh•SYAUπ] *n* F
reputation; repute

requête [ru•KEHT] *n* F request

requin [re•KAπ] *n* M shark

réseau [rai•ZO] *n* M network

réservation
[rai•ZEHR•vah•SYAUπ] *n* F
reservation

réserve [rai•ZEHRV] *n* F
reserve; caution; modesty;
stock; stockroom

réservé [rai•zehr•VEH] *adj*
withdrawn; modest; shy

réserves [rai•zerv] *npl* F store;
hoard

réservoir [rai•sehr•VWAHR] *n*
M reservoir; tank; well; ~
d'essence\ gas tank (auto)

résidence [rai•zee•DAHπS] *n* F
residence; home; dwelling

résider [rai•zee•DEH] *vi* reside;
live

résidu [rai•zee•DEW] *n* M
residue

résiduel -le [rai•zee•dew•EHL]
adj residual; vestigial

résignation
[rai•EEG•nah•SYAUπ] *n* F
resignation; quitting

résistance [rai•zee•STAHπS] *n*
F resistance

résistant [rai•sees•TAHπ] *adj*
tough; resistant

résister [rai•zee•STEH] *vt*
resist; withstand

résolu [rai•zau•LEW] *adj* intent;
resolute; stalwart

résolution
[rai•ZAU•lew•SYAUπ] *n* F
resolution

résonance [rai•zau•NAHπS] *n*
F resonance

résonant [rai•zau•NAHπ] *adj*
resonant; resounding

résoudre [rai•ZOODR] *vt*
resolve; solve

respect [reh•SPEH] *n* M
respect; ~ de soi\ self-respect

respectable
[reh•spehk•TAHBL] *adj*
respectable

respectif -ive [reh•spehk•TEEF]
[-TIVE] *adj* respective

respectueux -euse
[reh•spehk•TEWØ]
[-TEWØZ] *adj* MF respectful;
reverent~ des lois\
law-abiding

respirer [re•spee•REH] *vi*
breathe; inhale

responsabilité
[reh•SPAUHπ•sah•BEE•lee•TEH]
n F responsibility; liability

responsable
[reh•sphauπ•SAHBL] *adj* F
responsible

ressemblance
[ru•sahn•BLAHNS] *n* F
resemblance; likeness

ressembler [ru•sahπ•BLEH] *vi*
resemble

ressentiment
[ru•SAHN•tee•MAHπ] *n* M
resentment; *vi* ressentir

ressource [ru•SURS] *n* F
resource

restant [rehs•TAHπ] *n* M
remnant

restaurant [reh•staur•AHπ] *n*
M restaurant

restaurer [reh•stau•REH] *vt*
restore

reste [rest] *n* M remainder; rest

rester [re•STEH] *vt vi* remain;
stay

restes [rest] *npl* F left-overs;
ruins; remains

restitution
[reh•stee•tew•SYAUπ] *n* F
restitution; repayment

restoration
[reh•STAUR•ah•SYAUπ] *n* F
restoration

résultat [reh•zewl•TAH] *n* M
result ~s des élections\ returns
(election)

résumé [rai•zew•MAI] *n* M
summary; resume; en ~\ on
the whole; after all

retard [ru•TAHR] *n* M delay; slow-down; en ~\ late

rétarder [rai•tahr•DEH] *vt* retard

retenir [ru•te•NEER] *vt* detain; retain

retentissant [ruh•tahπ•tee•SAHπ] *adj* thunderous; echoing; loud

retentissement [ruh•tahπ•tees•MAHπ] *adj* thundering

retenir [ru•teh•NEER] *vt* retain; keep back; reserve

retenue [reht•NEW] *n* F reserve

rétiré [rai•tee•RAI] *adj* secluded

retirer [ru•teeur•EH] *vt* retract; withdraw

retomber [ru•tauπ•BEH] *vi* revert

retour [ru•TOOR] *n* M reutrn; reptition; être de ~\ be back; sans ~\ forever; ~ de flame\ backfire

retourner [ru•tur•NEH] *vi* revert; return; come back to

retraite [ruh•TREHT] *n* F withdrawal; retreat

rétrécir [rai•trai•SEER] *vt* shrink; reduce; lessen

rétroactif [reh•TRAU•ak•TEEF] *adj* retroactive

retrouver [ru•trew•VEH] *vt* retrieve; get back

réunion [reh•ew•NYAUπ] *n* F reunion; meeting

réunir [reh•ew•NEEUR] *vt* reunite; reunify

réussir [reh•ew•SEEUR] *vi* succeed; ~ à\ succeed at

revâsser [ru•vah•SAI] *vi* daydream; wool-gather (coll.)

rêve [rev] *n* dream; *vi* rêver (de)

réveil [rai•VAI] *n* M alarm clock

réveillé [rai•ve•YAI] *adj* awake

reveiller [reh•veh•YEH] *vt* wake; awaken

révélateur -euse [reh•veh•lah•TœR] [-ØZ] *adj* telling; revealing

révélation [rai•VAI•lah•SYAUπ] *n* F disclosure; revelation

révéler [rai•vai•LAI] *vt* disclose; reveal

revenir [rehv•NEEUR] *vt* come back; come again; haunt; cost; accrue; ~ à soi\ recover

revenu [re•vu•NEW] *n* M income; revenue

révérance [reh•veh•RAHπS] *n* F reverence; respect

révérer [rai•veh•REH] *vt* revere; respect

revers 1 [ru•VER] *n* M lapel

revers 2 [ru•VER] *n* setback; reverse

rêveur [re•VœR] *adj* dreamy

reviser [ru•vee•ZEH] *vt* overhaul; *vt* revise

révision [rai•vee•ZYAUπ] *n* F revision

révolution [reh•vau•lew•SYAUπ] *n* F revolution

révolutionnaire [reh•vau•LEW•syaun•NEHR] *adj* revolutionary

revolver 1 [re•vaul•VEH] *n* M
gun

révolver 2 [re•vaul•VEH] *vt*
revolve; turn

révoquer [reh•vau•KEH];
[ah•new•leh] *vt* revoke

revue [re•VEW] *n* F magazine

rez-de-chaussée
[re•du•sho•ZAI] *n* M ground
floor

rhétorique [reh•taur•EEK] *n* F
rhetoric

rhinocéros [ree•NAU•cehr•O] *n*
M rhinoceros

rhubarbe [rew•BAHRB] *n* F
rhubarb

rhum [ruhm] *n* M rum

rhume [rewm] *n* F cold

rhumatisme [rew•mah•TIZM]
n M rheumatism

riche [reesh] *adj inv* rich;
wealthy

richesse [ree•SHEHSH] *n* F
richness; wealth

ride [reed] *n* F wrinkle

rideau [ree•DO] *n* M curtain;
npl rideaux\ drapes

rider [reed•EH] *vt* wrinkle;
crease

ridicule [ree•dee•KEWL] *n* M
ridicule; *adj* ridiculous;
foolish; preposterous

ridiculiser
[ree•dee•KEW•lee•ZAI] *vt*
deride; ridicule

rien [ryahπ] *pron* nothing; ~ de
nothing

rigide [ree•ZHEED] *adj* rigid

rigidité [ree•ZHEE•dee•TAI] *n*
F rigidity

rigueur; [ree•GœR] *n* F rigor;
hardship; de ~\ necessary

rime [reem] n; *vt* F rhyme

rinçage [raπ•SAHZH] *n* M
rinse

rinser [raπ•SEH] *vt* rinse

riposte; [ree•PAUST] F retort;
reply; come-back (coll)

rire [reer] *vi n* M laugh;
laughter; *npl* ~s\ laughter

ris de veau [ree duh vo] *n* M
sweetbread

risque [reesk] *n* (prendre un
risque) M risk; gamble

risquer [ree•SKEH] *vt; vi*
venture; gamble; risk

rite [reet] *n* MF rite

rituel [ree•tew•EL] *n* M ritual

rivage [ree•VAHZH] *n* shore

rival -e [ree•VAHL] *n* MF
rival

rivaliser [ree•VAHL•ee•ZEH] *v*
vie; rival

rivalité [ree•VAHL•ee•TAI] *n* F
rivalry; competition (sport)

rivière [ree•vee•EHR] *n* M
river

rixe [reeks] *n* F brawl

riz [ree] *n* M rice

robe [raub] *n* F gown; costume;
dress; ~ du soir\ evening
gown

robinet [rau•bee•NAI] *n* M
faucet; spigot; tap

robuste [ro•BEWST] *adj* MF
robust; healthy; hardy

roc; roche [rauk]; [raush] *n* MF
rock

rocher [ro•SHEHR] *n* M
boulder

rôder [rau•DEH] *vi* prowl; skulk; wander

rôdeur [rau•DœR] *n* M prowler

roi [rwah] *n* M king

rôle [raul] *n* M role; character; roster; à tour de ~\ in turn

Romain -e [rau•MAπ]; [rau•MAN] *n* MF *adj* Roman

roman [rau•MAHπ] *n* novel; *adj* Romance (epoque de lettres)

romance [rau•MAHπS] *n* F romance

romancier [rau•mahπ•SYEH] *n* novelist

romantique [rau•mahπ•TEEK] *n* MF *adj* romanticist; romantic

romantisme [rau•mahπ•TEEZM] *n* M romanticism

rompre [raumpr] *vt* break; break off; snap; disrupt; break in; train; interrupt; upset; call off; ~ avec\ break up (avec qqn)

rond -de [rauπ]; [-nd] *adj* round; circular; plump; frank; open

rondelle [raun•DEHL] *n* F washer

ronger [rauπ•ZHAI] *vt* gnaw; chew; nibble; pick; fret; torment

ronronner [rauπ•rau•NAI] *vi* purr

rosaire [rau•ZEHR] *n* M rosary

rose 1 [rauz] *n* M pink

rose 2 [rauz] *n* (fleur) F rose

rosée [ro•ZAI] *n* F dew

rosser [rau•SEH] *vt* wallop; hit; strike

rossignol [rau•see•NYAUL] *n* M nightingale

rotatif [rau•tah•TIF] [-TEEV] *adj* rotary

rotation [rau•teh•SYAUπ] *n* F rotation

rôti [ro•TEE]*n*M roast ; *vt* rôtir

rotule [rau•TEWL] *n* M kneecap

roucouler [roo•koo•LAI] *vi* coo

roue [roo] *n* F wheel; faire la ~ strut; show off

roué [roo•AI] *adj* crafty; artful; *n* M rake; roué

rouer [roo•EH] *vi* thrash

rouet [roo•EH] *n* M spinning-wheel

rouge [roozh] *n* M *adj* red; ~ à lèvres\ lipstick; ~-gorge (oiseau)\ robin

rougeole [roo•ZHAUL] *n* F measles

rougir [roo•ZHEER] *vi* blush; redden

rouillé [rwee•YAI] *adj* rusty

rouille [rweel] *n* rust f; *vi* se rouiller

rouleau 1 [roo•LO] *n* coil (elec)

rouleau 2 [roo•LO] *n* scroll (papier)

Roumanie [roo•mah•NEE] *n* F Romania

route [root] *n* F road; route

routine [roo•TEEN] *n* F routine

rouvrir [roo•REEUR] *vt* reopen

roux m (rousse) [roo] *n* F *adj* redhead

royal [rwah•YAHL] *adj* regal; royal

royaume [rwah•YOM] *n* F
kingdom

ruban [rew•BAHπ] *n* M ribbon;
~ adhésif\ tape

rubis [rew•BEE] *n* M ruby

ruche [rewsh] *n* F beehive;
hive

rude [rewd] *adj* rugged; rough;
harsh; uneven

rue [rew] *n* F street; road;
way

ruer [rew•AI] *vi* fling; hurl;
kick; buck (cheval)

rugby [rewg•BEE] *n* M rugby

rugir [rew•ZHEEUR] *n* M *vt*
roar

ruine [rween] *n* F ruin; *vt*
ruiner

ruisseau [rwee•SO] *n* M brook;
creek; stream

rumeur [rew•MœR] *n* F
rumor

rupture [rewp•TEWR] *n* F
rupture; break; breach (of
contract)

rural [rew•RAHL] *adj* rural;
country

rusé 1 [rew•ZAI] *adj* crafty;
clever; tricky

rusé 2 [rew•ZAI] *adj* rueful;
sad; grieving

ruse [rewz] *n* F ruse; trick;
stealth; wile

rusé [rew•zai] *adj* cunning

russe [rews] *n* M Russian; *n*
MF (gens) Russe; (langue)
russe M

Russie [rew•SEE] *n* F Russia

rustique [rew•STEEK] *adj*
rustic

rustre [rewstr] *n* M lout

rythme [reetm] *n* M rhythm

S

sa [sah] poss *adj* his; her; its;
one's

sabbat [sah•BAH] *n* M
Sabbath

sable [sahbl] *n* M sand; gravel;
~ mouvants\ quicksand; *adj*
sablé

sablier [sah•BLYEH] *n*
hourglass

sabot [sah•BO] *n* M hoof;
wooden shoe; skid

sabotage [sah•bau•TAHZH] *n*
M sabotage *vt* saboter

sabots [sah•BO] *npl* M clogs

sac [sahk] *n* M bag; ~ à dos *n*
M backpack; knapsack; ~ à
main\ handbag; pocketbook;
purse

saccade [sah•KAHD] *n* F jerk;
jolt; fit; *adj* saccadé

sacerdoce [sah•ser•DAUS] *n* M
priesthood

sacré [sah•KRAI] *adj* sacred;
holy; consecrated

sacrement [sah•kru•MAHπ] *n*
M sacrament

sacrifice [sah•kree•FEES] *n*
sacrifice; *vt* sacrifier

sacristie [sah•kree•STEE] *n* F
vestry; sacristy

sadiste [sah•DEEST] *adj*
sadistic

safran [sah•FRAHπ] *n* M
saffron

sage [sahzh] *adj* sage; prudent;
wise *n* F sauge; ~-femme\
midwife

sagesse [sah•ZHEHS] *n* M
wisdom; goodness

saigner [se•NYAI] *vi vt* bleed

sain; -e [saπ]; [san] *adj*
wholesome; sound; healthy;
sane

saindoux [seπ•DOO] *n* lard

saint [saπ] *adj* holy; saintly *n* M
saint; ~ sanctifié *adj*\ hallowed

sainteté [saπ•tu•TAI] *n* F
holiness; sanctity

saisir [se•ZEER] *vt* grab; seize

saison [se•ZAUπ] *n* F season

saisonnier [se•zu•NYAI] *adj*
seasonal

salade [sah•LAHD] *n* F salad

saladier [sah•lah•DYAI] *n* M
salad bowl

salaire [sah•LEHR] *vt* M wages;
pay; salary; reward;
retribution

sale [sahl] *adj* filthy; grubby;
dirty; unclean

salé [sah•LAI] *adj* salty

saleté [sahl•TAI] *n* F dirt; filth

salive [sah•LEEV] *n* F saliva

salle [sahl] *n* F room; salon;
(hospital) ward; house; ~ à
manger\ dining room; ~
d'attente\ waiting-room; ~ de

bains\ bathroom; ~de classe\
classroom

salon [sah•LAUπ] *n* M parlor;
salon; sitting room; ~
d'essayage\ fitting room

salope [sah•LAUP] *n* F bitch

salopette [sah•lau•PET] *n* F
overalls

saluer [sah•lew•EH] *vt* greet;
salute; bow

salut 1 [sah•LEW] *n* M
salvation; safety; welfare

salut 2 [sah•LEW] *n* salute; *vt*
saluer

salutaire [sah•lew•TEHR] *adj*
beneficial; healthful

salutation
[sah•lew•tah•SYAUπ] *n* F
greeting

salve [sahl•VU] *n* F volley

samedi [sahm•DEE] *n* M
Saturday

sanction [sahπk•SYAUπ] *n* F
sanction; *vt* sanctionner

sandale [sahπ•DAHL] *n* F
sandal

sandwich [sahπ•dweesh] *n* M
sandwich

sang [sahπ] *n* M blood

sang-froid [sahπ•frwah] *n* M
composure; *adj* cold-blooded

sanglant [sahπ•GLAHπ] *adj*
bloody; gory

sanglier [saπ•glee•AI] *n* M boar

sanglot [sahng•GLO] *n* M sob;
vi sangloter

sangsue [sahπ•SEW] *n* F leech

sanitaire [sah•nee•tehr] *adj*
sanitary

sans [sahπ] *prep* without; free
from

santé 1 [sahπ•TAI] *excl* cheers

santé 2 [sahπ•TAI] *n* F health; ~ mentale\ sanity

saper [sah•PEH] *vt* undermine

saphir [sah•FEER] *n* M sapphire

sapin [sah•PAπ] *n* M fir

sarcastique [sahr•kah•STEEK] *adj* sarcastic

sarcelle [sahr•SEHL] *n* F teal

sarcler [sahr•KLEH] *vt* weed

Sardaigne [sahr•de•NYU] *n* F Sardinia

sardine [sahr•DEEN] *n* F sardine

Satan [sah•TAHπ] *n* M Satan

satellite [sah•tu•LEET] *n* M satellite

satin [sah•TAπ] *n* M satin

satire [sah•TEER] *n* F lampoon; satire

satisfaction [sah•TEES•fahk•SYAUπ] *n* F gratification; satisfaction

satisfaire [sah•tees•FEHR] *vt* indulge; satisfy

satisfaisant [sah•tees•fe•ZAHπ] *adj* satisfactory

satisfait [sah•tees•FEH] *adj* satisfied; ~ de soi\ self-righteous

saturer [sah•tew•rai] *vt* saturate

sauce [sos] *n* F sauce

saucisse [so•SEES] *n* F sausage

sauf [sof] *prep conj* except; *adj* safe; unhurt; unscathed

saule [saul] *n* M willow

saumon [so•MAUπ] *n* M salmon

sauna [so•NAH] *n* M sauna; steam bath

saut [so] *n* M jump; leap; spring; vault; omission; somersault

sauter [so•TAI] *vi* jump; leap bound; blow up; explode; ~ aux yeux\ be obvious; self-evident

sauterelle [so•te•REL] *n* F grasshopper

sauvage [so•VAHZ] *adj* wild; savage; wild; untamed

sauvegarde [sov•GAHRD] *n* safeguard; *vt* sauvegarder

sauver 1 [so•VEH] *vt* salvage; rescue; help; save

sauver 2 [so•VEH] *n* M savior;

sauver 3 [so•VEH] *n* F zest; flavor; savor

savoir [sah•VWAHR] *n* M learning; *vt* know

savoir-faire *n* M know-how

savon 1 [sah•VAUπ] *n* M soap

savon 2 [sah•VAUπ] *n* M rebuke

savourer [sah•voo•REH] *vt* savor

savoureux -euse [sah•voor•Ø]; [-ØZ] *adj* tasty

saxaphone [sahk•sah•FAUN] *n* M saxaphone

scalpel [skahl•PEL] *n* M scalpel

scalper [skahl•PEH] *vt* scalp

scandale [skahπ•DAHL] *n* M scandal

scandaleux [skahπ•dah•LØ] *adj* outrageous; shocking

scandaliser [skahn•DAH•lee•ZAI] *vt* scandalize

scandinave [skahπ•dee•NAHV] *adj* Scandinavian; *n* MF (gens) Scandinave Scandinavie [skahπ•DEE•nah•VEE] *n* F Scandinavia

scarabée [skah•rah•BAI] *n* M beetle

scénario [sai•nah•RYAU] *n* M scenario; script

scenteur [sahπ•TœR] *n* scent; perfume

sceptique [sep•TEEK] *n* MF skeptic; *adj* skeptical

schisme [skeezm] *n* M schism; rift

scie [see] *n* F saw; *vt* scier ~ à métaux\ hacksaw

science [see•AHπS] *n* F science

scientifique [syahπ•tee•FEEK] *adj* scientific; *n* MF scientist

scintillement [saπ•teey•MAHπ] *n* M glitter; *vi* scintiller

sciure [syewr] *n* F sawdust

scolaire [skau•LEHR] *adj* scholastic; anée ~\ school year

scone [skaun] *n* M scone

score [skaur] *n* score

scorpion [skaur•PYAUπ] *n* M scorpion

scrupule [skrew•PEWL] *n* M scruple

scruter [skrew•TEH] *vt* scrutinize; scan

scrutin [skrew•TEπ] *n* M ballot; vote

sculpter [skewlp•TEH] *vt vi* sculpt

sculpteur [skewlp•TœR] *n* M sculptor

sculpture [skewlp•TEWR] *n* F sculpture

se [suh] *refl pron* himself; herself; itself; oneself; *pl* themselves; each other; one another

séance [sai•AHπS] *n* M sitting; seat; session; séance

seau [so] *n* M bucket; pail

sec sèche [sek sesh] *adj* dried; dry

sécession [sai•se•SYAUπ] *n* F secession

sécheresse [saish•res] *n* drought

séchoir [sai•SHWAHR] *n* M dryer

secondaire [se•kauπ•DEHR] *adj* secondary

secouer [se•koo•EH] *vt* jiggle

secours [su•KUR] *n* M help; rescue; au ~!\ help!

secourir [suh•koo•REEUR] *vt* succor; give aid

secousse [se•koos] *n* F jolt, bump, shock

secourer [se•koo•REH] *vt* shake

secret [se•KREH] *adj* classified; secret; *n* M secrecy; secret

secrétaire [se•krai•TEHR] *n* MF secretary

sécréter [sai•krai•TEH] *v* secrete; hide

sécrétion [sai•krai•SYAUπ] *n* F secretion

sectaire [sek•TEHR] *adj* MF bigot

secte [sekt] *n* F sect

secteur [sek•TœR] *n* M sector

section [sek•SYAUπ] *vt*
section; segment; *vt*
sectionner

séculier [sai•kew•LYAI] *adj*
secular

sécurité [sai•KEW•ree•TAI] *n* F
safety; security

sédatif [sai•dah•TEEF] *n* M
sedative

sédiment [sai•dee•MAHπ] *n* M
sediment

séduction [sai•dewk•SYAUπ] *n*
F seduction

séduire [sai•DWEER] *vt* seduce

séduisant [sai•dwee•SAHπ] *adj*
glamorous; seductive;
tempting

seigle [segl] *n* M rye

seigneur [se•NYœR] *n* M lord;
le Seigneur

sein [seπ] *n* M bosom; breast

seize [sez] *num* sixteen

séjour [seh•ZHUR] *n* M
sojourn; trip; journey

sel [sel] *n* M salt; *vt* saler

sélectif [sai•lek•TEEF] *adj*
selective

sélection [sai•lek•SYAUπ].*n* F
selection

selle [sel] *n* F saddle; stool;
evacuation; *vt* (horse) seller

selon [se•LOπ] *prép* according;
~ que\ as

semaine [suh•MAN] *n* F week;
week's pay

semblable [sahπ•BLAHBL] *adj*
similar; resembling; *n* M
match; equal

semblant [sahπ•BLAHπ] *n*
semblance; resemblance

sembler [sahπ•BLEH] *vi* seem;
appear

semestre [se•MESTR] *n* M
semester

séminaire [sai•mee•NEHR] *n*
M seminary; seminar

semis [se•MEE] *n* F seedling

sénat [sai•NAH] *n* senate

sénateur [sai•nah•TœR] *n* M
senator

sénile [sai•NEEL] *adj* senile;
elderly

sens 1 [sahπs] *n* M sense;
feeling; sentiment; meaning; ~
dessus dessous\ topsy-turvy
M; avoir un ~\ make sense;
dans un ~\ in a sense

sens 2 [sahns] *n* drift (neige)

sensation [sahπ•sah•SYAUπ] *n*
F sensation; feeling

sensible [sahπ•SEEBL] *adj*
sensitive; sensible

sensuel [sahπ•sew•el] *adj*
sensual; voluptuous

sentier [sahn•TYEH] *n* M
footpath; trail; suivre le ~\
follow the trail

sentiment léger (de cupabilité)
[sahπ•tee•MAHπ leh•ZHEH]
n comp M twinge

sentiment [sahπ•tee•MAHπ] *n*
M sentiment; feeling

sentimental
[sahπ•tee•mahπ•TAHL] *adj*
sentimental

sentinelle [sahπ•tee•NEL] *n* F
sentry

séparation
[sai•pah•rah•SYAUπ] *n* F
parting; separation

séparé [sai•pah•RAI] *adj* estranged; separated; segregated; *vt* séparer; *vi* se séparer séparément [sai•pah•rai•MAHπ] *adv* separately

sept [set] *num* seven

septembre [sep•TAHπBR] *n* M September

septième [seh•TYEM] *num* seventh

septique [sep•TEEK] *adj* septic

sépulcre [sai•PEWLKR] *n* M sepulcher; grave; tomb

serein [se•RAπ] *adj* serene; peaceful

sergent [ser•ZHAHπ] *n* sergeant

série [sai•REE] *n* F series; break; succession; sequence

sérieusement [sai•ryØz•MAHπ] *adv* seriously

sérieux [sai•RYØ] *adj* serious; grave; earnest

seringue [seh•RAπG] *n* F syringe

serment [ser•MAHπ] *n* oath; sous ~\ under oath

sermon [ser•MAUπ] *n* M sermon

serpent [ser•PAHπ] *n* M serpent; ~ à sonnettes\ rattlesnake

serre [ser] *n* F greenhouse

serrer [se•REH] *vt* clench; squeeze; tighten

serrure [se•REWR] *n* lock; keyhole

sérum [sai•RœN] *n* serum

serveur; -euse [sehr•VœR]; [-VØZ] *n* MF waiter; waitress

service [ser•VEES] *n* service

serviette 1 [ser•VYET] *n* F briefcase

serviette 2 [ser•VYET] *n* F napkin; ~ hygiénique\ sanitary napkin

servile [ser•VEEL] *adj* menial; slavish

seuil [sœy] *n* M threshold

seul [sul] *adj adv* alone; unique; single; *adv* seulement

sève [sev] *vt* F stength, life; *n* saper\ sap

sévère [sai•VEHR] *adj* stern; harsh; severe; grim

sevrer [seh•VREH] *vt* wean

sexe [seks] *n* M sex

sexiste [sek•SEEST] *n* MF sexist

sexuel [sek•sew•EL] *adj* sexual

sexy [sek•SEE] *adj* sexy

seyant [se•YAHπ] *adj* becoming

shampooing [shahn•poo•ANG] *n* M shampoo

shérif [shai•REEF] *n* M sheriff

si [see] *conj* if; si que; soit que [see]; [~ kuh]; [swah kuh] *conj* whether

SIDA [SEE•dah] *n* M AIDS

siècle [sye•KL] *n* M century

siège 1 [syezh] *n* M siege

siège 2 [syezh] *n* seat

siffler [see•FLEH] *vi* hiss; whistle

signal [see•NYAHL] *n* M cue; signal

signature [see•nyah•TEWR] *n* F signature

signe [see•NYU] *n* M sign; road sign; ~ de tête\ nod

significatif [see•NYEE•fee•kah•TEEF] *adj* significant; important

signifier [see•nyee•FYAI] *vt* signify

silence [see•LAHπS] *n* M silence; hush

silencieux [see•lahπ•SYØ] *n* M silencer; *adj* soundless; quiet silent

silex [see•LEKS] *n* M flint; *n* F (of lighter) pierre

silhouette [see•loo•ET] *n* F silhouette

simple [saπpl] *adj* mere; simple; ordinary

simplement [saπ•pl•MÁHπ] *adv* merely; simply

simplicité [saπ•PLEE•see•TAI] *n* F simplicity

simplifier [saπ•plee•FYAI] *vt* simplify

simuler [see•mew•LEH] *vt* simulate

simultané [see•mewl•tah•NAI] *adj* simultaneous; at once

sincère [saπ•SEHR] *adj* sincere; earnest

sincérité [saπ•sai•ree•TAI] *n* F sincerity

singe [saπzh] *n* M ape; monkey

singulier [saπ•gew•LYEH] *n* M singular

sinistre [see•NEESTR] *adj* sinister; evil; wicked; left

sinus [see•NEW] *n* M sinus

siphon [see•FAUπ] *n* siphon; *vt* siphonner

sirène [see•REN] *n* F mermaid; siren

sirop [see•RO] *n* M syrup

situation [se•twah•SYAUπ] *n* F situation; site; location; place; predicament

situé [see•TWAI] *adj* situated; placed; located

six [sees] *num* six

ski [skee] *n* M ski; skiing; *vt* faire du ski\ skier

skieur [skee•œR] *n* M skier

smoking [smau•KING] *n* M tuxedo; dinner jacket

snob [snaub] *adj* stuck-up

sobre [saubr] *adj* sober

sobrement [sau•bruh•MAHπ] *adv* soberly

sobriété [sau•breey•eh•TAI] *n* sobriety

sociable [sau•seey•AHBL] *adj* sociable

social -e [sau•SEEYAHL] *adj* social

socialisme [sau•seeyahl•EEZM] *n* M socialism

socialiste [sau•seeyahl•EEST] *adj n* MF socialist

société [sau•seeyai•TAI] *n* F society; company; corporation

sociologie [sau•SEEYAU•lau•JEE] *n* F sociology

sodium [sau•DEEYM] *n* M sodium

sœur [sœr] *n* F sister

sofa [sau•FAH] *n* M sofa

soie [swah] *n* silk; *adj* en ~

soif [swahf] *n* F thirst

soigné [swah•NYAI] *adj* painstaking

soigner [swah•NYEH] *vt; vi*
tend; care for; take care of;
attend to

soigneux [swah•NYU] *adj*
careful

soin [swahπ] *n* M care

soir [swahr] *n* M tonight; night;
evening

soirée [swah•RAI] *n* evening;
evening party

soixante [swah•SAHπT] *num*
sixty

soixante-dix
[swah•sahπt•DEES] *n* seventy

sol [saul] *n* ground; floor; soil

solaire [sau•LEHR] *adj* solar

soldat [saul•DAH] *n* M soldier;
trooper

solennel [sau•leh•NEHL] *adj*
solemn

solennité [sau•LEH•nee•TEH]
n F solemnity

solicitation
[sau•LEE•see•tah•SYAUπ] *n*
F solicitation

solidarité
[sau•LEE•dehr•ee•TAI] *n* F
solidarity

solide [sau•LEED] *adj* solid;
sturdy

soliloque [sau•lee•LAUK] *n* M
soliloquy

solitaire [sau•lee•TEHR] *adj*
lone; solitary; lonely

solitude [sau•lee•TEWD] *n* F
loneliness; seclusion; solitude

solliciter [sau•lee•see•TEH] *vt*
solicit

solliciteur [sau•lee•see•TœR] *n*
M solicitor

solo [sau•LAU] *n* M solo; alone

solstice [saul•STEES] *n* M
solstice

solution [sau•lew•SYAUπ] *n* F
solution

sombre [sauπbr] *adj* somber;
dark

someiller [sau•me•YAI] *vi*
doze; sleep; nap

sommeil [sau•MEHY] *n* M
sleep

sommet [sau•MEH] *n* M
hilltop; M de colline *n*\ hilltop

somnolent [saum•nau•LAHπ]
adj drowsy; somnolent

somptueux [sauπ•TWØ] *adj*
plush; lavish

son 1 [sauπ] *n* M bran

son 2 [sauπ] *n* M sound

Son Altesse *n* highness

son (sa) ses *pron poss* its

sonate [sau•NAHT] *n* F sonata

songeur [sauπ•ZHœR] *adj*
pensive

sonner [sau•NEH] *vt comp* toll;
ring

sonnet [sau•NEH] *n* M sonnet

sonore [sau•NAUR] *adj*
sonorous

sophistication
[sau•FEE•stee•kah•SYAUπ]
adj F sophistication

sophistiqué
[sau•FEE•stee•KAI] *adj*
sophisticated

soprano [sau•prah•NO] *n* MF
soprano; treble voice

sorcier [saur•SYEH] *n* M
wizard; sorcerer

sorcière [saur•SYEHR] *n* F
witch

sordide [saur•DEED] *adj*
sleazy; sordid; squalid

sortie [saur•TEE] *n* F outing; ~
de bain\ bathrobe; ~ de
secours\ emergency exit

sortie [saur•TEE] *n* exit; *vi*
sortir

sottises [sau•TEES] *npl* F
nonsense

souburbain [soo•byr•BAπ] *adj;*
n comp F suburban

souche [soosh] *n* F stump;
(d'un arbre)

souci [soo•SEE] *n* marigold

soucier (de) [soo•CYEH] *vi*
care (about)

soucieux [soo•SYØ] *adj*
mindful

soucoupe [soo•KOOP] *n* F
saucer; ~ volante\ flying
saucer

soudain [soo•DAπ] *adj* sudden

soudainement;
[soo•dan•MAHπ] *adv*
suddenly

soudaineté [soo•dan•TAI] *n* F
suddenness

soude [sood] *n* F soda

souder [soo•DEH] *vt* solder;
weld

soudoyer [soo•dwah•YEH] *vt*
M bribe

souffle [soofl] *n* M breath

souffrance [soo•FRAHπS] *n* F
suffering

souffrir [soo•FREEUR] *vt*
suffer

souhait [sooeh] *n* M wish

souhaiter [soo•eh•TEH] *vi*
wish

souiller [swee•YAI] *vt* defile;
deface; soil

soulager [soo•lah•ZHEH] *vt*
relieve; alleviation; solace;
unburden

soulèvement [soo•lehv•MAHπ]
n M upheaval; uprising; riot;
revolt

soulever [soo•lu•VEH] *vt* boost;
vi pry

soulever [sool•VEH] *vt* heave;
vi se soulever

souligner [soo•lee•NYEH] *vt*
underline

soumettre [soo•MEHTR] *vt*
submit

soumission [soo•mee•SYAUπ]
n F subjection; submission

soupçon [soop•SAUπ] *n* M
suspicion; little bit

soupe [soop] *n* F soup

soupir [soo•PEER] *n* sigh; *vi*
soupirer

soupirail [soo•pee•RAHY] *n* M
vent

source [surs] *n* F source; well

sourcil [soor•SEEL] *n* M
eyebrow

sourd [soor] *adj* deaf; dull;
insensitive; dead; hollow

souricière [soo•ree•SYEHR] *n*
F mousetrap

sourire [soo•REER] *n* grin;
smile; *vt* sourire

souris [soo•REE] *n* M mouse

sous [soo] *prép* under; under;
beneath; below; on upon;
~vêtements; lingerie;
underclothes

sous-bois [soo-BWAH] *n* M
underbrush

sous-comité
ſsoo•kau•mee•TAI] *n* M
subcommittee

sous-estimer
[sooz•eh•stee•MEH] *vt*
underestimate

sous-location
[soo-lau•kah•syauπ] *n* F sublet

sous-lwer [soo-lweh] *vt* sublet

sous-marin [soo-mah•RAπ] *n*
M submarine

sous-payer [soo-peh•YEH] *vt*
underpay

sous-sol [soo•SOL] *n* M
basement

souscrire (un risque)
[soo•SKREEUR] *vt*
underwrite

soussigné -e [soo•see•NYEH]
adj undersigned

sousterrain -ne [soo•tehr•Aπ]
[-AN] *adj; n* M subterranean

soustraction
[soo•strahk•SYAUπ] *n* F
subtraction

soustraire [soo•STREHR] *vt*
subtract

soutenable [sootn•AHBL] *adj*
tenable

soutenir [soot•NEEUR] *vt*
uphold; support; sustain;
endure; abet

soutien [soo•TYAHπ] *n* M
support; prop; stay; supporter

souvenir [soov•NEER] *n* M
keepsake; recollection;
souvenir

souvent [soo•VAHπ] *adv* often

souverain -e [soo•VRAπ] *n*
MF sovereign

Soviet [sau•VEEYEHT] *n* M
Soviet

spacieux -euse [spah•see•Ø];
[spah•see•ØZ] *adj* roomy;
spacious

spasme [spahzm] *n* M spasm

spécieux -euse [speh•SEEYØ]
[-ØZ]; *adj* specious

spécifier [speh•see•FEEYEH] *vt*
specify

spécifique [speh•see•FEEK] *adj*
specific

spécimen [speh•see•MEHN] *n*
M specimen

spéctacle [spehk•TAHKL] *n* M
spectacle; show; play

spectateur -trice
[spek•tah•TœR] *n* MF
onlooker; spectator

spéculation
[speh•KEW•lah•SYAUπ] *n* F
venture (business);
speculation

spéculer [speh•kew•LEH] *vi*
speculate; guess

sperme [sperm] *n* M semen

sphére [sfehr] *n* F sphere

sphérique [sfehr•EEK] *adj*
spherical

spinal [spee•AHL] *adj* spinal

spirale [ahπ speeur•AHL] *adj n*
F spiral

spiritualité
[speeur•EE•tew•AH•lee•TEH]
n F spirituality

spirituel [speeur•EE•tew•EL]
adj spiritual; religious;
intellectual; witty

spiritueux [spee•REE•tew•Ø]*n*
M liquor; spirits

splendeur [splahπ•DœR] *n* F
grandeur; splendor

splendide [splehn•DEED] *adj*
splendid; marvelous;
wonderful

spontané [spauπ•tah•NAI] *adj*
spontaneous

spontanéité
[spauπ•TAH•nehyee•TAI] *n* F
spontaneity

sport [spaur] *n* M sport; sports
fan

sportif -ive [spaur•TEEF];
[-TEEV] *adj* sportsman

sprint [spreeπ] *n* M sprint
(sport)

squellette [ske•LET] *n* M
skeleton

stabiliser [stah•BEE•lee•ZEH]
vt stabilize

stabilité [stah•BEEIL•ee•TAI] *n*
F stability; steadiness

stade [stahd] *n* M stadium;
stage

stagnant [stah•NYAHπT] *adj*
stagnant; still; stale

standard [stahπ•DAHR] *n* M
switchboard; *adj* standard

standardiste
[stahπ•dahr•DEEST] *n* MF
telephone operator

starter [stahr•TEEH] *n* M choke
(of car)

stationnaire
[stah•SEEY•au•NEHR] *adj*
stationary; static

stationnement
[stah•syaun•MAHπ] *n* M
parking

statistique [stah•tee•STEEK] *n*
F statistics

statuaire [stah•tew•EHR] *n* F
statuary

statue [stah•TEW] *n* F statue;
sculpture

statut [stah•TEW] *n* M statute
(loi)

stencil [sten•SEEIL] *n* M stencil

sténographe
[steh•nau•GRAHF] *n* MF
stenographer

sténographie
[stai•nau•grah•FEE] *n* F
shorthand; stenography

stéréo [stair•ai•AU] *n* M stereo

stéréotype [stair•AI•au•TEEP]
n M stereotype

stérile [stair•EEIL] *adj* sterile;
barren

stériliser [stair•EEIL•ee•ZEH]
vt sterilize

stérilité [stair•EEIL•ee•TAI] *n* F
sterility; barrenness

sterling [stehr•LING] *n* M
sterling

stéthoscope [stai•taus•KAUP]
n M stethoscope

steward [stew•UHD] *n* M
steward (avion)

stimulant [stee•mew•LAHπ] *n*
M stimulant

stimulation
[stee•MEW•lah•SYAUπ] *n* F
stimulation

stimuler [stee•mew•LEH] *vt*
stimulate

stimulus [stee•mew•LEWS] *n*
M stimulus

stipuler [stee•pew•LEH] *vt*
stipulate; proscribe; specify;
contract

stockage [stauk•AHZH] *n* M
storage

stoïcisme [stau•ee•SEEZM] *n*
M stoicism

stoïque [stau•EEK] *adj* stoic

store [staur] *n* M window shade

strangulation
[strahπ•GEW•lah•SYAUπ] *n*
F strangulation

stratagème [strah•tah•ZHEM]
n M ploy

stratégie [strah•teh•ZHEE] *n* F
strategy

stratégique [strah•teh•ZHEEK]
adj strategic

stratosphère [strah•taus•FEHR]
n F stratosphere

stress [strehs] *n* MF stress;
tension

strict [strikt] *adj* strict

strident [stree•DAHπ] *adj*
strident; loud; grating; jarring;
shrill

strophe [strauf] *n* F stanza;
verse

structural [strewk•tew•RAHL]
adj structural

structure [strewk•TYR] *n* F
structure

stuc [stewk] *n* M stucco

stupéfier [stew•pai•fee•EH] *vt*
amaze; astonish; stupefy

stupeur [stew•PœR] *n* F stupor

stupide [stew•PEED] *adj*
stupid; dull; dim-witted;
fatuous

style [steeil] *n* M style; ~ de
vie\ lifestyle

stylo [stee•LAU] *n* pen;
fountain pen; ~ à bille\
ballpoint pen

subalterne [sewb•ahl•TEHRN]
adj (inv); *n* MF subordinate;
subaltern

subconscient
[sewb•kauπ•SYAHπ] *n* M
subconscious

subdivision
[sewb•dee•vee•ZYAUπ] *n* F
subdivision

subir [sew•BEEUR] *vt* undergo;
subject

subjectif -ive
[sewb•jehk•TEEF] [-TEEV]
adj subjective

subjonctif (mode)
[sewb•zhauπk•TEEF] *n* M
subjunctive

sublime [sew•BLEEM] *adj n* M
sublime; delightful

submerger [sewb•mehr•ZHEH]
vt submerge

subsister [sewb•see•STEH] *vi*
subsist

substance [sewb•STAHNS] *n* F
substance; ~ fluide\ slop; ~
visqueuse\ slime

substantiel
[sewb•stahπ•SEEYEHL] *adj*
substantial

substantif [sewb•stahπ•TEEF]
adj substantive

subtil [sewb•TEEIL] *adj* subtle;
shrewd; cunning

subvention
[sewb•vahπ•SYAUπ] *n* F
grant; subsidy

subventionner
[sewb•VAHπ•syau•NEH] *vt*
subsidize

subversif -ive
[sewb•vehr•SEEF] [-seev] *adj*
subversive

succès [sewk•SEH] *n* M success

succession [sewk•seh•SYAUπ] *n* F succession

succion [sewk•SYAUπ] *n* F suction

succomber [sew•kauπ•BEH] *vi* succumb

succulent [sew•kew•LAHπ] *adj* succulent; luscious; tasty

sucer [sew•SEH] *vt* suck; absorb; draw

sucette [sew•SET] *n* F lollipop

sucre [sewkr] *n* M sugar

sucré [sew•KRAI] *adj* sweet

sucrer [sew•KREH] *vt* sweeten; sugar

sucrier [sew•kree•YEH] *n* M sugar bowl

sud [sewd] *n* M south

sud-est [sewd-EHST] *n* M southeast

sud-ouest [sewd-WEST] *n* M southwest

Suède [swehd] *n* F Sweden

Suédois -se [sweh•DWAH]; [-dwahz] *n* MF Swede

suédois -se [sweh•DWAH]; [-dwahz] *adj* Swedish

sueur; suer [sew•œR]; [sew•EH] *n; vi* F sweat

suffice [sew•FEES] suffice; *vi* suffire

suffisance [sew•fee•SAHπS] *n* F sufficiency

suffisant [sew•fee•SAHπ] *adj* M adequate; sufficient

suffocation [sew•FAU•kah•SYAUπ] *n* F suffocation

suffoquer [sew•fau•KEH] *vt; vi* suffocate

suffrage [sew•FRAHZH] *n* M suffrage

suggérer [sewg•zhehr•EH] *vt* suggest; imply

suggestif -tive [sewg•zhehs•TEEF] [-TEEV] *adj* suggestive

suggestion [sewg•zhehs•TYAUπ] *n* F suggestion

suicide [swee•SEED] *n* M suicide

suie [swee] *n* F soot; tallow

suinter [swaπ•TEH] *vi* seep; ooze

Suisse [swees] *adj; n* MF Swiss; *n* F Switzerland

suite 1 [sweet] *n* F succession; following; pursuite; sequence; tout de ~\ at once; donner ~ à\ follow up en ~\ following

suite 2 [sweet] *n* F retinue; followers

suivant [swee•VAHπ] *adj* ensuing; following; proceeding

suivre [sweevr] *vt vi* follow

sujet [sew•ZHEH] *n* M subject; topic

superficiel [sew•PEHR•fee•SYEHL] *adj* superficial; skin-deep (coll)

supériorité [sew•PEH•ryaur•ee•TAI] *n* F vantage; advantage

supplémentaire [sew•PLAI•mahπ•TEHR] *adj* extra; spare

supplication [sew•PLEE•kah•SYAUπ] *n* plea; supplication

support [sew•PAUR] *n* support;
prop; holder

supposer [sew•pau•ZEH] *vt*
reckon; assume; suppose

supprimer [sew•pree•MEH] *vt*
delete

sur 1 [sewr] *prép* upon; on;
onto; above

sur 2 [sewr] *adj* sour; tart

sûr [sewr] *adj* sure; certain;
safe; secure; confident

sûreté [sew•reh•TAI] *n* F
safety; security; guarantee

surgir [sewr•ZHEER] *vt* rise;
surge

surmener [sewr•mu•NEH] *vt*
overwork

surmonter [sewr•mauπ•TEH] *vt*
overcome; surmount

surnom [sewr•NAUπ] *n*
nickname; *vt* surnommer

surpasser [sewr•pa•SEH] *vt*
surpass; overtake; excel; ~ en
nombre\ outnumber

surplus [sewr•PLEW] *n* M glut;
surplus

surréserver [sewr•rai•zer•VEH]
vt overbook

surtout [sewr•TOO] *adv*
mostly; espcially; chiefly

surveillant -e [syr•vehy•AHπ]
n MF timekeeper; surveyor

surveiller [sewr•ve•YEH] *vt*
oversee; watch

survie [syr•VEE] *n* F survival

survivant [syr•vee•VAHπ] *n*
MF survivor

survivre [syr•VEEVR] *vi*
survive; outlive

susceptibilité
[sew•SEP•tee•BEE•lee•TAI] *n*

F sensibilities; sensitivities;
susceptibilities

suspendre [sew•SPAHπDR] *vt*
suspend; hang

suspens [sews•PAHπ] *n* MF
suspense

sycomore (arbre)
[see•kau•MAUR] *n* M
sycamore

syllabe [see•LAHB] *n* F
syllable

syllogisme [see•lau•ZHEEZM]
n M syllogism

symbole [saπ•BAUL] *n* M
symbol

symbolique [saπ•bau•LEEK]
adj symbolic

symétrique [see•meh•TREEK]
adj symmetrical

symphonie [saπ•fau•NEE] *n* F
symphony

symptomatique
[saπp•TAU•mah•TEEK] *adj*
symptomatic

symptôme [saπp•TOM] *n* M
symptom

synagogue [see•nah•GAUG] *n*
F synagogue

synchroniser
[saπ•KRAU•nee•ZEH] *vt*
synchronize

syndic [saπ•DEEK] *n* MF
trustee

syndicat [saπ•dee•KAH] *n* M
labor union; syndicate; ~
ouvriert\ trade-union

synonyme [see•nau•NEEM] *n*
M synonym; *adj* synonymous

syntaxe [saπ•TAHKS] *n* F
syntax

synthèse [saπ•TEHZ] *n* F
synthesis
Syrie [see•REE] *n* F Syria
Syrien -nne [see•reey•Aπ];
[see•reey•EHN] *adj; n* MF
Syrian

systématique
[see•STEH•mah•TEEK] *adj*
systematic
systeme [see•STEHM] *n* M
system

T

tabac [tàh•BAH] *n* M tobacco;
~ à priser\ snuff
tabasser [tah•bah•SEH] *vt* beat
up
table [tahbl] *n* F table; ~
d'opération\ operating table; ~
de jeu\ card table
tableau [tah•BLO] *n* M picture;
painting; scene; sigh; board;
blackboard; bulletin board; ~
de bord\ dash (auto)
tabouret [tah•bu•REH] *n* M
stool
tabulaire [tah•bew•LEHR] *adj*
tabular
tache [tahsh] *n* F stain; ~ de
vin\ birthmark
tâche [tahsh] *n* F task; job
tachéomètre
[tah•KEH•au•MEHTR] *n* M
tachometer
tacheté [tahsh•TAI] *adj* spotted
tacite [tah•SEET] *adj* tacit;
quiet
taciturne [tah•see•TOORN] *adj*
taciturn
tact [takt] *n* MF tact
tactile [tahk•TEEIL] *adj* tactile

tactique [tahk•TEEK] *adj* M
tactical; *n* F tactics
taffetas [tahf•TAH] *n* M taffeta
taie f d'oreiller *n* pillowcase
taille [tahy] *n* F cutting; paring;
trimming; cut; shape; tally;
waist; figure; size; measure; ~
-crayons\ pencil sharpener
tailler [tai•YEH] *vt; vi* cut;
prune; trim; hack; whittle
tailleur [tahy•œR] *n* M tailor
talc [tahlk] *n* M talcum
talent; [tah•LAHπ] *n* M talent
tambour [tahπ•BOOR] *n* M
drummer; *vt vi* tambouriner
tamisser [tah•mee•SEH] *vt* sift
tampon [tahπ•PAUπ] *n* M
swab; stopper; plug; *vt*
tamponner
tandem [tahπ•DEHM] *n* M
tandem
tandis [tahπ•DEE] *adv*
meanwhile; ~ que *conj*
whereas
Tanger [tahπ•ZHEH] *n* M
Tangiers
tangeute [tahπ•GWET] *n* F
tangent

tangible [tahπ•ZHEEBL] *adj inv* tangible

tannerie [tah•nehr•EE] *n* F tannery

tantaliser [tahπ•TAH•lee•ZEH] *vt* tantalize; tempt; tease

tante [tahπt] *n* F aunt

tapageur [tah•pah•ZHœR] *adj* flashy

taper légèrement [tah•PEH leh•zhehr•MAHπ] *vt; vi* tap

tapioca [tah•pyau•KAH] *n* M tapioca

tapis [tah•PEE] *n* M carpet; rug; ~ roulant\ conveyer belt

tapisserie [tah•pees•REE] *n* F tapestry; ~ d'ameublement *n* F upholstery

tapoter [tah•pau•TEH] *vt; vi* tap

taquiner [tah•kee•NEH] *vt* tease; tempt

tarder [tahr•DEH] *vi* tarry; loiter; delay

tardif [tahr•DEEF] *adj* belated; late; tardy sluggish; backward

tarif [tah•reef] *n* M tariff; price

tarte [tahrt] *n* F tart

tartre [tahrtr] *n* M tartar

tas [tah] *n* heap; pile *vt* entasser

tasse [tahs] *n* F cup; mug; ~ à thé\ teacup; ~ de thé\ cup of tea

tâtonner [tah•tau•NEH] *vi* grope

tatouage [tah•TWAHZH] *n* M tattoo

tatouer [tah•TWEH] *vt* tattoo

taudis [to•DEE] *n* M hovel; slum

taureau [tau•RO] *n* M bull

taux [to] *n* M rate; fixed; rate; ~ de natalité\ birthrate

taverne [tah•VEHRN] *n* F tavern; bar; pub

taxe [tahks] *n* M tax; duty; rate; charge; - supplémentaire\ late fee

taxi [tahk•SEE] *n* M cab; taxi

Tchécoslovakie [chai•KAU•slau•va•KEE] *n* F Czechoslovakia

tchèque [chek] *n* M Tchèque *adj* Czech

te [tuh] *pers pron* you; to you

technicien -enne [tehk•nee•SYAπ] [-SYΛN] *n* MF technician

technique [tehk•NEEK] *adj* technical

teckel [te•KEL] *n* M dachsund

teint [taπ] *n* M complexion; color; tint

teinte [taπt] *n* F hue; tinge

teinter [taπ•TEH] *n; vt* F tint

teinture [taπ•TYR] *n* F tincture; dye

tel -le ; tellement; tant [tehl]; [tehl•MAHπ]; [tahπ] *adj; adv* such

télécommande [teh•LAI•kau•MAHπD] *n* F remote control

télégramme [teh•lai•GRAHM] *n* M telegram

télégraphe [teh•lai•GRAHF] *n* M telegraph

téléphone [tai•lai•FAUN] *n* phone; telephone; *vt* téléphoner à; *vi* téléphoner; ~ public\ pay phone

téléphoniste [tai•lai•faun•eest]
n MF telephone operator

téléscope [teh•lai•SKAUP] *n* M
telescope

téléviser [teh•lai•vee•ZEH] *vt*
televise

télévision [teh•lai•vee•ZYAUπ]
n F television; ~ en couleurs\
color television

témérité [teh•MAI•ree•TAI] *n*
F temerity

témoignage [tai•mwah•NAZH]
n M testimony

témoigner de
[tai•mwah•NYEH] *vi* vouch;
testify

témoin [tai•MWAHπ] *n* M
witness; ~ oculaire eye\
witness

tempe [tahπp] *n* F temple
(anat)

tempérament
[tahπ•PAI•rah•MAHπ] *n* M
disposition; temperament;
temper

température
[tahπ•PAI•rah•TYR] *n* F
temperature

tempête [tahπ•PEHT] *n* F
tempest; ~ de neige\ blizzard

tempêter [tahπ•pe•TAI] *vi* rant;
rave

temple [tahπpl] *n* M temple

temporel -le [tahπ•pau•REHL]
adj temporal

temps [tahπ] *n* M weather;
time; duration; period; au ~
jadis\ yore

tenace [teh•NAHS] *adj*
tenacious

ténacité [tai•NAH•see•TAI] *n* F
tenacity

tendance [tahπ•DAHπS] *n* F
tendency; trend

tendon [tahπ•DAUπ] *n* M
tendon

tendre [tahπdr] *vi* tend; stretch
(ses affaires); *adj* tender

tendresse [tahπ•DREHS] *n* F
tenderness

tendu -e [tahπ•DEW] *adj* tense

ténébreux [tai•nai•BRØ] *adj*
murky

tenir [teh•NEER] *vi* have; hold;
possess; seize; grasp; occupy;
take up; keep ~ tête à\ to
resist; ~ de la place\ take up
room

tennis [teh•NEES] *n* M tennis

ténor [tai•NAUR] *n* M tenor

tension [tahπ•SYAUπ] *n* F
strain; stress

tentant [teπ•TAUπ]] *adj*
inviting

tentation [tahπ•tah•SYAUπ] *n*
F temptation

tentative [tahπ•tu•TEEV] *n*
endeavor

tente [tahπt] *n* F tent

tenter [tahπ•TEH] *vt* tempt;
attempt

ténu [tai•NEW] *adj* tenuous

térébenthine
[tai•RAI•bahπ•TEEN] *n* F
turpentine

terme [tehrm]; *n* MF term

terminal [tehr•mee•NAHL] *adj*
n M terminal

terminer [tehr•mee•NEH] *vt*
terminate

ternir [tehr•NEEUR] *vt* tarnish

terrain [teh•RAπ] *n* M terrain

terrasse [teh•RAHS] *n* F terrace

terre [ter] *n* F earth; country; land

terrestre [teh•REHSTR] *adj* terrestrial; worldly; sophisticated

terreur [tehr•œR] *n* F terror

terrible [tehr•EEBL] *adj* terrible

terrier [te•RYER] *n* M burrow

terrifier [tehr•ee•fee•YEH] *vt* terrify

territoire [tehr•ee•TWAHR] *n* M territory

terroriser [tehr•AU•ree•ZEH] *vt* terrorize

tertre [tertr] *n* M mound

testament [teh•stah•MAHπ] *n* M testament; will

tétanos [tai•tah•NAUS] *n* M tetanus

têtard [te•TAHR] *n* M tadpole

tête [tet] *n* head; head-piece; carnium; leader; head of an establishment

têtu [te•TEW] *adj* headstrong; pig-headed; stubborn

texte [tehkst] *n* M text

textile [tehks•TEEIL] *n* M textile

texture [tek•STYR] *n* F texture

thé [tai] *n* M tea; tea party

théâtral [tai•ah•TRAHL] *adj* theatrical

théâtre [tai•AHTR] *n* M theater

théière [tai•YEHR] *n* F teapot

thème [tehm] *n* M theme

théologie [tai•AU•lau•ZHEE] *n* F theology

théorème [tai•au•REHM] *n* M theorem

théorie [tai•au•REE] *n* F theory

théorique [tai•au•REEK] *adj* theoretical

thérapeutique [tehr•AH•pew•TEEK] *adj* therapeutic

thermal [tehr•MAHL] *adj* thermal

thermomètre [tehr•mo•MEHTR] *n* M thermometer

thermostat [tehr•mo•STAH] *n* M thermostat

thèse [tehz] *n* F thesis

thon [tauπ] *n* M tuna

thym [taπ] *n* M thyme

tibia [tee•BYAH] *n* M shin; tibia

tiède [tyed] *adj* lukewarm; tepid

tige [teezh] *n* F stem; talk

tigre [teegr] *n* M tiger

tigresse [tee•GREHS] *n* F tigress

timide [tee•MEED] *adj* self-conscious; bashful; shy; timid

timoré [tee•maur•AI] *adj* timorous

timpani [teem•pah•NEE] *n* tympani

tinter [taπ•TEH] *vi* tinkle

tique [teek] *n* F tick (insect)

tiraillement [tee•rahy•MAHπ] *n* M pang

tire-bouchon m [teer-] *n* corksrew

tirelire [teer•LEER] *n* F piggybank

tirer [teeur•EH] *vt vi* tug; pull; tow; ~ brusquement\ yank

tiroir [tee•RWAHR] *n* M drawer

tisser [tee•SHE] *vt* weave

tissu [tee•SEW] *n* M fabric; web; tissue; cloth

titre [teetr] *n* M title; heading

tituber [tee•tew•BEH] *vi* totter; wobble; be unsteady

toboggan [to•bau•GHAπ] *n* M sled; toboggan; slide

toile [twahl] *n* F canvas; web; ~ à sangles\ webbing; ~ d'araignée\ cobweb

toilette [twah•LEHT] *n* F washing; dressing; dressing table; faire sa ~\ groom oneself

toilettes [twah•LEHT] *npl* toilet; lavatory

toison [twah•ZAUπ] *n* F fleece

toit [twah] *n* M roof

tolérable [tau•lehr•AHBL] *adj* tolerable

tolérance [tau•lehr•AHπS] *n* F tolerance

tolérant [tau•lehr•AHπ] *adj* tolerant

tolérer [tau•lair•EH] *vt* tolerate

tolérer excuser [tau•lai•RAI] *vt* condone

tollé [tau•LAI] *n* M outcry

tomate [tau•MAHT] *n* F tomato

tombe [tauπb] *n* M tomb; sepluchre

tombeau [tauπ•BO] *n* M tomb

tomber [tauπ•BEH] *vi* droop fall; sik; decay; ~ sur\ meet; ~ bien\ come at the right time; ~ mal\ to come at the wrong time; tombée du jour\ nightfall; laisser ~\ drop; throw down

tomperie [trauπ•pehr•EE] *n* F trickery; trumpery; cheap goods

ton [tauπ] *n* M tone; manner; style; ~ monocorde\ monotone

tondeuse [tauπ•DØZ] *n* f clippers; shears (elec) lawn mower

tondre; [tauπdr] *vt* mow; shear

tonic [tau•NEEK] *adj n* MF tonic

tonne [taun] *n* F ton

tonneau [tau•NO] *n* M cask; tun

tonnelet [taun•LEH] *n* keg

tonnerre [tau•NEHR] *n* M *vi* thunder

tonsure [tauπ•SYR] *n* F tonsure

topaze [tau•PAHZ] *n* F topaz

topographie [tau•PAU•grah•FEE] *n* F topography

torche [taursh] *n* F torch; flashlight; link; twist

torchon1 [taur•SHAUπ] *n* M wiper

torchon 2 [taur•SHAUπ]; *n* M towel

tordre [taurdr] *vt* wring; twist; *vt* wrench

tordu [taur•doo] *adj* wry

tornade [taur•NAHD] *n* F tornado

torpille [taur•PEEY] *n* F torpedo

torrent [tau•RAHπ] *n* M torrent; storm

torride [tau•REED] *adj inv* torrid; scorching

tortue [taur•TEW] *n* F tortoise; turtle

tortueux -euse [taur•TYØ] [-TYØZ] *adj* tortuous

tortueux -euse [taur•tew•Ø]; [-ØZ] *adj* winding

torture [taur•TYR] *n* F torture; *vt* torturer

total [tau•TAHL] *n* M total

totalement [tau•tahl•MAHπ]; *adv* totally; completely

totalitaire [tau•TAHL•ee•TEHR] *adj inv* totalitarian

totalité [tau•TAHL•ee•TEH] *n* F totality

toubillon [toor•bee•YAUNπ] *n* M whirlwind

touchant [too•SHAHπ] *adj* touching

toucher [too•SHEH] *vt vi n* M touch

touffe [toof] *n* F tuft (of wheat)

toujours [too•JOOR] *adv* always; ~ le même\ unchanging

toupet [too•PEH] *n* M gall

tour [tour] *n* M tower

tourbe [toorb] *n* F peat

tourbillon d'eau [toor•bee•auπ D'O] *n* M whirlpool

tourelle [toor•EHL] *n* F turret

tourisme [too•REEZM] *n* F sightseeing; *vt* faire du tourisme

touriste [toor•EEST] *n* MF tourist

tourment [toor•mahπ] *n* M torment

tourne-disque [toorn•DEESK] *n* M record player

tourner [toor•NEH] *vt* wind; turn

tournevis [toorn•VEE] *n* M screwdriver

tournoi [toor•NWAH] *n* M tournament

tournoyer [toor•nwah•YAI] *vi* gyrate; twirl; swirl; *vt* spin

tourte [toort] *n* F pie

toussoter [tou•sau•TEH] *vi* sputter

tout [too] *adj* -e -es; tous *adj* all; everything; ~ de suite; *adv* straightway; ~ éveillé\ wide awake; ~ le monde\ everybody; ~ neuf\ brand-new; ~ petit;\ tiny

tout ~ seul\ single-handed; alone; ~s les heures\ hourly

toux [too] *n* F cough; *vi* tousser

toxine [tauk•SEEN] *n* F toxin

toxique [tauk•SEEK] *adj inv* toxic; poisonous

tracasser [trah•kah•SEH] *vt* worry; bother

trace [trahs] *n* F *vt* trace

traceur [trah•SœR] *n* M tracer

trachée [trah•SHEH] *n* F trachea

tracteur [trahk•TœR] *n* M tractor

tradition [trah•dee•SYAUπ] *n* F tradition; custom

traditions [trah•dee•SYAUπ] *npl* F lore; folklore

traducteur -trice [trah•dewk•TœR] [-TREES] *n* MF translator

traduction [trah•dewk•SYAUπ] *n* F translation

traduire [trah•DWEEUR] *vt* translate

trafic [trah•FEEK] *n* MF traffic

tragédie [trah•zheh•DEE] *n* F
tragedy

tragique [trah•ZHEEK] *adj; n*
M tragic

trahir [trah•EER] *vt* betray;
double-cross

trahison [trah•ee•ZOπ] *n* M
betrayal; treason

train [traπ]; *n* M train; suite;
attendants; pace; rate; way
course; ~ de merchandises\
freight train; ~ d'atterrissage\
undercarriage; ~ voyageurs\
passenger train ; ~ express\
rapide\ express train

traineau [treh•no] *n* M sleigh

traînée [treh•NEH] *n* F streak

traîner [treh•NEH] *vi* loiter;
laze about; lug; linger; haul;
drag

trait [treh] *n* M pullig; arrow;
dart; stroke; streak; leash;
stretch; tout d'un ~\ at one
stretch

traite [treht] *n* M treaty;
compact; agreement; treatise

traitement [treht•MAHπ] *n* M
stipend; treatment

traiter [treh•TEH] *vt* transact

traître [tratr] *n* M betrayer

traître -tress [TREHTR]
[-TREHS] *adj n* MF
treacherous; dangerous; traitor

traîtrise [treh•TREEZ] *n* F
treachery

trajectoire
[trah•zhehk•TWAHR] *n* F
trajectory

tram [trahm] *n* M tram;
streetcar

tramway [trahm•WAI] *n* M
streetcar; tram

tranche [trahπsh] *n* F slice; en
~s\ in slices

tranchant [trahπ•SHAHπ] *adj*
sharp; trenchant

tranquille [trahπ•KEEIL]
adj tranquil; peaceful;
undisturbed

tranquillité
[trahπ•KEEIL•ee•TAI] *n* F
tranquillity

transaction
[trahπz•ahk•SYAUπ] *n* F
transaction

transcender [trahπ•sahπ•DEH]
vt transcend.

transcrire [trahπ•SKREEUR] *vt*
transcribe

transe [trahπs] *n* F trance

transept [trahπ•SEHPT] *n* M
transept

transfert [trahπs•FEHR] *n* MF
transfer; *vt* transférer;

transformateur
[trahπs•FAUR•mah•TœR] *n* M
transformer (elec)

transformation
[trahπs•FAUR•mah•SYAUπ]
n F transformation; change

transformer [trahπs•faur•MEH]
vt transform

transfusion
[trahπs•few•SYAUπ] *n* F
transfusion

transgresser [trahπs•greh•SEH]
vt transgress

transgression
[trahπs•greh•SYAUπ] *n* F
transgression

transir [trahπ•ZEER] *vt* chill;
paralyze

transit [trahπ•ZEET] *n* M
transit

transitif -ve [trahπ•see•TEEF]
[-TEEV] *adj* MF transitive

transition [trahπ•zee•SYAUπ]
n F transition

transitoire [trahπ•zee•TWAHR]
adj inv transient; transitory

translucide [trahπs•lew•SEED]
adj translucent

transmetteur
[trahπs•meh•TœR] *n* M
transmitter

transmettre [trahπs•MEHTR]
vt transmit; broadcast;
impart

transmission
[trahπs•mee•SYAUπ] *n* F
transmission

transparent -e
[trahπs•pah•RAHπ] [-RAHπT]
adj transparent

transpiration
[trahπs•PEEUR•ah•SYAUπ] *n*
F transpiration; perspiration

transpirer [trahπ•spee•REH] *vi*
perspire

transporté [trahπ•spaur•TAI]
adj elated; transported

transporter [trahπs•paur•TEH]
vt transport; waft

transposer [trahπs•pau•ZEH] *vt*
transpose

trapèze [trah•PEHZ] *n* M
trapeze

trappe [trahp] *n* F trap-door

trapu [trah•PEW] *adj* stocky;
husky

travail [trah•VAYH] *n* M work;
workmanship; job; labor; toil;
~ d'équippe\ teamwork

travailleur 1 [trah•vah•YœR]
adj hardworking

travailleur 2 -euse
[trah•vahy•ER]; [-ØZ] *n* MF
worker (office)

travaux [trah•VO] *n* M
chores

traversal -e
[trahπs•vehr•SAHL] *adj*
transverse

traverse [trah•VEHRS] *n* F
transom

traverser [trah•vehr•SEH] *vt*
traverse

trébucher [trai•bew•SHEH] *vi*
stumble

trèfle [trefl] *n* M clover;
shamrock; trefoil

treillage [trehy•AHZH] *n* M
trellis

treillis [tre•YEES] *n* lattice

treize [trehz] *npl adj* (inv) M
thirteen

treizième [treh•ZYHM] *adj n*
MF thirteenth

tremblant [trahπ•BLAHπ] *adj*
tremulous; trembling

tremblement [trahπ•bl•MAHπ]
n M tremor; ~ de terre\
earthquake

trembler [trahπ•BLEH] *vi*
tremble; *vt* drench; douse;
steep

trente [trahπt] *adj npl* MF
thirty

trente et unième [trahπt eh
ew•nee•YEHM] *adj n* MF
thirty-first

trentième [trahπ•TYEHM] *adj n* MF thirtieth

trépied [trai•PYEH] *n* M tripod

très [treh] *adv* very

trésor [trai•ZAUR] *n* M treasure

trésorier -ière [trai•zaur•YEH] [-YEHR] *n* MF treasurer

tressaillir [tre•sah•YEER] *vi* flinch

tresse [tres] *n* (*vt* tresser) F braid

tréteau [trai•TO] *n* M trestle

trève [trehv] *n* F truce

triangle [tree•ahπgl] *n* M triangle

tribord [tree•BAUR] *adj n* M starboard (naut)

tribu [tree•BEW] *n* M tribe

tribunal [tree•bew•NAHL] *n* M tribunal

tribune [tree•BEWN] *n* F tribune

tributaire [tree•bew•TEHR] *adj* tributary

tricheur [tree•SHUR] *n* M cheater

tricot [tree•KAU] *n* M jersey; knitting; ~ de corps\ undershirt

tricoter [tre•kau•TEH] *vt vi* knit

trille [treey] *n* M trill

trimestriel [tree•me•STRYEL] *adj* quarterly

trio [tree•O] *n* M trio

triomphalement [tree•AUπ•fahl•MAHπ] *adv* triumphantly

triomphant [tree•auπ•FAHπ] *adj* triumphant

triomphe [tree•AUπF] *n* M triumph; *vt* triompher

triple [treepl] *adj inv* treble; triple

triste [treest] *adj* sad; sorrowful; glum

tristesse [tree•STES] *n* F sadness; gloom

trivial [tree•vy•AHL] *adj* trivial; mere; inconsequential

trois [trwah] *adj* (inv); *n* MF three; ~ fois *adv comp* thrice; three times

troisième [trah•ZYEHM] *adj n* MF third

troisièmement [trah•zyehm•MAHπ] *adv* M thirdly

trombone (mus) [trauπ•BAUN] *n* M trombone

tromper [trauπ•PEH] *vt vi* deceive; trick; cheat; hoodwink

tromperie [trauπ•pe•REE] *n* F deceit; deception

trompette [trauπ•PEHT] *n* F trumpet

trompeur [trauπ•PŒR] *adj* deceitful; misleading

tronc [trauπ] *n* M trunk

tronçoneuse [trauπ•sau•NUZ] *n* F chain saw

trône [tron] *n* M throne

trop [tro] *adv* too much; too many; too; over; overly; overmuch; exccess; de ~\ superfluous; ~ cuire\ overdo; ~ gros\ overweight; ~ petit\ undersized; ~ plein\ overflowing

trophée [trau•FAI] *n* M trophy

tropique [trau•PEEK] *n* M *adj* tropic

trot [tro] *n* M trot

trotter [trau•TEH] *vi* trot

trottoir [trau•TWAHR] *n* M sidewalk

trou [troo] *n* hole; gap

trouble [troobl] *adj* muddy; murky; cloudy; overcast; dim; dull; confused; *n* M confusion; disorder; turmoil

troubler [troo•BLEH] *vt* perturb; bother; trouble

troupeau [troo•PO] *n* M herd

troupes (mil) [troop] *npl* F troops

trousse [troos] *n* F kit

trousseau [troo•SO] *n* M trousseau

trouvaille [troo•VEY] *n*F discovery; find

trouver [troo•VEH] *vt* locate; find; objects ~s\ lost and found; *vi* se trouver\ to find oneself

trucs [trewk] *n* M thing; gadget; stuff

truelle [trew•EHL] *n* F trowel

tsar [tsahr] *n* M czar

tu; toi [tew]; [twah] *pron sujet; pron dém* you; thou

tube [tewb] *n* M tube

tuberculeux -euse [tew•BEHR•kew•LØ] [-LØZ] *adj* tubercular

tuberculose [tew•BEHR•kew•LAUZ] *n* F tuberculosis

tubes [tewb] *npl* M tubing

tuer [tew•EH] *vt* slay; kill; murder

tulipe [tew•LEEP] *n* F tulip

tulle (tissu) [tewl] *n* M tulle

tumeur [tew•MœR] *n* F tumor

tumulte [tew•MEWLT] *n* M tumult; uproar

tumultueux -euse [tew•MEWL•tew•Ø] [-ØZ] *adj* tumultuous

tunique [tew•NEEK] *n* F tunic

tunnel [tew•NEHL] *n* M tunnel

turbine [toor•BEEN] *n* F turbine

Turc Turque [toork] *n* MF Turk

turc; turque [toork] *adj* Turkish

turf [tyrf] *n* MF turf

turpitude [tyr•pee•TEWD] *n* F turpitude

Turquie [toor•KEE] *n* F Turkey

turquoise [tyr•KWAHZ] *adj n* F turquoise

tuyau [tew•YO] *n* M flue; pipe; hose

tweed [tweed] *n* M tweed

type [teep] *n* M guy (coll); *n* MF type; sort

typhoïde [tee•fau•eed] *adj comp* typhoid; (fièvre typhoïde) typhoid fever

typhon [tee•FAUπ] *n* M typhoon

typhus [tee•FEWS] *n* M typhus

typique [tee•PEEK] *adj inv* typical

typographie [tee•PAU•grah•FEE] *n* F typography

tyran [tee•RAHπ] *n* M bully; tyrant

tyrannie [teeur•ah•NEE] *n* F
tyranny

tyrannique [teeur•rah•NEEK]
adj inv tyrannical

U

ulcération
[ewl•sehr•ah•SYAUπ] *n* F
ulceration

ulcère [ewl•SEHR] *n* M ulcer;
sore

ultérieur [ewl•tehr•YœR] *adj*
ulterior; subsequent

un une [uhñ] [oon] indef art
one; a; an *adj pron* one;
first; ~ autre\ another; un à
un\ one by one; un de ses
jours\ sometime; une fois\ one
time

unanime [ew•nah•NEEM] *adj*
inv unanimous

unanimité
[ew•NAH•nee•mee•TAI] *n* F
unanimity

unique [ew•NEEK] *adj* only;
sole; single; fils ~\ only son;
sens ~\ one way

unir [ew•NEER] *vt* merge;
unify; unite; join; combine

uranium [yr•ah•NYAUM] *n* M
uranium

urbain -e [yr•BAπ] [-BAN] *adj*
urban

urgence [yr•ZHAHπS] *n* F
urgency

urgent [yr•ZHAHπ]
[-ZHAHπT] *adj* urgent;
pressing

urine [yr•EEN] *n* F urine

uriner [yr•ee•NEH] *vi* urinate

urne [yrn] *n* F urn

usage [ew•ZAHZH] *n* M
usage

usine [ew•SEEN] *n* F factory

ustensile [ews•tahπ•SEEUL] *n*
F utensil; tool

usuel [ew•zew•EHL] *adj* usual;
common

usure [ew•SYR] *n* F usury

usurien -ère [ew•syr•YEH]
[-EHR] *n* MF usurer

usurper [ew•syr•PEH] *vt*
usurp

utile [ew•TEEUL] *adj inv*
useful; relevant

utiliser [ew•TEE•lee•ZEH] *vt*
utilize; use

utilité [ew•TEE•lee•TEH] *n* F
usefulness; utility

uvule [ew•VEWL] *n* F
uvula

V

vacance [vah•KAHπS] *n* F
vacancy; space

vacances [vah•KAHπS] *npl* F
vacation

vacant [vah•KAHπ] *adj* vacant,
empty

vacarme [vah•KAHRM] *n* M
din; uproar

vaccin [vahk•SAπ] *n* M vaccine

vacciner [vahk•see•NEH] *vt*
vaccinate

vache [vahsh] *n* F cow.

vaciller [vah•see•YAI] *vi* flicker;
vacillate

vagabond [vah•gah•BAUπ] *n*
M hobo; wanderer

vague 1 [vahg] *n* F wave; ~ de
chaleur\ heatwave

vague 2 [vahg] *adj* faint; vague

vaillant -e [vahy•AHπ]
[-YAHNT] *adj* valiant; brave

vain [vaπ] *adj* fruitless; useless;
sterile

vaincre [veπkr] *vt* overpower;
vanquish

vainqueur [vaπ•KœR] *n* F
victor

vaisseau [veh•SO] *n* M vessel

vaisselle [ve•SEL] *n* F
crockery; tableware

val; vallée [vahl]; [vah•LEH] *n*
MF valley

valable [vah•LAHBL] *adj inv*
valid

valant -e [vah•LAHπ];
[-LAHπT] *adj* worth

valet [vah•LEH] *n* M valet;
servant; footman; groom

valeur [vah•LœR] *n* F valor;
value; worth; ~ marchande\
market value

valeureux -euse [vah•lœr•Ø]
[-ØZ] *adj* valorous;
courageous; brave

validité [vah•LEE•dee•TAI] *n* F
validity

vallonnée [vah•lau•NAI] *adj*
hilly; steep

valse [vahls] *n* F waltz; *vi*
valser

valve [vahlv] *n* F valve

vanille [vah•NY] *n* F vanilla

vanité [vah•nee•TAI] *n* F
conceit; vanity; tirer ~ de\ be
vain of

vaniteux [vah•nee•TØ] *adj*
conceited; vain

vanter [vahπ•TEH] *vt vi* vaunt;
extol; advocate; boost; se
vanter (de qqch)

vapeur [vah•PœR] *n* F steam;
vapor; ~ fumées\ fumes

vaporiser [vah•PAUR•ee•ZEH]
vt vaporize

variable [vah•RYAHBL] *adj
inv* variable

variance [vah•RYAHπS] *n* F
variance; difference

variation
[vah•REE•ah•SYAUπ] *n* F
variation

varicelle [vah•ree•SEL] *n* F
chicken pox

varié [vah•RYEH] *adj* varied

varier [vah•RYEH] *vt* vary

variété [vah•ryai•TAI] *n* F variety

vase 1 [vahz] *n* M vase

vase 2 [vahz] *n* silt

vaste [vahst] *adj inv* vast; wide

vautour [vau•TOOR] *n* M vulture

veau [vau] *n* M veal; calf

végétarien -ne [veh•ZHEH•tah•RYAπ] [-RYAN] *adj; n* MF vegetarian

végétation [veh•ZHEH•tah•SYAUπ] *n* F vegetation

végéter [veh•zheh•TEH] *vt* vegetate

véhémence [veh•eh•MAHπS] *n* F vehemence; passion

véhicule [veh•ee•KEWL] *n* M vehicle

veille 1 [vehy] *n* F eve

veille 2 [vehy] *n* F vigil; ~ mortuaire *n* F wake

veilleur [veh•YœR] *n* M watchman

veine [vehn] *n* F vein

veirge [vy•EHRZ] *n* F virgin

vélo [vai•LO] *n* M bike; bicycle

vélocité [vai•LAU•see•TAI] *n* F velocity; speed

velours [vuh•LœR] *n* M velvet

velu [ve•LEW] *adj* hairy; shaggy

venaison [vuh•neh•ZAUπ] *n* F venison

vendange [vahπ•DAπZH] *n* F vintage

vendeur [vahπ•DœR] *n* M salesman; representative

vendeuse [vahπ•DØZ] *n* F saleswoman; representative

vendre [vahπdr] *vt vi* sell; de ~\ for sale; ~ moins cher\ undersell

vendredi [vahπ•dr•DEE] *n* M Friday

vénérable [vai•nai•RAHBL] *adj inv* venerable; honorable

vénération [vai•NAI•rah•SYAUπ] *n* F veneration; honor

vénérer [vai•nai•REH] *vt* venerate; pay respects to; honor

vengeance [vahπ•ZHAHπS] *n* F vengeance; revenge

venger [vahπ•ZHAI] *vt* avenge; vindicate

venimeux -euse [vuh•nee•MØ] [-ØZ] *adj* venomous

venin [vuh•NAπ] *n* M venom

vent [vahπ] *n* M wind; air; emptiness; avoir ~ de\ get wind of (coll)

vente [vahπt] *n* F sale; selling; vent en gros\ wholesale; ~ au détail F retail; en ~\ on sale

venteux; -euse [vahπ•TØ]; [-ØZ] *adj* windy

ventilateur [vahπ•TEE•lah•TœR] *n* M ventilator; fan

ventilation [vahπ•TEE•lah•SYAUπ] *n* F ventilation

ventiler [vahπ•tee•leh] *vt* ventilate

ventre [vahπtr] *n* M belly; stomach

vêpres [vehpr] *npl* F vespers

ver [vehr] *n* M worm

véranda [vai•rahπ•DAH] *n* M porch; verandah

verbal [vehr•BAHL] *adj* verbal

verbe [vehrb] *n* M verb

verdict [vehr•DEEKT] *n* M verdict

verger [vehr•ZHE] *n* M orchard

vérification [vair•EE•fee•kah•SYAUπ] *n* F verification

verifier [ve•ree•FYAI] *vt* check; verify

véritable [vair•ee•TAHBL] *adj inv* veritable; real

vérité [vair•ee•TAI] *n* F truth

vermine [vehr•MEEN] *n* F vermin

vernaculaire [vehr•NAH•kew•LEHR] *adj n* M vernacular

vernis [vehr•NEE] *n* M varnish; *vt* vernir (bois ameublement)

verre [ver] *n* F glass; ~ à vin *n* wineglass

verrue [vehr•EW] *n* F wart

vers [vehr] *adv* towards; ~ l'est\ eastward; ~ l'intérieur\ inward; ~ l'ouest\ westward; ~ la maison; ~ son pays\ homeward

vers [vehr] *n* MF verse; stanza

versé [ver•SAI] *adj* conversant; versed

verser [vehr•SEH] *vt* tip; pour

version [vehr•ZYAUπ] *n* F version

vert [vert] *adj n* M green

vertèbre [vehr•TEBR] *n* F vertebra

vertical [vehr•tee•KAHL] *adj* vertical

vertige [vehr•TEEZH] *n* M vertigo

vertigineux [ver•TEE•zhee•NØ] *adj* dizzy

vertu [vehr•TEW] *n* F righteousness

vessie [ve•SEE] *n* F bladder

veste [vest] *n* F jacket

vestibule [veh•stee•BEWL] *n* M vestibule; hall

vestige [veh•STEEZH] *n* M vestige; remainder

vêtement [vet•MAHπ] *n* M garment

vêtements [vet•MAHπ] *npl* M clothes; clothing; wardrobe

vétérinaire [vai•TAI•ree•NEHR] *n* F veterinarian

vétérinarien [vai•TAI•ree•NEHR•e•EN] *adj* veterinary

veto [vee•to] *n* M veto

veuf [vØf] *n* M widower

veuve [vØv] *n* F widow

viaduc [vyah•DEWK] *n* M viaduct

viande [vyahπd] *n* F meat

viatiaque [vee•a•TEEK] *n* M viaticum

vibration [vee•brah•SYAUπ] *n* F vibration

vibrer [vee•BREH] *vi* vibrate

vicaire [vee•KER] *n* M curate

vice [vees] *n* M vice; evil

vicieux -euse [vee•SYØ]; [-ØZ] *adj* vicious

victime [veek•TEEM] *n* F
victim

victoire [veek•TWAH] *n* F
victory

victorieux -euse
[veek•taur•EEØ]; [-ØZ] *adj*
victorious

vide [veed] *adj* void; vacant,
empty; *vt* vider

videur [vee•DUR] *n* M bouncer

vie [vee] *n* life; lifetime;
existence; vitality; profession;
spirit; animation; noise;
gagner sa ~\ earn one's living

vieillesse [vye•YES] *n* F old
age

vieux [vyØ] *adj* M elderly; old

vif [veef] *adj* brisk; vivant;
frisky; vivacious; lively

vigilant [vee•zhee•LAHπ] *adj*
alert; vigilant; wary

vigne [veen] *n* F vine

vignobles [vee•NYOBL] *n* M
vineyard

vigoureux -euse [vee•goor•Ø];
[-ØZ] *adj* vigorous

vigueur [vee•GœR] *n* F vigor

vil [veel] *adj* vile; villainous

vilain [vee•LAπ] *n* M *adj* villain

vilenie [vee•NEE] *n* F villainy

villa [vee•LAH] *n* F villa

village [vee•LAHZ] *n* M
village; town

villageois [vee•lah•ZWAH] *n*
M villager

villageoise [vee•lah•ZWAHZ] *n*
F villager

ville [veey] *n* F city; town

vin [vaπ] *n* M wine

vinaigre [vee•HNEHGR] *n* M
vinegar

vinaigrette [vee•ne•GRET] *n* F
salad dressing

vindicatif -tive
[vaπ•DEE•kah•TIF]; [-TEEV]
adj vindictive

vingt [vaπ] *adj n* M twenty

vingtième [vaπ•TYEHM] *adj n*
MF twentieth

viol [vyaul] *n* M rape; violation

violation [vee•AU•lah•SYUπ] *n*
F violation

violence [vee•au•LANπ] *n* F
violence

violent [vee•au•LAHπ] *adj*
violent

violer [vee•au•LEH] *vt* violate;
rape

violet [vyau•LEH] *adj n* M
purple

violet; -te [vee•au•leh]; [-leht]
adj violet; violet (flower)

violeur [vyau•LœR] *n* M rapist

violincelle [vyau•lauπ•SEL] *n*
M cello

violon [vee•au•LAUπ] *n* M
violin

violoniste [vee•au•lahn•EEST]
n MF violinist

vipère [vee•PEHR] *n* F viper

virage [vee•RAZH] *n* M
turning; veering; bending;
turn; corner

virer [veeur•EH] *vi* veer

virginité [vee•ZHEE•nee•TAI]
n F virginity

virgule [veer•GEWL] *n* F
comma

viril [vee•REEL] *adj* virile;
potent; male; manly

virilité [vee•REE•lee•TAI] *n* F
virility

virtual -le [veer•tew•EHL] *adj* virtual

virulence [veer•riew•LAHNπ] *n* F virulence

virus [vee•REWS] *n* M virus

vis; [vee] *n* screw; *vt* visser; *vi* se visser

visa [vee•zah] *n* M visa

visage [vee•ZAHZ] *n* M visage; face

viscères [vee•SEHR] *npl* M viscera

viscosité [vees•KO•zee•TAI] *n* F viscosity

visibilité [vee•ZEE•bee•lee•TAI] *n* F visibility

visible [vee•ZEEBL] *adj* visible

visière [vee•zee•EHR] *n* F visor

vision [vee•SYAUπ] *n* F vision; sight

Visitation [vee•ZEET•tah•SYUπ] *n* F visitation (relig)

visite [vee•ZEET] *n* F visit; visitation; rendre ~ à qu'qun\ visit someone

visiter [vee•zee•TEH] *vt vi* visit

visiteur; -euse [vee•zee•TœR]; [-ØZ] *n* MF visitor

vison [vee•ZAUπ] *n* M mink

visser [vee•SEH] *vt* twist; bottle top

visuel -elle [vee•zew•EHL] *adj* visual

vital [vee•TAHL] *adj* vital; strong; minimum ~\ basic minimum

vitalité [vee•TAHL•lee•TA!] *n* F vitality

vitamine [vee•tah•meen] *n* F vitamin

vite [veet] *adj adv* swift; quick; quickly

vitesse [vee•TEHS] *n* F speed

vitreux [vee•TRØ] *adj* glassy; vitreous

vitriol [vee•tree•AUL] *n* M vitriol

viv; vive [veef]; [veev] *adj* vivid

vivacité [vee•VAH•see•TAI] *n* F vivacity

vivant [vee•VAHπ] *adj* alive; living; live (performance)

vivifiant [vee•vee•FYAHπ] *adj* invigorating; bracing

vocal [vau•KAUL] *adj* vocal

vocation [vo•kah•SYOπ] *n* F calling; vocation

vocaulaire [vo•KA•bew•LEHR] *n* M vocabulary

vogue [vaug] *n* F vogue

voie [vwah] *n* F way; highway; path; means; channel; ~ ferée\ railroad; railroad track; ~ navigable\ waterway; ~ publique\ thoroughfare

voile [vwahl] *n* M veil; sail; faire de la ~\ go sailing

voilé [vwah•LAI] *adj* warped

voiler [vwah•LEH] *vt* warp

voir [vwahr] *vt* see; behold; witness; faire ~\ show

voire [vwahr] *adv* indeed; even; in truth

voisin [vwah•ZAπ] *n* M neighbor; *adj* next-door

voisinage [vwah•zee•NAHZH] *n* M neighborhood

voiture [vwah•TEWR] *n* F car;
carriage; ~ d'occasion\ used
car

voix 1 [vwah] *n* F voice; à ~
basse\ whisper; à ~ haute\
aloud

voix 2 [vwah] *n* F vote

vol 1 [vaul] *n* M larceny;
robbery; theft; ~ à l'étalage\
shoplifting

vol 2 [vaul] *n* M flying; flight;
cover; ~ charter\ charter
flight; à ~ d'oiseau\ bird's eye
view

volaille [vau•LEY] *n* F fowl;
poultry

volan [vaul•KAHπ] *n* M
volcano

volatile [vaul•lah•TEEL] *adj*
volatile

volcanique [vaul•kah•NEEK]
adj volcanic

volée [vau•LAI] *n* F volley

voler [vau•LEH] *vt* rob; steal

volet [vau•LEH] *n* M shutter
(camera)

volonté [vau•lauπ•TAI] *n* F
will; ~\ willingly!

volontiers [vau•lauπ•TYER]
adv readily

volt [vault] *n* M volt

voltage [vaul•TAHZH] *n*
voltage

volume [vaul•EWM] *n* M
volume

voluntaire [vaul•lauπ•TEHR] *n*
MF volunteer; voluntary

volutueux -euse
[vaul•lewp•TYØ]; [-TYØZ]
adj voluptuous

vomir [vaum•MEER] *vt* M
vomit; throw up

vomitif [vaum•mee•TEEF] *n* M
vomit

vorace [vau•RAHS] *adj*
ravenous; voracious

votant [vau•TAHπ] *n* MF voter

vo [vau] *pron* yours

voter [vau•TEH] *vt; vi* vote

**votre; vos; à vous; le/la/les
vôtre** [vautr] *adj pron* your;
yours

vouloir [voo•LWAHR] *vt* want;
will

vous; tu [voo]; [too] *pron* you

vous-même; toi-même *pron*
yourself

voûté [voo•TAI] *adj* hunched

voûte [voot] *n* F vault

voyage [vwah•YAHZH] *n* M
journey; traveling; trip;
voyage; tour; travel; *vt vi*

voyager

voyageur -euse
[vwah•yah•ZHœR] [-ZHØZ] *n*
MF traveler

voyant [vwah•YAHπ] *adj*
gaudy; conspicuous

voyelle [vwah•YEHL] *n* F
vowel

voyou [vwah•YOO] *n* hoodlum;
thug

vrai -e [vreh] *adj* true; real;
truthful; correct; proper;
accurage; à ~ dire\ tell the
truth; être dans le ~\ to be (in
the) right

vraiment [vreh•MAHπ] *adv*
truly; really

vraisemblement
[vre•sahπbl•MAHπ] *adv*
presumably

vrille [vreey] *n* F tendril (bot)
vue [vew] *n* F eyesight; view;
vision; vista; sight; spectacle;
~ double
vulgaire [vewl•gehr] *adj* vulgar

vulgarité [vewl•GAH•ree•TAI]
n F vulgarity
vulnirable [vewl•neh•RAHBL]
adj vulnerable

W

wagon [vah•GAUπ] *n* M
carriage; coach; wagon; truck

whisky [wee•SKEE] *n* M
whiskey

X

xénophobe [zai•nau•FAUB] *n*
MF xenophobe
xénophobie
[zai•NAU•fau•BEE] *n* F
xenophobia

xylographie [zee•law•grah•fee]
n F xylography
xylophone [zee•lau•FAUN] *n*
M xylophone

Y

y [ee] *adv* there; here; hither;
there; within; *pron* to it; by it;
at it; in it; il y a\ there is;
there are

yacht [yaht] *n* M yacht
yeux [yœ] eyes\ *pl* oeil

Z

Zaïre [zehr] *n* M Zaire

zèbre [zehbr] *n* M zebra

zébrur [zeh•BROOR] *n* F welt (of skin)

zélé -e [zeh•LAI] *adj* zealous

zénith [zeh•NEET] *n* M zenith

zéphyr [zeh•FEEUR] *n* M zephyr

zeppelin [zeh•PLEHN] *n* M zeppelin

zéro [zeh•RAU] *n* M zero

zigzaguer [zeeg•zah•GEH] *vi* zigzag

zinc [zaπgk] *n* M zinc

zircon [zeeur•KAUπ] *n* M zircon

zodiacal -e [zau•dee•AHKL]; [AHL] *adj* zodiacal

zodiaque [zau•dee•AHK] *n* M zodiac

zone [zaun] *n* F zone

zoo [zo] *n* M zoo

zoologie [zo•lau•ZHEE] *n* F zoology

zoologique [zo•lau•ZHEEK] *adj inv* zoological

zygote [zee•GAUT] *n* M zygote

A

a [u or ai] (before vowel or silent 'h') an [en] *art* un (une); (expressing ratios per) 40 miles an hour\40 milles à l'heure; 30 cents a pound\30 cents la livre; twice a day\ deux fois par jour M

A.M. [am] (ante meridiem) du matin

abandon [u•BAN•dun] *vt* abandonner

abase [u•BAIS] *vt* abaisser

abbey [a•BEE] *n* abbaye F

abbreviate [u•BREE•vee•AIT] *vt* abréger

abbreviation [u•BREE•vee•AI•shn] *n* abréviation F

abdomen [AB•du•men] *n* abdomen M

abduct [ub•DUHKT] *vt* enlever; ravir

abet [u•BET] *vt* soutenir; encourager

abhor [ub•HAUR] *vt* abhorrer

abide (by) [u•BUYD] *vi* se conformer (à); respecter

ability [u•BI•li•tee] *n* capacité F; aptitude F

able [AI•bl] *adj* capable; to be ~ (to)\ pouvoir

abnormal [ab•NAUR•ml] *adj* anormal M

abode [u•BOD] *n* demeure F; residence F

abolish [u•BAH•lish] *vt* abolir

abominable [u•BAH•mi•nu•bl] *adj* abominable

abortion [u•BAUR•shn] *n* avorton M; se faire avorter M

about [u•BOUT] *prep* au sujet de sur; de quoi ce livre s'agit-il ?; *adv* (approximately) à peu près environ; vers 5 heures; sur le point de faire qqch

above [u•BUHV] *adv* au-dessus; *prep* au-dessus de; (in text) ci-dessus

abrupt [u•BRUHPT] *adj* brusque; (impolite; curt) abrupt M

absent [AB•sunt] *adj* absent M

absent-minded [-MUYN•did] *adj* distrait M

absolute [AB•su•LOOT] *adj* absolu M

absolutely [AB•su•LOOT•lee] *adv* absolument M

absorb [ub•ZAURB] *vt* absorber

abstain [ab•STAIN] *vi* s'abstenir (de)

absurd [ub•SURD] *adj*
absurde M

abundant [u•BUHN•dunt] *adj*
abondant M

abuse [u•BYOOS] *n*
maltraitement M; abus M;
injures *fpl*

abuse [u•BYOOZ] *vt* maltraiter
abuser de

abyss [u•BIS] *n* abîme M

academy [u•KA•du•mee] *n*
académie F école F

accent [AK•sent] *n* accent M

accept [ak•SEPT] *vt* accepter

access [AK•ses] *n* accès M

accident [AK•si•dunt] *n*
accident M; par hasard M

accidental [AK•si•DEN•tl] *adj*
accidentel M

accommodate
[uh•KAH•mu•DAIT] *vt*
accomoder obliger; (provide
lodging) loger

accompany [u•CUHM•pu•nee]
vt accompagner

accomplice [u•KAHM•plis] *n*
complice M

accomplish [u•KAHM•plish] *vt*
accomplir

accord [u•KAURD] *n* accord;
de son plein gré M

according [u•KAUR•ding] *prep*
selon d'après

accost [u•KAUST] *vt* accoster

account [u•KOUNT] *n*
compte F

accumulate
[u•KYOO•myu•LAIT] *vt*
accumuler; *vi* s'accumuler

accurate [A•kyu•ret] *adj* précis
exact M

accuse [u•KYOOZ] *vt* accuser

accustom [u•KUH•stum] *vt*
accoutumer; habituer; *vi*
s'accoutumer

ache [aik] *n* douleur F; mal M;
vi faire mal; j'ai mal à la
tête F

acid [A•sid] *adj n* acide M

acknowledge [ek•NAH•lij] *vt*
reconnaître

acquaintance [u•KWAIN•tuns]
n connaissance F

acquiesce [a•kwee•YES] *vi*
acquiescer

acquire [u•KWUYUR] *vt*
acquérir

acquit [u•KWIT] *vt* acquitter

acre [AI•kur] *n* acre F

acrid [A•krid] *adj* âcre M

across [u•KRAUS] *adv* en
travers; *prep* en travers de de
(on the other side of) l'autre
côté de; (in front of) en
face de

acrylic [u•KRI•lik] *adj n*
acrylique M

act [akt] *n* acte F action F;
(thea) acte F; *vi* agir; (thea)
jouer; *vt* jouer

action [AK•shn] *n* action\F;
prendre des mesures; agir

active [AK•tiv] *adj* actif; vif

actor [AK•tur] *n* akteur M

actress [AK•tris] *n* actrice F

actually [AK•chu•lee] *adv*
effectivement

acute [u•KYOOT] *adj* aigu M

adapt [u•DAPT] *vt* adapter; *vi*
s'adapter

add [ad] *vt* ajouter; additonner

addict [A•dict] *n* (drug etc) drogué M toxicomane mf; (sports) fanatique mf

addiction [u•DIK•shn] *n* dépendance F

addition [u•DI•shn] *n* addition F

additional [u•DI•shun•ul] *adj* accessoire M

address 1 [A•dres] *n* adresse F

address 2 [u•DRES] *vt* adresser

adequate [A•de•kwet] *adj* suffisant M

adjective [A•jik•tiv] *n* a djectif M

adjourn [u•JURN] *vt vi* ajourner

adjust [u•JUHST] *vt* ajuster

administer [ud•MI•ni•stur] *vt* administrer

admire [ud•MUYR] *vt* admirer

admission [ud•MI•shun] *n* admission F

admit [ud•MIT] *vt* (let enter) laisser entrer *vt* admettre

admonish [ud•MAH•nish] *vt* admonester

adolescence [A•du•LE•suns] *n* adolescence F

adopt [u•DAHPT] *vt* adopter

adoption [u•DÁHP•shun] *n* adoption F

adore [u•DAUR] *vt* adorer

adult [u•DUHLT] *n* adulte M; *adj* adulte; (material subject) pour adultes M

adultery [u•DUHL•tu•ree] *n* adultère M

advance [ed•VANS] *vt vi* avancer; *n* avance F; *adv* à l'avance

advantage [ed•VAN•tej] *n* avantage M; (sth) profiter de\ (sb) exploiter

advantageous [AD•VUN•TAI•jus] *adj* avantageux

Advent [AD•vent] *n* l'Avent M

adventure [ed•VEN•chur] *n* aventure F; *vt* aventurer F

adventurous [ed•VEN•chu•rus] *adj* aventureux M

adverb [AD•vurb] *n* adverbe M

adversity [ad•VUR•si•tee] *n* adversité F

advertise [AD•vur•TUYZ] *vt* annoncer faire de la publicité pour

advertisement [AD•vur•TUYZ•munt] *n* annonce F publicité F

advice [ad•VUYS] *n* conseil M avis M; prendre conseil M

advise [ad•VUYZ] *vt* conseiller donner avis; (alert) donner avis de; déconseiller qqn de qqch

affair [u•FAIR] *n* affaire F; liaison F F

affect [u•FEKT] *vt* affecter

affection [u•FEK•shn] *n* affection F

afford [uh•FAWRD] *vt* avoir les moyens d'acheter qqch

Afghanistan [af•GA•ni•STAN] *n* Afghanistan M

afraid (to be) [u•FRAID] *adj* peur (avoir)

Africa [A•fri•ku] *n* Afrique F

after [AF•tur] *prep adv* après; *conj* après que; après tout; après vous!; *adv* après

afternoon [AF•tur•NOON] *n*
après-midi M; bonjour M

again [uh•GEN] *adv* encore

against [uh•GENST] *prep adv*
contre

age [aij] *n* âge M

aged [AI•jud / aij'd] *adj* âgé M

agency [AI•jun•cee] *n* agence F

agenda [uh•JEN•duh] *n* ordre
du jour M

agent [AI•junt] *n* agent M

aggravate [A•gru•VAIT] *vt*
aggraver

aggressive [u•GRE•siv] *adj*
agressif

ago [uh•GO] *adv* il y a

agree [uh•GREE] *vi* d'accord
(être)

agreeable [u•GREE•u•bl] *adj*
agréable

agreement [u•GREE•munt] *n*
accord M

agriculture [A•gri•CUL•chur] *n*
agriculture F

ahead (of) [uh•HED] *adv*
(prep) devant

aid [aid] *n* aide F

AIDS [aids] *n* SIDA M

aim [aim] *n* but M; *vi* viser à

air [air] *n* air M

air-conditioning
[-kuhn•DI•shuh•ning] *n*
climatisation F

air-conditioned
[~-kuhn•DI•shuhnd] *adj*
climatisé

airmail [AIR•mail] *n* poste
aérienne F by ~ par avion

airplane [AIR•plain] *n* avion F

airport [AIR•paurt] *n*
aéroport M

airtight [AIR•tuyt] *adj*
hermétique

aisle [uyl] *n* allée F

ajar [uh•JAHR] *adj* entrouvert

alarm [u•LAHRM] *n* alarme *vt*
alarmer F

alarm clock [u•LARHRM
clahk] *n* réveil M

alas [uh•LAS] *excl* hélas

Albania [al•BAI•nee•yuh] *n*
Albanie F

album [AL•bum] *n* album M

alcohol [AL•ku•HAL] *n*
alcool M

alcoholic [AL•ku•HAU•lik] *adj*
n alcoolique

alert [uh•LUHRT] *adj* vigilant;
vt alerter

algebra [AL•je•bru] *n* algèbre F

Algeria [AL•jee•ree•yu] *n*
Algérie F

alibi [A•li•BUY] *n* alibi M

alike [uh•LUYK] *adj* pareil; le
même

alive [uh•LUYV] *adj* vivant

all [awl] *adj* tout; ~ at once\ tout
à coup; ~ right\bien; ~
over\fini

allegation [A•lu•GAI•shun] *n*
allégation F

allergic [u•LUR•jik] *adj*
allergique F

allergy [A•luhr•jee] *n* allergie F

alliance [u•LUY•yuns] *n*
alliance F; *n* entente F

allow [uh•LOW] *vt* permettre

allude [uh•LOOD] *vi* faire
allusion

allusion [u•LOO•zhuhn] *n*
allusion F

almost [AWL•most] *adv* presque

alone [uh•LON] *adj adv* seul

along [uh•LAWNG] *prep* le long de

aloud [uh•LOWD] *adv* à voix haute

alphabet [AL•fu•BET] *n* alphabet M

already [awl•RE•dee] *adv* déjà

alright [awl•RUYT] *adv* bien; (as answer) d'accord

also [AWL•so] *adv* aussi

alternate (with) [AUL•tur•NAIT] *vi* alterner (avec)

although [awl•THO] *conj* bien que

altogether [AWL•too•GE•thuhr] *adv* entièrement

always [AWL•waiz] *adv* toujours

am [am] present tense be *v* être

amateur [A•mu•CHUR] *adj n* amateur M

amaze [u•MAIZ] *vt* stupéfier; confondre

amazing [u•MAI•zing] *adj* étonnant

ambassador [am•BA•su•dur] *n* ambassadeur -drice MF

ambiguous [am•BI•gyoo•wus] *adj* ambigu (F:-ë)

ambitious [am•BI•shus] *adj* ambitieux

amend (law); amendment: amendment M [u•MEND] *vt* amender (loi); amendement M: amendment

America [u•ME•ri•ku] *n* Amérique

amnesty [AM•ni•stee] *n* amnistie F

among [u•MUHNG] *prep* parmi

amount [u•MOWNT] *n* quantité F; *vt* s'élever à; se chiffre

amuse [u•MYOOZ] *vt* amuser

analogy [u•NA•lu•jee] *n* analogie F

analysis [u•NA•lu•sis] *n* analyse F

analyze [A•nu•LUYZ] *vt* analyser

anarchy [A•nahr•kee] *n* anarchie F

ancestor [AN•SE•stur] *n* ancêtre M

anchor [AN•kur] *n* ancre F; *vt* ancrer; attacher

ancient [AIN•shunt] *adj* antique; ancien

and [and] or [end] *conj* et; de plus en plus; et ainsi de suite

angel [AIN•jul] *n* ange M

anger [ANG•gur] *n* colère F; *vt* fâcher mettre en colère

angle [ANG•gl] *n* angle M

angry [ANG•gree] *adj* faché en colère

anguish [AN•gwish] *n* angoisse; *vt* angoisser F

animal [A•ni•ml] *n* animal M

animate [A•ni•mut] *adj* animé

anniversary [A•ni•VUR•su•ree] *n* anniversaire F

announce [u•NOUNS] *vt* annoncer

annoy [u•NOI] *vt* agacer ennuyer

annoying [u•NOI•ying] *adj*
ennuyeux; agaçant

annual [A•nyoo•ul] *adj* annuel;
n (plant) plante F annuelle;
(periodical) publication F
annuelle

another [u•NUH•thur] *adj* un
autre

answer [AN•sur] *vt* répondre; *vi*
répondre à; *n* réponse F

ant [ant] *n* fourmi F

anthology [an•THAH•lu•jee] *n*
anthologie F

antique [an•TEEK] *adj* ancien

antisocial [AN•ti•SO•shul] *adj*
antisocial

anxiety [ang•ZUY•yu•tee] *n*
anxiété F

anxious [ANK•shus] *adj*
anxieux inquiet

any [E•nee] *adj* (interrogative)
du de la des; (following
negative) de: il n'y a pas de
qqch; (whichever) n'importe
quel; *pron* (in neg. sentences)
aucun je n'ai pas aucune idée;
en je n'en ai pas;
(interrogative) en est-ce que
vous en aimerais

anyone (anybody)
[E•nee•WUHN] *pron*
quelqu'un; n'importe qui; (in
neg. sentence) personne

anything [E•nee•THING] *pron*
quelque chose; n'importe
quoi; rien

anyway [E•nee•WAI] *adv* de
toute façon

anywhere [E•nee•WAIR] *adv*
quelque part; n'importe où;
(in neg. sentence) nulle part

apartment [u•PAHRT•munt] *n*
appartement M

ape [aip] *n* singe M

apologize [u•PAH•lu•JUYZ] *vi*
excuser

apology [u•PAH•lu•jee] *n*
excuses F

apparently [u•PA•runt•lee] *adv*
aparemment

appear [u•PEER] *vi* apparaître
se montrer; (seem) sembler
paraître

appearance [u•PEER•uns] *n*
apparition F; *n* (look)
apparence F

appetite [A•pu•TUYT] *n*
appétit M

appetizer [A•pu•TUY•zur] *n*
amuse-gueule M

applaud [u•PLAUD] *vt*
applaudir

apple [A•pl] *n* pomme F

application [A•pli•KAI•shn] *n*
application F; (for a job, etc.)
demande F; formulaire M de
demande

apply [uh•PLUY] *vt* appliquer;
vi (for a job etc) faire un
demande

appoint [u•POINT] *vt* nommer

appointment [u•POINT•ment]
n (to a position) nomination
F; (meeting) rendez-vous M;
prendre rendez-vous

appraisal [u•PRAI•zl] *n*
évaluation F

appraise [u•PRAIZ] *vt* estimer
évaluer

appreciate [u•PREE•shee•AIT]
vt apprécier

approach [u•PROCH] *vt*
approcher

appropriate [u•PRO•pree•IT]
adj approprié

approval [u•PROO•vl] *n*
approbation F

approve [uh•PROOV] *vt*
approuver

approximately
[u•PRAHK•su•mit•lee] *adv*
approximativement

apricot [A•pri•KAHT] *n*
abricot M

arbitrary [AHR•bi•TRE•ree]
adj arbitraire

arch [ahrch] *n* arc M

archaeology
[AHR•kee•AH•lu•jee] *n*
archéologie F

archaic [ahr•KAI•ik] *adj*
archaïque

architect [AHR•ki•TEKT]. *n*
architecte M

architecture
[AHR•ki•TEK•chur] *n*
architecture F

area [A•ree•u] *n* région F; (in
geometry) superficie F;
(approximately) environ F

argue [AHR•gyoo] *vt* discuter
(de); *vi* (to reason)
argumenter; se disputer (avec)

argument [AHR•gyu•mint] *n*
dispute F

arid [A•rid] *adj* aride

arm 1 [ahrm] *n* bras M

arm 2 [ahrm] *n* (weapon) arme
F; *vt* armer

armchair [AHRM•chair] *n*
fauteuil M

armor [AHR•mur] *n* armure F

army [AHR•mee] *n* armée F

aroma [u•RO•mu] *n* arôme M;
n odeur M

around [u•ROWND] *adv* (tout)
autour; se retourner; *prep*
autour de (approximately) à
peu près

arrange [u•RAINJ] *vt* arranger

arrangement [u•RAINJ•munt]
n arrangment M

arrest [u•REST] *vt* arrêter; *n*
arrestation F

arrival [u•RUY•vl] *n* arrivée F

arrive [u•RUYV] *vi* arriver

arrogant [A•ru•gent] *adj*
arrogant

arrow [A•ro] *n* flèche F

art [ahrt] *n* art M; *n* articie; M;
fine ~\a beaux-arts

article [AHR•ti•kl] *n* article M

articulate [ahr•TI•cyu•LAIT] *vt*
vi articuler

artificial [AHR•ti•FI•shl] *adj*
artificiel

artist [AHR•tist] *n* artiste M

as [az] *conj* (like) comme;
comme si; (while) au moment
que comme alors que à
mesure que; (because)
puisque comme; *adv* aussi
grand que; (like) comme;
quant à; autant que; autant de
qqch que; aussi; comme
d'habitude

ash [ash] *n* cendre F

ashamed (to be) [u•SHAIMD]
adj honte (avoir) F

ashtray [ASH•trai] *n*
cendrier M

aside [u•SUYD] *adv* de côté

ask [ask] *vt* demander

asleep [u•SLEEP] *adj* endormi; fall ~\s'endormir

asparagus [u•SPA•ru•gus] *n* asperges F

aspect [A•spekt] *n* aspect M

aspirin [A•sprin] *n* aspirine F

assassinate [u•SA•si•NAIT] *vt* assassiner

assassination [u•SA•si•NAI•shun] *n* assassinat

assemble [u•SEM•bl] *vt* assembler; *vi* s'assembler

assembly [u•SEM•blee] *n* (of group) assemblée F; (construction) assemblage M

assign [u•SUYN] *vt* assigner

associate [u•SO•shee•UT] *vt* associer; *n* associé M

association [u•SO•see•AI•shn] *n* association

assume [u•SOOM] *vt* supposer; prendre; s'emparer de

astonish [u•STAH•nish] *vt* stupéfier

astrology [u•STRAH•lu•jee] *n* astrologie F

astronaut [A•stru•NAHT] *n* astronaute MF

astronomy [a•STRAH•nu•mee] *n* astronomie F

at [at] *prep* (position; direction) à (au; à la; aux); chez Joseph; sur le conseil de; à midi; la nuit; à 4 heures; parfois

attach [u•TACH] *vt* attacher

attack [u•TAK] *vt* attaquer; *n* attaque F

attempt (to) [u•TEMPT] *vt* tenter (de) essayer (de); *n* tentative F

attend [u•TEND] *vt* assister à

attention [u•TEN•shn] *n* attention F

attentive [u•TEN•tiv] *adj* attentif

attic [A•tik] *n* grenier M

attitude [A•ti•TOOD] *n* attitude F

attract [u•TRAKT] *vt* attirer

attraction [u•TRAK•shn] *n* attraction F

attractive [u•TRAK•tiv] *adj* attirant

audience [AU•dee•uns] *n* of film public M; of TV téléspectateurs *npl;* of interview audience F

audition [au•DI•shun] *n* audition F

August [AU•gust] *n* aôut M

aunt [ant or ahnt] *n* tante F

Australia [au•STRAIL•yu] *n* Australie F

Austria [AU•stree•u] *n* Autriche F

authentic [au•THEN•tik] *adj* authentique

author [AU•thur] *n* auteur M

authority [u•THAU•ri•tee] *n* authorité F

autobiography [AU•to•buy•AH•gru•fee] *n* autobiographie F

autograph [AU•tu•GRAF] *n* autographe M

automatic [AU•to•MA•tik] *adj* automatique

autumn [AU•tum] *n* automne F

auxiliary [awg•ZIL•yu•ree] *adj n* auxiliaire M

available [u•VAI•lu•bl] *adj* disponible

avenge [u•VENJ] *vt* venger

avenue [A•vu•NYOO] *n* avenue F

average [A•vur•ij] *adj n* moyen; *vt* faire donner une moyenne de

avoid [u•VOID] *vt* éviter

awake [u•WAIK] *adj* réveillé; vigilant; *vi* exciter; se réviller

award [u•WAURD] *n vt* prix M; *vi* accorder; décider

aware [u•WAIR] *adj* conscient

away [u•WAI] *adv* au loin; go ~\s'en aller; right ~\ toute de suite

awe [au] *n* F crainte; terreur; *vi* inspirer de la crainte

awesome [AU•sum] *adj* impressionant

awful [AU•ful] *adj* affreux

awkward [AU•kwurd] *adj* maladroit

axe [ax] *n* hache F

axis [AK•sis] *n* axe M

axle [AK•sl] *n* essieu M

B

babble [BA•bl] *vi* babiller

baby [BAI•bee] *n* bébé M

bachelor [BA•chu•lur] *n* célibataire M

back [bak] *adv adj n vt* dos; revenir (revenir dans une heure); rentrer (dans la salle) M

background (in the) [BAK•grownd] *n* arrière-plan (à l') M

backlash [BAK•lash] *n* contrecoup M

backpack [BAK•pak] *n* sac à dos M

backward [BAK•wurd] *adv adj* en arrière; à la reverse

backyard [bak•YAHRD] *n* arrière-cour F

bacon [BAI•kun] *n* lard M

bad [bad] *adj* mauvais; m'chant; dangereux; ~ tempered\ acariâtre

badge [baj] *n* badge M

badly [BAD•lee] *adv* mal

bag [bag] *n* sac M; *n* valise M

baggage [BA•gij] *n* bagages M

bagpipes [BAG•puyps] *npl* cornemuse F

bail [bail] *n* caution F; on ~\ sous caution; (from detention) caution F; on ~\ sous caution; *vt* ~ out\ mettre en liberté sous caution; (water) vider; (from plane) sauter en parachute

bait [bait] *n* appât M; *vt* appâter

bake [baik] *vt* faire cuire au four; *vi* cuire au four

baker [BAI•kur] *n* boulanger M

bakery [BAI•ker•ee] *n* cuisson F; boulangerie F

balance [BA•luns] *n* équilibre M; (total) solde M; (scales) balance F; *vt* mettre en équilibre; équilibrer; (account) balancer; *vi* s'équilibrer

balance sheet [BA•lens sheet] *n* bilan M

balcony [BAL•ku•nee] *n* balcon M

bald [bauld] *adj* chauve

bale [baiul] *n* balle F; *vt* emballoter

balk [bauk] *vi* ~ at\ hésiter devant

ball [bawl] *n* balle F; (football) ballon M; (shape) boule F; (dance) bal M

ballad [BA•lud] *n* ballade F

ballerina [BA•lu•REE•nu] *n* ballerine F

ballet [BA•lai] *n* ballet M

balloon [bu•LOON] *n* ballon M

ballot [BA•lut] *n* scrutin M; *vt* cast a ~\voter

bamboo [bam•BOO] *n* bambou M

ban [ban] *n* interdiction; *vt* interdire F

banal [bu•NAL] *adj* banal

banana [bu•NA•nu] *n* banane F

band [band] *n* orchestre M; (of rock music) groupe M

bandage [BAN•dij] *n* bandage M

banish [BA•nish] *vt* bannir

bank [bank] *n* banque F

banknote [BANK•not] *n* billet M de banque

banker [BANG•kur] *n* banquier M

bankrupt [BANK•ruhpt] *adj* failli; go ~\faire faillite

bankruptcy [BANK•RUHPT•see] *n* faillite F

banner [BA•nur] *n* banderole F

banquet [BANG•kwet] *n* banquet M

banter [BAN•tur] *n* badinage M; *vt vi* badiner

baptism [BAP•tizm] *n* baptême M

baptize [bap•TUYZ] *vt* baptiser

bar [bahr] *n* bar (pub) M

barbarian [bahr•BE•ree•un] *adj n* barbare

barbed [bahrbd] *adj* barbelé

barber [BAHR•bur] *n* coiffeur M; *n* barbier M

bare [bair] *adj* nu

barefoot [BAIUR•fut] *adj adv* pieds nus; nu-pieds

barely [BAIR•lee] *adv* à peine

bargain [BAHR•gin] *n vi* occasion F; *vi* négocier

barge [bahrj] *n* péniche F

bark [bahrk] *n; ~ at\vi* (of dog) aboiement M; (of tree) écorce; *vi* (at) aboyer (après) M

barley [BAHR•lee] *n* orge F

barn [bahrn] *n* grange F

barometer [bu•RAH•mi•tur] *n* baromètre M

baroque [bu•ROK] *adj n* baroque M

barracks [BA•ruks] *npl* caserne F

barrel [BA•rul] *n* (of oil) baril
M; (of wine etc) tonneau M

barren [BA•run] *adj* stérile;
(land) aride

barricade [BA•ri•KAID] *n*
barricade F

barrier [BA•ree•ur] *n* barrière F

bartender [BAHR•TEN•dur] *n*
barman M

base [bais] *n* base F; *vi* ~ on\
baser sur fonder sur

baseball [BAIS•bawl] *n*
base-ball M

basement [BAIS•munt] *n*
sous-sol M

bashful [BASH•ful] *adj* timide

basic [BAI•sik] *adj* fondamental

basil [baizl] *n* basilic M

basis [BAI•sis] *n* base F

basket [BA•skit] *n* corbeille F;
n panier M

basketball [BA•skit•BAWL] *n*
basket M

bass (mus) [bais] *n* basse F

bassoon [bu•SOON] *n*
basson M

bastard [BA•sturd] *n* bâtard
(-e) MF

baste [baist] *vt* arroser

bat [bat] *n* (animal)
chauve-souris F; (for baseball)
batte F

bath [bath] *n* bain M

bathe [bayth] *vt* prendre un
bain

bather [BAI•thur] *n* baigneur M

bathing suit [BAI•thing ~] *n*
maillot de bain M

bathrobe [BATH•rob] *n* sortie
de bain F

bathroom [BATH•room] *n*
salle de bains F

bathtub [BATH•tuhb] *n*
baignoire F

baton [bu•TAHN] *n* for police:
bâton M-for conductor:
baguette F

battalion [bu•TA•lyun] *n*
bataillon M

batter [BA•tur] *n* pâte F; *vt*
frapper; heurter; démolir

battery [BA•tu•ree] *n* pile F

battle [batl] *n* bataille F; *n*
combat m; *vt* combattre;
se battre

battleship [BA•tl•SHIP] *n*
cuirassé M

bawdy [BAU•dee] *adj* paillard

bawl [baul] *vt vi* brailler; *n*
cri M

bay [bai] *n* baie F

bayonet [BAI•u•net] *n*
baïonnette F

bazaar [bu•ZAHR] *n* bazar M

BC (before Christ) [bee cee]
av. J.-C.

be [bee] *aux* v être; I am well\je
vais bien; I am hungry\J'ai
faim; it is fine;\ il fait beau

beach [beech] *n* plage; *vi* tirer
à sec

bead [beed] *n* perle F; *n*
grain M

beagle [BEE•gl] *n* beagle M

beak [beek] *n* bec M

beam [beem] *n* (of light) rayon
M; (of wood) poutre F; *vi*
rayonner M

bean [been] *n* haricot M

bear [bair] *n* ours M

beard [beerd] *n* barbe F

beast [beest] *n* bête F; *n* animal F

beastly [BEE•stlee] *adj* bestial

beat [beet] *vt* battre

beat up *vt* tabasser

beating 1 [BEE•ting] (heart wings etc) *n* battement M; (thrashing) raclée F

beating 2 [BEE•ting] (thrashing) *n* raclée F

beautiful [BYOO•ti•ful] *adj* beau belle

beauty [BYOO•tee] *n* beauté F

beaver [BEE•vur] *n* castor M

because [bi•CAWZ] *conj* parce que; ~ of *prep*\à cause de

beckon [BE•kun] *vt* faire signe à

become [bi•CUHM] *vi* devenir; convenir; aller bien à

becoming [bi•CUH•ming] *adj* seyant; convenable

bed [bed] *n* lit; *vi* go to ~\se coucher M

bedroom [BED•room] *n* chambre F

bee [bee] *n* abeille F

beech [beech] *n* hêtre M

beef [beef] *n* bœuf M

beehive [BEE•huyv] *n* ruche F

beer [bee'ur] *n* bière F

beet [beet] *n* betterave F

beetle [beetl] *n* scarabée M

before [bi•FAWR] *adv* avant; *prep* (in front of) devant; *conj* avant que ; avant de

befriend [bu•FREND] *vt* prendre en amitié

beg [beg] *vt* mendier; prier; soliciter; I ~ your pardon\ je vous demande pardon

beggar [BE•gur] *n* mendiant M

begin [bi•GIN] *vt vi* commencer; se metter à; to ~ with\pour commencer

beginner [bu•GI•nur] *n* débutant M

beginning [bi•GI•ning] *n* début M; *n* origine F

behalf [bi•HAF] *n* de la part de

behave [bi•HAIV] *vi* comporter; se conduire

behavior [bi•HAI•vyur] *n* comportement M

behead [bi•HED] *vt* décapiter

behind [bi•HUYND] *prep adv n* derrière; arrière; en arrière

beige [baizh] *adj n* beige M

being [BEE•ing] *n* être M; *n* existence F; *adj* existant

belated [bi•LAI•tid] *adj* tardif

belfry [BEL•free] *n* beffroi M

Belgian [BEL•jun] *adj* belge

Belgium [BEL•jum] *n* Belgique F

belief [bi•LEEF] *n* croyance F; *n* foi F; *n* conviction F

believe [bi•LEEV] *vt vi* croire

bell [bel] *n* cloche F (large); clochette F (small); sonnete F

bellow [BE•lo] *vi* mugir

belly [BE•lee] *n* ventre M

belong [bi•LAUNG] *vi* (ownership) appartenir à; (be a member of) faire partie de

beloved [bi•LUVHVD] *adj* bien-aimé; amoreux de

below [bi•LO] *adv* en dessous; *prep* sous au-dessous de

belt [belt] *n* ceinture F; *n* courroire (mech) M

bench [bench] *n* banc M

bend [bend] *vt* courber; *n* virage
M; *n* coude M

beneath [bi•NEETH] *adv* en
dessous; *prep* sous; au-dessous
de

benediction [BE•ni•DIK•shun]
n bénédiction F

benefactor [BE•ni•FAK•tur] *n*
bienfaiteur

beneficial [BE•nu•FI•shl] *adj*
salutaire; avagentaux

benefit [BE•ni•FIT] *n* avantage
M; of dans l'interêt de; *vt*
faire du bien à; *vi* profiter de

benign [bi•NUYN] *adj* bénin

bent [bent] *adj* courbé; *n*
penchant M; *n* inclination F

bequeath [bi•KWEETH] *vt*
léguer

beret [bu•RAI] *n* berét M

berry [BE•ree] *n* baie F

beside [bi•SUYD] *prep*
à côté de

besides [bi•SUYDS] *adv prep*
en plus; diaillerus; en outre

besiege [bi•SEEJ] *vt* assiéger

best [best] *adj* le meilleur/ la
meilleure le mieux

bestow [bi•STO] *vt* conférer;
accorder

bet [bet] *n* pari M; *vt* parier

betray [bi•TRAI] *vt* trahir

betrayal [bi•TRAI•ul] *n*
trahison M

betrayer [bi•TRAI•ur] *n*
traître M

better [BE•tur] *adj* meilleur;
adv mieux

between [bi•TWEEN] *prep adv*
entre

beverage [BE•vu•rij] *n*
boisson F

beware (of) [bi•WAIR] *vi*
méfier (de)

bewitching [bi•WI•ching] *adj*
ensorcelant; enchanté

beyond [bi•YAHND] *adv prep*
au delà; là-bas

bias [BUY•us] *n* préjugé M; *n*
biais M; *vi* influencer

biased [BUY•ust] *adj* partial

bib *n* bavette F

Bible [BUY•bl] *n* Bible F

bicker [BI•kur] *vi* chamailler

bicycle [BUY•si•kul] *n*
bicyclette F

bid [bid] *n vi* enchère F

big [big] *adj* grand; important

bigamy [BI•gu•mee] *n* bigamie F

bigot [BI•gut] *n* sectaire

bike [buyk] *n* vélo M

bikini [bi•KEE•nee] *n* bikini M

bile [buyl] *n* bile F

bilingual [BUY•LING•gwul]
adj bilingue

bill [bil] *n* facture F; addition F;
projet sm de loi; billet M be
banque; bec

billiards [BIL•yurdz] *n* billard M

billion [BIL•yun] *num* milliard M

bin [bin] *n* poubelle F (for
garbage)

binoculars [bi•NAH•kyu•lurz]
npl jumelles F

biography [buy•AH•gru•fee] *n*
biographie F

biology [buy•AH•lu•jee] *n*
biologie F

birch [burch] *n* bouleau M

bird [burd] *n* oiseau M

birdcage [BURD•kaig] *n* cage de oiseau F

birth [burth] *n* naissance F; *n* origine; F; *n* commencement M

birth control [birth kon•TROL] *n* contrôle M des naissances

birthday [BURTH•dai] *n* anniversaire F

birthmark [BURTH•mahrk] *n* tache de vin F

birthrate [BURTH•rait] *n* taux de natalité

bishop [BI•shup] *n* évêque M

bit *n* morceau M; fragment M; *adv* un peu

bitch [bich] *n* chienne; salope

bite [buyt] *vt* mordre

bite (insect snake) [buyt] *vt* piquer

bitter [BI•tur] *adj* amer (ère)

bitterness [BI•tur•NIS] *n* amertume F

blab [blab] *vi vt* jaser vi; ébruiter vt

black [blak] *adj n* noir M

blackberry [BLAK•BU•ree] *n* mûre F

blackbird [BLAK•burd] *n* merle M

blackboard [BLAK•baurd] *n* tableau noir M

blacken [BLA•kun] *vt* noircir

blackmail [BLAK•mail] *n* chantage M; *vt* faire chanter M

black market [blak MAHR•kit] *n* marché noir M

blacksmith [BLAK•smith] *n* forgeron M

bladder [BLA•dur] *n* vessie F

blade [blaid] *n* lame; brin feuille F

blame [blaim] *vt* blâmer; *n* blâme F

bland [bland] *adj* fade

blank [blank] *n* blanc M; *adj* balnc; vide; en blanc

blanket [BLANG•kit] *n* couverture F

blaspheme [blas•FEEM] *vt vi* blasphémer

blast [blast] *n* explosion; *vt* exploser; détruire

blatant [BLAI•tunt] *adj* flagrant

blaze [blaiz] *n* incendie F; fi flamber; respendir

bleach [bleech] *n* eau de Javel F

bleed [bleed] *vi vt* saigner

blemish [BLE•mish] *n* défaut; faute M

blend [blend] *vt* mélanger

bless [bles] *vt* bénir

blessing [BLE•sing] *n* bénédiction F

blind [bluynd] *adj* aveugle; window *n* ~\ abat jour M

blindfold [BLUYND•fold] *n* bandeau M

blindly [BLUYND•lee] *adv* aveuglément

blink [blink] *vt* clignoter

blinker (car) [BLING•kur] *n* oeillere M

bliss [blis] *n* félicité F

blister [BLI•stur] *n* ampoule F

blizzard [BLI•zurd] *n* tempête de neige

bloated [BLO•tid] *adj* bouffi; gonflé

block [blahk] *n* cube; pâté; bloc;
v bloquer; road ~\boucher)

blockade [blah•KAID] *n*
blocus M

blockage [BLAH•kij] *n*
blocage M

blonde [blahnd] *adj* blond

blood [bluhd] *n* sang M

bloody [BLUH•dee] *adj*
sanglant

bloom [bloom] *vi* fleurir; en
fleur

blossom [BLAH•sum] *n* fleur
M; *vi* fleurir

blouse [blous] *n* chemisier M

blow [blo] *vt* souffler *vt;* gonfler
vt; faire sauter *vt;* moucher *vi*
refl

bludgeon [BLUH•jn] *vt*
matraquer

blue [bloo] *adj n* bleu M

bluebird *n* oiseau M bleu

blueberry [BLOO•BE•ree] *n*
myrtille F

blueprint [BLOO•print] *n*
photocalque M

bluff [bluhf] *n* n bluff M; *vt vi*
bluffer

blunder [BLUHN•dur] *n* gaffe
F; *vi* faire une gaffe

blunt [bluhnt] *adj* (blade)
émoussé; (person) brusque

blurry [BLU•ree] *adj* brouillé

blush [bluhsh] *vi* rougir; *n*
rougeur F

boar [baur] *n* sanglier M

board 1 [baurd] *n* (of wood)
planche F; (administrative)
conseil M

board 2 [baurd] *vt* (ship plane)
monter à bord de; (train)
monter dans; à bord

boarding school [BAUR•ding
~] *n* internat M

boast [bost] *vi* se vanter

boat [bot] *n* (large) bateau M;
(small) canot M

boating [BO•ting] *n* canotage;
faire du canotage M

body [BAH•dee] *n* corps M

bodyguard
[BAH•dee•GAHRD] *n* garde
M du corps

bog [bahg] *n* marais M

boil [boil] *vt* faire bouillir; *vi*
bouillir M

boiled egg [boild ~] *n* œuf M
à la coque

boiling point [BOI•ling ~] *n*
(point d') ébullition F

boisterous [BOI•stu•rus] *adj*
bruyant

bold [bold] *adj* hardi

boldness [BOLD•nes] *n*
hardiesse F

bolt [bolt] *n* (of door window)
verrou; (screw) boulon M; *vt*
verouiller; boulonner

bomb [bahm] *n* bombe F; *vt*
bombarder F

bomb scare *n* alerte à la bombe

bombard [BAHM•bahrd] *vt*
bombarder

bomber [BAH•mur] *n*
bombardier (avion) M

bombing [BAH•ming] *n*
bombardement M

bond [bahnd] *n* lien; (title) bon
M; obligation F

bondage [BAHN•dij] *n*
esclavage M

bone [bon] *n* os; arête M; make
no ~s about\n'avoir pas de
scrupules à

bonfire [BAHN•fuyur] *n* feu M
de joie

bonnet [BAH•nit] *n* bonnet M

bonus [BO•nus] *n* prime;
boni M

boo [boo] *vt vi* huer; *excl* hue!

book [bük] *n* livre; registre; *vt;*
enregistrer

bookkeeper [BüK•KEE•pur] *n*
comptable

bookkeeping [BüK•KEE•ping]
n comptabilité F

bookstore [BüK•staur] *n*
librairie F

boom [boom] *vi n* gronder; *n*
(noise) grondement M; (in
market) boom M

boomerang [BOO•mu•RANG]
n boomerang M

boos [booz] *npl* huées F

boost [boost] *vt* soulever

boot [boot] *n* botte; F

booth [booth] *n* baraque F;
cabine F; isoloir M

booty [BOO•tee] *n* butin M

border [BAUR•dur] *n* frontière
F; bord M

bore [baur] *vt* ennuyer; *n* ennui;
importun M

boredom [BAUR•dum] *n*
ennui M

boring [BAU•ring] *adj*
ennuyeux; penible

born (to be) [baurn] *adj* naître
(être)

borough [BUH•ro] *n*
municipalité F

borrow [BAH•ro] *vt* emprunter

Bosnia [BAHZ•nee•u] *n*
Bosnie F

Bosnian [BAHZ•nee•un] *adj n*
bosniaque mf M

bosom [BU•zum] *n* sein M; ~
buddy\ami intime

boss [baus] *n* patron;
politicien M

botany [BAH•tu•nee] *n*
botanique F

both [both] *adj* les deux; *pron*
tous/toutes les deux

bother [BAH•thur] *vt* embêter;
n embêtement M

bottle [BAH•tl] *n* bouteille F; *vt*
mettre en bouteille F

bottom [BAH•tum] *n* fond;
prep au fond de M; ~s up\ à
la votre

boulder [BOL•dur] *n* rocher M

bounce [bouns] *vi vt* rebondir

bounce [bouns] *n* rebond M; *vt*
sauter; se jeter sur; expulser

bouncer [BOUN•sur] *n*
videur M

bound [bound] *adj* (to be ~
for) en route pour (être); à
destination de (être)

boundary [BOUN•du•ree] *n*
limite M

bout [bout] *n* combat M

bovine [BO•vuyn] *adj* bovin

bow 1 [bou] *vt vi n* incliner

bow 2 [bo] *n* nœud M (knot)

bow tie [BOW ty] *n* œud;
papillon M

bowels [boulz] *npl* intestins M

bowl [bol] *n* bol; (large)
jatte F M

bowling [BO•ling] *n*
bowling M

box 1 [bahks] *n* boîte F

box 2 [bahks] *vi* boxer F

box office [bahx AW•fis] *n*
bureau M de location

boxer [BAH•ksur] *n* boxeur M

boxing [BAH•ksing] *n* boxe F

boy [boi] *n* garçon M

boycott [BOI•kaht] *n vt* boycott

bra [brah] *n* soutien-gorge M

brace [brais] *n* (dental) appareil
M; (for back leg) appareil
orthopédique

bracelet [BRAI•slit] *n* bracelet

bracket (in writing) [BRA•kit]
n crochet M

brag [brag] *vi* se vanter

braid [braid] *n vt* tresse F

braille [brail] *n* braille M

brain [brain] *n* cerveau M;
cervelle F; ~ storm\idée de
gènie

brake [braik] *n vi* frein M

bran [bran] *n* son M

branch [branch] *n* branche;
agence F *vi* s'embrancher

brand [brand] *n* marque F

brand [brand] *vt* (cattle etc)
marquer au fer rouge F

brand-new [brand NOO] *adj*
tout neuf flambant neuf

brandy [BRAN•dee] *n*
cognac M

brash [brash] *adj* éffronté

brass [bras] *n* laiton M

brat [brat] *n* mioche

brave [braiv] *adj vt* brave; beau;
vt braver

bravery [BRAI•vu•ree] *n*
bravoure F

brawl [braul] *n* rixe F

brawn [braun] *n* muscle M

bray [brai] *vi* braire

breach (in wall) [breech] *n vt*
brèche F; (of contract) *n*
rupture (de contrat) F

bread [bred] *n* pain M

breadth [bredth] *n* largeur F

break 1 [braik] *vt vi* rompre
casser briser *vt;* casser briser
vi refl; tomber en panne;
prendre une pause; rompre
(avec qqn); entrer par
effraction

break 2 [braik] *n* rupture F;
in arm leg cassure F; from
work (short) pause F

breakdown (machine)
[BRAIK•doun] *n* panne F

breakfast [BREK•fust] *n* petit
déjeuner M

breast [brest] *n* sein M

breast (of bird) [brest] *n*
blanc M

breath [breth] *n* souffle M

breathe [breeth] *vi* respirer

breathless [BRETH•lis] *adj*
éssouflé

breed (animals) [breed] *n vt*
race F

breeding (plants; animals)
[BREE•ding] *n* élevage

breeze [breez] *n* brise F

brevity [BRE•vi•tee] *n*
brièveté F

brew [broo] *vt* faire *vt;* brasser
vt; faire infuser

brewer [BROO•ur] *n*
brasseur M

brewery [BROO•u•ree] *n*
brasserie F

bribe [bruyb] *n* pot-de-vin M; *vt*
soudoyer

brick [brik] *n* brique F

bridal [BRUY•dl] *adj* nuptial
bride [bruyd] *n* mariée F
bridegroom [BRUYD•groom]
    n marié M
bridesmaid [BRUYDZ•maid] *n*
    demoiselle F d'honneur
bridge [brij] *n* pont M
brief [breef] *adj* bref; *n* dossier;
    sommaire M
briefcase [BREEF•kais] *n*
    serviette F
briefly [BREE•flee] *adv*
    brièvement
bright [bruyt] *adj* brillant
brilliance [BRIL•lyuns] *n* éclat
    M; intelligence F
brilliant [BRIL•yunt] *adj*
    brillant
bring [bring] *vt* (person) amener
    (thing) apporter *vt;* person)
    ramener (thing) rapporter *vt;* (
    in conversation) soulever *vt*
brisk [brisk] *adj* vif
bristle [BRI•sl] *vi* hérisser
British [BRI•tish] *adj*
    britannique
broad [braud] *adj* large
broadcast [BRAUD•kast] *vt*
    radiodiffuser; téléviser
broadcast [BRAUD•kast] *n*
    émission F
brocade [bro•KAID] *n*
    brocart M
broccoli [BRAH•klee] *n*
    brocoli M
brochure [bro•SHUR] *n*
    brochure F
broil [broil] *vt* griller
broker [BRO•kur] *n* courtier M
bronze [brahnz] *n adj* bronze
brooch [broch] *n* broche F

brook [brük] *n* ruisseau M
broom [broom] *n* balai M
broth [brauth] *n* bouillon M
brothel [BRAH•thl] *n* bordel
brother [BRUH•thur] *n* frère M
brother-in-law
    [BRUH•thur•in•LAU] *n*
    beau-frère M
brown [braun] *adj n* brun M
bruise [brooz] *n vt* bleu M
brunette [broo•NET] *n*
    brunette F
brush [bruhsh] *n vt* brosse F;
    (of painter) pinceau M
Brussels [BRUH•slz] *n*
    Bruxelles F
brutal [BROO•tl] *adj* brutal
brute [broot] *n* brute F
bubble [BUH•bl] *n vi* bulle F
buck [buhk] *vi* ruer
bucket [BUH•kit] *n* seau M;
    baquet M
buckle [BUH•kl] *n vt* boucle F
bud [buhd] *n vi* bourgeon M
Buddhism [BOO•DI•zm] *n*
    bouddhisme M
budge [buhj] *vi vt* bouger
budget [BUH•jit] *n* budget M
buffalo [BUH•fu•LO] *n*
    buffle M
buffet [BUH•fai] *n* buffet M
bug [buhg] *n* (insect) punaise;
    (hidden microphone) micro
bugle [BYOO•gl] *n* clairon M
build [bild] *vt* bâtir; construire
builder [BIL•dur] *n*
    entrepreneur; constructeur M
building [BIL•ding] *n* bâtiment
    M; *adj* de construction à batir
bulb [buhlb] *n* (light~) ampoule
    F; (of plant) oignon

Bulgaria [BUHL•GAI•ree•u] *n* Bulgarie F

bulge [buhlj] *n* bosse F

bull [bül] *n* taureau M

bulldog [BüL•daug] *n* bouledogue M

bulldozer [BüL•do•zur] *n* bulldozer M

bullet [Bü•lit] *n* balle F

bulletin [Bü•lu•tin] *n* bulletin M

bully [Bü•lee] *n* tyran M

bumblebee [BUHM•bl•BEE] *n* bourdon M

bump [buhmp] *n vt* bosse F

bumper (of car) [BUHM•pur] *n* pare-chocs M

bun [buhn] *n* (bread) petit pain M; (in hair) chignon M

bunch [buhnch] *n* (of people) groupe M; (of flowers) bouquet M; (of keys) trousseau M; (of bananas) régime M

bundle [BUHN•dl] *n* paquet; (of papers) liasse M

bunk beds [buhnk ~] *npl* lits M superimposés

buoy [BOO•ee] *n* bouée F

burden [BUR•dn] *n vt* charge F

bureau [BYü•ro] *n* bureau; agence M

bureaucracy [byü•RAH•kru•see] *n* bureaucratie F

burglar [BUR•glur] *n* cambrioleur M

burial [BU•ree•ul] *n* enterrement M

Burma [BUR•mu] *n* Birmanie F

Burmese [bur•MEEZ] *adj* birman

burn [burn] *vi vt* brûler

burner [BUR•nur] *n* brûleur M

burrow [BUH•ro] *n vt* terrier M

burst [burst] *vt* éclater *vi* faire éclater *vt;* (balloon) crever *vt*

bury [BU•ree] *vt* enterrer

bus [buhs] *n* autobus; bus M

bush [büsh] *n* buisson M

bushel [Bü•shul] *n* boisseau M

business [BIZ•nis] *n* affaires F; negoce M; *adj* commercial

businessman –woman [BIZ•nis•MAN] *n* homme M d'affaires femme ~ F

bust (of statue) [buhst] *n* buste M

bustle [BUH•sl] *n vi* remue-ménage M

busy [BI•zee] *adj* occupé; diligent; laborieux

busybody [BIZ•ee•BAH•dee] *n* mouche F du coche

but [buht] *conj* mais; *n . . .* que; éxcept'; nothing ~\ rien que

butcher [BU•chur] *n* boucheur M

butcher (shop) [BUTCH•ur] *n* boucherie F

butler [BUHT•lur] *n* maître M d'hotel

butt (of cigarette) [buht] *n* mégot M

butter [BUH•tur] *n vt* beurre M

butterfly [BUH•tur•FLUY] *n* papillon M

buttock [BUH•tuk] *n* fesse F; *npl* derrière

button [BUH•tn] *n* bouton M

buy [buy] *vt* acheter

buyer [BUY•ur] *n* acheteur M

buzz (of insect) [buhz] *n*
bourdonnement M; *vi*
bourdonner M

by [buy] *prep* par; (near to)
prep près de; en à envers; sur;
one ~ one\un à un; ~
oneself\tout seul

C

cab [kab] *n* taxi M

cabbage [CA•bij] *n* chou M

cabin [CA•bin] *n* cabane F

cabinet [KA•bi•nit] *n* cabinet M

cable [KAI•bl] *n vi vt* câble M;
vt câbler

cackle [KA•kl] *vi* caqueter

cactus [KAK•tes] *n* cactus M

cadaver [ku•DA•vur] *n*
cadavre M

cadet [ku•DET] *n* cadet M

cafeteria [KA•fi•TEE•ree•u] *n*
cafétéria F

cage [kaij] *n* cage F

cake [kaik] *n* gâteau M; (soap)
pain M

calcium [KAL•see•um] *n*
calcium M

calculate [KAL•kyoo•LAIT] *vt*
calculer

calculator [KAL•kyoo•LAI•tur]
n calculatrice F

calendar [KA•lin•dur] *n*
calendrier M

calf [kaf] *n* veau; (of leg)
mollet M

call [caul] (by phone téléphoner)
vt n appeler (s: appel m);
~ for\demander

calling [KAU•ling] *n* vocation F

calm [kahm] *adj* calme

calm down [kalm down] *vt vi*
calmer

Cambodia [kam•BO•dyu] *n*
Camboge M

camel [KA•mul] *n* chameau M

cameo [KA•mee•O] *n* camée M

camera [KA•mu•ru] *n*
appareil M

cameraman [KA•mu•ru•MAN]
n cameraman M

camp [kamp] *n* camp M; *vi*
camper

campaign [kam•PAIN] *n vi*
campagne

campground [KAMP•ground]
n camping M

can 1 [kan] *n* (for drink food
garbage) boîte F; (for oil)
bidon M

can 2 [kan] *vi-aux* pouvoir;
(know how to) savoir

Canada [KA•nu•du] *n*
Canada M

canal [ku•NAL] *n* canal M

canary [ku•NA•ree] *n* canari M

cancel [KAN•suhl]
(appointment) *vt*
décommander annuler

cancer [KAN•sur] *n* cancer M

candid [KAN•did] *adj* franc;
ouvert

candidate [KAN•di•DUT] *n* candidat M

candle [KAN•dl] *n* bougie F

candor [KAN•dur] *n* franchise F

candy [KAN•dee] *n* bonbon M

cane [kain] *n* canne F; *vt* bâtoner

canine [KAI•nuyn] *adj* canin

cannibal [KA•ni•bl] *n* cannibale

cannon [KA•nun] *n* canon M

canoe [ku•NOO] *n* canoë M

canon [KA•nun] *n* canon M

canopy [KA•nu•pee] *n* baldaquin; dais M

canvas [KAN•vus] *n* toile F

canyon [KA•nyun] *n* cañon

cap [kap] *n* casquette F; *vt* surmounter; capsuler

capacity [ku•PA•ci•tee] *n* capacité F

cape 1 (clothing) [kaip] *n* cape F

cape 2 (geog.) [kaip] *n* cap M

caper [KAI•pur] *n* câpre F

capital [KA•pi•tl] *n* capitale; (letter) majuscule F F

capitalism [KA•pi•tu•LI•zm] *n* capitalisme M

capsule [KAP•sul] *n* capsule F

captain [KAP•tin] *n* capitaine M

caption [KAP•shun] *n* légende F

captive [KAP•tiv] *n* captif M

capture [KAP•chur] *vt n* capturer

car [kahr] *n* voiture F

carbon [KAHR•bun] *n* charbone M

carcass [KAHR•kus] *n* carcasse F

card [kahrd] *n* carte F

cardboard [KAHRD•baurd] *n* carton M

cardiac [KAHR•dee•AK] *adj* cardiaque

cardigan [KAHR•di•gun] *n* cardigan

cardinal [KAHR•di•nl] *n* cardinal M

care [kair] *n* soin M; (about); take ~ of\s'occuper de; I don't ~\ça m'est égal *vi* soucier (de)

career [ku•REER] *n* carrière; occupation F

carefree [KAIR•free] *adj* insouciant

careful [KAIR•ful] *adj* soigneux; be ~ !\fais attention!

careless [KAIR•lis] *adj* insouciant

caress [ku•RES] *vt* caresser; *n* caresse F

cargo [kahr•go] *n* cargaison M

Caribbean (Sea) [KU•ri•BEE•un] *n* Mer des Caraïbes

carnal [KAHR•nul] *adj* charnel

carnation [kahr•NAI•shun] *n* œillet M

carnival [KAHR•nu•vl] *n* carnaval M

carnivorous [kahr•NI•vu•rus] *adj* carnivore

carp [kahrp] *n* carpe F

carpenter [KAHR•pun•tur] *n* charpentier M

carpet [KAHR•put] *n* tapis M; *vi* couvrir d'un tapis

carriage [KA•rij] *n* voiture F

carrot [KA•rut] *n* carrotte F

carry [KA•ree] *vt* porter; emporter; ~ on continuer; ~ out\metter à exécution

cart [kahrt] *n* charrotte F; *vt* transporter

carton [KAHR•tn] *n* carton M

cartoon [kahr•TOON] *n* dessin animé M

carve [kahrv] *vt vi* (wood; stone) sculpter *vt;* (meat) découper *vt*

case [kais] *n* (box crate) caisse F; (for eyeglasses cigarettes etc) étui m; (law) affaire F M

case (in ~ of) [kais] *n* cas (en ~ de); in any ~\en tout cas; in case\au cas où M

cash [kash] *n* espèces F

cash register [kash RE•jis•tur] *n* caisse enregistreusé F

cask [kask] *n* tonneau M

casket [KA•skit] *n* cercueil

cassette [ku•SET] *n* cassette

cast 1 [kast] *n* (of actors) distribution F; (for broken limb) plâtre M F

cast 2 [kast] *vt* lancer; jeter

castle [KA•sl] *n* château M

casual [KA•zhoo•ul] *adj* désinvolte; sans cérémonie

cat [kat] *n* chat M

catalogue [KA•tu•LAHG] *n vt* catalogue; cataloguer *vt* M

catapult [KA•tu•PUHLT] *vt n* catapulter; catapulte F

cataract [KA•tu•RAKT] *n* cataract F

catastrophe [ku•TA•stru•fee] *n* catastrophe F

catch [kach] *vt* attraper

categorical [KA•tu•GAU•ri•kl] *adj* catégorique

category [KA•tu•GAU•ree] *n* catégorie F

cater (banquet etc) [KAI•tr] *vt* préparer des repas pour

caterpillar [KA•tur•PI•lur] *n* chenille F

cathedral [ku•THEE•drul] *n* cathédrale F

Catholic [KATH•lik] *adj n* catholique

cattle [KA•tl] *npl* bétail M

cauliflower [KAH•lee•FLOU•ur] *n* chou-fleur M

cause [kauz] *vt* causer; *n* cause F

caustic [KAU•stik] *adj* caustique

caution [KAU•shun] *n vt* prudence F; (warning) avertissement avertir *vt*

cautious [KAU•shus] *adj* prudent; en garde; circonspect

cavalry [KA•vl•ree] *n* cavalerie F

cave [kaiv] *n* caverne F

caveman [KAIV•man] *n* hommé des cavernes M

cavity [KA•vi•tee] *n* cavité F

cease [sees] *vt vi* cesser; arrêter; interrompre

cease-fire [CEES•FUYUR] *n* cessez-le-feu M

cedar [SEE•dur] *n* cèdre M

cede [seed] *vt vi* céder

cedilla [si•DI•lu] *n* cédille F

celebrate [SE•li•BRAIT] *vt vi*
célébrer *vt;* faire la fête *vi*

celebration [SE•li•BRAI•shun]
n célébration F

celebrity [si•LE•bri•tee] *n*
célébrité F

celibate [SE•li•but] *adj*
célibataire

cell [sel] *n* cellule F

cellar [SE•lur] *n* cave F

cello [CHE•lo] *n* violincelle M

Celtic [KEL•tik] *adj* celte

cement [si•MENT] *vt n*
cimenter; ciment M

cemetery [SE•mi•TE•ree] *n*
cimitière M

censor [SEN•sur] *n* censeur M;
vt censurer

censorship [SEN•sur•SHIP] *n*
censure F

census [SEN•sus] *n*
recensement M

centennial [sen•TEN•ee•ul] *n*
centenaire M

center [SEN•tur] *n* centre M

centigrade [SEN•ti•GRAID]
adj centigrade

centimeter [SEN•ti•MEE•tur] *n*
centimètre M

centipede [SEN•ti•PEED] *n*
mille-pattes M

central [SEN•trul] *adj* central

century [SEN•chu•ree] *n*
siècle M

ceramic [si•RA•mik] *adj*
céramique

cereal [SI•ree•ul] *n* céréale F

ceremony [SE•ri•MO•nee] *n*
cérémonie F

certain [SUR•tn] *adj* certain

certainly [SUR•tn•lee] *adv*
certainement

certainty [SUR•tn•tee] *n*
certitude F

certificate [sur•TI•fi•kut] *n*
certificat M

certify [SUR•tu•FUY] *vt*
certifier

chain [chain] *n vt* chaîne;
enchaîner *vt* F

chain saw [CHAIN sau] *n*
tronçoneuse F

chair [chair] *n* chaise F

chairman [CHAIR•mun] *n*
président M

chalk [chauk] *n* craie F

challenge [CHA•linj] *vt n*
défier *vt;* défi M

chamber [CHAIM•bur] *n*
chambre F

chameleon [ku•MEEL•yun] *n*
caméléon M

champagne [sham•PAIN] *n*
champagne M

champion [CHAM•pyun] *n*
champion M

chance [chans] *n* chance;
(opportunity) occasion F; *n*
hasard M; *adj* accidental; by
~\par hasard

chancellor [CHAN•su•lur] *n*
chancelier

change [chainj] *n vt vi*
changement M; changer *vi vt;*
(clothes) changer *vi refl;*
modifier; *n* la Bourse F

channel 1 (TV; radio)
[CHA•nul] *n* chaîne F

channel 2 (water) [CHA•nul] *n*
vt chenal M; canaliser *vt* M

chant (rel) [chant] *n vt vi*
psalmodie F; psalmodier
vt vi F

chaos [KAI•ahs] *n* chaos M

chapel [CHA•pl] *n* chapelle F

chaplain [CHA•plen] *n*
aumônier M

chapter [CHAP•tur] *n*
chapitre M

character [KA•ruk•tur] *n*
carectère; (in novel etc)
personnage M

characteristic
[KA•ruk•tu•RI•stik] *n adj*
characteristique

charcoal [CHAHR•col] *n*
charbon M de bois

charge [charj] *n* prix; *vi vt* faire
payer; payer; (elec) charge;
(attack) charger *vt;* (law)
accuser *vt;* charger de *vi* refl;
être responsable de M

charity [CHA•ru•tee] *n*
charité F

charm [chahrm] *n* charme M *vt*
charmer

charming [CHAHR•ming] *adj*
charmant

chart [chahrt] *n* graphique M

charter (flight) [CHAHR•tur] *n*
vol M charter

chase [chais] *n vt* poursuite;
poursuivre *vt;* chasser *vt* F

chasm [KA•zm] *n* abîme F

chaste [chaist] *adj* chaste

chastise [cha•STUYZ] *vt*
châtier

chastity [CHA•sti•tee] *n*
chasteté F

chat [chat] *vi* bavarder; *n*
bavardage F

chatterbox [CHA•tur•BAHKS]
n bavard M

chauffeur [SHO•fur] *n*
chauffeur M

cheap [cheep] *adj* bon marché

cheapen [CHEE•pn] *vt*
rabaisser

cheat [cheet] *vt vi* tromper; (on
test; in game) *vi* tricher

cheater [CHEE•tr] *n* tricheur M

check [chek] *vt* verifier F (bill)
n addition F (currency) *n*
cheque F

checkbook [CHEK•buk] *n*
chéquier M

checkers [CHEK•urz] *n* jeu M
de dames M

cheek [cheek] *n* joue F

cheer [cheer] *vt* acclamer;
encourage; *n* joie;
acclamation F

cheer up *vi* égayer

cheerful [CHEER•ful] *adj* gai

cheering [CHEE•ring] *n*
acclamations F

cheers (drinking toast) [cheerz]
excl santé

cheese [cheez] *n* fromage F

cheetah [CHEE•tu] *n*
guépard M

chef [shef] *n* chef de cuisine M

chemical [KE•mi•kul] *adj n*
chimique; produit M chimique

chemist [KE•mist] *n* chimiste

chemistry [KE•mi•stree] *n*
chimie F

cherish [CHE•rish] *vt* chérir;
nourrir

cherry [CHE•ree] *n* cerise F

chess [ches] *n* échecs M

chest [chest] (anat.) *n* poitrine F;
(box) caisse F

chest of drawers *n*
commode F

chestnut [CHEST•nuht] *n*
châtaigne F

chew [choo] *vt* mâcher

chick [chik] *n* oisillon

chicken [CHI•kin] *n* poulet M

chicken pox [~ pahks] *n*
varicelle F

chief [cheef] *n* chef M

child [chuyld] *n* enfant MF

childbirth [CHUYLD•burth] *n*
accouchement M

childhood [CHUYLD•hud] *n*
enfance F

childish [CHUYL•dish] *adj*
puéril; enfantin

Chile [CHI•lee] *n* Chili M

chill [chil] *n* frisson M;
froid M

chill [chil] *vi vt* (person) faire
frissoner *vt;* (with fright)
transir ; (wine food) refraichir
vi M

chills (med) [chilz] *n*
refroidissements M

chilly [CHI•lee] *adj* froid; be
~\avoir froid

chime [chuym] *n vi* carillon M;
carilloner *vi*

chimney [CHIM•nee] *n*
cheminée F

chimpanzee [chim•PAN•ZEE]
n chimpanzé M

chin [chin] *n* menton M

China 1 [CHUY•nu] *n* Chine F

china 2 [CHUY•nu] *n*
porcelaine F

Chinese [chuy•NEEZ] *adj*
chinois

chip 1 [chip] *n* (fragment) éclat
M; (in dish etc) ébruchure F;
(in gambling) jeton M

chip 2 [chip] *vt* ébrecher

chirp [churp] *vi* pépier

chisel [CHI•zl] *n vt* ciseau M;
ciseler *vt* M

chivalry [SHI•vl•ree] *n*
galanterie F

chive [chuyv] *n* civoulette F

chlorine [KLAU•reen] *n*
chlore M

chlorophyll [KLAU•ru•FIL] *n*
chlorophylle F

chocolate [CHAU•ku•lut] *n*
chocolat M

choice [chois] *n* choix M

choir [kwuyr] *n* chœur M

choke [chok] *vt* étrangler; (of
car) *n* starter M

cholera [KAH•lu•ru] *n*
choléra M

choose [chooz] *vi vt* choisir

chop 1 [chahp] *vt* (food)
hacher; (wood) couper

chop 2 (of meat) [chahp] *n*
côtelette F

chord [kaurd] *n* accord M

chores [chaurz] *npl* travaux M

chorus [KAU•rus] *n* chœur M

Christ [kruyst] *n* Christ M

christen [KRI•sn] *vt* baptiser

Christian [KRI•schun] *adj n*
chrétien

Christianity
[KRI•schee•A•nu•tee] *n*
christianisme M

Christmas [KRIS•mus] *n*
Noël M

chrome [krom] *n* chrome M
chronic [KRAH•nik] *adj* chronique
chronicle [KRAH•ni•kl] *n* chronique F; *vt* relater; narrer
chronological [KRAH•nu•LAH•ji•kl] *adj* chronologique
chrysanthemum [kri•SAN•thi•mum] *n* chrysanthème M
chubby [CHUH•bee] *adj* potelé
chuck [chuhk] *vt* lancer; jeter
chuckle [CHUH•kl] *vi* glousser
chunk [chuhnk] *n* gros morceau M
church [church] *n* église F
churn (butter) [churn] *vt* baratter
chute [shoot] *n* glissière F
cider [SUY•dur] *n* cidre M
cigar [si•GAHR] *n* cigare M
cigarette [SI•gu•RET] *n* cigarette F
cinder [SIN•dur] *n* cendre F
Cinderella [SIN•du•RE•lu] *n* Cendrillon F
cinema [SI•nu•mu] *n* cinéma M
cinnamon [SI•nu•mun] *n* cannelle F
circle [SUR•kl] *n* cercle M
circuit [SUR•kit] *n* circuit M
circular [SUR•cyu•lur] *adj* circulaire
circulate [SUR•kyu•LAIT] *vi vt* circuler; *vi* faire circuler
circulation [SUR•kyu•LAI•shun] *n* circulation F; (of periodical) tirage M

circumcision [SUR•cuhm•SI•zhun] *n* circoncision F
circumference [sur•CUHM•fu•runs] *n* circonférence F·
circumflex [SUR•cuhm•FLEKS] *adj* circonflex
circumstances [SUR•cum•STANS] *n* circonstance F
circus [SUR•kus] *n* cirque F
cite [suyt] *vt* citer
citizen [SI•ti•zn] *n* citoyen M
city [SI•tee] *n* ville; cité F
city hall [SIT•tee hall] *n* hôtel de ville
civic [SI•vik] *adj* civique
civil [SI•vl] *adj* civil; (polite) poli
civilian [si•VI•lyun] *n* civil M
civilization [SI•vi•li•ZAI•shun] *n* civilisation
civilize [SI•vi•LUYZ] *vt* civiliser
claim [klaim] *vt n* (assert) affirmer *vt;* (responsibility) revendiquer *vt;* (to hold that...) prétendre *vt;* (for payment) revendication F; (insurance) déclaration F de sinistre; (right) droit M; (assertion) affirmation F
clam [klam] *n* palourde F
clamor [CLA•mur] *n* cris M
clamp [klamp] *n vt* crampon M; cramponner
clan [klan] *n* clan M
clandestine [klan•DE•stin] *adj* clandestin

clap [klap] *vi* applaudir; ~ of thunder\coup de tonerre

clapping [KLA•ping] *n* applaudissements M

clarify [KLA•ri•FUY] *vt* clarifier

clarinet [KLA•ri•NET] *n* clarinette F

clarity [KLA•ri•tee] *n* clarté F

clash [klash] *n vi* (noise) choc M; (conflict) conflit M heurt M; *vi* se heurter; (colors) jurer

clasp 1 [klasp] *n* fermoir M; *vt* serrer

class 2 [klass] *n vt* classe; leçon F *vt* classier

classic [KLA•sik] *adj n* classique M

classical [KLA•si•kl] *adj* classique M

classified [KLA•si•FUYD] *adj* secret

classified ad *n* petite annonce F

classify [KLA•si•FUY] *vt* classifier

classroom [KLAS•rum] *n* salle de classe

clause [klauz] *n* clause; (in grammar) proposition F

claw [clau] *n* (of animal) griffe F; (of crab) pince F

claw (at) [clau] *vi* griffer

clay [klay] *n* argile F

clean [kleen] *adj* propre; *vt* nettoyer; faire la nettoyaage

cleaner [KLEE•nur] *n* nettoyeur M

cleaning lady [KLEE•ning LAI•dee] *n* femme de ménage F

cleanliness [KLEN•lee•nis] *n* propreté F

clear [kleer] *adj vt* clair; transparent; *vt* éclaircir; (way) dégager; (table) débarasser; (through customs) dédouaner; *vi* (to become clear) s'éclaircir

clearance [KLEE•runs] *n* autorisation F

clearing [KLEE•ring] *n* (in forest) clarrière F

clearly [KLEER•lee] *adv* clairement

cleavage [KLEE•vij] *n* clivage F

cleaver [KLEE•vur] *n* couperet M

clench [klench] *vt* serre; *n* crampon; rivet M

clergy [KLUR•jee] *n* clergé M

clerical [KLE•ri•kl] *adj* de bureau; (rel) clérical

clerk [clurk] *n* employé; (court) clerc M

clever [KLE•vur] *adj* habile; adroit; astucieux; (idea) ingénieux

client [KLUY•unt] *n* client -e MF

clientele [KLUY•un•TEL] *n* clientèle F

cliff [klif] *n* falaise F

climate [KLUY•mit] *n* climat M

climax [KLUY•maks] *n* apogée M

climb [cluym] *n* montée F; *vt vi* monter; grimper; gravir; descendre

cling [kling] *vi* accrocher

clinic [KLI•nik] *n* clinique F

clinical [KLI•ni•kl] *adj* clinique F

clip [klip] *n* (for paper) trombone M; (for hair) pince; *vt* (hair nails) couper; (hedge) tailler; attacher

clippers [KLI•purz] *npl* (for hair) tondeuse F; (for hedge) cisailles *fpl*

cloak [klok] *n* cape F; manteau M; *vt* couvrir d'un manteau; masquer

clock [klahk] *n* (large) horloge F; (small) pendule F

clockwise [KLAHK•wuyz] *adj adv* dans le sens des aiguilles d'une montre

clog [klahg] *vt vi* boucher

clogs [klahgz] *npl* sabots M

cloister [KLOI•stur] *n* cloître M

close 1 [klos] *adj adv adj* (near) proche (de) près (de); (friend) intime; tout près; (in competition) serré; *adv* près de près; (translation) fidèle; *adv prép* près de

close 2 [kloz] *vt vi vt* fermer; *vi* (shop) fermer; *vi refl* (lid; door; etc) fermer

closet [KLAH•zit] *n* placard; cabinet M

cloth [klauth] *n* tissu M étoffe F; (for cleaning) chiffon M M

clothe [kloth] *vt* habiller

clothes [klothz] *npl* vêtements; habits M

clothing [KLO•thing] *n* -clothes M

cloud [kloud] *n* nuage F

cloudy [KLOU•dee] *adj adj* nuageux; (liquid) trouble; *vi* se couvrir de nuages

clove [klov] *n* clou M de girofle; (of garlic) gousse F d'aile

clover [KLO•vur] *n* trèfle M

clown [kloun] *n* clown; *vi* faire le clown M

club [kluhb] *n vt n* (weapon) massue F; (organization) club M; (for golf) club M; (in playing cards) trèfle; *vt* matraquer

cluck [cluhk] *vi* glousser

clue [kloo] *n* indice M; (in crossword) définition F M

clump [kluhmp] *n* (of trees bushes; flowers) bouquet M; massif M

clumsy [KLUHM•zee] *adj* maladroit; gauche

cluster [KLUH•stur] *n* groupe M

clutch 1 [kluhch] *n* (of car) embrayage M

clutch 2 [kluhch] *vt* (~ at) *vi* agripper

clutter [KLUH•tur] *vt vt* encombrer; *n* encombrement M

coach 1 [koch] *n* (of bus) car M; (of train) voiture F; (of team) entraîneur M; *vt* entraîner; (prepare) préparer; (with horses) carrosse F; (of train) voiture F; (bus) car M

coach 2 (sports) [koch] *n* entraîneur M; *vt* entraîner

coal [kol] *n* charbon M

coarse [caurs] *adj* grossier

coast 1 [kost] *n* côte F

coast 2 [kost] *vi* descendre en roue libre

coat 1 [kot] *n* manteau M; (of paint) couche F; (of fur) pelage M

coat 2 [kot] *vt* couvrir; (with paint) enduire

coax [koks] *vt* persuader par des cajoleries

cobblestones [KAH•bl•STONZ] *npl* pavés M

cobweb [KAHB•web] *n* toile F d'araignée

cocaine [ko•KAIN] *n* cocaïne F

cock 1 [kahk] *n* coq M

cock 2 (a gun) [kahk] *vt* armer

cockroach [KAHK•roch] *n* cafard M

cocktail [KAHK•tail] *n* cocktail M

cocoa [KO•ko] *n* cacao M

coconut [KO•ku•nuht] *n* noix M de coco

cocoon [ku•KOON] *n* cocon M

cod [kahd] *n* morue F

code [kod] *n vt* code F; *vt* chiffrer

coerce [ko•URS] *vt* contraindre

coffee [KAU•fee] *n* café M

coffee break [KAU•fee braik] *n* pause-café F

coffee cup [KAU•fee kup] *n* tasse F à café

coffee pot [KAU•fee pot] *n* cafetière F

coffee shop [KAU•fee shop] *n* café M

coffin [KAU•fin] *n* cercueil M

coherent [ko•HEE•runt] *adj* cohérent

coil 1 [koil] *n* rouleau M; (elec) bobine F

coil 2 [koil] *vt vi refl* enrouler; (snake) lover

coin [koin] *n* pièce (de monnaie) F

coincide [KO•in•SUYD] *vi* coïncider

coincidence [ko•IN•si•duns] *n* coïncidence F

cold [kold] *adj n adj* froid; it's ~il fait froid; I am ~\ j'ai froid; *n* froid M; (illness) rhume M; (to catch a ~) attraper un rhume

cold-blooded [BLU•did] *adj adj* (person) de sang-froid; à sang-froid; *adv* (in cold blood) de sang-froid

collaborate [ku•LA•bu•RAIT] *vi* collaborer

collapse [ku•LAPS] *n* i effondrement; M écroulement M; *vi refl* effondre ;écrouler

collar [KAH•lur] *n* col M; (for dog) collier M

collateral [ku•LA•tu•rul] *n* nantissement M

colleague [KAH•leeg] *n* collègue

collect [KU•lekt] *vt* rassembler ramasser; (as hobby) collectionner; (money) recueiller; (taxes) percevoir; *vi refl* (to gather together) rassembler amasser

college [KAH•lij] *n* (school) école F; (electoral etc) collège M

collide (with) [ku•LUYD] *vi* entrer en collision (avec)

colloquial [ku•LO•kwee•ul] *adj* familier

colon [KO•lun] *n* (anat) côlon M; (grammar) deux-points M

colony [KAH•lu•nee] *n* colonie F

color [KUH•lur] *n* couleur F; *vt* colorer; (with crayon) colorier; (dye) teindre

color television [KUH•lor TEL•i•VI•shn] *n* télévision en couleurs

color-blind [KUH•lor blynd] *adj* daltonien

colorful [KUH•lur•ful] *adj* coloré

colossal [ku•LAH•sul] *adj* colossal

colt [kolt] *n* poulain M

column [KAH•luhm] *n* colonne; (of newspaper) rubrique F

coma [KO•mu] *n* coma M

comb [kom] *n* peigne F; *vt* peigner

combat [KAHM•bat] *n vt* combat M; *vt vi* combattre

combination [KAHM•bi•NAI•shn] *n* combinaison F

combine [kum•BUYN] *vt* combiner

come [kuhm] *vi* venir arriver; revenir; descendre (en bas); (en haut); entrer; (in conversation) survenir; (regain consciousness) revenir à soi; allez!; sortir (sun, moon, book) paraître; s'avancer; *vt* tomber sur; précéder; succeder

comeback [KUHM•bak] *n* rentrée F

comedian [ku•MEE•dee•un] *n* comique M; (in theater) comédien

comedy [KAH•mi•dee] *n* comédie F

comet [KAH•mit] *n* comète F

comfort [KUHM•furt] *n* confort M; *vt* consoler

comfortable [KUHMF•tur•bl] *adj* confortable

comic [KAH•mik] *n* comique M; *adj* comique; amusant

comics (comic strip) [KAH•miks] *npl* bande F dessinée

coming [KUH•ming] *adj* prochain à venir

comma [KAH•mu] *n* virgule F

command [ku•MAND] *n* ordre; commandement M; (of subject) maîtrise F; *vt* ordonner; commander; (~ respect) inspirer

commander [ku•MAN•dur] *n* commandant M

commence [ku•MENS] *vt vi* commencer

commend [ku•MEND] *vt* louer; recommander

comment [KAH•ment] *n vi* commentaire M; *vi* faire des commentaires sur; *vt* remarquer que

commerce [KAH•murs] *n* commerce M .

commercial [ku•MUR•shl] *n* annonce F publicitaire

commission [ku•MI•shn] *n* commission

commissioner [ku•MI•shu•nur] *n* commissaire M

commit [ku•MIT] *vt* (crime; sin; error; etc) commettre; (to mental hospital) interner; (sth/sb to sb's care) confier; (~ suicide) se suicider

committee [ku•MI•tee] *n* comité F

committment [ku•MIT•munt] *n* engagement M obligation F

commodity [ku•MAH•di•tee] *n* marchandise F

common [KAH•mun] *adj* (shared) commun; ordinaire; vulgaire

common sense [KAH•mun sens] *n* bon sens M

commonly [KAH•mun•lee] *adv* généralement

commonplace [KAH•mun•PLAIS] *adj* banal

commotion [ku•MO•shn] *n* commotion F

communicate [ku•MYOO•ni•KAIT] *vt vi* communiquer

communion [ku•MYOO•nyun] *n* communion F

communism [KAH•myu•NI•zm] *n* communisme M

communist [KAH•myu•nist] *adj n* communiste M

community [ku•MYOO•nu•tee] *n* communauté F

commute [ku•MYOOT] *vt vi* (law) commuer; *vi* (travel) faire la navette

compact [kahm•PAKT] *adj* compact; *n* (for cosmetics) poudrier M

compact disc [KAHM•pakt disk] *n* disque M compact

companion [kum•PA•nyun] *n* compagnon M; compagne F

company [KUHM•pu•nee] *n* compagnie; tenir compagnie à qqn F

compare [kum•PAIR] *vt* comparer

comparison [kum•PA•ri•sn] *n* comparaison F

compartment [kum•PAHRT•munt] *n* compartiment M

compass [KAHM•pus] *n* boussole F; (for drawing circles) compas M

compassion [kum•PA•shn] *n* compassion F

compassionate [kum•PA•shu•nit] *adj* compatissant

compatible [kum•PA•ti•bl] *adj* compatible

compel [kum•PEL] *vt* contraindre; obliger

compelling [kum•PE•ling] *adj* irrésistible

compensate [KAHM•pun•SAIT] *vt* dédommager; indemniser; *vi* compenser qqch

compensation [KAHM•pun•SAI•shn] *n* (payment) dédommagement M; (for sth) compensation F

compete [kum•PEET] *vi* concourir; faire concurrence

competence [KAHM•pi•tuns] *n* compétence; abilité F

competent [KAHM•pi•tunt] *adj*
compétent

competition
[KAHM•pu•TI•shn] *n* rivalité
F concurrence F (in sports
game) compétition F

competitive [kum•PE•tu•tiv]
adj (in business)
concurrentiel; (sport) de
compétition

complacent [kum•PLAI•sunt]
adj complaisant

complain [kum•PLAIN] *vi*
plaindre

complaint [kuhm•PLAINT] *n*
plainte F; (in shop etc)
reclamation F

complement [KAHM•pli•munt]
vt (to go well with) compléter

complete [kum•PLEET] *adj*
complet; *vt* compléter; (a
form) remplir; (finish)
achever

complex [kahm•PLEKS] *adj*
complexe; *n* complexe M

complexion [kum•PLEK•shn] *n*
teint M; complexion F

complicate [KAHM•pli•KAIT]
vt compliquer

complicated
[KAHM•pli•KAI•tid] *adj*
compliqué

compliment [KAHM•pli•ment]
n compliment M; *vt*
complimenter

comply [kum•PLUY] *vi* refl
conformer à

component [kum•PO•nunt] *n*
composant M

compose [kum•POZ] *vt*
composer; *vi refl* composer de

composer [kum•PO•zur] *n*
compositeur M

composition
[KAHM•pu•ZI•shn] *n*
composition F

composure [kum•PO•zhur] *n*
sang-froid M; calme F

compound [KAHM•pound] *adj*
composé; *n* composé M;
(land) enceinte F

comprehend
[KAHM•pree•HEND] *vt*
comprendre

comprehension
[KAHM•pree•HEN•shn] *vt*
comprendre

comprehensive
[KAHM•pree•HEN•siv] *adj*
complet; compréhensif;
détaillé; (insurance)
tous-risques

compress [kum•PRES] *vt*
comprimer

comprise [kum•PRUYZ] *vt* (be
~d of) comprendre

compromise
[KAHM•pru•MUYZ] *n vt vi*
compromis M; *vt* transiger; *vi*
compromettre

compulsive [kum•PUHL•siv]
adj (psych) compulsif;
(obligatory) obligatoire

computer [kum•PYOO•tur] *n*
ordinateur M

computerize
[kum•PYOO•tu•RUYZ] *vt*
informatiser

comrade [KAHM•rad] *n*
camarade MF

conceal [kun•SEEL] *vt*
dissimuler; cacher

concede [kun•SEED] *vt vi*
concéder

conceit [kun•SEET] *n* vanité F

conceited [kun•SEE•tid] *adj*
vaniteux

conceive [kun•SEEV] *vt vi*
concevoir

concentrate
[KAHN•sun•TRAIT] *v vi vt*
concentrer; *vi refl* concentrer
sur

concept [KAHN•sept] *n*
concept M; idée F

concern [kun•SURN] *n*
inquietude F souci M;
(business) affaire F; *vt*
(involve); no ~ of mine\ cela
ne me regarde pas; ~ed
about\se preoccuper de;
concerner; (worry) *refl*
inquieter

concerning [kun•SUR•ning]
prep en ce qui concerne;
concernant

concert [KAHN•surt] *n*
concert M

concession [kun•SE•shn] *n*
concession F

concise [kun•SUYS] *adj* concis

conclude [kun•KLOOD] *vt vi*
conclure

concrete [kahn•KREET] *adj n*
concret; *n* béton M

concur [kun•KUR] *vi* être
d'accord

condemn [kun•DEM] *vt*
condamner

condense [kun•DENS] *vt vi*
condenser

condescending
[KAHN•di•SEN•ding] *adj*
condescendant

condition [kun•DI•shn] *n*
condtion F; *vt* conditionner; à
condition de; à condition que

condolences [kun•DO•lun•ciz]
npl condoléances F

condone [kun•DON] *vt* tolérer
excuser

conduct [*n.* KAHN•duhkt *v.*
kun•DUHKT] *n* conduite F; *vt*
conduire; (mus) diriger; se
conduire

conductor [kun•DUHK•tur] *n*
(mus) chef M d'orchestre; (on
train) chef M de train; (elec)

cone [kon] *n* cône F; (for ice
cream) cornet M; pine ~\
pomme de pine M

confectionery
[kun•FEK•shu•NE•ree] *n*
confiserie F

confederation
[kun•FE•du•RAI•shn] *n*
confédération F

confer [kun•FUR] *vt vi* conférer

conference [KAHN•fu•runs] *n*
conférence F

confess [kun•FES] *vt vi*
confesser

confession [kun•FE•shn] *n*
confession F

confidant [KAHN•fi•DAHNT]
n confident M

confide [kun•FUYD] *vt vi*
confier

confidence [KAHN•fi•duns] *n*
confiance F; (secret)
confidence F; se confier à

confident [KAHN•fi•dunt] *adj*
sûr assuré

confidential
[KAHN•fi•DEN•shl] *adj*
confidentiel

confine [kun•FUYN] *vt* confiner
enfermer

confirm [kun•FURM] *vt*
confirmer

confirmation
[KAHN•fur•MAI•shn] *n*
confirmation F

confiscate [KAHN•fi•SKAIT]
vt confisquer

conflict [KUN•flikt] *n* conflit
M; *vi* être en conflit

conform [kun•FAURM] *vt vi*
conformer

conformist [kun•FAUR•mist]
adj n conformiste MF

confound [kun•FOUND] *vt*
confondre

confront [kun•FRUHNT] *vt*
confronter; (problem; danger;
etc) affronter faire face à

confuse [kun•FYOOZ] *vt*
confondre; (mix up)
embrouiller

confusing [kun•FYOO•zing]
adj embrouillant; déroutant

confusion [kun•FYOO•zhn] *n*
confusion F

congestion [kun•JES•chn] *n*
congestion; (traffic)
encombrement F

congratulate
[kung•GRA•chu•LAIT] *vt*
féliciter; (~ for sth) féliciter
de qqch

congregate
[KAHNG•gri•GAIT] *vi*
rassembler .

congregation
[KAHNG•gri•GAI•shn] *n*
assemblée F

conjugation
[KAHN•joo•GAI•shn] *n*
conjugaison F

conjunction [kun•JUHNK•shn]
n conjonction F

connect [ku•NEKT] *vt* joindre;
relier; (on telephone) mettre
en communication; (pipe
electricity) brancher

conquer [KAHGN•kur] *vt*
conquérir; (feelings) vaincre

conqueror [KAHNG•ku•rur] *n*
conquérant M

conquest [KAHNG•kwest] *n*
conquête F

conscience [KAHN•shuns] *n*
conscience F

conscientious
[KAHN•shee•EN•shus] *adj*
consciencieux

conscious [KAHN•shus] *adj*
conscient

consecrate [KAHN•se•KRAIT]
vt consacrer

consecutive [kun•SE•cyu•tiv]
adj consécutif

consent [kun•SENT] *n vi*
consentement M; *vi* consentir

consequence
[KAHN•si•KWENS] *n*
conséquence F

conservation
[KAHN•sur•VAI•shn] *n*
préservation F; protection F

conservative [kun•SUR•vu•tiv]
n adj conservaduer M; *adj*
traditionel (pol) conservadeur

consider [kun•SI•dr] *vt*
considérer; (take into account)
prendre en compte

considerable [kun•SI•du•ru•bl]
adj considérable

considerate [kun•SI•du•rit] *adj*
prévenant

considering [kun•SI•du•ring]
prep étant; donné

consist [kun•SIST] *vi* consister
en; consister à faire

consistency [kun•SI•stun•see] *n*
consistance F; cohérence F

consistent [kun•SIS•tunt] *adj*
conséquant; cohérent

consolation
[KAHN•su•LAI•shn] *n*
consolation F

console 1 [kun•SOL] *vt*
consoler

console 2 [KAHN•sol] *n*
console M

consolidate
[kun•SAH•lu•DAIT] *vt*
consolider

consonant [KAHN•su•nunt] *n*
consonne F

conspicuous [kun•SPI•kyoo•us]
adj voyant; se faire remarquer

conspiracy [kun•SPI•ru•see] *n*
conspiration F complot F

constant [KAHN•stunt] *n/adj*
constante F; *adj* constant;
incessant

constellation
[KAHN•stu•LAI•shn] *n*
constellation F

constituent [kun•STI•choo•int]
n constituant M; (pol)
electuer M

constitution
[KAHN•sti•TOO•shn] *n*
constitution F

constraint [kun•STRAINT] *n*
constrainte F; (restraint)
retenue F

construct [kun•STRUHKT] *vt*
construire; fabriquer

construe [kun•STROO] *vt*
interpréter

consulate [KAHN•su•lit] *n*
consulat M

consult [kun•SUHLT] *vt vi vt vi*
consulter; *vi refl* consulter

consume [kun•SOOM] *vt*
consommer

consumer [kun•SOOM•ur] *n*
consommateur

consummate
[KAHN•su•MAIT] *vt*
consommer

consumption
[kun•SUHMP•shn] *n*
consommation F; (med)
consomption F

contact [KAHN•takt] *vt*
contacter; prendre contact
avec; *vi* prendre contact; *n*
contact M

contagious [kun•TAI•jus] *adj*
contageux

contain [kun•TAIN] *vt* contenir;
enclore; inclure

container [kun•TAI•nur] *n*
récipient m; (for transport)
containeur M

contaminate
[kun•TA•mi•NAIT] *vt*
contaminer

contemplate
[KAHN•tum•PLAIT] *vt vi*
contempler; *vt* envisager

contemporary
[kun•TEM•pu•RE•ree] *adj n*
contemporain

contempt [kun•TEMPT] *n*
mépris M; outrage M à la
cour; mépriser

contemptible
[kun•TEMP•tu•bl] *adj*
méprisable

contend [kun•TEND] *vt*
prétendre que soutenir que; *vi*
lutter contre; rivaliser avec

content [kun•TENT] *adj*
content; satisfait; *vt* se
contenter de qqch

contents [KAHN•tents] *npl*
contenu M; table M de
matières

contest 1 [KAHN•test] *n*
concours

contest 2 [kun•TEST] *vt*
contester; disputer

context [KAHN•tekst] *n*
contexte M

continent [KAHN•ti•nunt] *n*
continent M

contingency [kun•TIN•jun•see]
n éventualité F

continual [kun•TI•nyoo•ul] *adj*
continuel

continually [kun•TI•nyoo•u•lee]
adv continuellement

continuation
[kun•TI•nyoo•AI•shn] *n*
continuation F

continue [kun•TI•nyoo] *v*
continuer; maintenir;
prolonger

contract 1 [KAHN•trakt] *n*
contrat M; *vt* contracter

contract 2 [kun•TRAKT] *vi* se
contracter

contraction [kun•TRAK•shn] *n*
contraction F

contradict [KAHN•tru•DIKT]
vt contredire

contradiction
[KAHN•tru•DIK•shn] *n*
contrediction F

contrary [KAHN•TRE•ree] *adj*
n contraire; au contraire

contrast [*n.* KAHN•trast *v.*
kun•TRAST] *n* contraste M;
par contraste avec; *vt*
contraster

contribute [kun•TRI•byoot] *vt*
vi contribuer; *vi* (to discussion;
report; etc) collaborer

contribution
[KAHN•tri•BYOO•shn] *n*
contribution F; (to discussion;
report; etc) collaboration F

contrive [kun•TRUYV] *vt*
inventer; *vi* s'arranger

control [kun•TROL] *vt* diriger;
(machinery) commander;
(restrain) (se) maîtriser; *n*
contrôle M; maîtrise F;
autorité F; *npl* ~s (machinery)
contrôles *fpl*

controller [kun•TRO•lur] *n*
contrôleur M

controversy
[KAHN•tru•VUR•see] *n*
controverse F; polémique F
dispute F

convalescence
[KAHN•vu•LE•suns] *n*
convalescence F

convalescent
[KAHN•vu•LE•sunt] *adj n*
convalescent M

convene [kun•VEEN] *vt*
convoquer assembler; *vi refl*
assembler

convenience [kun•VEE•nyuns] *n* commodité F; confort M; when it will be ~\quand cela vous convient

convenient [kun•VEE•nyunt] *adj* convenable; pratique; commode

convent [KAHN•vent] *n* couvent M

convention [kun•VEN•shn] *n* convention F assemblée F; (tradition practice) usage M

converge [kun•VURJ] *vi* converger

conversant [kun•VUR•sunt] *adj* versé (dans); au courant; de familier (avec)

conversation [KAHN•vur•SAI•shn] *n* conversation F

converse 1 [kun•VURS] *vi* converser

converse 2 [KAHN•vurs] *n* contraire M inverse M

conversion [kun•VUR•zhn] *n* conversion F

convert [n. KAHN•vurt v. kun•VURT] *n* converti M; *vt vi refl* convertir

convex [kahn•VEKS] *adj* convexe

convey [kun•VAI] *vt* (message idea etc) communiquer; (goods) transporter

conveyer belt [kun•VAI•ur ~] *n* tapis M roulant

convict [n. KAHN•vikt v. kun•VIKT] *n* forçat; *vt* condamner

convince [kun•VINS] *vt* convaincre; persuader

convincing [kun•VIN•sing] *adj* convaincant

convoy [KAHN•voi] *n* convoi M

coo [koo] *vi* roucouler

cook [kuk] *n* cuisinier M; *vt* faire cuire préparer; *vi* faire la cuisine cuisiner; (food) cuire

cookie [KU•kee] *n* biscuit; gateau; sec M

cooking [KU•king] *n* cuisine F

cool [kool] *adj* frais (fraîche); (weather) il fait frais; (relaxed) calme; (unfriendly) froid ; *vt vi* rafraîchir; refroidir

coolness [KOOL•nis] *n* fraîcheur F frais M; (person) sang-froid M

coop [koop] *n* poulailler M; (fig) claquemurer; enfermer

cooperate [ko•AH•pu•RAIT] *vi* coopérer; collaborer

cooperation [ko•AH•pu•RAI•shn] *n* coopération; collaboration F

coordinate [n. ko•AUR•di•nit v. ko•AUR•di•NAIT] *n* (on map, etc) coordonnée F; *vt* coordonner

coordination [ko•AUR•di•NAI•shn] *n* coordination F

cop [kahp] *n* flic M (coll)

cope [kop] *vi* tenir tête; à se débrouiller; faire face à

copious [KO•pee•us] *adj* copieux

copper [KAH•pur] *n* cuivre M

copy [KAH•pee] *n* copie F; (of book) exemplaire F; (of

periodical) numéro; *vt* copier;
imiter

copyright |KAH•pee•RUYT| *n*
copyright; droit M d'auteur;
propriété F littéraire; *vt*

coral |KAU•rul| *n* corail M

cord |kaurd| *n* corde: F cordon
M; (string) ficelle; (elec)
fil M

corduroy |KAUR•du•ROI| *n*
velours M côtelé

cork |kaurk| *n* liège F; (of
bottle) bouchon M

corkscrew |KAURK•skroo| *n*
tire-bouchon M

corn |kaurn| *n* maïs M; cob;
épi; de maïs; (on foot) cor M

corner |KAUR•nur| *n* coin M
angle M; (of market)
accaparement M; *vt* (animal)
acculer; (market) accaparer

cornice |KAUR•nis| *n*
corniche F

coronation |KAU•ru•NAI•shn|
n couronnement

coroner |KAU•ru•NUR| *n*
coroner

corporal |KAUR•pu•rul| *adj*
corporel; *n* caporel M

corporation
|KAUR•pu•RAI•shn| *n*
compagnie; société F

corpse |kaurps| *n* cadavre M

correct |ku•REKT| *adj* correct;
vt corriger

correction |ku•REK•shn| *n*
correction F

correctly |ku•REKT•lee| *adv*
correctement

correspond |KAU•ri•SPAHND|
vi correspondre

correspondence
|KAU•ri•SPAHN•duns| *n*
correspondance F

correspondent
|KAU•ri•SPAHN•dunt| *n*
correspondant M

corresponding
|KAUR•uh•SPAHN•ding| *adj*
correspondant

corridor |KAU•ri•daur| *n*
corridor M; couloir M

corrode |ku•ROD| *vt* corroder;
vi se corroder

corrosion |ku•RO•zhn| *n*
corrosion F

corrupt |ku•RUHPT| *adj*
corrompu; dépravé; *vt*
corrompre; dépraver

corruption |ku•RUHP•shn| *n*
corruption F

Corsica |KAUR•si•ku| *n*
Corse F

cosmetic |kahz•ME•tik| *n*
cosmétique; produit M de
beauté

cosmopolitan
|KAHZ•mu•PAH•li•tn| *adj n*
cosmopolite MF

cost |kaust| *n* coût M; (law)
dépens mpl; à tout prix; coûte;
que coûte; *vi vt* coûter

costly |KAUST•lee| *adj* coûteux

costume |KAH•styoom| *n*
costume M

cot |kaht| *n* petit lit M

cottage |KAH•tij| *n* cottage M;
chaumière F

cotton |KAH•tn| *n* coton M

couch |kouch| *n* canapé F

cough |kauf| *n* toux F; *vi*
tousser

council [KOUN•sl] *n* conseil M;
(Church) concile M

counsel [KOUN•sl] *n* conseil
M; (lawyer) avocat M; *vt*
conseiller

counselor [KOUN•su•lur] *n*
conseiller M

count [kount] *vt vi* compter; *vt*
compter sur; *n* compte M;
(noble title) comte M

counter [KOUN•tur] *n* comptoir
M; *vt* contrer; *vi* riposter par

counteract [KOUN•tur•AKT]
vt contrebalancer

counterfeit [KOUN•tur•FIT]
adj faux; *vt* contrefaire

counterpart
[KOUN•tur•PAHRT] *n*
équivalent M; (person)
homologue mf

countess [KOUN•tis] *n*
comtesse F

countless [KOUNT•lis] *adj*
innombrable

country [KUHN•tree] *n* pays
M; (rural area) campagne;
(region) région F

countryman [KUHN•tree•mun]
n (from the same country)
compatriote; paysan M

county [KOUN•tee] *n* comté M

coup [koo] *n* (military) coup M
d'État

couple [KUH•pl] *n* couple M;
paire F; deux; quelques

coupon [KOO•pahn] *n* coupon;
bon M

courage [KU•rij] *n* courage M

courageous [ku•RAI•jus] *adj*
courageux

courier [KU•ree•ur] *n* courrier;
messager M

course [kaurs] *n* cours M;
(direction) route F; (of meal)
plat M entrée F; (for golf etc)
terrain M; au cours de; *adv*
bien sûr naturellement; *vt vi*
courir

court [kaurt] *n* (law; sports, etc)
cour F; (votes, etc) briguer;
(date; woo) courtiser

courteous [KUR•tee•us] *adj*
courtois; poli

courtesy [KUR•ti•see] *n*
courtoisie F; politesse F

courtyard [KAURT•yahrd] *n*
cour F

cousin [KUH•zin] *n* cousin -e
MF

cove [kov] *n* crique; anse F

covenant [KUH•vu•nunt] *n*
contrat; pacte M; alliance F

cover [KUH•vur] *vt* couvrir;
(with insurance) couvrir;
(scandal etc) cacher; *n* (of
book bed) couverture F;
(insurance) couverture F; (lid)
couvercle M; (for furniture)
housse F; (shelter) abri M; se
mettre à l'abri; à l'abri

cover-up (scandal etc) *n*
étouffement M

coverage [KUH•vu•rij] *n* (of
news) reportage M

covering [KUH•vu•ring] *n*
(layer) couche F

covert [KO•vurt] *adj* clandestin;
caché

covet [KUH•vit] *vt* convoiter

cow [kou] *n* vache F

coward [KOU•urd] *n* lâche MF

cowardice [KOU•ur•dis] *n*
lâcheté

cowardly [KOU•urd•lee] *adj*
lâche

cowboy [KOU•boi] *n*
cow-boy M

cower [KOU•ur] *vi* se tapir

coy [koi] *adj* faussement; timide

cozy [KO•zee] *adj* douillet

crab [krab] *n* crabe M

crack [krak] *n* (in glass etc)
fêlure F; (in ground; wall
wood; etc) fissure F fente F;
(noise) craquement M; (of
whip) claquement; *vt* (a whip)
faire claquer; (glass; etc) fêler;
(wood; etc) fissurer; (egg; etc)
casser; *vi* (glass; etc) se fêler;
(wood; etc) se fissurer

cracker [KRA•kur] *n*
craquelin M

cradle [KRAI•dl] *n* berceau M;
vt bercer

craft [kraft] *n* (trade) métier M;
(ship) embarcation F

crafty [KRAF•tee] *adj* rusé

cram [kram] *vt* bourrer (qqch
de); fourrer (qqch dans); *vi*
(for exam) bachoter

cramp [kramp] *n* crampe F; *vt*
gêner entraver cramponner

cranberry [KRAN•BE•ree] *n*
canneberge F

crane [krain] *n* grue F

crank [krank] *n* manivelle F;
vilebrequin M

cranky [KRANG•kee] *adj*
grincheux fantasque

crape [kraip] *n* crêpe M

crash [krash] *n* (noise) fracas
M; (of car plane) accident M;

collision F; *vi* (plane)
s'écraser; (cars trains) se
percuter s'emboutir; (market)
s'effrondrer; *vt* (plane) écraser

crate [krait] *n* cageot M

crater [KRAI•tur] *n* cratère M

crave [kraiv] *vt* avoir grand
besoin de; avoir un besoin
maladif de

crawl [kraul] *vi* ramper se
traîner; (babies) aller à quatre
pattes; (cars traffic) avancer
au pas

crayfish [KRAI•fish] *n*
écrevisse F

crayon [KRAI•un] *n* crayon M

craze [kraiz] *n* engouement M;
mania F

crazy [KRAI•zee] *adj* foux
(folle); ~ about\être fou de

creak [kreek] *vi* craquer grincer

cream [kreem] *n* crème F

creamy [KREE•mee] *adj*
crémeux

create [kree•AIT] *vt* créer

creation [kree•AI•shn] *n*
création F

creative [kree•AI•tiv] *adj* créatif

creator [kree•AI•tur] *n*
créateur M

creature [KREE•chur] *n*
créature F

credible [KRE•di•bl] *adj*
croyable; plausible

credit [KRE•dit] *n* crédit M; à
crédit; (praise, recognition)
mérite F honneur M; faire
honneur à; *vt* reconnaître;
(banking) créditer

credit card [KRE•dit kard] *n*
carte de crédit F

creed [kreed] *n* croyance F; credo M

creek [kreek] *n* ruisseau M

creep [kreep] *vi* se glisser; (cars traffic) avancer au pas

crescent [KRE•snt] *n* croissant M

crest [krest] *n* krête F; (on coat of arms) timbre M

crevice [KRE•vis] *n* fissure F

crew [kroo] *n* équipage M

crib [krib] *n* berceau M

cricket [KRI•kit] *n* grillon M; (game) cricket M

crime [kruym] *n* crime M

criminal [KRI•me•nl] *adj n* criminel M

crimson [KRIM•sun] *adj* cramoisi

cringe [krinj] *vi* reculer

cripple [KRI•pl] *n* boiteux M; estropié M; *vt* estropier; paralyser

crisis [KRUY•sis] *n* crise F

crisp [krisp] *adj* croustillant; croquant; (weather) vif

criterion [kruy•TEER•ree•un] *n* critère M

critic [KRI•tik] *n* critique M

criticism [KRI•ti•SI•zm] *n* critique F

criticize [KRI•ti•SUYZ] *vt vi* critiquer

croak [krok] *vi* (frog) coasser; (crow) croasser

crochet [kro•SHAI] *n* crochet M

crockery [KRAH•ku•ree] *n* vaisselle F

crocodile [KRAH•ku•DUYL] *n* crocodile M

crook [kruk] *n* escroc M

crooked [KRU•kid] *adj* courbé; tordu; (dishonest) malhonnête

crop [krahp] *n* culture F; (amount harvested) recolte F

cross [kraus] *n* croix F; (hybrid) croisement M; *vt* traverser; (arms legs) croiser; rayer; biffer; barrer

cross-country [kros KUN•tree] *adj* (running) cross M; (skiing) ski M de fond

crossfire [KRAUS•fuyr] *n* feu M croisé

crossroads [KRAUS•rodz] *n* carrefour M

crossword (puzzle) [KRAUS•wurd] *npl* mots croisés M

crow [kro] *n* corneille F; à vol d'oiseau; *vi* (rooster) chanter

crowbar [KRO•bahr] *n* levier M

crowd [kroud] *n* foule F du monde M; *vi* affluer s'amasser s'attrouper; *vt* (area space etc) remplir

crown [kroun] *n* couronne F; *vt* couronner

crucial [KROO•shl] *adj* crucial

crucifix [KROO•si•FIKS] *n* crucifix M; the Crucifixion *n* la Crucifixion F

crude [krood] *adj* (manners; etc) grossier; (material oil etc) brut

cruel [krooul] *adj* cruel

cruise [krooz] *n* croisière F; *vt* (car) rouler; (ship) croiser

crumb [kruhm] *n* miette F

crumble [KRUHM•bl] *vt*
émettier; *vi* s'émittier;
(structure) s'écrouler; (stone
etc) s'effriter

crunch [kruhnch] *vt* croquer;
(underfoot) faire crisser

crusade [kroo•SAID] *n*
croisade F

crush [kruhsh] *n* have a ~ on\sb
avoir un béguin pour *vt*
écraser

crust [kruhst] *n* croûte F

crutch [kruhch] *n* béquille F

cry [kruy] *n* cri M; *vi* pleurer;
(shout) crier; *vt* crier

crystal [KRI•stl] *n* cristal M

Cuba [KYOO•bu] *n* Cuba M

Cuban [KYOO•bun] *adj* cubain;
n Cubain M

cube [kyoob] *n* cube M; *vt*
(math) élever au cube

cubic [KYOO•bik] *adj* cubique

cucumber [KYOO•kuhm•bur] *n*
concombre M

cuddle [KUH•dl] *vt* câliner;
caresser; ~ up\s'éteindre

cue [kyoo] *n* signal; indice M;
queue F de billard

cuff [kuhf] *n* poignet M; (of
pants) revers M; à
l'improviste; au pied levé

culinary [KUH•li•NE•ree] *adj*
culinaire

culminate [KUHL•mi•NAIT] *vi*
se terminer par

culprit [KUHL•prit] *n* coupable
MF

cult [kuhlt] *n* culte M

cultivate [KUHL•ti•VAIT] *vt*
cultiver

cultural [KUHL•chu•rul] *adj*
culturel

culture [KUHL•chur] *n*
culture F

cumulative [KYOO•myu•lu•tiv]
adj cumulatif

cunning [KUH•ning] *adj* rusé;
habile; astucieux

cup [kuhp] *n* tasse F; (prize)
coupe F

cupboard [KUH•burd] *n*
placard; buffet M

curate [KYOO•rit] *n* vicaire M

curb [kurb] *n* bord M du
trottoir; *vt* mettre un frein à

curdle [KUR•dl] *vt* cailler; *vi* se
cailler

cure [kyoour] *n* remède M; *vt*
guérir; (meat etc) saler

curfew [KUR•fyoo] *n*
couvre-feu F

curiosity
[KYOOUR•ree•AH•si•tee] *n*
curiosité F

curious [KYOOUR•ree•us] *adj*
curieux

curl [kurl] *n* boucle F; *vt vi*
(hair) friser boucler; *vi*
s'enrouler; se pelotonner

curly [KUR•lee] *adj* frisé bouclé

currant [KUH•runt] *n* raisin M
sec

currency [KU•run•see] *n*
monnaie F

current [KU•runt] *adj* actuel;
courant; *n* courant M

curry [KU•ree] *n* curry M

curse [kurs] *n* malédiction F
fléau F; (swearword) juron M;
vt maudire; *vi* jurer

curtail [kur•TAIL] *vt* écourter

curtain [KUR•tn] *n* rideau M

curve [kurv] *n* courbe F; (in road) tournant; *vi* faire une courbe

cushion [KU•shn] *n* coussin M; *vt* amortir

custard [KUH•sturd] *n* crème F anglaise

custodian [KUH•STO•dyun] *n* gardien M; conservateur M

custody [KUH•stu•dee] *n* (of child) garde F; emprisonnement M

custom [KUH•stum] *n* coutume F; douane F

customer [KUH•stu•mur] *n* client M

cut [kuht] *n* (in skin) coupure F; (of meat) morceau M; (in prices etc) reduction F; *vt* couper; (prices; etc) réduire; (shape sculpt) tailler

cute [kyoot] *adj* mignon

cutlery [KUHT•lu•ree] *n* couverts M

cutlet [KUHT•lit] *n* côtelette F

cycle [SUY•kl] *n* cycle M; *vi* faire de la bicyclette

cyclone [SUY•klon] *n* cyclone M

cylinder [SI•lin•dur] *n* cylindre M

cynic [SI•nik] *n* cynique MF

cynical [SI•ni•kl] *adj* cynique

cypress [SUY•pris] *n* cyprès M

cyst [sist] *n* kyste M

czar [zahr] *n* tsar M

Czech [chek] *adj* tchèque; *n* Tchèque M

Czechoslovakia [che•KO•slo•vah•KEE•uh] *n* Tchécoslovakie F

D

dachshund [DAHK•sund] *n* teckel M

dad [dad] *n* papa M

daffodil [DA•fu•DIL] *n* jonquille F

daily [DAI•lee] *adj* quotidien; journalier; *adv* quotidiennement; *n* (periodical) quotidien M

dairy [DAI•ree] *adj* laitier; *n* laiterie F

daisy [DAI•zee] *n* marguerite F; (wild) pâquerette F

dam [dam] *n* barrage M; *vt* construire un barrage M

damage [DA•mij] *n* dommage M; (fig) tort M; endommager

damp [damp] *adj* humide

dampen [DAM•pun] *vt* humecter

dance [dans] *n* danse F bal M; *vi* dancer

dancer [DAN•sur] *n* danseur M

dandelion [DAN•di•LUY•un] *n* pissenlit M

dandruff [DAN•druhf] *n*
pellicules F

danger [DAIN•jur] *n* danger M;
en danger; risquer de M

dangerous [DAIN•ju•rus] *adj*
dangereux

dangle [DANG•gl] *vt* balancer;
vi pendre

dare [dair] *n* défi M; *vi* oser; *vt*
défier qqn de faire qqch

daredevil [DAIR•DE•vl] *n*
casse-cou M

daring [DAI•ring] *adj*
audacieux

dark [dahrk] *adj* sombre;
obscur; (color) foncé;
commencer a faire nuit; *n*
dans le noir

darken [DAHR•kn] *vt*
assombrir; obscurcir; *vi*
s'assombrir; s'obscurcir

darkness [DAHRK•nis] *n*
obscurité F

darling [DAHR•ling] *adj n*
chéri M

darn [dahrn] *vt* repriser

dart [dahrt] *n* flèchette F

dash [dash] *n* (in punctuation)
tiret M; (of salt etc) pincée F;
vi se ruer vers

dashboard [DASH•baurd] *n*
tableau M de bord

data [DAI•tu] *n* données F

database [DAI•tu•BAIS] *n* base
de données F

date [dait] *n* date F;
(appointment) rendez-vous M;
(fruit) datte F; *vt* sortir avec;
adj démodé

daughter [DAU•tur] *n* fille F

daughter-in-law
[DAU•tur•in•LAU] *n*
belle-fille F

daunting [DAUN•ting] *adj*
intimidant

dawdle [DAU•dl] *vi* flâner

dawn [dawn] *n* aube F aurore F;
vi il est venu a mon esprit;
que

day [dai] *n* jour M journée F; la
veille; avant-hier M; le
lendemain; après-demain M

daybreak [DAI•braik] *n* lever
du jour M

daydream [DAI•dreem] *vi*
revâsser

daze [daiz] *n* in a ~\hébété; *vt*
étourdir

dazzle [DA•zl] *vt* éblouir

dead [ded] *adj* mort; *npl* les
morts M

deadline [DED•luyn] *n* date;
limite F

deadly [DED•lee] *adj* mortel

deaf [def] *adj* sourd

deafen [DE•fn] *vt* assourdir

deafening [DE•fu•ning] *adj*
assourdissant

deal [deel] *n* (agreement)
marché M; (bargain) affaire
F; *vt* (cards) donner
distribuer; *vi* s'occuper de; (in
business) traiter avec

dealer [DEE•lur] *n* marchand
M négociant M; (cards)
donneur M

dealings [DEE•lingz] *npl*
relations F; rapports M

dean [deen] *n* doyen M

dear [deer] *adj* cher; *n* chéri M

death [deth] *n* mort; peine F de mort F

debacle [du•BAH•kl] *n* débâcle F

debase [di•BAIS] *vt* avalir abaisser

debate [di•BAIT] *n* débat M; *vt vi* débattre

debauchery [di•BAU•chu•ree] *n* débauche F

debit [DE•bit] *n* débit M; débiter

debt [det] *n* dette F; *adj* endetté

debtor [DE•tur] *n* débiteur M

debut [DAI•byoo] *n* début; *vi* débuter

decade [DE•kaid] *n* décennie F

decadence [DE•ku•duns] *n* décadence F

decadent [DE•ku•dunt] *adj* décadent

decanter [di•KAN•tur] *n* carafe F

decay [di•KAY] *n* pourriture F; *vi* pourrir

deceased [di•SEEST] *adj* décéder; *n adj* défunt M

deceit [di•SEET] *n* tromperie F

deceitful [di•SEET•ful] *adj* trompeur

deceive [di•SEEV] *vt vi* tromper

December [di•SEM•bur] *n* décembre M

decency [DEE•sn•see] *n* décence F

decent [DEE•sunt] *adj* décent

deception [di•SEP•shn] *n* tromperie F

decide [di•SUYD] *vt* décider; *vi* décider; décider de faire qqch; ~on sth\ décider pour

decimal [DE•si•ml] *n* décimale F

decimate [DE•si•MAIT] *vt* décimer

decipher [di•SUY•fur] *vt* déchiffrer

decision [di•SI•zhn] *n* décision

decisive [di•SUY•siv] *adj* décisif

deck [dek] *n* (of cards) jeu M; (of ship) pont M; (of house) véranda F

declare [di•KLAIR] *vt* déclarer

decline [di•KLUYN] *n* déclin M; en déclin; *vt* refuser décliner; *vi* décliner

decode [dee•KOD] *vt* décoder

decompose [DEE•kum•POZ] *vi* se décomposer

decorate [DE•ku•RAIT] *vt* décorer

decoration [DE•ku•RAI•shn] *n* décoration F

decorum [di•KAU•rum] *n* décorum M

decoy [DEE•coi] *n* leurre M; (person) compère F

decrease [dee•CREES] *n* diminution F; *vt vi* diminuer

decree [di•KREE] *n* décret M; (law) arrêt M; *vt* décréter

decrepit [di•KRE•pit] *adj* décrepit

dedicate [DE•di•KAIT] *vt* dédier; (oneself etc) consacrer

dedication [DE•di•KAI•shn] *n* (of person) dévouement M; (of book etc) dédicace F

deduct [di•DUHKT] *vt* déduire

deduction [di•DUHK•shn] *n* déduction F

deed [deed] *n* action F; (law) titre

deem [deem] *vt* juger estimer

deep [deep] *adj* profond; *adv* profondément

deepen [DEEP•n] *vt* approfondir; *vi* s'approfondir

deer [deer] *n* cerf M

deface [di•FAIS] *vt* barbouiller

defamation [DE•fu•MAI•shn] *n* diffimation F

defame [di•FAIM] *vt* diffamer

default [di•FAULT] *n* défaut M; par défaut; *vi* faire défaut

defeat [di•FEET] *n* défaite F; *vt* battre vaincre

defect [*n.* DEE•fekt *v.* di•FEKT] *n* défaut M; *vi* faire défection

defend [di•FEND] *vt* défendre

defendant [di•FEN•dunt] *n* défenseur M

defense [di•FENS] *n* défense F

defensive [di•FEN•siv] *adj* défensif; *n* sur la défensive F

defer [di•FUR] *vt* différer; *vi* déferer (à)

defiance [di•FUY•uns] *n* défi M; au mépris de

deficiency [di•FI•shun•see] *n* manque F; insuffisance F; (of vitamins) carense F

deficient [di•FI•shunt] *adj* insuffisant

deficit [DE•fi•sit] *n* déficit M

defile [di•FUYL] *vt* souiller

define [di•FUYN] *vt* définir

definite [DE•fi•nit] *adj* déterminé; certain; (sure, clear) catégorique

definitely [DE•fi•nit•lee] *adv* sans aucune doute

definition [DE•fi•NI•shn] *n* définition

deflate [di•FLAIT] *vt* dégonfler; *vi* se dégonfler

deflect [di•FLEKT] *vt* dévier détourner

deformed [di•FAURMD] *adj* difforme

defraud [di•FRAUD] *vt* frauder

defrost [di•FRAUST] *vt* dégivrer; décongeler

deft [deft] *adj* adroit

defy [di•FUY] *vt* défier; défier de faire qqch

degenerate [*adj.* di•JE•nu•rit *v.* di•JE•nu•RAIT] *adj* dégénéré; *vi* dégénérer

degrading [di•GRAI•ding] *adj* dégradant

degree [di•GREE] *n* degré M; (academic) grade M universitaire licence F; jusqu'à un certain point

dehydrate [di•HUY•drait] *vt* déshydrater

deity [DAI•i•tee] *n* divinité F

dejected [di•JEK•tid] *adj* abattu; découragé

delay [di•LAI] *n* retard M; *vt* retarder; *vi* tarder (à + inf)

delegate [*n* DE•li•gut *v.* DE•li•GAIT] *n* délégué M; *vt* déléguer

delegation [DE•li•GAI•shn] *n* délégation F

delete [di•LEET] *vt* supprimer

deliberate [*adj.* di•LI•brut *v.* du•LI•bu•RAIT] *adj* délibéré; *vi* délibérer

deliberately [di•LI•brut•lee]
adv exprès

delicacy [DE•li•ku•see] *n* (food)
mets M délicat

delicate [DE•li•kut] *adj* délicat

delicatessen [DE•li•ku•TE•sun]
n épicerie F fine

delicious [di•LI•shus] *adj*
délicieux

delight [di•LUYT] *n* délice M;
vi prendre grand plaisir à

delighted [di•LUY•tid] *adj* ravi
de

delightful [di•LUYT•ful] *adj*
ravissant; délicieux

delinquent [di•LING•kwunt]
adj n délinquant M

delirious [di•LI•ree•us] *adj*
délirant

deliver [di•LI•vur] *vt* livrer;
(mail) distribuer; (baby)
mettre au monde; (liberate)
délivrer

delivery [di•LI•vu•ree] *n*
livraison F; (of baby)
accouchement M

deluge [DE•lyooj] *n* déluge M

delusion [di•LOO•zhn] *n*
illusion F

demagogue [DE•mu•GAHG] *n*
démagogue mf

demand [di•MAND] *n* exigence
F demande F; *vt* exiger;
réclamer

demanding [di•MAN•ding] *adj*
exigeant; (work etc)
astreignant

demeanor [di•MEE•nur] *n*
comportement M

demented [di•MEN•tid] *adj*
dément fou

demerit [di•ME•rit] *n*
démérite M

demobilize [di•MO•bi•LUYZ]
vt démobiliser

democracy [di•MAH•kru•see] *n*
démocratie F

democrat [DE•mu•KRAT] *n*
démocrate MF

democratic [DE•mu•KRA•tik]
adj démocratique

demolish [di•MAH•lish] *vt*
démolir

demonstrate
[DE•mun•STRAIT] *vt*
démontrer; *vi* (picket)
manifester

demonstration
[DE•mun•STRAI•shn] *n*
démonstration F; (picket)
manifestation F

demonstrative
[di•MAHN•stru•tiv] *adj*
démonstratif

demoralize
[di•MAU•ru•LUYZ] *vt*
démoraliser

demure [di•MYOOR] *adj*
modeste

den [den] *n* (room) cabinet M
de travail (of animal) antre M
tanière F

denial [di•NUYL] *n*
(deprivation) dénégation F;
(of accusation etc) démenti M

Denmark [DEN•mahrk] *n*
Danemark M

denounce [di•NOUNS] *vt*
dénoncer

dense [dens] *adj* dense; (stupid)
bouché

density [DEN•si•tee] *n*
densité F

dent [dent] *n* bosselure M; *vt* cabosser

dental [DEN•tl] *adj* dentaire

dentist [DEN•tist] *n* dentiste mf

deny [di•NUY] *vt* nier; (deprive) refuser

depart [di•PAHRT] *vi* partir; quitter

department [di•PAHRT•munt] *n* département M; ministère M; (in store) rayon

department store [dee•PART•mint stor] *n* grand magasin M

departure [di•PAHR•chur] *n* départ M

depend [di•PEND] *vi* dépendre de; (rely on) compter sur; ça dépend

dependable [di•PEND•u•bl] *adj* digne de confiance sûr

depict [di•PIKT] *vt* répresenter; (describe) dépeindre

deplete [di•PLEET] *vt* épuiser

deplorable [di•PLAU•ru•bl] *adj* déplorable

deplore [di•PLAUR] *vt* déplorer

deport [di•PAURT] *vt* expulser; déporter

depose [di•POZ] *vt* déposer

deposit [di•PAH•zit] *n* dépôt M; *vt* déposer

depot [DEE•po] *n* dépôt M; (train station) gare F

depreciate [di•PREE•shee•AIT] *vi* se déprécier

depress [di•PRES] *vt* déprimer; (prices) abaisser

depressed [di•PREST] *adj* déprimé; (area) en déclin

depressing [di•PRE•sing] *adj* déprimant

depression [di•PRE•shn] *n* dépression F

deprive [di•PRUYV] *vt* priver

depth [depth] *n* profondeur M; en profondeur; au coeur de au plus profond de

deputy [DE•pyu•tee] *n* député M

derail [di•RAIL] *vi* dérailler

deranged [di•RAINJD] *adj* dérangé

deride [di•RUYD] *vt* ridiculiser; railler

derive [di•RUYV] *vt* dériver; *vi* dériver (de); venir (de)

descend [di•SEND] *vt vi* descendre

descendant [di•SEN•dunt] *n* descendant M

descent [di•SENT] *n* descente F; d'originè (country *adj*)

describe [di•SKRUYB] *vt* décrire

description [di•SKRIP•shn] *n* description F

desert [*n.* DE•zurt *v.* di•ZURT] *n* désert M; *vt vi* déserter

deserter [di•ZUR•tur] *n* déserteur M

deserve [di•ZURV] *vt* mériter

deserving [di•ZUR•ving] *adj* méritant; (cause) méritoire

design [di•ZUYN] *n* (pattern details) dessin; (plan) dessein; plan M; *vi* avoir des desseins sur; *vt* dessiner inventer; (plan) concevoir

designate [DE•zig•NAIT] *vt* désigner

designer [di•ZUY•nur] *n*
dessinateur M; (fashion)
styliste MF

desirable [di•ZUY•ru•bl] *adj*
désirable

desire [di•ZUYUR] *n* désir M;
vt désirer

desist [di•SIST] *vi* cesser

desk [desk] *n* bureau M; (in
classroom) pupitre M

desolate [DE•su•lut] *adj* désolé;
(place) abandonné

despair [di•SPAIUR] *n*
désespoir M; *vi* (for)
désespérer (de)

desperate [DE•sprut] *adj*
désespéré

desperation [DI•spu•RAI•shn]
n désespoir M

despicable [di•SPI•ku•bl] *adj*
méprisable

despise [di•SPUYZ] *vt* mépriser

despite [di•SPUYT] *prep*
malgré; en dépit de

despondent [di•SPAHN•dunt]
adj découragé; abattu

despot [DE•sput] *n* despote M

dessert [di•ZURT] *n* dessert M

destination [DE•sti•NAI•shn] *n*
destination F

destiny [DE•sti•nee] *n*
destinée F

destitute [DE•sti•TOOT] *adj*
indigent

destroy [di•STROI] *vt* détruire

destruction [di•STRUHK•shn]
n destruction F

destructive [di•STRUHK•tiv]
adj destructeur F

detach [di•TACH] *vt* détacher

detail [DEE•tail] *n* détail M; in
~\en détail; *vt* détailler

detain [di•TAIN] *vt* retenir; (in
jail) détenir

detect [di•TEKT] *vt* déceler;
percevoir; (by radar etc)
détecter

detection [di•TEK•shn] *n*
découverte F détection F

detention [di•TEN•shn] *n*
détention F; (in school)
retenue F

deter [di•TUR] *vt* dissuader

detergent [di•TUR•junt] *n*
détergent

deteriorate
[di•TEER•ee•aur•AIT] *vi* se
détériorer

determination
[di•TUR•mi•NAI•shn] *n*
détermination F

determine [di•TUR•min] *vt*
déterminer; sth résoudre de
faire

detest [di•TEST] *vt* détester

detonate [DE•tu•NAIT] *vt* faire
détoner; *vi* détoner

detour [DEE•toor] *n* détour M

detract [di•TRAKT] *vt*
diminuer

detrimental [DE•tri•MEN•tl]
adj préjudiciable

devastate [DE•vu•STAIT] *vt*
dévaster; accabler

devastating [DE•vu•STAI•ting]
adj dévastateur

develop [di•VE•lup] *vt*
développer; (habit illness etc)
contracter; *vi* se développer

development [di•VE•lup•munt]
n développement M

deviate [DEE•vee•AIT] *vi*
dévier

device [di•VUYS] *n* appareil;
dispositif M

devil [de•vl] *n* diable M;
(Satan) le Diable

devious [DEE•vee•us] *adj*
détourné; (person) tortueux

devise [di•VUYZ] *vt* concevoir;
inventer

devoid [di•VOID] *adj* (of)
dénué (de)

devote [di•VOT] *vt* consacrer

devoted [di•VO•tud] *adj*
dévoué

devotion [di•VO•shn] *n*
dévouement M; (religious)
dévotion F

devour [di•VOUUR] *vt* dévorer

devout [di•VOUT] *adj* dévot

dew [doo] *n* rosée F

diabetes [DUY•u•BEE•teez] *n*
diabète M

diabetic [DUY•u•BE•tik] *adj n*
diabétique MF

diagnose [DUY•ug•NOS] *vt*
diagnostiquer

diagnosis [DUY•ug•NO•sis] *adj*
n diagnostic F

diagonal [duy•AG•nl] *adj*
diagonal; *n* diagonale F

diagram [DUY•u•GRAM] *n*
diagramme M

dial [duyul] *n* cadran M; *vt*
(number) composer

dialect [DUY•u•LEKT] *n*
dialecte M

dialog [DUY•u•LAHG] *n*
dialogue M

diameter [duy•A•mi•tur] *n*
diamètre M

diamond [DUY•mund] *n*
diamant; *npl* ~s (cards)
carreau M

diamond-shaped [-shaipt] *adj*
en losange

diary [DUY•u•ree] *n* journal M;
agenda M

dice [duys] (sing: die) *npl* dés
(dé); *vt* (cut) couper en dés

dictate [DIK•tait] *vt* dicter; *n*
précepte M

dictation [dik•TAI•shn] *n*
dictée F

dictator [DIK•TAI•tur] *n*
dictateur M

dictatorship
[dik•TAI•tur•SHIP] *n*
dictature F

dictionary [DIK•shu•NE•ree] *n*
dictionnaire M

did [did] *pt* fait

die [duy] *vi* mourir; se mourir;
mourir d'envie de; *n* (sing.
dice) dé M

diet [DUY•ut] *n* alimentation F
régime M; on a ~au régime;
vi suivre un régime

differ [DI•fur] *vi* différer; ne
pas être d'accord avec

difference [DI•fruns] *n*
différence F; it makes no ~\
cela ne fait pas rien

different [DI•frunt] *adj*
différent

differentiate
[DI•fu•REN•shee•ait] *vt*
différencier

difficult [DI•fi•kult] *adj* difficile

difficulty [DI•fi•kul•tee] *n*
difficulté F

diffuse [di•FYOOZ] *vt* diffuser

dig [dig] *vt* creuser; bêcher; déterrer; *vi* creuser; bêcher

digest [*n.* DUY•jest *v.* duy•JEST] *vt vi* digérer; *n* digest M

digestion [duy•JES•chn] *n* digestion F

digit [DI•jit] *n* chiffre M

digital [DI•ji•tl] *adj* digital M

dignified [DIG•ni•FUYD] *adj* digne

dignify [DIG•ni•FUY] *vt* honorer

dignity [DIG•ni•tee] *n* dignité F

digress [duy•GRES] *vt* (from) s'éloigner (de)

dilate [DUY•lait] *vt* dilater; *vi* se dilater

dilemma [di•LE•mu] *n* dilemne M

diligence [DI•li•juns] *n* assiduité F

diligent [DI•li•junt] *adj* assidu; appliqué

dilute [duy•LOOT] *adj* dilué; *vt* diluer

dim [dim] *adj* (light) faible; (memory) vague; (person) bouché; *vt* baisser; *vi* baisser affaiblir

dimension [di•MEN•shn] *n* dimension; à trois dimensions F

diminish [di•MI•nish] *vt vi* diminuer

dimple [DIM•pl] *n* fossette F

din [din] *n* vacarme M

dine [duyn] *vi* dîner

diner [DUY•nur] *n* café M; (person) dineur M

dinghy [DING•gee] *n* canot; youyou M

dingy [DIN•jee] *adj* miteux terne

dining room [DUY•ning—] *n* salle à manger .

dinner [DI•nur] *n* dîner; smoking M

dinosaur [DUY•nu•SAUR] *n* dinosaure M

diocese [DUY•u•seez] *n* diocèse M

dip [dip] *n* (in ground) déclivité F; (swim) baignade F; (for chips etc) sauce F; *vt* plonger; *vi* baisser descendre

diploma [di•PLO•mu] *n* diplôme M

diplomacy [di•PLO•mu•see] *n* diplomatie M

diplomat [DI•plu•MAT] *n* diplomate M

diplomatic [DI•plu•MA•tik] *adj* diplomatique; (person) diplomate

dire [duyur] *adj* extrême

direct [di•REKT] *adj* direct; *adv* directement; *vt* diriger; (order) ordonner

direction [di•REK•shn] *n* direction F; ~s\ indications *npl* F

directly [di•REKT•lee] *adv* directement; justement

director [di•REK•tur] *n* directeur M; (cinema tv) réalisateur M; (theater) metteur M en scène

directory [di•REK•tu•ree] *n* annuaire M

dirt [durt] *n* saleté F

dirty [DUR•tee] *adj* sale;
(vulgar) grossier

disabled [di•SAI•bld] *adj*
handicapé

disadvantage
[DI•sud•VAN•tij] *n*
désadvantage; désavantagé

disagree [DI•su•GREE] *vi* ne
pas être d'accord avec;
differer; se disputer

disagreement
[DI•su•GREE•munt] *n*
désaccord M; (dispute)
différend M

disappear [DI•su•PEEUR] *vi*
disparaître; *n* disparition F

disappoint [DI•su•POINT] *vt*
décevoir

disappointing
[DI•su•POIN•ting] *adj*
décevant

disappointment
[DI•su•POINT•munt] *n*
déception F

disapproval [DI•su•PROO•vl]
n désapprobation F

disapprove [DI•su•PROOV] *vi*
désapprouver qqch/qqn

disarm [di•SAHRM] *vt vi*
désarmer

disarray [DI•su•RAI] *n* en
désordre

disaster [di•ZA•stur] *n* désastre
M catastrophe F

disastrous [di•ZA•strus] *adj*
désastreux

disavow [DI•su•VOU] *vt*
désavouer

discard [di•SKAHRD] *vt* mettre
de côté

discern [di•SURN] *vt* discerner;
distinguer

discharge [*n.* DIS•charj *v.*
dis•CHARJ] *n* (release)
décharge F; (from military
etc) libération F renvoi M; (of
gun) décharge F; *vt* (patient)
renvoyer; (from military)
licencier; (of emission)
émettre

disciple [di•SUY•pl] *n*
disciple M

discipline [DI•si•plin] *n*
discipline F; *vt* discipliner

disclose [di•SKLOZ] *vt* révéler

disclosure [dis•KLO•zhur] *n*
révélation F

discomfort [di•SKUHM•furt] *n*
malaise M; (pain) douleur F

disconnect [DI•sku•NEKT] *vt*
disjoindre détacher; (electric
etc) débrancher

discord [DI•skaurd] *n* discorde
F dissension F

discount [DI•skount] *n* rabais
M remise F; *vt* escompter;
(ignore) ne pas tenir
compte de

discourage [di•SKU•rij] *vt*
décourager

discourse [di•SKAURS] *n*
discours M; dialogue M

discover [di•SKUH•vur] *vt*
découvrir

discovery [di•SKUH•vu•ree] *n*
découverte F

discredit [dis•KRE•dit] *n*
discrédit; *vt* discréditer

discreet [di•SKREET] *adj*
discret

discrepancy [di•SKRE•pun•see]
n divergence

discretion [di•SKRE•shn] *n*
discrétion; (opinion) jugement

discriminate
[di•SKRI•mi•NAIT] *vi*
(against) faire de la
discrimination contre;
(between) distinguer; établir
une distinction entre

discuss [di•SKUHS] *vt* discuter
de

discussion [di•SKUH•shn] *n*
discussion F

disdain [dis•DAIN] *n* dédain M

disease [di•ZEEZ] *n* maladie F

disengage [DI•sin•GAIJ] *vt*
dégager; (tech) débrayer

disfigure [dis•FI•gyur] *vt*
défigurer

disgrace [dis•GRAIS] *n* honte
F; *vt* faire honte; à déshonorer

disgraceful [dis•GRAIS•ful] *adj*
honteux; scandaleux

disgruntled [dis•GRUHN•tld]
adj mécontent

disguise [dis•GUYZ] *n*
déguisement M; *vt* déguiser;
en déguisé

disgust [dis•GUHST] *n* dégoût
M; *vt* dégoûter

disgusting [dis•GUH•sting] *adj*
degoûtant

dish [dish] *n* plat M; faire la
vaisselle

dishearten [dis•HAHR•tn] *vt*
décourager

dishevelled [di•SHE•vld] *adj*
échevelé

dishonest [dis•AH•nist] *adj*
malhonnête

dishonor [dis•AH•nur] *n*
déshonneur M; déshonorer

dishwasher [DISH•WAH•shur]
n lave-vaisselle M

disillusion [DIS•i•LOO•zhn] *n*
désillusion F

disinfect [DI•sin•FEKT] *vt*
désinfecter

disinfectant [DI•sin•FEK•tunt]
n désinfectant

disintegrate
[di•SIN•tu•GRAIT] *vi* se
désintégrer

disinterested [dis•IN•tru•stid]
adj désintéressé

disk [disk] *n* disque M

disk drive *n* lecteur M de
disques

dislike [di•SLUYK] *n* aversion
F; *vt* ne pas aimer

dislocate [DIS•lo•kait] *vt*
disloquer; (shoulder etc) se
démettre; se luxer

disloyal [dis•LOI•ul] *adj*
déloyal

dismal [DI•zml] *adj* lugubre;
morne

dismay [di•SMAI] *n*
consternation F; consterner

dismiss [dis•MIS] *vt* congédier
renvoyer; (law) rejeter; (idea
etc) écarter

dismissal [dis•MI•sl] *n* renvoi
M; (of idea etc) rejet M

dismount [dis•MOUNT] *vi*
descendre

disobedient
[DI•so•BEE•dee•unt] *adj*
désobéissant

disobey [DI•so•BAI] *vt*
désobéir à

disorder [di•SAUR•dur] *n*
désordre M; (med) trouble M

disorganized
[di•SAUR•gu•NUYZD] *adj*
désordonné

disoriented
[di•SAU•ree•EN•tud] *adj*
désorienté

disown [dis•ON] *vt* renier

disparaging [di•SPA•ru•jing]
adj désobligeant

dispassionate [di•SPA•shu•nit]
adj calme froid; impartial

dispel [di•SPEL] *vt* dissiper

dispense [di•SPENS] *vt*
distribuer; administrer;
(forego) se passer de

dispenser [di•SPEN•sur] *n*
distributeur M

disperse [di•SPURS] *vt*
disperser; (news etc)
disséminer; *vi* se disperser

displace [dis•PLAIS] *vt*
déplacer

display [di•SPLAI] *n* étalage M
exposition F; (of strength;
emotion; etc) manifestation F;
vt exposer; faire preuve de

displease [dis•PLEEZ] *vt*
déplaire à

displeased [dis•PLEEZD] *adj*
mécontent

disposal [di•SPO•zl] *n* (of
garbage) enlèvement M; at
one's ~à sa disposition

dispose [di•SPOZ] *vt* disposer;
(throw away) se débarrasser
de

disposed [di•SPOZD] *adj* (to)
disposé (à)

disposition [DI•spu•ZI•shn] *n*
témpéramant M·

disprove [dis•PROOV] *vt*
réfuter

dispute [di•SPYOOT] *n* dispute
M; (labor etc) conflit M; *vt*
contester discuter

disqualify [dis•KWAH•li•FUY]
vt (sports) disqualifier

disregard [DIS•ree•GAHRD] *n*
indifférance F; *vt* ne pas tenir
compte de

disreputable
[dis•RE•pyu•tu•bl] *adj* de
mauvaise réputation;
déshonorant

disrespect [DIS•ru•SPEKT] *n*
manque M de respect;
irrespecteux

disrupt [dis•RUHPT] *vt*
déranger; perturber;
interrompre

dissatisfy [di•SAT•is•FUY] *vt*
mécontenter

dissect [duy•SEKT] *vt* disséquer

dissemble [di•SEM•bl] *vt vi*
dissimuler

disseminate [di•SE•mi•NAIT]
vt disséminer

dissent [di•SENT] *n*
dissentiment; *vi* différer (de)

dissimulate [di•SI•myu•LAIT]
vt vi dissimuler

dissipate [DI•si•PAIT] *vt*
dissiper; *vi* se dissiper

dissociate [di•SO•shee•UT] *vt*
dissocier; *vi* se dissocier

dissolute [DI•su•LOOT] *adj*
dissolu

dissolve [di•ZAHLV] *vt*
dissoudre; *vi* se dissoudre

dissuade [di•SWAID] *vt* dissauder

distance [DI•stuns] *n* distance F; au loin; de loin

distant [DI•stunt] *adj* lointain; éloigné; (manner) distant

distaste [dis•TAIST] *n* dégoût M

distill [dis•TIL] *vt vi* distiller

distillery [dis•TI•lu•ree] *n* distillerie

distinct [dis•TINGKT] *adj* distinct

distinguish [di•STING•gwish] *vt* distinguer

distort [di•STAURT] *vt* déformer

distract [di•STRAKT] *vt* distraire

distraught [di•STRAUT] *adj* éperdu

distress [di•STRES] *n* détresse F; *vt* affliger

distribute [di•STRI•byoot] *vt* distribuer

distribution [DI•stri•BYOO•shn] *n* distribution F

district [DI•strikt] *n* (of country) région M; (of town) quartier F

distrust [dis•TRUST] *n* méfiance F; *vt* se méfier de

distrustful [dis•TRUST•ful] *adj* méfiant

disturb [di•STURB] *vt* déranger; troubler

disturbance [di•STUR•buns] *n* dérangement M; (fight) tapage M; (pol) troubles M *pl*

disturbing [di•STUR•bing] *adj* inquiétant; troublant

ditch [dich] *n* fossé M; *vt* abandonner

ditto [DI•to] *adv* idem

dive [duyv] *n* plongeon M; (of bird; plane) piqué M; (of submarine) plongée F; *vi* plonger; (bird; plane) piquer

diverge [di•VURJ] *vi* diverger

diverse [di•VURS] *adj* divers

diversify [di•VUR•si•FUY] *vt* diversifier; *vi* se diversifier

diversity [di•VUR•si•tee] *n* diversité F

divert [di•VURT] *vt* (detour) dévier; (funds) détourner

divide [di•VUYD] *vt* diviser; séparer; *vi* se diviser

divine [di•VUYN] *adj* divin

divinity [di•VI•ni•tee] *n* divinité F

division [di•VI•zhn] *n* division F; séparation F

divorce [di•VAURS] *n* divorce M; *vt* divorcer

divulge [di•VUHLJ] *vt* divulguer

dizzy [DI•zee] *adj* vertigineux; avoir la tête qui tourne

do [doo] *vt* faire; (fare) marcher; (suffice) suffire; supprimer ; (~ up) fermer (~ over) refaire; remettre à neuf; se contenter de; se passer de *vi* s'en passer; that will ~!\ça suffit!

docile [DAH•sul] *adj* docile

dock [dahk] *n* dock M; *vt* mettre à quai; *vi* se mettre à quai

doctor 1 [DAHK•tur] *n* docteur
M médecin M

doctor 2 [DAHK•tur] *vt*
falsifier; *vi* (food etc) altérer

doctorate [DAHK•tu•rut] *n*
doctorat M

doctrine [DAHK•trin] *n*
doctrine F

document [DAH•kyu•munt] *n*
document M; *vt* documenter

dodge [dahj] *vt* esquiver éviter;
vi s'esquiver

doe [do] *n* biche F

dog [daug] *n* chien M

dogma [DAUG•mu] *n*
dogme M

doings [DOO•ings] *npl*
actions F

dole [dol] *n* allocation F de
chômage; au chômage; *vt*
distribuer

doll [dahl] *n* poupée F

dollar [DAH•lur] *n* dollar M

dolphin [DAHL•fin] *n* dauphin

domain [do•MAIN] *n*
domaine M

dome [dom] *n* dôme M

domestic [du•ME•stik] *adj*
domestique; (not foreign)
intérieur; *n* domestique MF

dominant [DAH•mi•nunt] *adj*
dominant

dominate [DAH•mi•NAIT] *vt*
dominer

domineering
[DAH•mi•NEEU•ring] *adj*
dominateur

donate [do•NAIT] *vt* donner;
accorder; faire don de

donation [do•NAI•shn] *n*
don M

donkey [DAHNG•kee] *n* âne

donor [DO•nr] *n* (of blood etc)
donneur M; (to charity)
donateur M

doodle [DOO•dl] *vi* griffoner

doom [doom] *n* destin M;
ruine F

doomed [doomd] *adj* être voué
à l'échec

doomsday [DOOMZ•dai] *n* le
Jugement dernier

door [daur] *n* porte F

doormat [DAUR•mat] *n*
paillasson M

doorstep [DAUR•step] *n* pas M
de la porte

dope [dop] *n* idiot M; (drugs)
dope F

dormitory
[DAUR•mi•TAU•ree] *n*
dortoir M

dose [dos] *n* dose F

dot [daht] *n* point; *vt*
pointiller M

double [DUH•bl] *adj* double;
adv en deux; (twice the
amount) deux fois plus; *n*
double M; *vt* doubler

double vision [DUH•bl VI•shn]
n vue F double

double-breasted [-BRE•stid]
adj croisé

double-cross *vt* trahir

doubly [DUH•blee] *adv*
doublement

doubt [dout] *n* doute M;
without a ~\sans aucun doute;
vt douter

doubtful [DOUT•ful] *adj*
douteux incertain

dough [do] *n* pâte F

douse [dous] *vt* tremper; (fire) éteindre

dove [duhv] *n* colombe F

dove [dov] *pt a* dive

down [doun] *adv* en bas vers le bas; (costs) baisser; tomber; (costs) baisser; *prep* en bas de; descendre la rue; *adj* (sad) découragé; *n* (feathers) duvet M

down payment [doun PAI•mint] *n* acompte

downcast [DOUN•kast] *adj* démoralisé

downpour [DOUN•paur] *n* déluge M

downstairs [DOUN•STAIURZ] *adj* du bas; *adv* en bas; descendre (en bas)

downward [DOUN•wurd] *adj* descendant; *adv* vers le bas en bas

dowry [DOUU•ree] *n* dot F

doze [doz] *vi* someiller; *n* somme M

dozen [DUH•zn] *n* douzaine (de) F

draft [draft] *n* (document) brouillon M; (mil) conscription F; (slight wind) courant M d'air; *vt* (document) faire le brouillon; (mil) appeler

drag [drag] *vt vi* traîner; *vi* s'éterniser; *n* (bore) corvée; (of cigarette) bouffée; en travesti

dragon [DRA•gn] *n* dragon M

dragonfly [DRA•gn•FLUY] *n* libellule F

drain [drain] *n* égout M; (high expense) saignée F; *vt* (vegetables) égoutter; (land) drainer assécher; (exhaust) épuiser; *vi* s'écouler

drama [DRAH•mu] *n* drame M

dramatic [dru•MA•tik] *adj* dramatique

dramatist [DRAH•mu•tist] *n* dramatiste MF

dramatize [DRAH•mu•TUYZ] *vt* dramatiser

drape [draip] *vt* draper

drapes [draips] *npl* rideaux *mpl*

drastic [DRA•stik] *adj* drastique; sévère

draw [drau] *n* (tie) match M nul; *vt* dessiner; (weapon card etc) tirer; (attract) attirer; prolonger

drawer [draur] *n* tiroir M

drawing [DRAU•ing] *n* dessin

dread [dred] *n* épouvante F; *vt* redouter

dreadful [DRED•ful] *adj* épouvantable

dream [dreem] *n* rêve M; *vi* rêver (de)

dreamy [DREE•mee] *adj* rêveur; de réve

dreary [DREEU•ree] *adj* morne; triste

drench [drench] *vt* tremper

dress [dres] *n* robe F; (attire) costume M; *vt* habiller; s'habiller; *vi* s'habiller

dresser [DRE•sur] *n* commode F

dressing [DRE•sing] *n* (for salad) assaisonnement M

dried [druyd] *adj* sec (sèche);
(flowers) sèché

drift [drift] *n* sens M; (of snow)
congère; *vi* (boat) dériver;
(snow sand etc) s'amonceler

drill [dril] *n* perceuse F; (of
dentist) fraise F; (test run)
exercice M; *vt* percer; (tooth)
fraiser; (for oil etc) forer

drink [dringk] *n* boisson M; *vt*
vi boire

drip [drip] *n* goutte F; *vi*
goutter; tomber goutte à
goutte

drive [druyv] *n* promenade F;
(road) chaussée F; (ambition)
énergie F; (desire) désir M; *vt*
conduire; (push; guide)
pousser; (render) rendre; *vi*
conduire

drivel [DRI•vl] *n* idioties fpl

driver [DRUY•vur] *n*
conducteur M; chauffeur M;
(~'s license) *n* permis M de
conduire

drizzle [DRI•zl] *n* bruine F; *vi*
bruiner

drool [drool] *vi* baver

droop [droop] *vi* tomber;
s'affaisser

drop [drahp] *n* goutte F; (fall)
baisse F; *vt* laisser tomber;
(lower) baisser; déposer qqn;
vi tomber

drought [drout] *n* sécheresse

drove [drov] *pt a* drive

drown [droun] *vt* noyer; *vi* se
noyer

drowsy [DROU•zee] *adj*
somnolent

drug [druhg] *n* médicament M;
(narcotic) drogue F; *vt*
droguer

drug addict [druhg A•dikt] *n*
drogué toxicomane MF

druggist [DRUH•gist] *n*
pharmacien M

drum [druhm] *n* tambour M; *vt*
vi tambouriner

drummer [DRUH•mur] *n*
tambour M

drunk [druhngk] *adj* ivre soûl;
s'enivrer; *n* soûlard M
ivrogne M

drunkenness
[DRUHNG•kn•nis] *n* ivresse F

dry [druy] *adj* sec (sèche);
(land) asséché; (weather) sans
pluie; *vt vi* sécher essuyer

dryer [DRUY•ur] *n* séchoir M

dual [dooul] *adj* double

dubbed [duhbd] *adj* (film)
doublé; (named) surnommé

dubious [DOO•byus] *adj*
douteux; hésitant

Dublin [DUH•blin] *n* Dublin

duchess [DUH•chis] *n*
duchesse F

duck [duhk] *n* canard M; *vt*
(elude) esquiver; *vi* se baisser

duct [duhkt] *n* conduite F;
(anat) conduit M

due [doo] *adj* dû (due);
(suitable) qui convient; devoir
arriver; (book etc) devoir être
rapporté

duel [dooul] *n* duel M; *vi* se
battre en duel

duet [doo•ET] *n* duo M

duke [dook] *n* duc M

dull [duhl] *adj* ennuyeux;
(person) pénible; (knife)
émoussé

dumb [duhm] *adj* (mute) muet;
(stupid) bête

dumbfound [DUHM•found] *vt*
abasourdir

dummy [DUH•mee] *n*
mannequin M

dump [duhmp] *n* décharge M;
vt jeter; déposer

dunce [duns] *n* cancre M

dune [doon] *n* dune F

dung [duhng] *n* fumier M

dungeon [DUHN•jun] *n*
cachot M

duplicate [*adj* n. DOO•pli•kut
v. DOO•pli•KAIT] *adj* double;
n double M; *vt* faire un
double de

duplicity [doo•PLI•si•tee] *n*
duplicité F

durable [DOOU•ru•bl] *adj*
durable solide

duration [du•RAI•shn] *n*
durée F

dusk [duhsk] *n* crépuscule M

dust [duhst] *n* poussière F; *vt*
épousseter

dustpan [DUHST•pan] *n* pelle
à poussière F

Dutch [duhch] *adj* hollandais
néerlandais; *n* (lang)
hollandais M néerlandais M;
les Hollandais *npl* les
Néerlandais *npl*

duty [DOO•tee] *n* devoir M
fonctions fpl; (customs) droit
M; on ~\de garde de service;
off ~\libre pas de garde pas
de service

duty-free [DOO•tee free] *adj*
hors taxe exempt de douane

dwarf [dwaurf] *n* nain M; *vt*
écraser

dwell [dwel] *vi* habiter
demeurer; ~ on\s'arrêter sur

dwelling [DWE•ling] *n*
habitation F demeure F

dwindle [DWIN•dl] *vi* diminuer

dye [duy] *n* teinture F; *vt*
teindre

dying [DUY•ing] *adj* mourant;
moribund

dynamic [duy•NA•mik] *adj n*
dynamique F

dynamite [DUY•nu•MUYT] *n*
dynamite M; *vt* dynamiter

dynasty [DUY•nu•stee] *n*
dynastie F

E

elect [ee•LEKT] *vt* élire

each [eech] *adj* chaque; pron
chacun M; l'un l'autre les
uns les autres; ils se
connnaissent

eager [EE•gur] *adj* avide
impatient; avide de

eagle [EE•gl] *n* aigle M

ear [eeur] *n* oreille F; (of corn;
wheat) épi M

earlobe [eeur•LOB] *n* lobe M
de l'oreille

early [UR•lee] *adj* précoce; de
bonne heure; (ahead of
schedule) en avance; *adv* tôt
de bonne heure; (ahead of
schedule) en avance

earn [urn] *vt* gagner

earnest [UR•nist] *adj* sincère;
sérieux

earring [EEU•ring] *n* boucle F
d'oreille

earth [urth] *n* terre F

earthquake [URTH•kwaik] *n*
tremblement M de terre F

ease [eez] *n* facilité F aisance F;
facilement; à l'aise; ill at
~\mal à l'aise; *vt* calmer;
diminuer

easily [EE•zi•lee] *adv*
facilement

east [eest] *adj n* est M; the
~\l'est; *adv* aller à/vers l'est

Easter [EE•stur] *n* Pâques M

eastern [EE•sturn] *adj* de l'est
oriental

eastward [EEST•wurd] *adv*
vers l'est; à l'est

easy [EE•zee] *adj* facile; ne pas
se fatiguer

eat [eet] *vt vi* manger; *vt* ~
away\ronger

ebb [eb] *n reflux* M déclin M;
vi refluer; décliner

ebony [E•bu•nee] *adj* d'ébène;
n ébène F

eccentric [ek•SEN•trik] *adj n*
eccentrique MF

ecclesiastic
[ee•KLEE•zee•A•stik] *adj*
ecclésiastique

echo [E•ko] *n* écho M; *vt*
répéter; *vi* faire écho

eclipse [ee•KLIPS] *n* éclipse F;
vt éclipser

ecology [ee•KAH•lu•jee] *n*
écologie F

economic [E•ku•NAH•mik] *adj*
économique

economical [E•ku•NAH•mi•kl]
adj (thing) économique;
(person) économe

economics [E•ku•NAH•miks] *n*
eeconomie F politique

economy [ee•KAH•nu•mee] *n*
économie F

ecstasy [EK•stu•see] *n* extase F

ecstatic [ek•STA•tik] *adj*
extatique F

edge [ej] *n* bord M; (of blade)
tranchant M

edible [E•di•bl] *adj* comestible

edit [E•dit] *vt* éditer

edition [e•DI•shn] *n* édition F

editor [E•di•tur] *n* (of
magazine) directeur M; (of
newspaper) rédacteur; (of
book etc) éditeur

editorial [E•di•TAU•ree•ul] *adj*
n éditorial M

educate [E•ju•KAIT] *vt*
instruire

education [E•ju•KAI•shn] *n*
éducation F

educational [E•ju•KAI•shu•nl]
adj pédagogique; éducatif

eel [eeul] *n* anguille

effect [i•FEKT] *n* effet M; take
~\prendre effet; *vt* effectuer

effective [i•FEK•tiv] *adj*
efficace; ~ly\efficacement

efficiency [i•FI•shun•see] *n*
efficacité F

efficient [i•FI•shunt] *n* efficace

effort [E•furt] *n* effort M; faire
un effort

egg [eg] *n* œuf; ~ yolk\jaune M
d'œuf; ~ white\blanc M
d'œuf; *vt* pousser M

eggplant [EG•plant] *n*
aubergine F

ego [EE•go] *n* moi M

egotist [EE•go•tist] *n* égotiste
MF

Egypt [EE•jipt] *n* Égypte F

Egyptian [ee•JIP•shn] *adj*
égyptien; *n* Égyptien M

eight [ait] *num* huit

eighteen [ai•TEEN] *num*
dix-huit

eighteenth [ai•TEENTH] *num*
dix-huitième; see also eighth

eighth [aith] *num* huitième;
(following person's name)
huit; (in dates) le huit

eighty [AI•tee] *num*
quatre-vingts

either [EE•thur] *adj* l'un ou
l'autre; (in neg. construction)
ni l'un ni l'autre; de toute
façon; *adv* (in neg.
construction) non plus; *conj*
soit/ou . . . soit/ou . . .

eject [ee•JEKT] *vt* expulser;
(cassette etc) éjecter

elaborate [*adj* i•LA•brit *v.*
i•LA•bu•RAIT] *adj* détaillé; *vt*
élaborer; *vi* donner des détails

elastic [i•LA•stik] *adj n*
élastique M

elated [i•LAI•tid] *adj* transporté

elbow [EL•bo] *n* coude M

elder [EL•dur] *adj n* aîné M

elderly [EL•dur•lee] *adj* vieux;
âgé

elect [i•LEKT] *adj* élu; *vt* élire

election [i•LEK•shn] *n* élection

electric [i•LEK•trik] *adj*
électrique

electricity [i•LEK•TRI•si•tee] *n*
électricité

electrocute
[i•LEK•tru•KYOOT] *vt*
électrocuter

electronic [i•LEK•TRAH•nik]
adj électronique; ~
mail\courrier M électronique

elegance [E•li•guns] *n*
élégance F

elegant [E•li•gunt] *adj*
élégant F

element [E•li•munt] *n* élément
M; rudiments *npl;* (rain, etc)
les éléments *npl* M

elementary [E•li•MEN•tu•ree]
adj élémentaire

elephant [E•lu•fint] *n*
éléphant M

elevate [E•lu•VAIT] *vt* élever

elevator [E•li•VAI•tur] *n*
ascenseur M

eleven [i•LE•vn] num onze

eleventh [i•LE•vnth] num
onzième; see also eighth

elicit [i•LI•sit] *vt* obtenir

eligible [E•li•ju•bl] *adj* éligible;
admissible

eliminate [i•LI•mi•NAIT] *vt*
éliminer

elite [i•LEET] *adj* d'élite; *n*
élite F

elitist [i•LEE•tist] *adj n* élitiste
MF

elk [elk] *n* élan M

elm [elm] *n* orme M

elope [i•LOP] *vi* s'enfuir

eloquence [E•lu•kwuns] *n* éloquence F

eloquent [E•lu•kwunt] *adj* éloquent

else [els] *adv* autre; d'autre; autrement

elsewhere [ELS•waiur] *adv* ailleurs

elude [i•LOOD] *vt* échapper à; esquiver

emaciated [i•MAI•shee•AI•tid] *adj* émacié

emanate [E•mu•NAIT] *vi* émaner

emancipation [i•MAN•si•PAI•shn] *n* émancipation F

embankment [em•BANGK•munt] *n* (of road) remblai M; (of river) digue F

embargo [im•BAHR•go] *n* embargo M; *vt* mettre un embargo

embarrass [im•BA•rus] *vt* embarrasser

embarrassed [im•BA•rust] *adj* embarrassé

embarrassing [im•BA•ru•sing] *adj* embarrassant

embarrassment [im•BA•rus•munt] *n* embarras M

embassy [EM•bu•see] *n* ambassade F

embellish [im•BE•lish] *vt* embellir; orner

embers [EM•burz] *npl* braises F

embezzle [em•BE•zl] *vt* détourner

emblem [EM•blum] *n* emblème M

embody [im•BAH•dee] *vt* incarner; incorporer

embrace [im•BRAIS] *n* étreinte F; *vt* embrasser; *vi* s'embrasser

embroidery [im•BROI•du•ree] *n* broderie F

embryo [EM•bree•O] *n* embryon M

emerald [E•mu•ruld] *adj n* émeraude F

emerge [i•MURJ] *vi* émerger

emergency [i•MUR•jun•see] *adj* d'urgence; *n* urgence F; en cas d'urgence

emergency exit *n* sortie F de secours

emigrant [E•mi•grunt] *n* émigré M

emigrate [E•mi•GRAIT] *vi* émigrer M

eminence [E•mi•nuns] *n* éminence F; distinction F

eminent [E•mi•nunt] *adj* éminent

emissary [E•mi•SE•ree] *n* émissaire M

emission [i•MI•shn] *n* émission F

emit [i•MIT] *vt* émettre

emperor [EM•pu•rur] *n* empereur M

emphasis [EM•fu•sis] *n* accent M; insistance F

emphasize [EM•fu•SUYZ] *vt*
insister sur; souligner

empire [EM•puyur] *n* empire M

employ [em•PLOI] *vt* employer

employee [em•PLOI•YEE] *n*
employé M

employer [em•PLOI•yur] *n*
employeur M

employment [em•PLOI•munt]
n emploi M

empress [EM•pris] *n*
impératrice M

empty [EMP•tee] *adj* vide; *vt*
vider; *vi* se vider

emulate [E•myu•LAIT] *vt*
imiter

enable [e•NAI•bl] *vt* permettre
(à qqn de faire qqch)

enact [e•NAKT] *vt* (law)
promulguer; décréter

enamel [i•NA•ml] *n* émail M;
vt émailler

enamored [i•NA•murd] *adj*
épris de

encampment [en•KAMP•munt]
n campement M

enchant [en•CHANT] *vt*
enchanter

enclose [en•CLOZ] *vt* entourer;
(in letter) joindre; inclure

encompass [en•KAHM•pus] *vt*
inclure; incorporer

encore [AHN•kaur] *n* rappel M;
excl bis!

encounter [en•KOUN•tur] *n*
rencontre F; *vt* rencontrer

encourage [en•KU•rij] *vt*
encourager

encouragement
[en•KU•rij•munt] *n*
encouragement M

encroach [en•KROCH] *vi*
empiéter sur

encyclopedia
[en•SUY•klo•PEE•dee•u] *n*
encyclopédie F

end [end] *n* fin M; (in area
surface) bout M; extrémité F;
(in time) terme M; *vt* mettre
fin à terminer; *vi* se terminer
finir

endanger [en•DAIN•jur] *vt*
mettre en danger

endearing [en•DEEU•ring] *adj*
affectueux

endeavor [en•DE•vur] *n*
tentative F; *vi* ~ to\tenter de

ending [EN•ding] *n*
dénouement M

endless [END•lis] *adj*
interminable; sans fin

endorse [en•DAURS] *vt*
appuyer; annoncer son
approbation; (check) endosser

endurance [en•DU•runs] *n*
endurance

enemy [E•nu•mee] *n* ennemi M

energetic [E•nur•JE•tik] *adj*
énergique

energy [E•nur•jee] *n* énergie F

enforce [en•FAURS] *vt* faire
respecter; imposer

engage [en•GAIJ] *vt* engager

engaged [en•GAIJD] *adj* (for
marriage) fiancé; se fiancer

engagement [en•GAIJ•munt] *n*
rendez-vous M; (for marriage)
npl fiançailles F

engaging [en•GAI•jing] *adj*
engageant; attirant

engine [EN•jin] *n* moteur M

engineer [EN•ji•NEEUR] *n*
ingénieur M; (of train)
mécanicien M

engineering
[EN•ji•NEEU•ring] *n*
ingénierie

England [ING•glund] *n*
Angleterre F

English [ING•glish] *adj* anglais;
n Anglais M; *npl* les Anglais

engrave [en•GRAIV] *vt* graver

engraving [en•GRAI•ving] *n*
gravure F

engulf [en•GUHLF] *vt* engloutir

enhance [en•HANS] *vt*
rehausser

enigma [i•NIG•mu] *n* énigme F

enjoy [en•JOI] *vt* prendre plaisir
à; ~ o.s. s'amuser

enjoyable [en•JOI•u•bl] *adj*
agréable; plaisant

enlarge [en•LAHRJ] *vt*
agrandir; *vi* s'agrandir

enlighten [en•LUY•tn] *vt*
éclairer

Enlightenment
[en•LUY•tn•munt] *n* the ~\ le
Siècle des lumières

enlist [en•LIST] *vt* enrôler;
(services etc) : *vi* s'enrôler

enormous [i•NAUR•mus] *adj*
énorme

enough [i•NUHF] *adj* assez de;
pron assez; *adv* assez; (rather
quite) plûtot; *excl* ~!\assez!

enrage [en•RAIJ] *vt* mettre en
rage

enrich [en•RICH] *vt* enrichir

enroll [en•ROL] *vt* inscrire; *vi*
s'inscrire

enslave [en•SLAIV] *vt* asservir

ensuing [en•SOO•ing] *adj*
suivant

ensure [en•SHOOUR] *vt*
assurer

entail [en•TAIL] *vt* entraîner;
inclure

enter [EN•tur] *vt* entrer dans;
(register) s'inscrire à; ~ sb/sth
into sth\ inscrire qqn/qqch à
qqch; *vi* entrer s'inscrire

enterprise [EN•tur•PRUYZ] *n*
entreprise F

enterprising
[EN•tur•PRUY•zing] *adj*
entreprenant

entertain [EN•tur•TAIN] *vt*
divertir amuser; (host)
recevoir; (idea) considérer

entertaining
[EN•tur•TAI•ning] *adj*
amusant; divertissant

entertainment
[EN•tur•TAIN•munt] *n*
amusement M; divertissement
M; (show) spectacle M

enthusiasm
[en•THOO•zee•A•zm] *n*
enthousiasme M

enthusiastic
[en•THOO•zee•A•stik] *n*
enthousiaste M

enticing [en•TUY•sing] *adj*
attirant; attrayant

entire [en•TUYUR] *adj* entier

entirely [en•TUYUR•lee] *adv*
entièrement

entirety [en•TUYUR•tee] *n* en
entier

entitled [en•TUY•tld] *adj* avoir
le droit à; (named) intitulé

entity [EN•ti•tee] *n* entité F

entrance [*n.* EN•truns *v* en•TRANS] *n* entrée F; *vt* enchanter; ravir

entry [EN•tree] *n* entrée F; (in register) inscription F

enumerate [i•NOO•mu•RAIT] *vt* énumérer

envelop [en•VE•luhp] *vt* envelopper

envelope [EN•vu•LOP] *n* enveloppe F

envious [EN•vee•us] *adj* envieux

environment [en•VUY•run•munt] *n* environnement M; (surroundings) milieu M

envoy [EN•voi] *n* envoyé M; émissaire M

envy [EN•vee] *n* envie F; *vt* envier

epic [E•pik] *adj* épique; *n* épopée F

epidemic [E•pi•DE•mik] *n* épidémie F

episode [E•pi•SOD] *n* épisode M

epistle [i•PI•sl] *n* épître F

epitaph [E•pi•TAF] *n* épitaphe F

epitome [e•PI•tu•mee] *n* modèle M; quintessence F

epoch [E•puk] *n* époque

equal [EE•kwul] *adj* égal; *n* égal M; *vt* égaler

equality [ee•KWAH•li•tee] *n* égalité F

equally [EE•kwu•lee] *adv* également; (before *adj* in comparison) tout aussi

equation [ee•KWAI•zhn] *n* équation F

equator [ee•KWAI•tur] *n* équateur M

equip [i•KWIP] *vt* équiper; munir de

equipment [i•KWIP•munt] *n* équipement M

equivalent [i•KWI•vu•lunt] *adj n* équivalent M

era [E•ru] *n* ère F époque F

eradicate [i•RA•di•KAIT] *vt* éradiquer

erase [i•RAIS] *vt* effacer; (with eraser) gommer

eraser [i•RAI•sur] *n* gomme F

erect [i•REKT] *adj* droit; *vt* construire; (monument) ériger

erection [i•REK•shn] *n* érection F; (of building) construction F

erode [i•ROD] *vt* éroder; diminuer; *vi* s'éroder

erosion [i•RO•zhn] *n* érosion F

err [er] *vi* se tromper

errand [E•rund] *n* course F; faire une course

error [E•rur] *n* erreur F

erudite [ER•yu•DUYT] *adj* érudit

erupt [i•RUHPT] *vi* entrer en éruption; (fight etc) éclater

eruption [i•RUHP•shn] *n* éruption F

escalate [E•sku•LAIT] *vt* intensifier; *vi* s'intensifier

escalator [E•sku•LAI•tur] *n* escalier; M roulant

escape [e•SKAIP] *n* évasion F fuite F; *vt* échapper à; *vi* s'échapper fuir; (from jail) s'évader

escort [n. E•skaurt v. e•SKAURT] n escorte F; vt escorter

especially [e•SPE•shu•lee] adv paticulièrement; surtout

espionage [E•spee•u•NAHZH] n espionnage M

essay [E•sai] n essai M

essence [E•suns] n essence F

essential [e•SEN•shl] adj essenciel F

essentially [e•SEN•shu•lee] adv essenciellement F

establish [e•STA•blish] vt établir

establishment [e•STA•blish•munt] n établissement M; l'Establishment M

estate [e•STAIT] n (land) domaine F; (possessions) npl biens M

esteem [e•STEEM] n estime F; vt estimer

estimate [n. E•sti•mut v. E•sti•MAIT] n évaluation F; (appraisal) devis M; vt estimer; évaluer

estranged [e•STRAINJD] adj séparé

eternal [i•TUR•nl] adj éternel

eternity [i•TUR•ni•tee] n éternité F

ethic [E•thik] n éthique F; morale F

ethical [E•thi•kl] adj moral

Ethiopia [EE•thee•O•pee•u] n Éthiopie

ethnic [ETH•nik] adj ethnique

etiquette [E•ti•kut] n étiquette F; convenances fpl

eulogy [YOO•lu•jee] n éloge M; panégyrique F

euphemism [YOO•fu•MI•zm] n euphémisme M

Europe [YOO•rup] n Europe F

European [YU•ru•PEE•un] adj européen; n Européen M F

European Community [YOOR•e•PEE•en kuh•MYU•ni•tee] n the ~\la Communauté européene F

euthanasia [YOO•thu•NAI•zhu] n euthanasie F

evacuate [i•VA•kyoo•AIT] vt évacuer; vi s'évacuer

evade [i•VAID] vt échapper à; esquiver

evaluate [i•VAL•yoo•AIT] vt évaluer

evaporate [i•VA•pu•RAIT] vt faire évaporer; vi s'évaporer

evasive [i•VAI•siv] adj évasif

eve [eev] n veille F

even [EE•vn] adj égal regulier; (number) pair; se venger de; adv même; (in comparison) encore plus/moins; conj même si; bien que

evening [EEV•ning] n soir M; (duration) soirée F; (regularly) le soir

evening gown [EEV•ning gown] n robe F du soir

event [i•VENT] n événement M; de toute façon; en cas de

eventual [i•VEN•chu•ul] adj final

eventually [i•VEN•chuu•lee] adv finalement

ever [E•vur] *adv* jamais; (all the time) toujours; as-tu déjà . . .?; depuis; *conj* depuis que

evergreen [E•vur•GREEN] *n* arbre M à feuilles persistantes

every [E•vree] *adj* chaque; tous les (toutes les)

everybody [E•vree•BUH•dee] *pron* tout le monde

everyday [E•vree•DAI] *adj* quotidien

everyone [E•vree•wuhn] *pron* tout le monde; chacun; tous

everything [E•vree•THING] *pron* tout

everywhere [E•vree•WAIUR] *adv* partout

evict [i•VIKT] *vt* expulser

evidence [E•vi•duns] *n* preuve F; (testimony) temoignage M

evident [E•vi•dunt] *adj* évident

evil [EE•vl] *adj* mauvais; *n* mal M

evoke [i•VOK] *vt* évoquer

evolution [E•vu•LOO•shn] *n* évolution F

evolve [i•VAHLV] *vi* évoluer se développer

ewe [yoo] *n* brebis F

exact [eg•ZAKT] *adj* exact; précis; *vt* (information etc) exiger

exaggerate [eg•ZA•ju•RAIT] *vt vi* exagérer

exaggeration [eg•ZA•ju•RAI•shn] *n* exagération

exalt [eg•ZAULT] *vt* élever; (in worship) exalter

exam [eg•ZAM] *n abbr of* examination

examination [eg•ZA•mi•NAI•shn] *n* examen; take an ~\passer un examen M

examine [eg•ZA•min] *vt* examiner M

example [eg•ZAM•pl] *n* exemple M; for ~\par exemple

exasperate [eg•ZA•spu•RAIT] *vt* exaspérer

excavate [EK•sku•VAIT] *vt* creuser excaver

exceed [ek•SEED] *vt* dépasser excéder

excel [ek•SEL] *vi* exceller

excellence [EK•su•luns] *n* excellence

excellent [EK•su•lunt] *adj* excellent

except [ek•SEPT] *prep conj* sauf

exception [ek•SEP•shn] *n* exception F; à l'exception de; objecter

exceptional [ek•SEP•shu•nl] *adj* exceptionel

excerpt [EK•surpt] *n* extrait M

excess [EK•ses] *adj* excédentaire; *n* excès M

excessive [ek•SE•siv] *adj* excessif

exchange [eks•CHAINJ] *n* échange M; *vt* échanger

excite [ek•SUYT] *vt* exciter; s'exciter

excited [ek•SUY•tid] *adj* excité

exciting [ek•SUY•ting] *adj* passionnant

exclaim [ek•SKLAIM] *vi* s'exclamer; s'écrier

exclamation point
[EK•sklu•MAI•shn ~] *n* point
d'exclamation M

exclude [ek•SKLOOD] *vt*
exclure

excrement [EK•skri•munt] *n*
excrément M

excursion [ek•SKUR•zhn] *n*
excursion F

excuse [*n.* ek•SKYOOS *v.*
ek•SKYOOZ] *n* excuse F; *vt*
excuser; excusez-moi pardon
je m'excuse

execute [EK•si•KYOOT] *vt*
exécuter

execution [EK•si•KYOO•shn] *n*
exécution F

executioner
[EK•si•KYOO•shu•nur] *n*
bourreau F

executive [eg•ZE•kyu•tiv] *adj*
exécutif; *n* exécutif M;
directeur MF

exemplary [eg•ZEM•plu•ree]
adj exemplaire

exemplify [eg•ZEM•pli•FUY]
vt exemplifier

exempt [eg•ZEMPT] *adj*
exempt; *vt* exempter

exercise [EK•sur•SUYZ] *n*
exercice F; *vt* exercer; *vi*
prendre de l'exercice
s'entraîner

exert [eg•ZURT] *vt* exercer

exhale [eks•HAIL] *vt* exhaler;
vi expirer

exhaust [eg•ZAUST] *n* (of car;
etc) gaz M d'échappement; *vt*
épuiser

exhausted [eg•ZAU•stid] *adj*
épuisé

exhaustion [eg•ZAUS•chn] *n*
épuisement M

exhibit [eg•ZI•bit] *n* exposition
F; *vt* exposer

exhilarating
[eg•ZI•lu•RAI•ting] *adj*
grisant; stimulant

exile [EG•zuyl] *n* exil M; exilé
M; *vt* exiler

exist [eg•ZIST] *vi* exister

existence [eg•ZI•stuns] *n*
existence F

exit [EG•zit] *n* sortie F; *vi* sortir

exodus [EK•su•dus] *n* exode M

exonerate [eg•ZAH•nu•RAIT]
vt disculper de

exotic [eg•ZAH•tik] *adj*
exotique

expand [ek•SPAND] *vt*
développer; accroître; étendre;
(metal; etc) dilater; *vi*
s'étendre; (business; etc) se
développer s'accroître; (metal;
etc) se dilater

expansion [ek•SPAN•shn] *n*
développement M
accroissement M; (metal; etc)
dilatation F

expect [ek•SPEKT] *vt*
s'attendre à; compter sur;
(insist) exiger; (await)
attendre

expectation
[EK•SPEK•TAI•shn] *n* espoir
M; espérance F

expecting [ek•SPEK•ting] *adj*
(pregnant) enceinte

expedition [EK•spu•DI•shn] *n*
expédition F

expel [ek•SPEL] *vt* expulser;
(from school) renvoyer

expend [ek•SPEND] vt
dépenser

expenditure [ek•SPEN•di•chur]
n dépense F

expense [ek•SPENS] n dépense
F; frais npl M; aux frais de;
aux dépens de qqn

expensive [ek•SPEN•siv] adj
cher; coûteux; (tastes)
dispendieux

experience
[ek•SPEEU•ree•uns] n
expérience F; vt éprouver;
(difficulties) se heurter à

experienced
[ek•SPEEU•ree•unst] adj
expérimenté

experiment [ek•SPE•ri•munt] n
expérience F; vt faire une
expérience expérimenter

expert [EK•spurt] adj n
expert M

expire [ek•SPUYUR] vi expirer

explain [ek•SPLAIN] vt
expliquer; vi s'expliquer

explanation
[EK•splu•NAI•shn] n
explication F

explode [ek•SPLOD] vt faire
exploser; vi exploser

exploit [n. EK•sploit v.
ek•SPLOIT] n exploit M; vt
exploiter

exploration [EK•splu•RAI•shn]
n exploration F

explore [ek•SPLAUR] vt vi
explorer

explorer [ek•SPLAU•rur] n
exploreur M

export 1 [EK•spaurt] n
exportation F

export 2 [ek•SPAURT] vt vi
exporter

expose [ek•SPOZ] vt exposer;
(the truth; etc) révéler;
(unmask) demasquer

exposure [ek•SPO•zhur] n
exposition F; (publicity)
publicité F

express [ek•SPRES] adj exprès;
(train route) express; n (train)
express M; adv exprès; vt
exprimer

expression [ek•SPRE•shn] n
expression F

expressive [ek•SPRE•siv] adj
expressif

exquisite [ek•SKWI•zit] adj
exquis

extend [ek•STEND] vt étendre;
prolonger; (offer) offrir; vi
s'étendre

extension [ek•STEN•shn] n
prolongement; (of stay)
prolongation F; (of building)
agrandissement M; (of phone)
poste M

extensive [ek•STEN•siv] adj
considérable vaste étendu

extent [ek•STENT] n étendue
F; dans une certaine mesure

exterior [ek•STEEU•ree•ur] adj
n extérieur M

exterminate
[ek•STUR•mi•NAIT] vt
exterminer

external [ek•STUR•nl] adj
externe

extinct [ek•STINGKT] adj
disparu; éteint

extinguish [ek•STING•gwish]
vt éteindre

extort [ek•STAURT] *vt* extorquer qqch à qqn

extra [EK•stru] *adj* supplémentaire; *adv* (extremely) extra; *n* supplément

extract [*n.* EK•strakt *v.* ek•STRAKT] *n* extrait M; *vt* extraire; (tooth) arracher

extradite [EK•stru•DUYT] *vt* extrader

extraordinary [ek•STRAU•di•NE•ree] *adj* extraordinaire

extravagance [ek•STRA•vu•guns] *n* extravagance; prodigalité

extravagant [ek•STRA•vu•gunt] *adj* extravagant; (tastes) dispendieux

extreme [ek•STREEM] *adj n* extrême M

extremist [ek•STREE•mist] *adj n* extrémiste M

extrovert [EK•stru•VURT] *adj n* extroverti M

exuberant [eg•ZOO•bu•runt] *adj* exubérant

exult [eg•ZUHLT] *vi* exulter

eye [uy] *n* œil M (~s yeux mpl); surveiller; (of needle) chas M; *vt* regarder

eyewitness [uy•WIT•nis] *n* témoin M oculaire F

eyeball [UY•baul] *n* globe M oculaire M

eyebrow [UY•brou] *n* sourcil M

eyelash [UY•lash] *n* cil M

eyelid [UY•lid] *n* paupière F

eyesight [UY•suyt] *n* vue F

F

fable [FAI•bl] *n* fable F

fabric [FA•brik] *n* tissu M; textile M; édifice M

fabricate [FA•bri•KAIT] *vt* fabriquer

fabulous [FA•byu•lus] *adj* fabuleux; (excl) formidable

facade [fu•SAHD] *n* façade F

face [fais] *n* visage M figure M; devant; *vt* faire face à; (house, etc) donner à (fears problems etc) affronter

facet [FA•sit] *n* facette F

facetious [fu•SEE•shus] *n* facétieux

facilities [fu•SI•li•tees] *npl* installations F; équipement M

facing [FAI•sing] *prep* en face de

fact [fakt] *n* fait M; en fait

factor [FAK•tur] *n* facteur M

factory [FAK•tu•ree] *n* usine F; fabrique F

faculty [FA•kul•tee] *n* faculté; (in school) corps M enseignant F

fad [fad] *n* engouement M; marotte F

fade [faid] *vt* décolorer; *vi* se décolorer; diminuer

fail [fail] *vt* (test) rater; *vi* échouer

failure [FAIL•yur] *n* échec M; (person) raté; (of machine) défaillance

faint [faint] *adj* vague; faible; *vi* s'évanouir

fair [faiur] *adj* juste; équitable; (complexion) clair; *n* fête

fairy [FAIU•ree] *n* fée F

fairy tale [FAIR•ée tail] *n* conté de fées M

faith [faith] *n* foi F; confiance F

faithful [FAITH•ful] *adj* fidèle

fake [faik] *adj n* faux; artificiel

falcon [FAL•kn] *n* faucon M

fall [faul] *n* automne M; *vi* tomber; (prices etc) baisser; (~ in love) tomber amoureux; (~ sick) tomber malade

false [fauls] *adj* faux (fausse)

falsify [FAUL•si•FUY] *vt* falsifier

falter [FAUL•tur] *vi* chanceler; hésiter

fame [faim] *n* gloire F renommée F

famed [faimd] *adj* renommé

familiar [fu•MI•lyur] *adj* familier; be ~ with\connaître

familiarize [fu•MI•lyu•RUYZ] *vt* familiariser

family [FA•mu•lee] *n* famille F

famine [FA•min] *n* famine F

famished [FA•misht] *adj* affamé

famous [FAI•mus] *adj* célèbre

fan [fan] *n* ventilateur M; (of paper) éventail MF; (of sports celebrity etc) fan M; *vt* éventer

fanatic [fu•NA•tik] *n* fanatique MF

fancy [FAN•see] *adj* fin; de luxe; *n* envie; *vt* (like) avoir le goût de

fang [fang] *n* croc M; (of snake) crochet M

fantastic [fan•TA•stik] *adj* fantastique

fantasy [FAN•tu•see] *n* rêve M; fantaisie F

far [fahr] *adj* lointain éloigné; *adv* loin; au loin; de loin; as ~ as\autant que farce [fahrs] *n* farce F

fare 1 [faiur] *n* prix M du billet; (bill of ~) menu; carte

fare 2 [faiur] *v* voyager; se porter

farewell [faiur•WEL] *n* adieu M

farm [fahrm] *n* ferme F; *vt* cultiver

farmer [FAHR•mur] *n* fermier M

farming [FAHR•ming] *n* agriculture F

farther [FAHR•thur] *adj* plus lointain; *adv* plus loin

farthest [FAHR•thist] *adj adv* superlative; le plus loin

fascinate [FA•si•NAIT] *vt* fasciner

fascinating [FA•si•NAI•ting] *adj* fascinant

fascination [FA•si•NAI•shn] *n* fascination F

fascism [FA•shi•zm] *n*
fascisme M

fashion [FA•shn] *n* mode F;
(way) façon F; *vt* façonner

fashionable [FA•shu•nu•bl] *adj*
à la mode

fast 1 [fast] *adj* rapide; *adv* vite

fast 2 [fast] *n* jeûne M; *vi*
jeûner

fasten [FA•sun] *vt* (coat etc)
fermer; (seatbelt) attacher; *vi*
s'attacher

fastidious [fa•STI•dee•us] *adj*
exigeant méticuleux

fat [fat] *adj* gros; (food) gras;
get ~\grossir; *n* graisse F

fatal [FAI•tl] *adj* fatal; (illness)
mortel

fate [fait] *n* destin M; (one's)
sort M

fateful [FAIT•ful] *adj* fatidique

father [FAH•thur] *n* père M

father-in-law
[FA•thur•in•LAU] *n* beau-père
M

fatherland [FAH•thur•LAND]
n patrie F

fatherly [FAH•thur•lee] *adj*
paternel

fathom [FA•thum] *n* brasse F;
vt sonder; comprendre

fatigue [fu•TEEG] *n* fatigue F

fatten [FA•tun] *vt* engraisser

fatuous [FA•chu•us] *adj* stupide

faucet [FAU•sit] *n* robinet M

fault [fault] *n* faute F; (defect)
défaut M; (it's my ~) c'est de
ma faute; (geo) faille F; *vt*
prendre en défaut blâmer

faulty [FAUL•tee] *adj*
défectueux

fauna [FAU•nu] *n* faune F

favor [FAI•vur] *n* faveur F;
service M; rendre un service
à; *vt* favoriser

favorable [FAI•vru•bl] *adj*
favorable

favorite [FAI•vrit] *adj n*
favori M

fawn [faun] *n* faon M; *vi* ~
on\flatter

fear [feeur] *n* peur F crainte M;
for ~ of\de peur de; de peur
que; *vt* craindre; avoir peur de

fearful [FEEUR•ful] *adj*
(afraid) craintif; (frightening)
effrayant affreux

fearless [FEEUR•lis] *adj*
intrépide

feasible [FEE•zu•bl] *adj*
faisable

feast [feest] *n* festin M; *vt* se
régaler de; *vi* festoyer

feat [feet] *n* exploit M

feather [FE•thur] *n* plume F

feature [FEE•chur] *n* trait M
carécteristique M; (film)
grand film M; *vt* présenter

February [FE•broo•U•ree] *n*
février M

federal [FE•du•rul] *adj* fédéral

federation [FE•du•RAI•shn] *n*
fédération F

fee [fee] *n* frais *mpl* prix M; (of
doctor etc) honoraires *npl* M

feeble [FEE•bl] *adj* faible

feed [feed] *n* (silage) nourriture
F pâture F; *vt* nourrir; donner
à manger; *vi* se nourrir de

feel [feeul] *n* sensation F; *vt*
sentir; toucher; palper; *vi* se
sentir; avoir froid/chaud

feeling [FEEU•ling] *n* sentiment
M; sensation F; *npl*
~s\sensibilité F; *npl*
sentiments M

feign [fain] *vt* feindre

fell [fel] *pt* a fall

fellow [FE•lo] *n* compagnon M;
homme M; (guy) type M;
(member) membre M

fellowship [FE•lo•SHIP] *n*
amitié F; (group)
association F

felon [FE•lun] *n* criminel

felony [FE•lu•nee] *n* crime M

felt [felt] *n* feutre M; *pt* a feel

female [FEE•mail] *adj* féminin;
(animal) femelle; *n* femelle F

feminine [FE•mi•nin] *adj*
féminin; *n* (in grammar)
féminin M

fence [fens] *n* clôture F; *vi*
(sport) faire de l'escrime

fencing [FEN•sing] *n* escrime F

fend [fend] *vi* se débrouiller; *vt*
parer

fender [FEN•dur] *n* (around
wheel) gardeboue M;
(bumper) pare-chocs M

ferment [*n.* FUR•ment *v.*
fur•MENT] *n* agitation F; *vt*
faire fermenter; *vi* fermenter

fern [furn] *n* fougère F

ferocious [fu•RO•shus] *adj*
féroce

ferret [FE•rit] *n* furet M; *vt*
dénicher

ferry [FE•ree] *n* ferry; *vt*
transporter M

fertile [FUR•tl] *adj* fertile;
(woman) fécond

fertility [fur•TI•li•tee] *n* fertilité
F; fécondité F

fertilize [FUR•ti•LUYZ] *vt*
fertiliser

fertilizer [FUR•ti•LUY•zur] *n*
engrais M

fervent [FUR•vunt] *adj* fervent

festival [FE•sti•vl] *n* festival M

festive [FE•stiv] *adj* joyeux; de
fête

fetch [fech] *vt* aller chercher;
rapporter

fetus [FEE•tus] *n* fœtus M

feud [fyood] *n* dispute F
querelle F; *vi* se quereller

feudal [FYOO•dl] *adj* féodal

fever [FEE•vur] *n* fièvre F

feverish [FEE•vu•rish] *adj*
fiévreux F

few [fyoo] *adj* peu de; *pron* peu
M; quelques-uns M
quelques-unes F

fiancé [fee•ahn•SAI] *n* fiancé M

fiancée [fee•ahn•SAI] *n*
fiancée F

fib [fib] *n* bobard M; *vi* raconter
des bobards

fiber [FUY•bur] *n* fibre F

fickle [FI•kl] *adj* inconstant;
capricieux

fiction [FIK•shn] *n* fiction F

fiddle [FI•dl] *n* violon M; *vi*
jouer du violon; (toy with) *vt*
tripoter

fidelity [fi•DE•li•tee] *n*
fidélité F

fidget [FI•jit] *vi* se trémousser

field [feeuld] *n* champ M; (area
of knowledge) domaine M;
(for football etc) terrain M

fiend [feend] *n* démon M

fiendish [FEEN•dish] *adj* diabolique

fierce [feeurs] *adj* féroce; violent

fiery [FUYU•ree] *adj* brûlant; ardent; (temper) fougeux

fifteen [fif•TEEN] *num* quinze

fifteenth [fif•TEENTH] *num* quinzième (see also eighth)

fifth [fifth] *num* cinquième (see also eighth)

fiftieth [FIF•tee•ith] *num* cinquantième

fifty [FIF•tee] *num* cinquante

fig [fig] *n* figue F

fight [fuyt] *n* bagarre F; (mil) combat M; (struggle) lutte F; *vt* combattre; lutter contre; *vi* se battre

figurative [FI•gyu•ru•tiv] *adj* figuré

figure [FI•gyur] *n* figure F; (number calculation) chiffre; (body outline) forme F silhouette F; (body shape health) ligne M; *vt* (assume believe) penser; résoudre comprendre

file [fuyul] *n* dossier M; (tool) lime F; en file indienne; *vt* classer; (with tool) limer

fill [fil] *vt* remplir; (hole) boucher; (form) remplir

fillet [fi•LAI] *n* filet F

filling [FI•ling] *n* (in tooth) plombage F; (in cake; etc) garniture F

film [film] *n* film M; (of camera) pellicule F; *vt* filmer

filter [FIL•tur] *n* filtre M; *vt* filtrer

filth [filth] *n* saleté F

filthy [FIL•thee] *adj* sale

fin [fin] *n* (of fish) nageoire F

final [FUY•nl] *adj* final; dernier; *n* finale M; ~s \ examens à la fin du semestre

finally [FUY•nu•lee] *adv* enfin; finalement

finance [fuy•NANS] *n* finance F; *npl* finances *fpl;* *vt* financer

financial [fuy•NAN•shl] *adj* financier

finch [finch] *n* pinson M

find [fuynd] *n* trouvaille F; trouver; se renseigner sur; déclarer coupable

fine [fuyn] *adj* beau (belle); (thin detailed) fin délicat; *adv* (well) bien; *n* (penalty charge) amende F; *vt* condamner à une amende

finger [FING•gur] *n* doigt M

fingerprint [FING•gur•PRINT] *n* empreinte F digitale

fingertip [FING•gur•TIP] *n* bout M du doigt

finish [FI•nish] *n* fin F; (of furniture) finition; ~ line\ arrivée F; *vt* finir terminer; *vi* finir se terminer

Finland [FIN•lund] *n* Finlande F

Finn [fin] *n* Finlandais F

Finnish [FI•nish] *adj* finlandais; *n* (language) finnois M F

fir [fur] *n* sapin M

fire [fuyur] *n* feu M; (blaze) incendie M; en feu; mettre le feu à; prendre feu; *vt* (gun etc) tirer; (employee) renvoyer

fire station [fuyur STAI•shn] *n* caserne F de pompiers F

fireman [FUYUR•man] *n* pompier M

fireplace [FUYUR•plais] *n* cheminée F

firewood [FUYUR•wud] *n* bois M de chauffage

fireworks [FUYUR•wurks] *npl* feu M d'artifice

firm [furm] *adj* ferme; *n* firme F

first [furst] *adj* premier; *adv* en premier premièrement; d'abord; *n* premier M

first aid [FURST AID] *npl* premiers secours M

first name [FURST NAIM] *n* prénom

first-class [FURST•KLASS] *adj* de première classe

firsthand [FURST•HAND] *adj adv* de premier main

fiscal [FI•skl] *adj* fiscal

fish [fish] *n* poisson M; *vt vi* pêcher

fisherman [FI•shur•mun] *n* pêcheur M

fishing [FI•shing] *n* go ~\ aller à la pêche; *n* canne F à pêche

fission [FI•shn] *n* fission F

fissure [FI•shur] *n* fissure F

fist [fist] *n* poignet M

fit [fit] *adj* convenable; (healthy) en forme; apte à; *n* (attack) accès M; crise F; (of coughing etc) quinte F; *vt* (clothes) aller à; *vi* (be suitable, go ~clothes etc) aller

fitting room [FI•ting ~] *n* salon M d'essayage

five [fuyv] *num* cinq

fix [fiks] *vt* fixer; (contest etc) arranger

fixation [fik•SAI•shn] *n* fixation F

fixed [fikst] *adj* fixe; (contest etc) arrangé

fizz [fiz] *n* pétillement M; *vi* pétiller

flag [flag] *n* drapeau; *vt* héler M

flagpole [FLAG•pol] *n* mât M

flagrant [FLAI•grunt] *adj* flagrant; criant

flair [flaiur] *n* flair M

flake [flaik] *n* (of snow) flocon M; (of paint etc) écaille; *vi* s'écailler F

flame [flaim] *n* flamme F

flamingo [flu•MING•go] *n* flamant M

flammable [FLA•mu•bl] *adj* inflammable M

flank [flangk] *n* flanc M; *vt* flanquer; flanqué de

flannel [FLA•nl] *n* flanelle F

flap [flap] *n* (of envelope pocket) rabat M; *vt vi* (wings) battre; *vi* (flag) claquer

flare [flaiur] *n* fusée F éclairante; *vi* (fire) s'embrasser; (anger) s'emporter

flash [flash] *n* (of light) éclat M; (of lightning) éclair M; (of camera) flash M; en un clin d'œil; *vt* projeter; (blink) clignoter; *vi* (sparkle) briller

flashback [FLASH•bak] *n* flashback M

flashlight [FLASH•luyt] *n*
lampe de poche F

flashy [FLA•shee] *adj* tapageur;
tape-à-l'œil (inv)

flask [flask] *n* bouteille; F
flacon M

flat [flat] *adj* plat; (tire)
dégonflé; (soda) éventé;
(voice) faux; (denial; refusal)
net; *n* (tire) crevaison F

flatten [FLA•tn] *vt* aplatir

flatter [FLA•tur] *vt* flatter

flattering [FLA•tu•ring] *adj*
flatteur

flattery [FLA•tu•ree] *n*
flatterie F

flaunt [flaunt] *vt* faire étalage
de

flavor [FLAI•vur] *n* saveur F
goût M; (of ice cream)
parfum M; *vt* parfumer

flaw [flau] *n* défaut M

flax [flaks] *n* lin M

flea [flee] *n* puce F

fleck [flek] *n* moucheture F;
particule F

flee [flee] *vt vi* fuir

fleece [flees] *n* toison F

fleet [fleet] *n* (of ships) flotte F

flesh [flesh] *n* chair; *vt*
assouvir

fleshy [FLE•shee] *adj* charnu

flex [fleks] *vt vi* fléchir

flexible [FLEK•si•bl] *adj*
flexible

flicker [FLI•kur] *vi* vaciller

flight [fluyt] *n* (of plane) vol
M; (of bird) volée F; (escape)
fuite F; (of stairs) escalier M

flimsy [FLIM•zee] *adj* peu
solide; (excuse) pauvre

flinch [flinch] *vi* tressaillir;
reculer

fling [fling] *vt* lancer

flint [flint] *n* silex M; (of
lighter) pierre F

flip [flip] *n* petit coup M;
chiquenaude F; *vt* faire sauter;
jouer à pile ou face

flippant [FLI•punt] *adj*
désinvolte

flirt [flurt] *n* flirt M; *vi* flirter

float [flot] *n* (in parade) char
M; (for fishing) flotteur M; *vt*
faire flotter; *vi* flotter

flock [flahk] *n* (of birds) vol M;
(of sheep) troupeau M; *vi*
s'attrouper

flog [flahg] *vt* flageller fouetter

flogging [FLAH•ging] *n*
fouet M

flood [fluhd] *n* inondation F;
(widespread ~ from rain)
déluge F; *vt* inonder

floodlight [FLUHD•luyt] *n*
projecteur

floor [flaur] *n* sol M; (of
building) étage F; (of ocean)
fond M; avoir la parole; *vt*
terrasser

flora [FLAU•ru] *n* flore F

florist [FLAU•rist] *n* fleuriste
MF

floss [flaus] *n* bourre F

flounder [FLOUN•dur] *n* flet
M; *vi* patauger

flour [flouur] *n* farine F

flourish [FLU•rish] *vi*
prospérer; (plants) venir bien

flout [flout] *vt* se moquer de

flow [flo] *n* (of tide) flux M;
(of words; blood) flot M;

(movement – of water news) circulation F; *vi* couler; (of blood) circuler

flower [flouur] *n* fleur M; *vi* fleurir

flown [flon] *pp* a fly

flu [floo] *n* grippe F

fluctuate [FLUHK•chu•AIT] *vi* fluctuer

flue [floo] *n* tuyau M

fluency [FLOO•un•see] *n* aisance F

fluent [FLOO•unt] *adj* coulant (speech) couramment

fluff [fluf] *n* duvet M; peluche; *vt* rendre duveteux; rendre pelucheux

fluid [FLOO•id] *adj n* fluide M

fluke [flook] *n* coup M de veine

flunky [FLUHNG•kee] *n* laquais M

fluorescent [flau•RE•sunt] *adj* fluorescent

fluoride [FLAU•ruyd] *n* fluorure M

flurry [FLU•ree] *n* (of snow) rafale F

flush [fluhsh] *adj* au ras de; (toilet) tirer la chasse d'eau; (blush) rougir

fluster [FLUH•stur] *vt* énerver; troubler

flute [floot] *n* flûte F

flutter [FLUH•tur] *n* (of wings) battement M; *vi* voleter; (wings) battre

fly [fluy] *n* (insect) mouche F; (of pants) braguette; *vt* faire voler; (pilot a plane) faire voler un avion; (carry by plane) transporter par avion;

vi (bird plane) voler; (travel by plane) voyager en avion

flying saucer [FLUY•ing ~] *n* soucoupe F volante

foam [fom] *n* mousse F; *vi* mousser

focal [FO•kl] *adj* focal; foyer M; (of topic; etc) point M central

focus [FO•kus] *n* foyer M; (of lens) mise F au point; *vt* mettre au point; *vi* (eyes) accommoder

fodder [FAH•dur] *n* fourrage M

foe [fo] *n* ennemi M

fog [fahg] *n* brouillard M

foil [foiul] *n* papier M d'aluminium; *vt* déjouer

fold [fold] *n* pli M; *vt* plier; (arms) croiser; *vi* se plier; (fail – business) s'écrouler

foliage [FO•lee•ij] *n* feuillage M

folk [fok] *adj* (music art) folklorique; *npl* gens *mpl*

follow [FAH•lo] *vt vi* suivre

follower [FAH•lo•ur] *n* disciple MF

following [FAH•lo•ing] *adj* suivant; *npl* admirateurs; disciples M

folly [FAH•lee] *n* folie F

foment [FO•ment] *vt* fomenter

fond [fahnd] *adj* affectueux; tendre; avoir le goût de; aimer

fondle [FAHN•dl] *vt* caresser

font [fahnt] *n* (baptismal) fonts *mpl;* (type of print) police F

food [food] *n* nourriture F

fool [fooul] *n* idiot M; (jester) fou M; *vt* duper

foolish [FOOU•lish] *adj*
ridicule; insensé

foolproof [FOOUL•proof] *adj*
infaillible

foot [fut] *n* pied M; (bottom)
bas M; à pied

football [FUT•baul] *n* football
M foot M; (American)
football américain; (ball)
ballon M

footnote [FUT•not] *n* note F
(en bas de page)

footpath [FUT•path] *n* sentier

footprint [FUT•print] *n*
empreinte F (de pied)

footstep [FUT•step] *n* pas M

for [faur] *prep* pour; (out of due
to) par; (duration) pendant
cinq jours/milles; (since) j'ai
travaillé depuis des années;
c'est l'heure de

forage [FAU•rij] *n* fourrage M;
vt vi fourrager

forbid [faur•BID] *vt* interdire
défendre; interdire/défendre à
qqn de faire qqch

force [faurs] *n* force F; de force;
(law) en vigueur; *vt* forcer

forceful [FAURS•ful] *adj*
énergique

forceps [FAUR•seps] *npl*
forceps M

ford [faurd] *n* gué M

forearm [FAUR•ahrm] *n*
avant-bras M

forecast [FAUR•kast] *n*
prévision F; (weather)
prévisions météorologique; *vt*
prévoir

forefather [FAUR•fah•thur] *n*
ancêtre

forego [faur•GO] *vt* renoncer à;
skip over\ sauter

foreground [FAUR•ground] *n*
premier plan M

forehead [FAUR•hed] *n*
front M

foreign [FAU•run] *adj* étranger;
(trade) extérieur

foreigner [FAU•ru•nur] *n*
étranger M

foreman [FAUR•mun] *n*
contremaître M

foremost [FAUR•most] *adj*
premier; principal; tout
d'abord

forerunner [FAUR•ruh•nur] *n*
précurseur

foresee [faur•SEE] *vt* prévoir

foreshadow [faur•SHA•do] *vt*
présager

foresight [FAUR•suyt] *n*
prévoyance F

forest [FAU•rist] *n* forêt F

foretell [faur•TEL] *vt* prédire

forever [fu•RE•vur] *adv* pour
toujours

foreword [FAUR•wurd] *n*
avant-propos M

forfeit [FAUR•fit] *n* (in sports)
gage M; *vt* perdre

forge [faurj] *n* forge F; *vt* (iron
etc) forger; (signature)
contrefaire; (document)
fabriquer

forget [faur•GET] *vt vi* oublier;
oublier de faire

forgetful [faur•GET•fl] *adj*
distrait

forgive [faur•GIV] *vt*
pardonner; ~ sb for sth\
pardonner qqch à qqn

fork [faurk] *n* fourchette F; (in road) bifurcation F; *vi* (road) bifurquer

forlorn [faur•LAURN] *adj* malheureux; (hope plan) désespéré

form [faurm] *n* forme F; (document) formulaire M; *vt* former; *vi* se former

formal [FAUR•ml] *adj* (attire) de cérémonie; (dinner) officiel; (person) cérémonieux

formality [faur•MA•li•tee] *n* formalité F

former [FAUR•mur] *adj* ancien; *n* celui-là (celle-là); celui-ci (celle-ci)

formidable [FAUR•mi•du•bl] *adj* redoutable

formula [FAUR•myu•lu] *n* formule F

forsake [faur•SAIK] *vt* abandonner

forsaken [faur•SAI•kn] *adj* abandonné

fort [faurt] *n* fort M

forth [faurth] *adv* en avant; et ainsi de suite

forthcoming [faurth•CUH•ming] *adj* à venir; (person) ouvert

fortification [FAUR•ti•fi•KAI•shn] *n* fortification F

fortify [FAUR•ti•FUY] *vt* fortifier

fortitude [FAUR•ti•TOOD] *n* force F d'âme

fortnight [FAURT•nuyt] *n* quinze jours *mpl* quinzaine F

fortress [FAUR•tris] *n* forteresse F

fortuitous [faur•TOO•i•tus] *adj* fortuit

fortunate [FAUR•chu•nut] *adj* heureux; avoir de la chance

fortunately [FAUR•chu•nut•lee] *adv* heureusement

fortune [FAUR•chun] *n* fortune F; (luck) chance F; ~teller\diseuse F de bonne aventure

forty [FAUR•tee] *num* quarante (see also eighty)

forward [FAUR•wurd] *adj* en avant; (bold rude) effronté; *adv* en avant; *vt* faire suivre

fossil [FAH•sl] *n* fossile F

foster [FAH•stur] *adj* (parent) adoptif; (child) adopté; *vt* élever; (idea; etc) entretenir

foul [foul] *adj* (food smell etc) infect; (language) ordurier; *n* (in sports) faute F;

found [found] *vt pt* a find; *vt* fonder

foundation [foun•DAI•shn] *n* fondation F; (basis) base F

founder [FOUN•dr] *n* fondateur F

fountain [FOUN•tuhn] *n* fontaine F

four [faur] *num* quatre

fourteen [faur•TEEN] *num* quatorze

fourth [faurth] *num* quatrième

fowl [foul] *n* volaille F

fox [fahks] *n* renard M

fraction [FRAK•shn] *n* fraction F

fracture [FRAK•chur] *n*
fracture F; *vt* fracturer

fragile [FRA•jul] *adj* fragile

fragment [FRAG•munt] *n*
fragment M

fragrance [FRAI•gruns] *n*
parfum M

fragrant [FRAI•grunt] *adj*
parfumé

frame [fraim] *n* cadre M; (of
stucture body) charpente F;
(of glasses) monture F; *vt*
encadrer

franc [frangk] *n* franc M

France [frans] *n* France F

franchise [FRAN•chuyz] *n*
franchise F; droit de vote M

frank [frangk] *adj* franc; *vt*
affranchir

frantic [FRAN•tik] *adj*
frénétique

fraternal [fru•TUR•nl] *adj*
fraternel

fraternity [fru•TUR•ni•tee] *n*
confrérie F; (ideal)
fraternité F

fraud [fraud] *n* fraude F
supercherie F; (person)
imposteur M

fraudulent [FRAU•dyu•lunt]
adj frauduleux

frayed [fraid] *adj* (person)
énervé; (cloth) effiloché

freak [freek] *adj* monstre M

free [free] *adj* libre; (no charge)
gratuit; gratuitement; *vt* libérer

free speech [FREE SPEECH] *n*
librerté de la parole F

free trade [FREE TRAID] *n*
libre-échange M

free will [FREE WILL] *n* libre
arbitre M; de son propre gré

freedom [FREE•duhm] *n*
liberté F

freeze [freez] *vt* geler; (food)
congeler; (prices; etc) bloquer;
vi se geler; se congeler; *n* (of
winter) gel M; (prices; etc)
blocage F

freezer [FREE•zur] *n*
congélateur M

freight [frait] *n* fret

French [french] *adj* français; *n*
(language) français M; *n*
(people) Français M

french fries [~ fruyz] *npl*
frites *fpl*

frenzy [FREN•zee] *n* frénésie F

frequency [FREE•kwun•see] *n*
fréquence F

frequent [*adj.* FREE•kwunt *v.*
free•KWENT] *adj* fréquent; *vt*
fréquenter F

fresh [fresh] *adj* frais

freshen [FRE•shn] *vt* refraîchir;
faire un brin de toilette

freshman [FRESH•mun] *n*
étudiant de première année M

freshness [FRESH•nus] *n*
fraîcheur F

freshwater [FRESH•WAU•tur]
adj d'eau douce

fret [fret] *vi* se tracasser

friar [fruyur] *n* frère M

friction [FRIK•shn] *n* friction F

Friday [FRUY•dai] *n* vendredi
M; on ~s\le vendredi

friend [frend] *n* ami M

friendly [FREND•lee] *adj*
amical

friendship [FREND•ship] *n*
amitié F

fright [fruyt] *n* peur F

frighten [FRUY•tn] *vt* effrayer
faire peur à

frightening [FRUY•tu•ning]
adj effrayant

frigid [FRI•jid] *adj* glacial;
(sexually) frigide

fringe [frinj] *n* frange F; ~
benefits*npl* avantages M
sociaux

frisk [frisk] *vt* fouiller

frisky [FRI•skee] *adj* vif

frivolous [FRI•vu•lus] *adj*
frivole

frog [frahg] *n* grenouille F

frolic [FRAH•lik] *vi* folâtrer

from [fruhm] *prep* de; à partir
de; venir de; (according to)
d'après ce que j'ai appris; (as
soon as) dès que je;
depuis jusqu'à

front [fruhnt] *adj* de devant;
(first) premier; *adv* devant; *n*
avant M; (of stucture) devant
M; (of weather of battle) front
M; *prep* devant

front door [FRUNT DOR] *n*
porte F d'entrée

frontier [fruhn•TEER] *n*
frontière F

frost [fraust] *n* gel M; *vt* (cake)
glacer

frostbite [FRAUST•buyt] *n*
gelure F

froth [frauth] *n* (of beer)
mousse F; (of waves)
écume F

frown [froun] *n* froncement M
de sourcils; *vi* froncer les
sourcils

frugal [FROO•gl] *adj* économe;
(meal) frugal

fruit [froot] *n* fruit M

fruitless [FROOT•lis] *adj* vain;
stérile

frustrate [FRUH•strait] *vt*
frustrer

frustration [fruh•STRAI•shn] *n*
frustration F

fry [fruy] *vt vi* frire

fudge [fuj] *n* fondant M de
chocalat

fuel [fyooul] *n* combustible M;
(for car) carburant M; *vt*
alimenter

fugitive [FYOO•ju•tiv] *n*
fugitif M

fulfill [ful•FIL] *vt* réaliser;
(responsibilities) remplir

fulfillment [ful•FIL•munt] *n*
réalisation F; (satisafaction)
satisfaction

full [ful] *adj* plein; complet

full moon [FUL MOON] *n*
pleine lune F

full-time [ful•TUYM] *adj adv* à
temps plein

fumble [FUHM•bl] *vt* laisser
tomber; *vi* ~ for
words\\bégayer

fumes [fyoomz] *npl* vapeurs;
fumées F

fumigate [FYOO•mi•GAIT] *vt*
fumiger

fun [fuhn] *adj* amusant; *n*
amusement M; have
~\\s'amuser; make ~ of\\se
moquer de

function [FUNGK•shn] *n*
fonction F; (event) réception
F; *vi* fonctionner

fund [fuhnd] *n* fonds M; *vt*
  financer
fundamental
  [FUHN•du•MEN•tl] *adj*
  fondamental
funeral [FYOO•nu•rul] *n*
  enterrement M; obsèques *fpl*
fungus [FUNG•gus] *n*
  champignon M
funnel [FUH•nl] *n* entonnoir M
funny [FUH•nee] *adj* drôle;
  amusant; (strange) curieux
fur [fur] *n* fourrure F
furious [FYOOU•ree•us] *adj*
  furieux
furnace [FUR•nis] *n*
  fourneau M
furnish [FUR•nish] *vt* meubler;
  (supply) fournir
furniture [FUR•ni•chur] *n*
  meubles *mpl;* meuble M
furry [FU•ree] *adj* à fourrure
further [FUR•thur] *adj* plus
  loin; (advice; reading; etc)

supplementaire; *adv* plus loin;
  vt faire avancer
furthermore
  [FUR•thur•MAUR] *adv* de
  plus
furthest [FUR•thist] *adj adv*
  superl a far; le plus loin
furtive [FUR•tiv] *adj* furtif
fury [FYUR•ee] *n* fureur F
fuse [fyooz] *n* fusible M plomb
  M; (of explosive) détonateur
  M amorce F; *vt vi* (melt)
  fondre; (combine) fusionner
fusion [FYOO•zhn] *n* fusion F
fuss [fuhs] *n* façons; (pouting;
  complaining) histoires F;
  make a ~\faire des histoires
futile [FYOO•tl] *adj* futile; vain
future [FYOO•chur] *adj* futur;
  n avenir; (grammar) futur M;
  in the ~\à l'avenir
fuzzy [FUH•zee] *adj* (hair)
  crépu; (image; memory) flou

G

gable [GAI•bl] *n* pignon
gadget [GA•jit] *n* gadget M
Gaelic [GAIU•lik] *adj n*
  gaélique M
gag [gag] *n* bâillon M; (joke)
  gag M blague F; *vt* bâillonner
gage (gauge) [gaij] *n* jauge F
  mesure F; *vt* jauger mesurer
gain [gain] *n* gain M; *vt* gagner;
  (weight) prendre
gait [gait] *n* démarche F

gale [gaiul] *n* coup M de vent
gall [gaul] *n* (audacity)
  toupet M
gallant [GA•lunt] *adj*
  courageux; (chivalrous) galant
gallery [GA•lu•ree] *n* galerie F;
  (for art) musée M
galley [GA•lee] *n* galère F
gallon [GA•ln] *n* gallon M
gallop [GA•lup] *n* galop M; *vi*
  galoper

gallows [GA•loz] *npl* potence F; gibet M

gamble [GAM•bl] *n* risque M; *vi* jouer (de l'argent); jouer de l'argent sur

game [gaim] *n* jeu M; match M; (of hunting) gibier M

gang [gang] *n* bande F; *vi* (~ up on) se liguer contre

gangster [GANG•stur] *n* gangster M

gangway [GANG•wai] *n* (of ship) paserelle F

gap [gap] *n* trou M; (in story etc) lacune F

gape [gaip] *vi* bâiller; regarder; bouche; bée

gaping [GAI•ping] *adj* (hole wound etc) béant

garage [gu•RAHZH] *n* garage M

garbage [GAHR•bij] *npl* détritus M: ordures F

garbage can *n* poubelle F

garden [GAHR•dn] *n* jardin M; *vi* jardiner

gargle [GAHR•gl] *vi* se gargariser

gargoyle [GAHR•goil] *n* gargouille F

garland [GAHR•lund] *n* guirlande F

garlic [GAHR•lik] *n* ail M

garment [GAHR•munt] *n* vêtement M

garnish [GAHR•nish] *n* garniture F; *vt* garnir

garrison [GA•ri•sn] *n* garnison

garter [GAHR•tr] *n* (for stockings) jarretière F

gas [gas] *n* gaz M; (gasoline) essence F; *vt* gazer

gaseous [GA•shs] *adj* gazeux

gasket [GA•skit] *n* joint M

gasoline [GA•su•LEEN] *n* essence F

gasp [gasp] *vi* haleter; ~ from surprise\ avoir le souffle coupé

gate [gait] *n* barrière F; (of airport) porte F

gather [GA•thur] *vi* ramasser; (flowers; fruit) cueillir; (people) rassembler; *vi* se rassembler

gathering [GA•thu•ring] *n* rassemblement M

gaudy [GAU•dee] *adj* voyant criard

gaunt [gaunt] *adj* décharné

gauntlet [GAUNT•lit] *n* gantelet M; jeter le gant

gauze [gauz] *n* gaze F

gay [gai] *adj* gai; joyeux; (homosexual) homo; gai

gaze [gaiz] *n* regard M fixe; *vi* regarder fixement

gazette [gu•ZET] *n* gazette F

gear [geeur] *n* équipement M; (of car) vitesse F;

gelatin [JE•lu•tin] *n* gélatine F

gem [jem] *n* pierre F précieuse gemme F

gender [JEN•dur] *n* genre M

gene [jeen] *n* gène M

general [JE•nu•rl] *adj n* général M; (in ~) en général

generalization [JEN•ru•li•ZAI•shn] *n* généralisation

generalize [JE•nu•ru•LUYZ] *vt*
généraliser

generally [JE•nu•ru•lee] *adv*
généralement; en général

generate [JE•nu•RAIT] *vt*
(create) générer engendrer;
(electricity) produire

generation [JE•nu•RAI•shn] *n*
génération F

generator [JE•nu•RAI•tur] *n*
(of electricity) génératrice F

generosity [JE•nu•RAH•si•tee]
n générosité F

generous [JE•nu•rus] *adj*
généreux

genetic [ji•NE•tik] *adj*
génétique; *n* génétique F

genial [JEE•nyul] *adj* cordial

genital [JE•ni•tl] *adj* génital; ~s
npl organes *mpl* génitaux

genius [JEE•nyus] *n* génie M

gentle [JEN•tl] *adj* doux

gentleman [JEN•tl•mun] *n*
monsieur M; (in behavior)
gentleman M

gently [JENT•lee] *adv*
doucement

gentry [JEN•tree] *n* petite
noblesse F

genuine [JE•nyoo•in] *adj*
authentique; (person) sincère

geography [jee•AH•gru•fee] *n*
géographie F

geology [jee•AH•lu•jee] *n*
géologie F

geometric [JEE•u•ME•trik] *adj*
géométrique

geometry [jee•AH•mu•tree] *n*
géométrie F

germ [jerm] *n* germe M

German [JER•mun] *adj*
allemand; *n* (person)
Allemand M; (language)
allemand M

Germany [JER•mu•nee] *n*
Allemagne F

germinate [JER•mi•NAIT] *vi*
germer

gesticulate [je•STI•kyu•LAIT]
vi gesticuler

gesture [JES•chur] *n* geste M;
vi faire signe à

get [get] *vt* obtenir; recevoir;
avoir; (understand)
comprendre; (a cold) etc)
attraper; (become) devenir se
faire + *adj/inf*; (bus train)
prendre; monter dans; partir
de; (arrive) arriver à/en; *vi* se
lever; monter; descendre;
rentrer; il me faut aller

ghastly [GAST•lee] *adj* affreux
horrible

ghost [gost] *n* fantôme M

giant [JUY•unt] *adj n* géant M

gibberish [JI•bu•rish] *n*
charabia M

giddy [GI•dee] *adj* étourdi

gift [gift] *n* cadeau M; (talent)
don M

gifted [GIF•tid] *adj* doué

gigantic [juy•GAN•tik] *adj*
gigantesque

giggle [GI•gl] *vi* glousser

gilded [GIL•did] *adj* doré

gills [gilz] *npl* branchies F

gin [jin] *n* gin M

ginger [JIN•jur] *n* gingembre M

gingerbread [JIN•jur•BRED] *n*
pain d'épice M

gingerly [JIN•jur•lee] *adv* délicatement

gipsy [JIP•see] *n* a gypsy M

giraffe [ji•RAF] *n* girafe F

girder [GUR•dur] *n* poutrelle F

girdle [GUR•dl] *n* ceinture F; (corset) gaine F

girl [gurl] *n* fille F

girlfriend [GURL•frend] *n* petite amie F

girth [gurth] *n* circonférence F; (of horse) sangle F

gist [jist] *n* essentiel M

give [giv] *vt* donner; rendre; (quit) arrêter; *vi* (surrender) se rendre

given [GI•vn] *prep* etant; donné

glacier [GLAI•shur] *n* glacier M

glad [glad] *adj* content

gladly [GLAD•lee] *adv* avec plaisir

glamor [GLA•mur] *n* charme F; prestige M

glamorous [GLA•mu•rus] *adj* séduisant

glance [glans] *n* regard M coup M d'œil; *vi* ~ at\jeter un coup d'œil sur

gland [gland] *n* glande F

glare [glaiur] *n* regard M mauvais; (from light) lumière F éblouissante; *vi* regarder d'un air furieux; éblouir

glaring [GLAIU•ring] *n* (light) éblouissant; (extremely obvious) flagrant

glass [glas] *n* verre F; (of window; etc) vitre F

glasses [GLA•siz] *npl* lunettes F

glassy [GLA•see] *adj* vitreux

glaze [glaiz] *n* (of pottery) vernis M; (of pastry) glaçage M; *vt* vernisser; glacer

gleam [gleem] *n* lueur F; *vi* luire; (eyes) briller

glean [gleen] *vt* glaner

glee [glee] *n* joie F

glib [glib] *adj* désinvolte

glide [gluyd] *vi* (move easily) glisser; (plane) planer

glimmer [GLI•mur] *n* lueur F faible

glimpse [glimps] *n* aperçu M; *vt* apercevoir

glisten [GLI•sn] *vi* luire; briller

glitter [GLI•tur] *n* scintillement M; *vi* scintiller

gloat [glot] *vi* se réjouir

global [GLO•bl] *adj* (shape) global; (worldwide) mondial M

globe [glob] *n* globe M

gloom [gloom] *n* tristesse F

gloomy [GLOO•mee] *n* triste; (place) lugubre F

glorify [GLAU•ri•FUY] *vt* glorifier

glorious [GLAU•ree•us] *adj* glorieux; (excellent) splendide; magnifique

glory [GLAU•ree] *n* gloire F

gloss [glaus] *n* lustre M

glossary [GLAU•su•ree] *n* glossaire M

glossy [GLAU•see] *adj* lustré M

glove [gluhv] *n* gant M

glow [glo] *n* lueur F; (of fire; etc) rougeoiment M; *vi* rougeoyer

glowing [GLO•wing] *adj* chaleureux

glucose [GLOO•kos] *n*
glucose M

glue [gloo] *n* colle F; *vt* coller

glum [gluhm] *adj* triste; morne

glut [gluht] *n* surplus M

glutton [GLUH•tn] *n*
glouton M

gluttonous [GLUH•tu•nus] *adj*
glouton

gluttony [GLUH•tu•nee] *n*
gloutonnerie F

gnarled [nahrld] *adj* noueux

gnash [nash] *vt* grincer les
dents

gnat [nat] *n* moucheron M

gnaw [nau] *vt* ronger

go o *vi* aller; (leave) partir;
(function) marcher; (become)
devenir; (match) aller (avec);
~ in\entrer; ~ away\s'en aller;
~ up\monter; ~ on\continuer;
~ out\sortir; ~ back\retourner;
~ through\(undergo) subir; ~
without\se passe de; let's
~!\allons-y!; ~ ahead!\vas-y!

go-between
[GO•buh•TWEEN] *n*
intermédiaire MF

goal [goul] *n* but M

goat [got] *n* chèvre F

gobble [GAH•bl] *vt* engloutir

goblin [GAH•blin] *n* lutin M

God [gahd] *n* Dieu M; god\
dieu M

goddaughter
[GAHD•DAU•tur] *n* filleule F

goddess [GAH•dis] *n* déesse F

godfather [GAHD•FAH•thur] *n*
parrain M

godless [GAHD•lis] *adj* athée

godmother
[GAHD•MUH•thur] *n*
marraine F

godsend [GAHD•send] *n*
aubaine F

godson [GAHD•suhn] *n*
filleul M

goggles [GAH•glz] *npl*
lunettes *fpl*

gold [gould] *n* or M; (made of)
en or

gold-plated [GOLD•PLAI•tid]
adj plaqué d'or

golden [GOL•dn] *adj* (color)
doré; (in substance) en or

goldfish [GOLD•fish] *n* poisson
M rouge

golf [gahlf] *n* golf M

gong [gahng] *n* gong M

good [gud] *adj* bon (bonne);
(child) sage; (kind) genial;
pour de bon; c'est un plaisir
de; très bien!; (useless) ne
servir à rien; be ~ to\être bon
à; être bon en; *n* bien M;
marchandises *fpl* biens M; ~
morning, etc\bonjour; bonjour;
bonsoir; bonsoir; (at bedtime)
bonne nuit; au revoir;
goodbye\ adieu

good-looking [GUD•LU•king]
adj beau (belle); joli

goose [goos] *n* oie F

gore [gaur] *vt* encorner

gorge [gaurj] *n* gorge F; *vt* se
bourrer de qqch

gorgeous [GAUR•jus] *adj*
magnifique splendide

gorilla [gu•RI•lu] *n* gorille M

gory [GAU•ree] *adj* sanglant

gospel [GAH•spl] *n* évangile
M; the Gospel\ l'Evangile M

gossip [GAH•sip] *n* commérage
M; (person) commère F; *vi*
(chat) bavarder; (with malice)
cancaner

gothic [GAH•thik] *adj* gothique

gourd [gaurd] *n* gourde F

gout [gout] *n* goutte F

govern [GUH•vurn] *vt vi*
gouverner

governess [GUH•vur•nis] *n*
gouvernante F

government [GUH•vurn•munt]
n gouvernement M

governor [GUH•vur•nur] *n*
gouverneur M

gown [goun] *n* robe F

grab [grab] *vt* saisir

grace [grais] *n* grâce F; *vt*
honorer

graceful [GRAIS•ful] *adj*
gracieux

gracious [GRAI•shus] *adj*
courtois

grade [graid] *n* qualité F;
calibre M; (year in school)
classe F; (on test) note F; *vt*
classer; calibrer; (exams; etc)
noter

grade school [GRAID skool] *n*
école F primaire

gradual [GRA•joo•ul] *adj*
graduel

graduate [*n*. GRA•joo•it *v*.
GRA•joo•AIT] *n* diplômé M;
vi recevoir son diplôme; (from
high school) recevoir son
baccalauréat

graduation [GRA•joo•AI•shn]
n remise F de diplômes

graft [graft] *n* greffe F; *vt*
greffer

grain [grain] *n* grain M; (wheat
corn etc) céréales *fpl;* (of
wood) fil M

gram [gram] *n* gramme M

grammar [GRA•mur] *n*
grammaire F

grammatical [gru•MA•ti•kl]
adj grammatical

granary [GRAI•nu•ree] *n*
grenier M

grand [grand] *adj* (large) grand;
(plans; etc) grandiose;
(excellent) magnifique

granddaughter
[GRAN•DAU•tur] *n*
petite-fille F

grandeur [GRAN•jur] *n*
splendeur F

grandfather
[GRAND•FAH•thur] *n*
grand-père M

grandiose [GRAN•dee•OS] *adj*
grandiose; pompeux

grandma [GRAND•mah] *n*
mémé F

grandmother
[GRAND•MUH•thur] *n*
grand-mère F

grandpa [GRAND•pah] *n*
pépé M

grandparents
[GRAND•PA•runts] *npl*
grands-parents M

grandson [GRAND•suhn] *n*
petit-fils M

granite [GRA•nit] *n* granit M

grant [grant] *n* subvention F;
(for student) bourse F; *vt*
accorder; (admit) admettre

granule [GRA•nyoo•ul] *n*
granule M

grape [graip] *n* raisin M

grapefruit [GRAIP•froot] *n*
pamplemousse M

graph [graf] *n* graphique M

graphic [GRA•fik] *adj*
graphique; (descriptive)
vivant; *npl* graphique F

grapple [GRA•pl] *vi* lutter
avec; être aux prises avec

grasp [grasp] *n* prise F; (of
subject) compréhension F; *vt*
saisir; comprendre

grasping [GRA•sping] *adj*
avide

grass [gras] *n* herbe F

grasshopper [GRAS•HAH•pur]
n sauterelle F

grassy [GRA•see] *adj* herbeux

grate [grait] *n* grille F; *vt*
(food) râper; (nerves etc)
grincer

grateful [GRAIT•ful] *adj*
reconnaissant

grater [GRAI•tur] *n* râpe F

gratification
[GRA•ti•fi•KAI•shn] *n*
satisfaction F

grating [GRAI•ting] *n* grille F;
adj grinçant

gratitude [GRA•ti•TOOD] *n*
reconnaissance F

gratuity [gru•TOO•i•tee] *n*
pourboire M

grave [graiv] *adj* grave; *n*
tombe F

gravel [GRA•vl] *n* gravier M;
npl gravillons M

gravity [GRA•vi•tee] *n* gravité
F; pesanteur F

gravy [GRAI•vee] *n* jus M (de
viande); sauce F

gray [grai] *adj n* gris M; *vi*
grissonner

graze [graiz] *vt* paître; (skin)
écorcher; *vi* paître

grease [grees] *n* graisse F; (for
machine) lubrifiant M; *vt*
graisser; lubrifier

great [grait] *adj* (large) grand;
(excellent) génial

Great Britain [~ BRI•tn] *n*
Grande-Bretagne F

great-granddaughter
[GRAIT•GRAN•DAW•tur]
arrière-petite-fille F

great-grandfather
[GRAIT•GRAND•FA•thur] *n*
arrière-grand-père M

great-grandmother
[GRAIT•GRAND•MU•thur] *n*
arrière-grand-mère F

great-grandparents
[GRAIT•GRAND•PAI•rintz]
npl arrière-grands-parents *mpl*

great-grandson
[GRAIT•GRAND•son] *n*
arrière-petit-fils M

greatness [GRAIT•nis] *n*
grandeur F

Greece [grees] *n* Grèce F

greed [greed] *n* avidité F

greedy [GREE•dee] *adj* avide

Greek [greek] *adj* grec; *n*
(person) Grec M (Grecque);
(language) grec M

green [green] *adj n* vert M

greenhouse [GREEN•hous] *n*
serre F

Greenland [GREEN•lund] *n*
Groenland M

greens [greenz] *npl* légumes M

greet [greet] *vt* saluer; (at door) acueiller

greeting [GREE•ting] *n* salutation F

grenade [gru•NAID] *n* grenade F

greyhound [GRAI•hound] *n* lévrier M

grid [grid] *n* grille F; (elec) réseau M

grief [greef] *n* chagrin M

grievance [GREE•vuns] *n* doléance F

grieve [greev] *vt* pleurer; *vi* être en deuil

grievous [GREE•vus] *adj* grave

grill [gril] *n* gril M; *vt* faire griller; *vi* griller

grille [gril] *n* grillage M

grim [grim] *adj* sévère; sinistre; (sad) morne

grimace [GRI•mus] *n* grimace F; *vi* grimacer

grime [gruym] *n* crasse F

grimy [GRUY•mee] *adj* crasseux F

grin [grin] *n* sourire M; *vi* sourire

grind [gruynd] *vt* moudre; (teeth) grincer

grinder [GRUYN•dur] *n* moulin M

grip [grip] *n* prise F; *vt* saisir

gripe [gruyp] *n* plainte F; *vi* rouspéter (contre)

grisly [GRIZ•lee] *adj* macabre

gristle [GRI•sl] *n* cartilage M

grit [grit] *n* gravillon M; (courage) cran M; *vt* sabler; (teeth) serrer les dents

groan [gron] *n* gémissement M; *vi* gémir

groceries [GROS•reez] *npl* provisions F

grocery [GROS•ree] *n* épicerie F

groin [groin] *n* aine F

groom [groom] *n* marié; *vt* (horse) panser; (prepare) préparer

groove [groov] *n* rainure F; (of record) sillon M; *vt* canneler

grope [grop] *vi* tâtonner; chercher à tâtons

gross [gros] *adj* (sum) brut; (blatant) flagrant; (rude) grossier; *n* grosse F

grotesque [gro•TESK] *adj* grotesque

grouch [grouch] *n* grognon M

ground [ground] *n* sol M terre F; (coffee) marc M; *vt* ~ in/on\fonder sur baser sur; *npl* (area) terrain M; (around building) parc M; (basis) *npl* motifs M

ground floor [GROUND FLOR] *n* rez-de-chaussée M

groundless [GROUND•lis] *adj* sans fondement

group [groop] *n* groupe F; *vt* grouper; *vi* se grouper

grove [grov] *n* bosquet M

grovel [GRAH•vl] *vi* ramper

grow [gro] *vt* faire pousser; cultiver; *vi* (plant) pousser; (person; animal) grandir; (organization) s'agrandir; (increase) augmenter s'accroître; (become) devenir

growl [grouul] *n* grognement M; *vi* grogner

growth [groth] *n* croissance F; (of plants) pousse F; (medical) grosseur F tumeur F

grub [gruhb] *n* (insect) larve F; (food) bouffe F

grubby [GRUH•bee] *adj* sale

grudge [gruhj] *n* rancune F; garder rancune à

grueling [GROOU•ling] *adj* éreintant

gruff [gruhf] *adj* bourru; brusque

grumble [GRUHM•bl] *vi* grommeler; rouspéter

grumpy [GRUHM•pee] *adj* maussade

grunt [gruhnt] *n* grognement M; grogner

guarantee [GA•run•TEE] *n* garantie F; *vt* garantir

guard [gahrd] *n* garde M; (organization) garde F; on ~\de garde; *vt* garder; défendre: protéger

guardien [GAHR•dee•un] *n* gardien M; (of child) tuteur M

guerrilla [gu•RI•lu] *n* guérillero M

guess [ges] *n* conjecture F; *vt vi* deviner

guest [gest] *n* invité M; (at hotel) client M

guestroom [GEST•ROOM] *n* chambre d'amis F

guffaw [guh•FAU] *vi* pouffer de rire

guidance [GUY•duns] *npl* conseils M

guide [guyd] *n* guide M; *vt* guider; diriger

guild [gild] *n* guilde F

guile [guyul] *n* astuce F

guillotine [GI•lu•TEEN] *n* guillotine F

guilt [gilt] *n* culpabilité F

guilty [GIL•tee] *adj* coupable; reconnaître coupable/non coupable

guinea pig [GI•nee ~] *n* cobaye M

guise [guyz] *n* apparence F

guitar [gi•TAHR] *n* guitare F

gulf [guhlf] *n* (abyss) gouffre M; (body of water) golfe F

gull [guhl] *n* mouette F

gullet [GUH•lit] *n* gosier M

gullible [GUH•li•bl] *adj* crédule

gully [GUH•lee] *n* ravin M

gulp [guhlp] *n* bouchée F; gorgée F; *vt* avaler

gum [guhm] *n* gomme F; gencives *fpl*

gun [guhn] *n* revolver M; pistolet M; fusil M; canon M; pistolet M

gunfire [GUHN•fuyur] *npl* coups de feu M

gunpoint [GUHN•point] *n* sous la menace d'un pistolet/fusil

gunpowder [GUHN•pow•dur] *n* poudre à canon F

gunshot [GUHN•shaht] *n* coup M de feu

gurgle [GUR•gl] *vi* gargouiller

gush [guhsh] *n* jaillisement M; *vi* jaillir

gusset [GUH•sit] *n* gousset M

gust [guhst] *n* (of wind) rafale F; (of smoke) bouffée F

gut [guht] *n* intestin M; cran M;
vt vider

gutter [GUH•tur] *n* gouttière F;
caniveau M

guy [guy] *n* type M

guzzle [GUH•zl] *vt* lamper; *vi*
s'empiffrer

gym [jim] *n* gymnase M

gymnasium [jim•NAI•zee•um]
n gymnase M

gymnast [JIM•nust] *n* gymnaste
mf

gymnastics [jim•NA•stiks] *npl*
gymnastique F

Gypsy [JIP•see] *n* gitan M

gyrate [JUY•rait] *vi* tournoyer

H

habit [HA•bit] *n* habitude F;
habit M

habitual [hu•BI•choo•ul] *adj*
habituel

hack [hak] *vt* tailler; pirater

hackneyed [HAK•need] *adj*
banal rebattu usé

hacksaw [HAK•sau] *n* scie F à
métaux

haggard [HA•gurd] *adj* abattu
hagard

haggle [HA•gl] *vi* marchander

hail [haiul] *n* grêle F; *vt* héler;
vi grêler

hailstone [HAIUL•ston] *n*
grêlon M

hair [haiur] *npl* cheveux M; (of
skin; animal) poils M; (single
hair) cheveu M; poil M

hairbrush [HAIUR•bruhsh] *n*
brosse F à cheveux

haircut [HAIUR•kuht] *n* coupe
F de cheveux

hairdresser [HAIUR•DRE•sur]
n coiffeur M

hairless [HAIUR•lis] *adj*
chauve; sans cheveux; sans
poils

hairpin [HAIUR•pin] *n* épingle
M à cheveux

hairspray [HAIUR•sprai] *n*
laque F

hairstyle [HAIUR•stuyul] *n*
coiffure F

hairy [HAIUR•ee] *adj* velu
poilu; chevelu

Haiti [HAI•tee] *n* Haïti M

half [haf] *adj* demi: *adv* à
moitié à demi; moitié-moitié;
six heures et demie; la demie;
n moitié F; en deux

half-hearted [~ HAR•tid] *adj*
sans enthousiasme

half hour [HAF OUR] *n*
demi-heure F

half-mast [HAF•MAST] *adj* en
berne

half-price [HAF•PRUYS] *adj* à
moitié prix

halfway [HAF•WAI] *adj adv* à
mi-chemin

halibut [HA•li•but] *n* flétan M

hall [haul] *n* vestibule M;
couloir M; salle F

hallowed [HA•lod] *adj* saint
sanctifié

Halloween [HAH•lo•WEEN] *n*
Halloween F veille M de la
Toussaint

hallucinate [hu•LOO•si•NAIT]
vi avoir des hallucinations

hallucination
[hu•LOO•si•NAI•shn] *n*
hallucination F

hallway [HAUL•wai] *n*
couloir M

halo [HAI•lo] *n* auréole F; (of
moon etc) halo M

halt [hault] *n* halte F; *vt* faire
arrêter; *vi* s'arrêter

halter [HAUL•tur] *n* licou M

halve [hav] *vt* diviser en deux;
reduire de moitié

ham [ham] *n* jambon

hamburger [HAM•BUR•gur] *n*
hamburger M

hamlet [HAM•lit] *n* hameau M

hammer [HA•mur] *n* marteau
M; *vt* marteler; enfoncer

hammock [HA•muk] *n*
hamac M

hamper [HAM•pur] *n* coffre M
à linge; *vt* gêner

hand [hand] *n* main F; (worker)
ouvrier M; on the . . . d'une
côté . . . de l'autre côté . . .; *vt*
passer; transmettre; distribuer;
céder; remettre; lend a ~\
donner un coup de main

handbag [HAND•bag] *n* sac M
à main

handcuff [HAND•kuhf] *npl*
menottes F; *vt* mettre les
menottes à

handful [HAND•ful] *n*
poignée F

handicap [HAN•dee•KAP] *n*
handicap

handicapped
[HAN•dee•KAPT] *adj*
handicapé

handkerchief [HANG•kur•chif]
n mouchoir M

handle [HAN•dl] *n* anse F;
manche F; poignée F; *vt*
manier; s'occuper de

handmade [HAND•MAID] *adj*
fait à la main

handshake [HAND•shaik] *n*
poignée de main F

handwriting
[HAND•WRUY•ting] *n*
écriture F

handy [HAN•dee] *adj* pratique;
adroit

hang [hang] *vt* pendre; accrcher;
pendre; *vi* pendre; ~ out/
around\traîner;~on\s'accrocher;
attendre; ~ up\raccrocher

hang-up [HANG•uhp] *n*
complexe M

hangar [HANG•ur] *n* hangar

hanger [HANG•ur] *n* cintre M

hangman [HANG•man] *n*
bourreau M

hangover [HANG•O•vur] *n*
gueule de bois F

haphazard [hap•HA•zurd] *adj*
au hasard

hapless [HAP•lis] *adj*
malchanceux

happen [HA•pn] *vi* se passer;
arriver; se produire; qu'est-ce
que t'a arrivé

happening [HA•pu•ning] *n*
événement M

happily [HA•pi•lee] *adv*
joyeusement; heureusement

happiness [HA•pee•nis] *n*
bonheur F

happy [HA•pee] *adj* heureux
content

harass [hu•RAS] *vt* harceler

harassment [hu•RAS•munt] *n*
harcelement M

harbor [HAHR•bur] *n* port M;
vt garder; héberger

hard [hahrd] *adj* dur; difficile;
adv dur; sérieusement; avec
effort; fort

harden [HAR•din] *vt* durcir;
endurcir; *vi* se durcir;
s'endurcir

hardly [HARD•lee] *adv* à peine;
ne . . . guère; presque jamais

hardship [HAHRD•ship] *n*
épreuves *fpl*

hardware [HAHRD•waiur] *n*
quincaillerie F; (of computers)
hardware M

hardworking
[HARD•WUR•king] *adj*
travailleur

hardy [HAHR•dee] *adj* robuste;
résistant

hare [haiur] *n* lièvre M

harm [hahrm] *n* mal M; tort M;
vt faire du mal à; faire du
tort à

harmful [HAHRM•ful] *adj*
nuisible

harmless [HAHRM•lis] *adj*
innocent; pas méchant

harmonica [hahr•MAH•ni•ku] *n*
harmonica M

harmonious [hahr•MO•nee•us]
adj harmonieux

harmonize [HAHR•mu•NUYZ]
vt harmoniser; *vi*
s'harmoniser F

harmony [HAHR•mu•nee] *n*
harmonie F

harness [HAHR•nis] *n* harnais;
vt harnacher; exploiter

harp [hahrp] *n* harpe F

harpoon [hahr•POON] *n*
harpon M; *vt* harponner

harpsichord
[HARP•si•KAURD] *n*
clavecin M

harsh [hahrsh] *adj* sévère; cruel
rude; criard

harvest [HAHR•vist] *n* moisson
F; récolte F; *vt* moissonner;
récolter

hassle [HA•sl] *n* embêtement
M; *vt* embêter

haste [haist] *n* hâte F; in ~\ à la
hâte

hasten [HAI•sn] *vt* hâter; *vi* se
hâter

hastily [HAI•sti•lee] *adv* à la
hâte

hat [hat] *n* chapeau M

hatch [hach] *vt* faire éclore; *vi*
éclore

hatchet [HA•chit] *n* hachette F

hate [hait] *n* haine F; *vt* haïr;
détester

hateful [HAIT•ful] *adj* odieux

hatred [HAI•trid] *n* haine F

haughty [HAU•tee] *adj* hautain

haul [haul] *vt* traîner tirer

haunt [haunt] *vt* hanter

have [hav] aux verb avoir; être;
vt avoir; prendre; faire

qqch à qqn; *vi* devoir; être
obligé de; ~ to\ il me faut /il
faut que je; porter

haven [HAI•vn] *n* havre M

havoc [HA•vuk] *npl* ravages M;
vt ravager

hawk [hauk] *n* faucon

hay [hai] *n* foin M

haystack [HAI•stak] *n* meule F
de foin

hazard [HA•zurd] *n* hasard M;
vt hasarder

hazardous [HA•zur•dus] *adj*
hasardeux; dangereux

haze [haiz] *n* brume F

hazelnut [HAI•zl•NUHT] *n*
noisette F

hazy [HAI•zee] *adj* brumeux;
(memory) vague

he [hee] *pers pron* il;
(emphatic) lui

head [hed] *n* tête F; (of table
bed etc) tête F; (of lettuce)
pomme F; (person in charge)
chef M; *adj* principal; *vt* (list)
être en tête de; (be in charge
of) être à la tête de; pile ou
face

headache [HE•daik] *n* mal M
de tête; avoir un mal à la tête

heading [HE•ding] *n* titre M;
(of letter) entête M

headlight [HED•luyt] *n*
phare M

headline [HED•luyn] *n*
manchette

headphones [HED•fonz] *npl*
casque F

headquarters
[HED•KAUR•turz] *npl* (of

business) siège M central;
(military) quartier M géneral

headrest [HED•rest] *n*
appui-tête M

headstrong [HED•straung] *adj*
têtu

headway [HED•wai] *n*
progrès M

heal [heeul] *vt* guérir; *vi* se
guérir

health [helth] *n* santé F

healthy [HEL•thee] *adj* sain en
bonne santé

heap [heep] *n* tas M; *vt* entasser

hear [heeur] *vt* entendre; *vi*
entendre; entendre parler
que . . .

hearing [HEEU•ring] *n* ouïe F;
(in court) audience F

hearsay [HEEUR•sai] *n*
ouï-dire M

hearse [hurs] *n* corbillard M

heart [hahrt] *n* cœur M; briser
le cœur à qqn

heart attack [HART a•TAK] *n*
crise F cardiaque

heartbeat [HAHRT•beet] *n*
battement M de cœur

heartbroken
[HAHRT•BRO•kn] *adj* navré
avec le cœur brisé

hearth [hahrth] *n* foyer M

heartless [HAHRT•lis] *adj* sans
cœur

heartwarming
[HAHRT•WAR•ming] *adj*
réconfortant; chaleureux

hearty [HAHR•tee] *adj* cordial;
(appetite) robuste

heat [heet] *n* chaleur F; in ~\en
chaleur *vt* chauffer; (room)

réchauffer; *vi* chauffer; se
réchauffer

heater [HEE•tur] *n* appareil M
de chauffage

heather [HE•thur] *n* bruyère F

heating [HEE•ting] *n*
chauffage M

heat wave [HEET WAIV] *n*
vague F de chaleur

heave [heev] *vt* soulever; *vi* se
soulever

heaven [HE•vn] *n* paradis M
ciel M; the ~s*npl* les cieux M

heavenly [HE•vn•lee] *adj*
celestial; (excellent) divin
magnifique

heavily [HE•vu•lee] *adv*
lourdement; (rain etc) fort;
(sleep) profondement

heavy [HE•vee] *adj* lourd; (rain
etc) gros; (sleep) profond

heckle [HE•kl] *vt* interpeller

hectic [HEK•tik] *adj* agité;
mouvementé

hedge [hej] *n* haie F

hedgehog [HEJ•hahg] *n*
hérisson M

heed [heed] *vt* tenir compte de

height [huyt] *n* (of stucture)
hauteur F; (of person) taille F;
(of plane) altidude F; (of
career etc) sommet M

heighten [HUY•tn] *vt* hausser;
rehausser; (increase)
augmenter; *vi* se rehausser;
augmenter

heir [aiur] *n* héritier M

heiress [AIU•ress] *n* héritière F

heirloom [AIUR•loom] *n*
meuble M (or bijou M) de
famille M

helicopter [HE•li•KAHP•tur] *n*
hélicoptère M

hell [hel] *n* enfer M; va te faire
voir!

hellish [HE•lish] *adj* infernal

hello [hu•LO] *excl* bonjour!; (on
telephone) âllo!

helm [helm] *n* barre F; tenir la
barre

helmet [HEL•mit] *n* casque F

help [help] *n* aide F;
(employee) employé M; *vt vi*
aider; au secours!; vous
désirez?; servez-vous!

helper [HEL•pur] *n* aide *mf;*
assistant M

helping [HEL•ping] *n* (of food)
portion F

helpless [HELP•lis] *adj*
impuissant F

hem [hem] *n* ourlet M; *vt* ourler

hemisphere [HE•mis•FEEUR]
n hémisphère M

hemorrhage [HE•mu•rij] *n*
hémorragie F

hemorrhoids [HE•mu•roidz]
npl hémorroïdes F

hen [hen] *n* poule F

henhouse [HEN•hous] *n*
poulailler M

hence [hens] *adv* d'où

henceforth [HENS•faurth] *adv*
dorénavant; désormais

her [hur] *pers pron* (direct obj)
la; (in comparison after prep)
elle; (indirecet obj) lui; *poss
pron* son (sa) ses

herald [HE•ruld] *n* héraut M; *vt*
annoncer

heraldry [HE•rul•dree] *n*
héraldique F

herb [urb] *n* herbe F

herbal [UR•bl] *adj* d'herbes

herd [hurd] *n* troupeau M; *vt* mener

here [heeur] *adv* ici; voici; ça et là

hereby [heeur•BUY] *adv* par le (la)

hereditary [he•RE•di•TE•ree] *adj* héréditaire

heredity [he•RE•di•tee] *n* hérédité F

herein [heeur•IN] *adv* (enclosed ~) ci-joint; dedans

heresy [HE•ru•see] *n* hérésie F

herewith [heeur•WITH] *adv* ci-joint

heritage [HE•ri•tij] *n* héritage M

hermit [HUR•mit] *n* ermite M

hernia [HUR•nee•u] *n* hernie F

hero [HEEU•ro] *n* héros M

heroic [hu•RO•ik] *adj* héroïque

heroin [HE•ro•in] *n* héroïne F

heroine [HE•ro•in] *n* héroïne F

heroism [HE•ro•I•zm] *n* héroïsme M

heron [HE•run] *n* héron M

herring [HE•ring] *n* hareng M

hers [hurz] *poss pron* le sien (la sienne) les siens (les siennes); c'est à elle/c'est le sien

herself [hur•SELF] *pron* (reflexive) se; (after prep) elle; (emphatic) elle-même

hesitant [HE•zi•tunt] *adj* hésitant

hesitate [HE•zi•TAIT] *vi* (to) hésiter (à)

hesitation [HE•zi•TAI•shn] *n* hésitation F

heterosexual [HE•tu•ro•SEK•shoo•ul] *adj n* hétérosexuel M

hexagon [HEK•su•GAHN] *n* hexagone M

hey [hai] *excl* hé

heyday [HAI•dai] *n* âge M d'or; apogée M

hibernate [HUY•bur•NAIT] *vi* hiberner

hibernation [HUY•bur•NAI•shn] *n* hibernation F

hiccup [HI•kuhp] *n* hoquet M; have the ~a\svoir le hoquet; *vi* hoqueter

hidden [HI•dn] *adj* caché

hide [huyd] *n* (skin) peau F; *vt* cacher; *vi* se cacher

hideous [HI•dee•us] *adj* hideux

hiding [HUY•ding] *n* se tenir caché

hiding place *n* cachette F

hierarchy [HUYU•RAHR•kee] *n* hiérarchie F

high [huy] *adj* haut; (speed) grand; (price) élevé; (sound) aigu; (tipsy) gris; *adv* haut; quatre pieds de haut

high school *n* école F secondaire; (French equiv) lycée M

highlight [HUY•luyt] *n* point culminant M; *vt* souligner

highly [HUY•lee] *adj* très; *adv* hautement; fortement; penser du bien de

highness [HUY•nis] *n* Son Altesse

highway [HUY•wai] *n* autoroute F

hike [huyk] *n* randonnée F; *vi*
faire une (des) randonnée(s);
aller au pied

hilarious [hi•LAU•ree•us] *adj*
hilarant

hill [hil] *n* colline F; (slope)
côte F

hillside [HIL•suyd] *n* coteau M

hilltop [HIL•tahp] *n* sommet M
de colline

hilly [HI•lee] *adj* vallonnée

hilt [hilt] *n* garde F; à fond

him [him] *pers pron* (direct obj)
le; (in comparison after prep)
lui; (indirecet obj) lui

himself [him•SELF] *pron*
(reflexive) se; (after prep) lui;
(emphatic) lui-même

hind [huynd] *adj* de derrière; *n*
biche F

hinder [HIN•dur] *vt* gêner;
(impede) empêcher

hindrance [HIN•druns] *n* gêne
F obstacle M

Hindu [HIN•doo] *adj* hindou; *n*
Hindou M

hinge [hinj] *n* charnière F; *vi*
dépendre de

hint (of flavor) soupçon M; *vt*
insinuer que; *vi* faire allusion à

hip [hip] *n* hanche F

hippopotamus
[HI•pu•PAH•tu•mus] *n*
hippopatame M

hire [huyur] *vt* employer
engager; (rent) louer

his [huiz] *poss adj* son (sa) ses;
poss pron le sien (la sienne)
les siens (les siennes); c'est à
lui/c'est le sien

Hispanic [hi•SPAN•ik] *n adj*
Hispanique; hispanique MF

hiss [his] *vi* siffler

historian [hi•STAU•ree•un] *n*
historien M

historic [hi•STAU•rik] *adj*
historique

history [HI•stu•ree] *n* histoire F;
(of person) passé M

hit [hit] *n* coup M; (success)
succès M; *vt* frapper; (in
accident) heurter

hitch [hich] *vt* accrocher;
remonter; *vi* (hitchhike) faire
du stop

hitchhike [HICH•huyk] *vi* faire
de l'auto-stop faire du stop

hitchhiker [HICH•HUY•kur] *n*
auto-stoppeur M

hitherto [HI•thur•TOO] *adv*
jusqu'ici

hive [huyv] *n* ruche F; *npl*
urticaire F

hoard [haurd] *npl* réserves F; *vt*
ammasser

hoarse [haurs] *adj* (voice)
enroué; (tone) rauque

hoax [hoks] *n* canular M

hobble [HAH•bl] *vi* boitiller

hobby [HAH•bee] *n*
passe-temps M

hobo [HO•bo] *n* vagabond M

hockey [HAH•kee] *n* hockey M

hocus-pocus [HO•kus•PO•kus]
n passe-passe M

hoe [ho] *n* houe F binette F; *vt*
biner

hog [hahg] *n* cochon M

hoist [hoist] *vt* hisser

hold [hold] *n* prise; *vt* avoir;
tenir; (contain) contenir; (in

jail) détenir; (support) soutenir; retenir; lever; tendre; *vi* tenir; (wait) attendre; ~ on\durer

holder [HOL•dur] *n* support M; (of ticket land) détenteur M; (of title office) titulaire mf

holding [HOL•ding] *n* possession F; (in stocks etc) *npl* intérêts M; (farm) ferme F

holdup [HOLD•uhp] *n* (robbery) holdup M; (delay) retard M

hole [hol] *n* trou

holiday [HAH•li•DAI] *n* jour M férié

holiness [HO•lee•nis] *n* sainteté F

Holland [HAH•lund] *n* Hollande F

hollow [HAH•lo] *adj n* creux M; *vt* creuser

holly [HAH•lee] *n* houx M

holocaust [HAH•lu•KAUST] *n* holocauste M

holster [HOL•stur] *n* étui M

holy [HO•lee] *adj* saint

home [hom] *n* maison F foyer M; chez soi à la maison

homeland [HOM•land] *n* patrie F

homeless [HOM•lis] *adj* sans abri; *npl* les sans-abri M

homely [HOM•lee] *adj* laid; ordinaire

homemade [HOM•MAID] *adj* fait à la maison

homesick [HOM•sik] *n* nostalgique; be ~\avoir le mal du pays M

homeward [HOM•wurd] *adv* vers la maison; vers son pays

homework [HOM•wurk] *npl* devoirs M

homicide [HAH•mi•SUYD] *n* homicide M

homosexual [HO•mo•SEK•shoo•ul] *adj n* homosexuel M

honest [AH•nist] *adj* honnête; (sincere) franc; sincère

honesty [AH•ni•stee] *n* honnêteté F

honey [HU•nee] *n* miel

honeymoon [HUH•nee•MOON] *n* lune F de miel

honk [hahngk] *vi* klaxonner

honor [AH•nur] *n* honneur F; in ~ of\ en l'honneur de; *vt* honorer

honorable [AH•nu•ru•bl] *adj* honorable

honorary [AH•nu•RE•ree] *adj* honoraire

hood [hud] *n* capuchon M; (of stove) hotte F; (of car) capot M; (criminal) voyou M

hoodlum [HUD•lum] *n* voyou M truand

hoodwink [HUD•wingk] *vt* tromper

hoof [huf] *n* sabot M

hook [huk] *n* crochet M; (for fishing) hameçon M; (on dress) agrafe F; *vt* accrocher; agrafer; (fish) prendre

hooky [HU•kee] *n* faire l'école buissonière

hoop [hoop] *n* cerceau M

hoot [hoot] *n* (of owl)
hululement M; *vi* hululer

hop [hahp] *n* saut M; *vi* sauter;
(gingerly) sautiller

hope [hop] *n* espoir M; *vi*
espérer; espérer bien; espérer
que non; espérer qqch

hopeful [HOP•ful] *adj* plein
d'espoir

hopeless [HOP•lis] *adj*
désespéré

horizon [hu•RUY•zn] *n* horizon

horizontal [HAU•ri•ZAHN•tl]
adj horizontal

hormone [HAUR•mon] *n*
hormone F

horn [haurn] *n* (of animal)
corne F; (musical) cor M; (of
car) klaxon M

hornet [HAUR•nit] *n* frelon

horoscope [HAU•ru•SKOP] *n*
horoscope M

horrible [HAU•ri•bl] *adj*
horrible

horrid [HAU•rid] *adj* horrible;
méchant

horrify [HAU•ri•FUY] *vt*
horrifier

horror [HAU•rur] *n* horreur F;
film M d'épouvante

horse [haurs] *n* cheval M

horseback [HAURS•bak] *adj*
adv à cheval

horsepower
[HAURS•POU•wur] *n*
puissance F en chevaux

horseradish [HAURS•RA•dish]
n raifort M

horseshoe [HAURS•shoo] *n* fer
M à cheval

hose [hoz] *n* tuyau M; *vt* arroser
au jet

hosiery [HO•zhu•ree] *n*
bonneterie F

hospitable [hah•SPI•tu•bl] *adj*
hospitalier

hospital [HAH•spi•tl] *n*
hôspital M

hospitality
[HAH•spi•TA•li•tee] *n*
hospitalité F

host [host] *n* hôte M

hostage [HAH•stij] *n* otage M

hostess [HO•stis] *n* hôtesse F

hostile [HAH•stul] *adj* hostile

hostility [hah•STI•li•tee] *n*
hostilité F

hot [haht] *adj* chaud; (spicy)
épicé; j'ai chaud; il fait chaud

hot dog [HAHT daug] *n*
hot-dog M

hot plate [HAHT plait] *n*
chauffe-plats M

hot-tempered
[HOT•TEM•purd] *adj*
colérique; irascible

hotel [ho•TEL] *n* hôtel M

hound [hound] *n* chien M de
chasse; chien M courant; *vt*
poursuivre

hour [ouur] *n* heure F

hourglass [OUUR•glas] *n*
sablier

hourly [OUUR•lee] *adj adv*
toutes les heures

house [*n.* hous *v.* houz] *n*
maison F; (theater) salle F; *vt*
loger; héberger

housekeeper [HOUS•KEE•pur]
n gouvernante F

housekeeping
[HOUS•KEE•ping] *n*
ménage M

housewife [HOUS•wuyf] *n*
ménagère F; femme F au
foyer

housework [HOUS•wurk] *n*
ménage M

housing [HOU•zing] *n*
logement M

hovel [HUH•vl] *n* taudis M

hover [HUH•vur] *vi* planer

how [hou] *adv* comment;
combien (de)? combien ça
coûte?; (with adjectives) quel
+ noun; quel âge as-tu? quel
est la longeur de ça?; *excl*
comme c'est génial; que c'est
génial; (since when) depuis
combien de temps . . . ?

however [hou•E•vur] *conj*
cependant pourtant; *adv* de
quelque manière que; (with
adj) si . . . que

howl [houl] *n* hurlement M; *vi*
hurler

hub [huhb] *n* centre M; (of
wheel) moyeu M

hubcap [HUHB•kap] *n*
enjoliveur

huddle [HUH•dl] *vi* se blottir
(les uns contre les autres)

hue [hyoo] *n* teinte F

huff [huhf] *n* froissé

hug [huhg] *n* étreinte F; *vt*
éteindre; (wall, etc) serrer

huge [hyooj] *adj* énorme

hull [huhl] *n* coque F

hum [huhm] *vt* fredonner; *vi*
fredonner; (machine) vrombir;

human [HYOO•mun] *adj n*
humain M

human being *n* être humain M

human rights *npl* droits M de
l'homme M

humane [hyoo•MAIN] *adj*
humain

humanitarian
[hyoo•MA•ni•TA•ree•un] *adj*
humanitaire

humanity [hyoo•MA•ni•TEE] *n*
humanité F

humble [HUHM•bl] *adj*
humble; *vt* humilier

humid [HYOO•mid] *adj* humide

humidity [hyoo•MI•di•tee] *n*
humidité F

humiliate [hyoo•MI•lee•AIT] *n*
humilier F

humiliation
[hyoo•MI•lee•AI•shn] *n*
humiliation F

humility [hyoo•MI•li•tee] *n*
humilité F

hummingbird
[HUH•ming•BYRD] *n*
oiseau-mouche

humor [HYOO•mur] *n* humour
M; (mood) humeur F; *vt*
accéder à

humorous [HYOO•mu•rus] *adj*
humoristique; drôle

hump [huhmp] *n* brosse F

hunch [huhnch] *n* (feeling)
pressentiment M; intuitition F

hunchback [HUHNCH•bak] *n*
bossu M

hunched [huhnchd] *adj* voûté

hundred [HUHN•drud] *num*
cent; des centaines

hundredth [HUHN•druth] *num*
centième (see also fifth)

Hungarian
[HUNG•GAU•ree•un] *adj*
hongrois; *n* Hongrois M;
(language) hongrois M

Hungary [HUNG•gu•ree] *n*
Hongrie F

hunger [HUNG•gur] *n* faim F;
vt avoir faim de

hungry [HUNG•gree] *adj* avoir
faim

hunt [huhnt] *n* chasse F;
(search) recherche F; *vt*
chasser; (for person)
poursuivre; (search for)
chercher; *vi* chasser

hunter [HUHN•tur] *n*
chasseur M

hurdle [HUR•dl] *n* obstacle M;
(of running track) haie F; *vt*
sauter

hurl [hurl] *vt* lancer

hurricane [HU•ri•KAIN] *n*
ouragan M

hurried [HU•reed] *adj* précipité;
pressé

hurriedly [HU•red•lee] *adv*
précipitamment

hurry [HU•ree] *n* hâte F; être
pressé; *vt* (person) faire
presser; (process etc) presser;
vi se presser se dépêcher

hurt [hurt] *vt* blesser; faire mal
à; se faire mal à la main/le
dos; *vi* faire mal; *adj* blessé

hurtful [HURT•ful] *adj* blessant

husband [HUHZ•bund] *n*
mari M

hush [huhsh] *n* silence M; *vt*
faire taire; chut!

husk [huhsk] *n* (of seed corn)
enveloppe F

husky [HUH•skee] *adj* rauque;
n chien M eskimau

hustle [HUH•sl] *n* (rush)
bousculade F; *vt* bousculer

hut [huht] *n* hutte F

hutch [huhch] *n* clapier M

hyacinth [HUY•u•SINTH] *n*
jacinthe F

hybrid [HUY•brid] *adj n*
hybride M

hydrant [HUY•drunt] *n* bouche
F d'incendie

hydraulic [huy•DRAU•lik] *adj*
hydraulique

hydrogen [HUY•dru•jun] *n*
hydrogène M

hyena [huy•EE•nu] *n* hyène F

hygiene [HUY•jeen] *n*
hygiène F

hymn [him] *n* hymne M

hyperactive [HUY•pur•AK•tiv]
adj hyperactif

hyphen [HUY•fn] *n* trait M
d'union

hypnosis [hip•NO•sis] *n*
hypnose F; en état d'hypnose

hypnotic [hip•NAH•tik] *adj*
hypnotique

hypnotize [HIP•nu•TUYZ] *vt*
hypnotiser

hypocrisy [hi•PAH•kri•see] *n*
hypocrisie F

hypocrite [HI•pu•KRIT] *n*
hypocrite MF

hypocritical [HI•pu•KRI•ti•kl]
adj hypocrite

hypothesis [huy•PAH•thi•sis] *n*
hypothèse F

hypothetical
[HUY•pu•THE•ti•kl] *adj*
hypothétique MF

hysterical [hi•STE•ri•kl] *adj*
hystérique

hysterics [hi•STE•riks] *npl* crise
F de nerfs

I

I [uy] *pers pron* je; (before
vowel) j'; (emphatic) moi
ice [uys] *n* glace F; (on road)
verglas M; *vt* (pastry) glacer;
vi geler; (window etc) se
givrer
ice cube [UYS KYUB] *n*
glaçon M
ice skating [UYS SKAI•ting] *n*
patinage M (sur glace)
ice-cream [uys•KREEM] *n*
glace F
ice-skate [UY•skait] *n* patin à
glace M; *vi* faire du patin à
glace
iceberg [UYS•burg] *n*
iceberg M
Iceland [UYS•lund] *n* Islande F
icing [UY•sing] *n* glaçage M
icy [UY•see] *adj* glacial; (road)
verglacé
idea [uy•DEE•u] *n* idée F
ideal [uy•DEEIL] *adj n* idéal M
idealism [uy•DEEIL•izm] *n*
idéalisme M
idealistic [uy•DEEU•LI•stik]
adj idéaliste
identical [uy•DEN•ti•kl] *adj*
identique
identification
[uy•DEN•ti•fi•KAI•shn] *n*

identification F; (papers) pièce
F d'identité
identify [uy•DEN•ti•FUY] *vt*
identifier; associer qqn/qqch
avec qqn/qqch; *vi* s'identifier
identity [uy•DEN•ti•tee] *n*
identité
ideology [UY•dee•AH•lu•jee] *n*
idéologie F
idiot [I•dee•ut] *n* idiot M;
imbécile MF
idiotic [I•dee•AH•tik] *n* idiot
idle [UY•dl] *adj* (still)
désœuvré; (lazy) oisif; (threat
attempt) vain; (machine) en
repos; *vi* tourner au ralenti
idole
idol [UY•dl] *n* idole F
idolize [UY•du•LUYZ] *vt*
idolâtrer
if [if] *conj* si; comme si; sinon;
si seulement
ignite [ig•NUYT] *vt* mettre le
feu à enflammer; *vi* prendre
feu s'enflammer
ignition [ig•NI•shn] *n* ignition
F; (of car) allumage M;
mettre le contact
ignorance [IG•nu•runs] *n*
ignorance F

ignorant [IG•nu•runt] *adj*
ignorant

ignore [ig•NAUR] *vt* ne pas
tenir compte de; (person) faire
semblant de ne pas voir

ill [il] *adj* malade; become ~\
tomber malade

ill at ease [ILL at EEZ] *adj* mal
à l'aise

ill will *n* animosité F

illegal [i•LEE•gl] *adj* illégal

illegitimate [I•li•JI•ti•mut] *adj*
illégitime

illicit [i•LI•sit] *adj* illicite

illiteracy [i•LI•tu•ru•see] *n*
illetrisme M
analphabétisme M

illiterate [i•LI•tu•rut] *adj* illetré;
analphabète

illness [IL•nis] *n* maladie F

illogical [i•LAH•ji•kl] *adj*
illogique

illuminate [i•LOO•mi•NAIT] *vt*
éclairer

illusion [i•LOO•zhn] *n*
illusion F

illustrate [I•lu•STRAIT] *vt*
illustrer

illustration [I•lu•STRAI•shn] *n*
illustration F

illustrious [i•LUH•stree•us] *adj*
illustre

image [I•mij] *n* image F;
(appearance reputation) image
F de marque

imagery [I•mu•jree] *npl*
images F

imaginary [i•MA•ji•NE•ree] *adj*
imaginaire

imagination [i•MA•ji•NAI•shn]
n imagination F

imaginative [i•MA•ji•nu•tiv]
adj imaginatif; (person) plein
d'imagination

imagine [i•MA•jin] *vt*
s'imaginer; (suppose)
imaginer

imbalance [im•BA•luns] *n*
déséquilibre M

imbecile [IM•bu•sil] *n* imbécile
MF

imitate [I•mi•TAIT] *vt* imiter

imitation [I•mi•TAI•shn] *n*
imitation F

immaculate [i•MA•kyu•lut] *adj*
impeccable; (rel) immaculé

immaterial [I•mu•TEEU•ree•ul]
adj insignifiant

immature [I•mu•CHOOUR] *adj*
qui manque de maturité;
prématuré

immediate [i•MEE•dee•ut] *adj*
immédiat

immediately
[i•MEE•dee•ut•lee] *adv*
immédiatement; toute de suite;
(directly) directement

immense [i•MENS] *adj*
immense

immerse [i•MURS] *vt* immerger
plonger; se plonger dans

immigrant [I•mi•grunt] *n*
immigré

immigration [I•mi•GRAI•shn]
n immigration F

imminent [I•mi•nunt] *adj*
imminent

immobile [i•MO•bl] *adj*
immobile

immobilize [i•MO•bi•LUYZ] *vt*
immobiliser

immoral [i•MAU•rl] *adj*
immoral

immorality [I•mau•RA•li•tee] *n*
immoralité F

immortal [i•MAUR•tl] *adj*
immortel

immortality
[I•MAUR•TA•li•tee] *n*
immortalité F

immune [i•MYOON] *adj*
immunisé

immunity [i•MYOO•ni•tee] *n*
immunité F

immunize [I•myu•NUYZ] *vt*
immuniser

imp [imp] *n* lutin M

impact [*n* IM•pakt *v.* im•PAKT]
n impact M; *vt* (have an
influence on) effectuer;
influencer

impair [im•PAIUR] *vt* (~ one's
hearing) affaiblir;
endommager

impart [im•PAHRT] *vt* (~
knowledge) transmettre;
donner

impartial [im•PAHR•shl] *adj*
impartial

impassioned [im•PASH•nd]
adj (give an ~ plea)
passionné; ardent

impatience [im•PAI•shns] *n*
impatience F

impatient [im•PAI•shnt] *adj*
impatient; s'impatienter

impeach [im•PEECH] *vt* (~ a
President) accuser

impede [im•PEED] gêner;
empêcher

impediment [im•PE•di•munt] *n*
obstacle M

impel [im•PEL] *vt* inciter; être
incliné à

imperative [im•PE•ru•tiv] *adj*
impératif nécessaire; *n*
(grammar) impératif M

imperfect [im•PUR•fikt] *adj*
imparfait

imperial [im•PEEU•ree•ul] *adj*
impérial

imperious [im•PEEU•ree•us]
adj impérieux

impersonal [im•PUR•su•nl] *adj*
impersonel

impersonate
[im•PUR•so•NAIT] *vt* imiter

impertinent [im•PUR•ti•nunt]
adj impertinent

impervious [im•PUR•vee•us]
adj imperméable

impetuous [im•PE•choo•us] *adj*
impétueux

impetus [IM•pit•tus] *n*
impulsion F

implant [im•PLANT] *vt*
implanter

implement [*n* IM•pli•munt *v.*
IM•pli•MENT] *n* outil M;
instrument; *vt* exécuter réaliser

implicate [IM•pli•KAIT] *vt*
impliquer

implicit [im•PLI•sit] *adj*
implicite

implore [im•PLAUR] *vt*
implorer

imply [im•PLUY] *vt* insinuer;
suggérer

impolite [IM•pu•LUYT] *adj*
impoli

import [*n.* IM•paurt *v.*
im•PAURT] *n* importation F;
vt importer

importance [im•PAUR•tuns] *n*
importance F

important [im•PAUR•tunt] *adj*
important

impose [im•POZ] *vt* (on)
imposer (à); (inconvenience)
abuser de

impossible [im•PAH•si•bl] *adj*
impossible

impostor [im•PAH•stur] *n*
imposteur M

impotent [IM•pu•tunt] *adj*
impuissant

impress [im•PRES] *vt*
impressionner

impression [im•PRE•shn] *n*
impression; avoir l'impression
que F

impressive [im•PRE•siv] *adj*
impressionnant

imprint [*n.* IM•print *v.*
im•PRINT] *n* empreinte F; *vt*
imprimer

imprison [im•PRI•zn] *vt*
emprissonner

improbable [im•PRAH•bu•bl]
adj improbable;
invraisemblable

improper [im•PRAH•pur] *adj*
impropre

improve [im•PROOV] *vt*
améliorer; *vi* s'améliorer

improvement
[im•PROOV•munt] *n*
amélioration F

improvise [IM•pruh•VUYZ] *vt*
vi improviser

imprudent [im•PROO•dunt] *adj*
imprudent

impudent [IM•pyu•dunt] *adj*
impudent

impulsive [im•PUHL•siv] *adj*
impulsif

impunity [im•PYOO•ni•tee] *n*
avec impunité F

impure [im•PYUR] *adj* impur

impurity [im•PYU•ri•tee] *n*
impureté F

in [inside] *prep* (the car is ~ the
garage) dans

in love (with) *adj* amoureux
(de)

in-laws [IN•lauz] *npl*
belle-famille F beaux-parents
M

inability [I•nu•BI•li•tee] *n*
incapacité

inaccurate [in•A•kyu•rut] *adj*
inexact

inactive [in•AK•tiv] *adj* inactif

inadequate [in•A•du•kwit] *adj*
insuffissant

inadvertent [IN•ud•VER•tunt]
adj fait par inadvertence

inane [i•NAIN] *adj* inepte;
absurde; stupide

inanimate [in•AN•uh•muht]
inanimé

inappropriate
[IN•u•PRO•pree•ut] *adj* mal à
propos

inauguration
[i•NAU•gyu•RAI•shn] *n*
inauguration F; (of president
etc) investiture F

incapable [in•KAI•pu•bl] *adj*
incapable

incense [*n.* IN•sens *v.* in•SENS]
n encens M; rendre furieux

incentive [in•SEN•tiv] *n* (have
an ~ to lose weight)
motivation F

incessant [in•SE•sunt] *adj*
incessant

inch [inch] *n* pouce
(centimètres) M

incident [IN•si•dunt] *n* incident

incidental [IN•si•DEN•tl] *adj*
(~ expenses) (~ meeting)
occasionné par; par hasard

incite [in•SYT] *vt* inciter

incline [in•KLUYN] *vt* (be ~ed
to gossip) (he ~ed his body
against the wall) (s')incliner;
pencher

include [in•KLOOD] *vt* inclure

including [in•KLOO•ding] *prep*
y compris

income [IN•kuhm] *n* revenu M

income tax *n* impôt M sur le
revenu

incomparable
[in•KAHM•pru•bl] *adj*
incomparable sans pareil

incompatible
[IN•kum•PA•ti•bl] *adj*
incompatible

incompetent
[in•KAHM•pu•tunt] *adj*
incompétent

incomplete [IN•kum•PLEET]
adj incomplet

inconsiderate
[IN•kun•SI•du•rut] *adj*
iconsideré

inconsistent [IN•kun•SIS•tnt]
adj inconsistant; (story etc)
inconséquant

inconspicuous
[IN•kun•SPI•kyoo•us] *adj*
discret

inconvenient
[IN•kun•VEE•nyunt] *adj*
inopportun

incorporate
[in•KAUR•pu•RAIT] *vt*
incorporer

incorrect [IN•ku•REKT] *adj*
incorrect

increase [*n.* IN•krees *v.*
in•KREES] *n* augmentation F;
vt vi augmenter

increasingly
[in•KREE•sing•lee] *adv* de
plus en plus

incredible [in•KRE•di•bl] *adj*
incroyable

incredulous [in•KRE•dyu•lus]
adj incrédule

incriminate [in•KRI•mi•NAIT]
vt incriminer

incur [in•KUR] *vt* encourir

incurable [in•KYOOU•ru•bl]
adj incurable; inguérissable

incursion [in•KUR•zhn] *n*
incursion F

indebted [in•DE•tid] *adj*
redevable

indecent [in•DEE•sunt] *adj*
indécent

indeed [in•DEED] *adv* en effet;
excl ~!\vraiment!

indefinite [in•DE•fi•nit] *adj*
indefini

indemnity [in•DEM•ni•tee] *n*
indemnité F

indent [in•DENT] *vt* entailler

independence
[IN•du•PEN•duns] *n*
indépendence F

independent
[IN•du•PEN•dunt] *adj*
indépendent

indestructible
[IN•di•STRUHK•ti•bl] *adj*
indestructible

index [in•DEKS] *n* index M

index finger *n* index M

India [IN•dee•u] *n* Inde F

Indian [IN•dee•un] *adj* indien; *n* Indien

indicate [IN•di•KAIT] *vt* indiquer

indicator [IN•di•KAI•tur] *n* indicateur

indict [in•DUYT] *vt* accuser

indifferent [in•DI•fu•runt] *adj* indifférent

indigenous [in•DI•ji•nus] *adj* indigène

indigestion [in•di•JES•chn] *n* indigestion F

indignant [in•DIG•nunt] *adj* indigné; s'indigner

indigo [IN•di•GO] *adj n* indigo

indirect [IN•di•REKT] *adj* indirect

indiscreet [IN•di•SKREET] *adj* indiscret

indispensable [IN•di•SPEN•su•bl] *adj* indispensable

indispose [IN•di•SPOZ] *vi* indisposer

indistinct [IN•di•STINKT]·*adj* indistinct

individual [IN•di•VI•joo•ul] *adj* individuel; *n* individu M

indoctrinate [in•DAHK•tri•NAIT] *vt* indoctriner

Indonesia [IN•do•NEE•zhu] *n* Indonésie F

indoor [IN•DAUR] *adj* d'intérieur; *adv* à l'intérieur

induce [in•DOOS] *vt* pousser (qq'un) à (faire qqch)

induct [in•DUHKT] *vt* initier

indulge [in•DUHLJ] *vt* satisfaire

industrial [in•DUH•stree•ul] *adj* industriel

industrious [in•DUH•stree•us] *adj* industrieux

industry [IN•duh•stree] *n* industrie F

inebriated [i•NEE•bree•AI•tid] *adj* ivre

ineffective [IN•u•FEK•tiv] *adj* inefficace

inequality [IN•ee•KWAH•li•tee] *n* inégalité F

inevitable [i•NE•vi•tu•bl] *adj* inévitable

inexpensive [IN•ek•SPEN•siv] *adj* pas cher

inexperienced [IN•ek•SPEEU•ree•unst] *adj* inexpérimenté

infallible [in•FA•li•bl] *adj* infaillible

infamous [IN•fu•mus] *adj* infâme

infancy [IN•fun•see] *n* petite enfance F

infant [IN•funt] *n* petit enfant M

infantry [IN•fun•tree] *n* infanterie F

infect [in•FEKT] *vt* infecter

infection [in•FEK•shn] *n* infection F

infectious [in•FEK•shus] *adj* infectueux

infer [in•FUR] *vt* déduire

inferior [in•FEEU•ree•ur] *adj n* inférieur M

infidelity [IN•fi•DE•li•tee] *n*
infidelité F

infinite [IN•fi•nit] *adj* infini

infinitive [in•FI•ni•tiv] *adj n*
infinitif M

infinity [in•FI•ni•tee] *n*
infinité F

infirmity [in•FUR•mi•tee] *n*
infirmité F

inflame [in•FLAIM] *vt*
enflammer

inflate [in•FLAIT] *vt* gonfler

inflation [in•FLAI•shn] *n*
inflation F

inflection [in•FLEK•shn] *n*
inflexion F

inflict [in•FLIKT] *vt* infliger

influence [IN•FLOO•uns] *n*
influence F; *vt* influencer

influenza [IN•floo•EN•zu] *n*
grippe F

influx [IN•fluhks] *n* afflux M

inform [in•FAURM] *vt*
informer qqn de qqch
renseigner qqn sur qqch; *vi*
informer contre qqn

informal [in•FAUR•ml] *adj*
familier non officiel

information [IN•fur•MAI•shn]
npl renseignements M;
information F; (piece of)
renseignement M

infringe [in•FRINJ] *vt*
enfreindre; *vi* empiéter sur

infuriate [in•FYU•ree•AIT] *vt*
rendre furieux

ingenious [in•JEE•nyus] *adj*
ingénieux

ingratitude [in•GRA•ti•TOOD]
n ingratitude F

ingredient [in•GREE•dee•unt]
n ingrédient M

inhabit [in•HA•bit] *vt* habiter

inhale [in•HAIUL] *vt* inhaler;
(smoke) avaler

inherent [in•HE•runt] *adj*
inhérent

inherit [in•HE•rit] *vt* hériter

inheritance [in•HE•ri•tuns] *n*
héritage M

inhibit [in•HI•bit] *vt* inhiber

inhuman [in•HYOO•mun] *adj*
inhumain

initial [i•NI•shl] *adj* initial; *n*
initiale; *vt* parafer

initiate [i•NI•shee•AIT] *vt*
initier; commencer

inject [in•JEKT] *vt* injecter

injure [IN•jur] *vt* blesser

injury [IN•ju•ree] *n* blessure F

injustice [in•JUH•stis] *n*
injustesse F

ink [ingk] *n* encre F

inmate [IN•mait] *n* détenu M

inmost [IN•most] *adj* (the
astonomer was able to observe
the ~ regions of outer space)
le plus profond; les
profondeurs F

inn [in] *n* auberge F

innate [i•NAIT] *adj* inné

inner [I•nur] *adj* intérieur

innkeeper [IN•KEE•pur] *n*
aubergiste MF

innocence [I•nu•suns] *n*
innocence F

innocent [I•nu•sunt] *adj*
innocent

innovation [I•nu•VAI•shn] *n*
innovation F

innuendo [IN•yoo•EN•do] *n*
insinuation F

inoculate [i•NAH•kyu•LAIT] *vt*
inoculer

inorganic [IN•aur•GA•nik] *adj*
inorganique

inquire [in•KWUY•ur] *vi*
demander; se renseigner sur

inquiry [in•KWU•ree] *n*
demande; (investigation)
investigation F enquête F

inquisition [IN•kwi•ZI•shn] *n*
investigation F; l'Inquisition F

inquisitive [in•KWI•zi•tiv] *adj*
curieux

insane [in•SAIN] *adj* fou (folle)

insanity [in•SA•ni•tee] *n* folie F

insatiable [in•SAI•shu•bl] *adj*
insatiable

inscription [in•SKRIP•shn] *n*
inscription F

insect [IN•sekt] *n* insecte M

insecticide [in•SEK•ti•SUYD] *n*
insecticide M

insecure [IN•su•CYUR] *adj* peu
sûr; (person) anxieux; inquiet

insensitive [in•SEN•si•tiv] *adj*
insensible

inseparable [in•SE•pru•bl] *adj*
inséparable

insert [in•SURT] *vt* insérer

inside [in•SUYD] *adj* intérieur;
adv dédans à l'intérieur; *n*
intérieur M

insight [IN•suyt] *n* perspicacité
F; (knowledge idea) aperçu M

insignificant
[IN•sig•NI•fi•kunt] *adj*
insignifiant

insipid [in•SI•pid] *adj* insipide

insist [in•SIST] *vi* insister pour;
(claim) affirmer

insistent [in•SI•stunt] *adj*
insistant

insolent [IN•su•lunt] *adj*
insolent

insomnia [in•SAHM•nee•u] *n*
insomnie F

inspect [in•SPEKT] *vt* inpecter
examiner

inspection [in•SPEK•shn] *n*
inspection F examen M

inspector [in•SPEK•tur] *n*
inspecteur M

inspiration [IN•spu•RAI•shn] *n*
inspiration F

inspire [in•SPUY•ur] *vt* inspirer

install [in•STAUL] *vt* installer

installation [IN•stu•LAI•shn] *n*
installation F

instance [IN•stuns] *n* exemple
M; par exemple

instant [IN•stunt] *adj*
instantané; immédiat; (coffee)
soluble; *n* instant M

instead [in•STED] *adv* plûtot;
au lieu de

instigate [IN•sti•GAIT] *vt*
inciter; provoquer

instill [in•STIL] *vt* instiller qqch
à qqn

instinct [IN•stingkt] *n*
instinct M

institute [IN•sti•TOOT] *n*
insitut M; *vt* instituer

instruct [in•STRUHKT] *vt*
instruire

instruction [in•STRUHK•shn] *n*
instruction F; *npl* ~s\directives
F instructions F

instructor [in•STRUHK•tor] *n*
instructeur M

instrument [IN•stru•munt] *n*
instrument M

insufficient [IN•su•FI•shunt]
adj insuffissant

insulate [IN•su•LAIT] *vt* isoler

insulation [IN•su•LAI•shn] *n*
isolation F; (against cold)
calorifugeage M

insult [*n*. IN•suhlt *v*. in•SUHLT]
n insulte F; *vt* insulter

insurance [in•SHOOU•runs] *n*
assurance F

insure [in•SHOOUR] *vt* assurer

intact [in•TAKT] *adj* intact

integral [IN•tu•grul] *adj*
intégral

integration [IN•tu•GRAI•shn]
n intégration F

integrity [in•TE•gri•tee] *n*
intégrité F

intellectual [IN•tu•LEK•chu•ul]
adj n intellectuel M

intelligence [in•TE•li•juns] *n*
intelligence F

intelligent [in•TE•li•junt] *adj*
intelligent

intend [in•TEND] *vt* avoir
l'intention de

intense [in•TENS] *adj* intense

intensify [in•TEN•si•FUY] *vt*
intensifier

intensity [in•TEN•si•tee] *n*
intensité F

intensive [in•TEN•siv] *adj*
intensif

intent [in•TENT] *adj* resolu à;
n intention F

intention [in•TEN•shn] *n*
intention F

intentional [in•TEN•shu•nl] *adj*
intentionnel F

intercept [IN•tur•SEPT] *n*
intercepter

interchange [*n*. IN•tur•chainj *v*.
in•tur•CHAINJ] *n* échange M;
vt échanger

intercom [IN•tur•KAHM] *n*
interphone M

intercourse [IN•tur•KAURS] *n*
rapports *mpl*

interest [IN•trust] *n* intérêt M;
(business) intérêts *mpl*; *vt*
intéresser; be ~ed
in\s'intéresser de

interesting [IN•tru•sting] *adj*
intéressant

interfere [IN•tur•FEEUR] *vi*
s'immiscer dans

interference
[IN•tur•FEEU•runs] *n*
intrusion F; (on radio tv)
parasites *mpl*

interim [IN•tu•rim] *adj*
provisoire; *n* intérim M

interior [in•TEEU•ree•ur] adj' *n*
intérieur M

interlock [IN•tur•LAHK] *vi*
s'enclencher

intermediate
[IN•tur•MEE•dee•ut] *adj*
intermédiaire; (course etc)
moyen

interminable
[in•TUR•mi•nu•bl] *adj*
interminable

intermission [IN•tur•MI•shn] *n*
entracte M

intern [IN•turn] *n* interne MF;
vt interner

internal [in•TUR•nl] *adj*
interne; (affairs; politics)
intérieur

international
[IN•tur•NA•shu•nl] *adj*
international

interpret [in•TUR•prit] *vt*
interpréter; *vi* faire l'interprète

interpretation
[in•TUR•pru•TAI•shn] *n*
interprétation F

interpreter [in•TUR•pri•tur] *n*
interprète MF

interrogate [in•TE•ru•GAIT] *vt*
interroger

interrogation
[in•TE•ru•GAI•shn] *n*
interrogatoire M;
interrogation F

interrupt [IN•tu•RUHPT] *vt vi*
interrompre

interruption [IN•tu•RUHP•shn]
n interruption F

intersect [IN•tur•SEKT] *vt*
croiser; couper; *vi* se croiser
se couper

intersection [IN•tur•SEK•shn]
n intersection F; (of roads)
carrefour M

intertwine [IN•tur•TWUYN] *vt*
entrelacer; vo s'entrelacer

interval [IN•tur•vl] *n* intervalle
M; par intervalles

intervene [IN•tur•VEEN] *vt*
intervenir

intervention [IN•tur•VEN•shn]
n intervention

interview [IN•tur•VYOO] *n*
entrevue F; *vt* avoir une
entrevue avec; interviewer

intestine [in•TE•stin] *n*
intestin M

intimacy [IN•ti•mu•see] *n*
intimité F

intimate [*adj.* IN•ti•mit *v.*
IN•ti•MAIT] *adj* intime; *vt*
laisser entendre faire savoir

into [IN•too] *prep* dans; à;
(change turn) en

intolerable [in•TAH•lu•ru•bl]
adj intolérable

intolerance [in•TAH•lu•runs] *n*
intolérance F

intolerant [in•TAH•lu•runt] *adj*
intolérant

intoxicated
[in•TAHK•si•KAI•tid] *adj* ivre

intravenous [IN•tru•VEE•nus]
adj intraveineux

intricate [IN•tri•kut] *adj*
compliqué

intrigue [in•TREEG] *n* intrigue
F; *vt* intriguer

introduce [IN•tru•DOOS] *vt*
présenter; introduire

introduction
[IN•tru•DUHK•shn] *n*
introduction F; présentation F

introvert [IN•tru•VURT] *n*
introverti M

introverted [IN•tru•VUR•tid]
adj introverti

intrude [in•TROOD] *vi* faire
intrusion

intruder [in•TROO•dur] *n*
intrus M

intrusion [in•TROO•zhn] *n*
intrusion F

intuition [IN•too•I•shn] *n*
intuition F

inundate [I•nun•DAIT] *vt*
inonder

invade [in•VAID] *vt* envahir

invalid [*adj.* in•VA•lid *n.*
IN•vu•lid] *adj* non valide; *n*
invalide MF

invaluable [in•VA•lyu•bl] *adj*
inestimable

invariably [in•VA•ryu•blee] *adv*
invariablement

invasion [in•VAI•zhn] *n*
invasion F

invent [in•VENT] *vt* inventer

invention [in•VEN•shn] *n*
invention F

inventive [in•VEN•tiv] *adj*
inventif

inventor [in•VEN•tur] *n*
inventeur M

inventory [IN•vun•TAU•ree] *n*
inventaire M

invest [in•VEST] *vt vi* investir

investigate [in•VE•sti•GAIT]
vt faire une enquête sur

investigation
[in•VE•sti•GAI•shn] *n* enquête
F investigation F

investment [in•VEST•munt]
n investissement M
placement M

investor [in•VE•stur] *n*
investisseur M

invigorating
[in•VI•gu•RAI•ting] *adj*
vivifiant

invincible [in•VIN•si•bl] *adj*
invincible

invisible [in•VI•zi•bl] *adj*
invisible

invitation [IN•vi•TAI•shn] *n*
invitation F

invite [in•VUYT] *vt* inviter

inviting [in•VUY•ting] *adj*
attrayant; tentant

invoice [IN•vois] *n* facture F

invoke [in•VOK] *vt* invoquer

involuntary
[in•VAH•lun•TE•ree] *adj*
involontaire

involve [in•VAHLV] *vt* (entail)
nécessiter; (include) faire
participer qqn à

involvement
[in•VAHLV•munt] *n*
participation (à)

inward [IN•wurd] *adj adv* vers
l'intérieur

iodine [UY•u•DUYN] *n* iode M

Iran [uy•RAN] *n* Iran M

Iranian [uy•RAI•nyun] *adj*
iranien; *n* Iranien M M

Iraq [uy•RAK] *n* Irak M

Iraqi [uy•RA•kee] *adj* irakien; *n*
Irakien M M

Ireland [UYUR•lund] *n*
Irlande F

iris [UY•ris] *n* iris M

Irish [UY•rish] *adj* irlandais; *n*
(person) Irlandais M;
(language) irlandais M

iron [UY•urn] *n* fer M; (for
pressing) fer M à repasser; *vt*
repasser

ironic [UY•RAH•nik] *adj*
ironique

ironing [UY•ur•ning] *n*
repassage M

irony [UY•ru•nee] *n* ironie F

irrational [i•RA•shu•nl] *adj*
irrationel

irregular [i•RE•gyu•lur] *adj*
irrégulier

irregularity
  [i•RE•gyu•LA•ri•tee] *n*
  irrégularité F
irrelevant [i•RE•lu•vunt] *adj*
  sans rapport F
irreparable [i•RE•pru•bl] *adj*
  irréparable
irreplaceable [i•ri•PLAI•su•bl]
  adj irremplaçable
irresistible [I•ru•ZI•stu•bl] *adj*
  irrésistible
irresponsible
  [I•ri•SPAHN•su•bl] *adj*
  irresponsable
irrigate [I•ri•GAIT] *vt* irriguer
irrigation [I•ri•GAI•shn] *n*
  irrigation F
irritable [I•ri•tu•bl] *adj* irritable
irritate [I•ri•TAIT] *vt* irriter
irritating [I•ri•TAI•ting] *adj*
  irritant
Islam [iz•LAHM] *n* islam M
island [UY•lund] *n* île F
isle [uyul] *n* île F
isolate [UY•su•LAIT] *vt* isoler
isolation [UY•su•LAI•shn] *n*
  isolation F
issue [I•shoo] *n* question F; en
  question; (of newspaper etc)
  numéro M; (of banknotes etc)
  émission F; *vt* (decree etc)
  donner faire; (distribute)

distribuer; (banknotes etc)
  émettre
it *pron* (specific subject) il
  (elle); (as dir obj) le (la) l';
  (as ind obj) lui; here il est or
  c'est ici; (after preps) en; y;
  (impersonal) il; il pleut/fait
  chaud; il est trois heures; qui
  est-ce? c'est lui
Italian [i•TAL•yun] *adj* italien;
  n (person) Italien M;
  (language) italien M
italic [uy•TA•lik] *adj* italique;
  npl italiques F
itch [ich] *n* démangeaison F; *vi*
  (subj: part of body)
  démanger; mon pied me
  démange
itchy [I•chee] *adj* qui démange
item [UY•tum] *n* article M; (on
  agenda) question F point M
itemize [UY•tu•MUYZ] *vt*
  détailler
itinerary [uy•TI•nu•RE•ree] *n*
  itinéraire M
its [its] *poss pron* son (sa) ses
itself [it•SELF] *pron* (reflexive)
  se; (after prep) soi;
  (emphatic) lui-même
  (elle-même)
ivory [UY•vree] *n* ivoire
ivy [UY•vee] *n* lierre M

J

jab [jab] *n* coup M; *vt* enfoncer
  qqch dans

jack [jak] *n* (tool) cric M; (of
  playing cards) valet; *vt*
  soulever au cric

jackal [JA•kl] *n* chacal M

jacket [JA•kit] *n* veste F

jackhammer [JAK•HA•mur] *n* marteau-piqueur M

jackpot [JAK•paht] *n* gros lot M

jaded [JAI•did] *adj* éreinté

jagged [JA•gid] *adj* dentelé

jail [jaiul] *n* prison F; *vt* emprissonner

jam [jam] *n* confiture F; (in traffic) embouteillage M; be in a ~\être dans le pétrin; *vt* (obstruct) encombrer; (machine etc) bloquer coincer; (radio) brouiller; ~ sth into\ entasser qqch dans; *vi* (machine door etc) se coincer se bloquer

janitor [JA•ni•tur] *n* concierge M

January [JA•nyoo•E•ree] *n* janvier M

Japan [ju•PAN] *n* Japon M

Japanese [JA•pu•NEEZ] *adj* japonais; *n* (person) Japonais M; (language) japonais M

jar [jahr] *n* pot M

jargon [JAHR•gun] *n* jargon M

jaundice [JAUN•dis] *n* jaunisse F

javelin [JA•vu•lin] *n* javelot M

jaw [jau] *n* mâchoire F

jay [jai] *n* geai M

jazz [jaz] *n* jazz M

jealous [JE•lus] *adj* jaloux

jealousy [JE•lu•see] *n* jalousie F

jeans [jeenz] *npl* (blue-)jean M

jeep [jeep] *n* jeep F

jeer [jeeur] *vi* huer; railler

jelly [JE•lee] *n* gelée F

jellyfish [JE•lee•FISH] *n* méduse F

jeopardize [JE•pur•DUYZ] *vt* mettre en danger

jerk [jurk] *n* saccade F secousse F; (person) mufle M; *vt* donner une secousse à; *vi* (vehicle) cahoter

jersey [JUR•zee] *n* tricot M

jest [jest] *n* plaisanterie F

jet [jet] *n* jet M

jetty [JE•tee] *n* jetée F

Jew [joo] *n* Juif M

jewel [jooul] *n* bijou M

jeweler [JOOU•lur] *n* bijoutier M; (shop) bijouterie F

jewelry [JOOUL•ree] *npl* bijoux M

Jewish [JOO•ish] *adj* juif

jig [jig] *n* gigue F

jiggle [JI•gl] *vt* secouer (doucement)

jigsaw (puzzle) [JIG•sau] *n* puzzle M

jilt [jilt] *vt* laisser tomber

jingle [JING•gl] *n* (of glass metal etc) cliquetis M; (of bell) tintement M; (song) petit couplet; *vi* (bell) tinter; (glass metal etc) cliqueter

job [jahb] *n* travail M; (employment) emploi M poste M

jockey [JAH•kee] *n* jockey M

jog [jahg] *vi* faire du jogging

jogging [JAH•ging] *n* jogging M

join *vt* unir joindre; (club) s'inscrire à; (meet up with) retrouver rejoindre; *vi* (come together) se joindre; (club) s'incrire; ~ **in** vi participer; ~ **up** vi s'engager

joint adj commun; collectif joint; n joint M; (knee; elbow; etc) articulation F; (place) bouge M; (of marijuana) joint M

joint account n compte M joint

joke [jok] n blague F; plaisanterie; jouer un tour à; vi blaguer plaisanter

joker [JO•kur] n blagueur M plaisantin M; (of playing cards) joker M

jolly [JAH•lee] adj gai enjoué

jolt [jolt] n choc M; (shake) secousse F; vt (upset; disturb) bouleverser; (shake) secouer

jot [jaht] vt noter

journal [JUR•nl] n journal M

journalism [JUR•nu•LI•zm] n journalisme M

journalist [JUR•nu•list] n journaliste MF

journey [JUR•nee] n voyage M

jovial [JO•vyul] adj jovial

joy [joi] n joie F

joyful [JOI•ful] adj joyeux

jubilant [JOO•bi•lunt] adj réjoui

judge [juhj] n juge M; vt vi juger

judicial [joo•DI•shl] adj judiciaire

judicious [joo•DI•shus] adj judicieux

jug [juhg] n pot

juggle [JUH•gl] vt jongler avec; vi jongler

juggler [JUH•glur] n jongleur M

juice [joos] n jus M

juicy [JOO•see] adj juteux

jukebox [JOOK•bahks] n juke-box

July [ju•LUY] n juillet M

jump [juhmp] n saut M bond M; vt (over sth) sauter franchir; vi sauter bondir; (from fear etc) sursauter; (increase greatly) monter en flèche

junction [JUHNGK•shn] n (of railroad) embranchement M

June [joon] n juin M

jungle [JUHNG•gl] n jungle F

junior [JOO•nyur] adj jeune; (after name) junior; n cadet M (cadette); he's 3 years my ~\il est mon cadet de 3 ans; (in university) étudiant M de deuxième année

junk [juhngk] n bric-à-brac M

jurisdiction [JOOU•ris•DIK•shn] n juridiction F

juror [JOOU•rur] n juré M

jury [JOOU•ree] n jury M

just [juhst] adj juste; adv il vient d'arriver; (only merely) seulement; ne . . . que; exactement comme; au moment où je partais; (right now) j'allais juste le faire; (in comparison) tout aussi . . . que

justice [JUH•stis] n justesse F

Justice of the Peace n juge de paix M

justify [JUH•sti•FUY] vt justifier

juvenile [JOO•vu•NUYUL] *adj*
  juvénile; (behavior) puéril; *n*
  adolescent M

juxtapose [JUHK•stu•POZ] *vt*
  juxtaposer

K

kaleidoscope
  [ku•LUY•du•SKOP] *n*
  kaléidoscope M
kangaroo [KANG•gu•ROO] *n*
  kangourou M
keen *adj* (interest; mind; etc)
  vif; (eyesight) perçant
keep *vt* garder; (maintain)
  tenir; (raise—animals) élever;
  ~ sth cold\tenir qqch au
  frioid; ~ sb from doing
  sth\empêcher qqn de faire
  qqch; *vi* (remain) rester;
  (food) se conserver;
  (continue) ~ talking\
  continuer à parler; ~
  on\vicontinuer; ~ out*vt*
  empêcher d'entrer; ~
  out\défense d'entrer; ~
  up*vt* maintenir; ~ up
  with\aller aussi vite que
keeper [KEE•pur] *n*
  gardien M
keeping [KEE•ping] *n* garde;
  être conforme à
keepsake [KEEP•saik] *n*
  souvenir
keg *n* tonnelet
kennel [KE•nl] *n* niche
Kenya [KE•nyu] *n* Kenya M

kernel [KUR•nl] *n* amande F
kerosene [KE•ru•SEEN] *n*
  kérosène M
ketchup [KE•chup] *n*
  ketchup M
kettle [KE•tl] *n* bouilloire F
key [kee] *n* clé F clef F; (of
  piano typewriter etc)
  touche F; (of map) legende
  F; *adj* clé
key ring *n* porte-clés M
keyboard [KEE•baurd] *n*
  clavier M
khaki [KA•kee] *adj* kaki; *n*
  (color) kaki M
kick [kik] *n* coup de pied; M
  s'amuser de qqch; por
  s'amuser; *vt* donner un coup
  de pied à; chasser jeter dehors
kid [kid] *n* (child) gosse mf;
  gamin M; (young goat)
  chevreau M; *vt* blaguer
  plaisanter
kidnap [KID•nap] *n* kidnapper;
  enlever
kidnaping [KID•na•ping] *n*
  enlèvement
kidnapper [KID•na•pur] *n*
  ravisseur M
kidney [KID•nee] *n* rein M;
  (culinary) rognon M

kill [kil] *vt* tuer; (plans; etc) détruire

killer [KI•lur] *n* meurtrier M; tueur M

kiln [kiln] *n* four M

kilogram [KI•lu•GRAM] *n* kilogramme M

kilometer [ki•LAH•mi•tur] *n* kilomètre M

kilowatt [KI•lu•WAHT] *n* kilowatt

kilt *n* kilt M

kin *npl* parents M

kind [kuynd] *adj* gentil; aimable; *n* sorte F espèce F genre M; *adv* ~ of\un peu

kindergarten [KIN•dur•GAHR•tn] *n* jardin M d'enfants

kindle [KIN•dl] *vt* allumer

kindly [KUYND•lee] *adj* bienveillant; *adv* avec bienveillance/gentillesse

kindness [KUYND•nis] *n* gentillesse F

king *n* roi M

kingdom [KING•dum] *n* royaume F; (of biology) règne

kinky [KING•kee] *adj* bizarre

kiss [kis] *n* baiser M; give a ~ to\donner un baiser ~a; *vt* embrasser; *vi* s'embrasser

kit *n* trousse F; (for assembly) kit M

kitchen [KI•chn] *n* cuisine F

kitchen sink *n* évier M

kite [kuyt] *n* cerf-volant M

kitten [KI•tn] *n* chaton M

knack [nak] *n* avoir le coup pour

knapsack [NAP•sak] *n* sac M à dos

knead [need] *vt* pétrir

knee [nee] *n* genou

kneecap [NEE•kap] *n* rotule M

kneel [neeul] *vi* s'agenouiller se mettre à genoux

knife [nuyf] *n* couteau M; *vt* poignarder

knight [nuyt] *n* chevalier M; (of chess) cavalier; *vt* faire chevalier

knit [nit] *vt vi* tricoter

knitting [NI•ting] *n* tricot M

knob [nahb] *n* (of door) poignée F; (of radio tv etc) bouton M

knock [nahk] *n* coup M; *vi* frapper heurter; *vt* renverser; assomer

knocker [NAH•kur] *n* heurtoir M

knot [naht] *n* nœud M; *vt* nouer

know [no] *vy* savoir; (be familiar with) connaître; ~ how to do sth\savoir faire qqch; ~ about/of sb/sth\être courant de qqn/qqch

know-how [NO•hou] *n* savoir-faire

know-it-all [NO•it•ALL] *n* je-sais-tout MF

knowledge [NAH•lij] *n* connaissance F; savoir M

knuckle [NUH•kl] *n* articulation F du doigt

Korea [ku•REE•u] *n* Corée F

kosher [KO•shur] *adj* kasher

Kuwait [ku•WAIT] *n* Koweït M

L

lab *n* labo M

label [LAI•bl] *n* étiquette F; *vt* étiquer

labor [LAI•bur] *n* travail M; (workforce) main-d'œuvre F; (childbirth) travail M (d'enfant); *vi* travailler; ~ over*vi* peiner sur

Labor Party *n* parti M travailliste

labor union *n* syndicat M

laboratory [LA•bru•TAU•ree] *n* laboratoire M

laborer [LAI•bu•rur] *n* manœuvre M

lace [lais] *n* dentelle F; (of shoe) lacet M; *vt* lacer

lack [lak] *n* manque M; *vt* manquer de; *vi* manquer

lacquer [LA•kur] *n* lácque; *vt* lacquer M

ladder [LA•dur] *n* échelle F

ladle [LAI•dl] *n* louche F; *vt* servir (à la louche)

lady [LAI•dee] *n* dame F

lag *vi* (falter do poorly) être en retard; ~ behind\traîner

lagoon [lu•GOON] *n* lagune F

lair [laiur] *n* antre M; repaire M

lake [laik] *n* lac M

lamb [lam] *n* agneau M

lame [laim] *adj* boiteux

lament [lu•MENT] *n* lamentation F; *vt* se lamenter sur

laminate [LA•mi•NAIT] *vt* laminer

lamp *n* lampe F

lamp shade *n* abat-jour M

lamp-post *n* lampadaire; feu (l'autoroute) M

lampoon [lam•POON] *n* satire F

lance [lans] *n* lance F

land *n* terre F; (country) pays M; (property) terres *fpl;* *vt* (ship) débarquer; (plane) atterrir; (acquire) décrocher; *vi* débarquer atterrir; ~ up*vi* atterrir

landing [LAN•ding] *n* (of plane) atterrissage M; (of stairs) palier M

landlady [LAND•LAI•dee] *n* propriétaire F

landlord [LAND•laurd] *n* propriétaire M

landmark [LAND•mahrk] *n* point M de repère

landowner [LAND•O•nur] *n* propriétaire MF foncier(-ère)

landslide [LAND•sluyd] *n* glissement M de terrain

lane [lain] *n* (in city) ruelle F; (in country) chemin M; (of cars in traffic) voie F file F

language [LANG•gwj] *n* langage M; langue F

languid [LANG•gwid] *adj* languissant

lantern [LAN•turn] *n* lanterne F

lap [lap] *n* sur les genoux; (in race) tour de piste M; *vt*

(drink) laper; (in race)
prendre un tour à
lapel [lu•PEL] *n* revers M
lapse [laps] *n* défaillance F; (in
time) laps de temps M; *vi*
(expire – license etc) se
périmer
larceny [LAHR•su•nee] *n* vol M
lard [lahrd] *n* saindoux
large [lahrj] *n* grand; (person
animal) gros; at ~\ en liberté
largely [LAHRJ•lee] *adv* en
grande partie
lark [lahrk] *n* alouette F; (joke)
blague F
lash *n* (of eye) cil M; (of whip)
coup M de fouet; *vt* fouetter;
~ out at\attaquer
last *adj* dernier; hier soir; *adv*
en dernier; *vi* durer
last name *n* nom M de famille
lasting [LA•sting] *adj* durable
latch [lach] *n* loquet M
late [lait] *adj* en retard; tardif;
(recently deceased) feu;
(former) ancien; in ~
March\vers le fin de mars; *adv*
en retard; tard
latent [LAI•tunt] *adj* latent
lather [LA•thur] *n* mousse F
(de savon)
Latin [LA•tin] *adj n* latin M
Latin America *n* Amérique F
latine M
latitude [LA•ti•TOOD] *n*
latitude F
latter [LA•tur] *adj* dernier;
(second) deuxième; *n* the
~\celui-ci (celle-ci)
lattice [LA•tis] *n* treillis M;
treillage M

Latvia [LAHT•vee•u] *n*
Lettonie F
laugh [laf] *vi n* rire M
laughter [LAF•tur] *n* rire M;
npl rires M
launch [launch] *n* lancement; *vt*
lancer
launder [LAUN•dur] *vt* blanchir
laundry [LAUN•dree] *n*
linge M
laurel [LAU•rl] *n* laurier M
lava [LAH•vu] *n* lave F
lavatory [LA•vu•TAU•ree] *npl*
toilettes F
lavish [LA•vish] *adj* somptueux;
(very generous) ~
with\prodigue de; *vt* ~ sth on
sb\prodiguer qqch à qqn
law [lau] *n* loi F; (subject of
study) droit M; against the
~\contraire à la loi
law school *n* faculté F de droit
law-abiding [~ a•BUY•ding]
adj respectueux des lois
lawful [LAU•ful] *adj* légal
lawn [laun] *n* pelouse F
lawn mower [~ MO•wur] *n*
tondeuse F à gazon
lawsuit [LAU•soot] *n* procès M
lawyer [LAU•yur] *n* (in court)
avocat M; (of company)
juriste M; (for sales wills)
notaire M
lax [laks] *adj* relâché
laxative [LAK•su•tiv] *n*
laxatif M
lay [lai] *adj* (not clergy) laïque;
vt mettre poser; (egg) pondre;
(trap) tendre; *vi* ~
aside\mettre de côté; ~ off
(employees)\licencier

layer [LAI•ur] *n* couche F;
(level) niveau M

layout [LAI•out] *n* agencement
M plan M; (of page) mise F
en page

lazy [LAI•zee] *adj* paresseux

lead 1 [leed] *n* tête; en tête;
(role) rôle M principal; *vt*
mener; (guide) guider; *vi*
mener conduire; (be winning)
être en tête; (result in)
aboutir à

lead 2 [lead] *n* plomb M; (in
pencil) mine F

leader [LEE•dur] *n* chef M;
(political) leader M;

leadership [LEE•dur•SHIP] *n*
direction F; *npl* qualités F de
chef

leading [LEE•ding] *adj*
principal; (front) en tête

leaf [leef] *n* feuille F; (of table)
rallonge F; *vi* ~
through\feuilleter

league [leeg] *n* ligue F; (in
sports) championat M

leak [leek] *n* fuite F; *vt*
(information) divilguer; *vt* fuir

lean [leen] *adj* maigre; *vt* s'
appuyer; *vi* (bend slope) se
pencer; s'appuyer sur/contre

leap [leep] *n* saut M bond M; *vi*
sauter; bondir

leap year *n* année F bissextile

learn [lurn] *vt vi* apprendre;
apprendre à faire qqch

learning [LUR•ning] *n*
savoir M

lease [lees] *n* bail M; *vt* louer

leash [leesh] *n* laisse F

least [leest] *adj* le (la) moindre
le (la) plus petit(e); *pron* le
mons; *adv* au moins

leather [LE•thur] *n* cuir M

leave [leev] *n* congé M;
(military) permission F; *vt*
laisser; (go away from)
quitter; *vi* partir

Lebanon [LE•bu•nahn] *n*
Liban M

lecherous [LE•chu•rus] *adj*
lubrique

lecture [LEK•chur] *n*
conférence F; (of professor)
cours M (magistral); give a ~
on\faire une conférence sur; *vt*
~ on\faire un cours sur;
(scold) reprimander

ledge [lej] *n* (of window)
rebord M; (of mountain)
corniche F

ledger [LE•jur] *n* grand livre M

leech [leech] *n* sangsue F

leek [leek] *n* poireau M

leer [leeur] *n* regard M mauvais;
vi ~ at\regarder d'un air
mauvais

left [left] *pt pp* a leave *adj*
gauche; *adv* à gauche; *n*
gauche M; the Left la Gauche

left-handed [~ HAN•did] *adj*
gaucher

left-overs [LEFT•O•vurz] *npl*
restes F

left-wing [LEFT•WING] *adj* de
gauche

leftist [LEF•tist] *adj n*
gauchiste M

leg [leg] *n* jambe F; (of animal)
patte F; (of furniture) pied M;
(of trip etc) étape F; (of

chicken) cuisse F; (of lamb) gigot M

legacy [LE•gu•see] *n* legs M héritage M

legal [LEE•gl] *adj* légal

legalize [LEE•gu•LUYZ] *vt* légaliser

legend [LE•jund] *n* légende F

legendary [LE•jun•DE•ree] *adj* légendaire

legible [LE•ji•bl] *adj* lisible

legislation [LE•jis•LAI•shn] *n* législation F

legislature [LE•jis•LAI•chur] *n* corps législatif M

legitimate [lu•JI•tu•mit] *adj* légitime

leisure [LEE•zhur] *n* loisir M; à loisir M

lemon [LE•mun] *n* citron M

lemonade [LE•mu•NAID] *n* citronnade F

lend [lend] *vt* prêter

length [length] *n* longeur F; (piece of board, pipe, etc) morceau M bout M

lengthen [LENG•thun] *vt* rallonger; (process duration) prolonger; *vi* s'allonger

lens [lenz] *n* lentille F; loupe F; (of glasses) verre M; (of camera) objectif M

Lent [lent] *n* Carême M

leopard [LE•purd] *n* léopard M

leper [LE•pur] *n* lépreux M

leprosy [LE•pru•see] *n* lèpre F

lesbian [LEZ•bee•un] *n* lesbienne F

less [les] *adj* moins de; *adv* *pron* moins; ~ than\moins que; ~ than (+ number)\moins de

lessen [LE•sn] *vt* diminuer atténuer; *vi* diminuer s'atténuer

lesser [LE•sur] *adj* moindre; à un degré moindre

lesson [LE•sn] *n* leçon F

let *vt* laisser; faire savoir qqch à qqn; lâcher; allons-y!; voyons; *vi* s'arrêter

lethal [LEE•thl] *adj* mortel fatal

lethargy [LE•thur•jee] *n* léthargie F

letter [LE•tur] *n* lettre F

lettuce [LE•tus] *n* laitue F salade F

level [LE•vl] *adj* horizontal; (even flat) plat plan; *n* niveau M; *vt* niveler aplanir; (destroy) raser; ~ off\ *vi* se stabiliser

lever [LE•vur] *n* levier M

levy [LE•vee] *n* impôt M; *vt* prélever; percevoir

lewd [lood] *adj* obscène

liability [LUY•u•BI•li•tee] *n* responsabilité F

liable [LUY•u•bl] *adj* susceptible de faire qqch; être sujet de qqch; responsable de

liaison [LEE•ai•ZAUN] *n* liaison F

liar [LUY•ur] *n* menteur M

libel [LUY•bl] *n* diffamation F; *vt* diffamer

liberal [LI•brul] *adj* *n* libéral M

liberate [LI•bu•RAIT] *vt* libérer M

liberation [LI•bu•RAI•shn] *n* libération F

liberty [LI•bur•tee] *n* liberté F

librarian [luy•BRE•ree•un] *n*
bibliothécaire MF

library [LUY•BRE•ree] *n*
bibliothèque F

Libya [LI•bee•u] *n* Libye F

license [LUY•sns] *n* permis M
autorisation F; driver's
~\permis M de conduire; (in
business) licence F; *vt*
autoriser

lick [lik] *vt* lécher

lid [lid] *n* couvercle M

lie [luy] *n* mensonge M; *vi*
mentir; (rest on one's back)
être couché/allongé; (be
located) se trouver; ~ down*vi*
se coucher s'allonger

lieutenant [loo•TE•nunt] *n*
lieutenant M

life [luyf] *n* vie

life expectancy [~ ek•SPEK•
ten•cee] *n* espérance F
de vie

life jacket *n* gilet de
sauvetage M

life sentence *n* condamnation F
à perpétuité

lifeboat [LUYF•bot] *n* canot M
de sauvetage

lifeless [LUYF•lis] *adj* sans vie
inanimé; (boring) qui manque
de vie

lifelike [LUYF•luyk] *adj* qui
semble vivant

lifelong [LUYF•laung] *adj* de
toujours

lifespan [LUYF•span] *n* durée
F de vie

lifestyle [LUYF•stuyul] *n* style
M de vie

lift [*n* emmener; *vt* lever;
soulever; *vi* se lever

ligament [LI•guh•mint] *n*
ligament M

light [luyt] *adj* (bright) clair; (in
weight) léger; *n* lumière F;
(lamp) lampe F; (for cigarette
fire) feu M; do you have a
~?\avez-vous un feu; ?; *vt*
(with fire flame) allumer
mettre feu à; (turn on light)
éclairer; *vi* ~ up
(illuminate)\éclairer;
(expression face) s'éclairer

lighten [LUY•tn] *vt* (weight
work) alléger; (brighten)
éclaircir

lighter [LUY•tur] *n* briquet M

lighthouse [LUYT•haus] *n*
phare M

lighting [LUY•ting] *n*
éclairage M

lightly [LUYT•lee] *adv*
légèrement

lightness [LUYT•nis] *n*
légèreté F

lightning [LUYT•ning] *n* éclair
M; foudre F

likable [LUY•ku•bl] *adj*
agréable

like [luyk] *n* préférence F goût
M; ~s *npl*\ préférences *fpl*
goûts *mpl*; *vt* aimer aimer
bien; *prep* comme; look
~\ressembler

likely [LUYK•lee] *adj* probable;
risquer de faire qqch

likeness [LUYK•nis] *n*
ressemblence F

likewise [LUYK•wuyz] *adv* de
même

liking [LUY•king] *n* affection F; goût M de qqch

limb [lim] *n* (arm leg) membre M; (of tree) branche F

limbo [LIM•bo] *npl* limbes M

lime [luym] *n* (fruit) lime F; (mineral) chaux F

limelight [LUYM•luyt] *n* au premier plan

limit [LI•mit] *n* limite F; *vt* limiter

limitation [LI•mi•TAI•shn] *n* limitation F

limousine [LI•mu•ZEEN] *n* limousine F

limp *adj* mou (molle); *n* boiter; *vi* boiter

line [luyn] *n* ligne; (of people) file F queue F; (of poem) vers M; (row) rangée F; (of string rope) corde F; (for fishing) ligne F; faire la queue; *vt* (box) tapisser; (clothes) doubler; *vt* aligner; *vi* faire la queue

linen [LI•nun] *n* lin M; (sheets napkins etc) linge F

linger [LING•gur] *vi* traîner; (persist) persister

lingerie [LAHN•zhu•RAI] *n* sous-vêtements; lingerie MF

lingo [LING•go] *n* jargon M

linguistics [ling•GWI•stiks] *n* linguistique F

lining [LUY•ning] *n* doublure F

link [lingk] *n* (of chain) maillon M; (connection) lien M; *vt* relier lier

lint [lint] *n* charpie F

lion [LUY•un] *n* lion M

lioness [LUY•u•nes] *n* lionne F

lip *n* lèvre F; (of container) rebord M

lip-read [LIP•reed] *vt* lire sur les lèvres

lipstick [LIP•stik] *n* rouge M à lèvres

liquid [LI•kwid] *adj n* liquide M

liquidate [LI•kwi•DAIT] *vt* liquider

liquor [LI•kur] *n* spiritueux M alcool M

list *n* liste F; *vt* faire la liste de; (enumerate) énumérer

listen [LI•sn] *vi* écouter; écouter qqn/qqch

listener [LI•su•nur] *n* auditeur M

literal [LI•tu•rl] *adj* littéral

literary [LI•tu•RE•ree] *adj* littéraire

literature [LI•tu•ru•CHUR] *n* littérature F

litigation [LI•ti•GAI•shn] *n* litige M

litter [LI•tur] *n* détritus *mpl;* ordures *fpl;* (for cat) portée F

little [LI•tl] *adj* petit; (small amount) peu de; *adv* peu un peu; *n* a ~ un peu

live [adj. luyv v. liv] *adj* vivant; (performance) en public; (tv radio) en direct; *vi* vivre; (reside) habiter; vivre de

lively [LUYV•lee] *adj* vif animé

liven [LUY•vn] *vt* animer

liver [LI•vur] *n* foie M

livery [LI•vu•ree] *n* livrée F

livestock [LUYV•stahk] *n* bétail M

livid [LI•vid] *adj* furieux

living [LI•ving] *adj* vivant; *n* gagner sa vie; faire dans la vie

lizard [LI•zurd] *n* lézard M

load [lod] *n* (burden; cargo; etc) charge F chargement M; (a lot) des tas *mpl* de; *vt* charger

loaf [lof] *n* pain; *vi* traîner M

loafer [LO•fur] *n* mocassin M

loan [lon] *n* prêt M; *vt* prêter

loathe [loth] *vt* détester

loathsome [LOTH•sum] *adj* répugnant

lobby [LAH•bee] *n* (of building) hall M; (political) lobby M; groupe M de pression; *vt* faire pression sur

lobe [lob] *n* lobe M

lobster [LAHB•stur] *n* homard M

local [LO•kl] *adj* local

locality [lo•KA•li•tee] *n* région F; endroit M

locate [LO•kait] *vt* trouver; se trouver être situé

location [lo•KAI•shn] *n* emplacement M; (film) en extérieur

lock [lahk] *n* serrure F; (of hair) mèche F; (of canal) écluse F; *vt* fermer à clef; *vi* (wheels) *n* bloquer; ~ in*vt* enfermer; ~ out\ *vt* enfermer dehors; ~ up*vt* enfermer; (imprison) mettre en prison

locomotive [LO•ku•MO•tiv] *n* locomotive F

locust [LO•kust] *n* locuste F

lodge [lahj] *n* pavillon M; (club) loge F; *vt* porter plainte; *vi* loger chez

lodger [LAH•jur] *n* locataire MF

lodgings [LAH•jingz] *n* chambre

loft [lauft] *n* grenier M

log [lahg] *n* bûche F; (book – of ship) journal M de bord; (– of plane) carnet M de vol

logic [LAH•jik] *n* logique F

logical [LAH•ji•kl] *adj* logique

logo [LO•go] *n* logo M

loin *n* filet M

loiter [LOI•tur] *vi* traîner

lollipop [LAH•lee•PAHP] *n* sucette F

London [LUHN•dn] *n* Londres

lone [lon] *adj* solitaire

loneliness [LON•lee•nis] *n* solitude F

lonely [LON•lee] *adj* solitaire seul

long [laung] *adj* long; quelle est la longeur de . . .?; (duration) quelle est la durée de . . .?; long de 2 miles; qui dure 2 heures; *adv* longtemps; ne . . . plus; *conj* pourvu que; *vi* avoir très envie de faire qqch; *vt* désirer

longitude [LAUN•ji•TOOD] *n* longitude F

look [luk] *n* regard; jeter un regard; (appearance) air M aspect M; *vi* regarder; (search) chercher; (seem) sembler; *vt* regarder; *vt* ressembler; *vt* chercher; *vt* s'occuper de; attendre avec impatience; *vt* admirer; *vt* dédaigner; *vt* faire attention à; (person) guetter

loom *n* métier M à tisser; *vi* surgir

loony [LOO•nee] *adj* cinglé

loop *n* boucle

loophole [LOOP•houl] *n* échappatoire F

loose [loos] *adj* (screw assembly) desserré; (clothes) ample; (rocks pole etc) branlant; (sexually) facile; (lifestyle) dissolu; (translation) approximatif

loosely [LOOS•lee] *adv* approximativement; (not tightly) sans serrer

loosen [LOO•sn] *vt* deserrer; défaire; délier; *vi* se deserrer; se défaire; se délier

loot *n* butin M; *vt* piller

lord [laurd] *n* seigneur M; le Seigneur

lore [laur] *n* traditions

lose [looz] *vt* perdre; (pursuers) semer; *vi* perdre; be/get ~ se\perdre

loss [laus] *n* perte F; être perplexe

lost [laust] *adj* perdu; get ~!

lot [laht] *n* beaucoup (de); (destiny) sort M; (land) terrain; (for parking) parking M

lotion [LO•shn] *n* lotion F

loud *adj* bruyant; (clothes) voyant; *adv* (speak) fort

loudspeaker [LOUD•SPEE•kur] *n* haut-parleur M

lounge [lounj] *n* salon M; *vi* se prélasser

louse [lous] *n* pou M

lout [lout] *n* rustre M

lovable [LUH•vu•bl] *adj* adorable

love [luhv] *n* amour M; être amoureux de; tomber amoureux de; faire l'amour; *vt* aimer

love affair *n* liaison F

lovely [LUHV•lee] *adj* charmant; séduisant

lover [LUH•vur] *n* amant M; (of sports; nature; etc) amoureux M

low [lo] *adj* bas; (collar) décolleté; (depressed) déprimé; *adv* bas

lower [LO•ur] *adj* plus bas; *vt* abaisser; baisser

lowly [LO•lee] *adj* humble modeste

loyal [LOI•ul] *adj* loyal

loyalty [LOI•ul•tee] *n* loyauté F

lubricant [LOO•bri•kunt] *n* lubrifiant M

lubricate [LOO•bri•KAIT] *vt* lubrifier

lucid [LOO•sid] *adj* lucide

luck [luhk] *n* chance F; malchance F; bonne chance!

luckily [LUH•ku•lee] *adv* heureusement

lucky [LUH•kee] *adj* avoir de la chance; (fortunate) heureux; (charm etc) qui porte bonheur

ludicrous [LOO•di•krus] *adj* absurde

lug [luhg] *vt* traîner

luggage [LUH•gij] *npl* bagages M

lukewarm [LOOK•WAURM] *adj* tiède

lull [luhl] *n* (in storm) accalmie F; (in conversation) arrêt M; *vt* (baby) bercer

lullaby [LUH•lu•BUY] *n* berceuse F

lumber [LUHM•bur] *n* bois M de charpente

lumberjack [LUHM•bur•JAK] *n* bûcheron M

luminous [LOO•mi•nus] *adj* lumineux

lump [luhmp] *n* morceau M; (in sauce) grumeau M; (on skin) grosseur F; *vt* ~ together\réunir

lunar [LOO•nur] *adj* lunaire

lunatic [LOO•nu•TIK] *n* fou M (folle)

lunch [luhnch] *n* déjeuner M; *vi* déjeuner

lunch hour *n* pause F de midi

lung [luhng] *n* poumon M

lunge [luhnj] *vi* s'elancer sur

lurch [lurch] *n* écart M brusque; (of car) embardée F; *vi* tituber

lure [loour] *n* appât M; *vt* persuader; attirer par la ruse

lurid [LU•rid] *adj* affreux

lurk [lurk] *vi* se cacher

luscious [LUH•shs] *adj* succulent; (sexually) appétissant

lust [luhst] *n* désir M; *vt* convoiter; désirer

luster [LUH•stur] *n* lustre M brillant M

luxurious [luhg•ZHU•ree•us] *adj* luxueux

luxury [LUHK•shu•ree] *adj* de luxe; *n* luxe M

lying [LUY•ing] *npl* mensonges F

lynch [linch] *vt* lyncher

lyric [LEEU•rik] *adj* lyrique

lyrical [LEEU•ri•kl] *adj* lyrique

lyrics [LEEU•riks] *npl* paroles F

M

macaroni [MA•ku•RO•nee] *n* macaroni M

machete [mu•SHE•tee] *n* machette F

machine [mu•SHEEN] *n* machine F

machine gun *n* mitrailleuse F

machinery [mu•SHEE•nu•ree] *n* machinerie F: (parts of) mécanisme M

mackerel [MA•krul] *n* maquereau M

mad *adj* furieux fâché; (insane) fou; ~ about\fou de; go ~\devenir fou

madam [MU•dam] *n* madame F; (unmarried) mademoiselle F

madden [MA•dn] *vt* exaspérer; rendre fou

madly [MAD•lee] *adv* follement; follement amoureux de

madman [MAD•man] *n* fou M

madness [MAD•nis] *n* folie F

magazine [MA•gu•ZEEN] *n* revue F

magic [MA•jik] *adj* magique enchanté; *n* magie F; enchantement M

magical [MA•ji•kl] *adj* magique; enchanté

magician [ma•JI•shn] *n* magicien

magistrate [MA•ji•STRAIT] *n* magistrat M; juge M

magnet [MAG•nit] *n* aimant M

magnetic [mag•NE•tik] *adj* magnétique

magnificence [mag•NI•fi•suns] *n* magnificence F

magnificent [mag•NI•fi•sunt] *adj* magnifique

magnify [MAG•ni•FUY] *vt* grossir

magnifying glass [MAG•ni•FUY•ing ~] *n* loupe

magnitude [MAG•ni•TOOD] *n* ampleur F; grandeur F

mahogany [mu•HAH•gu•nee] *n* acajou M

maid [maid] *n* domestique F

maiden name [MAI•dn ~] *n* nom M de jeune fille

mail [maiul] *n* courrier M; (service) poste F; *vt* poster; envoyer

mailbox [MAIUL•bahks] *n* boîte F aux lettres

mailman [MAIUL•man] *n* facteur M

maim [maim] *vt* estropier

main [main] *adj* principal; *n* (pipe) conduite; F principale

main course *n* plat M principal

mainland [MAIN•land] *n* continent

maintain [main•TAIN] *vt* maintenir

maintenance [MAIN•tu•nuns] *n* maintien M; (of machine etc) maintenance F

majestic [mu•JE•stik] *adj* majéstueux

majesty [MA•ji•stee] *n* majesté F; Sa Majesté le Roi; Sa Majesté la Reine

major [MAI•jur] *adj* majeur; *n* (of air force) commandant M; (of infantry) chef M de bataillon

majority [mu•JAU•ri•tee] *n* majorité F

make [maik] *vt* faire; fabriquer; *n* marque F; rendre qqn; faire faire qqch à qqn; prendre une decision; en or/bois

makeup [MAI•kuhp] *n* maquillage M

male [maiul] *adj* mâle; (sex) masculin; *n* mâle M

malice [MA•lis] *n* méchanceté F malice F

malicious [mu•LI•shus] *adj* méchant

malign [mu•LUYN] *vt* diffamer; calomnier

malignant [mu•LIG•nunt] *adj* malin -igne

mallet [MA•lit] *n* maillet M

malpractice [MAL•PRAK•tis] *n* faute F professionelle; négligence F

mammal [MA•ml] *n* mammifère M

mammoth [MA•muth] *adj* géant; *n* mammouth M

man [man] *n* homme M

manage [MA•nij] *vt* gérer; *vi* (cope) se débrouiller

management [MA•nij•munt] *n* administration F direction F; (maintenance) gestion F

manager [MA•ni•jur] *n* directeur M; (of hotel) gérant M

mandate [MAN•dait] *n* mandat M

mandatory [MAN•du•TAU•ree] *adj* obligatoire

mane [main] *n* crinière F

maneuver [mu•NOO•vur] *n* manœuvre F; *vt vi* manœuvrer

manhood [MAN•hud] *n* âge M d'homme

mania [MAI•nee•u] *n* manie F

manicure [MA•ni•KYUR] *n* manucure F

manifest [MA•ni•FEST] *adj* manifeste; *vt* manifester

manipulate [mu•NI•pyu•LAIT] *vt* manipuler

mankind [MAN•KUYND] *n* humanité F

manner [MA•nur] *n* manière F; (behavior) attitude F; ~s\ *npl* manières

manor [MA•nur] *n* manoir M

manpower [MAN•pouur] *n* main-d'œuvre F

mansion [MAN•shn] *n* château M

manslaughter [MAN•SLAU•tur] *n* homicide M involontaire

mantelpiece [MAN•tl•PEES] *n* cheminée F

manual [MA•nyoo•ul] *adj n* manuel M

manufacture [MA•nyu•FAK•chur] *n* fabrication F; *vt* fabriquer

manufacturer [MA•nyu•FAK•chu•rur] *n* fabricant M

manure [mu•NOOUR] *n* fumier

manuscript [MA•nyu•SKRIPT] *n* manuscrit M

many [ME•nee] *adj* beaucoup de; trop de; combien (de); autant de . . . que . . . ; autant de; *pron* beaucoup

map *n* carte F

maple [MAI•pl] *n* érable M

mar [mahr] *vt* gâter

marathon [MA•ru•THAHN] *n* marathon M

marble [MAHR•bl] *n* (stone) marbre M; (toy) bille M

march [mahrch] *n* marche F; *vi* marcher au pas

March [mahrch] *n* mars M

mare [maiur] *n* jument M

margarine [MAHR•ju•rin] *n* margarine F

margin [MAHR•jin] *n* marge F

marginal [MAHR•ji•nl] *adj* marginal

marigold [MA•ri•GOLD] *n* souci

marijuana [MA•ri•WAH•nu] *n* marijuana F

marinate [MA•ri•NAIT] *vt* faire mariner

marine [mu•REEN] *adj n* marine M

mark [mahrk] *n* marque F; (in school) note F; *vt* marquer; (exams etc) noter corriger

marker [MAHR•kur] *n* (pen) repère

market [MAHR•kit] *n* marché M; *vt* commercialiser

market value *n* valeur F marchande

marmalade [MAHR•mu•LAID] *n* confiture F d'oranges

maroon [mu•ROON] *adj* bordeaux

marriage [MA•rij] *n* mariage M

married [MA•reed] *adj* marié

marry [MA•ree] *vt* épouser; (subj: priest justice of the peace etc) marier; *vi* se marier

Mars [mahrz] *n* Mars F

marsh [mahrsh] *n* marais M marécage M

marshal [MAHR•shl] *n* maréchal M

marshy [MAHR•shee] *adj* marécageux

martial [MAHR•shl] *adj* martial

martyr [MAHR•tur] *n* martyr M; *vt* ma yriser

marvel [MAHR•vl] *n* merveille F; *vi* (at) s'émerveiller (de)

marvelous [MAHR•vu•lus] *adj* merveilleux

mascara [ma•SKA•ru] *n* mascara M

masculine [MA•skyu•lin] *adj* masculin

mash *vt* faire en purée

mask *n* masque M; *vt* masquer

mason [MAI•sn] *n* maçon

masquerade [MA•sku•RAID] *n* mascarade F; *vi* se faire passer pour

mass *n* masse F; (rel) messe F; *vi* se masser

massacre [MA•su•kr] *n* massacre M; *vt* massacrer

massage [mu•SAHZH] *n* massage M; *vt* masser

massive [MA•siv] *adj* massif

mast *n* mât M

master [MA•stur] *adj n* maître M; maîtriser

masterpiece [MA•stur•PEES] *n* chef-d'œuvre M

mat *n* (petit) tapis M; (at door) paillason M

match [mach] *n* allumette F; (game) match M; (equal) égal M; *vt* assortir; égaler; (go with) aller avec; *vi* s'assortir

mate [mait] *n* mâle M; femelle F; *vt* (animals) accoupler; *vi* s'accoupler

material [mu•TEEU•ree•ul] *adj* matériel; *n* matière F; (fabric) tissu M; (for article etc) natériaux *mpl*

materialist [mu•TEEU•ree•u•list] *n* matérialiste MF

materialistic [mu•TEEU•ree•u•LI•stik] *adj* matérialiste

maternal [mu•TUR•nl] *adj* maternel

mathematics [MA•thu•MA•tiks] *npl* mathématiques F

matriculation [mu•TRI•kyu•LAI•shn] *n* inscription F

matrimony [MA•tri•MO•nee] *n* marriage M

matrix [MAI•triks] *n* matrice F

matter [MA•tur] *n* matière F;
(subject) affaire F question F;
what's the ~?\qu'est-ce qu'il y
a?; *vi* importer; no ~
what\quoiqu'il arrive

mattress [MA•tris] *n* matelas M

mature [mu•CHOOUR] *adj*
mûr; *vt* mûrir

maturity [mu•CHOOU•ri•tee] *n*
maturité F

maximum [MAK•si•mum] *adj*
n maximum M

may [mai] modal v pouvoir;
puis-je . . .

May [mai] *n* mai M

mayonnaise [MAI•u•NAIZ] *n*
mayonnaise F

mayor [MAI•yur] *n* maire M

maze [maiz] *n* labyrinthe M

me [mee] *pers pron* (direct &
indirect) me; (emphatic; after
prep; in comparison) moi

meadow [ME•do] *n* pré M

meager [MEE•gr] *adj* maigre

meal [meeul] *n* repas M

mean [meen] *adj* mesquin
méchant; (average) moyen; *n*
(math) moyenne F; *vt* vouloir
dire; (intend) ~ to do\avoir
l'intention de faire; meant
for\destiné à

meaning [MEE•ning] *n* sens M
signification F

means [meenz] (way) moyen
M; *npl* (resources)
moyens M

meantime [MEEN•tuym] *adv*
pendant ce temps; en
attendant

meanwhile [MEEN•wuyul] *adv*
pendant ce temps

measles [MEE•zlz] *n*
rougeole F

measure [ME•zhur] *n* mesure
F; *vt vi* mesurer

measurement [ME•zhur•munt]
n mesure F

meat [meet] *n* viande F

meatball [MEET•baul] *n*
boulette F de viande

mechanic [mu•KA•nik] *n*
mécanicien M; *n* mécanique F

mechanical [mu•KA•ni•kl] *adj*
mécanique

mechanism [ME•ku•NI•zm] *n*
mécanisme M

medal [ME•dl] *n* médaille F

medallion [mu•DAHL•yun] *n*
médaillon M

meddle [ME•dl] *vi* se mêler de

media [MEE•dee•u] *npl*
médias M

mediate [MEE•dee•AIT] *vt*
servir de médiateur

mediator [MEE•dee•AI•tur] *n*
médiateur M

medical [ME•di•kl] *adj* médical

medicate [ME•di•KAIT] *vt*
médicamenter

medicine [ME•di•sin] *n*
médicine F; (drug)
médicament M

medieval [mi•DEE•vl] *adj*
médiéval

mediocre [MEE•dee•O•kr] *adj*
médiocre

meditate [ME•di•TAIT] *vi*
méditer qqch

medium [MEE•dee•um] *adj*
moyen; *n* (means) moyen M;
(psychic) médium

meek *adj* doux

meet *vt* rencontrer; (planned) retrouver; (for first time) faire la connaissance de; *vi* se rencontrer; se retrouver; (gather) se réunir

meeting [MEE•ting] *n* rencontre F; (of organization) réunion F; (appointment) rendez-vous M; (business) conférence F

megaphone [ME•gu•FON] *n* porte-voix M

melancholy [ME•lun•KAH•lee] *adj* mélancolique; *n* mélancolie F

mellow [ME•lo] *adj* doux; (taste) moelleux; *vi* s'adoucir

melody [ME•lu•dee] *n* mélodie F

melon [ME•lun] *n* melon M

melt *vt* faire fondre; *vi* fondre

member [MEM•bur] *n* membre

membership [MEM•bur•SHIP] *n* adhésion

memo [ME•mo] *n* note F

memoirs [MEM•wahrz] *npl* mémoires F

memorial [me•MAU•ree•ul] *adj* commemoratif; *n* mémorial M

memorize [ME•mu•RUYZ] *vt* apprendre par cœur

memory [ME•mu•ree] *n* mémoire F

menace [ME•nus] *n* menace F; *vt* menacer

menacing [ME•nu•sing] *adj* menaçant

mend *vt* réparer; (clothes) raccommoder

menial [MEEN•yul] *adj* servile

menopause [ME•nu•PAUZ] *n* ménopause F

menstruation [MEN•stroo•AI•shn] *n* menstruation F

mental [MEN•tl] *adj* mental

mentality [men•TA•li•tee] *n* mentalité F

mention [MEN•chn] *vt* mentionner

menu [ME•nyoo] *n* menu M carte F

mercenary [MUR•su•NE•ree] *adj n* mercenaire M

merchandise [MUR•chun•DUYS] *npl* marchandises F

merchant [MUR•chunt] *n* marchand M; négociant M

merciful [MUR•si•ful] *adj* miséricordiaux

merciless [MUR•si•lis] *adj* impitoyable; sans pitié

mercury [MUR•kyu•ree] *n* mercure M; Mercure F

mercy [MUR•see] *n* pitié F merci F; à la merci de

mere [meeur] *adj* simple

merely [MEEUR•lee] *adv* simplement

merge [murj] *vt* unir; (business) fusionner; *vi* se fondre; se fusionner; (roads) converger

merger [MUR•jur] *n* fusion F

merit [ME•rit] *n* mérite M; *vt* mériter

mermaid [MUR•maid] *n* sirène F

merry [ME•ree] *adj* gai; joyeux

merry-go-round [ME•ree•go•ROUND] *n* manège

mesh *n* maille F; filet M; *vi* (gears) s'engrener

mesmerize [MEZ•mu•RUYZ] *vt* hypnotiser

mess [mes] *n* gâchis M désordre M; (military) mess M; *vt* ~ up\gâcher; mettre en désordre

message [ME•sij] *n* message M

messenger [ME•sin•jur] *n* messager M

messy [ME•see] *adj* en désordre; sale

metal [ME•tl] *n* métal M

metallic [mu•TA•lik] *adj* métallique

metaphor [ME•tu•FAUR] *n* métaphore F

meteor [MEE•tee•ur] *n* météore M

meteorology [MEE•tee•u•RAH•lu•jee] *n* météorologie F

meter [MEE•tur] *n* compteur M; (unit of measure) mètre M

method [ME•thud] *n* méthode F

meticulous [mu•TI•kyu•lus] *adj* méticuleux

metric [ME•trik] *adj* métrique

metropolitan [ME•tru•PAH•li•tun] *adj* métropolitain

Mexican [MEK•si•kun] *adj* mexicain; *n* Mexicain M

Mexico [MEK•si•KO] *n* Mexique M

mice [myz] *npl* a mouse

microchip [MUY•cro•CHIP] *n* puce F

microphone [MUY•kru•FON] *n* microphone M

microscope [MUY•kru•SKOP] *n* microscope M

microscopic [MUY•kru•SKO•pik] *adj* microscopique M

microwave [MUY•kru•WAIV] *n* four M à micro-ondes M

mid *adj adv* à mi-chemin; mi-mars; *n* midi M; milieu m/cœur M de l'été

middle [MI•dl] *adj* du milieu; *n* milieu M centre M; au milieu

Middle Ages *npl* moyen-âge M

middle class *n* classe F moyenne bourgeoisie F

Middle East *n* Moyen-Orient M

midnight [MID•nuyt] *n* minuit M

midst [midst] *n* au milieu de; in the ~ of\en train de

midwife [MID•wuyf] *n* sage-femme F

might 1 [muyt] *modal v* c'est possible qu'il + *ind/fut/past;* il peut que j'aille; il peut-être veut

might 2 [muyt] *n* force F puissance F

mighty [MUY•tee] *adj* puissant

migraine [MUY•grain] *n* migraine F

migrant [MUY•grunt] *adj* (bird) migrateur; (person) migrant; (worker) saisonnier

migrate [MUY•grait] *vi* (bird) migrer; (person) émigrer

mild [muyuld] *adj* doux

mildew [MIL•doo] *n* moississure F

mile [muyul] *n* mile M

militant [MI•li•tunt] *adj n*
militant M

military [MI•li•TE•ree] *adj*
militaire; *npl* les militaires M

militia [mi•LI•shu] *n* milice F

milk [milk] *n* lait M; *vt* (cow)
traire

mill [mil] *n* moulin M; *vt*
moudre

millenium [mi•LE•nee•um] *n*
millénaire M

million [MIL•yun] *num* million
M; des milliers de

millionaire [MIL•yu•NAIUR] *n*
millionaire MF

mimic [MI•mik] *n* imitateur M;
vt imiter mimer

mince [mins] *vt* hacher

mind [muynd] *n* esprit M; *vt*
(take care of) s'occuper de;
(bother) cela vous dérange si;
I don't ~\ça m'est égal; don't
~ it\ne t'en fais pas

mindful [MUYND•ful] *adj*
soucieux; attentif

mine [muyn] *n* le mien (la
mienne) les miens (les
miennes); it's ~\c'est à moi; *n*
(quarry etc) mine F; *vt*
(substance) extraire; (area)
miner

mineral [MI•nu•rul] *adj n*
minéral M

mingle [MING•gl] *vi* (with) se
mêler (à)

miniature [MI•nu•CHUR] *adj n*
miniature F

minimize [MI•ni•MUYZ] *vt*
minimiser

minimum [MI•ni•mum] *adj n*
minimum M

mining [MUY•ning] *n*
exploitation F minière

minister [MI•ni•stur] *n* ministre
M; (rel) pasteur M; *vi* ~
to\subvenir à

ministry [MI•ni•stree] *n*
ministère M; (rel) pastorat M

mink [mingk] *n* vison M

minor [MUY•nur] *adj n*
mineur M

minority [muy•NAU•ri•tee] *n*
minorité F

mint *n* (plant) menthe F;
(candy) bonbon M à la
menthe; hôtel M de la
Monnaie; *vt* (coins) battre

minus [MUY•nus] *prep* moins;
adj négatif; *n* moins M

minute [*adj.* muy•NYOOT *n.*
MI•nit] *adj* miniscule minime;
n minute M

miracle [MI•ru•kl] *n* miracle M

miraculous [mi•RA•kyu•lus]
adj miraculeux M

mirage [mi•RAHZH] *n*
mirage M

mirror [MI•rur] *n* miroir M
glace F; *vt* refléter

misanthrope [mi•SAN•throp] *n*
misanthrope MF

misappropriation
[mis•U•PRO•pree•AI•shn] *n*
détournement M de fonds

misbehave [MIS•bee•HAIV] *vi*
se conduire mal

miscarriage [MIS•KA•rij] *n*
(medical) fausse couche F;
(law) erreur F judiciaire

miscellaneous
[MI•su•LAI•nee•us] *adj* divers

mischief [MIS•chif] *n* mal M;
dommage M; (of child) *npl;*
sottises F

mischievous [MIS•chi•vus] *adj*
malicieux; méchant; (child)
espiègle

misconception
[MIS•kun•SEP•shn] *vt*
conception F erronée

misconduct [mis•KAHN•duhkt]
n mauvaise conduite F

misconstrue [mis•KUN•stroo]
vt mal interpréter

miscount [mis•KOUNT] *vt vi*
mal compter

misdeed [mis•DEED] *n*
méfait M

misdemeanor
[MIS•du•MEE•nur] *n* délit M
infraction F

miser [MUY•zur] *n* avare MF

miserable [MIZ•ru•bl] *adj*
misérable; (unhappy)
malheureux

miserly [MUY•zur•lee] *adj*
avare

misery [MI•zu•ree] *n* misère F;
(sorrow) tristesse F

misfire [mis•FUYUR] *vi* rater

misfit [MIS•fit] *n* inadapté M

misfortune [MIS•FAUR•chun]
n malchance F

misgivings [MIS•GI•vingz] *npl*
doutes F; soupçons M

mishap [MIS•hap] *n*
mésaventure F

misinform [MIS•in•FAURM] *vt*
mal renseigner

misjudge [mis•JUHJ] *vt*
méjuger; (evaluate
incorrectly) mal évaluer

misleading [MIS•LEE•ding]
adj trompeur

misplace [mis•PLAIS] *vt* égarer

misprint [MIS•print] *n* faute F
d'impression

Miss [mis] *n* Mademoiselle F

miss [mis] *vt* manquer rater;
(long for) I ~ it\cela me
manque; *vi* manquer

missile [MI•sul] *n* missile M

missing [MI•sing] *adj* (lost)
égaré; (absent) absent
manquant

mission [MI•shn] *n* mission F

missionary [MI•shu•NE•ree] *n*
missionaire MF

misspell [mis•SPEL] *vt* mal
orthographier

mist *n* brume F

mistake [mi•STAIK] *n* erreur F;
par erreur; se tromper; *vt*
prendre pour

mistaken [mi•STAI•kn] *adj*
érroné; se tromper

mister [MI•stur] *n* Monsieur M

mistreat [mis•TREET] *vt*
maltraiter

mistress [MI•strus] *n*
maîtresse F

mistrust [mis•TRUHST] *n*
méfiance F; *vt* se méfier de

misty [MI•stee] *adj* brumeux

misunderstand
[mis•UHN•dur•STAND] *vt*
mal comprendre

misunderstanding
[mis•UHN•dur•STAN•ding] *n*
malentendu M

misuse [*n.* mis•YOOS *v.*
mis•YOOZ] *n* mauvais emploi

M; (of authority etc) abus M;
vt mal employer; abuser de

mitigating [MI•ti•GAI•ting] *adj*
atténuant

mitten [MI•tn] *n* moufle F

mix [miks] *vt* mélanger; *vi* se
mélanger; *n* mélange M; ~
up*vt* confondre

mixture [MIKS•chur] *n*
mélange M

moan [mon] *n* gémissement M;
vi gémir

moat [mot] *n* fossé douves M
npl`

mob [mahb] *n* foule F; la
populace F

mobile [MO•bl] *adj* mobile

mobilize [MO•bu•LUYZ] *vt*
mobiliser

mock [mahk] *vt* se moquer de

mockery [MAH•ku•ree] *n*
moquerie F raillerie

mode [mod] *n* mode M

model [MAH•dl] *adj* modèle; *n*
modèle M; mannequin M; *vt*
modeler

moderate [*adj. n.* MAH•du•rit
v. MAH•du•RAIT] *adj n*
modéré M; *vt* modérer; *vi* se
modérer

moderation
[MAH•du•RAI•shn] *n* avec
modération

modern [MAH•durn] *adj*
moderne

modernize [MAH•dur•NUYZ]
vt moderniser

modest [MAH•dist] *adj*
modeste

modesty [MAH•di•stee] *n*
modestie F

modify [MAH•di•FUY] *vt*
modifier

moist *adj* moite; humide

moisten [MOI•sn] *vt* humecter

moisture [MOIS•chur] *n*
humidité F

molar [MO•lur] *n* molaire F

molasses [mu•LA•sis] *n*
mélasse F

mold *n* moisissure F; (shape)
moule M; *vt* mouler

mole [mol] *n* (animal) taupe F;
(on skin) grain M de beauté

molest [mu•LEST] *vt* (bother)
molester

mollusk [MAH•lusk] *n*
mollusque M

molten [MOL•tn] *adj* fondu

mcment [MO•munt] *n*
moment M

momentary [MO•mun•TE•ree]
adj momentané

momentous [mo•MEN•tus] *adj*
important; capital

monarch [MAH•nahrk] *n*
monarque M

monarchy [MAH•nahr•kee] *n*
monarchie F

monastery [MAH•nu•STE•ree]
n monastère M

Monday [MUHN•dai] *n*
lundi M

monetary [MAH•nu•TE•ree]
adj monétaire

money [MUH•nee] *n* argent;
gagner de l'argent M

mongrel [MAHN•grul] *n* (dog)
bâtard

monk [muhngk] *n* moine M

monkey [MUHNG•kee] *n*
singe M

monologue [MAH•nu•LAHG]
n monologue M

monopolize
[mu•NAH•pu•LUYZ] *vt*
monopoliser

monopoly [mu•NAH•pu•lee] *n*
monopole M

monotone [MAH•nu•TON] *n*
ton M; monocorde M

monotonous [mu•NAH•tu•nus]
adj monotone

monotony [mu•NAH•tu•nee] *n*
monotonie

monsoon [mahn•SOON] *n*
mousson M

monster [MAHN•stur] *n*
monstre M

monstrosity
[mahn•STRAH•si•tee] *n*
monstruosité F

monstrous [MAHN•strus] *adj*
monstrueux F

month [muhnth] *n* mois

monthly [MUHNTH•lee] *adj n*
mensuel M; *adv*
mensuellement

monument [MAH•nyu•munt] *n*
monument

monumental
[MAH•nyu•MEN•tl] *adj*
monumental

moo *n* meuglement M; *vi*
meugler; beugler

mood *n* humeur F; in a good
~\de bonne humeur

moody [MOO•dee] *adj* de
mauvaise humeur

moon *n* lune F

moonlight [MOON•luyt] *n*
clair M de lune; *vi* travailler
de noir

moor [moour] *n* lande F
bruyère F

Moor [moour] *n* Maure M

mop [mahp] *n* balai M à laver;
vt éponger; laver; (one's
brow) essuyer

mope [mop] *vi* avoir le cafard

moral [MAU•rul] *adj* moral; *n*
morale F; ~s\npl moralité F

morale [mau•RAL] *n* moral M

morality [mu•RA•li•tee] *n*
moralité F

morbid [MAUR•bid] *adj*
morbide

more [maur] *adj* plus (de)
davantage; encore de qqch;
adv plus davantage; encore
une fois; plus que

moreover [mau•RO•vur] *adv* de
plus

morgue [maurg] *n* morgue F

morning [MAUR•ning] *n* matin
M; matinée F; le matin;
bonjour

Morocco [mu•RAH•ko] *n*
Maroc M

moron [MAU•rahn] *n* minus M
crétin M

morsel [MAUR•sl] *n*
morceau M

mortal [MAUR•tl] *adj n*
mortel M

mortality [maur•TA•li•tee] *n*
mortalité F

mortar [MAUR•tur] *n* mortier

mortgage [MAUR•gij] *n*
hypothèque F; *vt* hypothèquer

mortify [MAUR•ti•FUY] *vt*
mortifier

mosaic [mo•ZAI•ik] *n*
mosaïque F

Moscow [MAH•skou] *n*
Moscou

mosque [mahsk] *n* mosquée F

mosquito [mu•SKEE•to] *n*
moustique

moss [maus] *n* mousse F

most *adj* la plupart de; le plus
de; *pron* la plupart; *adv* le
plus

mostly [MOST•lee] *adv* surtout
por la plupart

moth [mauth] *n* papillon M de
nuit; (in clothes) mite F

mother [MUH•thur] *n* mère F;
vt dorloter

mother-in-law
[MUH•thur•in•LAU] *n*
belle-mère F

motherhood [MUH•thur•HUD]
n maternité F

motherly [MUH•thur•lee] *adj*
maternel

motif [mo•TEEF] *n* motif

motion [MO•shn] *n* mouvement
M; (proposal) motion F; *vt* ~
to\faire signe à

motivate [MO•ti•VAIT] *vt*
motiver

motivation [MO•ti•VAI•shn] *n*
motivation F

motive [MO•tiv] *n* motif M

motor [MO•tur] *n* moteur F

motorboat [MO•tur•BOT] *n*
canot M automobile

motorcycle [MO•tur•SUY•kl] *n*
moto M

motto [MAH•to] *n* devise F

mound *n* tertre M monticule M;
(of clothes; garbage; etc) tas M

mount *n* (structure) monture F;
(hill) mont M; (of machine)

support M; (of painting)
carton M de montage; *vt*
monter (sur); *vi* monter

mountain [MOUN•tn] *n*
montagne F

mountaineer
[MOUN•tu•NEEUR] *n*
alpiniste MF

mountainous [MOUN•tu•nus]
adj montaigneux

mourn [maurn] *vt* pleurer

mourning [MAUR•ning] *n*
deuil M; in ~\en deuil M

mouse [mous] *n* souris M

mousetrap [MOUS•trap] *n*
souricière F

mousse [moos] *n* mousse F

moustache [MUH•stash] *n*
moustache F

mouth *n* bouche F; (of animal)
gueule F; (of river)
embouchure F

mouthful [mouth•ful] *n*
bouchée F

mouthwash [MOUTH•wahsh]
n eau F dentifrice

movable [MOO•vu•bl] *adj*
mobile

move [moov] *n* mouvement M;
(change of residence)
déménagement M; (in game)
coup M; *vt* bouger déplacer;
(feelings) émouvoir; *vi* bouger
remuer se déplacer; (change
residence) déménager; ~ in\
emménager; ~ out\déménager;
~ over\se pousser; ~ up\
avancer; ~ away\ s'éloigner; ~
back\reculer

movement [MOOV•munt] *n*
mouvement M

movie [MOO•vee] *n* film M; le cinéma M

moving [MOO•ving] *adj* (touching) émouvant

mow [mo] *vt* tondre; faucher

much [muhch] *adj* beaucoup de; trop de; how ~\ combien (de); as ~\ autant de . . . que . . . ; autant de; *pron* beaucoup

mucous [MYOO•kus] *n* mucus M

mud [muhd] *n* boue F

muddle [MUH•dl] *n* fouillis M désordre M; *vt* embrouiller

muddy [MUH•dee] *adj* boueux

muffin [MUH•fin] *n* muffin M

muffle [MUH•fl] *vt* (sound) assourdir; (face) emmitoufler

mug [muhg] *n* tasse F; (face expression) gueule F; *vt* agresser

mule [myooul] *n* mule F

multiple [MUHL•ti•pl] *adj n* multiple M

multiplication [MUHL•ti•pli•KAI•shn] *n* multiplication F

multiply [MUHL•ti•PLUY] *vt* multiplier; *vi* se multiplier

multitude [MUHL•ti•TOOD] *n* multitude F

mumble [MUHM•bl] *vt vi* marmotter

mummy [MUH•mee] *n* momie F

mumps [muhmps] *npl* oreillons M

munch [muhnch] *vt vi* croquer; mâcher

mundane [muhn•DAIN] *adj* banal

municipal [myoo•NI•si•pl] *adj* municipal

municipality [myoo•NI•si•PA•li•tee] *n* municipalité

mural [MYOOU•rul] *n* peinture F murale

murder [MUR•dur] *n* meurtre F; *vt* assassiner

murderer [MUR•du•rur] *n* meurtrier M assassin M

murderous [MUR•du•rus] *adj* meurtrier

murky [MUR•kee] *adj* ténébreux obscur

murmur [MUR•mur] *n* murmure M; *vt vi* murmurer

muscle [MUH•sl] *n* muscle M

muscular [MUH•skyu•lur] *adj* musculaire; (person) musclé

muse [myooz] *n* muse F; *vi* méditer

museum [myoo•ZEE•um] *n* musée M

mushroom [MUHSH•rum] *n* champignon

music [MYOO•zik] *n* musique F

musical [MYOO•zi•kl] *adj* musical; *n* comédie F musicale F

musician [myoo•ZI•shn] *n* musicien

Muslim [MUHZ•lim] *adj* musulman; *n* Musulman M

mussel [MUH•sl] *n* moule F

must [muhst] *modal v* devoir I ~\ il me faut *or* il faut que je

mustache [MUH•stash] *n* a moustache M

mustard [MUH•sturd] *n* moutarde F

muster [MUH•stur] *vt*
rassembler

musty [MUH•stee] *adj* de
moisi

mute [myoot] *adj n* muet M

mutilate [MYOO•ti•LAIT] *vt*
mutiler

mutiny [MYOO•ti•nee] *n*
mutinerie F

mutter [MUH•tur] *vt vi*
marmonner

mutton [MUH•tn] *n*
mouton M

mutual [MYOO•choo•ul]
adj mutuel; (friend etc)
commun

muzzle [MUH•zl] *n* museau M;
vt museler

my [muy] *poss adj* mon (ma)
mes

myself [muy•SELF] *pron*
(reflexive) me; (after prep)
moi; (emphatic) moi-même

mysterious [mi•STEEU•ree•us]
adj mystérieux

mystery [MI•stu•ree] *n*
mystère M

mystic [MI•stik] *n*
mystique M

mystical [MI•sti•kl] *adj*
mystique

myth [mith] *n* mythe M

mythical [MI•thi•kl] *adj*
mythique F

mythology [mi•THAH•lu•jee]
n mythologie F

N

nab *vt* attraper; pincer

nag *vt* gronder; harceler

nail [naiul] *n* clou M; (of finger)
ongle M; *vt* clouer; ~ in\
enfoncer

naive [nuy•EEV] *adj* naïf

naked [NAI•kid] *adj* nu

nakedness [NAI•kid•nis] *n*
nudité F

name [naim] *n* nom M;
comment vous appelez-vous?;
à son nom; *vt* nommer

namely [NAIM•lee] *adv* à
savoir

nap *n* petit somme M; faire un
petit somme

napkin [NAP•kin] *n* serviette F

narcotic [nahr•KAH•tik] *adj n*
narcotique M

narrate [NA•rait] *vt* raconter;
narrer

narration [na•RAI•shn] *n*
narration

narrative [NA•ru•tiv] *adj*
narratif; *n* récit M

narrator [na•RAI•tur] *n*
narrateur M

narrow [NA•ro] *adj* étroit; *vi* se
rétrécir

narrow-minded
[NAI•row•MUYN•did] *adj*
borné

nasal [NAI•zl] *adj* nasal

nasturtium [nu•STUR•shum] *n* capucine F

nasty [NA•stee] *adj* méchant; (unpleasant) désagréable mauvais; (disgusting) dégoûtant

nation [NAI•shn] *n* nation F

national [NA•shu•nl] *adj* national

nationality [NA•shu•NA•li•tee] *n* nationalalité F

nationalize [NA•shu•nu•LUYZ] *vt* nationaliser

native [NAI•tiv] *adj* indigène; originaire de; (common to area country) natal; (language) maternel; *n* autochtone MF; (in colonized land) indigène MF

Nativity [nu•TI•vi•tee] *n* Nativité F

natural [NA•chrul] *adj* naturel

naturalize [NA•chru•LUYZ] *vt* naturaliser

naturally [NA•chru•lee] *adv* naturellement

nature [NA•chur] *n* nature; caractère F

naughty [NAU•tee] *adj* (child) vilain; (book etc) risqué

nausea [NAU•zee•u] *n* nausée F

nauseate [NAU•zee•AIT] *vt* écœurer; dégoûter

nauseous [NAU•shus] *adj* nauséeux

naval [NAI•vl] *adj* naval

navel [NAI•vl] *n* nombril

navigate [NA•vi•GAIT] *vt* (plane) piloter; (boat) gouverner; *vi* naviguer

navigation [NA•vi•GAI•shn] *n* navigation

navigator [NA•vi•GAI•tur] *n* navigateur

navy [NAI•vee] *adj* (color) bleu marine; *n* marine F

near [neeur] *adj* proche; *adv* près; *prep* près de; come ~\ s'approcher; *vt* approcher de

nearsighted [NEEUR•suy•tid] *adj* myope

nearby [neeur•BUY] *adj* proche; *adv* près

nearly [NEEUR•lee] *adv* presque

neat [neet] *adj* net; en ordre; soigné

necessary [NE•su•SE•ree] *adj* nécessaire

necessity [nu•SE•si•tee] *n* nécessité F

neck [nek] *n* cou M; (of bottle) col M goulot M; (of shirt) encolure F

need *n* besoin M; *vt* avoir besoin de

needle [NEE•dl] *n* aiguille F; *vt* asticoter

needless [NEED•lis] *adj* inutile

needy [NEE•dee] *adj* nécessiteux

negative [NE•gu•tiv] *adj* négatif; *n* (of photo) négatif M; (grammar) négation F

neglect [ni•GLEKT] *n* négligence F; *vt* négliger

negligence [NE•gli•juns] *n* négligence F

negligent [NE•gli•junt] *adj*
négligent

negotiate [ni•GO•shee•AIT] *vt*
vi négocier

negotiation
[ni•GO•shee•AI•shn] *n*
négociation F

Negro [NEE•gro] *adj n* nègre M

neigh [nai] *n* hennissement M;
vi hennir

neighbor [NAI•bur] *n* voisin M

neighborhood [NAI•bur•HUD]
n voisinage M; quartier M

neither [NEE•thur] *adj* ni; ni
l'un ni l'autre; *adv*
ni; . . . ni . . . ni . . . ; *conj* non
plus; moi non plus; *pron* ni
l'un ni l'autre; aucun

nephew [NE•fyoo] *n* neveu M

Neptune [NEP•toon] *n*
Neptune F

nerve [nurv] *n* nerf M;
(courage) courage M; get on
one's ~s\taper sur les nerfs de
qqn; have ~\avoir le trac

nervous [NUR•vus] *adj*
nerveux; (apprehensive)
inquiet

nest *n* nid M; *vi* nicher

net *adj* net; *n* filet M; *vt* (fish
etc) prendre au filet

Netherlands [NE•thur•lundz]
npl Pays-Bas *mpl*

nettle [NE•tl] *n* ortie F

network [NET•wurk] *n*
réseau M

neurosis [nu•RO•sis] *n*
névrose F

neurotic [nu•RAH•tik] *adj n*
névrosé M

neuter [NOO•tur] *adj* neutre; *vt*
châtrer

neutral [NOO•trul] *adj* neutre;
n (gear) poit M mort

neutrality [noo•TRA•li•tee] *n*
neutralité F

neutralize [NOO•tru•LUYZ] *vt*
neutraliser

never [NE•vr] *adv* (ne . . .)
jamais

nevertheless [NE•vur•thu•LES]
adv néanmoins

new [noo] *adj* nouveau; (brand
new) neuf

New Year *n* nouvel an M;
bonne année; jour M de l'an;
la Saint-Sylvestre F

newly [NOO•lee] *adv*
nouvellement

news [nooz] *npl* nouvelle(s) F;
(show) informations F

newscast [NOOZ•kast] *n*
informations *fpl*

newsletter [NOOZ•le•tur] *n*
bulletin M

newspaper [NOOZ•pai•pur] *n*
journal M

next [nekst] *adj* prochain
suivant; *adv* ensuite; *prep* ~
to\ à côté de; excl ~!\ au
suivant!

next-door [NEXT•DOR] *adj*
voisin; *adv* à côté

nibble [NI•bl] *vt* grignoter

nice [nuys] *adj* (person) gentil;
sympathique; (day event etc)
agréable beau; bon

nicely [NUYS•lee] *adv*
gentiment; agréablement;
bien

niche [nich] *n* niche F

nick [nik] *n* (cut; scratch)
entaille F; *vt* entailler; in the
~ of time\ à point nommé

nickname [NIK•naim] *n*
surnom M; *vt* surnommer

nicotine [NI•ku•TEEN] *n*
nicotine F

niece [nees] *n* nièce F

night [nuyt] *n* nuit F; at ~\ la
nuit; (evening) soir

nightclub [NUYT•kluhb] *n*
boîte F de nuit

nightfall [NUYT•faul] *n*
tombée F du jour

nightgown [NUYT•goun] *n*
chemise F de nuit

nightingale [NUY•tin•GAIUL]
n rossignol M

nightly [NUYT•lee] *adj* de
toutes le nuits/tous les soirs;
adv toutes les nuits/tous les
soirs

nightmare [NUYT•maiur] *n*
cauchemar M

nimble [NIM•bl] *adj* agile

nine [nuyn] *num* neuf

nineteen [nuyn•TEEN] *num*
dix-neuf

ninety [NUYN•tee] *num*
quatre-vingts-dix

ninth [nuynth] *num* neuvième

nipple [NI•pl] *n* mamelon M;
(of bottle) tétine F

nitrogen [NUY•tru•jun] *n*
azote M

no *adv* non; non merci; (in
comparison) pas plus grand;
adj aucun pas de; défense de
fumer; *n* non M

nobility [no•BI•li•tee] *n*
noblesse F

noble [NO•bl] *adj* noble

nobody [NO•bu•dee] *pron*
personne (ne) F; (as object)
ne . . . personne; *n* zéro M

nocturnal [nahk•TUR•nl] *adj*
nocturne

nod [nahd] *n* signe M de tête; *vi*
faire un signe de tête; (in
affirmation) faire un signe de
tête que oui

noise [noiz] *n* bruit M

noisy [NOY•zee] *adj* bruyant

nominal [NAH•mi•nul] *adj*
nominal; (in name) de nom

nominate [NAH•mi•NAIT] *vt*
proposer; (appoint elect)
nommer

nomination
[NAH•mi•NAI•shn] *n*
proposition F; nomination F

nonchalant
[NAHN•shu•LAHNT] *adj*
nonchalant

nonconformist
[NAHN•kun•FAUR•mist] *adj*
n non-conformiste MF

none [nuhn] *pron adj* aucun;
(person) personne nul

nonentity [NAHN•EN•ti•tee] *n*
nullité F zéro M

nonetheless [NUHN•thu•LES]
adv néanmoins

nonfiction [nahn•FIK•shn] *n*
ouvrages romanesques M

nonsense [NAHN•sens] *npl*
absurdités F bêtises F
sottises F

nonsmoker [NAHN•SMO•kur]
n non-fumeur M

nonstop [NAHN•STAHP] *adj*
sans arrêt; (trip) direct; *adv*
sans arrêt M

noodles [NOO•dlz] *npl* nouilles *fpl*

noon *n* midi M

noose [noos] *n* nœud M coulant; (of hangman) corde F

nor [naur] *conj* ni; moi non plus

norm [naurm] *n* norme F

normal [NAUR•ml] *adj* normal

normally [NAUR•mu•lee] *adv* normalement

north [naurth] *adj* nord du nord; *adv* au nord vers le nord; *n* nord; ~-east/-west\ *n* nord-est/-ouest M; *adv* vers e/au nord-est/-ouest

North America *n* Amérique F du Nord

North Pole *n* pôle M Nord

northern [NAUR•thurn] *adj* du nord

Northern Ireland *n* Irlande F du Nord

northward(s) [NAURTH•wurd(z)] *adv* vers le nord

Norwegian [naur•WEE•jun] *adj* norvègien; *n* Norvègien M; (language) norvègien M

Norway [NAUR•wai] *n* Norvège F

nose [noz] *n* nez M

nostalgia [nah•STAL•ju] *n* nostalgie F

nostril [NAH•stril] *n* narine F

nosy [NO•zee] *adj* fouinard

not [naht] *adv* pas; ne . . . pas; pas encore; pas du tout; j'espère que non

notable [NO•tu•bl] *adj* notable

notably [NO•tu•blee] *adv* notamment

notary [NO•tu•ree] *n* notaire M

notch [nahch] *n* entaille F; encoche F; (of belt) cran M

note [not] *n* note F; (brief letter) mot M; (currency) billet M; *vt* remarquer noter

notebook [NOT•buk] *n* cahier

noteworthy [NOT•wur•thee] *adj* remarquable

nothing [NUH•thing] *pron* rien (ne); (as object) ne . . . rien; ~ interesting\ rien d'interésant; ~ but\ rien que

notice [NO•tis] *n* avis M; (in news) annonce F; *vt* remarquer s'apercevoir de

noticeable [NO•ti•su•bl] *adj* perceptible visible

notify [NO•ti•FUY] *vt* aviser; avertir

notion [NO•shn] *n* idée F notion F

notoriety [NO•tu•RUY•u•tee] *n* notoriété

notorious [no•TAU•ree•us] *adj* notoire

notwithstanding [NAHT•with•STAN•ding] *adv* néanmoins; *prep* malgré

noun *n* nom M

nourish [NU•rish] *vt* nourrir

nourishing [NU•ri•shing] *adj* nourrissant

nourishment [NU•rish•munt] *n* nourriture F

novel [NAH•vl] *n* roman M; *adj* nouveau original

novelist [NAH•vu•list] *n* romancier

novelty [NAH•vul•tee] *n* nouveauté F

November [no•VEM•bur] *n*
novembre M

novice [NAH•vis] *n* novice MF

now [nau] *adv* maintenant; de
temps en temps; dorénavant à
partir de maintenant; *conj*
maintenant que; jusqu'ici

nowhere [NO•waiur] *adv* nulle
part

noxious [NAHK•shus] *adj* nocif

nozzle [NAH•zl] *n* (of hose)
ajutage M; jet M; lance F

nuance [NOO•ahns] *n* nuance F

nuclear [NOO•klee•ur] *adj*
nucléaire

nucleus [NOO•klee•us] *n*
noyau M

nude [nood] *adj n* nu M

nudge [nuhj] *n* (petit) coup M
de coude; *vt* pousser du coude

nudist [NOO•dist] *n* nudiste MF

nudity [NOO•di•tee] *n* nudité F

nuisance [NOO•suns] *n* ennui
M plaie F; it's a ~\ c'est
ennuyeux

null [nuhl] *adj* nul; et non avenu

nullify [NUH•li•FUY] *vt*
annuler

numb [nuhm] *adj* engourdi;
(from cold) transi; *vt*
engourdir; *vi* s'engourdir

number [NUHM•bur] *n* nombre
M; (of phone address) numéro
M; (numeral) chiffre M; *vt*
(count) compter; (give a
number to) numéroter

numeral [NOO•mu•rul] *n*
chiffre M

numerous [NOO•mu•rus] *adj*
nombreux

nuptial [NUHP•shl] *adj* nuptial

nurse [nurs] *n* infirmière F; *vt*
(care for) soigner; (object:
baby) allaiter

nursery [NUR•su•ree] *n*
chambre F d'enfants; (for
plants) pépinière F

nursery rhyme *n* comptine F

nurture [NUR•chur] *vt* élever

nut [nuht] *n* noix M; noisette F;
(for bolt) écrou M; (crazed
person) dingue M

nutcrackers [NUHT•kra•kurz]
npl casse-noix M;
casse-noisette M

nutrition [noo•TRI•shn] *n*
nutrition F

nutritious [noo•TRI•shus] *adj*
nutritif; nourissant F

nylon [NUY•lahn] *n* nylon M

nymph [nimf] *n* nymphe F

O

o'clock [u•KLAHK] *adv* une
heure; cinq heures

oak [ok] *n* chêne M; *adj* en
chêne

oar [aur] *n* rame F; aviron M

oasis [o•AI•sis] *n* oasis F

oath [oth] *n* serment M; under
~\ sous serment

oatmeal [OT•meeul] *npl*
flocons M d'acoine

oats [ots] *npl* avoine F

obedience [o•BEE•dee•uns] *n*
obéissance F

obedient [o•BEE•dee•unt] *adj*
obéissant

obese [o•BEES] *adj* obèse; gros

obey [o•BAI] *vt* obéir à; *vi*
obéir

obituary [o•BI•choo•E•ree] *n*
nécrologie F

object [*n.* AHB•jekt *v.*
ub•JEKT] *n* objet M; (goal)
but M; (grammar)
complément M d'objet; *vi*
s'opposer à

objection [ub•JEK•shn] *n*
objection F

objective [ub•JEK•tiv] *adj n*
objectif M

obligation [AH•bli•GAI•shn] *n*
obligation F

obligatory [u•BLI•gu•TAU•ree]
adj obligatoire

oblige [u•BLUYJ] *vt* obliger

obliging [u•BLUY•jing] *adj*
obligeant

oblique [o•BLEEK] *adj* oblique

obliterate [u•BLI•tu•RAIT] *vt*
effacer; obliterer

oblivion [u•BLI•vee•un] *n*
oubli M

oblivious [u•BLI•vee•us] *adj*
oublieux

obnoxious [ub•NAHK•shus]
adj odieux

obscene [ub•SEEN] *adj*
obscène

obscenity [ub•SE•ni•tee] *n*
obscénité F

obscure [ub•SKYOOUR] *adj*
obscur; *vt* obscurcir

obscurity [ub•SKYU•ri•tee] *n*
obscurity F

observance [ub•ZUR•vuns] *n*
observation F

observant [ub•ZUR•vunt] *adj*
observateur

observation [AHB•sur•VAI•shn]
n observation F

observatory
[ub•ZUR•vuh•TAUR•ee] *n*
observatoire M

observe [ub•ZURV] *vt*
observer; (comment)
remarquer

observer [ub•ZUR•vur] *adj*
observateur M

obsess [ub•SES] *vt* obséder

obsession [ub•SE•shn] *n*
obsession

obsessive [ub•SE•siv] *adj*
obsédant

obsolete [AHB•su•LEET] *adj*
obsolète

obstacle [AHB•stu•kl] *n*
obstacle M

obstinacy [AHB•sti•nu•see] *n*
obstination F

obstinate [AHB•sti•nit] *adj*
obstiné

obstruct [ub•STRUHKT] *vt*
obstruer; encombrer; boucher

obstruction [ub•STRUHK•shn]
n obstruction; (in road)
encombrement M

obtain [ub•TAIN] *vt* obtenir

obtuse [ub•TOOS] *adj* obtus

obvious [AHB•vee•us] *adj*
évident

obviously [AHB•vee•us•lee] *adj*
évidemment

occasion [u•KAI•zhn] *n*
occasion F; (event)
événement M

occasional [u•KAI•zhu•nl] *adj*
occasionnel

occasionally
[u•KAI•zhu•nu•lee] *adv* de
temps en temps

occult [u•KUHLT] *adj* occulte

occupant [AH•kyu•punt] *n*
occupant M

occupation
[AH•kew•PAI•shun] *n* (I'm a
carpenter by ~) métier;
profession MF

occupy [AH•kyu•PUY] *vt*
occuper; s'occuper de qqch

occur [u•KUR] *vi* se produire;
se présenter; avoir lieu; qqch
est venue à mon esprit

occurrence [u•KU•runs] *n*
événement M

ocean [O•shn] *n* océan M

octagon [AHK•tu•GAHN] *n*
octagone M

October [ahk•TO•bur] *n*
octobre M

octopus [AHK•tu•puś] *n*
pieuvre F

odd [ahd] *adj* étrange; (number)
impair; ~s\ chances *fpl*

oddity [AH•di•tee] *n*
bizzarrerie F

odious [O•dee•us] *adj* odieux

odor [O•dur] *n* odeur F

of [uhv] *prep* de; du (de la) des;
en de

off [auf] *adj* (light) éteint;
(motor electricity) coupé;
(calculation) inexact;
(cancelled) annulé; day ~\

jour M de congé; *prep* de; *adv*
(discount) 25% ~\ 25% de
rabais

offend [u•FEND] *vt* offenser

offense [u•FENS] *n* offense F;
(crime) délit M

offensive [u•FEN•siv] *adj*
insultant; impoli; (attack)
offensif; *n* offensive F

offer [AU•fur] *n* offre F; *vt*
offrir

offering [AU•fu•ring] *n* offre F

offhand [AUF•HAND] *adj*
cavalier; improvisé; *adv*
cavalièrement

office [AU•fis] *n* bureau M;
(post function) fonction F;
office M; (department) agence
F; office M ministère M

officer [AU•fi•sur] *n* officier M;
(police) agent M

official [u•FI•shl] *adj* officiel; *n*
fonctionnaire MF

offspring [AUF•spring] *n*
rejeton M

offstage [AUF•STAIJ] *adj adv*
dans les coulisses

often [AU•fn] *adv* souvent; how
~ ?\ combien de fois?

oil [oiul] *n* huile F; (petroleum)
pétrole; *vt* graisser

oily [OIU•lee] *adj* huileux; (skin
clothes) graisseux; (food)
grais

ointment [OINT•munt] *n*
pommade F

old *adj* vieux (vielle); (former)
ancien; I'm 26 years ~ j'ai 26
ans; how ~ are you?\ quel âge
avez-vous?; grow ~\ vieillir

old age *n* vieillesse F

old-fashioned
[OLD•FA•shund] *adj* démodé;
(manner; style) vieux jeu F

olive [AH•liv] *adj n* olive F

omelet [AHM•lit] *n* omelette F

omen [O•mn] *n* augure M
présage M

ominous [AH•mi•nus] *adj*
menaçant

omission [o•MI•shn] *n*
omission F

omit [o•MIT] *vt* omettre

omnipotent [ahm•NI•pu•tunt]
adj omnipotent

on [ahn] *prep* sur dessus; à; en;
(about) sur; ~ Friday\
vendredi; ~ line\ en ligne; ~
leaving (upon)\ en sortant; *adj*
(electricity) allumé; *adv* from
now ~\ dorénavant; come ~!\
allons donc!; have ~ (wear)\
porter

once [wuhns] *adv* une fois; de
temps en temps; il était une
fois; (right away) toute de
suite; (simultaneously) à la
fois

one [wuhn] *num* un(e); *impers
pron* on; lequel (laquelle)?;
lesquels (lesquelles)?; celui-ci
(celle-ci); celui-là (celle-là)

one-sided [WUHN•SUY•did]
adj partial

one-way [WUHN•WAI] *adj*
(road) à sens unique

oneself [wuhn•SELF] *pron*
(reflexive) se; (after prep) soi;
(emphatic) soi-même

onion [UH•nyun] *n* oignon M

onlooker [AHN•lu•kur] *n*
spectateur M

only [ON•lee] *adj* seul unique;
adv seulement ne . . . que

onslaught [AHN•slaut] *n*
attaque F

onward [AHN•wurd] *adv* en
avant

ooze [ooz] *vi* suinter; filtrer

opal [O•pl] *n* opale F

opaque [o•PAIK] *adj* opaque

open [O•pn] *adj* ouvert;
(meeting etc) public; (person;
attitude) franc sincère; *vt*
ouvrir; *vi* (store etc) ouvrir;
(door) s'ouvrir

open-minded
[O•pn•MUYN•did] *adj*
impartial; à l'esprit ouvert

opening [O•pu•ning] *adj*
préliminaire; *n* ouverture F;
(vacancy) vacance F

openly [O•pn•lee] *adv*
ouvertement; franchement

opera [AH•pru] *n* opéra M

operate [AH•pu•RAIT] *vt*
opérer; (machine) faire
marcher; *vi* (machine etc)
s'opérer; (surgeon) opérer

operation [AH•pu•RAI•shn] *n*
opération F; (of machine)
marche F fonctionnement M

operator [AH•pu•RAI•tur] *n*
opérateur M; (of telephone)
standardiste MF téléphoniste
MF

opinion [u•PI•nyun] *n* opinion
F; avis M; in my ~\ à mon
avis

opinionated
[u•PI•nyu•NAI•tid] *adj*
opinionâtre

opponent [u•PO•nunt] *n*
adversaire MF

opportune [AH•pur•TOON]
adj opportun

opportunist
[AH•pur•TOO•nist] *n*
opportuniste MF

opportunity
[AH•pur•TOON•ah•tee] *n*
occasion F

oppose [u•POZ] *vt* s'opposer à

opposed [u•POZD] *adj* opposé;
par opposition à

opposing [u•PO•zing] *adj*
opposé

opposite [AH•pu•sit] *adj*
opposé contraire; (across)
d'en face; *prep* en face de; *n*
opposé M contraire M

opposition [AH•pu•ZI•shn] *n*
opposition

oppress [u•PRES] *vt* oprimer;
(be unbearable to) opresser

oppression [u•PRE•shn] *n*
oppression F

oppressive [u•PRE•siv] *adj*
oppressif; (unbearable)
étouffant; accablant

opt [ahpt] *vi* opter pour; choisir
de

optical [AHP•ti•kl] *adj* optique

optician [ahp•TI•shn] *n*
opticien M

optimism [AHP•ti•MI•zm] *n*
optimisme M

optimist [AHP•ti•mist] *n*
optimiste MF

optimistic [AHP•ti•MI•stik] *adj*
optimistique

option [AHP•shn] *n* option F;
choix M

optional [AHP•shu•nl] *adj*
facultatif

opulence [AH•pyu•luns] *n*
opulence F

opulent [AH•pyu•lunt] *adj*
opulent

or [aur] *conj* ou; (in negative)
ni; ou . . . ou . . . or soit . . .
soit . . . ; (otherwise) sinon

oracle [AU•ru•kl] *n* oracle M

orange [AU•runj] *adj* orange; *n*
(color) orange M; (fruit)
orange F

orator [AU•rai•tur] *n* orateur M

oratory [AU•ru•TAU•ree] *n*
discours M

orbit [AUR•bit] *n* orbite F sur
orbite; *vt* orbiter

orchard [AUR•churd] *n*
verger M

orchestra [AUR•ku•stru] *n*
orchestre M

orchestral [aur•KE•strul] *adj*
orchestral M

orchid [AUR•kid] *n* orchidée

order [AUR•dur] *n* ordre M (in
business restaurant)
commande F; pour; pour que;
prendre une commande; *vt*
ordonner; commander

orderly [AUR•dur•lee] *adj*
ordonné; en ordre

ordinarily [AUR•di•NE•ri•lee]
adv d'habitude; ordinairement;
d'habitude

ordinary [AUR•di•NE•ree] *adj*
ordinaire

ore [aur] *n* minerai M

oregano [au•RE•gu•NO] *n*
origan M

organ [AUR•gn] *n* organe M;
(music) orgue M

organic [aur•GA•nik] *adj*
organique; (food) biologique

organism [AUR•gu•NI•zm] *n*
organisme M

organization
[AUR•gu•ni•ZAI•shn] *n*
organisation F

organize [AUR•gu•NUYZ] *vt*
organiser

orgasm [AUR•ga•zm] *n*
orgasme M

orgy [AUR•gee] *n* orgie F

oriental [AU•ree•EN•tl] *n*
oriental

orientate [AU•ree•un•TAIT] *vt*
orienter

orientation
[AU•ree•un•TAI•shn] *n*
orientation F

orifice [AU•ri•fis] *n* orifice M

origin [AU•ri•jin] *n* origine F

original [u•RI•ji•nl] *adj n*
original M

originality [u•RI•ji•NA•li•tee] *n*
originalité M

originally [u•RI•ji•nu•lee] *adv*
originallement

originate [u•RIJ•i•NAIT] *vi* ~
from\ être originaire de

ornament [AUR•nu•munt] *n*
ornement M

ornamental [AUR•nu•MEN•tl]
adj décoratif

ornate [aur•NAIT] *adj* ornée

orphan [AUR•fn] *n* orphelin M

orphanage [AUR•fu•nij] *n*
orphelinat M

orthodox [AUR•thu•DAHKS]
adj orthodoxe

oscillate [AH•si•LAIT] *vi*
osciller

ostensible [ah•STEN•si•bl] *adj*
prétendu

ostentatious
[AH•stun•TAI•shus] *adj*
ostentatoire; prétentieux

ostrich [AHS•trich] *n*
autruche F

other [UH•thur] *adj* autre;
l'autre; *pron* l'autre; ~s\
d'autres; les autres; *adv*
autrement que

otherwise [UH•thur•WUYZ]
adv autrement; *conj* sinon

otter [AH•tur] *n* loutre F

ought [aut] aux *v* devoir; je
dois faire qqch il faudrait
que je fasse qqch

ounce [ouns] *n* once F

our [ouur] *poss adj* notre nos *pl*

ours [ouurz] *poss pron* le (la)
nôtre les nôtres *pl*

ourselves [ouur•SELVZ] *pron
pl* (*reflexive after prep*) nous;
(*emphatic*) nous-mêmes

oust *vt* évincer

out *adv* (to go ~ of the house)
(to go ~ with friends) dehors;
à l'extérieur; sortir

outbreak [OUT•braik] *n*
eruption F; (of dispute riot)
déclenchement MF

outburst [OUT•burst] *n*
explosion F; éclat M

outcast [OUT•kast] *n* paria M

outcome [OUT•kuhm] *n* issue
F résultat M

outcry [OUT•kruy] *n* tollé M

outdated [out•DAI•tid] *adj*
démodé

outdoor [OUT•dauur] *adj* de/en
plein air

outdoors [out•DAUURZ] *adv*
dehors

outer [OU•tur] *adj* extérieur

outfit [OUT•fit] *n* (clothes)
tenue F; (organization)
équipe F

outgoing [OUT•go•ing] *adj*
(friendly) ouvert; (leaving)
sortant

outhouse [OUT•hous] *n*
appentis M

outing [OU•ting] *n* sortie F

outlaw [n. OUT•lau v.
OUT•lau] *n* hors-la-loi M; *vt*
mettre hors la loi

outlet [OUT•let] *n* (electric)
prise F (de courant);
(emotional) exutoire M;
(shop) point M de vente

outline [OUT•luyn] *n*
(summary) grandes lignes *fpl*;
(shape) contour M; *vt*
(summarize) esquisser

outlive [out•LIV] *vt* survivre à

outlook [OUT•luk] *n* attitude F
perspective F

outmoded [out•MO•did] *adj*
démodé

outnumber [out•NUHM•bur] *vt*
surpasser en nombre

output [OUT•put] *n* production
F; (computer) sortie F

outrage [OUT•raij] *n* atrocité
F; scandale M; *vt* outrager

outrageous [out•RAI•jus] *adj*
scandaleux; (shocking)
choquant

outright [out•RUYT] *adj*
catégorique; *adv*
catégoriquement

outset [OUT•set] *n* début M

outside [*adj prep n.* out•SUYD
adv. out•SUYD] *adj* extérieur;
adv dehors à l'extérieur; *n*
extérieur M; *prep* en dehors
de à l'extérieur de; (apart
from) à part

outsider [out•SUY•dur] *n*
étranger; (in race)
outsider M

outskirts [OUT•skurts] *npl*
faubourgs M

outspoken [out•SPO•kn] *adj*
franc; ouvert

outstanding [out•STAN•ding]
adj exceptionnel; (debt)
impayé

outward [OUT•wurd] *adj*
extérieur

outwardly [OUT•wurd•lee] *adv*
en apparence

outweigh [out•WAI] *vt*
l'emporter sur

outwit [out•WIT] *vt* se montrer
plus malin que

oval [O•vl] *adj n* ovale M

ovary [O•vu•ree] *n* ovaire M

ovation [o•VAI•shn] *n*
ovation F

oven [UH•vn] *n* four M

over [O•vr] *adj* fini; *adv* ici;
là-bas; *prep* au-dessus de; (on
top of) sur; (on the other side
of) par-dessus; (more than)
plus de; *adv prep* partout

overall [*adj.* o•vur•AUL *adv.*
o•vur•AUL] *adj* d'ensemble;
adv en général

overalls [O•vur•aulz] *npl*
salopette F

overbearing [o•vur•BAIU•ring] *adj* autoritaire

overboard [O•vur•baurd] *adv* par-dessus bord

overbook [o•vur•BUK] *vt* surréserver

overcast [O•vur•kast] *adj* couvert

overcharge [o•vur•CHAHRJ] *vt* faire payer qqch trop cher à qqn

overcoat [O•vur•kot] *n* pardessus M

overcome [o•vur•KUHM] *vt* surmonter; être accablé de

overdo [o•vur•DOO] *vt* trop faire; (food) faire trop cuire

overdraw [o•vur•DRAU] *vt* (account) tirer à découvert

overdrawn [o•vur•DRAUN] *adj* à découvert

overflow [*n.* O•vur•flo *v.* O•vur•FLO] *n* trop-plein M; *vi* déborder

overgrown [o•vur•GRON] *adj* (garden) envahi par la végétation

overhaul [O•vur•HAUL] *vt* reviser

overhear [o•vur•HEEUR] *vt* entendre par hasard

overjoyed [o•vur•JOID] *adj* ravi

overlap [o•vur•LAP] *vt* se chevaucher

overlook [o•vur•LUK] *vt* oublier; négliger; (forgive) fermer les yeux sur

overnight [*adj.* o•vur•NUYT *adv.* o•vur•NUYT] *adj* de nuit; d'une nuit; *adv* la nuit

overpower [o•vur•POU•ur] *vt* vaincre

overrun [o•vur•RUHN] *adj* envahi de; (infested) infesté (de)

overseas [o•vur•SEEZ] *adj adv* d'outre-mer à l'étranger

oversee [o•vur•SEE] *vt* surveiller; donner sur

overseer [O•vur•see•ur] *n* contremaître M

overshadow [o•vur•SHA•do] *vt* éclipser

overstep [o•vur•STEP] *vt* dépasser

overtake [o•vur•TAIK] *vt* dépasser; doubler

overthrow [o•vur•THRO] *vt* renverser

overtime [O•vur•tuym] *npl* heures F supplémentaires

overture [O•vur•chur] *n* ouverture

overweight [o•vur•WAIT] *adj* trop gros; excédent

overwhelm [o•vur•WELM] *vt* accabler

overwhelming [o•vur•WEL•ming] *adj* accablant; (desire) irrésistible; (defeat) écrasant

overwork [o•vur•WURK] *vt* surmener

owe [o] *vt* devoir

owl [ouul] *n* hibou M

own [on] *adj* propre; *pron* le (la) mien (ne); *adv* tout seul; *vt* posséder; *vi* avouer

owner [O•nur] *n* propriétaire MF

ownership [O•nur•SHIP] *n*
possession F
ox [ahks] *n* bœuf M

oxygen [AHK•si•jun] *n*
oxygène M
oyster [OI•stur] *n* huître M

P

pace [pais] *n* pas M; (rate
speed) vitesse F
Pacific [pu•SI•fik] *adj* le
Pacifique l'océan Pacifique
pacify [PA•si•FUY] *adj* apaiser;
(nation) pacifier
pack [pak] *n* paquet M; (bag)
sac M; (of dogs) meute F; (of
wolves) bande F; *vt* faire ses
bagages; (clothes) emballer;
(fill) remplir; *vi* faire ses
bagages; *vt* entasser
package [PA•kij] *n* colis M;
paquet M
packet [PA•kit] *n* paquet M
packing [PA•king] *n*
emballage M
pact [pakt] *n* pacte M
pad *n* (for writing) bloc M; *vt*
rembourrer
padding [PA•ding] *n*
rembourrage M
paddle [PA•dl] *n* (oar) pagaie
F; *vt* pagayer
padlock [PAD•lahk] *n*
cadenas M
pagan [PAI•gn] *adj n* païen M
page [paij] *n* page M; *vt* (call)
appeler
pail [paiul] *n* seau M
pain *n* douleur F be in ~\ *vi*
souffrir; avoir mal

painful [PAIN•ful] *adj*
douloureux; (difficult) pénible
painkiller [PAIN•ki•lur] *n*
calmant M
painless [PAIN•lis] *adj* indolore
painstaking [PAIN•STAI•king]
adj soigné
paint [paint] *n* peinture F; *vt vi*
peindre
paintbrush [PAINT•bruhsh] *n*
pinceau M
painter [PAIN•tur] *n* peintre M
painting [PAIN•ting] *n*
(process) peinture F; (picture)
tableau M
pair [paiur] *n* (of shoes etc)
paire F; (of people) couple M;
a ~ of pants\ un pantalon
pajamas [pu•JA•muz] *npl*
pyjama M
Pakistan [PA•ki•STAN] *n*
Pakistan M
pal *n* copain M (copine)
palace [PA•lis] *n* palais M
palatable [PA•li•tu•bl] *adj*
agréable
palate [PA•lit] *n* palais M
pale [paiul] *adj* pâle; grow ~\
pâlir
Palestine [PA•li•STUYN] *n*
Palestine F
palette [PA•lit] *n* palette F

palm [pahm] *n* (of hand) paume F; (leaf) palme F; (tree) palmier M

Palm Sunday *n* le dimanche des Rameaux

palpable [PAL•pu•bl] *adj* palpable; évident manifeste

paltry [PAUL•tree] *adj* dérisoire

pamper [PAM•pur] *vt* dorloter

pamphlet [PAM•flit] *n* brochure F

pan *n* casserole F; poêle F

panacea [PA•nu•SEE•u] *n* panacée F

Panama [PA•nu•MAH] *n* Panama M

pancake [PAN•kaik] *n* crêpe F

panda [PAN•du] *n* panda M

pane [pain] *n* carreau M vitre F

panel [PA•nl] *n* panneau M; (comittee) comité F

pang *n* tiraillement M

panic [PA•nik] *n* panique F; *vi* paniquer; s'affoler

pansy [PAN•zee] *n* pensée F

pant *vi* haleter

panther [PAN•thur] *n* panthère F

panties [PAN•teez] *npl* culotte F

pantyhose [PAN•tee•HOZ] *n* collant M

pantry [PAN•tree] *n* garde-manger M

pants *npl* pantalon M

papa [PAH•pu] *n* papa M

papal [PAI•pl] *adj* papal

paper [PAI•pur] *adj* de or en papier; *n* papier M; (newspaper) journal

paperback [PAI•pur•BAK] *n* livre M de poche

par [pahr] *n* (golf) par M; à égalité avec

parable [PA•ru•bl] *n* parabole F

parachute [PA•ru•SHOOT] *n* parachute M; *vi* sauter en parachute

parade [pu•RAID] *n* parade F; (military) défilé; *vt* (show off) faire étalage de; *vi* défiler

paradise [PA•ru•DUYS] *n* paradis M

paradox [PA•ru•DAHKS] *n* paradoxe M

paragraph [PA•ru•GRAF] *n* paragraphe M

Paraguay [PA•ru•GWAI] *n* Paraguay M

parakeet [PA•ru•KEET] *n* perruche F

parallel [PA•ru•LEL] *adj* parallèle; *n* parallèle F; (geography) parallèle M

paralysis [pu•RA•lu•sis] *n* paralysie F

paralyze [PA•ru•LUYZ] *vt* paralyser

paranoid [PA•ru•NOID] *adj* paranoïaque

paraphernalia [PA•ru•fu•NAIU•lyu] *n* attirail

parasite [PA•ru•SUYT] *n* parasite M

parasol [PA•ru•SAUL] *n* ombrelle F; parasol M

parcel [PAHR•sl] *n* colis M paquet M

parched [pahrchd] *adj* desséché; (person) assoiffé

parchment [PAHRCH•munt] *n*
parchemin M

pardon [PAHR•dn] *n* pardon
M; (for crime) grâce F; *vt*
pardonner à; gracier

parent [pa•runt] *n* père M mère
F; *npl* parents M

parenthesis [pu•REN•thu•sis] *n*
(*pl* parentheses) paranthèse F

parish [PA•rish] *adj* paroissal; *n*
paroisse F

park [pahrk] *n* parc M; *vt* garer;
vi se garer

parking [PAHR•king] *n*
stationnement M

parking lot *n* parking M

parlance [PAHR•luns] *n*
langage M

parliament [PAHR•lu•munt] *n*
parlement M

parliamentary
[PAHR•lu•MEN•tu•ree] *adj*
parlementaire M

parlor [PAHR•lur] *n* salon M

parochial [pu•RO•kee•ul] *adj*
paroissial

parody [PA•ru•dee] *n* parodie
F; *vt* parodier

parole [pu•ROUL] *n* en liberté
conditionelle

parrot [PA•rut] *n* perroquet M

parsley [PAHR•slee] *n* persil M

parsnip [PAR•snip] *n* panais M

parson [PAHR•sn] *n* pasteur M

part [pahrt] *n* partie F; (role)
rôle M; (participation)
participation F à; (in hair) raie
F; *adv* in ~\ en partie; in large
~\ en grande partie; *vt* se
séparer; *vt* se défaire de

part-time [PAHRT•TUYM] *adj*
adv à temps partiel à
mi-temps

partial [PAHR•shl] *adj* partiel;
(biased) partial

partiality [PAHR•shee•A•li•tee]
n (favorable bias) partialité F

partially [PAHR•shu•lee] *adv*
partiellement

participant [pahr•TI•si•punt] *n*
participant M

participate [pahr•TI•si•PAIT] *vi*
participer; participer à

participation
[pahr•TI•si•PAI•shn] *n*
participation F

particle [PAHR•ti•kl] *n*
particule F

particular [pur•TI•kyu•lur] *adj*
particulier

particularly
[pur•TI•kyu•lur•lee] *adv*
particulièrement

parting [PAHR•ting] *n*
séparation F

partisan [PAHR•ti•sun] *adj n*
partisan M

partition [pahr•TI•shn] *n*
cloison M; (of nation) partage
M; *vt* cloisoner; (nation)
partager

partly [PAHRT•lee] *adv* en
partie

partner [PAHRT•nur] *n*
partenaire MF; (business)
associé M

partnership
[PAHRT•nur•SHIP] *n*
association F

partridge [PAHR•trij] *n*
perdrix F

party [PAHR•tee] *n* fête F;
(political) parti M; (group)
groupe M

pass [pas] *n* (sports) passe F;
(in mountains) col M; (for
entry) laissez-passer M; make
a ~ at\ sb faire des avances à
qqn; *vt* passer; (walking)
croiser; (in car) doubler
dépasser; (law) voter; (exam)
réussir à; ~ away\ *vi* mourir;
~ out\ *vt* distribuer; *vi*
s'évanouir; ~ up\ *vt* laisser
passer

passage [PA•sij] *n* (hallway)
couloir M; (of book)
passage M

passenger [PA•sin•jur] *n*
passager

passerby [PA•sur•BUY] *n*
passant M

passion [PA•shn] *n* passion F

passionate [PA•shu•nit] *adj*
passioné

passive [PA•siv] *adj* passif

passport [PAS•paurt] *n*
passeport M

password [PAS•wurd] *n* mot M
de passe

past *adj* passé; (former) ancien;
(of time in the ~ two years)
depuis les derniers deux ans;
n passé M; *prep* au dela de;
après

pasta [PAH•stu] *n* pâtes *fpl*

paste [paist] *n* pâte F; (glue)
colle F; *vt* coller

pastel [pa•STEL] *adj n*
pastel M

pasteurize [PAS•chu•RUYZ] *vt*
pasteuriser

pastime [PAS•tuym] *n*
passe-temps M

pastor [PA•stur] *n* pasteur M

pastry [PAI•stree] *n* pâte F;
(cake) pâtisserie F

pastry shop *n* pâtiserrie F

pasture [PAS•chur] *n*
pâturage M

pat *n* peite tape F; *vt* donner
une petite tape à

patch [pach] *n* (on clothes)
pièce F; (of land) parcelle F;
vt rapiécer; ~ up\ *vt* réparer;
(dispute) régler

pâté [pa•TAI] *n* pâté M

patent [PA•tunt] *adj* manifeste;
n brevet M (d'invention); *vt*
faire breveter

patent leather *n* cuir M verni

paternal [pu•TUR•nl] *adj*
paternel

paternity [pu•TUR•ni•tee] *n*
paternité F

path *n* chemin M sentier M;
(trajectory) trajectoire F

pathetic [pu•THE•tik] *adj*
pitoyable

pathology [pa•THAH•lu•jee] *n*
pathologie F

pathway [PATH•wai] *n* chemin
M; sentier M

patience [PAI•shns] *n*
patience F

patient [PAI•shnt] *adj n*
patient M

patriot [PAI•tree•ut] *n* patriote
MF

patriotic [PAI•tree•AH•tik] *adj*
patriotique; (person) patriote

patriotism [PAI•tree•u•TI•zm]
n patriotisme M

patrol [pu•TROUL] *n* patrouille F; *vt* patrouiller dans

patron [PAI•trun] *n* client; (benefactor) patron M; (of arts) mécène M

patronize [PAI•tru•NUYZ] *vt* patronner; (condescend) traiter avec condescendance

patronizing [PAI•tru•NUY•zing] *adj* condescendant; de condescendance

patter [PA•tur] *n* (sound) crépitement

pattern [PA•turn] *n* modèle M; (design) motif M; (of actions etc) mode M; (sewing) patron M

pause [pauz] *n* pause F arrêt M; *vi* faire une pause s'arrêter

pave [paiv] *vt* paver; ouvrir la voie à

pavement [PAIV•munt] *n* pavé M; (roadway) chaussée F

pavilion [pu•VIL•yun] *n* pavillon M

paw [pau] *n* patte F

pawn [paun] *n* pion M; *vt* mettre en gage

pawnbroker [PAUN•bro•kur] *n* prêteur M sur gages

pawnshop [PAUN•shahp] *n* mont-de-piété M

pay [pai] *n* paie F; *vi* payer; (be worthwhile) être rentable; ~ attention\ prêter attention; ~ a visit\ rendre visite; ~ back\ *vt* rembourser; ~ off\ *vt* (bribe) soudoyer; ~ up\ *vt* régler; *vi* payer

pay phone *n* téléphone M public

payable [PAI•yu•bl] *adj* payable

paycheck [PAI•chek] *n* paie F

payment [PAI•munt] *n* paiement M

payroll [PAI•roul] *n* registre M du personnel

pea [pee] *n* pois M; *npl* petits pois M

peace [pees] *n* paix F; (calm) calme M; faire la paix

peaceful [PEES•ful] *adj* paisible; (nation) pacifique

peach [peech] *n* pêche F

peacock [PEE•cahk] *n* paon M

peak [peek] *n* sommet; ~ of\ apogée M

peal [peeul] *n* (of bell) carillon M; (of thunder, sound) coup M

peanut [PEE•nuht] *n* cacahuète F

peanut butter *n* beurre M de cacahuète

pear [paiur] *n* poire F

pearl [purl] *n* perle F

peasant [PE•znt] *n* paysan M

peat [peet] *n* tourbe F

pebble [PE•bl] *n* galet M caillou M

peck [pek] *n* (of bird) coup M de bec; (kiss) bise F; *vt* donner un coup de bec à

peculiar [pi•KYOOU•lyur] *adj* curieux; particulier à

pedal [PE•dl] *n* pédale F; *vi* pédaler

pedant [PE•dunt] *n* pédant M

pedantic [pi•DAN•tik] *adj* pédant

peddle [PE•dl] *vt* colporter; *vi* faire le colportage

pedestal [PE•du•stl] *n* piédestal M

pedestrian [pi•DE•stree•un] *n* piéton M

pedigree [PE•di•GREE] *adj* de race; *n* pedigree M; (of person) ascendance F

peek *vi* jeter un coup d'œil furtif

peel [peeul] *n* peau F; (of citrus fruit) écorce F; *vt* éplucher; *vi* (paint) s'écailler; (wallpaper) se décoller

peep *n* coup M d'œil furtif; (sound) pépiement M

peephole [PEEP•houl] *n* judas M

peer [peeur] *n* pair M; *vi* scruter; regarder attentivement

peg *n* (hook) cheville F

pellet [PE•lit] *n* boulette F; (for gun) plomb M

pelt *n* peau M; *vt* bombarder qqn (de)

pen *n* stylo M; (for animals) parc M

penal [PEE•nl] *adj* pénal

penalty [PE•nl•tee] *n* pénalité F; (fine) amende M; (sports) pénalisation F; (kick: soccer) penalty M

penance [PE•nuns] *n* pénitence F

penchant [PEN•chnt] *n* penchant; inclination MF

pencil [PEN•sl] *n* crayon M

pencil sharpener *n* taille-crayon M

pendant [PEN•dnt] *n* pendentif M

pending [PEN•ding] *adj* imminent; *prep* en attendant

pendulum [PEN•dyu•lum] *n* pendule M; (of clock) balancier M

penetrate [PE•nu•TRAIT] *vt* pénétrer dans

penguin [PENG•gwin] *n* manchot M

penicillin [PE•ni•SI•lin] *n* pénicilline F

peninsula [pu•NIN•su•lu] *n* péninsule F

penis [PEE•nis] *n* pénis M

pennant [PE•nunt] *n* fanion M

penniless [PE•nee•lis] *adj* sans le sou

penny [PE•nee] *n* cent M

pension [PEN•shn] *n* pension F

pensive [PEN•siv] *adj* songeur

penthouse [PENT•haus] *n* appartement M de luxe (en attique)

people [PEE•pl] *npl* gens *mpl*; (persons) personnes *fpl*; (nation race) peuple M; a lot of ~\ beaucoup de monde; *vt* peupler

pepper [PE•pur] *n* poivre M; (vegetable) poivron M; *vt* poivrer

peppermint [PE•pur•mint] *n* menthe F poivrée; (candy) bonbon M à la menthe

per [pur] *prep* par; à; ten miles ~ hour\ 10 miles à l'heure; le livre; ~ par personne/jour

perceive [pur•SEEV] *vt*
percevoir; (notice)
s'apercevoir de

percent [pur•SENT] *adv* pour
cent

percentage [pur•SEN•tij] *n*
pourcentage M

perception [pur•SEP•shn] *n*
perception F; (understanding)
perspicacité F

perch [purch] *n* (fish) perche F;
(of bird) perchoir M; *vi* se
percher

perennial [pu•RE•nee•ul] *adj*
perpétuel; (plant) vivace; *n*
plante F vivace

perfect [*adj.* PUR•fikt *v.*
pur•FEKT] *adj* parfait; *vt*
parfaire mettre au point

perfection [pur•FEK•shn] *n*
perfection F

perfectionist
[pur•FEK•shu•nist] *n*
perfectionniste MF

perfectly [PUR•fikt•lee] *adv*
parfaitement F

perforate [PUR•fu•RAIT] *vt*
perforer

perform [pur•FAURM] *vi* (duty
task) exécuter; remplir; (play
concert) jouer; *vi* jouer

performance [pur•FAUR•mns]
n exécution; (show)
représantation; (of artist)
interprétation F; (of car)
performance F

perfume [PUR•fyoom] *n*
parfœn M; parfum M; *vt*
parfumer

perhaps [pur•HAPS] *adv*
peut-être

peril [PE•ril] *n* péril M

perimeter [pu•RI•mi•tur] *n*
périmètre M

period [PEEU•ree•ud] *n* période
MF; (in history) époque F;
(grammar) point M;
(menstruation) règles *fpl*

periodic [PI•ree•AH•dik] *adj*
périodique

periodical [PI•ree•AH•di•kl] *n*
périodique M

perish [PE•rish] *vi* périr;
(decay) se détériorer

perjury [PUR•ju•ree] *n* parjure
M; (in court) faux
témoignage M

perm [purm] *n* permanente F

permanent [PUR•mi•nunt] *adj*
permanent F

permeate [PUR•mee•AIT] *vt*
s'infiltrer dans pénétrer; *vi*
s'infiltrer

permission [pur•MI•shn] *n*
permission F

permit [*n.* PUR•mit *v.* pur•MIT]
n permis M; *vt* permettre;
permettre à qqn de faire qqch

perpendicular
[PUR•pn•DI•kyu•lur] *adj n*
perpendiculaire F

perpetrate [PUR•pu•TRAIT] *vt*
perpétrer

perpetual [pur•PE•choo•ul] *adj*
perpétuel

perplex [pur•PLEKS] *vt* rendre
perplexe; confuser

perplexed [pur•PLEKST] *adj*
perplexe

persecute [PUR•si•KYOOT] *vt*
persécuter

perseverance
[PUR•si•VEEU•rns] *n*
persévérance F

persevere [PUR•si•VEEUR] *vi*
persévérer

Persian Gulf [PUR•zhn ~] *n* le
golfe Persique

persist [pur•SIST] *vi* persister à
faire qqch

persistence [pur•SI•stns] *n*
persistance F

persistent [pur•SI•stnt] *adj*
persistant F

person [PUR•sn] *n* personne F;
en personne

personal [PUR•su•nl] *adj*
personnel

personality [PUR•su•NA•li•tee]
n personnalité F

personnel [PUR•su•NEL] *n*
personnel M

perspective [pur•SPEK•tiv] *n*
perspective F

perspiration
[PUR•spu•RAI•shn] *n*
transpiration; (sweat) sueur F

perspire [pur•SPUYUR] *vi*
transpirer

persuade [pur•SWAID] *vt*
persuader

persuasion [pur•SWAI•zhn] *n*
persuasion F; conviction F

persuasive [pur•SWAI•siv] *adj*
persuasif

pertain [pur•TAIN] *vi* être
relatif à

pertinent [PUR•ti•nunt] *adj*
pertinent

perturb [pur•TURB] *vt* troubler

perverse [pur•VURS] *adj*
pervers

pervert [*n.* PUR•vurt *v.*
pur•VURT] *n* pervers M; *vt*
(facts story) déformer;
(sexually) pervertir

pessimism [PE•si•MI•zm] *n*
pessimisme M

pessimist [PE•si•mist] *n*
pessimiste MF

pessimistic [PE•si•MI•stik] *adj*
pessimiste

pest *n* insecte nuisible;
(person) fléau

pester [PE•stur] *vt* harceler

pet *n* animal M (familier); *vt*
caresser; *vi* se peloter se
caresser

petal [PE•tl] *n* pétale M

petition [pu•TI•shn] *n*
pétition F

petrified [PE•tri•FUYD] *adj*
petrifié

petroleum [pu•TRO•lee•um] *n*
pétrole M

petty [PE•tee] *adj* (person)
mesquin; (unimportant)
insignifiant

pew [pyoo] *n* banc M (d'église)

phantom [FAN•tum] *n* fantôme

pharmacist [FAHR•mu•sist] *n*
pharmacien

pharmacy [FAHR•mu•see] *n*
pharmacie F

phase [faiz] *n* phase F; *vt* ~ in\
introduire/supprimer
progressivement

phenomenon
[fu•NAH•mu•NAHN] *n*
phénomène F

philosopher [fi•LAH•su•fur] *n*
philosophe MF

philosophical [FI•lu•SAH•fi•kl] *adj* philosophique

philosophy [fi•LAH•su•fee] *n* philosophie F

phone [fon] *n* téléphone M; au téléphone; *vt* téléphoner à; *vi* téléphoner

phone booth *n* cabine F téléphonique

phone call *n* coup M de fil

phonetics [fu•NE•tiks] *n* phonétique F

phony [FO•nee] *adj* (counterfeit) bidon faux; (person) pas franc; *n* (person) poseur M

photo [FO•to] *n* photo M

photograph [FO•tu•graf] *n* photographie F; take a ~ of\ sb/sth prendre qqn/qqch en photo; *vt* photographier

photographer [fu•TAH•gru•fur] *n* photographe MF

photography [fu•TAH•gru•fee] *n* photagraphie

phrase [fraiz] *n* expression F; *vt* exprimer

physical [FI•zi•kl] *adj* physique; *n* (examination) visite F médicale

physician [fi•ZI•shn] *n* médecin M

physicist [FI•zi•sist] *n* physicien

physics [FI•ziks] *n* physique F

physique [fi•ZEEK] *n* physique M

pianist [pee•U•nist] *n* pianiste MF

piano [pee•A•no] *n* piano M

pick [pik] *n* choix M; (tool) pioche F pic M; choisir; (flowers) cueillir; (lock) crocheter; ~ one's nose\ se décrotter le nez; ~ one's teeth\ se curer les dents; ~ on\ *vt* harceler; ~ out\ *vt* choisir; ~ up\ *vt* ramasser; (in car) prendre; (learn) apprendre; (speed) prendre de la vitesse

picket [PI•kit] *n* piquet M de grève; *vt* mettre un piquet de grève devant

pickle [PI•kl] *npl* pickles M; *vt* conserver dans du vinaigre/de la saumure

pickpocket [PIK•PAH•kit] *n* pickpocket M

picnic [PIK•nik] *n* pique-nique M; *vi* piqueniquer

picture [PIK•chur] *n* dessin M; (painting) peinture F tableau M; (photo) photo F; (mental) image F; take a ~ of sb/sth\ prendre qqn/qqch en photo; *vt* imaginer; (depict) représenter

picturesque [PIK•chu•RESK] *adj* pittoresque

pie [puy] *n* tourte F

piece [pees] *n* morceau M; (of string) bout M; (article) article M; ~ of advice\ conseil M; ~ together\ *vt* rassembler

pier [peeur] *n* jetée F

pierce [peeurs] *vt* percer transpercer

pig *n* cochon M porc M

pig-headed [PIG•HE•did] *adj* têtu

pigeon [PI•jn] *n* pigeon M

piggybank [PI•gee•BANGK] *n*
tirelire F

pigment [PIG•munt] *n*
pigment M

pigsty [PIG•stuy] *n* porcherie F

pile [puyul] *n* tas M; *vt* entasser;
vt entasser; *vi* s'accumuler

pilgrim [PIL•grim] *n* pèlerin M

pilgrimage [PIL•gri•mij] *n*
pèlerinage M

pill [pil] *n* pilule F

pillar [PI•lur] *n* pilier M

pillow [PI•lo] *n* oreiller M

pillowcase [PI•lo•KAIS] *n* taie
F d'oreiller

pilot [PUY•lut] *n* pilote M; *vt*
piloter

pimp *n* maquereau M
souteneur M

pimple [PIM•pl] *n* bouton

pin *n* épingle F; (for plug) fiche
F; (of machine device)
cheville F; ~s and needles\
fourmis; *vt* épingler; ~ sth on
sb\ mettre qqch sur le dos de
qqn

pinch [pinch] *n* pincement M;
(of salt etc) pincée F; *vt*
pincer

pine [puyn] *n* pin M

pink [pingk] adk *n* rose M

pinnacle [PI•nu•kl] *n* (of life
etc) apogée F

pint [puynt] *n* pinte F; (of beer)
demi M

pioneer [PUY•u•NEEUR] *n*
pionnier M; *vt* explorer

pious [PUY•us] *adj* pieux

pipe [puyp] *n* tuyau M conduite
F; (for smoking) pipe F; *vt*

amener par tuyau; ~ down\ *vi*
se taire

pique [peek] *n* dépit

pirate [PUY•rit] *adj* (casettes
etc) pirate; *n* pirate M; *vt*
(computers etc) pirater

pistol [PI•stl] *n* pistolet M

piston [PI•stn] *n* piston M

pitch [pich] *n* lancement M;
(sound) ton M; (in selling
advertising) baratin M; *vt*
lancer; (tent) dresser; (ball)
rebondir

pitcher [PI•chur] *n* cruche F;
(in baseball) lanceur M

pitchfork [PICH•faurk] *n*
fourche F

piteous [PI•tee•us] *adj*
pitoyable

pitiful [PI•ti•ful] *adj* pitoyable;
(performance; explanation;
etc) lamentable

pitiless [PI•tee•lis] *adj*
impitoyable; sans pitié

pity [PI•tee] *n* pitié F; what a ~\
quel dommage; *vt* plaindre

pivot [PI•vut] *n* pivot M

placard [PLA•kurd] *n* placard
M affiche F

placate [PLAI•kait] *vt* apaiser

place [plais] *n* lieu M endroit
M; (position rank) place F;
take ~\ avoir lieu; in the first
~\ premièrement; at my ~\
chez moi; in ~\ a sa place; out
of ~\ pas à sa place; *vt* mettre
placer; (identify) situer

placid [PLA•sid] *adj* calme;
(person) placide

plague [plaig] *n* peste F; *vt*
tourmenter

plaid [plad] *n* plaid; *adj* de plaid

plain *adj* simple ordinaire; (frank) franc; (patternless) uni; (unattractive) quelquonque; *n* plaine M

plainly [plain•lee] *adv* clairement; (frankly) carrément

plaintiff [PLAIN•tif] *n* plaignant demandeur M

plan *n* plan projet M; *vt* préparer; ~ to (intend to)\ projeter de

plane [plain] *adj* plan; *n* avion; (math) plan M; (tool) rabot M

planet [PLA•nit] *n* planète F

plank [plangk] *n* planche F

planning [PLA•ning] *n* planification F

plant *n* plante F; (factory) usine F; *vt* planter; (bomb) poser

plantation [plan•TAI•shn] *n* plantation F

plaque [plak] *n* plaque F; (on teeth) plaque F dentaire

plaster [PLA•stur] *n* plâtre M; *vt* plâtrer; *vt* couvrir de

plastic [PLA•stik] *adj n* plastique M

plate [plait] *n* assiette F; (sheet of metal) plaque F

plateau [pla•TO] *n* plateau M

plated [PLAI•tid] *adj* plaqué; plaqué d'or

platform [PLAT•faurm] *n* (at meeting) tribune F; (for train of political party) plate-forme F

platinum [PLAT•num] *n* platine M

platter [PLA•tur] *n* plat M

play [plai] *n* jeu M; (theater) pièce F; *vt* (instrument) jouer de; (opponent) jouer contre; (game) jouer à; (role part) jouer; *vi* jouer

playboy [PLAI•boi] *n* playboy M

player [PLAI•ur] *n* joueur M; (theater) acteur M

playful [PLAI•ful] *adj* enjoué

playground [PLAI•ground] *n* cour F de récréation

plaything [PLAI•thing] *n* jouet M

playwright [PLAI•ruyt] *n* dramaturge M

plea [plee] *n* supplication F; (call) appel M; (court) défense

plead [pleed] *vt* plaider; *vi* (court) plaider; implorer qqn

pleasant [PLE•znt] *adj* agréable

please [pleez] *vt* plaire à; *vi* plaire; *adv* s'il vous (te) plaît

pleased [pleezd] *adj* content; enchanté

pleasing [PLEE•zing] *adj* plaisant

pleasure [PLE•zhur] *n* plaisir M; avec plaisir; je vous en (t'en) prie

pleat [pleet] *n* pli M; *vt* plisser

pledge [plej] *n* promesse F; (binding) gage M; *vt* promettre; (pawn) mettre en gage

plentiful [PLEN•ti•ful] *adj* abondant

plenty [PLEN•tee] *n* beaucoup de

pliable [PLUY•u•bl] *adj* pliable

pliers [PLUY•urz] *npl* pinces F

plight [pluyt] *n* situation F critique; état F

plod [plahd] *vi* ~ along\ marcher lentement

plot [plaht] *n* complot M; (of story) intrigue F; (of land) lopin M; *vt* comploter; (on map graph) marquer; *vi* comploter

plow [plou] *n* charrue F; *vt* labourer

ploy [ploi] *n* stratagème M

pluck [pluhk] *vt* (chicken) plumer F; (eyebrow) épiler; (fruit) cueillir; (guitar etc) pincer

plug [pluhg] *n* (electric) prise F (de courant); (for drain) bonde F; *vt* (hole) boucher; ~ in\ *vt* brancher

plum [pluhm] *n* prune F

plumber [PLUH•mur] *n* plombier

plumbing [PLUH•ming] *n* (piping & trade) plomberie F

plume [ploom] *n* plume F

plump [pluhmp] *adj* bien; en chair

plunder [PLUHN•dur] *vt* piller

plunge [pluhnj] *n* plongeon M; (of prices; sales; etc) dégringolade F; *vt* plonger; *vi* plonger; dégringoler

plunger [PLUHN•jur] *n* débouchoir M à ventouse

plural [PLOOU•rl] *adj n* pluriel M

plus [pluhs] *n* (sign) signe M plus; (advantage) plus M; *prep* et

plush [pluhsh] *n* sompteux

ply [pluy] *vt* (in wool) pli M; (of wood) fil M; *vt* (trade) exercer

plywood [PLUY•wud] *n* contreplaqué M

pneumonia [noo•MO•nyu] *n* pneumonie F

poach [poch] *vt* (in cooking) pocher; (hunt illegally) chasser/pêcher sans permis; *vi* braconner

pocket [PAH•kit] *n* poche F; *vt* empocher

pocketbook [PAH•kit•BUK] *n* sac M à main

pocketknife [PAH•kit•NUYF] *n* canif

pod [pahd] *n* cosse F

poem [pom] *n* poème F

poet [PO•it] *n* poète

poetic [po•E•tik] *adj* poétique

poetry [PO•e•tree] *n* poésie F

point *n* pointe F; (in space) endroit M; (moment) moment M; (in scale score) point M; (purpose) raison F objet M; make a ~\ faire une remarque; get the ~\ saisir comprendre; on the ~ of\ sur le point de; there's no point in doing sth\ cela ne sert à rien de faire qqch; (decimals) [5.3] 5 ~ 3\ 5 virgule 3; *vt* ~ sth at (gun etc)\ braquer qqch sur; *vi* ~at sth\ montrer qqch du doigt: ~ out\ indiquer souligner

point of view *n* point M de vue

pointed [POIN•tid] *adj* pointu; (conversation etc) incisif

pointer [POIN•tur] *n* (stick)
baguette F; (help; advice)
conseil M

pointless [POINT•lis] *adj*
inutile vain

poise [poiz] *n* calme M

poison [POI•zn] *n* poison M; *vt*
empoisonner

poisoning [POI•zu•ning] *n*
empoisonnement M; food ~\
intoxication F alimentaire

poisonous [POI•zu•nus] *adj*
toxique; (plant substance)
vénéneux; (snake) venimeux

poke [pok] *vt* pousser du doigt;
(fire) tisonner; ~ around\ *vt*
fureter

poker [PO•kur] *n* (game) poker
M; (for fire) tisonnier M

Poland [PO•lund] *n* Polande F

polar [PO•lur] *adj* polaire

pole [poul] *n* mât M; perche F;
(north; south) pôle M

Pole [poul] *n* Polonais M

police [pu•LEES] *npl* police F;
vt maintenir l'ordre dans

police officer *n* policier M; flic
(coll)

police station *n* commisariat M

policeman [pu•LEES•man] *n*
agent M de police

policewoman
[pu•LEES•WU•mun] *n* femme
F agent de police

policy [PAH•li•see] *n* politique
F; (of insurance etc) police F

Polish [PO•lish] *adj* polonais;
(lang) polonais M

polish [PAH•lish] *n* (for floor
etc) cire F; (for shoes) cirage
M; (shine) lustre M; (of

person) raffinement M; *vt*
cirer; (shine) astiquer; faire
briller

polite [pu•LUYT] *adj* poli

politeness [pu•LUYT•nis] *n*
politesse F

political [pu•LI•ti•kl] *adj*
politique

politician [PAH•li•TI•shn] *n*
homme m/femme F politique

politics [PAH•li•TIKS] *n*
politique F

poll [poul] *n* vote; (for
information opinions) sondage
M; *vt* sonder

pollen [PAH•ln] *n* pollen M

pollute [pu•LOOT] *vt* polluer

pollution [pu•LOO•shn] *n*
pollution F

polo [PO•lo] *n* polo M

Polynesia [PAH•li•i•NEE•zhu] *n*
Polynésie F

pomp [pahmp] *n* pompe F

pompous [PAHM•pus] *adj*
pompeux

pond [pahnd] *n* étang M; (pool)
mare F

ponder [PAHN•dur] *vt*
considérer; peser (de)

pony [PO•nee] *n* poney M

ponytail [PO•nee•TAIUL] *n*
queue-de-cheval M

poodle [POO•dl] *n* caniche M

pool [pooul] *n* (for swimming)
piscine F; (pond) mare F; (of
rain) flaque F; (billiards)
billard M (américain); (in
betting) cagnotte F; *vt* mettre
en commun

poor [poour] *adj* pauvre; (attempt
at work etc) médiocre

mauvais; the ~\ *npl* les pauvres M

pop [pahp] *n* (music) pop M; (noise) pan M; (father) papa M; *vt* faire éclater; (put) fourrer; *vi* éclater; (button) sauter; ~ up\ *vi* surgir

pope [pop] *n* pape M

poplar [PAHP•lur] *n* peuplier M

poppy [PAH•pee] *n* coquelicot M; pavot M

populace [PAH•pyu•lus] *n* peuple M

popular [PAH•pyu•lur] *adj* populaire

popularity [PAH•pyu•LA•ri•tee] *n* popularité F

popularize [PAH•pyu•lu•RUYZ] *vt* populariser

populate [PAH•pyu•LAIT] *vt* peupler

population [PAH•pyu•LAI•shn] *n* population F

porcelain [PAURS•lun] *n* porcelaine F

porch [paurch] *n* véranda M

porcupine [PAUR•kyu•PUYN] *n* porc-épic M

pore [paur] *n* pore M

pork [paurk] *n* porc M

pornography [paur•NAH•gru•fee] *n* pornagraphie F

porous [PAU•rus] *adj* poreμx

porpoise [PAUR•pus] *n* marsouin M

porridge [PAU•rij] *n* porridge

port [paurt] *n* port M; (wine) porto M; (side of ship) bâbord M

portable [PAUR•tu•bl] *adj* portatif

porter [PAUR•tur] *n* porteur M

portfolio [paurt•FO•lee•O] *n* portefeuille M; (of artist) portfolio M

porthole [PAURT•houl] *n* hublot M

portion [PAUR•shn] *n* portion F

portly [PAURT•lee] *adj* corpulent

portrait [PAUR•trit] *n* portrait M

portray [paur•TRAI] *vt* dépeindre; représenter

portrayal [paur•TRAI•ul] *n* portrait M

Portugal [PAUR•chu•gl] *n* Portugal M

Portuguese [PAUR•chu•geez] *adj* portugais; *n* (person) Portugais M; (language) portugais M

postdate [post•DAIT] *vt* postdater

pose [poz] *n* pose F; *vt vi* poser; se faire passer pour

position [pu•ZI•shn] *n* position F; (job) poste M; *vt* placer

positive [PAH•zi•tiv] *adj* positif; (certain) sûr; (definite clear) précis

possess [pu•ZES] *vt* posséder

possession [pu•ZE•shn] *n* possession

possibility [PAH•si•BI•li•tee] *n* possibilité F

possible [PAH•si•bl] *adj*
possible

possibly [PAH•si•blee] *adv*
peut-être

post *n* (pole) poteau M; (job)
poste M; (mail) courrier M; *vt*
(mail) poster; (sign notice)
afficher; ~ office\ *n* poste F

postcard [POST•kard] *n* carte F
postale

postage [PO•stij] *n*
affranchissement M

postal [PO•stl] *adj* postal

poster [PO•stur] *n* affiche F

posterior [pah•STEEU•ree•ur]
adj n postérieur M

posthumous [PAH•styu•mus]
adj posthume

postman [POST•man] *n*
facteur M

postpone [post•PON] *vt*
remettre

posture [PAHS•chur] *vt*
posture F

pot [paht] *n* marmite F casserole
F; (for plant) pot M;
(marijauna) herbe F; *vt* mettre
en pot

potassium [pu•TA•see•um] *n*
potassium M

potato [pu•TAI•to] *n* pomme F
de terre

potent [PO•tunt] *adj* puissant;
(drink) fort

potential [pu•TEN•shl] *adj n*
potentiel M

potentially [pu•TEN•shu•lee]
adv potentiellement M

pothole [PAHT•houl] *n*
nide-poule M

potion [PO•shn] *n* breuvage M

pottery [PAH•tu•ree] *n*
poterie F

pouch *n* (of kangaroo etc)
poche M; (bag) petit sac M

poultry [POUL•tree] *n*
volaille F

pounce [pouns] *vi* bondir sur;
(capture) saisir

pound *n* (weight & currency)
livre F; (for dogs) fourrière F;
vt (strike) marteler; (crush)
piler

pour [paur] *vt* verser; *vi* couler
à flots; (rain) pleuvoir à verse;
(crowd) entrer/sortir en
masse; *vt* vider

pout [pout] *vi* faire la moue

poverty [PAH•vur•tee] *n*
pauvreté F

powder [POU•dur] *n* poudre F;
vt (face etc) poudrer

powdered [POU•durd] *adj* en
poudre

power [POU•ur] *n* (authority
ability) pouvoir M; (strength)
puissance F; (energy) énérgie
F; au pouvoir; en son pouvoir;
vt faire marcher

powerful [POU•ur•ful] *adj*
puissant

powerless [POU•ur•lis] *adj*
impuissant

practical [PRAK•ti•kl] *adj*
pratique

practical joke *n* farce F

practice [PRAK•tis] *n* pratique
F; (of skill) répétition F;
(training: sport) entraînement
M; (business profession)
cabinet M; (of profession)
exercice M; in ~\ en pratique;

out of ~\ rouillé; *vt* (sport)
s'entraîner à; (skill) s'exercer
à; (religion tradition)
pratiquer; *vi* s'entraîner;
s'exercer

practicing [PRAK•ti•sing] *adj*
(religious) pratiquant

prairie [PRAIU•ree] *n* prairie F

praise [praiz] *npl* louange(s)
F; éloge(s) M; *vt* louer
faire l'éloge de

prance [prans] *vi* (horse)
caracoler; (person) se pavaner

prank [prangk] *n* farce F

pray [prai] *vi* prier

prayer [praiur] *n* prière F

preach [preech] *vt vi* prêcher

preacher [PREE•chur] *n*
prédicateur M

precarious [pri•KA•ree•us] *adj*
précaire

precaution [pree•KAU•shn] *n*
précaution F

precede [pri•SEED] *vt* précéder

precedence [PRE•si•duns] *n*
préséance F; avoir la
préséance sur

precedent [PRE•si•dunt] *n*
précédent

precious [PRE•shus] *adj*
précieux

precipitate [pri•SI•pi•TAIT] *vt*
précipiter

precipitation
[pri•SI•pi•TAI•shn] *n*
précipitation F

precise [pri•SUYS] *adj* précis

precisely [pri•SUYS•lee] *adv*
précisément

precision [pri•SI•zhn] *n*
précision F

preclude [pri•KLOOD] *vt*
(exclude) exclure; (prevent)
empêcher

precocious [pri•KO•shus] *adj*
précoce

predator [PRE•du•tur] *n*
prédateur M

predecessor [PRE•di•SE•sur] *n*
prédécesseur M

predestined [pree•DES•tind]
adj prédestiné

predicament [pri•DI•ku•munt]
n situation F difficile; état F

predicate [PRE•di•kit] *adj n*
attribut M

predict [pri•DIKT] *vt* prédire

predictable [pri•DIK•tu•bl] *adj*
prévisible F

prediction [pri•DIK•shn] *n*
prédiction F

predisposed [PREE•dis•POZD]
adj ~ to\ prédisposé ~a

predominant
[pri•DAH•mi•nunt] *adj*
prédominant

preface [PRE•fus] *n* préface F

prefer [pri•FUR] *vt* préférer

preferable [PRE•fru•bl] *adj*
préférable

preferably [PRE•fru•blee] *adv*
de préférance

preference [PRE•fruns] *n*
préférence F

preferential [PRE•fu•REN•shl]
adj préférentiel

prefix [PREE•fiks] *n* préfixe M

pregnancy [PREG•nun•see] *n*
grossesse F

pregnant [PREG•nunt] *adj*
enceinte; (animal) pleine

prejudice [PRE•ju•dis] *npl*
préjugé(s) M; (harm)
préjudice M; *vt* influencer

prejudiced [PRE•ju•dist] *adj*
qui a des préjugés; partial

preliminary [pri•LI•mi•NE•ree]
adj préliminaire

prelude [PRAI•lood] *n*
prélude M

premarital [pree•MA•ri•tl] *adj*
avant le mariage

premature
[PREE•mu•CHOOUR] *adj*
prématuré

premier [pre•MEEUR] *adj*
premier; *n* premier ministre M

premiere [pri•MEEUR] *n*
première F

premise [PRE•mis] *n* prémisse
F; locaux M

premium [PREE•mee•um] *n*
prime M

premonition [PRE•mu•NI•shn]
n prémonition F

preoccupied
[pree•AH•kyu•PUYD] *adj*
préoccupé; préoccupé de

prepaid [pree•PAID] *adj* payé
d'avance

preparation [PRE•pu•RAI•shn]
n préparation F; ~s\
préparatifs M

prepare [pri•PAIUR] *vt*
préparer; *vi* se préparer

preposition [PRE•pu•ZI•shn] *n*
préposition F

preposterous [pri•PAH•stu•rus]
adj absurde ridicule

prerequisite [pri•RE•kwi•zit] *n*
contion F préalable

prerogative [pru•RAH•gu•tuv]
n prérogative F

prescribe [pri•SKRUYB] *vt*
prescrire

prescription [pri•SKRIP•shn] *n*
prescription F; (of doctor)
ordonnance F; (medicine)
medicament

presence [PRE•zns] *n*
présence F

present [*adj n.* PRE•znt *v.*
pri•ZENT] *adj* (time) actuel;
(not absent) présent; *n* (time)
présent M; (gift) cadeau M;
(grammar) présent M; *vt*
présenter

presentable [pri•ZEN•tu•bl] *n*
présentable

presentation
[PRE•zn•TAI•shn] *n*
présentation F; (speech report)
exposé M

presently [PRE•znt•lee] *adv*
actuellement

preserve [pri•ZURV] *vt*
proteger; conserver;
(maintain) maintenir; *npl* (of
fruit) confiture F

president [PRE•zi•dunt] *n*
président

presidential [PRE•zi•DEN•shl]
adj présidentiel

press [pres] *n* (machine tool)
presse F; (the media) presse
F; (for wire) pressoir M; *vt*
(push) appuyer sur; (squeeze)
presser; (iron) repasser;
(encourage urge) presser; *vi*
appuyer; se presser; ~ for\ *vt*
faire pression pour; ~ on\ *vi*
continuer

pressing [PRE•sing] *adj* urgent;
n repassage M

pressure [PRE•shur] *n* pression
F; *vt* faire pression sur

prestige [pre•STEEZH] *n*
prestige M

presumably [pri•ZOO•mu•blee]
adj vraisemblement

presume [pri•ZOOM] *vt*
présumer; supposer

presumption [pri•ZUMP•shn]
n présomption F

pretend [pri•TEND] *vi* faire
semblant; faire semblant de
faire qqch

pretension [pri•TEN•shn] *n*
prétention F

pretentious [pri•TEN•shus] *adj*
prétentieux

pretext [PREE•tekst] *n*
prétexte M

pretty [PRI•tee] *adj* joli; *adv*
assez

prevail [pri•VAIUL] *vi*
prévaloir l'emporter; (be
common abundant) avoir
cours

prevailing [pree•VAIU•ling]
adj dominant

prevalent [PRE•vu•lunt] *adj*
répandu; courant

prevent [pri•VENT] *vt*
empêcher; empêcher de faire

preventive [pri•VEN•tiv] *adj*
préventif

preview [PREE•vyoo] *n*
avant-première F

previous [PREE•vee•us] *adj*
précédent; antérieur

prey [prai] *n* proie F

price [pruys] *n* prix M; *vt* fixer
le prix de

priceless [PRUYS•lis] *asj*
inestimable

prick [prik] *vt* piquer; ~ up
your ears\ se dresser l'oreille

pride [pruyd] *n* fierté F;
orgueil M

priest [preest] *n* prêtre M

priesthood [PREEST•hud] *n*
sacerdoce M

prim [prim] *adj* guindé

primarily [pruy•ME•ri•lee] *adv*
premièrement

primary [PRUY•me•ree] *adj*
premier principal; *n* (in
elections) primaire F

primate [PRUY•mait] *n* primate
M; (of Church) primat M

prime [pruym] *adj* primordial
fondamental; (condition)
excellent; *n* be in one's ~\
être dans la fleur de la vie; *vt*
(paint) apprêter

primer [PRUY•mur] *n* (paint)
apprêt M

primitive [PRI•mi•tiv] *adj*
primitif

primrose [PRIM•roz] *n*
primevère F

prince [prins] *n* prince M

princess [PRIN•ses] *n*
princesse F

principal [PRIN•si•pl] *adj*
principal; *n* directeur M

principle [PRIN•si•pl] *n*
principe M

print *n* empreinte F; (writing)
caractères *fpl*; (fabric)
imprimé M; (art) gravure F;
in ~\ disponible; out of ~\

épuisé; *vt* imprimer; (publish) publier; (write) écrire à caractères d'imprimerie; *vi* imprimer

printer [PRIN•tur] *n* imprimeur M; (machine) imprimante F

printing [PRIN•ting] *n* impression

prior [PRUY•ur] *adj* antérieur; précédent; *prep* avant; avant de faire qqch

priority [pruy•AU•ri•tee] *n* priorité F; avoir la priorité (sur)

prism [PRI•zm] *n* prisme M

prison [PRI•zn] *n* prison F

prisoner [PRI•zu•nur] *n* prisonnier

privacy [PRUY•vu•see] *n* intimité F

private [PRUY•vit] *adj* privé; (personal) personnel; en privé F

privation [pruy•VAI•shn] *n* privation F

privilege [PRIV•lij] *n* privilège M

prize [pruyz] *adj* parfait; (animal) primé; *n* prix; *vt* priser

pro *n* (professional) pro M ~s and cons\ le pour et le contre

probability [PRAH•bu•BI•li•tee] *n* probabilité F

probable [PRAH•bu•bl] *adj* probable F

probably [PRAH•bu•blee] *adv* probablement F

probation [pro•BAI•shn] *n* (new employee) à l'essai; (criminal) en liberté surveillée

probe [prob] *n* (enquiry) enquête F; (medical satellite) sonde F; *vt* sonder

problem [PRAH•blum] *n* problème M; no ~ !\ pas de problème!

procedure [pru•SEE•jur] *n* procédure F

proceed [pru•SEED] *vi* avancer; continuer; se mettre à faire qqch

proceeding [pru•SEE•ding] *adj* suivant; *npl* (court) poursuites F

proceeds [PRO•seedz] *npl* recette F

process [PRAH•ses] *n* processus M; (method) procédé M; *vt* traiter

procession [pru•SE•shn] *n* procession F cortège M

proclaim [pru•CLAIM] *vt* proclamer

procrastinate [pru•KRA•sti•NAIT] *vi* faire traîner les choses

procure [pru•KYOOUR] *vt* procurer; (for oneself) se procurer

prod [prahd] *vt* pousser

prodigal [PRAH•di•gl] *adj* prodigue

prodigy [PRAH•di•jee] *n* prodige M

produce [*n.* PRO•doos *v.* pru•DOOS] *npl* produits M; *vt* produire; (reveal) présenter; (cause) causer; (theater) mettre en scène

producer [pru•DOO•sur] *n* (manufacturer filmmaker)

producteur M; (theater)
metteur M en scène

product [PRAH•duhkt] *n*
produit M

production [pru•DUHK•shn] *n*
production F; (theater) mise F
en scène

productive [pru•DUHK•tiv] *adj*
productif; (experience
conversation) fructueux

profane [pru•FAIN] *adj* impie

profession [pru•FE•shn] *n*
profession F

professional [pru•FE•shu•nl]
adj n professionnel M

professor [pru•FE•sur] *n*
professeur M

proficiency [pru•FI•shn•see] *n*
compétence F; aptitude F

profile [PRO•fuyul] *n* profil M

profit [PRAH•fit] *n* bénéfice M
profit M; *vi* profiter

profitable [PRAH•fi•tu•bl] *adj*
rentable lucratif; (experience
etc) profitable

profound [pro•FOUND] *adj*
profond

profuse [pru•FYOOS] *adj*
abondant

program [PRO•gram] *n*
programme M; (tv radio
show) émission F; *vt*
programmer

progress [*n.* PRAH•gres *v.*
pru•GRES] *n* progrès M;
make ~\ faire des progrès; in
~\ en cours; *vi* progresser
avancer

progressive [pru•GRE•siv] *adj*
(movement change) progessif;
(person) progressiste

prohibit [pru•HI•bit] *vt*
interdire; prohiber; défendre

prohibition [PRO•hi•BI•shn] *n*
prohibition F interdiction F

project [*n.* PRAH•jekt *v.*
pru•JEKT] *n* projet M; *vt*
projeter; (estimate) prévoir
estimer

projection [pru•JEK•shn] *n*
projection F; (estimation)
prévision F

proletariat [PRO•lu•TA•ree•ut]
n prolétariat M

prolong [pro•LAUNG] *vt*
prolonger

promenade
[PRAH•mu•NAHD] *n*
promenade F

prominent [PRAH•mi•nunt] *adj*
proéminent; (important)
important

promiscuous
[pru•MI•skyoo•us] *adj* de
mœurs légères

promise [PRAH•mis] *n*
promesse F; *vt vi* promettre; ~
sb sth\ promettre qqch à qqn

promising [PRAH•mi•sing] *adj*
prometteur

promote [pru•MOT] *vt*
promouvoir

promoter [pru•MO•tur] *n*
organisateur M

promotion [pru•MO•shn] *n*
promotion F

prompt [prahmpt] *adj* prompt
rapide; *n* (theater) réplique F;
vt provoquer

promptly [PRAHMPT•lee] *adv*
promptement rapidement

prone [pron] *adj* enclin à

prong [prahng] *n* (of fork etc)
dent M

pronoun [PRO•noun] *n*
pronom M

pronounce [pru•NOUNS] *vt*
prononcer

pronounced [pru•NOUNST]
adj prononcé

pronunciation
[pru•NUHN•see•AI•shn] *n*
prononciation F

proof *n* preuve F; (printing)
épreuve F; (alcohol) degré M

prop [prahp] *n* support M étai
M; *vt* soutenir étayer; *npl*
accessoires M

propaganda
[PRAH•pu•GAN•du] *n*
propagande F

propel [pru•PEL] *vt* propulser;
(cause) causer

propeller [pru•PE•lur] *n*
hélice F

proper [PRAH•pur] *adj*
(appropriate) approprié;
proprié; (suitable) convenable;
(correct) correct; (real) vrai

properly [PRAH•pur•lee] *adv*
correctement; convenablement

property [PRAH•pur•tee] *npl*
(possessions) biens propriété
F; (land) terres F; (aspect;
feature) propriété

prophecy [PRAH•fi•see] *n*
prophétie F

prophesy [PRAH•fi•SUY] *vt*
prédire

prophet [PRAH•fit] *n*
prophète M

proportion [pru•PAUR•shn] *n*
proportion F; (part) part F
partie F

proposal [pru•PO•zl] *n*
proposition F; (of marriage)
demande F en mariage

propose [pru•POZ] *vt* proposer;
(a toast) porter; *vi* faire une
demande en mariage

proposition [PRAH•pu•ZI•shn]
n proposition F

proprietor [pru•PRUY•u•tur] *n*
propriétaire MF

prose [proz] *n* prose F

prosecute [PRAH•si•KYOOT]
vt poursuivre (en justice)

prosecution
[PRAH•si•KYOO•shn] *npl*
poursuites F (judiciaires);
(lawyers) partie M plaignant

prosecutor
[PRAH•si•KYOO•tur] *n*
plaignant M

prospect [PRAH•spekt] *n*
possibilité F; *vt vi* prospecter

prospective [pru•SPEK•tiv] *adj*
éventuel

prosper [PRAH•spur] *vi*
prospérer

prosperity [prah•SPE•ri•tee] *n*
prospérité F

prosperous [PRAH•spu•rus]
adj prospère

prostitute [PRAH•sti•TOOT] *n*
prostituée F

protect [pru•TEKT] *vt* protéger

protection [pru•TEK•shn] *n*
protection F

protective [pru•TEK•tiv] *adj*
protecteur; (coating etc) de
protection

protein [PRO•teen] *n* protéine F

protest [*n.* PRO•test *v.*
pru•TEST] *n* protestation F;

(march) manifestation; *vt*
protester contre; *vi* protester
Protestant [PRAH•ti•stunt] *adj*
n protestant M
protester [pro•TE•stur] *n*
nanifestant M
protrude [pru•TROOD] *vt*
dépasser; avancer
proud *adj* fier; (conceited)
orgueilleux
prove [proov] *vt* prouver
proverb [PRAH•vurb] *n*
proverbe M
provide [pru•VUYD] *vt* fournir;
fournir qqch à qqn; *vt*
subvenir aux besoins de
provided [pru•VUY•did] *conj*
pourvu que; *adj* fourné
providing [pru•VUY•ding] *conj*
pourvu que
province [PRAH•vins] *n*
province F
provincial [pru•VIN•shl] *adj*
provincial
provision [pru•VI•zhn] *n*
provision F; (in contract etc)
clause F
provoke [pru•VOK] *vt*
provoquer; (annoy) contrarier
prowess [PROU•is] *n*
prouesse F
prowl [prouul] *vi* rôder
prowler [PROU•lur] *n*
rôdeur M
proximity [prahk•SI•mi•tee] *n*
proximité F
prude [prood] *n* prude F
prudent [PROO•dnt] *adj*
prudent
prudish [PROO•dish] *adj*
prude F

prune [proon] *n* pruneau M; *vt*
tailler
pry [pruy] (~ cap off bottle) *vt;*
(~ into neighbor's business)
vt; vi soulever
psalm [sahm] *n* psaume M
pseudonym [SOO•du•NIM] *n*
pseudonyme M
psyche [SUY•kee] *n* psyché F
psychiatrist [suy•KUY•a•trist]
n psychiatre MF
psychiatry [suy•KUY•a•tree] *n*
psychiatrie F
psychic [SUY•kik] *n* médium M
psychological
[SUY•ku•LAH•ji•kl] *n*
psychologique
psychologist [suy•KAH•lu•jist]
n psychologue MF
psychology [suy•KAH•lu•jee] *n*
psychologie
psychotic [suy•KAH•tik] *adj n*
psychotique F
pub [puhb] *n* pub M; café M;
taverne F
puberty [PYOO•bur•tee] *n*
puberté F
pubic [PYOO•bik] *adj* de pubis
public [PUH•blik] *adj* public
(publique); *n* public M
publication [PUH•bli•KAI•shn]
n publication F
publicity [puh•BLI•si•tee] *n*
publicité F
publicize [PUH•bli•SUYZ] *vt*
faire connaître au public
publish [PUH•blish] *vt* publier
publisher [PUH•bli•shur] *n*
éditeur
puck [puhk] *n* (of hockey)
palet M

pucker [PUH•kur] *vt* plisser

pudding [PU•ding] *n* dessert crémeux M

puddle [PUH•dl] *n* flaque F

puff [puhf] *n* (of smoke) bouffée F; *vt* (cigarette etc) tirer sur; *vi* (pant) haleter

pull [pul] *n* influence F; tirer sur qqch; *vt* tirer; (muscle) se froisser; *vi* tirer; *vt* séparer; *vt* tirer sur; *vt* baiser; (demolish) démolir; *vi* (car) se ranger; *vt* enlever ôter; (attempt etc) réussir; *vi* (withdraw) se retirer; (car) déboîter; (train) démarrer; *vi* (car) se ranger; *vi* s'en sortir; *vt* remonter; *vi* s'arrêter

pulley [PU•lee] *n* poulie F

pulp [puhlp] *n* pulpe F

pulpit [PUHL•pit] *n* chaire F

pulsate [PUHL•sait] *vi* battre; (music) vibrer

pulse [puhls] *n* pouls M; *vi* battre

pulverize [PUHL•vu•RUYZ] *vt* pulvériser

pumice [PUH•mis] *n* pierre F ponce

pump [puhmp] *n* pompe F; (shoe) escarpin M; *vt* pomper; ~ up\ *vt* gonfler

pumpkin [PUHMP•kin] *n* potiron

pun [puhn] *n* jeu M de mots; calembour M

punch [puhnch] *n* coup M de poing; (drink) punch M; *vt* donner un coup de poing à; (paper) poinçonner perforer

punctual [PUHNGK•choo•ul] *adj* ponctuel

punctuation [PUHNGK•choo•AI•shn] *n* ponctuation F

puncture [PUHNGK•chur] *n* crevaison F; *vt* crever

punish [PUH•nish] *vt* punir

punishment [PUH•nish•munt] *n* punition F châtiment M

punk [puhngk] *adj* punk; *n* (music) punk M; (person) punk MF

pupil [PYOO•pl] *n* élève MF; (of eye) pupille F

puppet [PUH•pit] *n* marionette F; (controlled person) pantin M

puppy [PUH•pee] *n* chiot M; petit chien M

purchase [PUR•chis] *n* achat M; *vt* acheter

pure [pyoour] *adj* pur

purgatory [PUR•gu•TAU•ree] *n* purgatoire M

purge [purj] *n* purge F; *vt* purger

purify [PYOOU•ri•FUY] *vt* purifier

puritan [PYU•ri•tun] *adj n* puritain M

purity [PYOOU•ri•tee] *n* pureté F

purple [PUR•pl] *adj n* violet M

purpose [PUR•pus] *n* raison F; (objective) but M objet M; on ~\ *adv* exprès

purr [pur] *vi* ronronner

purse [purs] *n* sac M à main; *vt* (lips) pincer

pursue [pur•SOO] *vt* poursuivre

pursuit [pur•SOOT] *n* poursuite F; (endeavor) occupation F

push *n* poussée F; *vt* pousser; (button) appuyer sur; (advertise) faire de la publicité pour; *vi* pousser; appuyer; ~ around\ *vt* harceler; ~ in\ *vt* enfoncer; ~ off\ *vi* filer; ~ on\ *vi* continuer; ~ for\ *vt* faire pression pour

put *vt* mettre poser placer; (express) *vt* exprimer; ~ across\ *vt* communiquer; ~ back\ *vt* remettre; ~ down\ *vt* déposer; (suppress) réprimer; (insult) insulter; ~ off\ *vt* (postpone) remettre à plus tard; ~ on\ (clothes) mettre; (tape record etc) mettre; ~ out\ *vt* (disturb impose) déranger; ~ up with\ supporter

putrid [PYOO•trid] *adj* putride

putty [PUH•tee] *n* mastic M

puzzle [PUH•zl] *n* (game) casse-tête M; (jigsaw) puzzle M; (mystery) énigme F; *vt* rendre perplexe

pyramid [PI•ru•MID] *n* pyramide F

python [PUY•thahn] *n* python

Q

quack [kwak] *n* (of duck) coin-coin M; (doctor) charlatan M

quadruple [kwah•DROO•pl] *vt vi* quadrupler

quadruplets [kwah•DROO•plits] *npl* quadruplés M

quagmire [KWAG•muyur] *n* bourbier

quail [kwaiul] *n* caille F

quaint [kwaint] *adj* pittoresque

quake [kwaik] *n* tremblement M de terre; *vi* trembler

qualification [KWAH•li•fi•KAI•shn] *n* qualification F compétence F; (degree) diplôme M; (condition) réserve F

qualify [KWAH•li•FUY] *vt* qualifier; *vi* remplir les conditions reqises pour; (in race etc) se qualifier

quality [KWAH•li•tee] *n* qualité F

qualm [kwahm] *n* doute F

quantity [KWAHN•ti•tee] *n* quantité F

quarantine [KWAU•run•TEEN] *n* quarantaine F; *vt* mettre en quarantaine

quarrel [KWAU•rl] *n* querrelle F; *vi* se quereller

quarry [KWAU•ree] *n* carrière F

quart [kwaurt] *n* (liter) litre M

quarter [KWAUR•tur] *n* quart
•M; (coin) pièce F de 25 cents;
~ past five\ cinq heures et
quart; ~ to five\ cinq heures
moins quart; (neighborhood)
quartier M; *vt* partager en
quatre; ~s *npl*\ quartiers *mpl*

quarterly [KWAUR•tur•lee] *adj*
trimestriel; *n* publication F
trimestrielle

quartet [kwaur•TET] *n*
quatuor M

quartz [kwaurts] *n* quartz M

quay [kee] *n* quai M

queasy [KWEE•zee] *adj* avoir
mal à l'estomac

queen [kween] *n* reine F; (in
cards) dame F

quell [kwell] *vt* réprimer

quench [kwench] *vt* (fire)
éteindre; se désaltérer

query [KWE•ree] *n* question F

quest [kwest] *n* quête F

question [KWES•chn] *n*
question; poser une question;
en question; *vt* questionner F;
~ mark\ *n* point M
d'interrogation

questionable
[KWES•chu•nu•bl] *adj*
(arguable) discutable;
(suspicious) douteux

questionnaire
[KWES•chu•NAIUR] *n*
questionnaire F

quibble [KWI•bl] *vi* chicaner a
propos de

quiche [keesh] *n* quiche F

quick [kwik] *adj* rapide;
prompte; *adv* vite rapidement

quicken [KWI•kn] *vt* accélerer;
vi s'accélerer

quickly [KWIK•lee] *adv* vite;
rapidement

quicksand [KWIK•sand] *npl*
sables M mouvants

quiet [KWUY•it] *adj* tranquille;
calme; (silent) silencieux; be
~!\ tais-toi!; *n* tranquillité F
calme M; *vt* ~ down\ calmer;
vi se calmer

quietly [KWUY•it•lee] *adv*
calmement; silencieusement;
(speak) doucement

quilt [kwilt] *n* édedron M

quinine [KWUY•nuyn] *n*
quinine F

quintet [kwin•TET] *n* quintelle
F

quintuplets [kwin•TUH•plits] *n*
quintuplés *mpl*

quit [kwit] *vt* (give up) arrêter
de; (job) qùitter; *vi* (give up)
abandonner; (resign)
démissioner

quite [kwuyt] *adv* plutôt assez;
(very) très; (completely) tout
à fait

quiver [KWI•vur] *n* frisson M;
vi frissonner

quiz [kwiz] *n* quiz M; petit
examen M; *vt* interroger

quota [KWO•tu] *n* quota M

quotation [kwo•TAI•shn] *n*
citation F; (estimate) devis M

quotation marks *npl*
guillemets M

quote [kwot] *n* citation F;
(estimate) devis M; *vt* citer

quotient [KWO•shnt] *n*
quotient M

R

rabbi [RA•buy] *n* rabbin M

rabbit [RA•bit] *n* lapin M

rabble [RA•bl] *n* cohue F;
(people) populace F

rabid [RA•bid] *adj* enragé

rabies [RAI•beez] *n* rage F

raccoon [ra•KOON] *n* raton M
laveur

race [rais] *n* course F; (ethnic)
race F; *vt* faire la course avec;
(engine) emballer; *vi* courir

racetrack [RAIS•trak] *n* piste F

racism [RAI•si•zm] *n*
racisme M

racist [RAI•sist] *adj n* raciste
MF

rack [rak] *n* (for luggage)
porte-bagages M; (for dishes
cups etc) égouttoir M; (shelf)
étagère F

racket [RA•kit] *n* racquette F;
(noise) vacarme F tapage M;
(illegal business) racket M

racketeer [RAK•uh•TEEUR] *n*
vi racketteur M

radiant [RAI•dee•unt] *adj*
radieux; rayonnant

radiation [RAI•dee•AI•shn] *n*
radiation F

radiator [RAI•dee•AI•tur] *n*
radiateur M

radical [RA•di•kl] *adj n*
radical M

radio [RAI•dee•O] *n* radio M

radioactive [RAI•dee•o•AK•tiv]
adj radioactif

radiology [RAI•dee•AH•lu•jee]
n radiologie F

radish [RA•dish] *n* radis M

radius [RAI•dee•us] *n* rayon M

raffle [RA•fl] *n* loterie F; *vt*
play a ~\ mettre en loterie

raft *n* radeau

rafter [RAF•tur] *n* chevron M

rag *n* chiffon M; (newspaper)
torchon M; ~s (clothes)\ *npl*
haillons M

rage [raij] *n* rage F; *vi* (person)
être furieux; (storm) faire rage

ragged [RA•gid] *adj* en haillons

raid *n* (military) raid M; (by
police) descente F; *vt* faire un
raid sur; faire une descente
dans

rail [raiul] *n* garde-fou M; (of
stairs) rampe; (of railroad)
rail M

railing [RAIU•ling] *n* garde-fou
M; (of stairs) rampe

railroad [RAIUL•rod] *n* chemin
M de fer; ~ station\ gare F; ~
track\ voie F ferée

rain *n* pluie F; *vi* pleuvoir; il
pleut

rainbow [RAIN•bo] *n* arc-en
ciel M

raindrop [RAIN•drahp] *n*
goutte F de pluie

rainfall [RAIN•fauul] *n* chute F
de pluie; (total) hauteur F de
précipitations

rainy [RAI•nee] *adj* pluveux

raise [raiz] *n* augmentation F; *vt* lever; (increase) augmenter; (rear) élever; (money) se procurer; ~ one's voice\ élever la voix; (question subject) soulever

raisin [RAI•zin] *n* raisin M sec

rake [raik] *n* râteau M; *vt* (ground) ratisser; (leaves) râteler

rally [RA•lee] *n* (meeting) rassemblement M; (protest) manifestation F; *vi* se ralier

ram *n* belier M; (crash into) emboutir; (push) tasser

ramble [RAM•bl] *n* (walk) randonnée F; *vi* faire une randonée; (speak) radoter

ramp [ramp] *n* rampe

rampage [RAM•paij] *n* se dechaîner

rancid [RAN•sid] *n* rance

random [RAN•dum] *adj* fait au hasard; *n* au hasard

range [rainj] *n* (scope) portée F; (of mountains) chaîne F; (stove) fourneau F; (farm) (grand) pâturage M; (of choices) gamme F; *vt* mettre en rang; *vi* (vary) varier

rank [rangk] *n* rang M; (military) grade M; *vt* classer; *vi* aller de pair avec; compter parmi

ransack [RAN•sak] *vt* piller; fouiller dans saccager

ransom [RAN•sum] *n* rançon M; hold ~\ mettre à rançon; *vt* rançonner

rant *vi* tempêter

rap *n* (music) rap M; *vt* frapper sur; taper sur

rape [raip] *n* viol M; *vt* violer

rapid [RA•pid] *adj* rapide; *npl* rapides M

rapist [RAI•pist] *n* violeur M

rapport [ru•PAUR] *n* rapport M

rapture [RAP•chur] *n* ravissement M

rare [raiur] *adj* rare; (steak, etc) saignant

rarely [RAIUR•lee] *adv* rarement

rarity [RA•ri•tee] *n* rareté F

rascal [RA•skl] *n* polisson M

raspberry [RAZ•be•ree] *n* framboise F

rat *n* rat M

rate [rait] *n* taux M; (speed) vitesse F; (price) tarif M; at any ~\ en tout cas; *vt* classer; considérer

rather [RA•thur] *adv* plutôt; plutôt que; I would ~\ j'aimerais mieux

ratify [RA•ti•FUY] *vt* ratifier

rating [RAI•ting] *n* cote F; classement M

ratio [RAI•shee•O] *n* proportion F

ration [RA•shn] *n* ration F; *vt* rationer

rational [RA•shu•nl] *adj* rationnel

rattle [RA•tl] *n* (noise) cliquetis M; (of motor engine) bruit M de ferraille; (toy) rochet M; *vt* affoler; *vi* cliqueter; faire un bruit de ferraille

rattlesnake [RA•tl•SNAIK] *n* serpent M à sonnettes

ravage [RA•vij] *n* ravage M; *vt* ravager

rave [raiv] *vi* tempêter contre; s'extasier

raven [RAI•vn] *n* corbeau M

ravenous [RA•vu•nus] *adj* vorace

ravine [ru•VEEN] *n* ravin M

ravishing [RA•vi•shing] *adj* ravissant

raw [rau] *adj* (food) cru; (untreated) brut; (weather) froid

raw material *n* matière F première

ray [rai] *n* rayon M

raze [raiz] *vt* raser

razor [RAI•zur] *n* rasoir M

razor blade *n* lame F de rasoir M

reach [reech] *n* portée F atteinte F; à portée; hors de portée; *vt* atteindre; (place) arriver à; (decision) parvenir à; *vi* s'étendre

react [ree•AKT] *vi* réagir

reaction [ree•AK•shn] *n* réaction F

reactionary [ree•AK•shu•NE•ree] *adj n* réactionnaire MF

read [reed] *vt* lire; parcourir; (gauge meter) indiquer; *vi* lire

reader [REE•dur] *n* lecteur M

readily [RE•di•lee] *adv* volontiers

reading [REE•ding] *n* lecture F

readjust [REE•u•JUHST] *vt* rajuster; *vi* réadapter

ready [RE•dee] *adj* prêt; se préparer

real [reeul] *adj* véritable vrai; réel

real estate *n* biens *mpl* immobiliers

realism [REEU•LI•zm] *n* réalisme M

realist [REEU•list] *n* réaliste MF

realistic [reeu•LI•stik] *adj* réaliste; (likely) vraisemblable

reality [ree•A•li•tee] *n* réalité F

realization [REEU•li•ZAI•shn] *n* réalisation F

realize [REEU•LUYZ] *vt* se rendre compte de; (make real) réaliser

really [REEU•lee] *adv* vraiment; vraiment?

realm [relm] *n* domaine M; (kingdom) royaume M

realtor [REEUL•tur] *n* agent M immobilier

reap [reep] *vt* moissonner; (benefit profit) récolter

reappear [REE•u•PEEUR] *vi* réapparaître reparaître

rear [reeur] *adj* arrière de derrière; *n* arrière M; (buttocks) derrière M; *vt* élever

reason [REE•zn] *n* raison F; *vi* raisonner

reasonable [REE•zu•nu•bl] *adj* raisonnnable

reasonably [REE•zu•nu•blee] *adv* raisonnablement; assez bien

reasoning [REE•zu•ning] *n* raisonnement M

reassure [REE•u•SHOOUR] *vt* rassurer

rebate [REE•bait] *n* rabais M

rebel [adj n. RE•bl v. ri•BEL]
adj n rebelle MF; *vi* rebeller

rebellion [ri•BEL•yun] *n*
rébellion F

rebellious [ri•BEL•yus] *adj*
rebelle

rebirth [REE•burth] *n*
renaissance F

rebound [REE•bound] *n* rebond
M; *vi* rebondir

rebuild [ree•BILD] *vt*
reconstruire

rebuke [ri•BYOOK] *n*
réprimande F; *vt* réprimander

recall [REE•kaul] *n* rappel M; *vt*
rappeler; (remember) se
rappeler

recede [ri•SEED] *vi* s'éloigner

receding [ri•SEE•ding] *adj*
(hairline) dégarni

receipt [ri•SEET] *n* réception F;
(record of purchase) reçu M

receive [ri•SEEV] *vt* recevoir

receiver [ri•SEE•vur] *n* (of
telephone radio) récepteur M

recent [REE•snt] *adj* récent

recently [REE•snt•lee] *adv*
récemmment

receptacle [ri•SEP•ti•kl] *n*
récipient

reception [ri•SEP•shn] *n*
réception F

recess [REE•ses] *n* (at school)
récréation F; (of court)
ajournement M; (of congress
parliament etc) vacances *fpl*

recession [ri•SE•shn] *n*
récession F

recipe [RE•si•pee] *n* recette F

recipient [ri•SI•pee•unt] *n*
bénéficiaire mf; (of award)
récipiendaire mf

reciprocal [ri•SI•pru•kl] *adj*
réciproque

recital [ri•SUY•tl] *n* récital

recite [ri•SUYT] *vt* réciter

reckless [REK•lis] *adj*
imprudent insouciant

recklessness [REK•lis] *n*
imprudence F insouciance F

reckon [RE•kn] *vt* (suppose)
supposer; imaginer; (consider)
considérer

reclaim [ri•KLAIM] *vt*
réclamer; (land) amender

recline [ri•KLUYN] *vi* être
allongé

recluse [RE•kloos] *n* reclus M

recognition [RE•kug•NI•shn] *n*
reconnaissance F

recognizable
[RE•kug•NUY•zu•bl] *adj*
reconnaissable

recognize [RE•kug•NUYZ] *vt*
reconnaître

recoil [n. REE•koiul v.
ri•KOIUL] *n* (of gun) recul
M; *vi* reculer

recollect [RE•ku•LEKT] *vt* se
rappeler

recollection [RE•ku•LEK•shn]
n souvenir M

recommend [RE•ku•MEND] *vt*
recommander

recommendation
[RE•ku•men•DAI•shn] *n*
recommandation F

reconcile [RE•kun•SUYUL] *vt*
(people) réconcilier; (plans

etc) concilier; ~ oneself to
sth\ se résigner à qqch

reconciliation
[RE•kun•SI•lee•AI•shn] *n*
réconciliation F

reconnaissance
[ri•KAH•ni•suns] *n*
reconnaissance F

reconsider [REE•kun•SI•dur] *vt*
reconsidérer

reconstruct
[REE•kun•STRUHKT] *vt*
reconstuire; (crime scene)
reconstituer

record [adj n. RE•kurd v.
ri•KAURD] *n* record; *n* (file)
dossier M; (album) disque M;
(highest lowest etc) record M;
(register) registre M; (report)
rapport M; break a ~\ battre
un record; *vt* (on tape etc)
enregistrer; (write down)
noter

record player *n* tourne-disque
M

recording [ri•KAUR•ding] *n*
enregistrement M

recount [ri•KOUNT] *vt* (tell)
raconter; (count again)
recompter

recourse [REE•kaurs] *n*
recours M

recover [ri•KUH•vur] *vt* (replace; recover) recouvrir; (get
back) récuperer; *vi* (get well)
se rétablir; (from shock
hardship) se remettre;
(economy; nation) se redresser

recovery [ri•KUH•vu•ree] *n*
récupération F; (from illness)

rétablissement M; (economy
etc) redressement;

recreation [RE•kree•AI•shn] *n*
récréation F

recruit [ri•KROOT] *n* recrue F;
vt vi recruter

rectangle [REK•TANG•gl] *n*
rectangle M

rectify [REK•ti•FUY] *vt* rectifier

rectory [REK•tu•ree] *n*
presbytère M

recuperate [ri•KOO•pu•RAIT]
vi se rétablir

recurring [ri•KU•ring] *adj*
périodique; fréquent

red *adj* rouge; (hair) roux
(rousse); *n* rouge M

Red Cross *n* Croix-Rouge F

red-hot [RED•HOT] *n* chauffé
au rouge; brûlant

redden [RE•dn] *vt vi* rougir

redeem [ri•DEEM] *vt*
rembourser; (from
pawnbroker) dégager

redeemer [ri•DEE•mur] *n*
sauveur M; R~\
Rédempteur M

redeeming [ri•DEE•ming] *adj*
qui rachète

redemption [ri•DEM•shn] *n*
rédemption

redhead [RED•hed] *n* roux M
(rousse)

redheaded [RED•he•dud] *adj*
roux (rousse)

redo [ree•DOO] *vt* refaire

reduce [ri•DOOS] *vt* réduire

reduction [ri•DUHK•shn] *n*
réduction F; (discount)
rabais M

reed *n* (plant) roseau M

reef *n* récif M écueil M

reek *vi* puer qqch

reel [reeul] *n* bobine F; (of fishing) moulinet M; *vt* bobiner; *vi* (waver sway) chanceler; *vt* remonter

refer [ri•FUR] *vt* adresser or envoyer qqn à; *vt* parler de; (consult) se référer à; (concern) concerner

referee [RE•fu•REE] *n* arbitre M; *vt* arbitrer; *vi* être arbitre

reference [RE•fruns] *n* (for information) référence F; (mention) mention F allusion F; (for job) référence F; (person) répondant M

referendum [RE•fu•REN•dum] *n* référendum M

refill [n. REE•fil v. ree•FIL] *n* (for pen etc) recharge F; *vt* remplir à nouveau

refine [ri•FUYN] *vt* raffiner

refined [ri•FUYND] *adj* raffiné

refinery [ri•FUY•nu•ree] *n* raffinerie F

reflect [ri•FLEKT] *vt* réfléchir; (show) refléter; *vi* (think) réfléchir

reflection [ri•FLEK•shn] *n* réflexion F; (image) reflet M; (sign) signe M; (thought) réflexion F

reflexive [ri•FLEK•siv] *adj* (grammar) réfléchi; *n* (verb) verbe M pronominal réfléchi

reform [ri•FAURM] *n* réforme F; *vt* réformer

Reformation [RE•fur•MAI•shn] *n* la Réforme

refrain [ri•FRAIN] *n* refrain M; s'abstenir de

refresh [ri•FRESH] *vt* rafraîchir

refreshing [ri•FRE•shing] *adj* agréable; (drink) refraîchissant

refreshments [ri•FRESH•munts] *npl* rafraîchissements mpl

refrigerator [ri•FRI•ju•RAI•tur] *n* réfrigérateur M; frigidaire M

refuel [ree•FYOOUL] *vi* se ravitailler en carburant

refuge [RE•fyooj] *n* refuge M; se réfugier

refund [n. REE•fuhnd v. ri•FUHND] *n* remboursement M; *vt* rembourser

refusal [ri•FYOO•zl] *n* refus M

refuse [ri•FYOOZ] *vt vi* refuser; refuser de faire qqch

refute [ri•FYOOT] *vt* réfuter

regal [REE•gl] *adj* royal

regard [ri•GAHRD] *n* respect M estime F; à cet égard; *vt* considérer; *prep* en ce qui concerne

regarding [ri•GAHR•ding] *prep* en ce qui concerne

regardless [ri•GAHRD•lis] *adv* quand même; *prep* sans se soucier de

regime [ri•ZHEEM] *n* régime M

regiment [RE•ji•munt] *n* régiment M

region [REE•jn] *n* région F

register [RE•gi•stur] *n* registre M; *vt* enregistrer; incrire; (officially) déclarer; *vi* s'inscire

registration [RE•ji•STRAI•shn]
n inscription F
enregistrement M

regret [ri•GRET] *n* regret M; *vt*
regretter

regular [RE•gyu•lur] *adj*
régulier; (size) standard;
(usual) habituel; (ordinary)
ordinaire; *n* (bar customer)
habitué

regularly [RE•gyu•lur•lee] *adv*
régulièrement

regulate [RE•gyu•LAIT] *vt*
régler

regulation [RE•gyu•LAI•shn] *n*
réglementation F

rehabilitate
[REE•hu•BI•li•TAIT] *vt*
(patient) rééduquer; (criminal)
réhabiliter

rehearsal [ri•HUR•sl] *n*
répétition F

rehearse [ri•HURS] *vt vi*
répéter

reign [rain] *n* règne M; *vi*
régner

reimburse [REE•im•BURS] *vt*
rembourser

reindeer [RAIN•deeur] *n*
renne M

reinforce [REE•in•FAURS] *vt*
renforcer

reinforcement
[REE•in•FAURS•munt] *n*
renforcement M; *npl*
renforts M

reiterate [ree•I•tu•RAIT] *vt*
réitérer

reject [ri•JEKT] *vt* rejeter;
refuser

rejection [ri•JEK•shn] *n* rejet
M; refus M

rejoice [ri•JOIS] *vt* se réjouir
(de)

rejuvenate [ri•JOO•vu•NAIT]
vt rejeunir

relapse [ri•LAPS] *n* rechute F

relate [ri•LAIT] *vt* établir un
rapport entre; (tell) raconter;
(report) rapporter; *vt* se
rapporter à; (understand)
s'entendre

related [ri•LAI•tid] *adj* lié;
(relatives) apparenté

relation [ri•LAI•shn] *n* rapport;
(relative) parent M; ~s *npl*
(relationship)\ relations *fpl*

relationship [ri•LAI•shn•SHIP]
n relations *fpl*; (romantic)
liaison F; (connection) lien M

relative [RE•lu•tiv] *adj* relatif;
n parent M

relatively [RE•lu•tiv•lee] *adv*
relativement

relax [ri•LAKS] *vt* détendre
relaxer; (law etc) relâcher; *vi*
se détendre; se relâcher

relaxation [ri•LAK•SAI•shn] *n*
relaxation F; détente F

relaxed [ri•LAKST] *adj*
détendu

release [ri•LEES] *n* libération;
(publication) sortie F; (of
record) nouveau disque M;
(of gas) émission F; (for
press) communiqué M; *vt*
(free) libérer; (publication)
sortir; (news) publier;
(untangle unstick etc) dégager

relent [ri•LENT] *vi* se laisser
fléchir

relentless [ri•LENT•lis] *adj*
implacable

relevant [RE•lu•vunt] *adj* utile;
important

reliable [ri•LUY•u•bl] *adj*
fiable; sérieux

relief [ri•LEEF] *n* (from pain
problems) soulagement M;
(help) assistance F

relieve [ri•LEEV] *n* (from pain
problems) soulager; (take over
for) relayer; (help) secourir

religion [ri•LI•jn] *n* religion F

religious [ri•LI•jus] *adj*
religieux

relinquish [ri•LING•kwish] *vt*
abandonner; (claim etc)
renoncer à

relish [RE•lish] *n* condiment M;
vt se délecter à

reluctant [ri•LUHK•tunt] *adj*
peu disposé

reluctantly [ri•LUHK•tunt•lee]
adv à contre-cœur

rely [ri•LUY] *vt* compter sur;
(be dependent on) dépendre
sur

remain [ri•MAIN] *vt vi* rester

remainder [ri•MAIN•dur] *n*
reste M

remains [ri•MAINZ] *npl* restes
M; (ruins) ruines F

remark [ri•MAHRK] *n*
remarque F; *vt* faire remarquer

remarkable [ri•MAHR•ku•bl]
adj remarquable

remedy [RE•mi•dee] *n* remède
M; *vt* remédier à

remember [ri•MEM•bur] *vt* se
souvenir de se rappeler; *vi* se
souvenir se rappeler

remind [ri•MUYND] *vt* rappeler
qqch à qqn; rappeler à qqn de
faire qqch

reminisce [RE•mi•NIS] *vi*
raconter des souvenirs

remiss [ri•MIS] *adj* négligent

remit [ri•MIT] *vt* (~ a debt); (~
a sum of money) remettre;
envoyer

remnant [REM•nunt] *n* (~s of
my memory) restant;
vestiges M

remodel [ree•MAH•dl] *vt*
remodeler

remorse [ri•MAURS] *n*
remords M

remote [ri•MOT] *adj* distant;
éloigné

remote control *n*
télécommande F

removal [ri•MOO•vl] *n* (of an
object of make-up)
enlèvement M

remove [ri•MOOV] *vt* enlever

removed [ri•MOOVD] *adj*
éloigné; distant

renaissance [RE•nai•SAHNS] *n*
renaissance F

render [REN•dur] *vt* rendre

renew [ri•NOO] *vt* renouveler

renewal [ri•NOOUL] *n*
renouvelement M

renovate [REN•o•VAIT] *vt*
rénover

renown [ri•NOUN] *n*
renommée F

rent *n* loyer (valeur locative)
M; *vt* louer (~ un
appartement)

rental [REN•tl] *adj* (a ~
apartment) ce qui concerne le
loyer la valeur locative

reopen [ree•O•pn] *vt* rouvrir

repair [ri•PAIUR] *vt* réparer M

reparation [RE•pur•AI•shun] *n* réparation; rémunération F

repay [ree•PAI] *vt* rembourser

repeal [ri•PEEIL] *vt* annuler; révoquer

repeat [ri•PEET] *vt* répéter

repel [ri•PEL] *vt* repousser; dégoûter

repent [ri•PENT] *vi* se repentir

repetition [RE•pu•TI•shun] *n* répétition M

replace [ri•PLAIS] *vt* remplacer; replacer

replenish [ri•PLEN•ish] *vt* réapprovisionner; remplir

replica [REP•li•kuh] *n* réplique F

reply [ri•PLUY] *n; vi* (~ to a question) réponse; répondre F

report [ri•PAURT] *n* rapport conte rendu M; *vt; vi* annoncer; rapporter; rendre compte

reporter [ri•PAUR•tur] *n* reporter; journaliste M

repose [ri•POZ] *vt* reposer ; *vi* se reposer

represent [RE•pri•ZENT] *vt* représenter

representation [RE•pri•ZEN•TAI•shun] *n* représentation F

representative [RE•pri•ZEN•tah•tiv] *n* représentatif -ive MF

repress [ri•PRES] *vt* réprimer; refouler

reprimand [RE•pre•MAND] n; *vt* réprimande; réprimander F

reproach [ri•PRAUCH] *n; vt* reproche; reprocher M

reproduce [REE•pro•DOOS] *vt* reproduire

reproduction [REE•pro•DUK•shun] *n* reproduction F

reproof [ri•PROOF] *n* reproche; critique péjorative MF

reprove [ri•PROOV] *vt* reprocher

reptile [REP•tuyul] *n* reptile M

republic [ri•PUHB•lik] *n* république F

republican [ri•PUB•li•can] *n; adj* républicain MF

repudiate [ri•PYOO•dee•AIT] *vt* renier

repugnant [ri•PUG•nent] *adj* répugnant

repulse [ri•PULS] *vt* dégoûter

repulsive [ri•PUHL•siv] *adj* répugnant

reputable [RE•pyoo•tah•bl] *adj* honorable; avoir une bonne réputation

reputation [RE•pyoo•TAI•shun] *n* réputation F

repute [ri•PYOOT] *n* réputation F

request [ri•KWEST] *n* requête F

require [ri•KWUYUR] *vt* exiger

requirement [ri•KWUYUR•ment] *n* exigence; nécessité F

rescue [RES•kyoo] *n vt* secours; sauver M

research [REE•surch] *n; vt* recherche; rechercher F

resemblance [ri•ZEM•blens] *n*
ressemblance F

resemble [ri•ZEM•bl] *vt* (she ~
her mother) ressembler

resent [ri•ZENT] *vt* en vouloir
à; s'offenser de

resentful [ri•ZENT•ful] *adj*
ressentiment M

reservation
[RE•zur•VEH•shun] *n*
réservation F

reserve [ri•SURV] *n; vt*
retenue; retenir F

reside [ri•ZUYD] *vi* résider

residence [REZ•i•dens] *n*
résidence F

residue [REZ•i•DYOO] *n*
résidu M

resign [ri•ZUYN] *vi*
démissionner

resignation [REZ•ig•NAI•shun]
n résignation F

resist [ri•ZIST] *vt* résister

resistance [ri•ZI•stans] *n*
résistance F

resolute [RE•zo•LYOOT] *adj*
résolu; déterminé

resolution [RE•zo•LYOO•shun]
n résolution F

resolve [ri•SOULV] *vt* résoudre

resonance [REZ•uh•nens] *n*
résonance F

resonant [REZ•uh•nent] *adj*
résonant

resort [ri•ZAURT] *n* ressource
M as a last ~\ en dernier
ressort; *vi* recourtir à

resource [REE•saurs] *n*
ressource F

respect [ru•SPEKT] *n; vt*
respect M

respectable [ru•SPEHK•tuhbl]
adj respectable

respectful [ru•SPEHKT•ful] *adj*
respecteux -euse MF

respective [ru•SPEHK•tiv] *adj*
respectif -ive MF

respite [ruh•SPUYT] *n* répit;
pause MF

respond [ri•SPAHND] *vi*
répondre

response [ri•SPAHNS] *n*
réponse F

responsibility
[ri•SPAHN•suh•BIL•i•tee] *n*
responsabilité F

responsible [ri•SPAHN•si•bl]
adj responsable F

rest *n; vt* pause; détente F

restaurant [RES•trahnt] *n*
restaurant M

restful [REST•ful] *adj* paisible;
calmant

restitution
[RE•sti•TYOO•shun] *n*
restitution F

restless [REST•les] *adj* agité;
impatient

restlessness [REST•les•nes] *n*
agitation F

restoration [RES•taur•AI•shun]
n restoration F

restore [ri•STAUR] *vt* restaurer;
rétablir

restrain [ri•STRAIN] *vt*
empêcher

restrict [ri•STRIKT] *vt* limiter;
contraindre

restriction [ri•STRIK•shun] *n*
limitation; contrainte F

result [ri•ZULT] *n* résultat M;
vi resulter

resume [re•zyoom] *n* résumé; *vt* reprendre

resuscitate [ri•SUH•suh•TAIT] *vt* ranimer

retail [REE•taiil] *adj* vente au détail F

retailer [REE•tai•lur] *n* détaillant -e MF

retaliate [ri•TAL•ee•AIT] *n* se venger

retaliation [ri•TAL•ee•AI•shun] *n* réprésailles; vengeance F

retard [ri•TAHRD] *vt* rétarder

retinue [REH•ti•NYOO] *n* suite; cortège

retire [ri•TUYUR] *vi* (~ from a job) prendre sa retraite

retirement [ri•TUYR•ment] *n* retraite F

retort [ri•TAURT] *n vi vt* riposte; rétorquer F

retract [ri•TRAKT] (~ one's words) *vt* retirer

retreat [ri•TREET] *n vi* retraite; asile; céder *vi* F

retrieve [ri•TREEV] *vt* retrouver

retroactive [REH•trau•AK•tiv] *adj* rétroactif

return [ri•TURN] *n vt vi* retour; rendre; revenir

return address *n* adresse de l'expéditeur F

returns (election) [ri•TURNZ (i•LEHK•shun)] *n* résultats des élections M

reunion [ree•YOO•nyun] *n* (family ~) réunion F

reunite [REE•yoo•NUYT] *vt* réunir

reveal [ri•VEEIL] *vt* révéler

revelation [RE•vuh•LAI•shun] *n* révélation F

revelry [REV•ul•ree] *n* festivités; gaieté F

revenge [ri•VENJ] *n* vengeance F; *vt* (se) venger

revenue [REV•uh•NYOO] *n* chiffre d'affaires F

revere [ree•VEEUR] *vt* révérer; vénérer

reverence [REH•vur•ens] *n* révérance; vénération F

reverend [REV•rend] *n* (priest minister) pasteur; curé M

reverent [REV•rent] *adj* respectueux -euse

reverse [ri•VURS] *n; adj; vt* contraire (n/adj); inverse (n/adj); renverser (vt) M

revert [ri•VURT] *vi* retomber dans/en; retourner à

review [ri•VYOO] *n* (book ~); *vt* (~ a play movie) conte rendu (d'un livre); critique (littéraire); faire la critique (d'un livre d'un film d'un pièce théâtrale) MF

revile [ri•VUYUL] *vt* insulter; décrier

revise [ri•VUYZ] *vt* réviser; corriger

revision [ri•VI•zhun] *n* révision F

revival [ri•VUY•vl] *n* récuperation (d'une personne); renaissance F

revoke [ri•VOK] *vt* révoquer; annuler (un cours universitaire)

revolt [ri•VOLT] *n* soulevement; révolte MF ; *vi*

se revolter revolution
[rev•u•lyoo•shun] *n*
révolution F

revolutionary
[REV•uh•LYOO•shuh•NAIUR•ee]
adj révolutionnaire

revolve [ri•VAULV] *vi vt*
révolver; tourner

reward [ri•WAURD] *n*
récompense F

rewrite [n. REE•ruyt vt.
ree•RUYT] *n; vt* récrire

rhetoric [REH•taur•ik] *n*
rhétorique F

rheumatism [ROO•muh•TIZM]
n rhumatisme M

rhinoceros [ruy•NAH•sur•us] *n*
rhinocéros M

rhubarb [RYOO•bahrb] *n*
rhubarbe F

rhyme [ruym] *n; vt* rime F

rhythm [rithm] *n* rythme M

rib *n* côte F

ribbon [RI•bn] *n* ruban M

rice [ruys] *n* riz M

rich *n adj* riche M

richness [RICH•nes] *n*
richesse F

rid *vt vi* se débarrasser (de)

riddle [ridl] *n* énigme F

ride [ruyd] *n* (go for a ~ in the
car); *vt* (~ a horse); faire une
promenade en voiture; monter
à cheval

ride (bicycle) [ruyd (BUY•sikl)]
vt monter sur une bicyclette F

ride (horseback) [ruyd
(HAURS•bak)] *vt* monter à
cheval M

rider [RUY•dur] *n* cavalier;
(document) annexe MF

ridge [rij] *n* crête F

ridicule [RI•di•KYOOL] *n; vt*
ridicule M

ridiculous [ri•DI•kyoo•lus] *adj*
ridicule

rifle [ruyfl] *n* fusil M

rig *n* matériel nautique; *vt.*
truquer M

right [ruyt] *npl* droit (les droits
de l'homme); be ~\ avoir
raison; ~ away *adv*\ sur le
champ; tout de suite MF

right-hand [RUYT•hand] *adj*
droit

righteous [RUY•chus] *adj* juste

righteousness [RUY•chis•nus]
n vertu F

rigid [RI•jid] *adj* rigide

rigidity [ri•JI•di•tee] *n* rigidité F

rigor [RI•gur] *n* rigueur;
sévérité F

rim *n* bord M

rind [ruynd] *n* (orange ~) peau
(d'une orange); écorce (d'un
tronc d'un arbre) F

ring *n* sonnerie MF; *n* cercle M

rink *n* (skating ~) patinoire F

rinse [rins] *n vt* rinçage;
rinser M

riot [ruyit] *n* soulèvement;
émeutte MF

ripe [ruyp] *adj* mûr

ripple [ripl] *n* miriade; *vt*
ondulation; onduler F

rise [ruyz] *n* ascension; monté
F; *vi* se relever (du lit)

risk [risk] *n* risque M; *vt* risquer

rite [ruyt] *n* rite (cérémonie
d'initiation) MF

ritual [RI•tyool] *n* rituel M

rival [ruyvl] *n vt* (~ sb) rival -e
MF

rivalry [RUYVL•ree] *n*
rivalité F

river [RI•vur] *n* rivière M

road [rod] *n* route; rue F

roam [raum] *vi* parcourir; errer

roar [raur] *n* rugir M; *vt vi*
rugir hurler M

roast [rost] *n; vt* rôti; rôtir M

rob [rahb] *vt* voler

robber [RAH•bur] *n* bandit;
voleur -euse MF

robbery [RAH•bur•ee] *n* vol M

robe [rob] *n* (bath~) peignoir
(de chambre) M

robin [RAH•bin] *n* (bird)
rouge-gorge M

robust [ro•BUST] *adj* robuste
MF

rock [rahk] *n; roc; roche MF; *vt*
blanacer; chanceler; ~ to
sleep\ bercer

rocker [RAH•kur] *n* fauteuil à
basculer M

rocket [RAH•kit] *n* fusée F

rocking [RAH•king] *n*
balancement M

rocking chair *n* fauteuil à
basculer M

rocky [RAH•kee] *adj* pierreux;
rocheux

rod [rahd] *n* (fishing ~) barre;
canne F

role [roul] *n* (a ~ in a play or a
movie) rôle

roll [roul] *n* (bread ~); petit
pain; rouleau (paper) M

Roman [RO•man] *n; adj* (~
soldier) Romain -e MF

romance [ro•MANS] *n*
romance F

Romania [ro•MAI•nee•u] *n*
Roumanie F

romantic [ro•MAN•tik] *adj* (~
Period in lit.) romantique MF

romanticism
[ro•MAN•ti•SIZM] *n*
romantisme M

romanticist [ro•MAN•ti•sist] *n*
romantique MF

romp [rahmp] *vi* s'ébattre; *vt*
jouer

roof *n* toit M

room *n* l'espace; chambre
(d'hôtel); pièce MF; *vt* faire
l'espace

roommate [ROO•mait] *n*
camarade de chambre MF

roomy [ROO•mee] *adj* spacieux
-euse

roost *n; vi* perchoir (d'un
oiseau); se percher M

root *n* racine F

rope [rop] *n vt* (~ a calf)
corde F

rosary [RAU•zur•ee] *n* (~
beads) rosaire M

rose [roz] *n* (flower) rose F

rosy [RO•zee] *adj* (~ cheeks);
rose

rot [raht] *n; vi* pourriture; su
pourrir F

rotary [RO•duh•ree] *adj* rotatif

rotation [ro•TAI•shun] *n*
rotation F

rotten [RAH•tn] *adj* (~ apple
or orange) pourri

rough [ruf] *adj* (~ skin or
hands) rude; parcheminée;
(difficult) difficil

rough draft *n* brouillon M

rough estimate *n* devis approximatif M

round *adj* rond -e

rouse [rouz] *vt* inciter; (wake) réveiller

route [rout] or [root] *n* (bus ~) itinéraire; route; direction MF

routine [roo•TEEN] *n; adj* routine F

row [ro] *n* rangée in a ~\ à la rame F; *vt* (boat) se queller

royal [roil] *adj* royal

rub *n; vt* frotter

rubdown [RUB•doun] *n* se frictionner

rubber [RUH•bur] *n* caoutchouc M

rubbish [RUH•bish] *npl* détritus; ordures MF

rubble [RUH•bl] *n* décombres (pl) M

ruby [ROO•bee] rubis

rudder [RUH•dur] *n* gouvernail M

rude [rood] *adj* impoli; (word) grossier

rueful [RYOO•ful] *adj* rusé

rug [ruhg] *n* tapis M

rugby [RUHG•bee] *n* rugby

rugged [RUH•gid] *adj* rude (inv); bourru (personne)

ruin [roon] *n* ruine F; *vt* ruiner; (spoil dirty) abîmer

rule [rool] *n* règle F; (regulation) règlement M; (of government etc) autorité F; as a ~\ en règle générale; *vt* gouverner; (control) dominer; (decide) décider; (court) statuer

rum [ruhm] *n* rhum M

rumble [RUHM•bl] *n* grondement M; *vi* gronder

rummage [RUH•mij] *vi* fouiller dans

rumor [ROO•mur] *n* rumeur F

rump [ruhmp] *n* (of animal) croupe F

rumple [RHUM•pl] *vt* froisser

run [ruhn] *vt vi* courir

run-down [RUN-DOUN] *adj* épuisé ; surmené

runaway [RUHN•u•WAI] *adj* fou (folle); (horse) emballé; *n* fuyard M

runner [RUH•nur] *n* coureur M; (of drawer) coulisseau M; (for carpet) chemin M

running [RUH•ning] *n* courant -e MF

runt [ruhnt] *n* avorton M

runway [RUHN•wai] *n* piste F

rupture [RUHP•chur] *n* rupture F

rural [ROOU•rl] *adj* rural

ruse [rooz] *n* ruse F

rush [ruhsh] *n* hâte F; (of crowd) ruée F bousculade; (plant) jonc M; *vt* (person) bousculer; (send) envoyer or transporter d'urgence; *vi* se dépêcher

rush hour *npl* heures F de pointe or d'affluence

Russia [RUH•shu] *n* Russie

Russian [RUH•shn] *adj* russe; (person) Russe MF; (language) russe M

rust [ruhst] *n* rouille F; *vi* se rouiller

rustic [RUH•stik] *adj* rustique

rusty [RUH•stee] *adj* rouillé
rut [ruht] *n* ornière F;
suivre l'ornière;
s'encroûter

ruthless [ROOTH•lis] *adj*
impitoyable sans pitié
rye [ruy] *n* seigle M; (bread)
pain M de seigle

S

Sabbath [SA•buth] *n* sabbat M
sabotage [SA•bu•TAHZH] *n*
sabotage M; *vt* sabotager
sack [sak] *n* sac M; *vt* renvoyer
sacrament [SA•kru•munt] *n*
sacrement M
sacred [SAI•krid] *adj* sacré
sacrifice [SA•kri•FUYS] *n*
sacrifice M; *vt* sacrifier
sad *adj* triste
sadden [SA•dn] *vt* attrister
saddle [SA•dl] *n* selle; *vt*
(horse) seller
sadistic [su•DI•stik] *adj* sadiste
sadness [SAD•nis] *n* tristesse F
safe [saif] *adj* sans danger; (out
of danger) hors de danger;
(careful) prudent; (bet etc)
sûr; ~ and sound\ sain(e) et
sauf(sauve); *n* coffre-fort M
safeguard [SAIF•gahrd] *n*
sauvegarde F; *vt* sauvegarder
safely [SAIF•lee] *adv* sans
danger; sans risque; (arrive) à
bon port
safety [SAIF•tee] *n* sécurité F
safety pin *n* épingle M de
sûreté or de nourrice
saffron [SA•frun] *n* safran M
sag *vi* s'affaisser fléchir
sage [saij] *adj* sage; *n* sauge F

sail [saiul] *n* voile F; *vt* piloter
manœuvrer; *vi* aller en bateau;
(boat) naviguer; (as sport)
faire de la voile; (leave port)
prendre la mer
sailboat [SAIUL•bot] *n* bateau
M à voile; voilier M
sailing [SAIU•ling] *n* voile F;
faire de la voile
sailor [SAIU•lur] *n* marin M
matelot M
saint *n* saint M
saintly [SAINT•lee] *adj* saint M
sake [saik] *n* par égard pour; for
God's ~\ pour l'amour de
Dieu
salad [SA•lid] *n* salade F
salad bowl *n* saladier M
salad dressing *n* vinaigrette F
salary [SA•lu•ree] *n* salaire M
traitement M
sale [saiul] *n* vente F; (at
discounted prices) soldes *mpl;*
on ~\ en vente; for ~\ à
vendre;
salesman [SAIULZ•man] *n*
vendeur M; (representative)
représentant M de commerce
saleswoman
[SAIULZ•WU•mun] *n*

vendeuse F; (representative)
représentante e de commerce

saliva [su•LUY•vu] *n* salive F

salmon [SA•mun] *n* saumon M

salon [su•LAHN] *n* salon M

salt [sault] *n* sel M; *vt* saler

saltwater [SAULT•WAU•tur] *n*
eau M de mer; *adj* de mer

salty [SAUL•tee] *adj* salé

salute [su•LOOT] *n* salut M; *vt*
saluer

salvage [SAL•vij] *vt* sauver

salvation [sal•VAI•shn] *n*
salut M

same [saim] *adj* même; *pron* le
même (la même); les mêmes;
do the ~\ faire de même; *adv*
the ~\ de la même manière

sample [SAM•pl] *n* échantillon
M; *vt* (taste) goûter

sanction [SANGK•shn] *n*
sanction F; *vt* sanctionner

sanctity [SANGK•ti•tee] *n*
sainteté F

sanctuary
[SANGK•choo•E•ree] *n* (for
wildlife) réserve F; (refuge)
asile M

sand *n* sable M; *vt* poncer

sandal [SAN•dl] *n* sandale F

sandpaper [SAND•PAI•pur] *n*
papier M de verre

sandwich [SAND•wich] *n*
sandwich M; *vt* intercaler

sandy [SAN•dee] *n* (soil)
sableux; (color) sable

sane [sain] *adj* sain d'esprit

sanitary [SA•ni•TE•ree] *adj*
sanitaire; (clean) hygiénique

sanitary napkin *n* serviette F
hygiénique

sanity [SA•ni•tee] *n* santé F
mentale; (levelheadedness)
bon sens M

Santa Claus [SAN•tu•KLAUZ]
n le Père Noël M

sap *n* sève F; *vt* (stength life)
saper

sapling [SAP•ling] *n* jeune
arbre M

sapphire [SA•fuyur] *n* saphir M

sarcastic [sahr•KA•stik] *adj*
sarcastique

sardine [sahr•DEEN] *n*
sardine F

Sardinia [sahr•DEE•nyu] *n*
Sardaigne F

sash *n* écharpe F

Satan [SAI•tn] *n* Satan M

satellite [SA•tu•LUYT] *n*
satellite M

satin [SA•tin] *n* satin M; *adj* de
or en satin

satire [SA•tuyur] *n* satire F

satisfaction [SA•tis•FAK•shn]
n satisfaction F

satisfactory
[SA•tis•FAK•tu•ree] *adj*
satisfaisant

satisfy [SA•tis•FUY] *vt*
satisfaire

saturate [SA•chu•RAIT] *vt*
saturer (de)

Saturday [SA•tur•dai] *n* samedi
M; on ~\ le Samedi

sauce [saus] *n* sauce F

saucer [SAU•sur] *n* soucoupe F

Saudi Arabia [SAU•dee
u•RAI•bee•u] *n* Arabie F
Saoudite F

sauna [SAU•nu] *n* sauna M

sausage [SAU•sij] *n* saucisse F

savage [SA•vij] *adj* sauvage;
(brutal) brutal; *n* sauvage MF;
vt attaquer férocement

save [saiv] *vt* (rescue) sauver;
(money) mettre de côté
économiser; (time) gagner;
(computers) sauvegarder; *vi*
mettre de l'argent de côté

savings [SA•vingz] *npl*
économies F

savings account *n* compte M
d'épargne

savior [SAI•vyur] *n* sauveur M

savor [SAI•vur] *vt* savourer

saw [sau] *n* scie F; *vt* scier

sawdust [SAU•duhst] *n* sciure

saxaphone [SAK•su•FON] *n*
saxaphone M

say [sai] *vi* dire; c'est-à-dire; *n*
have a ~ in sth avoir son mot
à dire sur qqch; dire ce que
on a à dire

scab [skab] *n* croûte F;
(strikebreaker) jaune M

scaffold [SKA•fuld] *n*
échafaud M

scaffolding [SKA•ful•ding] *n*
échafaudage M

scald [skauld] *vt* ébouillanter

scale [skaiul] *n* (of fish) écaille
F; (of map etc) échelle F;
(music) gamme F; *vt* (climb)
escalader; ~s *npl* balance F

scallop [SKA•lup] *n* coquille F
Saint-Jacques

scalp [skalp] *n* cuir M chevelu;
vt scalper

scalpel [SKAL•pl] *n* scalpel M

scan [skan] *vt* scruter; (by
radar) balayer; (computers)
faire un scannage de

scandal [SKAN•dl] *n*
scandale M

scandalize [SKAN•du•LUYZ]
vt scandaliser

Scandinavia
[SKAN•di•NAI•vee•u] *n*
Scandinavie F

Scandinavian
[SKAN•di•NAI•vee•un] *adj*
scandinave; *n* (person)
Scandinave MF

scapegoat [SKAIP•got] *n* bouc
M émissaire

scar [skahr] *n* cicatrice F

scarce [skaiurs] *adj* rare peu
abondant

scare [skaiur] *n* panique; *vt*
effrayer faire peur à

scarf [skahrf] *n* écharpe F

scarlet [SKAHR•lit] *adj n*
écarlate F

scary [SKAIU•ree] *adj* effrayant

scathing [SKAI•thing] *adj*
acerbe; cinglant

scatter [SKA•tur] *vt* éparpiller;
vi se disperser

scavenger [SKA•vin•jur] *n*
éboueur M; (animal) animal
M nécrophage

scenario [si•NAH•ree•O] *n*
scénario M

scene [seen] *n* (in book play
etc) scène F; (place) lieu M;
(sight) spectacle M vue F;
behind the ~s\ dans les
coulisses

scenery [SEE•nu•ree] *n* (of
country) paysage M; (theater)
décor M

scent [sent] *n* scenteur F parfum
M; (of animal) odeur F

schedule [SKE•joo•ul] *n* programme M plan M; (of train bus etc) horaire M; in ~\ à l'heure (prévue); ahead of/behind ~\ en avance/en retard; *vt* prévoir

scheme [skeem] *n* projet M plan M; (plot) complot M; *vt vi* comploter

schism [SKI•zm] *n* schisme M

scholar [SKAH•lur] *n* érudit M savant M

scholarly [SKAH•lur•lee] *adj* érudit savant

scholarship [SKAH•lur•ship] *n* (grant) bourse F (d'études)

scholastic [sku•LA•stik] *adj* scolaire

school [skooul] *n* école F; (secondary) lycée M collège M; (university) université F

school year *n* année F scolaire

schoolteacher [SKOOUL•TEE•chur] *n* instituteur M; professeur M

science [SUY•uns] *n* science F

scientific [SUY•un•TI•fik] *adj* scientifique

scientist [SUY•un•tist] *n* scientifique MF

scissors [SI•zurz] *npl* ciseaux M

scoff [skauf] *vi* se moquer de

scold [skold] *vt* gronder

scone [skon] *n* scone M

scoop [skoop] *n* pelle F (à main); (for ice cream) cuiller F à glace; (of ice cream) boule F; (news story) scoop M; *vt* prendre avec une pelle à main

scope [skop] *n* portée F; (opportunity) occasion F; (of talent skills) compétence F

scorch [skaurch] *vt* brûler; (land) dessécher

score [skaur] *n* score M; (music) partition F; keep ~\ compter les points; *vt vi* marquer

scorn [skaurn] *n* mépris dédain M; *vt* mépriser dédaigner

scorpion [SKAUR•pee•un] *n* scorpion M

Scot [skaht] *n* Écossais M

Scotch [skahch] *adj* écossais; *n* (whiskey) scotch M

Scotland [SKAHT•lund] *n* Écosse F

Scottish [SKAH•tish] *adj* écossais

scoundrel [SKOUN•drul] *n* coquin -e; scélérat -e MF

scour [skouur] *vt* récurer; (search) parcourir

scourge [skurj] *n* fléau M

scout [skout] *n* (military) éclaireur M; (boy scout) scout M; *vt* explorer

scowl [skoul] *n; vt* faire une grimace; froncer le sourcil F

scramble [SKRAM•bl] *n; vi* mêlée; brouiller F

scrap [skrap] *n* morceau (de papier); bout (de pain) M

scrape [skraip] *vt* gratter

scraper [SKRAIP•r] *n* grattoir M

scratch [skrach] *n; vt* griffe; gratter; se gratter F

scrawl [skrahl] *n; vt; vi* griffonage; griffonner M

scream [skreem] *n vi* cri; crier (des ordres) à qq'un M

screech [skreech] *vt* hurler; *vi* (tires) crisser

screen [skreen] *n* écran M paravent M; (of tv) écran M; *vt* masquer cacher; (for film) projeter; (candidate etc) filtrer

screw [skroo] *n* vis; *vt* visser; *vi* se visser; ~ up *vt* (ruin)\ bousiller

screwdriver [SKROO•DRUY•vur] *n* tournevis M

scribble [SKRI•bl] *vt vi* gribouiller griffonner

script [skript] *n* scénario M; (handwriting) écriture F script

scripture [SKRIP•chur] *n* Écriture F Sainte

scroll [skroul] *n* rouleau M; *vt* (computers) faire défiler

scrub [skruhb] *n* (plants) brousailles *fpl*; *vt* nettoyer (laver) à la brosse; (pots pans etc) récurer

scruple [SKROO•pl] *n* scrupule M

scrutinize [SKROO•ti•NUYZ] *vt* scruter

scrutiny [SKROO•ti•nee] *n* examen M attentif

sculpt [skuhlpt] *vt vi* sculpter

sculptor [SKUHLP•tur] *n* sculpteur M

sculpture [SKUHLP•chur] *n* sculpture F

scum [skuhm] *n* (on water etc) écume F; (person) salaud M; (people) rebut M

scurrilous [SKU•ri•lus] *adj* calomnieux

scythe [suyth] *n* faux F; *vt* faucher

sea [see] *n* mer F; par mer; à bord de la mer; *adj* de mer marin; maritime

seal [seeul] *n* (animal) phoque F; (stamp) cachet M sceau M; *vt* (envelope) coller; (letter) sceller; (entry) boucher; *vt* interdire l'accès de

seam [seem] *n* couture F

search [surch] *n* (for person thing) recherche(s) *fpl*; (of area) fouille F; *vt* (area) fouiller; *vi* chercher

search warrant *n* mandat M de perquisition

seasick [SEE•sik] *adj* avoir le mal de mer

season [SEE•zn] *n* saison F; *vt* assaisonner; relever

seasonal [SEE•zu•nl] *adj* saisonnier

seasoned [SEE•znd] *adj* (experienced) expérimenté

seasoning [SEE•zu•ning] *n* assaisonnement M

seat [seet] *n* siège M; (in bus train) place F; (in theater) fauteil M; *vt* faire asseoir

secede [si•SEED] *vt* faire sécession

secession [si•SE•shn] *n* sécession F

secluded [si•KLOO•did] *adj* retiré à l'écart

seclusion [si•KLOO•zhn] *n* solitude F

second [SE•kund] *num*
deuxième; *n* seconde F; *vt* (in
meeting) appuyer

second hand *n* (of clock)
trotteuse

second thought *n* réflexion
faite; *npl* doutes

second-hand [SE•kund•HAND]
adj adv d'occasion

second-rate [SE•kond•RAIT]
adj de deuxième ordre

secondary [SE•kun•DE•ree] *adj*
secondaire

secrecy [SEE•kru•see] *n*
secret M

secret [SEE•krit] *adj n* secret M

secretary [SE•kri•TE•ree] *n*
secrétaire MF; (politics)
ministre M

secrete [si•KREET] *v* sécréter

secretion [si•KREE•shn] *n*
sécrétion F

secretive [SEE•kri•tiv] *adj*
dissimulé

sect [sekt] *n* secte F

section [SEK•shn] *n* section F;
(of law contract) article M;
(of road) tronçon M; *vt*
sectionner

sector [SEK•tur] *n* secteur M

secular [SE•kyu•lur] *adj*
séculier; laïque;

secure [si•KYOOUR] *n*
(person) sécurisé; (fixed) fixe;
(job etc) en lieu sûr; *vt* fixer;
(acquire) acquérir; (safeguard)
sauvegarder

security [si•KYOOU•ri•tee] *n*
sécurité F; *npl* titres M

sedate [si•DAIT] *adj* posé; *vt*
donner un sédatif à

sedative [SE•du•tiv] *n*
sédatif M

sediment [SE•di•munt] *n*
sédiment M

seduce [si•DOOS] *vt* séduire

seduction [si•DUHK•shn] *n*
séduction F

seductive [si•DUHK•tiv] *adj*
séduisant

see *vt* voir; assurer que;
reconduire qqn jusq'à la porte;
excl à bientôt! tout à l'heure!;
vi voir; (understand) voir; *vt*
s'occuper de; *vt* voir clair
dans; (project) mener à bonne
fin; *prep* vu que

seed *n* graine F; (of idea etc)
germem

seedling [SEED•ling] *n* semis
M jeune plante F

seedy [SEE•dee] *adj* miteux

seek *vt* chercher rechercher;
(intend) chercher à

seem *vi* sembler paraître;
(describing mood state) avoir
l'air

seemingly [SEE•ming•lee] *adv*
apparemment

seep *vi* suinter

seesaw [SEE•sau] *n* bascule F

seethe [seeth] *vi* ~ (with)
bouillir (de)

segment [SEG•munt] *n* section
F partie F

segregate [SE•gri•GAIT] *vt*
séparer

seize [seez] *vt* saisir; attraper;
(take capture) s'emparer de;
vi (engine) se gripper

seizure [SEE•zhur] *n* crise F
attaque F; (taking) prise

seldom [SEL•dum] *adv*
rarement

select [si•LEKT] *adj* choisi;
d'élite; *vt* sélectionner

selection [si•LEK•shn] *n*
sélection F

selective [si•LEK•tiv] *adj*
sélectif

self *n* moi M

self-centered [SELF•SEN•turd]
adj égocentrique

self-confidence *adj* confidence
F en soi

self-confident
[SELF•KON•fi•dint] *adj* sûr
de soi

self-conscious
[SELF•KON•shus] *adj* timide

self-control [SELF•kon•TROL]
n maîtrise F de soi

self-defense [SELF•dee•FENZ]
n autodéfense F

self-discipline *n*
autodiscipline F

self-esteem *n* estime F de soi

self-evident *adj* qui va de soi

self-interset *n* intérêt M
personnel

self-portrait *n* autoportrait M

self-respect *n* respect M de soi

self-righteous *adj* satisfait
de soi

self-taught [SELF•TAUT] *adj*
autodidacte

selfish [SEL•fish] *adj* égoïste

selfishness [SEL•fish•nis] *n*
égoïsme M

selfless [SEL•flis] *adj*
désintéressé

sell [sel] *vt* vendre; *vi* vendre;
(product) se vendre; ~ out

(betray)\ trahir; the show is
sold out\ il ne rest plus de
billets

semblance [SEM•bluns] *n*
semblant

semen [SEE•mun] *n* sperme M

semester [su•ME•stur] *n*
semestre M

semicolon [SE•mee•KO•lun] *n*
point-virgule M

seminar [SE•mi•NAHR] *n*
séminaire M

seminary [SE•mi•NE•ree] *n*
séminaire M

senate [SE•nit] *n* sénat

senator [SE•nu•tur] *n* sénateur

send *vt* envoyer; envoyer qqn
chercher qqch; *vt* faire venir

sender [SEN•dur] *n*
expéditeur M

senile [SEE•nuyul] *adj* sénile

senior [SEE•nyur] *adj* (at job)
qui a plus d'ancienneté;
(older) ainé; (rank) supérieur;
n ainé M; (in school)
grand M

senior citizen *n* personne F
âgée

seniority [si•NYAU•ri•tee] *n*
ancienneté

sensation [sen•SAI•shn] *n*
sensation F

sense [sens] *n* sens M; (feeling)
sentiment M; make ~\ avoir
un sens; (be logical) être
logique; in a ~\ dans un sens;
vt sentir

senseless [SENS•lis] *adj*
insensible; (unconscious) sans
connaissance

sensibilities [SEN•si•BI•li•teez]
npl susceptibilité F

sensible [SEN•si•bl] *adj*
raisonnable

sensitive [SEN•si•tiv] *adj*
sensible; (conversation etc)
délicat

sensual [SEN•shoo•ul] *adj*
sensuel

sentence [SEN•tuns] *n* phrase
F; (judgement) condamnation
F sentence F; *vt* condamner

sentiment [SEN•ti•munt] *n*
sentiment M; (opinion)
opinion F; avis M

sentimental [SEN•ti•MEN•tl]
adj sentimental

sentry [SEN•tree] *n* sentinelle F

separate [adj. SE•prut v.
SE•pu•RAIT] *adj* séparé; *vt*
séparer; *vi* se séparer

separately [SE•prut•lee] *adv*
séparément

separation [SE•pu•RAI•shn] *n*
séparation F

September [sep•TEM•bur] *n*
septembre M

septic [SEP•tik] *adj* septique

septic tank *n* fosse F septique

sepulcher [SE•pul•kur] *n*
sépulcre M

sequel [SEE•kwul] *n*
conséquence F; (of film etc)
suite F

sequence [SEE•kwuns] *n* ordre
M; suite F

serene [su•REEN] *adj* serein
paisible

sergeant [SAHR•junt] *n* sergent
M; (in police) brigadier M

serial [SEEU•ree•ul] *n*
feuilleton M

series [SEEU•reez] *n* série F

serious [SEEU•ree•us] *adj*
sérieux; grave

seriously [SEEU•ree•us•lee] *adv*
sérieusement

sermon [SUR•mun] *n*
sermon M

serpent [SUR•punt] *n*
serpent M

serum [SEEU•rum] *n* sérum

servant [SUR•vunt] *n*
domestique MF

serve [surv] *n* (tennis) service
M; *vt* servir; (purpose) servir
à; (sentence) faire purger;
c'est bien fait pour toi; *vi*
servir; (tennis) servir

service [SUR•vis] *n* service M;
en/hors service; (of car)
révision F; *vt* (car) réviser

session [SE•shn] *n* séance;
(semester) semestre M

set *adj* fixe; (ready) prêt; résolu
à faire qqch; *n* série F;
(theater) scène M; (film)
plateau M; (tv) poste M; (of
tools etc) jeu M; (tennis) set
M; (collection) collection F;
vt mettre placer poser;
(adjust) régler; (fix; plan)
fixer; *vt* mettre de côté; *vt*
retarder; *vt* (explode) faire
exploser; *vt* disposer; *vi*
entreprendre de faire qqch; *vt*
(assemble) assembler; (install)
installer; (organization)
fonder; (frame) monter un
coup contre

setback [SET•bak] *n* revers M
contretemps M

setting [SE•ting] *n* cadre M; (of
device machine) réglage M

settle [SE•tl] *vt* régler; (calm)
calmer; *vi* (make one's home)
s'installer se fixer; (dust) se
poser; ~ for *vt* se contenter
de; ~ on *vt* se décider pour;
~ down *vi* se calmer

settlement [SE•tl•munt] *n*
colonie F; (agreement)
accord M

seven [SE•vn] *num* sept

seventeen [SE•vn•TEEN] *num*
dix-sept

seventh [SE•vnth] *num*
septième

seventy [SE•vn•tee] *n*
soixante-dix

sever [SE•vur] *vt* couper;
(relations) rompre

several [SE•vrul] *adj pron*
plusieurs

severe [su•VEEUR] *adj* sévère;
(serious) grave; (weather)
rude

sew [so] *vt vi* coudre; *vt*
recoudre

sewer [SOO•ur] *n* égout M

sewing [SO•ing] *n* couture F

sewing machine *n* machine F
à coudre

sex [seks] *n* sexe M; avoir des
rapports (sexuels) avec

sexist [SEK•sist] *n* sexiste MF

sexual [SEK•shoo•ul] *adj* sexuel

sexual harassment *n*
harcelement M sexuel

sexual intercourse *npl*
rapports M (sexuels)

sexy [SEK•see] *adj* sexy

shabby [SHA•bee] *adj* miteux;
(clothes) élimé; (behavior)
méprisable

shack [shak] *n* cabane F hutte F

shackles [SHA•klz] *npl* entraves
fpl

shade [shaid] *n* ombre F; (of
lamp) abat-jour M; (color)
nuance F ton M; (of window)
store M; *vt* abriter; nuancer

shadow [SHA•do] *n* ombre F

shady [SHAI•dee] *adj* ombragé;
(person) louche

shaft *n* (of mine) puits; (of
light) rayon M; (of car etc)
arbre M; (of elevator) cage F

shaggy [SHA•gee] *adj* hirsute

shake [shaik] *n* secousse F; *vt*
secouer; (bottle) agiter; ~ sb's
hand\ serrer la main à qqn; ~
hands\ se serrer la main; *vi*
trembler; ~s *npl*
tremblements

shall [shal] *aux v* (expressing
future tense) j'irai;
(expressing command) tu vas
aller!; (as question) ~ I do
sth?\ est-ce que vous aimeriez
que je fasse qqch?

shallow [SHA•lo] *adj* peu
profond; (person
conversation) superficiel

shame [shaim] *n* honte; *vt* faire
honte à; quel dommage!

shameful [SHAIM•ful] *adj*
honteux scandaleux

shameless [SHAIM•lis] *adj*
éhonté effronté

shampoo [sham•POO] *n*
shampooing M; *vt* faire un
shampooing à

shamrock [SHAM•rahk] *n* trèfle M

shark [shahrk] *n* requin M

sharp [shahrp] *adj* (blade) tranchant; (point) aigu; (teeth) pointu; (outline) net; (person pain) vif; (sound eyesight) perçant; *n* (music) dièse M; *adv* 3 o'clock ~\ 3 heures pile or tapantes

shatter [SHA•tur] *vt* briser fracasser; *vi* se briser se fracasser

shave [shaiv] *vt* raser; *vi* se raser

shaving [SHAI•ving] *n* rasage M

shaving cream *n* crème F a raser

shawl [shaul] *n* châle M

she [shee] pers *pron* elle

shear [sheeur] *vt* (sheep) tondre; (for plants) *npl* cisaille F

shed *n* remise F; *vt* (fur skin leaves) perdre; (tears) verser répandre

sheep [sheep] *n* mouton

shelf *n* étagère F rayon M

shell [shel] *n* (on beach) coquillage M (of egg nut) coquille F; (of turtle crab) carapace F; *vt* (nuts crabs etc) décortiquer; (egg) écaler

shelter [SHEL•tur] *n* abri M; *vt* abriter protéger; (criminal) cacher

shepherd [SHE•purd] *n* berger M; *vt* guider conduire

sheriff [SHE•rif] *n* shérif M

shield [sheeuld] *n* bouclier M; *vt* protéger

shift *n* changement M; (work time) poste M; (of workers) équipe F; *vt* déplacer; (change) changer; *vi* changer; (move) changer de place; (wind) changer; (in car) changer de vitesse

shimmer [SHI•mur] *vi* miroiter

shin *n* tibia M

shine [shuyn] *n* brillant M éclat M; *vt* faire briller; ~ a light on sth\ éclairer qqch; *vi* briller

shingle [SHING•gl] *n* (on roof) bardeau M; zona M

shiny [SHUY•nee] *adj* brillant

ship *n* bateau M; (large) navire M; *vt* transporter; (send) expédier

shirk [shurk] *vt* se dérober à

shirt [shurt] *n* chemise F

shit *n* merde M; *excl* merde!

shiver [SHI•vur] *n* frisson M; *vi* frissonner

shock [shahk] *n* (impact & emotional) choc M; (electric) secousse F; *vt* choquer

shock absorber *n* amortisseur

shoe [shoo] *n* chaussure F soulier M

shoe polish *n* cirage M

shoo *excl* ouste!

shoot *n* (of plant) pousse F; *vt* tuer (or blesser) d'un coup de feu; (sports) tirer; *vi* tirer sur; (sports) tirer

shooting [SHOO•ting] *n* (murder) meurtre M

shooting star *n* étoile F filante

shop [shahp] *n* magasin M; *vi* faire ses courses or achats

shoplifting [SHAHP•LIF•ting] *n* vol M à l'étalage

shopper [SHAH•pur] *n* personne F qui fait ses courses

shopping [SHAH•ping] *npl* achats M; aller faire ses courses or achats

shopping center *n* centre M commercial

shore [shaur] *n* rivage M bord M

short [shaurt] *adj* (in time) court bref; (not tall) court; diminutif de; *npl* short M; *adv* bref

short story *n* nouvelle •

short-tempered [~ TEM•purd] *adj* emporté

shortage [SHAUR•tij] *n* manque M

shortcomings [SHAURT•KUH•mingz] *npl* défauts mpl

shortcut [SHAURT•kuht] *n* raccourci

shorten [SHAUR•tn] *vt* raccourcir

shorthand [SHAURT•hand] *n* sténographie F

shortly [SHAURT•lee] *adv* bientôt

shot [shaht] *n* (of gun) coup M de feu; (sports) coup M; (photograph) photo F; (injection) piqûre F; (try) coup M

shotgun [SHAHT•guhn] *n* fusil M de chasse

should [shud] *v aux* devoir; je devrais partir; il devrait être à la maison maintenant

shoulder [SHOUL•dur] *n* épaule F; *vt* endosser

shout *n* cri M; *vt vi* crier

shove [shuhv] *vt* pousser; *vt* (pack into) fourrer dans

shovel [SHUH•vl] *n* pelle F; *vt* pelleter

show [sho] *n* démonstration F; (exposition) exposition F; (play) spectacle M; (on tv) émission F; (film) séance F; *vt* montrer; (humor courage) faire preuve de; (film) projeter; *vi* se voir être visible; *vt* faire entrer; *vt* faire étalage de; *vi* crâner; *vi vt* embarrasser; *vi* (arrive) s'amener

show business *n* le monde M du spectacle

show-off [SHO•auf] *n* m'as-tu-vu M

shower [SHOU•ur] *n* douche F; (rain) averse F; prendre une douche; *vt* combler qqn de; *vi* se doucher

showing [SHO•ing] *n* (of film) projection F

shred *n* (piece) lambeau M; (of evidence) parcelle F; *vt* (food) râper; (paper) couper en lambeaux

shrewd [shrood] *adj* astucieux

shriek [shreek] *n* hurlement M; *vt vi* hurler

shrill [shril] *adj* perçant; aigu

shrimp *n* crevette F grise

shrine [shruyn] *n* lieu M saint

shrink [shringk] *vt* rétrécir; *vi*
rétrécir; (income etc) se
réduire; ~ from sth\ reculer
devant qqch; *n*
(psychoanalyst) psychanalyste
MF

shrivel [SHRI•vl] *vt* flétrir; *vi* se
flétrir

shroud *n* linceul M; *vt*
enveloppé de

shrub [shruhb] *n* arbuste M

shudder [SHUH•dur] *vi* frémir;
frissonner

shuffle [SHUH•fl] *vt* (cards)
battre; traîner les pieds

shun [shuhn] *vt* éviter fuir

shut [shuht] *adj* fermé; *vt*
fermer; *vi* se fermer; (store)
fermer; *vt vi* fermer; *vt* couper
arrêter; *vi* se taire

shutter [SHUH•tur] *n* volet M;
(of camera) obturateur M

shuttle [SHUH•tl] *n* navette F

shy [shuy] *adj* timide

sick [sik] *adj* malade; (joke)
macabre; en avoir marre de

sicken [SI•kn] *vt* écœurer

sickening [SI•ku•ning] *adj*
écœurant

sickle [SI•kl] *n* faucille F

sickly [SI•klee] *adj* maladif

sickness [SIK•nis] *n* maladie F

side [suyd] *adj* (door etc)
latéral; *n* côté M; côté à côté;
(of road; river) bord M; (of
mountain) flanc M; (in
disagreement) camp M;
prendre le parti de qqn; *vi*
prendre le parti de qqn

side effect *n* effet M secondaire

sidetrack [SUYD•trak] *vt* faire
dévier

sidewalk [SUYD•wauk] *n*
trottoir M

sideways [SUYD•waiz] *adj adv*
de côté

siding [SUY•ding] *n* voie F de
garage

siege [seej] *n* siège M

sieve [seev] *n* (for flour) tamis
M; (for liquid) passoire F

sift *vt* tamisser; (explanation)
passe au cible

sigh [suy] *n* soupir M; *vi*
soupirer pousser un soupir

sight [suyt] *adj* vue F;
(spectacle) spectacle M

sightseeing [SUYT•SEE•ing] *n*
tourisme M; faire du tourisme

sign [suyn] *n* signe M; enseigne
F; (on road) panneau M; *vt*
signer; (military) engager; *vi*
s'engager; (for course)
s'inscrire

signal [SIG•nl] *n* signal M; *vt*
faire signe à; *vi* (in car)
clignoter

signature [SIG•nu•CHUR] *n*
signature F

significance [sig•NI•fi•kuns] *n*
signification F; importance F

significant [si•NI•fi•kunt] *adj*
significatif; important;
(amount) considérable

signify [SIG•ni•FUY] *vt*
signifier

silence [SUY•luns] *n* silence M;
vt faire taire réduire au
silence F

silencer [SUY•lun•sur] *n*
silencieux M

silent [SUY•lunt] *n* silencieux;
(film) muet F

silhouette [SI•loo•WET] *n*
silhouette F

silk *n* soie F; *adj* de or en soie

sill [sil] *n* rebord M

silly [SI•lee] *adj* bête sot stupide

silt *n* vase F limon M

silver [SIL•vur] *n* argent M; *adj*
(color) argenté; (in substance)
de or en argent

silverware [SIL•vur•WAIUR] *n*
argenterie F

similar [SI•mi•lur] *adj*
semblable

similarly [SI•mi•lur•lee] *adv* de
la même façon

simmer [SI•mur] *vt* faire cuire à
feu doux mijoter; *vi* cuire à
feu doux mijoter

simple [SIM•pl] *adj* simple

simplicity [sim•PLI•si•tee] *n*
simplicité F

simplify [SIM•pli•FUY] *vt*
simplifier

simply [SIM•plee] *adv*
simplement

simulate [SI•myu•LAT] *vt*
simuler

simultaneous
[SUY•mul•TAÏ•nee•us] *adj*
simultané

sin *n* péche F; *vi* pécher

since [sins] *adj prep* depuis;
conj depuis que; (because)
puisque

sincere [sin•SEEUR] *adj* sincère

sincerity [sin•SE•ri•tee] *n*
sincérité F

sing *vt vi* chanter

singe [sinj] *vt* brûler légèrement

single [SIN•gl] *n* seul unique;
(person) célibataire; ~ out\ *vt*
choisir; distinguer

single-handed [~ HAN•did]
adv tout seul

singular [SING•gyu•lur] *adj n*
singulier M

sinister [SI•ni•stur] *adj* sinistre

sink [singk] *n* évier M; (of
bathroom) lavabo M; *vt* (ship)
couler; *vi* couler sombrer; ~ in
vt\ pénétrer

sinner [SI•nur] *n* pécheur M

sinus [SUY•nus] *n* sinus M

sip *n* petite gorgée F; *vt* boire à
petites gorgées

siphon [SUY•fn] *n* siphon M; *vt*
siphonner

sir [sur] *n* monsieur

siren [SUYU•run] *n* sirène F

sirloin [SUR•loin] *n* aloyau M

sister [SI•stur] *n* sœur F

sister-in-law [SIS•tur•in•LAU]
n belle-sœur F

sit *vi* s'asseoir; (committee etc)
siéger; ~ down *vi*\ s'asseoir

site [suyt] *n* emplacement M
site M; (of building)
chantier M

sitting [SI•ting] (meeting) *n*
séance F

sitting-room *n* salon M

situated [SI•choo•AI•tid] *adj*
situé

situation [SI•choo•AI•shn] *n*
situation F

six [siks] *num* six (see also five)

sixteen [sik•STEEN] *num* seize
(see also five)

sixty [SIK•stee] *num* soixante;
npl les anées F soixante

size [suyz] *n* taille; (of building) dimensions; (of shoe) pointure F; *vt* jauger

sizzle [SI•zl] *vi* grésiller

skate [skait] *n* patin M; *vi* patiner; (roller-skate) faire du patin à roulettes

skateboard [SKAIT•baurd] *n* planche F à roulettes

skater [SKAI•tur] *n* patineur M; (roller skater) patineur M à roulettes

skating [SKAI•ting] *n* patinage M; (on roller skates) patinage M à roulettes

skating rink [~ ringk] *n* patinoire F

skeleton [SKE•li•tn] *n* squellette M

skeptic [SKEP•tik] *n* sceptique MF

skeptical [SKEP•ti•kl] *n* sceptique

sketch [skech] *n* croquis M esquisse F; (theater) sketch M; *vt* faire un croquis de dessiner

ski [skee] *n* ski M; *vi* faire du ski; skier

skid *n* dérapage M; *vi* déraper

skier [SKEE•ur] *n* skieur M

skiing [SKEE•ing] *n* ski M; faire du ski; skier

skill [skil] *n* compétance F

skilled [skild] *adj* habile; versé; compétant

skillet [SKIL•it] *n* poêle à frire F

skillful [SKIL•fl] *adj* expert ; adroit

skim *vt* (~ a magazine or a newspaper) feuilleter

skin *n* peau F

skin-deep [SKIN•DEEP] *adj* superficiel

skinny [SKI•nee] *adj* maigre

skip *n vt vi* saut; *vi* passer; *vi* gambader M

skipper [SKI•pur] *n* capitaine M

skirmish [SKUR•mish] *n* accrochage F

skirt [skurt] *n* jupe F

skit *n* impromptu; parodie MF

skittish [ski•dish] *adj* frivole

skulk [skuhlk] *vi* rôder

skull [skuhl] *n* crâne M

skunk [skuhnk] *n* (animal) moufette F

sky [skuy] *n* ciel M

skylight [SKUY•luyt] *n* lucarne F

skyscraper [SKUY•SKRAI•pur] *n* gratte-ciel (inv) M

slab *n* bloc; plaque MF

slack [slak] *n adj* laisse-aller; lâche M

slacken [SLA•kn] *vt* détendre

slacker [SLA•kur] *n* fainéant M

slam *vt* claquer

slander [SLAN•dur] *n; vt* calomnie F; calomnier

slang *n* argot M

slant *n vt vi* en bias; inclinaison MF

slap *n vt* gifle F

slash *n vt* coup de couteau; balafre (au visage) MF

slat *n* latte F

slate [slait] *n vi* (~ for government office) destiner à

slaughter [SLAU•tur] *n; vt*
massacre; massacrer; abattre
(un animal) M

slave [slaiv] *n* esclave MF

slavish [SLAI•vish] *adj* servile

slay [slai] *vt* tuer

sleazy [SLEE•zee] *adj* sordide

sled *n vi* (~ down the hill)
faire de la luge F

sledge [slej] *n; vi* luge F

sleek *adj* luisant

sleep *n; vi* sommeil (n); dormir;
s'endormir M

sleeper [SLEE•pur] *n; adj*
(succès inattendu surtout un
film/this movie was a ~); (~
car) d'un train dormeur;
canapé-lit; traverse (dans un
train) MF

sleepiness [SLEE•pee•nes] *n*
envie de dormir F

sleeping [SLEE•ping] *adj*
endormi

sleepless [SLEEP•les] *adj* sans
dormi; qui ne dort pas

sleepy [SLEE•pee] *adj* avoir
sommeil M

sleet *n vi* neige fondue F

sleeve [sleev] *n* manche F

sleigh [slai] *n* traineau M

sleight [slait] *n* dextérité; ruse F

sleuth [slooth] *n* détective M

slice [sluys] *n* tranche; *vt* couper
en tranches F

slick [slik] *adj* chic; lisse; rusé

slicker [SLI•kur] *n* arnaquer;
combinard -e M

slide [sluyd] *n vi* toboggan;
glisser M

slight [sluyt] *adj* léger -ère

slightly [SLUYT•lee] *adv*
légèrement

slim *adj* mince

slime [sluym] *n* substance
visqueuse F

sling *n; vt* écharpe (pour un
bras brisé); lancer (vt) F

slink [slingk] *vi* (~ into a room)
se glisser (dans une pièce);
s'éclipser

slip *n* (woman's petticoat);
(men's brief); *vt vi* (~ on
ice) *n* sous-vêtement; *vt vi*
glisser sur la glace M

slipper [SLI•pur] *n* pantoufle F

slippery [SLIP•ree] *adj* glissant

slit *n* fente F; fendre; *vt* inciser

slither [SLI•thur] *vi* ramper

sliver [SLI•vur] *n* [éclat] M

slobber [SLAH•bur] *vi* baver

slogan [SLO•gan] *n* devise F

slop [slahp] *n* substance
fluide/inappétissante /sale; un
mauvais repas (institutionnel)
F; *vi* renverser (une tasse de
café sur la table)

slope [slop] *n* pente; inclin F

small [smaul] *ad* petit; peu
nombreux; bref a ~ matter\
peu de chose

smart *ad* viv; chich; intelligent;
vi picoter; cuire

smell [smehl] *vi* sentir; flairer; *n*
odeur F; parum; odorat M

smile [smyul] *n* sourire M; *vt*
sourire

smiling [SMYUL•ing] *adj*
souriant; agréable

smoke [smok] *n* fumé F *vt vi*
fumer; enfumer; no smoking;
défense de fumer

smooth *adj* uni; lisse; glabre; *vt* polir; lisser; ~ talker beau parleur

smother [SMU•ther] *vt* étouffer

smuggle [SMUH•gl] *vt* faire de la contrebande

smut [smuht] *n* tache noire; nielle F

snack [snak] *n* casse-croûte M

snake [snaik] *n* serpent; vipère F

snap *vt* birser; *vi* se caser (whip) faire claquer (dog) happer; *adj* bruque; instantané; ~ one's fingers\ faire la nique; ~ at\ essayer de mordere; rembarrer

stach [snach] *vt* empoigner; enlever

sneak [sneek] *vt* se glisser furitvemen; *n* sournois; fureteur M

sneakers [SNEE•kurs] *n* espadrilles; chauseurs de tennis F

sneeze [sneez] *vt* éternuer; *n* éternuement M

snooze [snooz] *vt* faire un somme; *n* somme M

snore [snor] *vt* ronfler; *n* ronflement M

snort [snaurt] *n* museau; groin M *vt* grogner

snout [snaut] *n* museau (d'un animal) M

snow [sno] *n* neige F; *vi* neiger

snowball [SNO•baul] *n* boule de neige F

snowdrift [SNO•drift] *n* congère F

snowfall [SNO•faul] *n* chute de neige F

snowflake [SNO•flaik] *n* flocon de neige M

snowplow [SNO•plou] *n* chasse-neige M

snub *vt* rebuffade F

snuff [snuf] *n* tabac à priser M

snug *adj* confortable

so *conj* et puis? (so what?); c'est tellement bon ou si bon (it's so good); tant de travail! (so much. work!)

soak [sok] *vt vi* (~ in water) faire tremper

soap *n* savon M

soar [saur] *vi* (~ in the air) monter en flèche F

sob [sahb] *n; vi* sanglot; sangloter M

sober [SO•bur] *adj* sobre

soberly [SO•bur•lee] *adv* sobrement

sobriety [so•BRUYY•uh•tee] *n* sobriété

sociable [SO•shah•bl] *adj* sociable

social [SO•shul] *n* (church ~); *adj* (~ pressures) social

socialism [SO•shul•IZM] *n* socialisme M

socialist [SO•shul•ist] adj; *n* socialiste MF

society [so•SUY•eh•tee] *n* société F

sociology [SO•see•YAHL•uh•jee] *n* sociologie F

sock [sahk] *n vt* (~ sb in a brawl); *vi* chaussette F

socket [SAH•keht] *n* douille F

sod [sahd] *n* motte F

soda [so•dah] *n* soude; eau de seltz F

sodium [SO•deeyuhm] *n* sodium M

sofa [SO•fah] *n* sofa; canapé M

soft [sauft] *adj* doux

soften [SAU•fn] *vt* adoucir

softness [SAUFT•nes] *n* douceur F

soil *n* sol; terre MF

sojourn [SO•jurn] *n* séjour M

solace [SAHL•is] *n* consolation F

solar [SO•lur] *adj* solaire

solder [SOL•dur] *vt* souder

soldier [SOL•jur] *n* soldat M

sole [sol] *adj* seul; unique

solemn [SAH•lehm] *adj* solennel

solemnity [suh•LEM•ni•tee] *n* solennité F

solicit [suh•LI•sit] *vt* solliciter

solicitation [suh•LI•si•TAI•shun] *n* solictation F

solicitor [suh•LI•si•tur] *n* solliciteur M

solid [SAHL•id] *adj* solide

solidarity [SAH•li•DAIUR•i•tee] *n* solidarité F

solidify [suh•LI•di•FUY] *vt* se solidifier

soliloquy [suh•LIL•uh•kwee] *n* soliloque M

solitary [SAH•li•TAIUR•ee] *adj* solitaire

solitude [SAH•li•TYOOD] *n* solitude F

solo [SO•lo] *n* solo M

solstice [SAHL•stis] *n* solstice M

solution [so•LYOO•shun] *n* solution F

solve [sahlv] *vt* résoudre

solvent [SAHL•vent] *n* dissolvant M

somber [SAHM•bur] *adj* sombre

some [suhm] *adj* quelques-uns; quelques-unes quantité indéfinie; un peu; du des prendre du; chercher des

somebody [SUHM•buh•dee] *pron* quelqu'un; quelqu'une MF

somehow [SUHM•hou] *adv* d'une façon ou d'une autre

someone [SUHM•wuhn] *pron* quelqu'un; quelqu'une MF

somersault [SUH•mur•SAULT] *n* culbute F

something [SUHM•thing] *n pron* quelque chose M

sometime [SUHM•tuym] *adv* un de ses jours M

sometimes [SUHM•tuymz] *adv* quelquefois

somewhat [SUHM•whut] *adv* quelque peu; un peu M

somewhere [SUHM•waiur] *adv* quelque part

somnolent [SAHM•no•lent] *adj* somnolent

son [suhn] *n* fils M

son-in-law [SUHN•in•LAU] *n* gendre; beau-fils M

sonata [suh•NAH•duh] *n* sonate F

song [saung] *n* chanson F

song-bird [SAUNG•burd] *n*
oiseau chanteur M

song-writer
[SAUNG•RUY•tur] *n*
compositeur -trice MF

sonnet [SAH•neht] *n* sonnet M

sonorous [suh•NUR•us] *adj*
sonore

soon *adv* bientôt

soot [sut] *n* suie F

soothe [sooth] *vt* apaiser

sooty [SU•dee] *adj* plein de
suie F

sop [sahp] *adj* trempé *vt*
éponger

sophisticated
[so•FI•sti•KAI•tud] *adj*
sophistiqué

sophistication
[suh•FIS•ti•KAI•shun] *n*
sophistication F

sophomore [SAUF•maur] *n*
étudiant(e) de seconde année
(high school) MF

soprano [so•PRA•no] *n* soprano
MF

sorcerer [SAUR•sur•ur] *n*
sorcier -ière MF

sordid [SAUR•did] *adj* sordide

sore [saur] *adj* douleureux; *n*
blessure; plaie F

sorrow [SAH•ro] *n* douleur F

sorrowful [SAH•ruh•fl] *adj*
triste

sorry [SAH•ree] *adj* désolé

sort [saurt] *n* type; sorte; espèce
MF; *vt* sorter

soul [sol] *n* âme F

sound [saund] *n* son; bruit M

soundless [SAUND•les] *adj*
silencieux

soundproof [SAUND•proof]
adj insonorisé

soup [soop] *n* soupe F

sour *adj* aigre

source [saurs] *n* source F

south [sauth] *n* sud M

South America *n* amérique du
sud F

southeast [south•EEST] *n*
sud-est M

southerner [SUH•thur•nur] *n*
personne F qui vient du sud;
personne qui est originaire du
sud F

southward [SOUTH•waurd]
adj au sud M

southwest [south•WEST] *n*
sud-ouest M

souvenir [SOO•vuh•NEEUR] *n*
souvenir M

sovereign [SUH•vruhn] *n*
souverain -e MF

soviet [SAU•vee•yeht] *n*
Soviet M

sow 1 [saui *n* truie (animal) F

sow 2 [so] *vt* semer

space [spais] *n* espace M

spacious [SPAI•shus] *adj*
spacieux -euse

spade [spaid] *n* (a tool) pique
(cartes); bêche (outil) MF

span *n; vt n* durée; *vt* s'
étendre F

Spaniard [SPA•nyurd] *n*
Espagnol -e MF

Spanish [SPA•nish] *adj*
espagnol

spank [spangk] *vt* fesser

spanking [SPANGK•ing] *n*
fessée

spar [spahr] *vi n* faire un assaut amical M

spare [spaiur] *adj* supplémentaire; *n* extra; *vt* épargner

spark [spahrk] *n; vt n* étincelle; *vt* provoquer F

spark plug *n* bougie (voiture) F

sparkle [SPAHR•kl] *n vi* étincelement M; *vi* étinceler; briller M

sparkling [SPAHRK•ling] *adj* étincelant; scintillant

sparrow [SPAIUR•o] *n* (bird) moineau M

sparse [spahrs] *adj* épar

spasm [spazm] *n* spasme M

spat *vt; vi* (pt of spit) craché -e

spatter [SPA•dur] *vt* éclabousser

spawn [spaun] *n vt* engendrer; produire (oeufs)

speak [speek] *vi* parler (à qq'un)

speaker [SPEE•kur] *n n* orateur -trice mf; *n* conférencier -ère MF

spear [speeur] *n* lance F

special [SPEH•shul] *adj* exceptionnel ; unique

specialist [SPEH•shul•ist] *n* expert M; spécialiste mf

specialize [SPEH•shul•UYZ] *vi* se spécialiser (dans)

species [SPEE•sheez] *n* espèce F

specific [spuh•SI•ik] *adj* spécifique

specify [SPEH•si•FUY] *vt* spécifier

specimen [SPE•si•min] *n* spécimen M

specious [SPEE•shus] *adj* spécieux ; trompeur

speckle [spehkl] *n; vt n* moucheture F; petite tache F; *vt* tacheter F

spectacle [SPEK•tuhkl] *n* spéctacle M

spectacular [spek•TAK•yuh•lur] adj; *n adj* spectaculaire; *n* superproduction F

spectator [SPEK•TAI•tur] *n* spectateur -trice MF

spectrum [SPEK•trum] *n* gamme (de produits) F

speculate [SPE•kyoo•LAIT] *vi* (~ on the stock market) spéculer (sur qq ch); s'interroger (sur)

speculation [SPEH•kyoo•LAI•shun] *n* spéculation; conjecture F

speech *n* discours; parole MF

speed *n* vitesse F *vi* se dépêcher

speed limit *n* limitation de vitesse F

speedily [SPEE•di•lee] *adv* rapidement; vite

speedy [SPEE•dee] *adj* rapide; vite

spell [spel] *n* charme F *vt* épeler

spellbound [SPEHL•bound] *adj* charmé; envoûté; ensorcelé

spelling book *n* abécédaire M

spend *vt* dépenser

spendthrift [SPEND•thrift] *n* dépensier -ère MF

spew [spyoo] *vi* gicler

sphere [sfeeur] *n* sphére; domaine F

spherical [SFEEUR•i•kl] *adj* sphérique

spice [spuys] *n* épice F

spider [SPUY•dur] *n* araignée F

spigot [SPIG•it] *n* robinet M

spike [spuyk] (~ a drink with alcohol) *n* pointe F; *vt* arroser (une boisson) d'alcool F

spill [spil] *vt* renverser; *vi* déborder

spin *vt* tournoyer

spinach [SPIN•ich] *npl* épinards M

spinal [SPUY•nl] *adj* spinal

spinal column *n* colonne vertébrale F

spinal cord *n* moelle épinière M

spinner [SPIN•ur] *n* fileur -euse MF

spinning-wheel [SPIN•ing ~] *n* rouet M

spinster [SPIN•stur] *n* vieille fille; célibataire F

spiral [SPUY•rl] *adj*; *n* spirale F

spire [spuyur] *n* flèche F

spirit [SPEEUR•it] *n* esprit M

spirited [SPEEUR•i•ted] *adj* animé

spiritual [SPEEUR•i•chooul] *adj n* spirituel

spirituality [SPEEUR•i•choo•AL•i•tee] *n* spiritualité F

spit *n* crachet M; *vi* cracher M

spite [spuyt] *n* dépit M

spitting [SPIT•ing] *n* l'acte de cracher; *adj* (be the ~ image of sb); être le portrait craché

splash *n* plouf (l'eau) M; *vi* ploufer

spleen *n* rate (anat) F

splendid [SPLEN•did] *adj* splendide

splendor [SPLEN•daur] *n* splendeur F

splice [spluys] *vt* (~ film); (~ a rope) coller (un film); épisser (une corde)

splint [splint] *n* attelle F

splinter [SPLIN•tur] *n* (~ of wood) echarde F

split *vt* cliver; fendre; partager

spoil *vt* pourrir (la nourriture); gâter (un enfant); gacher (une vue)

spoke [spok] *n* rayon (de roue) M; *vi* (pt of to speak)

spokesperson [SPAUKS•PUR•sn] *n* porte-parole M

sponge [spuhnj] *n* éponge F

sponge cake *n* gâteau de Savoie M

sponger [SPUHN•jur] *n* parasite M

sponsor [SPAHN•sur] *n; vt n* sponsor M (d'une émission télévisée); *n* commanditaire mf (d'un artiste); *n* parrain m/marraine F (d'un(e) enfant) MF

spontaneity [SPAHN•tah•NEHY•i•dee] *n* spontanéité F

spontaneous [spahn•TAI•neeyus] *adj* spontané

spook [spyook] *n; vt* (~ sb)
fantôme M

spool *n* bobine (de fil) F

spoon *n* cuillère F

spoonful [SPOON•ful] *n*
cuillerée F

sport [spaurt] *n* sport M

sportsman [SPAURTS•mun] *n*
sportif -ive

spot [spaht] *n; pois* M (animal);
tache F (animal); *vt* tacheter;
apercevoir (qq'un au loin) MF

spotted [SPAH•ted] *adj*
tacheté; moucheté

spouse [spaus] *n* époux -se; M
mari F femme MF

spout *n* bec M

sprain *n; vt* (~ an ankle) *vt* se
fouler; *n* faire une à la
cheville F

sprawl [spraul] *vi* s'étaler

spray [sprai] *n; vt n* aérosol M;
vt vaporiser; *vt* pulvériser; M

sprayer [spraiur] *n* atomiseur M

spread [spred] *n* de terre;
tartiner F; *vt* étaler

spree *n* (shopping ~) faire des
dans les magasins F

sprig *n* brin M

sprightly [SPRUYT•lee] *adv*
alerte

spring *n* printemps (la saison)
vi (~ into action) passer
rapidement à l'action (n); *vi*
bondir (sur qq'un/qqch);
bondir (de joie) M

sprinkle [SPRING•kl] *vt*
parsemer

sprint *n vi* sprint (sport) M

sprout *n* (alfalfa ~s); *vt vi* (*n*)
pousse F; (*n*) germe F; (*vt vi*)
pousser; germer

spruce [spryoos] *n* épine F; *vt*
raffraîchir

spun [spuhn] *pt and pp* spin;
adj filé

spur *n* éperon M

spurn *vt* rejeter

spurt *vi* (~ out) jaillir

sputter [SPUH•tur] *vi* toussoter

spy [spuy] *n* espion -nne MF; *vt*
espionner MF

spy [spuy] *n* espion -nne MF

squabble [SKWAH•bl] *n vi*
dispute; querelle; se disputer F

squad [skwahd] *n* escouade
(mil); section; brigade (corps
de police) F

squadron [SKWAH•drun] *n*
escadron (aviation); escadrille
(marine) MF

squalid [SKWAH•lid] *adj*
sordide

squall [skwahl] *n vi* (*n*) rafale
de pluie; *vi* hurler F

squander [SKWAHN•dur] *vt vt*
gaspiller; *vt* dissiper (n
l'héritage m) M

square [skwehr] *n* carré M; *adj*
carré; vrai; on the ~ honnête;
~ oneself se mettre en règle

squash [skwahsh] *n* (the game
of ~); *vt* (n) jouer au squash
(game); (vt) écraser M

squat [skwaht] *vi* s'accroupir

squawk [skauk] *n* criaillement
M (d'un oiseau); *vi*
criailler M

squeak [skweek] *n* grincement
M; *vi* grincer M

squeal [skweeil] *vi* (~ on sb)
crisser (n freins mpl); (vt)
pousser un petit (n) cri M; *vi*

moucharder ou informer
(péj) M

squeamish [SKWEE•mish] *adj*
hypersensible

squeeze [skweez] *vt* serrer

squelch [skwelch] *n; vi* (the
snow ~ed under my feet as I
walked through the yard) *vi*
s'écraser (la neige s'écrasait
sous mes pieds pendant que je
traversait le jardin)

squint [skwint] *n; vi n* regard
M louche; *vi* loucher M

squire [skwuyur] *n* propriétaire
d'un domaine

squirm [skwurm] *vi* se tortiller

squirrel [skwurl] *n* écureuil M

squirt [skwurt] *n; vt* faire gicler
(*n* liquide m); faire jaillir (*n*
crème f)

stab *vt* (~ sb with a knife); *vi*
(take a ~ at something/essayer
de faire qqch) *vt* poignarder
(qq'un avec un couteau)

stability [stuh•BIL•i•dee] *n*
stabilité F

stabilize [STAI•buhl•UYZ] *vt*
stabiliser

stable [STAI•bl] *adj; n adj*
stable stationnaire; *n*
écurie F

stable [STAI•bl] *n; adj* écurie;
stationnaire F

stack [stak] *n; vt n* pile F; *vt*
empiler (des boites; meubles;
etc) F

stadium [STAI•deey•uhm] *n*
stade M

staff [staf] *n* (work force); *vt* (~
an office) *n* personnel M; *n*
bâton M; *n* houlette F (de

berger); *vt* fournir le
personnel d'une compagnie
d'une société MF

stag *n* cerf M

stag party *n* réunion F entre
hommes F

stage [staij] *n* (~ of
development); scène (théâtre)
stade (du développement) M

stage door *n* entrée F des
artistes F

stage fright *n* avoir le trac M

stage-struck [STAIJ•struhk]
adj se dit d'une personne qui
rêve de faire du théâtre

stagger [STA•gur] *vi* chanceler

stagnant [STAG•nùnnt] *adj*
stagnant; confiné (air)

staid [staid] *adj* rangé; en ordre

stain [stain] *adj n* tache F

stainless [STAIN•les] *adj*
inoxydable

stair *npl* escalier; escaliers M

stairs [stehrz] *npl* escaliers M

stake [staik] *n* pieu M

stale [staiil] *adj* (~ bread) rassis

stalk [stauk] *n; trognon M; n*
tige F (d'une plante); *vi* rôder
dans

stalk [stauk] *n; vt* tige (d'une
plante); rôder (dans) F

stall [stahl] *n* (horse's ~); *vt* (~
a vehicle); *vi* (~ for time) *n*
étal M (cheval); caler (dans
une véhicule); gagner (du
temps)

stallion [STAL•yuhn] *n*
étalon M

stalwart [STAHL•wurt] *adj*
résolu

stamina [STAM•i•nah] *n*
endurance F

stammer [STA•mur] *n; vt; vi n*
bégaiement M; *vt vi*
bégayer M

stamp *n;* timbre M; *vt*
tramponer

stampede [stam•PEED] *n*
débandade F *vt; vi* s'enfuir; se
précipiter

stanch or staunch [stanch];
[staunch] *adj* loyal

stand *n* kiosque M; venir àla
barre F (au tribunal); *vi* se
mettre debout

standard [STAN•durd] *adj; n*
adj normal; *adj n*
classique M

standardization
[STAN•dur•di•ZAI•shun] *n*
(~ of prices) normalisation F

standardize
[STAN•dur•DUYZ] *vt*
normaliser

standing [STAND•ing] *n*
réputation F

stanza [STAN•zah] *n* strophe F

staple [STAI•pl] *n* agrafe F;
allment de base M; *vt* agrafer

star [stahr] *n* étoile F; *vt* jouer
le rôle principal

starboard [STAHR•baurd] adj;
n (to ~); *vt* (to ~ the helm)
tribord (naut) M

starch [stahrch] *n; vt* (~ a shirt)
amidon; amidonner M

stark [stahrk] *adj* désclé; austère

start [stahrt] *vt* commencer (à
faire qqch)

starting [STAHR•ting] *n*
commencement M

starting point *n* point de
départ M

startle [STAHR•dl] *vt* étonner

starvation [stahr•VAI•shun] *n*
faim F

starve [stahrv] *adj* affamé;
laisser mourir de faim; *vi*
souffrir de la faim

state [stait] *n; vt n* état M; *vt*
dire (qqch à qq'un) M

stately [STAIT•lee] *adj*
majestueux -euse

statement [STAIT•muhnt] *n*
déclaration F

stateroom [STAIT•room] *n n*
salon M de réception
(bâtiment); *n* cabine F de
grand luxe (navire) MF

statesman [STAITS•muhn] *n*
homme d'Etat M

static [STA•dik] *adj*
stationnaire; *n* statique F

station [STAI•shun] *n* gare F

stationary [STAI•shi•NAI•ree]
adj stationnaire; immobile

stationery
[STAI•shun•NAI•ree] *n*
papeterie F

statistics [stah•TI•stiks] *npl*
statistique F

statuary [STA•choo•AIUR•ee]
n statuaire F

statue [STA•choo] *n* statue;
sculpture F

status [STA•tus] *n* (marital ~)
rang; position (sociale); *n*
situation F de famille MF

statute [STA•choot] *n* statut M

staunch *adj* loyal; dévoué

stay [stai] *vi* rester

stead [sted] *n* (to go in sb's ~)
au lieu M de; à la place F de
MF

steadfast [sted•fast] *adj*
inébranlable

steadily [STED•i•lee] *adv*
régulièrement

steadiness [STEH•dee•nes] *n*
stabilité F

steady [STE•dee] *adj* régulier
-ière

steak [staik] *n* bifteck M

steal [steeil] *vt* voler

stealth [stelth] *n* ruse F

steam [steem] *n* vapeur F

steam engine *n* moteur à
vapeur M

steamboat [STEEM•bot] *n*
bâteau à vapeur M

steamer [STEE•mur] *n* marmite
à vapeur F

steamship [STEEM•ship] *n*
navire à vapeur M

steed *n* coursier M

steel [steel] *n* àcier M; stainless
~ *n* acier inoxydable M

steep 1 *adj* raide

steep 2 *vt* tremper M

steeple [stee•pl] *n* clocher M

steer 1 *vt* conduire (une
voiture)

steer 2 *n* boeuf M

stem 1 *n* tige F

stem 2 *vt vi* arrêter (qqch ou
qq'un); être le résultat de F

stench [stench] *n* puanteur F

stencil [STEN•sul] *n* stencil M

stenographer
[ste•NAH•gruh•fur] *n*
sténographe MF

stenography
[ste•NAH•gru•fee] *n*
sténographie F

step *n* pas; marche (escalier)
MF; *vt* marcher

stepchild [STEP•chuyld] *n*
beau-fils; belle-fille MF

stepdaughter [STEP•DAU•tur]
n beau-fille F

stepfather [STEP•FA•thur]
beau-père M

stepladder [STEP•LA•dur] *n*
escabeau M

stepmother [STEP•MUH•thur]
n belle-mère F

stepson [STEP•suhn] *n*
beau-fils M

stereo [STAIR•ree•O] *n*
stéréo M

stereotype
[STAIR•ree•o•TUYP] *n*
stéréotype M

sterile [STAIR•ruyl] *adj* stérile

sterility [stair•RI•li•tee] *n*
stérilité F

sterilize [STAIR•ri•LUYZ] *vt*
stériliser

sterling [STUR•ling] *n*
sterling M

stern [sturn] *adj* sévère

stethoscope
[STETH•uh•SKOP] *n*
stéthoscope M

stevedore [STE•vu•DOR] *n*
docker M

stew [stoo] *n* ragoût M

steward [STOO•wurd] *n*
steward (avion) M

stewardess [STOO•wur•des] *n*
hôtesse F

stick 1 [stik] *n* branche F

stick 2 [stik] vt coller

stiff [stif] adj raide

stiffen [STIF•fin] vt; vi raidir; se raidir

stiffness [STIF•nes] n raideur F

stifle [STUY•fl] vt étouffer

stigma [STIG•muh] n honte (avoir honte) F

still 1 [stil] adj immobile

still 2 [stil] adv encore; toujours

stillness [STIL•nes] n immobilité; tranquillité F

stilt n échasse F

stimulant [STIM•yoo•lint] n stimulant M

stimulate [STIM•yoo•LAIT] vt stimuler

stimulation [STIM•yoo•LAI•shn] n stimulation F

stimulus [STIM•yoo•lus] n stimulus M

sting n piqûre; vt piquer F

stinginess [STIN•jee•nes] n avarice; avare F

stingy [STIN•jee] adj avare

stink n puanteur F; vt empester (une salle)

stint n période de travail F

stipend [STUY•pend] n traitement M

stipulate [STIP•yoo•LAIT] vt stipuler

stir [stur] vt vi remuer

stirring [STUR•ring] adj; n passionant; sentiment M

stirrup [STUR•rip] n étrier M

stitch [stich] n vt point; coudre M

stock [stok] n vt réserve; part; approvisionner F

Stock Exchange n bourse F

stock market n bourse F

stockade [stah•KAID] n palissade F

stockbroker [STAHK•BRO•kur] n agent de change M

stockholder [STAHK•HOL•dur] n actionnaire MF

stocking [STAHK•king] n bas (femmes); chaussettes MF

stockroom [STAHK•room] n réserve F

stocky [STAHK•kee] adj trapu

stockyards [STAHK•yardz] n parc à bestiaux M

stoic [STO•ik] adj stoïque

stoicism [STO•i•SIZM] n stoïcisme M

stoke [stok] vt alimenter (un feu)

stole [stol] n vt étole; volé (pp de voler) F

stolid [STAH•lid] adj impassible

stomach [STUH•mik] n estomac; ventre M

stomachache [STUH•mik•AIK] n (avoir) mal au ventre ou mal de ventre M

stone [ston] n pierre F

stonework [STON•wurk] n maçonnerie F

stony [STO•nee] adj pierreux -euse; cailouteux -euse

stooge [stooj] n laquais M

stool n tabouret M

stool pigeon n mouchard -e MF

stoop n porche; vi se pencher; s'accroupir M

stop [stahp] n vt; vi arrêt; arrêter; s'arrêter M

stoppage [STAH•pij] n arrêt; interruption MF

stopper [STAH•pur] n bouchon M

stopwatch [STAHP•wahtch] n chronomètre M

storage [STOR•aij] n stockage M

store [stor] n vt magasin; entreposer MF

storekeeper [STOR•KEE•pur] n commerçant -e MF

stork n cigogne F

storm n orage M

stormy [STOR•mee] adj orageux -euse

story 1 [STO•ree] n conte; histoire MF

story 2 [STO•ree] n étage (d'un immeuble) M

stout adj corpulent

stove [stov] n poêle M

stow [sto] vi ranger

straddle [STRAD•dl] vt chevaucher

straggle [STRAG•gl] vi s'étendre

straight [strait] adj droit

straighten [STRAI•tin] vt redresser

straightforward [STRAIT•FOR•wurd] adj direct

straightway [STRAIT•WAI] adv tout de suite; sur le champ

strain n tension; vt tendre; faire égoutter (légumes) F

strainer [STRAI•nur] n passoire F

strait n détroit M

strand 1 n mèche (des cheveux) F

strand 2 vt; vi échouer (un navire)

strange [strainj] adj étrange

strangeness [STRAINJ•nes] n étrangeté F

stranger [STRAIN•jur] n étranger -ère MF

strangle [STRAN•gl] vt étrangler

strangulate [STRAN•gyu•LAIT] vt étrangler

strangulation [STRAN•gyu•LAI•shn] n strangulation F

strap n courroie; bande F; vt attacher

strategic [struh•TEE•jik] adj stratégique

strategy [stra•TI•jee] n stratégie F

stratosphere [STRA•to•SFEER] n stratosphère F

straw [strau] n paille F

strawberry [STRAU•bair•ree] n fraise F

stray [strai] adj n vi errant -e; errer MF

stray bullet n balle perdue F

streak [streek] n vt traînée; traîner F

stream [streem] n courant; ruisseau M

streamer [STREE•mur] *n*
banderole F

streamlined [streem•luynd] *n*
forme profilée F

street *n* rue F

street door *n* porte sur la rue F

streetcar [STREET•kahr] *n*
tramway M

strength *n* pouvoir; puissance
MF

strengthen [STRENGTH•en] *vt*
fortifier

strenuous [STREN•yoo•us] *adj*
ardu

stress [stres] *n* stress; tension
MF

stretch [strech] *vt* tendre
(l'élastique); s'étendre (une
personne)

stretcher [STRECH•chur] *n*
brancard (méd) M

strew [stroo] *vt* répandre

strict [strikt] *adj* strict; sévère

stride [struyd] *n* (prendre un)
grand pas M

strident [STRUY•dint] *adj*
strident

strife [struyf] *npl* dissensions;
querelles F

strike [struyk] *n vt* (donner un)
coup; grève; frapper MF

striker [STRUY•kur] *n* gréviste
MF

striking [STRUY•king] *adj*
frappant

string *n* ficelle F

strip 1 *n* morceau (de papier);
bande MF

strip 2 *v* dévêtir (vêtements);
dépouiller (qq'un de ses
droits); se dévêtir

stripe [struyp] *n* raie; rayer F

strive [struyv] *vi* s'acharner à

stroke 1 [strok] *n* attaque
d'apoplexie F

stroke 2 [strok] *vt* caresser

stroll [strol] *n vi* petite
promenade; flaner F

strong *adj* fort; puissant

stronghold [STRONG•hold] *n*
bastion; forteresse MF

strongly [STRONG•lee] *adj*
fortement; avec force

structural [STRUK•chur•ul] *adj*
structural; architectural

structure [STRUK•chur] *n*
structure F

struggle [STRUH•gl] *n; vt*
lutte; lutter F

strut [struht] *n vi* démarche
fière; se pavener F

stub [stuhb] *n* bout (d'une
cigarette) M

stubble [STUHB•bl] *n* chaume;
barbe de plusieurs jours MF

stubborn [STUHB•born] *adj*
têtu ; obstiné

stubbornness
[STUHB•born•nes] *n*
obstination F

stucco [STUH•ko] *n* stuc M

stuck-up [STUH•KUHP] *adj*
snob (*inv*); prétentieux -euse

stud 1 [stuhd] *n* étalon (cheval);
clou M

stud 2 [stuhd] *vt* parsemer (de)

student [STOO•dent] *n* étudiant
-e MF

studio [STOO•dee•o] *n*
atelier M

study [STUH•dee] *vt* étudier

stuff [stuhf] *n vt* trucs; étoffe; bourrer MF

stuffing [STUHF•fing] *n* bourre; farce (cuisine) F

stuffy [STUH•fee] *adj* mal ventilé; stagnant

stumble [STUHMB•bl] *vi* trébucher

stump [stuhmp] *n* souche (d'un arbre) F

stun [stuhn] *vt* choquer; étonner

stunt [stuhnt] *n* exploit spectaculaire M

stunt [stuhnt] *vt* empêcher de croître

stupefy [STOO•pi•FUY] *vt* stupéfier

stupendous [stoo•PEN•dus] *adj* prodigieux -euse

stupid [STOO•pid] *adj* bête; stupide

stupidity [stoo•PI•di•tee] *n* bêtise; stupidité F

stupor [STOO•pur] *n* stupeur F

sturdy [STUR•dee] *adj* solide

sturgeon [STUR•jun] *n* esturgeon M

stutter [STUH•tur] *n vt vi* bégaiment; bégayer M

sty 1 [stuy] *n* porcherie (cochons) F

sty 2 [stuy] *n* orgelet (à l'oeil) M

style [stuyl] *n* style (d'un roman) M

stylish [STUY•lish] *n* à la mode F

subcommittee [SUHB•ko•MI•tee] *n* sous-comité M

subconscious [suhb•KON•shus] *n* subconscient (Id freudien) M

subdivision [SUHB•di•VI•shn] *n* subdivision F

subdue [suhb•DOO] *vt* maîtriser; contrôler

subject [n. SUHB•jekt v. suhb•JEKT] *n vt* sujet; soumettre M

subjection [suhb•JEK•shn] *n* soumission F

subjective [suhb•JEK•tiv] *adj* subjectif -ive

subjugate [SUHB•juh•GAIT] *vt* assujettir; soumettre

subjunctive [suhb•JUNK•tiv] *n* subjonctif (mode) M

sublet [SUHB•LET] *n vt* sous-location; sous-louer F

sublime [suhb•LUYM] *adj n* sublime M

submachine gun *n* mitraillete F

submarine [SUHB•muh•REEN] *n* sous-marin M

submerge [suhb•MURJ] *vt* submerger

submission [suhb•MI•shn] *n* soumission F

submit [suhb•MIT] *vt* soumettre

subordinate [suhb•BOR•di•nit] *adj* (inv); *n* subalterne MF

subpoena [suh•PEE•nuh] *n* citation (jur) F

subscribe [suhb•SKRUYB] *vi* s'abonner à

subscriber [suhb•SKRUY•bur] *adj; n* abonné –e MF

subscription [suhb•SKRIP•shn] *n* abonnement M

subsequent [SUHB•se•kwent] *adj* ultérieur [-eure]

subservient [suhb•SUR•vee•ent] *adj* obséquieux -euse

subside [suhb•SUYD] *vi* baisser; cesser

subsidize [SUHB•si•DUYZ] *vt* subventionner

subsist [suhb•SIST] *vi* subsister

substance [SUHB•stenz] *n* substance F

substantial [suhb•STAN•shul] *adj* substantiel

substantive [SUHB•stan•tiv] *adj* substantif -ive

subterranean [SUHB•tur•RAI•nee•yen] *adj; n* sousterrain -ne M

subtle [SUH•tl] *adj* subtil

subtract [suhb•TRAKT] *vt* soustraire

subtraction [suhb•TRAK•shn] *n* soustraction F

suburb [SUH•burb] *n* (en) banlieue F

suburban [suh•BUR•ban] *adj; n comp* souburbain; de banlieue F

subversive [suhb•VUR•siv] *adj* subversif -ive

subway [SUHB•wai] *n* métro M

succeed [suhk•SEED] *vi* réussir (à)

success [suhk•SES] *n* succès M

successful [suhk•SES•fl] *adj* qui réussit

succession [suhk•SES•shn] *n* succession; suite F

succor [SUHK•or] *vt* aider; secourir

succulent [SUHK•yoo•lint] *adj* succulent

succumb [suh•KUM] *vi* succomber

such [suhch] *adj; adv* tel -le (une telle personne); tellement; tant

suck [suhk] *vt* sucer

suction [SUHK•shn] *n* succion F

sudden [SUH•din] *adj* soudain

suddenly [SUH•din•lee] *adv* soudainement; tout d'un coup

suddenness [SUH•din•nes] *n* soudaineté E

suds [suhdz] *n comp* eau de savon F

sue [soo] *vt comp* intenter un procès (jur)

suet [SOO•it] *n* graisse de rognon F

suffer [SUHF•fur] *vt* souffrir

suffering [SUHF•fring] *n* souffrance F

suffice [suh•FUYZ] *vi* suffire suffice

sufficiency [suh•FI•shen•see] *n* suffisance F

sufficient [suh•FI•shent] *adj* suffisant

suffocate [SUH•fo•KAIT] *vt vi* suffoquer

suffocation [SUH•fo•KAI•shn] *n* suffocation F

suffrage [SUH•frij] *n* suffrage M

suffuse [suh•FYUZ] *vt vi* répandre; se répandre sur

sugar [SHOO•gur] *n* sucre M; (lump) *n comp* morceau de sucre M

sugar bowl [SHUG•gr BOL] *n* sucrier M

suggest [sug•JEST] *vt* suggérer

suggestion [sug•JES•shn] *n* suggestion F

suggestive [sug•JES•tiv] *adj* suggestif -ve

suicide [SOO•i•SUYD] *n* suicide M

suit [soot] *n* costume (man's); tailleur (woman's) M

suitcase [SOOT•kais] *n* valise F

suite [sweet] *n* suite F

sulk [suhlk] *vt* brouder

sullen [SUH•len] *adj* maussade; refrongé

sultan [SUHL•tin] *n* sultan M

sum [suhm] *n* somme F; calcul (math) M

summarize [SUHM•may•RUYZ] *vi* résumer; récapituler

summer [SUHM•mur] *n* été M

summit [SUHM•mit] *n* sommet M

summon [SUH•mun] *vt* faire venir; convoquer; mander

summons [SUH•munz] *n* sommation F; assignation F (law)

sun [suhn] *n* soleil M

sunny [SUHN•nee] *adj* esoleillé

sunbathe [SUHN•bayth] *vi* prendre un bain de soleil

sunbeam [SUHN•beem] *n* rayon de soleil M

sunburn [SUHN•birn] *n* bronzage (tan); coup de soleil (burn) M

Sunday [SUHN•dai] *n* dimanche M

sunflower [SUHN•flouur] *n* tournesol M

sunglasses [SUHN•glah•sez] *npl* lunettes de soleil F

sunlight [SUHN•luyt] *n* soleil M

sunshine [SUHN•shyn] *n* soleil M

super [SOO•pur] *adj* superbe

superficial [SOO•pur•FI•shul] *adj* superficiel

superintendent [SOO•pur•in•TEN•dunt] *n* directeur -trice M F

superior [soo•PEE•ree•ur] *adj* supérieur

superlative [soo•PUR•la•tiv] *adj* suprême; sans pareil

supermarket [SOO•pur•MAHR•ket] *n* supermarché M

supernatural [SOO•pur•NA•chur•el] *adj* spuernaturel

supersede [SOO•pur•SEED] *vt* remplacer; supplanter

superstition [SOO•pur•STI•shun] *n* superstition F

supervise [SOO•pur•VUYZ] *vt* surveiller; diriger

supervision [SOO•pur•VI•zhun] *n* surveillance; direction F

supper [SUH•pur] *n* souper; diner M

supplement [SUH•pluh•munt] *n* supplèment M: *vt* augmenter

supply [suh•PLUY] *n* provision F

supplies [suh•PLYUZ] *npl*
provisions F; materiel M

suppose [suh•POZ] *vi* supposer

suppress [suh•PRES] *vt*
suprimer; réprimer; étouffer
(yawn)

supreme [suh•PREEM] *adj*
suprème

sure [shoor] *adj* sûr; certain;
make ~\ s'assurer

surely [SHOOR•lee] *adv*
sûrment

surf *n* ressac M; écume
(foam) F

surf-board [SURF•baurd] *n*
plance de surf F

surface [SUR•fas] *n* suface F;
on the ~\ en apparence; *vt*
revèrtir; faire surface
(swimmer)

surge [surj] *n* vague; montée F;
vi déferler

surgeon [SUR•jun] *n*
chirugien M

surgery [SUR•jur•ee] *n*
chirugie F

surgical [SUR•ji•kul] *adj*
chirugical

surly [SUR•lee] *adj* revèche

surmount [sur•MOWNT] *vi*
surmonter

surname [SUR•naym] *n* nom
de famille M

surpass [sur•PAS] *vt* surpasser;
dépasser

surplus [SUR•plus] *n* surplus;
excédent M; *adj* en surplus

surprise [sur•PRYZ] *n* surprise
F; *adj* inattendu; *vt*
supprendre; étonner

surrealism [sur•REE•uh•LIZM]
n surréalisme M

surrealistic
[sur•REE•uh•LIS•tic] *adj*
surréaliste

surrender [sur•REN•dur] *vt*
(se) rendre; remettre (items);
renoncer à; abandonner;
n reddition; remise;
renonciation F

surreptitious [SU•rep•TI•shus]
adj subreptice

surround [su•ROWND] *vt vi*
entourer; encercler; *n*
bordure F

surrounding [su•ROWN•ding]
adj environant

surroundings
[su•ROWN•dingz] *npl*
alentours M

survey 1 [SIR•veh] *n* vue
général; enquête F; levé
(land) M

survey 2 [sir•VEH] *vi* passer en
revue; inspecter; arpenter
(land)

survival [sur•VUYV•l] *n*
survie F

survive [sur•VUYV] *vi* survivre

survivor [sur•VUY•vur] *adj n*
survivant MF

susceptibility
[suh•SEP•ti•BI•li•tee] *n*
prédisposition; susceptibilité F

susceptible [suh•SEP•ti•bl] *adj*
prédisposé; susceptible

suspect [adj., n. SUHS•pekt, v.
suhs•PEKT] *adj n vt vi*
suspect; soupçonner MF

suspend [suhs•SPEND] *vt*
suspendre

suspenders [suhs•SPEN•durz] *npl* bretelles F

suspense [suhs•SPENZ] *n* suspens; incertitude MF

suspicion [suhs•SPI•shn] *n* soupçon M

sustain [suh•STAIN] *vt* entretenir; soutenir

sustenance [SUH•ste•nenz] *n* nourriture F

suture [SOO•chur] *n* (point de) suture F

swab *n* tampon M

swagger [SWAG•gur] *vi* se pavaner

swain *n* jeune paysan M

swallow 1 [SWAH•lo] *n* hirondelle (oiseau) F

swallow 2 [SWAH•lo] *vt* avaler

swamp *n* marais M

swan [swahn] *n* cygne M

swap [swahp] *n vt* échange; échanger M

swarm *n vi* essaim (d'abeilles); entrer/sortir en masse M

swarthy [SWAR•thee] *adj* basané

swat *vt* écraser (une mouche)

swathe [swath] *vt* emmailloter

sway [swai] *vt comp* faire osciller

swear [swair] *vi* jurer

sweat [swet] *n; vi* sueur; suer F

sweater [SWET•tur] *n* pull-over; chandail M

Swede [sweed] *n* Suédois -se MF

Sweden [SWEED•din] *n* Suède F

Swedish [SWEED•dish] *adj* suédois -se

sweep *vt* balayer

sweeper [SWEEP•pur] *n* balayeur -euse MF

sweeping [SWEEP•ping] *n* comp; *n* d'un geste large; balayage M

sweet *adj* sucré; doué

sweet potato *n* patate douce F

sweetbread [SWEET•bred] *n* ris de veau M

sweeten [SWEET•tin] *vt* sucrer

sweetness [SWEET•nis] *n* goût sucré (aliment); douceur MF

swell *adj vt vi* chouette; gonfler; se gonfler

swelling *n* enflure F

swelter [SWEL•tur] *vi* étouffer de chaleur

swerve [swurv] *vi* dévier; virer

swift *adj; adv* vite (lecture vite d'un livre); (manger vite)

swiftness [SWIFT•nes] *n* rapidité F

swim *vi* nager

swimmer [SWIM•mur] *n* nageur -euse MF

swimming [SWIM•ming] *n* natation F

swimming pool *n* piscine F

swimsuit [SWIM•soot] *n* maillot de bain M

swindle [SWIN•dl] *n; vt* escroquerie; escroquer F

swing *vt vi* balancer; se balancer; *n* balançoire F

swipe [swuyp] *n comp; vt* donner un coup à qq'un; frapper; faucher M

swirl [swurl] *vi* tournoyer; tourbillonner

Swiss *adj; n* Suisse MF

switch *vt* échanger
switchboard [SWITCH•bord] *n*
  standard M
Switzerland [SWIT•zur•land] *n*
  Suisse F
swivel [SWI•vul] *vt vi* pivoter
swivel chair *n* fauteuil/chaise
  pivotant(e) MF
swoon *vi* se pâner
swoop *vi* comp descendre en
  piqué
sword [sord] *n* épée F
sycamore [SI•ki•MOR] *n*
  sycomore (arbre) M
syllable [SI•li•bl] *n* syllabe F
syllogism [SI•lo•JIZM] *n*
  syllogisme M
symbol [SIM•buhl] *n*
  symbole M
symbolic [sim•BAH•lik] *adj*
  symbolique
symmetrical [sim•ME•tri•kuhl]
  adj symétrique
sympathetic
  [SIM•puh•THE•tik] *adj*
  compatissant
sympathy [SIM•puh•thee] *n*
  compassion F

symphony [SIM•fo•nee] *n*
  symphonie F
symptom [SIMP•tum] *n*
  symptôme M
symptomatic
  [SIMP•to•MA•tik] *adj*
  symptomatique
synagogue [SI•no•GOG] *n*
  synagogue F
synchronize [SIN•kro•NUYZ]
  vt synchroniser
syndicate [SIN•di•kit] *n* comp
  syndicat (ouvrier);
  groupement de sociétés;
  groupe de grand banditisme M
synonym [SI•ni•NIM] *n*
  synonyme M
synonymous [si•NON•ni•mus]
  adj synonyme
syntax [SIN•tax] *n* syntaxe F
synthesis [SIN•thuh•sis] *n*
  synthèse F
Syria [SEE•ree•uh] *n* Syrie F
Syrian [SEE•ree•yen] *adj n*
  Syrien -nne MF
syringe [sir•RINJ] *n* seringue F
syrup [SEER•rup] *n* sirop M
system [SIS•tim] *n* systeme M
systematic [SIS•te•MA•tik] *adj*
  systématique

T

tab *n* étiquette F
table [TAI•bl] *n* table F
table (card) *n* table de jeu F
table (operating) *n* table
  d'opération F

tablet [TAB•lit] *n* comprimé;
  pilule; plaque MF
tableware [TAI•bl•WAIR] *n*
  vaisselle F
tabloid [TAB•bloyd] *n* journal M

tabular [TAB•yoo•lar] *adj*
tabulaire

tabulate [TAB•yoo•LAIT] *vt*
vi comp classifier (les
résultats); mettre sous forme
de table

tachometer [ta•KO•mu•tur] *n*
tachéomètre M

tacit [TA•sit] *adj* tacite

taciturn [TA•si•TURN] *adj*
taciturne

tack [tak] *n vt* punaise;•
clouer F

tackle [TAK•kl] *vt* attaquer
(travail); plaquer (football) M

tackle (fishing) [TAK•kl] *n*
comp matériel de pêche M

tact [takt] *n* tact; diplomatie MF

tactical [TAK•ti•kul] *adj*
tactique M

tactics [TAK•tix] *n* tactique F

tactile [TAK•tul] *adj* tactile

tadpole [TAD•pol] *n* têtard M

taffeta [TA•fit•tuh] *n* taffetas M

tag 1 *n* étiquette F

tag 2 *vt* étiqueter

tail *n; vt* queue; suivre F

tailor [TAI•lur] *n* tailleur M

taint *vt* entâcher

take [taik] *vt* prendre; saisir;
conduire; ~ walk\ faire; ~
care\ prendre garde; ~ in\
faire entrer; ~ into account\
tenir compte; ~ notice\ prêter
attention à; ~ out\ faire sortir

talcum [TAL•kum] *n* talc M

tale [tail] *n* conte M

talent *n* talent; don M

talk [tauk] *vi* parler; causer; *n*
conversation F bavardage F

talkative [TAUK•uh•tiv] *adj*
loquace; bavard

talker [TAU•kur] *n* orateur
-trice (conférencier -cière) MF

talking [TAU•king] *n* discours;
conversation MF

tall *adj* grand

tallow [TA•lo] *n* suie F

tally [TA•lee] *n* compte;
enregistrement M

Tam o' Shanter
[TAM•o•SHAN•tur] *n* béret
écossais M

tame [taim] *adj* domestiqué

tamper [TAM•pur] *vt; vi*
altérer; toucher à

tan *n* bronzage M

tandem [TAN•dim] *n*
tandem M

tangent [TAN•jent] *n*
tangeute F

tangerine [TAN•juh•REEN] *n*
mandarine F

tangible [TAN•juh•bl] *adj* (inv)
tangible

Tangiers [tan•JEERZ] *n*
Tanger M

tangle [TANG•gl] *vt*
embrouiller

tank *n* citerne F

tank (gasoline) *n* réservoir
d'essence M

tanker [TANK•kur] *n*
navire-citerne;
camion-citerne M

tannery [TAN•nur•ree] *n*
tannerie F

tantalize [TAN•tuh•LUYZ] *vt*
tantaliser; taquiner

tantrum [TAN•trum] *n* crise de
colère F

tap 1 *n* robinet (lavabo) M

tap 2 *vt vi* taper légèrement; tapoter

tape [taip] *n* ruban adhésif M

taper [TAI•pur] *vt* effiler

tapestry [TA•pe•stree] *n* tapisserie F

tapioca *n* tapioca M

tar *n* goudron M

tardy [TAR•dee] *n* comp en retard M

tare [tair] *n* comp; *n* poids à vide; tare MF

target [TAR•git] *n* cible F

tariff [TAIR•rif] *npl* tarif; prix; taux M

tarnish [TAR•nish] *vt* ternir

tarpaulin [tar•PO•lin] *n* bâche F

tarry [TAIR•ree] *vi* tarder

tart *n* tarte F; *adj* acide; piquant

tart *adj* aigre M

tartar [TAR•tur] *n* tartre M

task *n* tâche F

tassel [TA•suhl] *n* gland M

taste [taist] *vt* goût; goûter M

tasteless [TAIST•les] *adj*; *n* comp fade (aliment); de mauvais goût (commentaire) M

tasty [TAI•stee] *adj* savoureux -euse

tattered [TAT•turd] *npl* comp en haillons M

tattle [TAT•tl] *vi* babiller

tattletale [TAT•tl•TAIL] *n* babillard -e MF

tattoo 1 [tat•TOO] *n* tatouage M

tattoo 2 [tat•TOO] *vt* tatouer

taught [taut] adj; pp enseigner enseigné

taunt *n; vt* raillerie; railler F

tavern [TA•vurn] *n* taverne F

tax *n* impôts; taux; taxer M

tax (income) *n* impôt sur le revenue M

tax (non-resident) *n* taxe de séjour M

taxi [TAX•see] *n; comp* taxi; transporter en taxi M

taxpayer [TAX•PAI•ur] *n* contribuable MF

tea [tee] *n* thé M

tea party *n* thé M

teach [teech] *vt* enseigner

teacher [TEE•chur] *n* professeur (homme) (une femme) professeur; enseignant -e (collège université); instituteur -trice (école maternelle école élémentaire) MF

teaching [TEE•ching] *n* enseignment M

teacup [TEE•kup] *n comp* tasse à thé F

teakettle [TEE•KET•tl] *n* bouilloire F

teal [teel] *n* sarcelle F

team [teem] *n* équippe F

teamwork [TEEM•wurk] *n comp* travail d'équippe M

teapot [TEE•pot] *n* théière F

tear 1 [tayr] *n; vt* déchirure; déchirer F

tear 2 [teer] *n* larme F

tease [teez] *vt* taquiner

teaspoon [TEE•spoon] *n* cuillère à café F

technical [TEK•ni•kul] *adj* technique

technician [tek•NI•shn] *n*
technicien -enne MF

tedious [TEE•dee•is] *adj* (*inv*)
ennuyeux -euse; pénible

teem *vi* grouiller

teens [teenz] *npl* jeunes;
adolescentes MF

teethe *npl* dents F

telegram [TEL•le•GRAM] *n*
télégramme M

telegraph [TEL•le•GRAF] *n*
télégraphe M

telephone [TEL•le•FON] *n*
téléphone; *tvi* éléphoner (à
qq'un) M

telephone number *n* comp
numéro de téléphone M

telephone operator *n*
standardiste; téléphoniste MF

telescope [TEL•le•SKOP] *n*
téléscope M

televise [TEL•le•VUYZ] *vt*
téléviser

television [TEL•le•VI•shn] *n*
télévision F

television set *n* comp poste de
télévison M

tell *vt* dire; raconter; montrer; I
am told on me dit

teller *n* caissier -ère MF

telling [TEL•ling] *adj* révélateur
-euse

telltale [TELL•tail] *adj n*
rapporteur -euse MF

temerity [te•MAIR•ri•tee] *n*
témérité F

temper [TEM•pur] *n*
tempérament M

temperament [TEM•pur•ment]
n disposition; nature F

temperance [TEM•prenz] *n*
modération F

temperate [TEM•pret] *adj*
mesuré

temperature
[TEM•pruh•CHUR] *n*
température F

tempest [TEM•pest] *n*
tempête F

tempestuous [tem•PES•chus]
adj orageux -euse

temple 1 [TEM•pl] *n* temple M

temple 2 [TEM•pl] *n* tempe
(anat) F

temporal [TEM•pruhl] *adj*
temporel -le

temporary [TEM•po•RAI•ree]
adj (inv); *n* provisoire;
intérim M

temporize [TEM•po•RUYZ] *vi*
comp; *vi* chercher à gagner du
temps; temporiser

tempt *vt* tenter; tantaliser

temptation [tem•TAI•shn] *n*
tentation F

tempting [TEMP•ting] *adj*
séduisant -e; tentant -e;
appétisant (aliment)

ten *adj n* dix M

tenable [TEN•uh•bl] *adj*
soutenable

tenacious [ten•AI•shus] *adj*
tenace

tenacity [ten•A•si•tee] *n*
ténacité F

tenant [TEN•nant] *n* locataire
MF

tend *vt; vi* soigner (qq'un);
veiller à (qq'un); *vi* tendre à
(ses affaires)

tendency [TEN•den•cee] *n*
tendance F

tender 1 [TEN•dur] *adj* tendre;
sensible

tender 2 [TEN•dur] *n* monnaie
légale F

tenderloin [TEN•dur•LOYN] *n*
filet M

tenderness [TEN•dur•nes] *n*
tendresse; sensibilité F

tendon [TEN•din] *n* tendon M

tendril [TEN•dril] *n* vrille
(bot) F

tenement [TEN•ne•mint] *n*
immeuble ancien; taudis M

tennis [TEN•nis] *n* tennis M

tenor [TEN•nor] *n* ténor M

tense 1 [tens] *adj* tendu; crispé

tense 2 [tens] *npl* les temps
grammaticaux M

tensile [TEN•sil] *adj* (inv)
extensible

tension [TEN•shun] *n* stress;
tension MF

tent *n* tente F

tentative [TEN•tuh•tiv] *adj*
provisoire; tentatif -tive

tenth *adj n* dixième MF

tenuous [TEN•yoo•us] *adj* ténu

tepid [TE•pid] *adj* (inv) tiède

term [turm] *n* terme; période
MF

terminal [TUR•min•nl] *adj; n*
terminal ; terminus (chemin
de fer) M

terminate [TUR•min•NAIT] *vt*
terminer

terrace [TAIR•res] *n* terrasse F

terrain [tair•RAIN] *n* terrain M

terrestrial [tair•RES•stree•ul]
adj terrestre

terrible [TAIR•uh•bl] *adj*
terrible

terrific [tuhr•RIF•fik] *adj*
formidable

terrify [TAIR•ri•FUY] *vt*
terrifier

territory [TAIR•ri•TO•ree] *n*
territoire M

terror [TAIR•ror] *n* terreur F

terrorize [TAIR•ro•RUYZ] *vt*
terroriser

terse [turz] *adj* laconique

test [test] *n* essai; analyse MF

test (blood) *n* analyse de
sang F

test tube *n* éprouvette F

testament [TES•tuh•mint] *n*
testament M

testify [TES•ti•FUY] *vt vi*
témoigner (de); porter
témoignage

testimony [TES•ti•MO•nee] *n*
témoignage M

tetanus [TE•tuh•nes] *n*
tétanos M

tether [TE•thur] *n; vt* longe;
attacher F

text *n* texte M

textbook [TEXT•bok] *n*
manuel scolaire; livre M

textile [TEX•tuyl] *n* textile M

texture [TEX•chur] *n* texture F

than *conj* que; de

thank *vt* remercier; s'en
prendre; *npl* merci M

thankful *adj* reconnaissant M

thankfully [THANK•fuh•lee]
prép comp avec
reconnaissance F

thankfulness *n* gratitude F

thankless [THANK•les] *adj*
ingrat

thanklessness
[THANK•les•nes] *n*
ingratitude F

thanksgiving [thanks•GI•ving]
n comp action de grâce; fête
nationale américaine F

that *conj* que

thatch *n* chaume M

thaw [thau] *vi* fondre

the [thuh] *article* (gramm)
le/la/les

theater [THEE•i•tir] *n*
théâtre M

theatrical [thee•A•trik•kl] *adj*
théâtral

theft *n* vol M

their [thair] *pron possessif*
leur -s

theirs [thairz] *pron possessif*
le leur/la leur/les leurs

them *pron disjonctif; pron
object direct; pron objet
indirect* eux elles; les; leur

theme [theem] *n* thème M

themselves [them•SELVZ]
pron emphatique eux-mêmes
elles-mêmes

then *adv* ensuite; puis

theology [thee•AH•lo•gee] *n*
théologie F

theorem [THEE•or•em] *n*
théorème M

theoretical [THEE•o•RE•tik•kl]
adj théorique

theory [THEE•or•ree] *n*
théorie F

therapeutic
[THAIR•uh•PYU•tik] *adj*
thérapeutique

there; over there [thair] *adv*
là; là-bas

thereabouts
[THAIR•uh•BOUTZ] *adv
comp* dans les environs

thereafter [thair•AF•tur] *adv
comp* par la suite

thereby [thair•BUY] *adv comp*
de ce fait

therefore [thair•FOR] *adv* donc

therein [thair•IN] *adv* à
l'intérieur

thereof [thair•OF] *adv* de cela;
en

thereon [thair•ON] *adv*
là-dessus

thereupon [THAIR•uh•PON]
adv là-dessus

thermal [THUR•muhl] *adj*
thermal

thermometer
[thur•MAH•mee•tur] *n*
thermomètre M

thermostat [THUR•mo•STAT]
n thermostat M

these [theez] *pron pl* dém inv;
pron dém M F ces (livres);
ceux-ci celles-ci

thesis [THEE•sis] *n* thèse F

they [thai] *pron poss pl* ils/elles

thick [thik] *adj* épais -se

thicken [THIK•ken] *vi*
s'épaissir

thickly *adv comp* en tranches
épaisses

thickness [THIK•nes] *n*
épaisseur F

thief [theef] *n* bandit; voleur -se
MF

thigh [thuy] *n* cuisse F

thimble [THIM•bl] *n* dé à coudre M

thin *adj* mince; maigre; fin; fluide; *vt* amincir; diluer

thing *n* chose F; affaire F

think *vt vi* penser; penser (à qqch)

thinker [THINK•kur] *n* penseur -euse; philosophe (inv) MF

thinking [THINK•king] *n* pensée F

thinly [THIN•lee] *adv* comp (coupé) en fines tranches (un gâteau); à peine voilé(e) (un sentiment)

thinness [THIN•nes] *n* minceur F

third [thurd] *adj n* troisième MF

thirdly [THURD•lee] *adv* troisièmement M

thirst [thurst] *n* soif F; be thirsty avoir soif

thirteen [thur•TEEN] *npl adj* (inv) treize M

thirteenth [thur•TEENTH] *adj; n* treizième MF

thirtieth [THUR•tee•eth] *adj; n* trentième MF

thirty [THUR•tee] *adj; npl* trente MF

thirty-first [THUR•tee•FURST] *adj; n* trente et unième MF

this *adj* ce cet; cette ;ce.. ci; cet; ~ day\ aujour d'hui

thistle [THIS•tl] *n* chardon M

thong *n* lanière F

thorn *n* épine F

thorough [THUR•ro] *adj* minutieux -euse

thoroughbred [THUR•ro•BRED] *n* pur-sang; bête de race MF

thoroughfare [THUR•ro•FAIR] *n* voie publique F

thoroughly [THUR•ro•lee] *adv* à fond

those [thoz] ces; ceux-là celles-là

thou tu; toi

though [tho] *adv* quoique

thought [thaut] *n* pensée F

thoughtful [THAUT•fl] *adj; n* comp attentif -ive; geste plein d'attention

thoughtfulness [THAUT•fl•nes] *n* prévanance F

thoughtless [THAUT•les] *adj* inconsidéré

thoughtlessness [THAUT•les•nes] *n* manque de prévanance M

thousand [THOU•zund] *adj n* mille MF

thousandth [THOU•zundth] *adj; n* millième MF

thrash *vi* comp rouer de coups

thread [thred] *n* fil M; *vt* enfiler

threadbare [THRED•bair] *adj* râpé

threat [thret] *n* menace F

threaten [THRET•tin] *vt* menacer

threatening [THRET•ning] *adj* menaçant

three *adj* (inv); *n* trois MF

thresh *vt* battre

threshing [THRESH•ing] *n* battage M

threshold [THRESH•hold] *n* seuil M

thrice [thruyz] *adv comp* trois fois

thrift *n comp* esprit d'économie M

thrill *n; vt* frisson; transporter; électriser M

thrive [thruyv] *vi* prospérer

throat [throt] *n* gorge F

throb [thrahb] *n vi* pulsation; palpiter F

throne [thron] *n* trône M

throng *n* foule F

throttle [THRAH•tl] *n* accélérateur (moteur) M

through [throo] *adv; adv comp* par; à travers (lieu)

throw [thro] *vt* jeter (qqch dans la poubelle)

throw out *vt* rejeter

throw up *vt* vomir; rejeter

thrush [thruhsh] *n* grive (oiseau) F

thrust [thruhst] *n comp; vt comp* idée centrale; pousser vivement (les bras) F

thug [thuhg] *n* voyou; petit(e) délinquant(e) MF

thumb [thuhmb] *n* pouce M
thumbtack *n* punaise F

thump *n comp* [thuhmp] bruit lourd M

thunder [THUHN•dur] *n vi* tonnerre (temps)/un tonnerre d'applaudissements; tonner M

thunderbolt [THUHN•dur•BOLT] *n comp* coup de tonnerre M

thunderclap [THUHN•dur•KLAP] *n comp* coup de tonnerre M

thundering [THUHN•dring] *n adj* retentissement; orageux (temps) M

thunderous [THUN•drus] *adj* retentissant; éclatant

thunderstorm [THUHN•dur•STORM] *n* orage M

Thursday [THURZ•dai] *n* jeudi M

thus [thuhs] *adv* ainsi; ainsi que; donc

thus far *adv comp* jusqu'à ce point-ci; jusqu'ici

thwart *vt* contarier

thyme [tuym] *n* thym M

tiara [tee•AHR•uh] *n* diadème M

tibia [ti•bee•uh] *n* tibia (anat) M

tick 1 [tik] *n* tique (insecte) F

tick 2 [tik] *vi comp* faire tic-tac

ticket [TIK•kit] *n* billet; ticket M

ticket office *n* guichet M

tickle [TIK•kl] *n vt vi* chatouillement; chatouiller (les pieds d'un bébé); faire plaisir à M

tidal [TUY•dl] *n comp* raz de marée; (des eaux) qui ont des marées M

tide [tuyd] *n* marée M

tidiness [TUY•dee•nes] *n* ordre (dans une pièce dans une salle); netteté (d'aspect) MF

tidings [TUY•dings] *npl* nouvelles joyeuses F

tidy [TUY•dee] *adj* net -te; propre

tie [tuy] *n vt* cravate; ficeler F

tie-up [TUY•uhp] *n* embouteillage (circulation) M

tier [teer] *n* rang M

tiger [TUY•gur] *n* tigre M

tight [tuyt] *adj* étroit (vêt); serré (corde)

tighten [TUY•tin] *vt* serrer; resserrer

tightness [TUYT•nes] *n* raideur F

tightwad [TUYT•wahd] *n* avare MF

tigress [TUY•gris] *n* tigresse F

tile [tuyl] *n* carreau M

till 1 [til] *prép* jusqu'à; jusqu'a ce que

till 2 [til] *n* caisse F

tilt *vt* incliner

timber [TIM•bur] *n* comp bois de charpente M

time [tuym] *n* heure (quelle heure est-il?); temps (prendre son temps)

timekeeper [TUYM•KEE•pur] *n* surveillant -e (personne); montre MF

timely [TUYM•lee] *adv* comp; *vi* comp à temps; tomber à un point opportun M

timepiece [TUYM•pees] *n* horloge; montre F

timer [TUY•mur] *n inv* compte-minutes M

timetable [TUYM•TAI•bl] *n* horaire M

timid [TI•mid] *adj inv* timide

timorous *adj* timoré

tin *n* étain M

tin can *n* boîte en fer F

tincture [TINK•chur] *n* teinture F

tinder [TIN•dur] *n* amadou M

tinfoil [TIN•foil] *n* papier d'aluminium M

tinge [tinj] *n* teinte F

tingle [TING•gl] *vi* fourmiller; frissoner

tinkle [TINK•kl] *vi* tinter

tinned [tind] *adv* comp en boîte; en conserve F

tinsel [TIN•sul] *npl* cheveux d'ange M

tint *n vt* teinte; teinter F

tiny [TUY•nee] *adj* tout petit; minuscule

tip 1 *n* bout (d'un langue); sommet (des arbres) M

tip 2 *vt* verser

tipsy [TIP•see] *vi* se griser

tiptoe [TIP•to] *n* comp sur la pointe des pieds F

tirade [TUY•raid] *n* diatribe F

tire 1 (flat) [tuyr] *n* pneu dégonflé ou à plat M

tire 2 (spare) [tuyr] *n* pneu de rechange M

tire 3 [tuyr] *vi* se fatiguer

tired [tuyrd] *adj* fatigué

tiredness [TUYRD•nes] *n* fatigue F

tireless [TUYR•les] *adj inv* inépuisable

tiresome [TUYR•sum] *adj* ennuyeux -euse

tissue [TI•shyoo] *n* tissu (anat); étoffe (matière) MF

tissue-paper *n* papier de soie M

tithe [tuyth] *n* dîme F

title [TUY•tl] *n* iota M

titular [TI•choo•lur] *adj* nominal

to [too] *prep* à ; vers; en; de; pur; jusque jusqu'à; afin de; envers

toad [tod] *n* crapaud M

toast [tost] *n* comp; *vi* comp pain grillé; boire à la santé de qq'un (à la vôtre!; tchin-tchin!) MF

tobacco [tuh•BAK•ko] *n* tabac M

tobacconist [tuh•BAK•ko•nist] *n* marchand -e de tabac MF

toboggan [tuh•BOG•gin] *n* luge F

today [too•DAI] *adv; n* aujourd'hui M

toe [to] *n* orteil M

toenail *n* ongle de pied M

together [too•GE•thur] *adv* ensemble

toil *n* travail; *vi* peiner M

toilet [TOI•let] *npl* toilettes

toilet paper *n* papier hygiénique M

toilet water *n* eau de toilette F

token [TO•kin] *n* jeton M

told *adj; vi* (pp de dire) dit

tolerable [TAH•lur•uh•bl] *adj* tolérable

tolerance [TAH•luh•renz] *n* tolérance F

tolerant [TAH•luh•rent] *adj* tolérant

tolerate [TAH•luh•RAIT] *vt* tolérer

toll 1 [tol] *n* nombre (de victimes) M

toll 2 [tol] *vt* comp sonner le glas pour qq'un

toll-bridge [TOL•brij] *n* péage M

tomato [to•MAI•to] *n* tomate F

tomb [toomb] *n* tombeau; tombe M

tombstone [TOOMB•ston] *n* pierre tombale F

tomcat [TAHM•kat] *n* chat matou M

tomorrow [too•MAH•ro] *adv; n* demain M

ton [tuhn] *n* tonne; tonneau F

tone [ton] *n* ton M

tongs [taungz] *n* pinces; pincettes (cheminée); tenailles (menuisier) F

tongue [tuhng] *n* langue F

tongue-tied [TUHNG•tuyd] *vt* comp perdre sa langue F

tonic [TAH•nik] tonic (boisson); tonique MF

tonight [too•NUYT] *n* soir; ce soir M

tonnage [TUH•nij] *n* poids total M

tonsil [TAHN•sil] *n* amygdale(s) F

tonsillitis [TAHN•si•LUY•tis] *n* (avoir une) angine F

tonsure [TAHN•shur] *n* tonsure F

too *adv* aussi; trop; de même

tool *n* outil M; instrument M

tooth *n* dent F

toothache [TOOTH•aik] *n* comp mal de dents; mal aux dents F

toothpaste [TOOTH•paist] *n* dentifrice M

toothpick [TOOTH•pik] *n* inv cure-dents M

top [tahp] haut; sommet; dessus (d'une table); dépasser M

topaz [TO•paz] *n* topaze F

topcoat [TAHP•kot] *n* manteau; pardessus M

topic [TAH•pik] *n* sujet M

topmost [TAHP•most] *n* mât de hune M

topography [tah•PAH•grah•fee] *n* topographie F

topple [TAH•pl] *vi* basculer

topsy-turvy [TAHP•zee•TUHR•vee] *adv* sens dessus dessous M

torch *n* torche F

torment [tor•MENT] *vt* tourment; torturer M

tormentor [tor•MENT•er] *n* persécuteur -trice MF

tornado [tor•NAI•do] *n* tornade F

torpedo [tor•PEE•do] *n* torpille F

torpid [TOR•pid] *adj* engourdi

torrent [TOR•rint] *n* torrent M

torrid [TOR•rid] *adj inv* torride

tortoise [TOR•tus] *n* tortue F

tortuous [TOR•choo•us] *adj* tortueux -euse

torture [TOR•chur] *n vt* torture; torturer F

torturer [TOR•chur•rur] *n* bourreau M

toss *vt* lancer; jeter

tot [taht] *n* petit –e enfant MF

total [TO•tl] *n* total M

totalitarian [to•TA•li•TAI•ree•yen] *adj inv* totalitaire

totality [to•TA•li•tee] *n* totalité F

totally [TO•tuh•lee] *adv* totalement; complètement

totter [TAH•tur] *vi* tituber

touch [tuhch] *vt* toucher; toucher à; toucher M

touching [TUHCH•ching] *adj* touchant

touchy [TUH•chee] *adj comp* suseptible (sur)

tough [tuhf] *adj* résistant; dur

toughen [TUH•fin] *vt* renforcer (matière); endurcir (personne)

toughness [TUHF•nis] *n* dureté; résistance F

tour [toor] *n; vt* voyage; visiter un pays étranger M

tourist [TOOR•rist] *n* touriste MF

tournament [TOOR•nuh•mint] *n* tournoi M

tow [to] *vt* tirer

towards [TOO•wahrdz] *adv* vers (direction); envers (attitude)

towel [TOW•wuhl] *n* torchon (pour vaisselle); essuie-main M

tower [TOW•wur] *n* clocher (église); tour M

towing [TOW•wing] *n* halage (barge); remorque (voiture) MF

town *n* village; ville MF

township *n* canton (suisse); commune MF

toxic [TOK•sik] *adj inv* toxique

toxin [TOK•sin] *n* toxine F

toy [toi] *n* jouet; jeu M

trace [trais] *n vt* trace; retrouver F

tracer [TRAI•sur] *n* traceur (pour dessins) M

trachea [TRAI•kee•uh] *n* trachée F

track [trak] *n vt* sentier (de montagne); suivre; filer M

tract [trakt] *n* étendue (d'un terrain) F

tractable [TRAK•tuh•bl] accommodant (pers); malléable (matière)

traction [TRAK•shn] *n* extension (méd) F

tractor [TRAK•tur] *n* tracteur M

trade [traid] *n* métier; commerce; M faire le commerce (de)

trade school *n* école professionnelle F

trade union *n* syndicat; ouvrier M

trademark [TRAID•mark] *n* marque de fabrique F

trader [TRAI•dur] *n* négociant -e; opérateur -trice en bourse MF

tradesman [TRAIDZ•man] *n* commerçant -e MF

tradewind [TRAID•wind] *n* alizé M

trading [TRAI•ding] *n* commerce; négoce M

tradition [truh•DI•shn] *n* tradition F

traffic [TRAF•fik] *n* trafic (clientèle); circulation (véhicules) MF

tragedy [TRA•ji•dee] *n* tragédie F

tragic [TRA•jik] *adj n* tragique M

trail [trail] sentier; piste; suivre la piste d'un criminel MF

trailer [TRAI•lur] *n* remorque; bande-annonce (cinéma/télé) F

train *n* train; métro M (express) *n* train express; rapide M

train (passenger) *n* train de voyageurs M

trainer [TRAI•nur] *n* entraîneur -euse (sport); dresseur -euse (animaux) MF

training [TRAI•ning] *n* dressage; formation (scolastique) MF

trainman [TRAIN•man] *n comp* membre de l'équipage qui travaille à bord d'un train MF

trait *n* trait M

traitor [TRAI•tor] *n* traître -tresse MF

trajectory [truh•JEK•to•ree] *n* trajectoire F

tram *n* tram ou tramway M

tramp *n* clochard -e MF

trample [TRAM•pl] *vt* piétiner

trance *n* transe F

tranquil [TRAN•kwil] *adj* tranquille F

tranquillity [tran•KWIL•li•tee] *n* tranquillité F

transact [tranz•AKT] *vt* traiter

transaction [tranz•AK•shn] *n* transaction F

transcend [tran•SEND] *vt* transcender

transcribe [tran•SCRUYB] *vt* transcrire

transept *n* transept M

transfer [TRANS•fur] transfert (de fonds); faire la correspondance (métro); transférer MF

transform [trans•FORM] *vt* transformer

transformation [TRANS•for•MAI•shn] *n* transformation F

transformer [trans•FOR•mur] *n* transformateur M

transfusion [trans•FYU•shn] *n* transfusion F

transgress [trans•GRES] *vt* transgresser

transgression [trans•GRE•shn] *n* transgression F

transient [TRAN•sint] *adj* inv transitoire

transit [TRANS•zit] *n* transit M

transition [trans•ZI•shn] *n* transition F

transitive [TRANS•zi•tiv] *adj* transitif -ve MF

translate [tran•SLAIT] *vt* traduire

translation [trans•SLAI•shn] *n* traduction F

translator [trans•SLAI•tur] *n* traducteur -trice MF

translucent [trans•LOO•sent] *adj* translucide

transmission [trans•MI•shn] *n* transmission F

transmit [trans•MIT] *vt* transmettre

transmitter [trans•MI•tur] *n* transmetteur; émetteur (radio télé) M

transom [TRANS•sum] *n* traverse d'imposte F

transparent [trans•PAIR•rent] *adj* transparent

transpiration [TRANS•pi•RAI•shn] *n* transpiration F

transpire [tran•SPUYR] *vi* se passer; apparaître; transpirer (physio bot)

transplant [trans•PLANT] *vt* greffe; transplanter F

transport [trans•PORT] *vt* transporter

transpose [trans•POZ] *vt* transposer

transverse [trans•VURZ] *adj* traversal

trap piège; piéger M

trapdoor [TRAP•DOR] *n* trappe F

trapeze [tra•PEEZ] *n* trapèze M

trappings [TRAP•pings] *npl* accessoires M

trash *npl* ordures F

travel [TRA•vul] *n* voyage F; voyager M

travel agency *n* agence de voyages F

traveler [TRA•vuh•lur] *n* voyageur -euse MF

traveling [TRA•vuh•ling] *n* voyage M

traverse [tra•VURZ] *vt* traverser

travesty [TRA•ve•stee] *n* pastiche (littér); parodie MF

tray [trai] *n* plateau M

treacherous [TRE•chur•us] *adj* traître -tress MF

treachery [TRE•chur•ree] *n*
traîtrise F

tread [tred] *vi* marcher; nager
en chien

treason [TREE•zun] *n*
trahison F

treasure [TRE•shur] *n* trésor M

treasurer [TRE•shuh•ur] *n*
trésorier -ière; directeur -trice
financier -ière MF

treasury [TRE•shuh•ree] *n*
ministère des finances;
trésorerie MF

treat [treet] gâterie; traiter (d'un
sujet dans une dissertation) F

treatise [TREE•tis] *n* traité M

treatment [TREET•mint] *n*
traitement M

treaty [TREE•tee] *n* traité
(pol) M

treble [TRE•bl] *adj* triple

treble clef *n* clef de sol F

treble voice *n* soprano M

tree *n* arbre M (family) *n* arbre
généalogique M

trefoil [TREE•foil] *n* trèfle (à
quartre feuilles) M

trellis [TRE•lis] *n* treillage (bot)
(dessin) M

tremble [TREM•bl] *vi* trembler

tremendous [tre•MEN•dus] *adj*
énorme

tremor [TRE•mur] *n*
tremblement (de terre) M

tremulous [TRE•myu•lus] *adj*
tremblant

trench *n* fossé; tranchée MF

trench coat *n* imperméable
(imper en abrégé fam) M

trend *n* tendance F

trespass [TRES•pas] *vi comp*
entrer dans une propriété
privée sans autorisation

trespasser [TRE•pa•sur] *n*
intrus -e MF

tress [tres] *n* mèche de
cheveux F

trestle [TRE•sl] *n* tréteau (pour
une table); supports
horizontaux; scène d'un petit
théâtre ambulant M

trial [truyl] *n* procès M

triangle [TRUY•an•gl] *n*
triangle M

tribe [truyb] *n* tribu M

tribulation [TRI•byu•LAI•shn]
npl malheurs M

tribunal [truy•BYU•nl] *n*
tribunal M

tribune [TRI•byun] *n* tribune F

tributary [TRI•byu•TAI•ree]
tributaire (de); dépendre (de)

trick [trik] ruse; jouer un tour à
qq'un F

trickery [TRIK•ree] *n*
tomperie F

trickle [TRIK•kl] filet; dégoutter
(goutte à goutte) M

tricky [TRIK•kee] *adj* rusé ;
fourbe (pers); épineux -euse
(tâche)

trifle [TRUY•fl] *n* petit rien;
bagatelle MF

trigger [TRI•gur] gâchette
(pistolet); provoquer F

trill *n* trille M

trim net -te; soigné (d'apparence
soignée); couper (les
cheveux)

trinket [TRINK•kit] *n*
bibelot M

trio [TREE•o] *n* trio M

trip *n* voyage M

triple [TRIP•pl] *adj inv* triple

tripod [TRUY•pod] *n* trépied M

trite [truyt] *adj* banal

triumph [TRUY•uhmf]
triomphe; vaincre;
triompher M

triumphant [truy•UHM•fint]
adj triomphant

triumphantly
[truy•UHM•fint•lee] *adv*
triomphalement

trivial [TRI•vee•ul] *adj* trivial

trolley [TRAH•lee] *n* chariot
(au supermarché) M

trombone [trahm•BON] *n*
trombone (mus) M

troop *n* escadron (mil); bande
MF

trooper [TROOP•pur] *n*
soldat M

troops *npl* troupes (mil) F

trophy [TRO•fee] *n* trophée M

tropic [TRAH•pik] *n* tropique
(Tropique du Capricorne) M

trot 1 [trot] *n* trot M

trot 2 [trot] *vi* trotter

trouble [TRUH•bl] *npl* ennuis;
problèmes M

troublemaker
[TRUH•bl•MAI•kur] *n*
provocateur -trice MF

troubleshooter
[TRUH•bl•SHOO•tur] *n*
expert (appelé en cas de
crise); médiateur -trice (pol)
MF

troublesome [TRUH•bl•suhm]
adj gênant

trough [trahf] *n* abreuvoir M

trousers [TROU•zurz] *n*
pantalon M

trousseau [troo•SO] *n*
trousseau M

trowel [TROU•wl] *n* truelle
(outil) F

truant [TROO•int] *n* élève
absentéiste MF

truce [trooz] *n* trève F

truck [truhk] *n* camion M

trudge [truhj] *vi* marcher
péniblement (en traînant les
pieds)

true [troo] *adj* vrai

truly [TROO•lee] *adv* vraiment

trump [truhmp] *n* atout
(cartes) M

trumpet [TRUHM•pit] *n*
trompette F

trunk [truhnk] *n* tronc (d'un
arbre ou d'un corps);
coffre M

truss [truhs] *vt* ligoter; garrotter

trust [truhst] confiance; faire
confiance à qq'un F

trustee [TRUHS•stee] *n* syndic
(banqueoroute); dépositaire;
curateur -trice (mineur);
administrateur -trice MF

trustworthy
[TRUSHST•wur•thee] loyal;
qq'un à qui on peut faire
confiance

trusty [TRUH•stee] *adj* loyal

truth [trooth] *n* vérité; vrai F

truthful [TROOTH•fl] *adj*
honnête

truthfulness [TROOTH•fl•nes]
n honnêteté; véracité F

try [truy] *vt* essai; essayer (de
faire qqch) M

trying [TRUY•ying] douloureux
-euse; pénible

tub [tuhb] *n* bain; tonneau (de
vin) M

tube [toob] *n* tube (de
dentifrice) M

tubercular [too•BUR•kyu•lur]
adj tuberculeux -euse

tuberculosis
[too•BUR•kyu•LO•sis] *n*
tuberculose F

tubing [TOO•bing] *npl* tubes M

tuck [tuk] *vi* rentrer

Tuesday [TOOZ•dai] mardi M

tuft [tuhft] *n* touffe (blé); huppe
(plumes) F

tug [tuhg] tirer (sur)

tuition [TOO•i•shn] *npl* comp
frais d'inscription M

tulip [TOO•lip] *n* tulipe F

tulle [tool] *n* tulle (tissu) M

tumble [TUHM•bl] chute; faire
une chute F

tumbler [TUHM•blur] *n*
gobelet M

tumor [TOO•mur] *n* tumeur F

tumult [TOO•muhlt] *n*
tumulte M

tumultuous
[too•MUHL•choo•us] *adj*
tumultueux -euse

tun *n* tonneau (liquide) M

tuna [TOO•nuh] *n* thon M

tune [toon] mélodie; accorder
(un piano) F

tunic [TOO•nik] *n* tunique F

tuning 1 [TOO•ning] *n* accord
(mus); mise au point
(machine cantine) MF

tuning 2 [TOO•ning] *n* réglage
(télé radio) M

tunnel [TUH•nuhl] *n* tunnel M

turbid [TUR•bid] *adj* trouble;
brouillé

turbine [TUR•buyn] *n* turbine F

turbulent [TUR•byu•lint] *adj*
agité

turf *n* turf (sport); motte (de
gazon) MF

turgid [TUR•jid] *adj*
boursouflé; gonflé -e (méd)

Turk *n* Turc Turque MF

turkey [TUR•kee] *n* dindon;
dinde (oiseau) MF

Turkey [TUR•kee] *n* Turquie F

Turkish *adj* turc; turque

turmoil *n* trouble; agitation MF

turn *vt vi* tourner; se retourner
n occasion F; *n* tour; tournant
M; ~ in\ rendre; ~ to\ avoir
recours de; in ~\ à tour de
rôle

turnip *n* navet M

turnover [TUR•NO•vur] *n*
renouvellement (de
personnel) M

turntable [TURN•TAI•bl]
platine F

turpentine [TUR•pin•TUYN] *n*
térébenthine F

turpitude [TUR•pi•TOOD] *n*
turpitude F

turquoise [TUR•koyz]
turquoise F

turret [TUR•rit] *n* tourelle F

turtle [TUR•tl] *n* tortue F

tusk [tuhsk] *n* défense
(éléphant) F

tutor [TOO•tur] précepteur
-trice (pour les enfants);
professeur particulier; donner
des cours particuliers MF

tuxedo [tuk•SEE•do] *n*
smoking M

twang *n* comp accent léger
régional M

tweed *n* tweed M

tweezers [TWEE•zurz] *n* pince
à épiler M

twelfth *adj; n* douzième MF

twelve [twelv] *adj n* douze M

twentieth [TWEN•tee•ith] *adj;
n* vingtième MF

twenty [TWEN•tee] *adj n*
vingt M

twice [twuys] *adj comp* deux
fois

twig *n* brendille (d'un arbre) F

twilight [TWUY•luyt] *n*
crépuscule M

twin *n* jumeau jumelle MF

twine [twuyn] *n* ficelle F

twinge [twinj] *n* comp
sentiment léger (de
cupabilité) M

twinkle [TWINK•kl] *vi*
étinceler

twinkling [TWINK•kling] *n*
étincellement (étoiles) M

twirl *vi* tournoyer (danse); faire
tournoyer (un objet)

twist *vt* visser (le couvercle
d'une bouteille)

twitch *n* comp avoir un tic M

twitter *n* gazouillement (d'un
oiseau) M

two [too] *adj; n* deux M

tympani [TIM•puh•nee] *n*
timpani

type [tuyp] *n vt vi* type;
espèce; taper (une lettre) MF

typewriter [TUYP•RUY•tur] *n*
machine à écrire F

typhoid [TUY•foyd] *adj* comp
typhoïde (fièvre typhoïde)

typhoon [tuy•FOON] *n*
typhon M

typhus [TUY•fus] *n* typhus M

typical [TI•pi•kl] *adj inv*
typique

typist [TUY•pist] *n*
dactylographe MF

typography
[tuy•PAH•gruh•fee] *n*
typographie F

tyrannical [teer•RA•ni•kl] *adj
inv* tyrannique

tyranny [TEER•ri•nee] *n*
tyrannie F

tyrant [TUY•rent] *n* tyran M

U

udder [UH•dur] *n* pis; mamelle
MF

ugliness [UH•glee•nes] *n*
laideur F

ugly [UH•glee] *adj* laid

ulcer [UHL•sur] *n* ulcère M

ulceration [UHL•sur•RAI•shn]
n ulcération F

ulterior [uhl•TEE•ree•ur] *adj*
ultérieur

ultimate [UHL•ti•mit] *adj n*
extrême M

ultimately [UHL•ti•mit•lee] *adv*
éventuellement

umbilicus [uhm•BI•li•kus] *n*
ombilic; nombril M

umbrage [UHM•brij] *n*
ombrage M

umbrella [uhm•BREL•luh] *n*
parapluie M

umpire [UHM•puyr] *n*
arbitre M

un - [uhn] préfix non (préfix
sans trait d'union)

unable [uhn•AI•bl] *adj inv*
incapable

unaccountable
[UHN•a•KOWN•tuh•bl] *adj
inv* inexplicable

unaccustomed
[UHN•a•KUH•stumd] *adj*
inaccoutumé; peu habitué

unacknowledged
[UHN•ak•NAH•lejd] *adj* non
reconnu

unaffected [UHN•a•FEK•ted]
adj non affecté

unanimity
[YOO•nuh•NI•mi•tee] *n*
unanimité F

unanimous [yoo•NA•ni•mus]
adj inv unanime

unapproachable
[UHN•a•PRO•chuh•bl] *adj inv*
inabordable

unarmed [uhn•ARMD] *adj* non
armé

unassailable
[UHN•a•SAIL•luh•bl] *adj inv*
inébranlable

unassuming
[UHN•uh•SOO•ming] *adj inv*
modeste

unattractive
[UHN•uh•TRAK•tiv] *adj inv*
désagréable (habit
personnalité); peu attrayant
(visage)

unavailable
[UHN•uh•VAI•luh•bl] *adj inv*
indisponible

unavoidable
[UHN•uh•VOY•duh•bl] *adj
inv* inévitable

unaware [UHN•uh•WAIR] *adj*
ignorant

unawares [UHN•uh•WAIRZ]
adv à son insu

unbalanced [uhn•BAL•enzd]
adj mal équilibré

unbearable [uhn•BAI•ruh•bl]
adj insupportable

unbecoming
[UHN•bee•KUH•ming] *adj*
peu convenable

unbelievable
[UHN•bee•LEE•vuh•bl] *adj*
incroyable

unbeliever [UHN•bee•LEE•vur]
n athée MF

unbelieving
[UHN•bee•LEE•ving] *adj inv*
incrédule

unbending [uhn•BEN•ding] *adj
inv* inflexible

unbiased [uhn•BUY•esd] *adj*
impartial

unbounded [uhn•BOUN•ded]
adj illimité

unbreakable
[uhn•BRAI•kuh•bl] *adj inv*
incassable

unbroken [uhn•BRO•ken] *adj*
non cassé

unburden [uhn•BUR•den] *vt*
comp soulager l'esprit

unbutton [uhn•BUH•ten] *vt*
déboutonner

uncanny [uhn•KA•nee] *adj*
mystérieux -euse

unceasing [uhn•SEE•sing] *adj*
incessant

uncertain [uhn•SUR•ten] *adj*
incertain

unchangeable
[uhn•CHAIN•juh•bl] *adj inv*
immuable

unchanged [uhn•CHAIN•jed]
toujours le même; sans
variation

uncharted [uhn•CHAHR•ted]
adj inexploré

uncivil [uhn•SI•vil] *adj* impoli

unclaimed [uhn•KLAI•med] *adj*
non réclamé

uncle [UHN•kl] *n* oncle M

unclean [uhn•KLEEN] *adj inv*
sale

uncomfortable
[uhn•KOM•for•tuh•bl] *adj* inv
inconfortable

uncommon [uhn•KAH•men]
adj inv rare; unique

uncompromising
[uhn•KOM•pro•MUY•zing]
adj intransigeant

unconcerned
[uhn•KUHN•surnd] *adj*
insouciant

unconditional
[UHN•kun•DI•shuh•nl] *adj*
inconditionnel -le

unconquered [uhn•KON•kurd]
adj invaincu

unconscious [uhn•KON•shus]
adj inconscient

unconsciousness
[uhn•KON•shus•nes] *n*
inconscience F

uncontrollable
[UHN•kuhn•TRO•luh•bl]
effréné (passion); irréprimable
(mouvement)

uncontrolled
[UHN•kuhn•TROLD] *adj*
incontrôlé

unconventional
[UHN•kuhn•VEN•shun•nl] *adj*
inv non conformiste

uncork [uhn•KORK] *vt*
déboucher

uncouth [uhn•KOOTH] *adj*
grossier -ière

uncover [uhn•KUH•vur] *vt*
découvrir

unction [UHNK•shun] *n*
onction F

unctuous [UHNK•shus] *adj*
onctueux -euse

uncultured [uhn•KUL•churd]
adj inv barbare; inculte

undeceive [UHN•dee•SEEV] *vt*
détromper

undecided
[UHN•dee•SUY•ded] *adj*
incertain; indécis

undeniable
[UHN•dee•NUY•uh•bl] *adj*
inv incontestable

under [UHN•dur] *prep* sous;
au-dessus; de; dans; en moins
de; *adv* dessous; *adj* inférieur

under structure *n*
infrastructure F

underbrush
[UHN•dur•BRUSH] *n*
sous-bois M

undercarriage
[UHN•dur•KAI•rij] *n* train
d'atterrissage M

underclothes
[UHN•dur•KLOTHZ] *npl* sous
vêtements; lingerie (fém) MF

underestimate
[UHN•dur•ES•ti•MAIT] *vt*
sous-estimer

underfed *adj* mal nourri

undergo [UHN•dur•GO] *vt*
subir

undergraduate
[UHN•dur•GRA•joo•wait] *n*
étudiant qui prépare sa license
MF

underground
[UHN•dur•GROWND] métro;
sous la terre M

underhanded
[UHN•dur•HAN•ded] *vi comp*
qui manque de personnel

underline [UHN•dur•LUYN] *vt*
souligner

underlying
[UHN•dur•LUY•ing] *adv*
comp à l'origine (de)

undermine [UHN•dur•MUYN]
vt saper

underneath
[UHN•dur•NEETH] dessous;
au-dessous de

underpay [UHN•dur•PAI] *vt*
sous-payer

undersell [UHN•dur•SEL] *vt*
comp vendre moins cher
(que)

undershirt [UHN•dur•SHURT]
n tricot de corps M

undersigned
[UHN•dur•SUYND] *adj*
soussigné

undersized [UHN•dur•SUYZD]
adj trop petit

understand [UHN•dur•STAND] *vt*
comprendre

understandable
[UHN•dur•STAN•duh•bl] *adj*
inv compréhensible

understanding
[UHN•dur•STAN•ding] *adj*
bienviellant (envers qq'un)

understate [UHN•dur•STAIT]
vt comp dire avec retenue

understudy
[UHN•dur•STUH•dee] *n*
doublure (théâtre) F

undertake [uhn•dur•TAIK] *vt*
entreprendre (une tâche)

undertaken
[UHN•dur•TAI•ken] *adj*
entrepris

undertaker [UHN•dur•TAI•kur]
n comp entrepreneur -euse des
pompes funèbres MF

undertaking
[UHN•dur•TAI•king] *n*
entreprise F

undertow [UHN•dur•TO] *n*
comp ton léger (parole) qui
révèle une attitude
quelconque; courant de retour
(vagues) M

underwear [UHN•dur•WAIR]
npl sous-vêtements (gén);
lingerie F

underworld
[UHN•dur•WURLD] *n*
pègre F

underwrite
[UHN•dur•WRUYT] *vt*
souscrire (un risque)

undeviating
[UHN•DEE•vee•AI•ting]
droit; rigide

undiscriminating
[UHN•di•SKRI•mi•NAI•ting]
adv comp sans discernement

undistinguished
[UHN•di•STIN•gwish•ed]
commun; médiocre

undisturbed
[UHN•di•STUR•bed] *adj inv*
tranquille

undo [uhn•DOO] *vt* défaire;
détacher; ruiner; perdre

undress [uhn•DRES] *vi* se
déshabiller

undue [uhn•DOO] *adj inv*
injustifiable

undulate [UHN•joo•LAIT] *vt vi*
onduler

undying [uhn•DUY•ing] *adj*
immortel -le

unearned [uhn•URN•ed] *adj*
non mérité

unearth [uhn•URTH] *vt*
déterrer

uneasily [uhn•EEZ•i•lee] *adv*
comp d'un air gêné

uneasy [uhn•EE•zee] *adj* gêné;
inquiet; inquiète

uneducated
[uhn•ED•joo•KAI•ted] sans
instruction; inculte

unemployed
[UHN•em•PLOID] *adj n*
chômeur -euse

unemployment
[UHN•em•PLOI•ment] *n*
chômage M

unending [uhn•EN•ding] *adj*
comp interminable; sans fin

unequal [uhn•EE•kwell] *adj*
inégal

uneven [uhn•EE•ven] *adj* inégal

unexpected
[UHN•ek•SPEK•tid] *adj*
inattendu

unfair [uhn•FAYR] *adj* injuste

unfaithful [uhn•FAYTH•ful]
adj infidèle

unfasten [uhn•FAS•sin] *vt*
défaire

unfinished [uhn•FIN•ishd] *adj*
inachevé; à finir

unfit [uhn•FIT] *adj* inapte;
impropre

unfold [uhn•FAULD] *vt* déplier;
exposer; se dérouler (story)

unfortunate
[uhn•FAUR•tchoo•net] *adj*
malheureux; fâcheux

unfriendly [uhn•FREND•lee]
adj froid; hostile

ungrateful [uhn•GRAYT•ful]
adj ingrat

unhappy [uhn•HA•pee] *adj*
triste; malheureux

unhappiness [uhn•HA•pee•nes]
n tristesse F

unhealthy [uhn•HEL•thee] *adj*
malsain; maladif (person)

unicorn [YOO•nuh•KAURN] *n*
licorne F

unidentified
[UHN•ay•DEN•ti•FUYD] *adj*
non identifié

uniform [YOO•ni•FAURM] *adj*
uniforme

unimportant
[UHN•im•PAUR•tant] *adj* peu
important

uninterested
[uhn•IN•ter•ehs•tid] *adj*
indifférent

union [YOO•nyuhn] *n* union F

unique [yoo•NEEK] *adj* unique

unison [YOO•ni•suhn] *n*
unisson M in ~\ en choeur

unit [YOO•nit] *n* unité F; bloc;
groupe M

unite [yoo•NUYT] *vi* (s') junir;
unifier

United Kingdom *n*
Royaume-Uni M

United Nations *n* Nations
Unies FPL

United States *n* Etats-Unis
MPL

universe [YOO•ni•VERS] *n*
univers M

universal [YOO•nee•VER•sal]
adj universel

university
[YOO•nee•VER•see•tee] *n*
université F; *adj* universitaire

unjust [uhn•JUHST] *adj* injuste

unkind [uhn•KUYND] *adj* peu
amiable; méchant; cruel

unkindess [ubn•KUYND•nes] *n*
méchanté F

unknown [uhn•NOHN] *adj*
inconnu

unless [uhn•LES] *conj* à moins
que

unlike [uhn•LYK] *adj*
dissemblable; different; *prep* à
la différence de

unlikely [uhn•LYK•lee] *adj* peu
probable; invraisemblable
(story)

unlimited [uhn•LIM•i•tud] ad
illimité

unload [uhn•LOHD] *vt*
décharge; se défaire de (get
rid of)

unlock [uhn•LAHK] *vt* ouvrir

unlucky [uhn•LUH•kee] *adj*
malchanceux; malhereux; qui
porte malheur (superstition)

unmarried [uhn•MA•reed] *adj*
célibataire

unnatural [uhn•NA•chur•el] *adj*
anormal; contre nature

unnecessary
[uhn•NE•si•SAY•ree] *adj*
inutile; superflu

unnoticed [uhn•NOH•tisd] ad
inaperçu

unoccupied
[uhn•AH•kyoo•PUYD] *adj*
inoccupé; libre (place)

unofficial [uhn•oh•FI•shul] *adj*
officieu; non officiel

unpack [uhn•PAK] *vt* défaire
(suitcase); déballer (contents)

unpaid [uhn•PAYD] *adj*
impayé; non acquitté; non
retribué (employee)

unpleasant [uhn•PLEH•zunt]
adj disagréable; déplaisant

unpopular [uhn•PAH•pyoo•lur]
adj impopulaire

unpredictable
[uhn•pree•DIC•tuh•bul] *adj*
imprévisable; incertain

unqualifed
[uhn•KWAH•li•FUYD] *adj*

non qualifié; non diplôme;
sans réserve

unravel [uhn•RA•vul] *vi*
(s')effiler; débrouiller
(mystery)

unreal [uhn•REEL] *adj* irréel

unreasonable
[un•REE•zu•nu•bl] *adj*
déraisonnable

unsuccessful
[UHN•suhk•SES•fl] raté (un
examen); échec M

unsuitable [uhn•SOO•tuh•bl]
adj inv inconvenable

unsuspected
[UHN•suh•SPEK•ted] *adj*
insoupçonné

unsuspecting
[UHN•suh•SPEK•ting] *vi*
comp (qq'un qui) ne se
redoute de rien

unthinkable
[uhn•THIN•kuh•bl] *adj inv*
inconcevable

unthinking [uhn•THIN•king]
adj étourdi

untidiness [uhn•TUY•dee•nes]
n désordre (une pièce) M

untie [uhn•TUY] *vt* dénouer

until [uhn•TIL] *prep* jusqu'à;
jusqu'à ce que (voir till)

untimely [uhn•TUYM•lee]
inopportun; prématurément

untiring [uhn•TUYR•ring] *adj
inv* infatigable

unto [UHN•too] *prep* jusqu'à

untold [uhn•TOLD] *adj* inouï;
jamais raconté

untouched [uhn•TUHCHD] *adj*
intact; non touché

untrained [uhn•TRAIYND]
non dressé; sans formation F

untried [uhn•TRUYD] *adj*
comp qui n'a pas été mis(e) à
l'épreuve

untroubled [uhn•TRUH•bld]
adj inv calme

untrue [uhn•TROO] *adj* faux
fausse

unused [uhn•YOOSD] *adj* neuf
-ve; inutilisé e

unveil [uhn•VAIYL] *vt* dévoiler

unwarranted
[uhn•WAH•ren•ted] *adj*
injustifié

unwary [uhn•WAI•ree] *adj*
imprudent

unwashed [uhn•WASHD] *adj*
non lavé

unwelcome [uhn•WEL•kom]
adj importun (cadeau pers)

unwholesome [uhn•HOL•sum]
adj malsain

unwieldy [uhn•WEEL•dee] *adj
inv* gauche (pers)

unwilling [uhn•WIL•ling] *adj
comp* de mauvaise volonté

unwillingness
[uhn•WIL•ling•nes] *n comp*
manque d'enthousiasme M

unwind [uhn•WUYND] *vt; vi*
dérouler; se détendre (pers)

unwise [uhn•WUYZ] *adj*
imprudent

unworthy [uhn•WUR•thee] *adj
inv* indigne

unwrap [uhn•RAP] *vt* défaire

unyielding [uhn•YEEL•ding]
adj inv inflexible

up [uhp] être debout (à 6 heures
du matin); vers le haut;
monter; veiller

up-to-date [UHP•to•DAIT] *adv* au courant

upbraid [uhp•BRAIYD] *vt* réprimander

upgrade [UHP•graid] *vt* améliorer (un produit)

upheaval [uhp•HEE•vul] *n* soulèvement M

uphill [UHP•hil] pénible (fig); en montant

uphold [uhp•HOLD] *vt* soutenir

upholster [uh•POL•stur] *vt* rembourrer

upholstery [uh•POL•stree] *n* comp tapisserie d'ameublement F

upkeep [UHP•keep] *n* entretien M

uplift [uhp•LIFT] *n* élévation F

upon [uh•PAHN] *prep* sur

upper [UH•pur] *adj* de dessus

upright [UHP•ruyt] droit; debout

uprising [UHP•ruy•zing] *n* soulèvement M

uproar [UHP•ror] *n* tumulte M

upset [uhp•SET] bouleversement; renverser M

upshot [UHP•shot] *n* fin F

upside [UHP•suyd] *n* dessus M

upstairs [uhp•STAIRZ] *adv* en haut

upstart [UHP•start] *n* parvenu -e MF

upward [UHP•wurd] *adj* ascendant

uranium [yur•AI•nee•um] *n* uranium M

urban [UR•bin] *adj* urbain

urchin *n* oursin (mer); gamin MF

urge [urj] impulsion; presser F

urgency [UR•jen•see] *n* urgence F

urgent [UR•jent] *adj* urgent

urgently [UR•jent•lee] *adv* instamment

urinate [YUR•i•NAIT] *vi* uriner; pisser

urine [YUR•rin] *n* urine F

urn *n* urne F

us [uhs] *pron pl* nous

usage [YOO•sej] *n* usage M; traitement M; usage; emploi; service M; consummation F;

use [yooz] emploi; utiliser M; of no ~\ inutile; make ~ of\ se servir; get used to\ être accoutumé à

used car [yoozd ~] *n* voiture d'occasion

used up *adj* épuisé

useful [YOOS•ful] *adj inv* utile

usefulness [YOOS•ful•nes] *n* utilité F

useless [YOOS•les] *adj inv* inutile

uselessness [YOOS•les•nes] *n* inutilité F

usher [UH•shur] *vt* placer (des spectateurs)

usual [YOO•zjuh•wuhl] *adj* usuel ̄-le; commun

usually [YOO•zjuh•wuh•lee] *adv* d'habitude

usurer [YOO•zjur•ur] *n* usurien -ère MF

usurp [yoo•SURP] *vt* usurper

usury [YOO•zjuh•ree] *n* usure F

utensil [yoo•TEN•sul] *n* ustensile F

utility [yoo•TI•li•tee] *n* utilité F

utilize [YOO•ti•LUYZ] *vt*
utiliser

utmost [UHT•most] le plus
grand(e); maximum M

utter [UHT•tur] absolu;
prononcer un mot ou des mots

utterance [UHT•tur•anz] *n*
expression verbale F

uvula [YOO•vyu•luh] *n* uvule F

V

vacancy [VAI•ken•see] *n*
vacance; lacune F

vacant [VAI•kint] vide; vacant

vacate [VAI•kait] *vt* quitter (un
lieu)

vacation [vai•KAI•shn] *npl*
vacances (être en vacances) F

vaccinate [VAK•zin•NAIT] *vt*
vacciner

vaccine [vak•SEEN] *n* vaccin M

vacillate [VA•sil•LAIT] *vi*
vaciller

vacuum [VA•kyum] *n*
aspirateur M

vagabond [VA•guh•BOND]
vagabond -e MF

vague [vaig] *adj* vague; pas
clair

vain *adj* vaniteux -euse

valentine [VA•len•TUYN]
n bien-aimé e; (le massacre
de la) Saint-Valentin
MF

valet [va•LAIT] *n* valet (de
chambre); pressing (de
l'hôtel) M

valiant [VA•lee•ent] *adj*
vaillant

valid [VA•lid] *adj inv* valable

validity [va•LI•di•tee] *n*
validité F

valise [va•LEES] *n* mallette F

valley [VAL•lee] *n* val; vallée
MF

valor [VA•lor] *n* valeur F

valorous [VA•lo•rus] *adj*
valeureux -euse; courageux
-euse

valuable [VAL•yoo•bl] *adj* cher
chère; précieux -euse

value [VAL•yoo] *n* valeur F;
(market) *n comp* valeur
marchande F

valve [valv] *n* valve F

van *n* camionnette F

vane [vain] (weather) *n*
gerouette F

vanilla [vuh•NIL•luh] *n*
vanille F

vanish [VA•nish] *vi* s'évanouir;
disparaître

vanity [VA•ni•tee] *n*
vanité F

vanquish [VAN•kwish] *vt*
vaincre (l'ennemi)

vantage [VAN•tij] *n* supériorité
F; avatnage M

vapid [VA•pid] *adj inv*
insipide

vapor [VAI•por] *n* vapeur;
fumée F

vaporize [VAI•po•RUYZ] *vt*
vaporiser

variable [VAIR•ree•uh•bl] *adj*
inv variable

variance [VAIR•ree•enz] *n*
variance; différence F

variation [VAIR•ree•AI•shn] *n*
variation F

varied [VAIR•reed] *adj* varié e

variegated
[VAI•re•uh•GAI•ted] *adj*
bigarré (vêtement, fleur)

variety [vuh•RUY•i•tee] *n*
variété F

various [VAIR•ee•us] *adj* divers

varnish [VAR•nish] vernis;
vernir (bois, ameublement) M

vary [VAIR•ree] *vt* varier

vase [vaiz] *n* vase M

vast *adj inv* vaste

vastness *n* immensité F

vat *n* cuve (pour le
blanchissage; réservoir) F

vaudeville [VAUD•vil] *n comp*
de music-hall; de
vaudeville M

vault 1 *n* voûte F

vault 2 *vi* sauter

vaunt *vt vi* vanter; se vanter (de
qqch)

veal [veel] *n* veau M

veer *vi* virer (vèhicule: vers ou
à); dévier (conversation: sur)

vegetable [VE•je•tuh•bl] *n*
légume F

vegetarian [VE•je•TAI•ree•en]
végétarien -ne MF

vegetate [VE•je•TAIT] *vt*
végéter

vegetation [VE•je•TAI•shn] *n*
végétation F

vehemence [VEE•him•menz] *n*
véhémence; ardeur F

vehicle [VEE•hi•kl] *n*
véhicule M

veil [vail] *n* voile M

vein [vain] *n* veine F

velocity [ve•LAH•si•tee] *n*
vélocité F

velvet [VEL•vit] de velours;
velours M

vendor 1 [VEN•dur] *n*
distributeur automatique
(machine); marchand -e (pers)
MF

vendor 2 (street) [ven•dur] *n*
marchand -e ambulant -e MF

veneer [vuh•NEER] *n*
placage M

venerable [VE•nur•ah•bl] *adj*
inv vénérable

venerate [VE•nur•RAIT] *vt*
vénérer

veneration [VE•nur•RAI•shn]
n vénération F

vengeance [VEN•jenz] *n*
vengeance F

venison [VE•ni•sun] *n*
venaison F

venom [VE•nuhm] *n* venin M

venomous [VE•nuh•mus] *adj*
venimeux -euse

vent *n* soupirail; décharger M

ventilate [VEN•ti•LAIT] *vt*
aérer; ventiler

ventilation [VEN•ti•LAI•shn] *n*
ventilation F

ventilator [VEN•ti•LAI•tur] *n*
ventilateur M

venture 1 [VEN•chur] *vt*
risquer; oser

venture 2 (business) [ven•chur] *n* spéculation F

venue [VEN•yoo] *n* lieu (du procès; de réunion)

verandah [vur•AN•duh] *n* véranda F

verb [vurb] *n* verbe M

verbal [VER•bul] *adj* verbal

verbose [vur•BOS] loquace; verbeux -euse

verdict [VUR•dikt] *n* verdict M

verge [vurj] au bord (des larmes); s'approcher (de)

verification [VAI•ri•fi•KAI•shn] *n* vérification F

verify [VAI•ri•FUY] *vt* vérifier

veritable [VAI•rih•ti•bl] *adj inv* véritable

vermin [VUR•min] *n* vermine (insectes; pers péj) F

vernacular [vur•NAK•kyu•lur] vernaculaire (langue vernaculaire); commun M

verse [vurz] *n* vers ou strophe (poésie) MF

versed [vurzd] *adj* versé e (dans)

version [VUR•shin] *n* version F

vertebra [VUR•ti•bruh] *n* vertèbre F

vertical [VUR•ti•kl] *adj* vertical

vertigo [VUR•ti•GO] *n* vertige M

very [VAIR•ree] *adv* très

vespers [VE•spurz] *npl* vêpres F

vessel *n* vaisseau; navire M

vest *n* gilet M

vestibule [VE•sti•BYUL] *n* vestibule M

vestige [VE•stij] *n* vestige (les derniers vestiges de son passé) M

vestigial [ve•STI•jul] *adj* résiduel -le

vestment [VEST•ment] *n* habit vêtement M

vestry [VES•stree] *n* sacristie F

veteran [VE•tur•rin] expérimenté; véteran M

veterinarian [VE•truh•NAI•ree•en] *n* vétérinarian F

veterinary [VE•truh•nai•ree] *adj* vétérinarien

veto [VEE•to] *n* veto M

vex *vt* ennuyer; vexer; fâcher

via [VEE•yuh] *prep* par

viaduct [VUY•uh•DUKT] *n* viaduc M

vial [vuyl] *n* ampule F

viands [VEE•endz] *npl* aliments

viaticum [vee•A•ti•kum] *n* viatiaque communion M

vibrate [VUY•brait] *vi* vibrer

vibration [vuy•BRAI•shn] *n* vibration F

vice 1 [vuyz] *n* vice M

vice 2 [vuyz] *n* débauche F

vicinity [ve•SIN•i•tee] *npl* environs M; *npl* alentours M

vicious [VI•shus] *adj* vicieux; -euse

victim [VIK•tim] *n* victime F

victor [VIK•tor] *n* vainqueur F

victorious [vik•TO•ree•us] *adj* victorieux; -euse

victory [VIK•tree] *n*
victoire F

victuals [VIK•chulz] *npl*
provisions; aliments F

vie [vuy] *v* rivaliser

view [vyu] *n* vue F; *vt* observer;
bird's eye~ à vol d'oiseau

vigil [VI•jil] *n* veille F

vigilant [VI•ji•lint] *adj* vigilant

vigor [VI•gor] *n* vigueur F

vigorous [VI•gur•us] *adj*
vigoureux; -euse

vile [vuyl] *adj* vil

villa [VI•luh] *n* villa F

village [VI•lij] *n* village M

villager [VI•li•jur] *n* villageois
M; villageoise F

villain [VI•lin] *adj* vilain;
coquin; *n* vilain M; manant M

villainous [VI•lin•nis] *adj* vil

villainy [VI•lin•nee] *n* vilenie F

vim *n* force F

vindicate [VIN•di•KAIT] *vt*
venger

vindictive [vin•DIK•tiv] *adj*
vindicatif -tive

vine [vuyn] *n* vigne F

vinegar [VI•ni•gur] *n*
vinaigre M

vineyard [VIN•yurd] *n*
vignobles M

vintage 1 [VIN•tij] *n*
vendange F

vintage 2 [VIN•tij] *n* crue; vind
du grand cru M

violate [VUY•uh•LAIT] *vt*
violer

violation [VUY•uh•LAI•shn] *n*
violation F

violence [VUY•uh•lenz] *n*
violence F

violent [VUY•uh•lent] *adj*
violent

violet [VUY•uh•let] *adj* violet;
-te ; *n* violette F

violin [VUY•uh•LIN] *n*
violon M

violinist [VUY•uh•LI•nist] *n*
violoniste MF

viper [VUY•pur] *n* vipère F

virgin [VUR•jin] *n* veirge F

virginity [vur•JI•ni•tee] *n*
virginité F

virile [VEER•rl] *adj* viril

virility [vur•RI•li•tee] *n*
virilité F

virtual [VUR•choo•ul] *adj*
virtual; -le

virtually [VUR•chuh•lee] *adv*
de fait

virulence [VEER•yoo•lenz] *n*
virulence F

virus [VUY•rus] *n* virus M

visa [VEE•zuh] *n* visa M

visage 1 [VI•sej] *n* visage M

visage 2 [VI•sej] *n* figure F

viscera [VI•suh•ruh] *npl*
viscères M

viscosity [vi•SKAH•si•tee] *n*
viscosité F   •

visibility [VI•si•BI•li•tee] *n*
visibilité F

visible [VI•si•bl] *adj* visible

vision [VI•shin] *n* vision F

visionary [VI•shin•NAI•ree] *n*
prophète M

visit 1 [VI•zit] *n* visite F

visit 2 [VI•zit] *vt* visiter;
~someone\ rendre visite à
qu'qun

visitation 1 [VI•zi•TAI•shn] *n*
visite F

visitation 2 [VI•zi•TAI•shn] *n*
Visitation (relig) F

visitor [VI•zi•tur] *n* visiteur;
-euse MF

visor [VUY•zur] *n*
visière F

vista [VI•stuh] *n* vue F

visual [VI•zjoo•ul] *adj* visuel;
-elle

visualize [VI•zjoo•LUYZ] *vt*
imaginer

vital [VUY•tl] *adj* vital

vitality [vuy•TA•li•tee] *n*
vitalité F

vitamin [VUY•tuh•min] *n*
vitamine F

vitreous [VI•tree•us] *adj*
vitreux; -euse

vitriol [VI•tree•ol] *n*
vitriol M

vivacious [vuh•VAI•shus] *adj*
vif; vive

vivacity [vuh•VA•si•tee] *n*
vivacité F

vivid [VI•vid] *adj* viv; vive

vocabulary
[vo•KA•byu•LAI•ree] *n*
vocaulaire M

vocal [VO•kul] *adj* vocal –e

vocation [vo•KAI•shn] *n*
vocation F

vogue [vog] *n* vogue F

voice [voiz] *n* voix F

void *adj* nul -le

void *adj* vide (invalid)

volatile [VAH•li•tl] *adj*
volatile

volcanic [vol•KA•nik] *adj*
volcanique

volcano [vol•KAI•no] *n*
volcan M

volley 1 [VAH•lee] *n*
volée F

volley 2 [VAH•lee] *n*
salve F

volt *n* volt M

voltage [VOL•tej] *n* voltage

volume [VAHL•yoom] *n*
volume M

voluntary [VAH•lun•TAI•ree]
adj voluntaire

volunteer [VAH•lun•TEER] *n*
voluntaire MF; *vt* s'engager

voluptuous [vuh•LUP•shus]
adj voluteux -euse

vomit [VAH•mit] *n* vomitif M;
vt vomir

voracious [vor•RAI•shus] *adj*
vorace

vote [vot] *n* scrutin M; *n*
voix F; *vt* voter; *n* votant -e
MF

voting [VO•ting] *n* srutin M

vouch [vouch] *vt* attester; *vi*
témoigner de

voucher [VOU•chur] *n* bonn de
garantie

vow *n* vœu M; *vt* jurer; faire un
vœu

vowel [VOU•wul] *n* voyelle F

voyage 1 [VOI•ij] *n* voyage M;
vi voyager

voyage 2 (maiden) [VOI•ij] *n*
première traversie F

vulgar [VUL•gur] *adj* vulgaire;
commun

vulgarity [vul•GAR•uh•tee] *n*
vulgarité F

vulnerable [VUHL•nur•uh•bl]
adj vulnirable

vulture [VUHL•chur] *n*
vautour M

W

wad [wahd] *n* bourre F

waddle [WAH•dl] *vi* se dahndiner

wade [waid] *vi* marcher dans l'eau

wafer [WAI•fur] *n* gaufrette F

waffle [WAH•fl] *n* gaufre F

waft [wahft] *vt* transporter

wag *vt* hocher (la queue d'un chien)

wage 1 [waij] *vt* engager; (as war) faire la guerre

wage 2 [waij] *vt* salaire M

wager [WAI•jur] *n* pari M

wagon [WAG•gin] *n* fourgon M

waif *n* épave F

wail *vt* gémir; hurler des cris plaintifs; *npl* lamentations F

waist *n* taille F

wait *vt* attendre; ~ on\ être aux ordres de

waiter [WAI•tur] *n* serveur -euse MF; *n* garçon (de café) M

waiting [WAI•ting] *n* attente F

waiting-room *n* salle d'attente F

waitress [WAI•tres] *n* serveuse F

waive [waiv] *vt* renoncer; abandoner (rights)

wake 1 [waik] *vt* reveiller; se réveiller

wake 2 [waik] *n* veillé mortuaire F

waken [WAI•kin] *vt* évailler

walk [wauk] *vt* marcher; aller à pied

wall [waul] *n* mur M

walled [wauld] *adj* entoure de murailles

wallet [WAU•lit] *n* porte feuille M

wallflower [WAUL•FLOU•wur] *vt comp* fair tapisserie

wallop [WHAU•lop] *vt* rosser

wallow [WHAU•lo] *vi* se vautrer

wallpaper [WAUL•PAI•pur] *n* papier peint M

walnut [WAUL•nut] *n* noix F

waltz 1 [wahlz] *n* valse F

waltz 2 [wahlz] *vi* valser

wan *adj inv* blême

wand *n* bâton M

wander [WAHN•dur] *vi* errer; rôder

wanderer [WAHN•dur•rur] *n* vagabond M

wane [wain] *n* déclin M; *vt* décliner

want [wahnt] *vt* manquer de; *vt* vouloir; *vi* faut de

wanton [WAHN•tin] *adj* folâtre

war *n* guerre F; *vt* gerroyer; faire la guerre

warble 1 [WAR•bl] *vi* gazouiller

warble 2 [WAR•bl] *n* gazouillis M

ward *n* pupille F; salle (hospital) F

warden *n* directeur -trice MF

wardrobe [WAUR•drob] *n* garde-robe (furniture) F; *npl* vêtments M

ware [wair] *npl* marchandises F

warehouse [WAIR•houz] *n* magasin M

warlike [WAUR•luyk] *adj* guerrier -ière

warm [waurm] *adj* chaud

warmth *n* chaleur F

warn *vt* avertir

warning [WAUR•ning] *n* avis M

warp *vt* voiler

warped [waurpt] *adj* perverti; *adj* voilé

warrant [WAUR•rint] *n* autorisation F; garantie F

warrior [WAUR•yur] *n* guerrier -ière MF

wart *n* verrue F

wary [WAIR•ree] *adj* hésitant; vigilant

wash *vt* laver

wash *vi* se laver

washer *n* rondelle F

washing *n* lavage M

washing-machine *n* machine à laver F

wasp [wahsp] *n* guêpe F

waste [waist] *n* gaspillage M; *vt* gaspiller

waste-paper basket [WAIST•PAI•pur ~] *n* corbeille à papier M

wasteful [WAIST•fl] *adv* de gaspillage

watch1 *n* montre F; horloge M

watch 2 *n* garde: surveillance; montre F; *vt* veiller; surveiller;

vt regarder (something); faire attention

watchdog [WATCH•daug] *n* chein de garde M

watchman *n* veilleur M

water [WAH•tur] *n* eau F; *vt* arroser (plants) F

water sports *npl* jeux nautiques M

watercolor [WA•tur•CUH•lur] *n* aquarelle F

waterfall [WA•tur•FAL] *n* chute d'eau F

waterproof *adj* imperméable

watertight [WA•tur•TUYT] *adj* étanche

waterway [WA•tur•WAI] *n* voie navigable F

watery [WA•tur•ree] *adj* détremé

wave [waiv] *n* vague; lame; onde F; *n comp* geste de la main M; *v* onduler; s'agiter; flotter

wavelength [WAIV•length] *n* longeur d'onde F

wavy [WAI•vee] *adj* ondulé (hair)

wax *n* cire F; *v* cirer

way [wai] *n* chemain M; en passant (by the ~) M; *vt* ceder (give ~) M

waylay [WAI•lai] *vt* attaquer

wayward [WAI•wurd] *adj* entrêté

we [wee] *pron* nous

weak [week] *adj* faible

weaken [WEE•kin] *vt* affaiblir

weakly [WEEK•lee] *adv* faiblement

wealth [welth] *n* richesse F

wealthy [WEL•thee] *adj inv*
riche

wean [ween] *vt* sevrer

weapon [WE•pun] *n* arme F

wear [wair] *vt* porter; user;
lasser épuisser; faire usage; *n*
détérioration F; usage M

weariness [WEE•ree•ness] *n*
fatigue F

wearisome [WEE•ree•some]
adj épuissant

weary [WEE•ree] *adj* épuissé

weasel [WEE•zul] *n* belette F

weather [WE•thur] *n* temps M

weather conditions *npl*
conditions atmosphériques F

weave [weev] *vt* tisser

web *n* toile F; tissu M; spider
~\ toile d'araignée

webbing [WEB•bing] *n* toile à
sangles F

wed *vi* se marier avec; *adj*
marié

wedded *adj* marié

wedding *npl* noces; nuptials F

wedge [wej] *n* cale F; *vt*
coincer

Wednesday [WENS•dai] *n*
mercredi M

weed *n* mauvaise herbe F;
chiendent F; sarcler

weedy [WEE•dee] *adj* envahi
par les herbes

week *n* semaine F

weekday [WEEK•dai] *n comp*
jour de semaine M

weekly [WEEK•lee] *adv*
hebdomadaire

weep *vi* plurer

weeping [WEE•ping] *adj*
pleureur

weevil [WEE•vul] *n*
charançon M

weigh [wai] *vt* péser

weight [wait] *n* poids M

weighty [WAI•tee] *adj* lourd

welcome [WEL•kum] *adj*
bienvenue

weld *vt* souder

welfare [WEL•fair] *n*
bien-être M

well 1 *adv* bien; je vais bien (I
am ~); *adj* bien; portant; en
bon état; get ~\ se rétablier;
aussi bien que (as well as)

well 2 *n* puits M; source F

well 3 (oil) *n* puits de pétrol M

well-being [WEL•BEE•ing] *n*
bien être

well-bred *adj* bien elevé

well-to-do [WEL•too•DOO]
adj aisé

welt *n* zébrur (of skin) F

werewolf [WAIR•wolf] *n* loup
garou M

west *n* ouest M

western [WES•turn] *adj* de
l'ouest

westerner [WES•tur•nur] *adj*
Occidental

westward [WEST•wurd] *adj*
vers l'ouest

wet *adj* mouillé

whack [wak] *n* claque F

whale [wail] *n* baleine F

wharf [warf] *n* quai M

what 1 [waht] *pron* quoi; ce
qui; ce que; qu'est-ce que

what 2 [waht] *adj* quel; quelle;
quelles

whatever [waht•E•vur] *pron
comp* quoi que; quel que;
quelle que soit

wheat [weet] *n* blé M

wheel [weel] *n* roue F

wheelbarrow [WEEL•BAIR•ro] *n* burette F

wheelchair [WEEL•chair] *n* fauteil roulant M

wheezy [WHEE•zee] *adj* asthmatique

when [wen] *adv* quand; lorsque; et alors que; où

whenever [we•NE•vur] *pron* chaque fois

where [wair] *adv* où

whereabouts [WAIR•uh•BOUTZ] *pron comp* où se trouve (something)

whereas [wair•AS] *conj* tandis que

whereby [wair•BUY] *pron* par; lequel

wherefore [WAIR•for] *conj comp* pour quel raison

wherever [wair•E•vur] *adv comp* par où

wherewithal [WAIR•wi•THAL] *n* moyens M

whet [wet] *vt* aiguiser

whether [WE•thur] *conj* si; si que; soit que

which [wich] que (object); qui (subject)

whichever [wich•E•vur] celui/celle qui

whiff [wif] *n* bouffée F

while [wuyl] *prep* pendant que

whim [wim] *n* caprice M

whimper [WIM•pur] *n* gémissement M

whimsical [WIM•si•kl] *adj* capricieux -euse

whine [wuyn] *vi* se plaindre; *n* pleurnicherie F

whip [wip] *n* fouet M; *vt* fouetter

whipping [WIP•ping] *n* coups de fouet

whir [wur] *n* bruissement M

whirl [wurl] *vi* se tourner

whirlpool [WURL•pool] *n* tourbillon d'eau M

whirlwind [WURL•wind] *n* toubillon M

whisk [wisk] *vi* aller vite (movement); *vi* épousseter; battre (eggs)

whisker [WIS•kur] *npl* moustaches F

whiskey [WIS•kee] *n* whisky M

whisper [WIS•pur] *n* murmure M; *n* chucotement M; *vt* chucoter; à voix basse

whistle [WIS•sl] *vi* siffler

whit [wit] *adv comp* petit peu

white [wuyt] *adj* blanc; blanche

whiten [wuy•tin] blanchir

whiteness [WUYT•nis] *n* blancheur F

whitewash [WUYT•wash] *n* blanc de chaux; M *vi* blanchir à la chaux

Whitsuntide [WIT•zun•tuyd] *n* Pentecôte F

whittle [WIT•tl] *vt* tailler (au couteau)

whiz [wiz] *vi* filer

who [hoo] *pron* qui; qui est-ce qui; celui qui

whole [hol] *adj* complet; complète

wholesale [HOL•sail] *n* vent en gros F

wholesome [HOL•sum] *adj* sain

wholly [HOL•lee] *adv* entièrement

whom [hoom] *pron* à qui

whomever [hoo•ME•vur] *pron* qui que soit

whoop [woop] *n* cri M

whore [hor] *n* putain F

whose [hooz] *pron* à qui; de qui

why [wuy] *adv* pourquoi

wick [wik] *n* mèche (bougie) F

wicked 1 [WIK•kid] *adj* méchant; mauvais

wickedness [WIK•kid•nes] *adj* méchanceté

wicker [WIK•kur] *n* osier M

wicket [WIK•kit] *n* guichet M

wide [wuyd] *adv* largement; loin

wide [wuyd] *adj* large; vaste; étendu

wide awake *adj comp* tout(e) éveillé(e)

widely [WUYD•lee] *adv* largement

widespread [WUYD•SPRED] *adj* répandu

widow [WI•do] *n* veuve F

widower [WI•do•wur] *n* veuf M

width *n* largeur F

wield [weeld] *vt* brandir (arms)

wife [wuyf] *n* femme; épouse; mariée F

wig *n* perruque F

wild [wuyld] *adj* sauvage

wile [wuyl] *n* ruse F

will [wil] *n* volonté F; *v* vouloir; ordonner; *n* testament; gre M

willful *adj* intentionnel

willing *adj* bien disposé; enclin à; prêt à

willingly [WIL•ling•lee] *adv* de bon coeur

willingness *n* bonne volonte F

willow [WIL•lo] *n* saule M

wilt *vi* se faner (plants etc)

wily [WUY•lee] *adj* ausucieux; -euse

win *vt* gagner; remporter

wince [winz] *vi* grimacer

winch *n* manivelle F

wind 1 [wind] *vt* tourner; enrouler

wind 2 [wind] *n* vent; air; soufle M

windfall [WIND•fal] *n* bonne aubaine F

winding [WUYN•ding] *adj* tortueux -euse

windmill [WIND•mill] *n* moulin à vent M

window [WIN•do] *n* fenêtre F

window shade *n* store M

windowsill [WIN•do•SIL] *n* rebord de fenêtre M

windshield [WIND•sheeld] *n* par brise M

windshield wiper *n* essuie glace M

windy [WIN•dee] *adj* venteux; -euse

wine [wuyn] *n* vin M

wine cellar *n* cave F

wineglass [WUYN•glas] *n* verre à vin

wing *n* aile F

winged [WING•gid] *adj* ailé

wink *n* clin d'oeil M

winner [WIN•ner] *n* gagnant MF

winning [WIN•ning] *adj* gagnant

winter [WIN•tur] *n* hiver M

wintry [WIN•tree] *adj comp* d'hiver

wipe [wuyp] *vt* essuyer

wiper [WUY•pur] *n* essuie-glace (car); *n* torchon; esuyer M

wire [wuyr] *n* fil de fer; fil métalique M

wireless [WUYR•les] sans fil M

wiry [WUYR•ree] *adj* nerveux -euse

wisdom [WIZ•dom] *n* sagesse M

wise [wuyz] *adj* sage; prudent; sensé

wiseacre [WUYZ•AI•kur] *n* bel-esprit

wisecrack [WUYZ•krak] *n* bon-mot M

wish 1 *n* souhait M

wish 2 *vt* souhaiter; vouloir (wish to)

wistful *adj* pensif; -ve

wit *n* esprit M

witch [wich] *n* sorcière F

with *prep* avec; de par; à; dans; parmi

withdraw [with•DRAU] *vt* retirer

withdrawal [with•DRAU•wul] *n* retraite F

withdrawn [with•DRAUN] *adj* réservé

wither [WI•thur] *vi* se faner (flower)

withhold refuser

within [wi•THIN] *adv* dedans; *prep* dans (place); *prep* en (time; ~ un heur)

without [wi•THOUT] *prep* sans

withstand [with•STAND] *vi* résister à

witness [WIT•nes] *n* témoin M

witticism [WIT•ti•CIZM] *n* bon mot M

witty [WI•tee] *adj* spirituel; -le

wizard [WIZ•zurd] *n* sorcier M

woe [wo] *n* douleur F

wolf *n* loup; louve MF

woman [WUH•man] *n* femme F

womanhood [WUH•min•HUD] *n* fémininité F

womanly [WUH•min•lee] *adj* féminin

womb [woom] *n* matrice F

won *adj* gagné; *pp* gagner

wonder [WUN•dur] *n* étonment; prodige; miracle M; *vt* se demander

wonderful [WUN•dur•fl] *adj* formidable; étonant

wonderfully [WUN•dur•ful•lee] *adj* admirablement

wont [wahnt] *n* coutume F

woo *v* faire la cour à

wood [wud] *n* bois M

woodland [WUD•land] *n* région boisé F

woodpecker [WUD•PEK•kur] *n* pic M

woodwork [WUD•wurk] *n*
menuiserie F
woodworker
[WUD•WUR•kur] *n*
menuisier M
woof (wool) [wuf wul] *n*
laine F
woolen [WUH•lin] *n comp* de
laine
woolly [WUH•lee] *adj* laineux
-euse
word [wurd] *n* mot ; vocable;
avis M; parole; nouvelle F
have words with\ se quareller
wore [wor] *adj* porté
wore [wor] *pp* porter
work. [wurk] *n* travail; ouvrage;
emploi M; oeuvre besogne F;
vt vi travailler; accomplir;
fonctionner
workday [WURK•dai] *n*
journée de travail F
worker 1 [WURK•ur] *n*
ouvrier; -iere (factory) M
worker 2 [WURK•ur] *n*
travailleur; -euse (office) M
working [WUR•king] *adj* ce
qui marche; fonctionner
workman [WURK•man] *n*
ouvreir; travailleur M
workmanship
[WURK•man•SHIP] *n*
travail M
workshop [WURK•shop] *n*
atelier M
world [wurld] *n* monde M
worldly [WURLD•lee] *adj inv*
terrestre; matérialiste
worm [wurm] *n* ver M
worry [WUR•ree] *n* inquiétude
F; *vi* s'inquiéter; *vt* tracasser

worse [wurz] *adj inv* pire
worship [WUR•ship] *vt* adorer
worshipper [WUR•ship•pur] *n*
adorateur; -trice MF
worst [wurst] *adj* pire (le/la)
worth [wurth] *n* valeur F; *adj*
valant
worthless [WURTH•les] *n*
comp sans valeur F
worthy [WUR•thee] *adj* digne
(de)
wound [woond] *n* blessure F
wrangle [RAN•gl] dispute;
disputer F
wrap [rap] *vt* enrouler; rouler;
emballer (gift)
wrapper [RAP•pur] *n* papier
d'emballage M
wrapping paper *n* papier
cadeau M
wrath [rath] *n* colère F
wreath [reeth] *n* guirlande M
wreck [rek] *n* épave;
naufrage M
wreck [rek] faire naufrager;
couler
wrench [rench] *n* clé F; *vt*
tordre; arracher
wrest [rest] *vt* arracher
wrestle [RES•tl] *vi* lutter
wretch [retch] *n* malheureur;
-euse MF
wretched [RETCH•chid] *adj*
inv misérable
wring [ring] *vt* tordre
wrinkle [RINK•kl] *n* ride F; *vt*
rider
wrist [rist] *n* poignet M
writ [rit] *n* ordonnance F
write [ruyt] *vt* écrire

writer [RUY•tur] *n*
écrivain M
writhe [ruyth] *vi* se
tordre (de)
writing [RUY•ting] *n*
écriture F

wrong [rong] *n comp* avoir tort
M; *adj* faux; erroné M; *adv*
mal; à tort M
wrought iron [ROUT I•urn] *n*
fer forgé M
wry [ruy] *adj* tordu; de travers

X

X-ray [X•rai] *n* radiographie F
xenophobe [ZEE•no•FOB] *n*
xénophobe MF
xenophobia *n* xénophobie F

xylography
[zuy•LOG•gruh•fee] *n*
xylographie F
xylophone [ZUY•luh•FON] *n*
xylophone M

Y

yacht [yaht] *n* yacht M
yam *n* patate douce F
yank *vt* tirer brusquement
yard [yahrd] *n* jardin M
yardstick [YAHRD•stik] *n*
mètre M
yawn [yaun] *vi* bâiller
yea [yai] *adv* oui
year [yeer] *n* an M
yearn [yurn] *vt* désirer
yearning [YUR•ning] *n*
désir M
yeast [yeest] *n* lehvure F
yell [yel] *vt* crier
yellow [YEL•lo] jaun F

yeoman [YO•min] *n*
quartier-maître M
yes *adv* oui
yesterday [YES•tur•dai] hier
yet *adj* encorse
yield [yeeld] *vi* céder; *n*
fléchissement M
yielding [YEEL•ding] *adj* inv
flexible
yoke [yok] *n* joug M
yolk [yok] *n* jaune (d'oeuf) M
yonder [YON•dur] *adv* là-bas
yore [yor] *n* au temps jadis M
you [yoo] *pron* vous; tu
young [yung] *adj* jeune

youngster [YUNG•stur] *n*
adolescent MF

your; yours [yor; yorz] votre;
vos; à vous; le/la/les vôtre

yourself [yor•SELF] *pron*
vous-même; toi-même

youth [yooth] *n* jeunesse;
adolescence F

youthful [YOOTH•fl] *adj inv*
jeune

Yuletide [YOOL•tuyd] *n*
Noël M

Z

Zaire [zah•EER] *n* Zaïre M

zeal [zeel] *n* ferveur F

zealot [ZE•lot] *n* fantatique

zealous [ZE•lus] *adj* zélé -ę

zebra [ZEE•bruh] *n* zèbre M

zenith [ZEE•nith] *n* zénith M

zephyr [ZE•fur] *n* zéphyr M

zeppelin [ZE•pi•lin] *n*
zeppelin M

zero [ZEE•ro] *n* zéro M

zest *n* saveur F

zigzag *vi* zigzaguer

zinc *n* zinc M

zip *vt* aller à toute vitesse; brûler
le pavé

zipper [ZIP•pur] *n* fernature à
crémaillère F

zircon *n* zircon M

zither [ZITH•thur] *n* cithare F

zodiac [ZO•dee•AK] *n*
zodiaque M

zodiacal [zo•DUY•i•kl] *adj*
zodiacal -e

zone [zon] *n* zone F

zoo *n* zoo M

zoological
[ZOO•uh•LAH•jik•kl] *adj inv*
zoologique

zoology [zoo•AH•lo•gee] *n*
zoologie F

zoom *vi comp* aller à toute
vitesse

zygote *n* zygote M